HOTEL MANAGEMENT
AND OPERATIONS
fourth edition

Ph.D.

agement

.D.

nt

, INC.

Library of Congress Cataloging-in-Publication Data:

Hotel management and operations / edited by Denney G. Rutherford, Ivar Haglund, and
    Michael J. O'Fallon. — 4th ed.
        p.   cm.
    Includes bibliographical references and index.
        ISBN-13: 978-0471-47065-6
        ISBN-10: 0-471-47065-1 (pbk.)
    1. Hotel management.   I.   Rutherford, Denney G., 1942–   II.   Haglund, Ivar.
    TX911.3.M27H663   2007
    647.94′068—dc22   2005011811

Printed in the United States of America

10   9   8   7   6   5   4   3   2

DEDICATION

The fourth edition of *Hotel Management and Operations* is hereby dedicated to all of those hospitality students who have enriched the lives of their guests by continuing to learn beyond their formal education. It is these professionals who constantly strive to find even better ways to give the gift of friendship. All the best to you.

D.G.R. and M.J.O'F 2005

CONTENTS

chapter 2 ORGANIZATION 69

chapter 3 GENERAL MANAGERS: A VIEW AT THE TOP 89

chapter 4 OPERATIONS: ROOMS 121

chapter 5 OPERATIONS: HOUSEKEEPING, ENGINEERING, AND SECURITY   167

chapter 6 FOOD AND BEVERAGE DIVISION   235

chapter 7 MARKETING AND ASSOCIATED ACTIVITIES   303

chapter 8 FINANCIAL CONTROL AND INFORMATION MANAGEMENT   365

chapter 9 HUMAN RESOURCES POLICY MANAGEMENT 415

PREFACE

As Denney would tell you, the first edition of this textbook project was originally born out of a range of frustrations. While there are many outstanding textbooks in the hotel management field that dealt with significant portions of operations, particularly housekeeping, front office, and food and beverage, there are very few that try to treat, in a balanced and in-depth way, each department in the hotel. One frustration was that some texts that dealt with these departments spent an inordinate amount of time focused on one aspect of the hotel operations—usually either front of the house, food and beverage or marketing. Other departments, for better or worse, were treated as minor players. Consequently, students and readers of such texts were given only a cursory introduction to the intricacies of these "minor" departments, their management, their people, and their interactive functions in the overall hotel organization.

Another frustration he encountered was using then currently available material to pro-mote the idea of critical thinking among students of hotel administration. Critical thinking refers to that process whereby the student is exposed to a number of different viewpoints within a theoretical structure, and from analysis of those viewpoints, becomes better able to synthesize a viewpoint about hotel operations that will enable them to intelligently approach whatever practical situations they may find themselves confronted with in the "real world."

There is a conventional wisdom that goes, "something may be okay in theory but it doesn't work in practice." Like economist Milton Friedman, we reject that statement. If theory doesn't work in practice, it is lousy theory. What professors need to guide students in understanding is that theory, (in the word of Friedman) explains, predicts, or controls, and does this in different ways given different variables in different organizations. This is another issue or frustration that subsequent editions have been designed to further address.

As we went about planning and designing the fourth edition of ***Hotel Management and Operations*** (HMO IV), we felt the need to continue to remind ourselves of the lessons of the frustrations listed above. We wanted to make sure the original idea behind this book did not get lost. By helping the reader gain an appreciation of what a *variety* of observers, thinkers, researchers, and commentators think about a topic, in this case, a hotel department, a student or hotel professional can feel better prepared to find ways to apply theory in a practical setting or situation. In the final analysis, it is up to you to make the best use of HMO IV, because like we state above, none of us knows it all. Good luck, it is our pleasure to do this work for you.

CONTRIBUTORS

Je'anna Abbott, University of Houston

Roy Alvarez, Senior Lecturer, Cornell University School of Hotel Administration

Peter C. Anderson, Anderson and Associates

Mario Arnaldo, Instructor, Travel Industry Management, Hawaii Pacific University, Honolulu, HI

Robert O. Balmer, General Manager, Doubletree Hotel, Bakersfield, California

James A. Bardi, Penn State Berks–Lehigh Valley College

Mark Beattie, Doctoral Student, Gonzaga University, Liberty Lake, WA

Cherylynn Becker, Richmond, Virginia

Rich Benninger, CMP, Executive Director of Catering of Catering and Convention Services, Caesar's Palace

Robert H. Bosselman, Dedman Chair of Hospitality Administration, Florida State University, Dedman Department of Hospitality Administration

Claudio Capaccioli, Deloitte and Touche Business Consulting Manager, Milan, Italy

Peter Cass, Crystal River, Florida

Paul Chappelle, Brand Revenue Manager, Red Lion Hotel and Inns, Vancouver, Washington

Beth G. Chung-Herrera, Associate Professor, College of Business, San Diego State University

Mark Conklin, Area Vice President, Western Europe, Marriott Hotels, Resorts, and Suites, Frankfort, Germany

Melissa Dallas, Florida Atlantic University, College of Business

Agnes Lee DeFranco, University of Houston, Conrad N. Hilton College

John Dew, Executive Consultant, Bellevue, Washington

Garry Dickover, General Manager, Convention Center Courtyard by Marriott, Las Vegas, Nevada

Michael J. Draeger, Controller, Dayton Depot Casino, Dayton, Nevada

Tom Dupar, Dupar Dynamics, Bellevue, Washington

Vince Eade, University of Nevada, Las Vegas Harrah School of Hotel Administration, Las Vegas, NV

Kurt Englund, Resort Manager, Four Seasons Resort Costa Rica at Peninsula Papagayo

Cathy A. Enz, Louis G. Shaeneman Professor of Innovation and Dynamic Management, Cornell University School of Hotel Administration

C. Lee Evans, Director of Purchasing, The Oasis Resort; Casa Blanca Spa and Golf and Virgin River Hotel and Casino

Emilio Fabico, Walt Disney World, Orlando, Florida

Gil B. Fried, Gil B. Fried and Associates, Risk Management Consultants, New Haven, CT

Jacinta Gau, Doctoral Student in Criminal Justice, Washington State University, Pullman, WA

Ajay Ghei, The World Bank Group

Bianca Grohmann, Assistant Professor of Marketing, Concordia University

Christian Hardigree, University of Nevada, Las Vegas Harrah School of Hotel Administration, Las Vegas, NV

Sharon K. Hodge, Assistant Professor, Love School of Business, Elon University

Earl D. Honeycutt Jr., Professor, Love School of Business, Elon University

Thomas Jones, University of Nevada, Las Vegas

John Lagazo, Director of Operations, The Madison Hotel, Rockville, MD

Melenie J. Lankau, Assistant Professor, Terry College of Business, University of Georgia

Stephen M. LeBruto, University of Central Florida

Valentino Luciani, Instructor, University of Nevada, Las Vegas

Vincent P. Magnini, Ph.D. candidate, Old Dominion University

Oliver Meinzer, Director of Operations, Newport Beach Marriott Suites, Newport Beach, CA

Susan V. Morris, Vice President, HQ Global Workplaces, Dallas, Texas

Suzanne K. Murrmann, Virginia Polytechnic Institute and State University, Department of Hospitality and Tourism Management

Arthur E. Nathan, New Product Thought Leader, Mellon HR Solutions

Eddystone C. Nebel III, Purdue University, Emeritus

Ellis Norman, University of Nevada, Las Vegas Harrah School of Hotel Administration, Las Vegas, NV

Peter O'Connor, Associate Professor, France's Institute de Management Hotelier International, Essec Business School, France

Bob Peckenpaugh, Hotel Manager, Rancho Bernardo Inn, San Diego, California

Gabriele Piccoli, Assistant Professor, Cornell University School of Hotel Adminstration

Dominic Provenzano, Director of Operations, Cleveland Marriott Downtown at Key Center, Cleveland, Ohio

William J. Quain, Florida International University, School of Hospitality Management

Clinton L. Rappole, University of Houston, Conrad N. Hilton College

Louis B. Richmond, President, Richmond Public Relations

Carl D. Riegel, Florida Atlantic University, Graduate School of Business

Gail Sammons, University of Nevada, Las Vegas Harrah School of Hotel Administration, Las Vegas, NV

ACKNOWLEDGMENTS

I sort of thought that by the time I reached the fourth edition, the project would have become easier. Well, it hasn't. The challenges of continual improvement—finding challenging and interesting material, presenting it in interesting ways, and trying to choose material that will transcend unanticipated events—get harder, not easier. While making the book was a team effort involving a wide range of professionals, all of its flaws, and there probably are more than a few, are solely my responsibility.

First of all, the authors of the various pieces included here who knowingly or unknowingly have contributed their thoughts, research, ideas, opinions, and expertise to this exercise in critical thinking about hotel departmental operations deserve recognition. Without the rich mixture of interest and talent extant in the hospitality profession and its educational establishment today, this collection of readings would not have been possible. It is my great good fortune that my

friends, colleagues, and former students could devote the time they did to contribute to this project. My badgering, cajoling, begging, and bribing aside, I think we're all still friends.

I want to particularly salute those who crafted custom pieces for this edition and those professionals who contributed "Day in the Life" and "As I See It" pieces. They have made this edition a richer and more user-friendly book. They also add a view of the real world that has been missing.

The support and encouragement of my colleagues at Washington State University was critical. Terry Umbreit, Director of the School of Hospitality Business Management, and a whole bunch of students all contributed to the success of this project with advice, counsel, and suggestions.

My good friend, colleague, and production assistant, Lillian Sugahara Jesse, helped me tremendously. Her magic with the computer literally saved this project by translating many files created in Adobe PDF or PageMaker for

Macintosh to something I could edit in Word. Because she kept accurate files of the manuscript of previous editions, we were able to overcome the problems attendant to the transfer of the project from Van Nostrand Rinehold to John Wiley & Sons. Lillian, you are the greatest.

Melissa Oliver, my editor at Wiley, provided needed support regarding material previously published by Wiley, and her willingness to discuss some of my off-the-wall ideas have truly made this a better project. Thanks, Melissa.

My wife and best friend, Sandy Sweeney, continues to provide the encouragement, support, and understanding she always does on big writing projects. Her understanding is particularly important when I disappear to work on "the book" when we could be doing other, more fun things. As with past editions, she does understand the rhythms of an author's life and endures losing me to "the book" with style and grace. The last two times I did this, we were moving—and surprise—it is happening again. I retired from Washington State University after 26 years in May 2004. We are in the process of building our retirement home in Port Townsend, Washington, and will be moving in July 2005, shortly after the book is due at the publisher. Building a house long distance has its own challenges, and with "the book," we have had to rely on Sandy for a lot of decisions. I love you, Sandy.

I also want to acknowledge the capable assistance of my colleague and former student, Michael O'Fallon. He is the author of the instructor's manual. Michael will co-author this and the next edition, after which the project will be all his.

Denney G. Rutherford

Spokane/Port Townsend, Washington 2005

chapter one
OVERVIEW

1.1 INTRODUCTION

The vast majority of research articles and essays in this book deal with one or more aspects of what has been called the art and science of modern hotel management. It should be noted that the word *modern* can be loaded with the potential of much misunderstanding. Hotels are changing and will continue to change. As a result, the techniques of management of modern hotels must adapt to changing circumstances. Subsequent sections of this book are designed to help the student and practitioner discover information, methods, and techniques for dealing with these changing circumstances.

▶ INFLUENCES

Like many other American businesses, hotels have been affected by shifts in emphasis among the country's living patterns. People and industry have moved from the so-called rust belt to the sun belt. The hotel business has been active in reborn and reconstructed central cities. The explosion of technology and information-based companies has concentrated human endeavor in technological corridors in California, Massachusetts, Washington, Texas, and North Carolina, to name a few such places. It can be safely said that where jobs are and major concentrations of economic activity occur, hotels will follow.

Among other current and ongoing influencers of hotel design, construction, marketing, and operation are the following. *Note:* This list is neither exhaustive nor exclusive.

- *Demographics* play a major role and will continue to be influential in the foreseeable future. As the baby boom generation and its children mature, the population of the country will for many years be older, healthier, and better educated than previous generations. These facts will present new challenges and opportunities to all business managers.

- *Technology*—in the form of computers, communication, personal devices, and laborsaving mechanical equipment—has had and will have a major effect on the way in which hotels are managed and operated. The speed with which information is accumulated, stored, manipulated, and transferred is such that today most travelers expect that the hotel rooms they rent will allow them to be as productive as they are in the office or at home. Increasingly, with portable computing, personal data assistants (PDAs), wireless communication, and virtually everything somehow connected to the Internet, hotels must provide services and access that allow guests seamless transition from the business, travel, or home environment to that of the hotel. Increasingly, entertainment must be fused with communication and productive processes.

- The concept of *market segmentation,* or ever-increasingly finely tuned market definitions, will dictate hotel structures and organizations, and management tactics designed to address those market segments have become even more important to the management of hospitality service businesses. With the increased power in the information and data manipulation realm, hotels have available to them ever-expanding databases about guests and are creating new products to attract those markets.

- One of the effects of the aging demographic is the emergence of *vacation re-sorts*—a modern incarnation of the time-share properties of several decades ago. Because these are being developed and operated by name hotel companies and are marketed to the affluent, healthy, well-educated population segment, resort managers have had to absorb new managerial realities.

- The well-documented change in the complexion of the *national economy* from one that emphasizes goods and, to a lesser extent, natural resources to one that emphasizes services has kindled new ideas about the way in which we manage the design and delivery of these services. Hotels, restaurants, and travel services are now seen as unique entities that dictate special kinds of managerial techniques and strategies.

- Changes in people's *travel patterns* have altered the way we manage our hotel properties. Deregulation of the airlines has driven a change in the way millions of people travel each year, given the hub-and-spoke design of airline services. Many hotel companies are now locating major hotel properties adjacent to hub air transport facilities, taking advantage of the fact that business travelers may not need to travel to a central business district (CBD) to accomplish their purpose in a given area. Meetings and conferences can now be scheduled within a five-minute limousine ride from the air terminal, and the business traveler can be headed for his or her next destination before the day is over without having to stay overnight in a CBD hotel.

- New *patterns of investment* in hotel facilities have emerged in the last two decades, and more attention is now paid to achieving optimum return on investment. Because people from outside the hotel industry are now participating in its financial structuring, hotel operations are no longer dependent on the vision of a single entrepreneur. Managers now must design tactics and strategies to achieve heretofore unanticipated financial goals. The same trend has also altered the complexion of management and organization of the modern hotel. This is especially true of publicly owned hotel firms, where Wall Street stock analysts heavily influence stock prices through expectations of quarterly revenues and profits. This puts pressure on hotel companies and their operations managers to perform, on a quarterly basis, in a way contrary to many managers' instincts.

Most of the foregoing issues and influences still operate (to a greater or lesser extent) on the organizational structures and strategies of the modern hotel. Since the last edition of this book, however, other phenomena of an economic, cultural, and social nature have come to the fore, complicating our view of hotel management. This furthers the argument that the hotel industry is a part of the greater economy and at the mercy of elements often completely out of its control.

The cyclical nature of the U.S. and international economies has recently affected significantly hotels' ability to respond to changing circumstances. In early 1993, for instance, employment growth was stagnant; corporate profits were low; the expansion of the gross national product (GNP) was only a marginal percentage above previous years; and travel in most segments was down due to corporate restructuring, downsizing, or reorganizing. Vast layoffs in the hundreds of thousands had been announced every month. While fuel prices continued to be relatively stable, consumer spending patterns and high employment growth had not materialized, particularly in light of corporate layoffs and the ongoing nervousness of consumers about whether or not their financial wherewithal was safe.

Now consider late 2000, when the third edition of this book was being written. Unemployment was at an all-time low; the Dow Jones Industrial Average was between 10,000 and 11,000; hotel occupancies had stabilized nationally in excess of 70 percent; and the federal government was running a surplus for the first time in the memory of most.

Then what happened? The terrorist attacks in New York and Washington, D.C., in 2001 changed the face of all business and travel, immediately and probably for the foreseeable future as well. Major airlines are in bankruptcy; hotels are struggling to achieve profitable occupancies; business travel is down; the high-tech stock market bubble burst; the country is at war in a number of locations; security has made travel more difficult, if not actually annoying; and people are nervous. Join this with an imbalance of trade, the outsourcing of jobs, and the largest federal deficits in history, and the face of the economy is challenging. This translates directly not only to business travel but personal and recreational travel as well. Finding ways to operate profitably in such an environment is the job of the next generation of hotel operators.

Among the predictions I made in the preceding edition was that cultural diversity will play a role in the management and organizational structure of the modern hotel in the United States. As surely as living patterns, economic cycles, and market segmentation have influenced the hotel industry, so will the change in ethnicity of the workforce. The cultural backgrounds that an increasingly diversified workforce will bring to hotel operations may be seen as a problem or a challenge—or both. To most operators, it will be seen as an opportunity to demonstrate to an increasingly diverse clientele that hotel companies are committed to hiring and training a workforce structure that mirrors society. I see no reason to change that prediction now; if anything, acculturation of the hospitality business will accelerate.

The legal and regulatory environments are increasingly important to all business managers, and hotel operators are no exception. Increasingly, operators must be aware of and alert to realms of risk that can engender lawsuits against them. Several articles and essays in this edition highlight these threats to hotels and their guests. It should be noted that present-day security concerns also have significantly affected the ways in which hotels are operated. Awareness of the risk environment and the regulatory realm are factors that affect a hotel's ability to compete in the early part of the twenty-first century. Essays and articles in the security section and the human resources section address this issue.

► INTRODUCTORY READINGS

I have attempted in this edition to present new and (sometimes) different takes on the hotel business. This section is also used to explore ideas that are new to the management process, and that—who knows?—may never completely catch on. Rather than focus exclusively on the operations of the major chains, the readings here are from the perspectives of operators, leaders, and experts such as regional operators, major industry consultants, and independent branded hotels.

John Dew, formerly president of Inn Ventures, a regional hotel management and development company that has built and operated many Marriott products, in addition to a proprietary hotel product, provides an insider's view of the steps needed to bring a hotel from conception to construction and operation. This unique view of hotel operations connects the concept of hotel development with the realities of day-to-day operation. It should help aspiring managers understand how the intricacies of the development process may influence the marketing and management of the hotel.

Peter Cass offers the reader insights, heretofore unavailable in books of this nature, into independently branded hotels that associate to provide market strength. He makes the case that the future success of independent hotels is linked to their ability to find ways to maintain their independence while sustaining competitive advantage in the luxury segment.

Because new construction of hotels diminished greatly after 9/11 but firms still needed to grow, rebranding existing properties generated a lot of growth activity. Rebranding is a complicated process that must be accomplished within critical time frames to coincide with marketing, financial, and operational variables. Tom Dupar is a seasoned veteran at this fascinating and important activity and has participated in rebranding operations around the world. His essay on the intricacies of rebranding was a mainstay in the previous edition of this book. Today's economic circumstances are different, and Dupar's business has changed its focus to opening new major projects. His piece serves as a useful companion to that of John Dew, and the two should be read together, with an eye toward comparing Dew's smaller project focus and Dupar's large projects.

Perhaps proving the axiom that "everything old is new again," the concept of health and wellness spas as a hotel and resort product has enjoyed a resurgence. Once the province of high-end hotels and resorts, the idea of being pampered in a spa has been added to the service mix in many more modest hotels and resorts. While the big-name spas at five-star properties still set the standard for pampering and pricing, the comfort of personal service in less lavish spas seems to appeal to the modern traveler as well. Peter Anderson's overview of the spa industry provides insights into this fascinating service product.

In addition to products, building, and re-branding, I have also chosen to include in the section two recently reviewed and studied ideas that may or may not be adopted across the industry.

At the end of this section are a number of suggested readings for the student who would like to gain more in-depth knowledge about the hospitality industry as a whole and specific historical antecedents. In particular, the books by Hilton and Jarman look closely at the intermachinations of the establishment by two early pioneers of the industry, one of whom, Conrad Hilton, lives on in an international, publicly traded company operated by one of his sons. E.M. Statler's contributions to the modern hotel business are legendary in that he is generally credited with founding and operating the first commercial hotel concept that recognized the realities of the early business traveler at the beginning of the twentieth century. The suggested articles are drawn from recently published historic overviews of the hotel side of the hospitality industry in the United States. They also highlight other major forces in the development of the modern hotel business.

1.2 THE HOTEL DEVELOPMENT PROCESS

John Dew

▶ INTRODUCTION

The bulldozers are working and a construction crane is being erected on that vacant lot you pass each day going to and from home. The sign on the fence states that a new hotel is being built with a planned opening date of spring 2007. If you have ever wondered just how that hotel was created, you may have wondered about some or all of the following questions:

- How did someone select that particular vacant lot?
- Who actually creates a new hotel?

- Who owns it?
- Where did they get the money to build it?
- How long does the process take from idea to grand opening day?
- Who selects the architect, the engineers, and the interior designer?
- Who manages the myriad details that go into the development of a new hotel?
- Who will manage the hotel once it's open?

We hope to address these and other questions you may have in this chapter.

► THE DEVELOPMENT COMPANY

The developer is the entrepreneur, the risk taker, who originates the idea for the hotel. Depending on the business structure selected, the developer often puts his or her personal wealth at risk when engaging in a hotel project. The developer, along with a small staff of people, networks with commercial real estate agents on the lookout for a suitable hotel site. Depending on the type of hotel to be developed, a site of at least two to four acres is required (for comparison, an acre is roughly the size of a football field). This property must be zoned by the city for a hotel, be visible from a freeway or major street arterial, and have city approval for such construction activities as curb cuts, left-hand turn lanes, and delivery truck access. Commercial realtors offer sites for the developer's consideration that include maps, aerial photos, and proof of hotel zoning.

Sometimes the developer views potential sites by driving around the neighborhood within five miles of the site or touring multiple sites by helicopter, noting where the potential guests live and work and where potential competing hotels are located.

The price per square foot of the land is considered. The higher the cost of land, the higher the rates the hotel will need to charge. Is the price too high for the average daily rate (ADR) in this particular market? Is it too low? Or is it acceptable? This is determined when the hotel financial pro forma budget document is created.

► THE FEASIBILITY STUDY

When the developer selects a site, a feasibility study is often commissioned to obtain an analysis of the site by an objective third party. Companies offer hotel feasibility studies for a fee and are experts in a particular market, or developers may use the consulting group of one of the major public accounting firms.

The company retained to do the feasibility study can spend up to several months gathering detailed data to see if, in their opinion, it makes economic sense to build the hotel. Their conclusion offers an objective third-party opinion as to whether the project is feasible, hence the term *feasibility study*. Generally, the feasibility study considers, evaluates, and makes recommendations about the project based on the following variables:

The Site

- Proper zoning
- Size in square feet/acres
- Visibility from arterials/freeways
- Traffic counts/patterns
- Accessibility from streets, freeways, airports, train stations, etc.
- Proximity to where potential guests live, travel, or work
- Barriers that discourage competition coming into the market, if any
- How adjacent property and businesses are utilized
- Master area development plans
- Local permitting process and the degree of difficulty for that particular city
- Impact fees charged by the city

The Economy of the Area

- Major employers, government agencies
- Business trends for each employer/agency
- Hotel needs and the demand for each
- Leisure travel demand in the area

- Nearby tourist attractions
- Visitor counts
- Conventions, trade shows, and meetings history

The Hotel Market

- The competitors, both existing and planned
- Historical occupancy of hotels in the area
- Historical average rate
- Proprietary data on area travel

Identification of Which Hotel Market Segment to Serve

- Full service
- Limited service
- Extended stay
- Luxury
- Midprice
- Economy
- Budget

Selection of Appropriate Hotel Design

- High-rise
- Midrise
- Garden apartment style
- Hybrid design

Selection of Appropriate Hotel Brand

- Franchised (Marriott, Sheraton, Hyatt, etc.)
- Licensed (Best Western, Guest Suites, etc.)
- Independent
- Independent with strategic market affiliation (Luxury Hotels of America, Historic Hotels of America, etc.)

Ten-year Projection

- Occupancy projection by year
- ADR by year
- Estimated cash generated for debt
- Estimated cash generated for distribution to investors
- Estimated cash-on-cash return (after-tax income divided by equity invested)
- Overall projected yield
- Projected internal rate of return
- Net present value of the project over each of the next ten years

Once the feasibility study is completed, the developer is prepared to move forward with the project. Often, at this stage of the process, the developer purchases an option on the land to tie it up until the remaining development steps can be completed—and to prevent the competition from purchasing it.

► CREATION OF THE OWNERSHIP ENTITY

An ownership entity (note that this is different than and separate from the development company) must be created to hold title to the land—and the hotel, once it's built. Considering the limitation of liability to the investors, tax consequences, estate implications for the investors, and potential requirements of the mortgage lender, a business structure is selected, normally in one of the following forms:

- Limited liability company (LLC)
- Limited partnership (LP)
- S corporation (formerly known as a *Sub-S corporation*)
- C corporation

► THE DEVELOPMENT AGREEMENT

The newly formed entity now enters into a development contract with the development company to take the project to completion. The development company charges a fee, approximately 3 percent of the total project cost, for this service. The agreement generally covers such variables as:

- Selection of architect/engineers
- Selection and supervision of a general contractor
- Processing all building and occupancy permits
- Raising all the equity money from investors
- Securing a construction mortgage loan
- Selecting a franchise company
- Securing the franchise
- Selecting an interior designer that meets franchise company requirements
- Purchasing all opening furniture, fixtures, equipment
- Selecting a management company to operate the hotel
- Liability for cost overruns

► SELECTING A FRANCHISE

Depending on the type of hotel to be built (based on the feasibility study), the developer recommends a franchise company to the hotel owner. A major consideration is the best franchise brand for the market segment to be served. Each franchise company has different franchise fees, royalty fees, and marketing/miscellaneous fees as part of its agreement structure with the operating company. Consideration must also be given to the brands already represented in the target market that may be available for franchise. The franchise company is approached and a franchise is requested, with the feasibility study offered as backup for the request.

The next step is for the franchise company to conduct an impact study of the market. This considers such matters as possible negative impact on existing hotels that carry the franchiser's flag. If the impact is judged to be insignificant, a franchise is usually granted to the ownership entity for a one-time fee of about $400 per room, depending on the franchise selected, with continuing royalty and marketing, usually based on a percentage of hotel revenue.

► SELECTING AN ARCHITECT

Because the final product of this process is a building the operator has to run as a hotel, the architect's experience in designing hotels, his or her experience with the prototypical drawings of the franchise selected, the fee, and his or her on-time record must be considered. Architect fees can run up to 5 percent of the total project cost but are often negotiated down, if the project is big enough. The firm's experience and record on similar projects are critical. The architect does not have to operate the hotel when it is completed. The developer wants the architect to design a hotel that will be easy to operate and maintain.

► SELECTING A GENERAL CONTRACTOR

Major consideration are the quality and reliability record of the general contractor and the firm's use of and relationships with the many subcontractors needed for a project as complex as a hotel. Again, experience in building the hotel type is important. It is hoped that the general contractor has learned from any mistakes made in building similar hotels. The general contractor and architect often bid the project as a team; this helps the developer determine the final cost. Often, up to a 10 percent contingency cost that allows for unforeseen circumstances is built into the project bidding process.

► FINANCING THE PROJECT

The following variables must be determined to qualify for financing:

- The cost of the land
- Design and construction cost of the building
- The cost of furniture, fixtures, equipment, and opening supplies
- Pre-opening marketing and labor costs
- A six-month operating capital cash reserve

The sum of these constitutes the total cost of the project for purposes of securing financing.

With this information, the ten-year operating pro forma budget is updated to reflect actual costs. It's now time to go to the money markets for construction financing. The terms and conditions of a construction loan can vary widely depending on the individual lender. Important terms that can affect the cost of the loan include:

- Personal guarantees by developers and/or equity partners/investors
- Loan origination fees
- Interest rate
- Required loan-to-value ratio
- Terms of repayment
- A requirement that interest/taxes be held in reserve
- Required debt service coverage ratios
- Length of the construction loan; length and costs of extensions

These are only a few of the considerations that must be analyzed when selecting a lender. The developer, on behalf of the owning entity, then approaches a number of lending institutions. The lending institutions analyze the deal and offer a proposed term sheet that answers all of the borrowers' questions. This allows the borrowers to select the lending institution with which they wish to work. The lender then commissions an appraisal of the project by an independent appraisal company such as Hospitality Valuation Services (HVS). Based on the appraisal, the lender issues a loan commitment for the project that usually offers up to 60 percent of the project cost. The balance must be raised as equity from investors.

► RAISING THE EQUITY INVESTMENT FUNDS

With the bank committed to about 60 percent of the cost, the remaining 40 percent must be raised in equity commitments by investors. To pursue these, the developer prepares an offering solicitation document that meets current securities and exchange law. The nature of this document depends on the type of business entity that was formed. For limited partnerships or limited liability companies, a private placement offering circular and project description is prepared. For S or C corporations, stock offerings are prepared for sale consistent with applicable federal and state securities laws.

The developer now contacts money sources that have risk capital available to invest. These can include:

- Individual investors
- Private asset managers
- Opportunity fund managers
- Venture capital fund managers

These potential investment sources are offered the opportunity to invest in the hotel. Based on their study and evaluation of the reports, documents, and studies detailed above, they decide whether or not to offer funding to the developer.

Once the loan is secured, the equity raised, and the building permit issued by the city, the land purchase option is exercised and the purchase is completed. Then the 12–16-month construction process begins. If the architect's plans work as intended, if the general contractor has no problems with subcontractors, unions, or permits, if all the furnishings, fixtures, and equipment arrive on time, if the weather cooperates, and if the employment market is such that human resources are sufficient to open a hotel, then congratulations! The hotel will open on time.

► SELECTING THE MANAGEMENT COMPANY

Often even before the construction activity commences, the owning entity selects an appropriate management company to manage the pre-opening, marketing and sales, selection and training of the opening staff, preparation of the operating budget, and day-to-day operations once the hotel is opened. Management companies charge 3–5 percent of revenue for this service. In recent years, management companies have charged 3–4 percent of revenue and 2–3 percent of gross operating profit so they can be measured and evaluated on both sales and profitability.

The franchise company may offer to provide management services to franchisees. Marriott International, Inc., for example, manages about 50 percent of all hotels that carry the Marriott flag under 20-year contracts. Independent management companies manage the remaining hotels under long-term management contracts of up to ten years' duration, often with several five-year renewal options.

► CONCLUSION

This is a largely linear explanation of the complicated process that a developer goes through in order to create a hotel. It has been described in a step-by-step process, but in reality, many of the steps are carried out concurrently to save time (and money). Nevertheless, the hotel development process takes about three years from original conception to first guest. It is important to remember that during the initial stages of the process, the developer can have as much as $1 million (U.S.) or more at risk in the process before a final go/no-go decision is reached. Only after the project is approved and all financing is in place can the developer start to recover up-front costs and collect development fees.

Hotel development with its component parts of hotel feasibility studies, hotel appraisal, hotel real estate finance, and hotel management are all among the career opportunities available to hotel and restaurant administration graduates.

► PUTTING IT ALL TOGETHER—THE STORY OF AN EXTENDED-STAY HOTEL DEVELOPMENT PROJECT

The City Development Commission in a Pacific Northwest community purchased a 1.55-acre parcel of riverfront land in the downtown area. The land was previously contaminated with industrial pollutants that made the parcel unsafe for habitation and construction. The City Development Commission used state, local, and federal grants to have the land decontaminated, created a master plan for the area, and then offered the parcel for sale and development.

The City Development Commission issued a request for proposal (RFP) that outlined the asking price of $2,076,240 ($30/sq. ft.) for the land and the design requirements set down by the Commission for a building that would fit the intended look and feel of

the area. The RFP was sent to many major hotel companies and commercial real estate brokers, asking prospective buyers to submit a purchase price bid along with a statement of the buyer's development history and ability to develop a hotel of the type envisioned by the Commission. It listed a closing date by which all bids had to be submitted.

An area commercial real estate broker contacted a hotel development and management company with a long history of developing and managing extended-stay hotels in the Pacific Northwest, including a property located in a similar setting to that being offered for sale. The commercial realtor offered to represent the developer in negotiations with the City Development Commission, which would be paying the real estate commission on the sale. An agreement was reached with the commercial real estate broker to represent the buyer to the seller, and the developer went to work in preparing a proposal.

The developer conducted a feasibility study to see all of the conditions in the marketplace that would be encouraging or discouraging to this development project. Studies were conducted to estimate how many room-nights were being sold within a five-mile radius, how many extended-stay room-nights were available in the market, how many hotel rooms existed, and how many were being planned over the following five years. From this, the developer was able to estimate the number of extended-stay room-nights available needed to produce an 82 percent occupancy with an average daily room rate of $141 when the hotel achieved stabilization three years after opening. That provided the basis for a ten-year revenue estimate.

The developer proposed a nine-floor, 258-suite extended-stay hotel with an indoor pool, spa, and exercise facility, a guest laundry, offices, meeting facilities, and a three-floor parking garage with parking for 193 automobiles, all at a total cost of $38 million, or $147,286 per suite.

The $38 million construction budget was broken down as follows:

Land	6.0%
Construction	66.0%
Office Equipment	1.4%
Furniture, Fixtures, Equipment	7.4%
Architecture/Engineering	2.8%
Permits/Fees/Environmental	2.8%
Appraisal/Legal/Tax/Insurance	1.3%
Pre-Opening Expenses	1.3%
Construction Loan Fee	1.1%
Developer Fee	2.8%
Construction Interest	2.8%
Working Capital	2.1%
Contingency	2.2%
Total	100%

The opening date for the hotel was projected at 27 months from the date of proposal acceptance.

The City Development Commission awarded the project to the developer, and work began.

First, an ownership limited liability company (LLC) was formed as the ownership entity that would hold title to the hotel.

The LLC, in turn, entered into a development and construction management agreement with the development company to manage the arrangements for financing and construction of the hotel.

The developer, as agent for the ownership LLC, also entered into a hotel management contract with a management company to manage the pre-opening marketing, pre-opening hiring and training, and the day-to-day operation of the hotel once it was opened. The arrangements called for the management company to be paid 3 percent of revenue and 2 percent of the net operating income for management services.

The ownership LLC then contacted a major hotel company and applied for a franchise to allow the development and operation of an extended-stay hotel. A 20-year franchise was granted with a fee of $400 per suite or, $102,800. This was to be followed by a 5 percent royalty and a 3 percent advertising fee once the hotel was open and operating.

The developer, acting as agent for the owner, prepared a private placement memorandum document seeking investments from accredited investors. These investors were primarily defined as people with a net worth of $1 million, or those with an income in excess of $200,000 over the previous two years and expecting an income in excess of $200,000 in the current year. (*Note:* Additional entities may also be defined as accredited investors by the Securities and Exchange Commission.)

The private placement memorandum offered $100,000 units of ownership to accredited investors, guaranteeing a 9 percent priority return on the investment and a combined 50 percent ownership in the hotel. A group of initial investors retained the other 50 percent in exchange for putting the project together. This effort was successful in raising 40 percent of the total cost of the hotel in anticipation that a lender would provide the remaining 60 percent in the form of a construction loan. In addition to the priority return, investors could expect to participate in any future capital gain realized should the hotel be sold.

The development company, continuing to function as agent for the owner, then sought a commercial bank to provide three-year construction financing for the project.

As $22,800,000, or 60 percent, of the $38 million development cost was to be borrowed, only major banks were considered as prospective lenders. The size of the construction loan was above the lending limits of most small regional banks. After a preconstruction appraisal by a third-party appraisal firm chosen by the lender confirmed the value at $38 million upon completion of construction, and for an origination fee of $400,000, a three-year construction loan was secured. The terms allowed the developer, as agent for the owner, to draw down the loan every 30 days after providing proof that funds had been properly disbursed in the construction process. The loan documents set an interest rate and also required that the ownership LLC seek a permanent mortgage prior to the three-year expiration date on the construction loan.

The development company then negotiated with and selected a general contractor with significant hotel construction experience who acted on behalf of the developer, as agent for the owner. The general contractor then selected design-build subcontractors and an interior designer to select colors, fabrics, furniture, fixtures, and equipment to meet the hotel franchise design requirements.

Building permits were applied for, and the building design was presented to the City Development Commission for its approval, along with other groups with a stake in the appearance of the finished building in relation to the area and neighborhood. With all of these approvals in place, construction commenced, and the hotel opened two years later.

▶ POSTSCRIPT

Three years after the hotel opened, the ownership LLC had the obligation to secure permanent financing on the hotel to replace the construction loan. The September 11, 2001, terrorist attacks on the World Trade Center and the Pentagon slowed travel throughout the United States. As a result, the hotel did not achieve the projected occupancy or average daily rate during the three-year construction loan period. An appraisal that was primarily based on the hotel's trailing 12-month net operating income produced a value about $2 million below the original construction cost. The bank that had provided the construction loan notified the owners that they did not wish to provide permanent financing under these circumstances. The owners were forced to conduct a search for a new mortgage bank. They were able to find a mortgage, but only after buying down the loan by $2 million to bring the loan-to-value ratio back to 40 percent equity and a loan at 60 percent of the appraised. This illustrates the risk that developers face when entering into a hotel project.

However, as hotel values historically peak and decline on about a ten-year cycle, the owners look forward to the option of selling the hotel on the next peak, which will allow them to capture the original projected return through capital appreciation. Hotel development and ownership is a high-risk, high-reward enterprise.

1.3 HOW WELL DOES THE BRANDED DISTRIBUTION COMPANY ALLOW INDEPENDENT HOTELS TO COMPETE WITH THE CHAINS?

Peter Cass

Dramatic changes have affected the hotel industry over the past 30 years. These changes have had a disproportionately high bearing on the independent hotel owner, who, in the face of increasing pressure from large, well-funded chains, struggles to maintain independence and to compete on the basis of distinctive hospitality and character.

Several organizations provide independent hotels and resorts with reservations and sales services. As competition has evolved and intensified, some of these organizations have modified their structure and enhanced their services to meet the changing needs of independent hotels and competitive market dynamics. Today, independent hotels may choose from among more than 20 such organizations delivering varying degrees of competitive advantage and ownership independence.

► A NEW MARKET MODEL

In the new millennium, the face of the global hospitality market continues to change at a rate never before seen. Four factors contribute to this rapidly changing environment:

- *The broadening and diversification of the global consumer market.* Both the demographic and psychographic characteristics of the global consumer market are growing and changing radically.

- *The rapid advancement and availability of technology.* This includes internal hotel operating systems, revenue management, direct-to-consumer communications and booking technology (Internet), marketing technology (customer databases), and telecommunications and automated sales systems that enable central sales offices to become revenue producers.

- *The growth and importance of global brands.* Recognized brand names and brand attributes are important in reaching diverse customer segments and in creating customer loyalty.

- *Consolidation of multiple brands under a single global management.* The management and leveraging of multiple brands use similar technology platforms and shared sales and marketing infrastructures to consolidate and direct consumer demand.

Some established ways of doing business—long-term, high-fee management contracts and franchises, a focus on traditional distribution channels, and traditional hospitality industry marketing techniques—are no longer effective in the new consumer-focused market. More and more hospitality marketing budgets are being directed toward technology-enabled customer booking and communication; this shift away from traditional hospitality marketing techniques is expected to evolve over several years and involve millions of U.S. dollars in telecommunication, e-commerce, data warehousing, and one-to-one marketing investment. The independent hotel or resort and many small branded management companies may not be able to fund this requirement.

However, this shift will not affect all independent hotels and resorts simultaneously. The first wave of change will hit the global business and city hotel market. This is primarily because of brand competition and the fact that the business travel distribution network is more structured and driven by multinational corporations desiring lower and more predictable costs. The second wave will affect the leisure market, and the changes could follow quickly. Leisure travel content, including packaging on the Internet, will increase rapidly as the presently fragmented leisure travel distribution network becomes more unified and efficient through consolidation.

The emergence of e-commerce modes in the hospitality industry is not eliminating the intermediary and empowering the individual property, as once thought; instead, it is creating new, more powerful intermediaries. Some of these evolve from the hospitality industry, while others are opportunistic e-commerce companies.

► MANAGEMENT COMPANIES AND FRANCHISES

In the 1970s, hotel chains continued to evolve as the need for capital to invest in additional properties restricted growth opportunities. This pressure bolstered the proliferation of the *management contract,* whereby the chain offers the hotel owner the rights to use its brand name and established facility and service standards as well as trained operations management and reservation and marketing services—for a significant fee, usually a percentage of gross sales. The pressure to grow also fostered the development of the franchise concept and franchise system in North America. The franchise differs from the management contract in that the owner is responsible for operations, including meeting the franchise standards.

The growth of management and franchise contracts has been remarkable, and today, according to a recent study, 75 percent of the hotel rooms in North America are covered by some form of branded franchise or professional management agreement (Travel Research International, 1999).

These new business structures continued to threaten the traditional independent owner by accelerating the growth of the chains' share of the lodging market. In response, the marketing/referral organizations formed in the 1960s began to offer a wider range of services. While these additional offerings leveraged linkages to the global distribution systems and led to strong relationships with travel agents, the consumer was largely ignored, and the organizations did little to generate consumer brand awareness.

In the United States, strong consumer branded operators are attracting increasing amounts of capital to fund their growth at the expense of unbranded operators (PricewaterhouseCoopers, 2000).

► BRAND DEVELOPMENT

As the consumer market became more diverse and the hospitality product more segmented, branding became increasingly important. By the late 1980s, without a recognized brand affiliation or a close relationship with the lending community, owners/developers found it difficult to obtain permanent financing on a new hotel or resort. Lenders, believing that an established brand provided greater economies of scale and established infrastructure, opted for the lower-risk alternative. In this brand-driven environment, the independent hotels' distinctive style and character became a competitive advantage, but only if they were able to meet recognized standards. As a result, the need for independent hotels to be associated with a clearly defined, trusted brand became more critical than ever.

In the late 1990s, independent hotels, particularly those in Europe, began to face the daunting costs of upgrading their technological infrastructure and facilities to accommodate changing consumer needs. Such upgrades as new property management systems, high-speed Internet access, two-line phones, in-room faxes, and leisure and health facilities became critical to maintaining competitiveness. When coupled with ever-increasing costs of consumer marketing, these costs put unprecedented strains on independent hotels' finances. As a result, these hotels became increasingly focused on leveraging greater returns from their reservation affiliation.

▶ RESERVATION AFFILIATIONS—A CHALLENGE TO EFFECTIVENESS

The relationship of independent hotels and resorts to reservation affiliations has been long and generally successful. These relationships operated best in a market environment that was stable, somewhat homogeneous in terms of demographic market segmentation, and where travel influencers played a dominant role in transient business, group, and leisure travel. Reservation affiliations are most effective in regional hospitality markets that do not have multiple brand competition and when the goals and objectives of the reservation organization are in alignment with the goals of the independent hotel owners. A contributing element to the attractiveness of reservation affiliations has always been the networking and camaraderie opportunities for the professional management at independent hotels.

Reservation affiliations focus on traditional channels of distribution. Access to the Global Distribution Systems (GDS) is no longer a competitive advantage; the GDS is a universal pipeline. The new competitive playing field is proprietary distribution channels leveraged by consumer segmentation, e-commerce technology and partners, and innovative customer management programs.

In the new technology-driven and consumer-empowered global market, the strength and effectiveness of reservation affiliations are challenged by new market and operating imperatives. The cost to compete against chains will grow exponentially. As competition intensifies, it is probable that local and regional market share at independent hotels and resorts will be drawn off by local and regional licensees of strong global brands. Independent hotels, therefore, need to draw more national and international business to fill occupancy gaps. This requirement runs counter to the established business model and capabilities of reservation affiliations.

The average room-night contribution of reservations companies to affiliated independent hotels is less than 5 percent of available rooms (Preferred Research).

At least four emerging factors are challenging the effectiveness of traditional reservation organizations:

1. The growing demographic and psychographic complexity of the global consumer market requires significant new expertise and resources in the area of segmentation and analysis.

2. The emergence of consumer direct-booking Internet technology requires significant new and ongoing investment.

3. The new marketplace requires innovative global brand management together with resources to establish and maintain a brand in the face of intense competition. To be competitive, a brand must attract new development and must therefore be strong enough to convince lenders to commit to permanent financing. Brand management also includes loyalty program management and the development of regional and global partners to strengthen and extend the effectiveness of the brand.

4. The corporate objectives and governance policies of traditional reservation organizations are influenced by the need to grow and meet shareholder profit requirements. These goals for growth can be at odds with the goals and expectations of independent hotel and resort members.

The traditional reservation affiliations must change not only their focus but also their structure if they want to succeed in this new competitive world.

The traditional reservation organization must be prepared to respond to competitive challenges by expanding resources and skills necessary to increase average room-night contribution to affiliated independent hotels to 15 percent—an average growth per member hotel of at least 200 percent over present performance levels (Preferred Research).

In response to this competitive environment and the need for more cooperative and focused business relationships, a new hospitality business structure is evolving for all scales of hotels: the branded distribution company.

► CHARACTERISTICS OF A BRANDED DISTRIBUTION COMPANY

The ideal branded distribution organization is a conventional equity company with ownership shared (in some cases) by the individual hotel owners, who have direct input into the corporation through an elected board of directors. This ownership structure creates a true operating partnership and a sharing of energies toward the common goal of creating value through increased brand awareness and room sales. Corporate profits must be adequate to maintain technical and managerial leadership and to support the shareholders' investment.

Unlike a reservations and representation company, a branded distribution corporation owns and builds a branded distribution network asset that, in turn, provides services as set out in the diagram below. The sole focus is performance for the affiliated independent hotels and resorts.

Joining such an organization is appropriate for independently owned and managed hotels and resorts that want to keep owner control but require effective and low-cost

Table 1.1 Hospitality Structures and Corresponding Brands

Types of Business Structure	Representation Firms (Group Meetings Only)	Reservation Services Only	Reservation/ Sales Affiliations	Branded Distribution Companies	Flagged and Franchise Management Companies
General Attributes	• Primarily Trade-Focused • Primary Reservation Technology • Disparate range of abilities in: —Management Expertise and Depth —Marketing, Sales, and Reservation Support			• Consumer & Trade-Focused • Performance Focused • Brand Management • Quality Standards and Assurance • Multiple Technologies • Integrated Marketing and Technology Solutions • Customer Recognition and Loyalty Programs • Full-Service Provider —Purchasing, Technology —Recruitment, Training —Consultative & Design Services • Management Expertise and Depth	
Examples of Organizations, Brands, and Management Companies	ALHI David Green Helms Briscoe Hinton/Grusich Krisam	Utell Flag Int'l Lexington Pegasus/ Rezsolutions Supranational TRUST	Concorde Golden Tulip Historic Hotels Leading Hotels of the World Relais and Chateaux Small Luxury Hotels Sterling SRS Hotels Steigenberger	Preferred Hotels and Resorts Worldwide (for profit) Best Western (not for profit) Summit	Accor brands Bass brands Carlson brands Cendant brands Choice brands Four Seasons Hilton brands Hyatt Mandarin Marriott brands Starwood brands Wyndham
Relationship of Hotel Owner to Structure	Client	Client	Member (some are Owners)	Member-Owner	Licensee
Owner Control	High	High	High	High	Low
Room-Night Production	Low	Low	Low-Medium	High	High
Consumer Focus	Low	Low	Low	High	High
Overall Fees	Low	Low	Low	Low	High

distribution, global consumer brand awareness, and group purchasing benefits without the encumbrances and costs of a traditional hotel chain franchise or management contract. Above all, it promises the independent hotel awareness of, and access to, their target consumer and rapidly emerging technology through cooperative ownership.

Table 1.1 shows a summary of the key characteristics of the various marketing business structures and suggests examples of corresponding brands.

▶ THE BENEFITS OF A BRANDED DISTRIBUTION COMPANY

This new business structure is attractive from an owner's or a developer's standpoint for a number of reasons, including:

- **Costs:** First, it requires less up-front cash; second, ongoing fees and reservation commissions are significantly lower than with either a pure franchise or management agreement. For example, a 9 or 10 percent franchise fee in many cases equals 50 percent of gross profits.

- **Contract terms:** The terms are typically shorter, easier to negotiate, and allow for substantial owner control over the operation, style, and character of the hotel. As a result, conflicts can be avoided, and the branded distribution contract can be completed and signed in as few as 45 days.

- **Marketing:** It frees hotel management from the daunting and increasingly expensive task of acquiring profitable new customers and allows them to focus their attention and operating skills on the de-

livery of an exceptional hospitality experience.

- **Common objectives:** Both the owner and the branded distribution company enter into the agreement with the same primary objective: revenue. The branded distribution company receives no revenue if it does not deliver to the hotel or resort. This shared goal strengthens and energizes the relationship between the two partners.

From a branded distribution company's standpoint, this structure allows the brand to expand faster because capital is not used to subsidize additional construction or to support an older business model. Instead, funds are used to build and maintain an up-to-date global distribution network and infrastructure composed of telecommunications, e-commerce functions, reservations software, data warehousing capability, and sales and marketing. The efficiency of the operation is assured by a focus that is almost entirely on the most important part of this business relationship—the generation of brand awareness and measurable room-night revenue for each affiliated hotel or resort.

Unlike hard flags, which focus primarily on hotel operations and asset management such as the Marriott or the Westin, and reservation affiliations, which focus on professional camaraderie and traditional distribution channels such as the Best Western, the branded distribution company is primarily market-focused; its full attention is on customer and travel influencer communication, relationship technology, and revenue streams. (*Note:* Travel influencers are the intermediaries between consumers and the travel product and include travel agents, etc.)

In contrast, asset management, profitability, and operating efficiency are the major concerns of management companies, which tend to be public companies with stockholder expectations that must be met. It is often the case that strategic asset management concerns conflict with day-to-day tactical operating needs. This is evident in Marriott's recent move to separate its ownership and operating divisions, to the benefit of both.

The same conflict can arise between the independent owners of a hotel property, who are focused on real estate concerns, and the management company they hire. Such misunderstandings can sour what should be a mutually supportive relationship. The fact that management contract fees are charged and collected, even when the cash flow is negative, does not create owner confidence in the partner. A franchise relationship can cause a similar conflict and put a financial and operating burden on an owner.

In contrast, participation of independent owner/operators as shareholders in a branded distribution company enables them to move beyond these concerns and focus on their operation and the consumer—the source of their revenue and the basis of their success.

► ARE THERE ANY DRAWBACKS TO A BRANDED DISTRIBUTION COMPANY?

The owners of property within a branded distribution company must relinquish a minimal amount of control and decision making, mainly in the areas of branding and quality assurance. In certain cases, member properties may have to adopt and maintain specific quality standards. In addition, they may also be required to demonstrate their affiliation with the branded distribution company through using its logo on marketing materials as well as participating in e-commerce and inventory management initiatives.

However, these drawbacks can actually enhance a hotel's operations and market positioning while allowing the hotel to maintain independent ownership and management.

► ENSURING COMPETITIVE ADVANTAGE

Independent hotels face significant risk in today's marketplace. Given the advances in technology and the profitability pressures put upon chain hotels by shareholders, competition for customers is intensifying. Keeping in step with competitive chain hotels presents a significant challenge to independent owners. To address this, they currently have several options outside of the branded distribution company, including representation firms, reservations services, flagged chains, and franchise management companies. However, given the economic, societal, and technological trends that are dramatically changing the hospitality industry, several of which are analyzed in this book, many of these old-economy options can offer only short-term solutions to long-term competitive pressures.

A branded distribution company has an inherent advantage going into this new competitive arena. Its sole focus is on customer acquisition and management, achieved through the development of new technologies. This competitive advantage extends to the independent hotel aligned with a branded distribution company. By providing the independent owner with a global brand and the technology and expertise to acquire profitable new customers, the branded distribution company enables the hotel management to focus its attention on the delivery of exceptional service and profits to the owners. This separation of skills, expertise, resources, and operating cultures in a cooperative business relationship provides a model and formula for success.

Independent hotels and resorts that align themselves with a branded distribution company will not only continue to operate profitably in the new global marketplace, but will also flourish.

1.4 THE ART AND SCIENCE OF OPENING A HOTEL

Tom Dupar

If you ever have the chance to be involved with opening a hotel, jump at the opportunity. Opening a hotel is one of the most rewarding jobs in the hospitality industry despite its frustrating and exhausting aspects.

Walk into any hotel, anywhere, and look around. Everything you see, hear, and feel, every detail, involved many people and countless decisions. I have been an operations project manager (OPM) since 1989 and have opened over 40 three-, four- and five-star hotels around the world. From Guam to Malta, Berlin to St. Louis, each project has been unique, each project has been the same, and each has been professionally rewarding.

The OPM is the third person hired, after the general manager and the director of marketing. The role of an OPM is to pull together the visions of the architect, interior designer, owner, operator, and others. When these visions are successfully melded, the hotel guest is satisfied, the owner makes money, and the architect and interior designer can add the project to their list of successful accomplishments.

The OPM oversees the following aspects of a project:

- Reviewing blueprints and specifications for the entire building
- Assisting with the creation of a model room
- Developing the pre-opening staff plan
- Developing and managing the pre-opening budget
- Developing the operational supplies and equipment budget (OS&E)
- Overseeing the purchasing, warehousing, delivery, and installation of the OS&E
- Developing the interior graphics package
- Coordinating the installation of third-party vendors

▶ BLUEPRINTS

The OPM's responsibilities start with the architectural blueprints. The focus is to ensure a good flow for guests, staff, and goods.

The bellperson bag storage room should be located between the porte cochere (entry) and the elevators and contain 1 square foot of space for each guest room.

If valet parking is offered, ensure that a convenient cashier's station is located near the porte cochere. Arrange for a key rack to hold the keys for each valet parking stall.

Given a 10,000-square-foot ballroom, the catering department can sell functions for 800+ for dinner. This requires 80 6-foot round tables, 800 chairs, a dais for the head table, a dance floor, and staging for the band. If sold for a 700-guest all-day meeting, the classroom setup requires 1,400 linear feet of narrow tables and 700 chairs. A short theater meeting setup for 1,000 requires 1,000 chairs, a podium, staging, and audio visual equipment. The same space accommodates a cocktail reception for 1,400 guests; this requires cocktail tables, portable bars, buffet stations, and so on. This all boils down to ensuring ample storage space for equipment not being used—at least 1,500 square feet.

Moving goods from the back of the house to the front requires careful planning to ensure that precious labor dollars are used efficiently. Are the rollaway beds, cribs, and high chairs stored near an elevator for quick delivery? The housekeeper closets should be centrally located on guest room floors to cut down on access time. A 6-foot, 2-cubic-yard garbage cart will not work if the elevator is only 5 feet deep.

If ice machines are offered for guest self-service, they must produce an ample supply (10 pounds per room per 24-hour period) for the number of guest rooms on that floor or floors. The ice machine room requires the proper utilities, including electricity, plumbing, lighting, and HVAC. Don't forget the sign on the outside of the room, which must meet ADA standards!

▶ MODEL ROOM

Build a typical king and double/double guest room close to the site so you can review every single item in them. Are ample electrical and telecom outlets placed exactly where the TV, lamps, clock radio, mini-bar, coffeemaker, hair dryer, Internet access, and telephones are located so the cords are hidden? Are spare outlets offered for guest use (computer, iron, etc.)? Is the closet rod hung so the ironing board organizer and iron board fit in the closet? Is the thermostat location convenient for guest access?

Are the case goods (dresser, nightstands, headboards, chairs, etc.), designed for commercial heavy-duty use? Will they hold up to abusive use? Do they have sharp corners that will snag guest clothing? Does the bedskirt hang ½ inch off the floor? Do the bedside lamps give off enough lumens so guests can read in bed? Does the room meet or exceed every operator brand standard?

These model rooms serve as sales tools for the sales and marketing staff selling group rooms up to three years before opening.

▶ PRE-OPENING STAFF PLAN

The pre-opening staffing begins with an organizational chart with all positions. Once the titles and staff counts by position are finalized, then spreadsheets are created to include the position titles, start dates, pay rates, bonus, transfer allowances, and number of full-time equivalents (FTEs) for all positions.

The pre-opening staff plan is a comprehensive document that states who is hired, when they start, how much they are paid, and whether or not they are allocated a relocation allowance and benefit costs. Each of these pieces is used to build the pre-opening staff plan budget. If hiring has already begun and the opening date changes, the budget must be amended. Hiring a position that does not conform to the plan, such as bringing on a renowned chef one month earlier than planned, also requires the budget be modified.

▶ PRE-OPENING BUDGET

The OPM develops and manages the pre-opening budget. This budget typically consists of three major categories; labor cost (40 percent), sales and marketing efforts (40 percent), and miscellaneous (20 percent).

The labor cost is taken directly from the pre-opening staff plan.

Sales and marketing activities comprise advertising, collateral, public relations, and travel to see clients.

Rounding out the budget are all of the miscellaneous items. These include office space rental before moving into the hotel, utilities (power, water, Internet, and telephone), human resources recruitment (ads, headhunters, drug testing, etc.), training materials, association dues, and licenses and permits (business, liquor, sales tax collection, etc.).

If the hotel opening date is delayed for any reason, the pre-opening budget is affected. Additional costs include labor, office rent, utilities, and marketing efforts. If the opening date changes within three weeks of the original plan, major costs are encountered, as most of the staff is already hired.

▶ OPERATIONAL SUPPLIES AND EQUIPMENT (OS&E)

The largest and most complex aspect of the OPM's responsibility is specifying, quantifying, and budgeting for the operational supplies and equipment (OS&E) list. This budget typically pencils out to $8,000 to $10,000 per guest room for a typical four-star property. The list of goods typically exceeds 2,500 line items. Add a little more for a full-service resort; deduct a little for an in-city business hotel.

The OS&E comprises all of the items that are not nailed down, with the exception of the furniture, fixtures, and equipment (FF&E). The FF&E is typically specified and ordered by the interior designer.

Typical guest room items include bedding (frames, box springs, mattresses, mattress pads, sheets, pillows, pillowcases, towels, etc.), clock radios, hangers, laundry bags, laundry tickets, iron, ironing board, ironing board organizer, luggage rack, guest amenities (soap, shampoo, lotion, etc.), hair dryer, shower curtains, and shower curtain hooks.

Housekeeping equipment includes vacuums (guest room and wide-area units), carpet shampooers, carpet extractors, housekeeper carts, laundry bins, garbage trucks, valet delivery carts, and shelving, to name a few of many items. Housekeeping must also keep an inventory of guest request items including humidifiers, dehumidifiers, cribs, high chairs, rollaway beds, bedboards, spare pillows, towels, amenities, refrigerators, laundry soap, and so on.

Food and beverage front-of-the-house items include flatware (knives, forks, and spoons), hollowware (serving trays, serving utensils, chafing dishes, sugar bowls and sauce boats, punch bowls), glassware, table linen, napkins, skirting, salt and pepper shakers, china, plate covers, espresso machines, menu covers and the list goes on and on.

Banquet items include all of the above plus tables, chairs, staging, staging steps and railings, dance floors, carts, carving boards, ice carving trays, flags, podiums, portable bars, ice bins, pianos, and tray jack stands.

The largest purchase order—typically over 100 pages long—is for a full-service kitchen and includes everything a chef needs to produce the menus being sold at the hotel. Every utensil, pot, pan, dish, and glass rack, warewashing chemicals, mops and buckets, specialty items (roller-docker, anyone?) must be reviewed by the chef, purchased, and delivered the day before the chef starts burning in the kitchen.

On the hotel administration side, the OPM specifies the office desks, chairs, cork and dry-erase boards, conference tables, filing cabinets, safes, bullet-proof window for the general cashier's office, fax machines, copiers, currency and coin trays, and a set of flags for the exterior flagpoles.

One of the largest and most complicated purchase orders is for staff uniforms. My recent Kona, Hawaii, project uniform purchase order was 68 pages long. The invoices covered over 100 pages!

Before quantifying uniform needs, many questions are asked. Do we need summer and winter uniforms? Will the uniforms be laundered by the hotel or the hotel associates? How many extra servers are needed for a capacity dinner function in the ballrooms? Is the intent to have a large percentage of part-time staff? Which uniforms need custom embroidery (restaurants, culinary, engineering, etc.)? What percentage of spare uniforms are needed in reserve?

Once these questions are answered, then the selection process begins. Operations and the interior designer review the look and feel the options available. Each position (housekeeper, bellperson, etc.) or similar position (front desk clerk/concierge) has different requirements. Housekeepers and bellpersons require durable uniforms that breathe and can handle lots of bending and stretching. The uniforms of the culinary and engineering staffs are often stained and must hold up to numerous launderings.

The uniform order is placed 90 to 120 days *before the first uniformed staff is hired.* To quantify the sizes required, a typical bell chart sizing curve is used for the particular country or region of the hotel. The uniforms are delivered and sorted prior to the individual fitting process. On the line staff's second day on the job, each individual is measured for uniforms. An army of seamstresses then takes the pants, jackets, and dresses and alters each piece for each associate. The fitted uniforms are issued a few days before opening day.

► PURCHASING, WAREHOUSING, DELIVERY, AND INSTALLATION OF THE OS&E

In an ideal process, the 500 purchase orders are issued beginning six months prior to opening. Each order is tracked to ensure it is delivered to the proper location on the desired date. Most goods are delivered to a local warehouse and pulled for delivery to the site as the general contractor completes construction and turns over areas. Some goods are shipped directly to the site to eliminate double handling. These large orders include bed sets (21 40-foot shipping containers for the Kona project), televisions (3 containers), banquet chairs (2 containers), banquet tables (3 containers), and guest room safes (1 container). The linen order for guest rooms and F&B are shipped to an off-site laundry facility for initial washing.

Once the goods are on site, they are typically staged in the largest ballroom for unpacking and distribution. The unpacking process requires a plethora of workers. For example, each clock radio must be unpacked, the electrical twist tie removed, the 9-volt battery installed, and the time set. Then the unit is placed in a guest room on the nightstand. For the 525-room Kona project, this task required two people for three eight-hour days. Once they completed this task, they spent the next five working days installing the 7,000+ shower curtain hooks, 525 shower curtains, and 525 shower liners. Then they unboxed 30,000 glasses and placed them in glass racks for washing. These kinds of tasks must be carried out for each of the 2,500 line items.

Once receiving and distribution begins on site, another element comes to the forefront: garbage. During the five-week Kona installation process, over 3 tons of packing material were generated *every day!* Making friends with the local waste-hauling service is a priority.

▶ INTERIOR GRAPHICS PACKAGE

The project manager reviews the interior graphics package for errors and omissions. This package includes every sign needed to direct guests and staff in front and back of the house areas. The recent Kona project included 1,600 signs, 98 percent of which were one of a kind. The text must be correct, the directional arrows must point the correct way, and most are required to include raised Braille text, per the ADA.

The OPM works with the marketing department to develop the identity for the unique areas within a property. These include the restaurants, bars, pools, spa, and retail areas. These logos are incorporated into the signage package, collateral (cocktail napkins, menus, check presenters, etc.), and uniforms.

▶ THIRD-PARTY VENDORS

Many third-party vendors must have access to the property prior to opening. The project manager schedules and directs all of these vendors, including the soft-drink vendor (who installs soda guns for the bars and vending machines for the guest floors), the coffee company (which must install and test equipment), the pay-per-view TV vendor (who must connect every television in the building and test the signal strength), the warewashing chemical vendor (who must install and calibrate the dishwashing machines), and the office furniture installer (who must assemble all office equipment). Among the other vendors are those dealing in copier services, postage machines, telephones, fitness center equipment, security systems, and first aid supplies.

These vendors are constantly informed when they can install their equipment based on the general contractor's completion dates. When the construction schedule changes, vendors must be updated so they show up when the area they need access to is ready.

▶ HUMAN RESOURCES

The OPM assists the human resources personnel during the last two months of pre-opening so that they have all of the tools they need to recruit and hire the staff. On average, the HR department interviews at least five applicants for every position. This works out to over 1,000 applicants for a typical 300-room four-star hotel. This process is referred to as the *mass hire.*

The mass hire is typically conducted over a two- or three-day period six weeks before opening. To interview this many job seekers, HR requires office space, reception space for up to 200 at one time, rest rooms, and break rooms for the interviewers. The OPM coordinates all of these details so that the operations team can focus on the recruitment.

Once the offer letters are accepted, all line associates start work about three weeks out. The first few days on the job are dedicated to group training, operational philosophies, code of conduct, and other general policies. On day three, divisional training takes place. In the second week of training, the staff is broken out into departmental or job-specific duties.

Departmental training includes teaching staff to make beds, clean a room, cook every menu item, the most efficient route to each guest room, and what to tell the guest en route to the room.

▶ OPENING DAY

The activity during the last 72 hours before the opening ceremonies is chaotic. This is the time that all hands are on deck. Sixteen-hour days are the norm. Rooms are cleaned. Housekeeping closets are stocked. Liquor and food storerooms are filled. The general contractor completes all small details such as paint touch-ups. Artwork and furnishings are installed in the public areas. Rehearsals are conducted for all aspects of the operation, including serving test meals and cocktails, guest check-ins and check-outs, and even such easy-to-overlook activities as valet parking and vacuuming the pool.

As soon as the general manger cuts the ceremonial ribbon, the OPM knows what kind of job has been done. The next step is to find the next project and do it all again!

1.5 ON-LINE PRICING: AN ANALYSIS OF HOTEL COMPANY PRACTICES

Peter O'Connor

The importance of electronic hotel-distribution routes has grown substantially in recent years. According to statistics quoted in the Horwath Worldwide Hotel Industry Studies, direct reservations fell from approximately 39 percent in 1995 to 33 percent in 1999, with the shift in sales going almost exclusively to electronic channels (O'Connor, 2001, 70–93). While hotels continue to make extensive use of travel-agent-oriented global distribution systems (GDSs), consumer adoption of the Internet as a reliable and secure commerce medium has prompted a change in the way in which hotel rooms are being distributed.

The Internet has dramatically changed the way people communicate, research information, and buy goods and services. Travel products in particular have proven to be suitable for sale on line. The typical Internet user—an affluent, frequent traveler who spends more than the average on leisure and entertainment—is an attractive market for travel suppliers (NFO Plog Research, 2000). Furthermore, from a consumer's perspective purchasing travel products on line has, in many instances, become faster, easier, and more convenient than contacting a travel agent or telephoning a supplier directly. As a result, on-line travel-related revenues are forecast to grow sharply. For example, according to a recent report by Jupiter Media Metrix, on-line travel sales will more than triple in the next five years—from US$18 billion in 2002 to US$64 billion in 2007 (Jupiter Media Metrix, 2001).

Booking volumes are also forecast to climb. The Travel Industry Association of America (TIAA) estimated that by the end of 2002 between 6 percent and 10 percent of all travel reservations would originate on the web (TIAA, 1998). If Jupiter's 2007 prediction comes true, travel will be the biggest selling on-line product, with a volume nearly double that of the current leading product, PC hardware (Forrester Research).

Price is key to selling successfully on line. Studies by Internet analysts Gomez and PhoCusWright, and also a study by TIAA, all identified price as being one of the key motivating factors that encourages consumers to purchase travel on line (Gomez.com, 2000; PhoCuSWright, 2001; TIAA, 2001). For example, the PhoCusWright study found that competitive pricing is the best way to attract customers (Pastore, 2001). When travelers who haven't bought on line were asked what would encourage them to do so, 64 percent said that saving money would make them more interested. No other benefit—whether saving time, getting bonus loyalty-club points, more control, or obtaining better information—came close to this level of response.

► HOTEL PRICING ON THE WEB

Yesawich, Pepperdine, and Brown found in a 2000 study that almost six out of ten leisure travelers now actively seek the "lowest possible price" for travel services (Yesawich, Pepperdine, and Brown, 2000). Similarly, a 2001 Forrester Research study found that 66 percent of all buyers had used an on-line discount in the previous 12 months to buy travel on line (Forrester Research, 2001), and a study by the Joint Hospitality Industry Congress found a real expectation among consumers that Internet prices would be lower than those available in the "bricks and mortar" world (Joint Hospitality Industry Congress, 2000).

Such a perception has developed for several reasons. First, many of the best-known Internet retailers (such as, for example, Amazon.com) initially competed with traditional outlets based, to a large extent, on price. Second, savvy consumers are aware that web-based distribution costs are lower than those of other channels (Nua, 1998). As Jack Geddes, Radisson Hotels Worldwide's managing director, sales and marketing Asia, has pointed out: "Consumers now understand that suppliers are cutting costs through this channel and expect savings to be passed on to them, as well as being rewarded for making the booking themselves" (Muqbil, 1998). Such expectations are being reinforced by the budget-airline sector, which offers substantial discounts for on-line bookings. Companies such as EasyJet, RyanAir, and Buzz estimate that by avoiding telesales and travel agents, they can achieve savings of up to 30 percent—which they pass on to customers in the form of lower fares (Cooke, 2000). Similar or even greater levels of savings can be made by hotel companies, as can be seen from the internal Accor figures in Table 1.2, which show how an 80- to 90-percent savings in transaction charges can be achieved by selling directly to the consumer on line. Finally, many hotels (and airlines) use the web to sell last-minute deals—packages at relatively low prices but with short lead times. While such promotions can help dispose of unsold inventory, they have also resulted in the public's associating rooms sold over the Internet with lower prices.

These factors have combined to make consumers associate on-line booking with good value, which in the consumer's mind translates into low prices. However, in the case of hotel brands' own web sites, industry practice frequently seems to be the opposite of theory. In a 1999 survey, for instance, a colleague and I found that rates obtained from the web site were usually substantially higher than those obtained by contacting the central reservations office (O'Connor and Horan, 1999). That study was limited, however, in that it focused only on direct sales over hotel chains' own branded web sites. Electronic distribution is rapidly evolving for hotels, and a large number of other on-line consumer-focused channels are now available, with most chains using multiple routes to reach the consumer (Castleberry *et al.*, 1998, 19–24).

Table 1.2 Reservation Cost by Distribution Channel

Route	Customer	Transaction Fee					Total Cost
		Traditional travel agent	**GDS**	**Switch**	**CRS**	**Hotel**	
Traditional route	**Customer**	$5.90	$3.20	$0.20	$4.20		$13.50
		Online travel agent	**GDS**	**Switch**	**CRS**	**Hotel**	
Online intermediary route	**Customer**	$3.00	$3.20	$0.20	$4.20		$10.50
Direct online route	**Customer**	**Hotel company website** $1.50				**Hotel**	$1.50

Source: Dresdner Kleinwort Benson/Accor, quoted in *Travel and Tourism Intelligence, The International Hotel Industry: Corporate Strategies and Global Opportunities* (London: Economic Intelligence Unit, 2001).

The availability of numerous points of sale poses some interesting questions. Foremost among these is: Is there consistency between the room availability and prices being offered over each of the channels? Unlike in the physical world, where a potential customer would have to telephone or visit several suppliers, comparison shopping on the web can generally be accomplished relatively quickly. Research has shown that consumers shopping for travel on line almost always check more than one site before purchasing. According to Jupiter Media Metrix (2001), just 10 percent of would-be guests visit only one site to book a hotel room, another 43 percent visit two or three sites, and 22 percent visit four or more sites. Because they check prices in several places, on-line purchasers have become increasingly intolerant of inconsistent information, and may react unfavorably to a firm's disparate rates by booking with the company's competitor. Two related questions, then, are:

1. If rates are not consistent across channels, is any one route consistently cheaper?

2. Is the company's approach to pricing logical from both the consumer's and the hotel's perspective?

In this paper, I seek to answer those questions.

▶ METHODOLOGY AND LIMITATIONS OF THE STUDY

Previous studies of hotels' Internet use have been limited. Murphy *et al.* (1996, 70–82) focused on rating the content of hotel web sites, while Van Hoof and Combrink (1998, 46–54) attempted to measure managers' perceptions of and attitudes toward the Internet. Web-reservations facilities were investigated in detail in the co-authored paper that I mentioned above (O'Connor and Horan, 1999). However, the issue of pricing over several distribution channels does not appear to have been the subject of extensive systematic research to date. The objective of this study, therefore, was to analyze the room rates being offered to consumers over multiple electronic distribution channels.

An exhaustive analysis of the rates being offered by all hotels would be virtually impossible. Those rates are constantly in flux, as hoteliers project occupancy rates and open or close rate classes accordingly (according to yield-management principles). I believe, however, that major international hotel chains' electronic-distribution activities are indicative of industry patterns, because recent research has shown that large companies are most active on the web—perhaps because their size often gives them an advantage in terms of technical expertise and financial resources. As a result, I decided to focus this study on the behavior of the top-50 international hotel brands. While this strategy means that the findings are not representative of the industry as a whole (and, therefore, not generally applicable), it does allow establishment of an accurate benchmark of trends as they currently stand. The companies were chosen based on the ranking of the top-50 hotel brands published in *Hotels* magazine in July 2000. Two of those companies (Disney and Club Med) were removed from the listing because they operate resorts and distribute their rooms largely as part of packages, which means that their products are not directly comparable to the rest of the industry. Furthermore, another three companies neither offered on-line reservations on their own web site nor were they listed on any of the other channels studied. Thus, the results discussed below reflect the findings from the 45 hotel brands for which consistent data could be found.

Five major types of electronic business-to-consumer distribution channels were identified from the literature, and leading examples of each category were selected for inclusion in the study. In addition to a chain's own web site (e.g., www.marriott.com), these comprised channels that draw their data and reservations engine from the GDS (i.e., Expedia and Travelocity); those that are based on the databases and reservation engine of the switch companies (namely, Travelweb); and pure web-based channels with an inventory and reservations database that is maintained on line (i.e., WorldRes). While not collectively exhaustive, these represent the majority of hotel-reservation sites. Omitted from the study were the auction-style web sites, such as Priceline.com, which are not comparable to typical booking approaches.

As another point of comparison, I incorporated voice channels into the study by analyzing the rates offered by the toll-free number to the central reservations service (CRS). Data were collected by repeatedly offering to reserve a standard double room for specified dates in a selected property from each of the brands using each of the distribution channels discussed above. Where the product requested was available on the system, both the number of rates displayed and the lowest rate available were recorded for analysis. To help ensure consistency, I ignored rates not available to the general public (e.g., corporate, military, AARP, and AAA), and analyzed only those rates that could be booked by a "normal" customer. After checking the web sites, I telephoned the hotel company's CRS to request the same booking. In that case, I recorded only the first rate quoted

by the agent, and I did not ask for a lower rate (nor did I record any subsequent offers after I demurred from making a reservation). Although better rates could probably be achieved by haggling, I decided that negotiating would leave no systematic way of consistently determining the lowest rate, depending as it does on the caller's persistence. The above process was repeated for five sets of alternative dates to reduce the possibility of error due to system malfunctions or other exceptional circumstances.

► SUMMARY OF RESEARCH FINDINGS

As can be seen from Table 1.3, each of the major hotel brands uses multiple simultaneous distribution channels. The most commonly available channels were voice (via the company's CRS) and electronic (through the company's corporate web site). The company that did not make a CRS number available was in the economy sector. Offering hotel rooms via the company web site is almost universal, all but one of the brands surveyed offering on-line reservations in this manner. It is interesting to note that this represents a considerable advancement when compared to surveys made only a few years ago, which found that only approximately 50 percent of the major hotel companies provided on-line reservations (O'Connor and Horan; Hensdill, 1998).

As shown in Table 1.3, hotel companies make less use of the other channels investigated. Approximately four-fifths of the major brands used the GDS-based intermediaries Expedia and Travelocity, three-quarters used Travelweb, and barely one-third used World-

Table 1.3 Channels Used by Major Hotel Brands (*n* = 45)

Channel	Number (*n*)	Percentage
Hotel company website	444	97%
Expedia	38	84%
Travelocity.com	35	78%
Travelweb	34	76%
WorldRes	14	31%
Voice (CRS)	44	97%

Res. These findings are not in themselves surprising. Both Expedia and Travelocity draw their data from the GDSs, where the majority of the hotel brands represented in this study (being major hotel companies) can reasonably expect to be represented. Similarly, Travelweb draws its data from THISCO (The Hotel Industry Switching Company), and thus any of the hotel brands that use this as their switch service could be expected to make inventory available for sale via Travelweb.

I found the chains' low usage of WorldRes surprising. With the exception of a company's own web site, using WorldRes has the lowest potential transaction cost and thus would appear to be an attractive channel for use by hotel companies. Examination of its property database reveals a large percentage of independent hotels, bed-and-breakfast inns, and small hotel chains. An unresolved question is why the major brands do not exploit this distribution channel.

► RATES AVAILABLE

Each of the electronic channels offered multiple rates. As can be seen from Table 1.4, each channel presented an average of five rates in response to the request, with more being offered to the customer by Travelocity than by the other channels surveyed.

Presenting a variety of rates to the customer has both positive and negative implications. From a positive perspective, it offers choices to potential customers, allowing them to match their needs with the products being sold. On the other hand, presenting a large number of rates without adequate differentiation between products can confuse customers regarding what they are getting for their money. This is best demonstrated by an example encountered in the study, where a property offered 17 different rates for a particular date on Travelweb, with few (if any) discernible differences in the room descriptions. Clearly such a scenario would be confusing and frustrating for any customer wishing to book that property.

Mean prices. It was difficult to make a general observation about which of the several channels is consistently least expensive on average, although Expedia's rates were marginally lower than those offered by other channels and WorldRes seemed to offer consistently higher rates than did the others (see Table 1.5). Indeed, all things considered, prices across each of the channels were comparable—with the average price for the

Table 1.4 Number of Rates Offered to the Customer

Channel	Mean	Standard Deviation
Hotel company website	4.27	3.6
Expedia	3.66	1.4
Travelocity.com	6.07	3.3
Travelweb	5.62	3.6
WorldRes	4.58	3.8
Voice (CRS)	1.00	—

requested room being in the range of US$163. It was interesting that Expedia's mean rates were lower, because as an on-line travel agency, it has a high distribution cost, and it would be logical to assume that rates offered over this channel would reflect the higher costs. By the same token, since WorldRes's transaction costs are relatively low in comparison with those offered by the other channels surveyed, hotels could potentially offer cheaper rates over this channel. In other words, what I found is that when selling hotel products on line, there does not appear to be a relationship between the cost of using the distribution channel and the rate offered. Illogically, the electronic channels with the highest transaction costs for the hotel seem to regularly offer the best value to the customer.

As will be discussed below, hoteliers need to rethink their current practices and take action if they are to benefit from the increasing market for on-line hotel-room sales.

Segment breakout. The foregoing discussion was based on an overall look at hotel-room sales distribution. If the brands studied are subdivided into classifications based on their targeted market segment, a different picture emerges. As can be seen from Table 1.6, hotels at the low end of the market are far more likely to offer consistent rates across all channels used. While it could be speculated that the reason for this might be that economy properties are more likely to have a single fixed price for their product irrespective of demand, it could also be due to a more consistent pricing strategy on the part of the ho-

Table 1.5 Average Rates Offered to the Customer

Channel	Mean	Standard Deviation
Hotel company website	$159	112
Expedia	$152	116
Travelocity.com	$166	134
Travelweb	$162	115
WorldRes	$181	168
Voice (CRS)	$163	117

Table 1.6 Market Sector Analysis (Lowest Rates)

| Channel | Percentage of cases where a channel offered the lowest rates | | | |
	Economy	Midprice	Luxury	Chi-squared
All rates equal	46%	21%	28%	0.016*
Hotel company website	26%	47%	14%	0.036*
Expedia	14%	11%	41%	0.030*
Travelocity.com	3%	5%	7%	0.750
Travelweb	9%	5%	7%	0.900
WorldRes	0%	0%	0%	—
Voice (CRS)	3%	11%	3%	0.600

*Indicates that the association is significant at the 95-percent confidence level.

tel companies involved when addressing a relatively price-sensitive market. Furthermore it can be seen that consumers at the low ends of the market are far more likely to obtain low rates through direct (company-owned) channels. For economy brands, direct sales over the company's own web site were lowest 26 percent of the time. When coupled with the 46 percent of cases where the same rate is offered irrespective of the channel used, that means that a consumer reserving an economy room will find the cheapest rate on the hotel company's web site nearly three times out of four. With mid-price products, the chain's web site is even more likely to give the best rate, offering the lowest rate nearly half of the time.

The situation is different at the upper end of the market. Luxury-hotel companies' web sites gave the cheapest rate in less than 10 percent of cases. Furthermore, Table 1.7 shows that the company's web site quoted the highest rate in over one-third of cases. Overall, the evidence seems to indicate that if you want to stay in up-market hotels, you should avoid booking on these hotels' web sites if you are searching for good value. Instead, the on-line intermediaries (in particular, Expedia) offer the highest probability of finding the best rate available for high-end properties, with an average savings of 5 percent available by booking through Expedia rather than on the company's own site.

Haggling required. It is also clear from the data that a hotel company's CRS is not the place to obtain the best rates, at least if one takes the first offer as I did for this study. Irrespective of the market segment, there is a higher probability of being quoted the highest rate through this channel, and bookings through this route were almost never the cheapest available. This finding, however, is to a large extent driven by my methodology. Indeed, in many cases, as soon as I indicated that I did not plan to make a booking at the quoted rate, the CRS associate quoted another, lower rate. This anecdotal finding suggests that negotiation might have resulted in lower prices. (This is a longstanding CRS practice; see Lewis and Roan, 1986).

Table 1.7 Market Sector Analysis (Highest Rates)

Channel	Percentage of cases where a channel offered the highest rates			
	Economy	Midprice	Luxury	Chi-squared
All rates equal	46%	21%	28%	0.016*
Hotel company website	14%	16%	34%	0.011*
Expedia	0%	21%	7%	0.017*
Travelocity.com	3%	5%	10%	0.450
Travelweb	0%	0%	0%	—
WorldRes	6%	0%	0%	0.240
Voice (CRS)	31%	37%	21%	0.440

*Indicates that the association is significant at the 95-percent confidence level.

▶ DAWN OF A NEW WAY

From the above discussion, it can be seen that both the range of channels through which hotels can be booked and the complexity of such channels have grown. This study represents a first attempt at documenting hotel companies' pricing practices over electronic routes. The study revealed that the majority of hotel brands now use simultaneous, multiple electronic channels of distribution, making their rooms available to a relatively wide audience. While the use of CRS-based reservations has fallen slightly, there has been a growth in the availability of hotel companies' own web sites, and a vast majority of companies that I studied now make their rooms available for sale in this manner. The differences between this study's findings and earlier published research indicate a major expansion in hotel chains' use of the web as a direct-sales medium, perhaps accompanied by a realization of the web's benefits in comparison with other, more traditional, electronic channels of distribution.

Most companies offer multiple rates to customers over each channel. It is interesting to note, however, the large number of companies that now offer consistent pricing across all channels. Previous research found less than 10 percent of companies had consistent pricing and cited the lack of integration among the various inventory databases used to manage inventory as a possible cause. Yet over one-third of the brands I studied now offer consistent pricing across multiple channels, indicating progress in the industry's management of electronic distribution.

Although no single channel consistently offers the lowest prices, in-depth analysis does reveal a link between pricing and the market being targeted. First, the lowest prices can rarely be obtained from the CRS (absent negotiation), irrespective of market segment. As compared to the first-offered CRS price, a would-be customer can save at least 5 percent by booking over any of the electronic channels I examined. From the data it can be seen that consumers are more likely to find the lowest prices on the hotel chains' own web sites in the economy and mid-price segments than will be found from those companies'

CRS or third-party web sites. So-called up-market hotel brands are, on the other hand, more likely to quote higher prices on their own web site than what they offer on other channels. Economy brands seem to be the only ones in the industry as a whole display-ing a logical on-line pricing strategy (in terms of the relationship between the cost of using a channel and the rates offered there) and also in terms of actively managing their channels of distribution.

Implications. First, it is clear that for those with a taste for upscale products, the hotel brand's own web site is not the place to shop, as better value can be obtained in most cases through other channels. More interesting, however, is the fact that, in general, prices have become more or less equal across many of the channels investigated, and by implica-tion, across many other electronic distribution channels as well. It is well established that time is a valuable commodity in today's soci-ety. Since the number and variety of ways that a consumer can book a hotel room has be-come undeniably manifold, the cost associ-ated with searching through even a small number of the many consumer-focused chan-nels currently available in the marketplace in an attempt to find a low price has increased. Given that this study has found that many of the rates being offered over alternative chan-nels are more or less the same for many ho-tels, customers should reconsider whether all that time and energy searching for the lowest rate is actually worthwhile.

The implications for the hotelier are more pressing. My findings suggest that many hotel chains are not actively managing the room rates being offered in their portfolio of elec-tronic distribution channels. Most companies offer multiple rates on each channel, which, as discussed earlier, can be beneficial as it gives a choice to the customer. Displaying too

many rates, though, can be counterproduc-tive, if the customer becomes overwhelmed. Presenting a small number of tightly defined rates would be the most appropriate solution. However, most companies currently display about five rates in response to a customer in-quiry, with others showing significantly more, usually with little or no apparent product dif-ferentiation. In addition, there appears to be inconsistency in terms of the rates being of-fered over electronic channels. In many cases, no clear or logical pricing strategy is appar-ent. The lowest prices are offered on channels with the highest transaction costs, and vice versa. A small number of companies offer consistent pricing irrespective of the channel being used to make the booking. Informal fol-low up with those companies revealed that they follow this strategy as they believe in the principle of one "correct" price for each cus-tomer. In this way, they do not have to address the issue of customer dissatisfaction as a re-sult of a person's being quoted a lower price for a room on a different channel after having already made a booking. However, such an approach ignores the issue of the cost of pro-cessing a booking over a particular channel. As was discussed earlier, such costs vary greatly depending to a large extent on the number of intermediaries between the sup-plier and the customer. The greater the num-ber of intermediaries, the greater the transaction cost and processing fees—and therefore the greater the distribution cost. This would seem to argue for having high rates on the channels that have high-cost structures and low prices on those with low-cost structures. Coupled with this matter is the fact that customers have become more knowledgeable about and comfortable with e-commerce issues in general, are more aware that distribution costs are lower in the virtual world than the bricks-and-mortar one, and thus increasingly expect to find the cheapest prices over electronic, and particularly direct electronic, routes. Put simply, when they go to a hotel company's web site, they expect to find the best value there. This study has shown that in many cases this is simply not the case, given that luxury hotels in particular tend to offer their highest rates over direct channels—and (ironically) their cheapest rates over the most expensive on-line intermediaries. Informal follow up to the study revealed that this may be due to the proactive approach of the on-line companies in contacting hotel companies on practically a daily basis and encouraging them to reduce their rates in return for better positioning on their search listings. In contrast, the rates on hotel companies' web sites go largely unmanaged, in many cases being set far in advance and not adjusted to reflect changing supply and demand.

Irrespective of its root cause, the behavior of hotel companies is driving Internet shoppers into the arms of the waiting on-line intermediaries, where in addition to consistently low prices, they also find wide product choice. Because of this, it's likely that many hotels are losing potential bookings to competitors as a result of consumers' migration toward the on-line travel sites that offer relatively low rates from many different hotel chains. Instead of being presented with a list of a chain's properties on a company's web site, prospective guests see a much wider variety of options from the on-line intermediary and may be tempted to book a competitor's room (especially if price becomes an issue). Once consumers conclude that they will usually find better prices on a third-party channel, they will make Expedia or Travelocity, for example, their first port of call for future bookings—threatening brand loyalty, driving up transaction fees, increasing reservation leakage, and strengthening the third parties' power to demand "special rates" or commission overrides for a company to gain premium positioning (or even inclusion) in their search listings. Hotel companies need to take urgent action if they are not to lose control over the sale of their own product. At the very least, this means offering consistent prices over all channels, but more probably means providing customers the lowest rate over their own web site. This would decrease guests' motivation to book on alternative electronic channels, would help build web-site traffic, and should help to decrease distribution costs.

1.6 CUSTOMER RELATIONSHIP MANAGEMENT—A DRIVER FOR CHANGE IN THE STRUCTURE OF THE U.S. LODGING INDUSTRY

Gabriele Piccoli, Peter O'Connor, Claudio Capaccioli, and Roy Alvarez

Note: Over the past two years, we have engaged in significant formal and informal discussion with senior executives from top hotel chains, management companies, and ownership groups. The propositions presented here are the fruit of these discussions as well as in-depth case studies of two of the largest U.S.–based hotel chains.

Customer Relationship Management (CRM)—a managerial philosophy that enables a firm to become intimately familiar with its customers—is currently gaining widespread popularity in many industries. Firms that embrace CRM strive to provide consistent and personal customer service over time and across multiple touch points. At first glance, the lodging sector, with its emphasis on customer service and multiplicity of customer touch points, seems ideally positioned to take advantage of CRM initiatives. We believe, however, that the current structure of the lodging industry gives rise to a "data-ownership dilemma," which appears to be limiting the adoption of a comprehensive CRM approach.[10] The three parties typically involved in running a hotel—the owner, the management company, and the brand (*Brand* refers to the franchiser that flags a given property (e.g., Hilton, Marriott, Six Continents)—have partially misaligned interests and, as a result, often resist sharing customer data, a prerequisite for successful CRM. (The recent slew of lawsuits between brands and ownership groups that allege data misuse confirms the often conflicted relationship between the entities; see Billing, 2002, for example.)

This paper highlights the data-ownership dilemma and outlines several possible future scenarios leading to its resolution. The first section introduces the CRM concept and discusses the potential benefits and risks it engenders. The second section examines the current structure of the U.S. lodging industry and outlines the complementary role of the three major industry players—owners, management companies, and brands. The following section demonstrates why the current structure of the lodging industry creates a barrier to successful CRM adoption by hotel companies. The effect of the "data-ownership dilemma" is discussed. The final section of the article presents alternative scenarios as to how the dilemma may be resolved.

▶ CUSTOMER RELATIONSHIP MANAGEMENT

Customer Relationship Management (CRM) is currently one of the hottest topics in the fields of business strategy, information technology, and marketing management (Hall, 2001, 24–27). Put simply, CRM is a management philosophy that calls for the reconfiguration of the firm's activities around the customer. CRM differs from traditional marketing initiatives (see Table 1.8) in that, while the latter take predominately a short-term, transaction approach, CRM focuses on maximizing revenue from each customer over the lifetime of the relationship by getting to know each one intimately (Wilson, Daniel, and McDonald, 2002, 193–219). CRM is also, by definition, a crossfunctional philosophy that calls for substantial business integration (Markus, 2000). Thus, to implement CRM successfully, a very different mindset is needed: The firm no longer markets to customers, but it fosters a relationship with them through programs that span marketing, operations, information systems, accounting, and other organizational functions.

One of the questions most often asked about CRM is, "why bother?" Changing an organization's philosophy and methods of operation is troublesome; developing and maintaining in-depth customer databases is expensive and the benefits of the approach are not guaranteed. Day, Dean, and Reynolds neatly summarize the benefits of using CRM

Table 1.8 Traditional Marketing Versus CRM Approach

Traditional Marketing		Customer Relationship Management
Transaction focus	←————————→	Customer focus
Short-term focus	←————————→	Lifetime focus
One transaction	←————————→	Multiple transactions
Broadcast approach	←————————→	Sniper approach
One-way, one-time communications	←————————→	Two-way, continuous dialog
Segment of many	←————————→	Segment of one

(Day, Dean and Reynolds, 1998, 828–837) First, by developing a closer relationship with customers, the firm may gain a competitive advantage and, through increased switching costs, may be able to defend it. Over time individual customers typically educate a company about their individual needs, wants, and preferences—a costly process that they are reluctant to repeat with a rival (Peppers and Rodgers, 1994, 6). Thus, getting to know customers intimately creates a barrier to imitation of the leader's strategy.

Second, effective CRM can lead to increased customer satisfaction. Properly implemented, the customer-company dialogue facilitates the tailoring of products and services closely to individual needs, and the development of new products and services to meet changing needs or even anticipate future needs (Palmer, 1994).

Third, using CRM techniques contributes to decreasing overall marketing expenditure. Acquiring new customers is estimated to be more expensive than keeping existing ones (Blattberg and Deighton, 1996, 136–144). Figures of between five and seven times as much have been quoted (Kotler, 1997). And, last,

developing a closer relationship with customers is thought to increase customer loyalty, and loyal customers are thought to stay with the firm longer, buy more from it, and buy more often (Dowling, 2002, 87–104). An oft-quoted statistic is that companies can improve profitability by between 25 and 85 percent by reducing customer defections by 5 percent (Reichheld and Sassre, 1990, 301–307). While the value of loyalty is currently being debated (Reinartz and Kumar, 2002, 4–12), for some time now lodging firms have been fostering loyalty through frequent-traveler programs and CRM may be seen as the logical next step.

The above arguments offered by CRM proponents suggest that CRM leads to higher profitability due to increased sales, declining customer acquisition costs, and increasing profitability of customers willing to pay a premium for "better" service. Figure 1.1 presents a graphical representation of how CRM is thought to work. The top row of effects leads to building relationships with customers and thus establishing customer loyalty. The bottom row lists well-accepted outcomes of data-mining activities. Together those two sets of

Figure 1.1   CRM Model

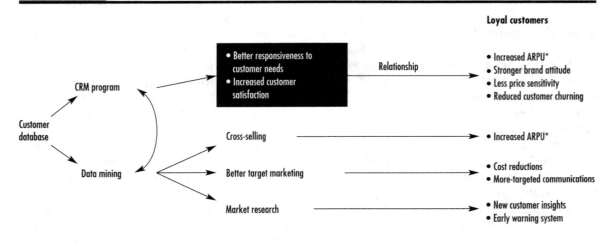

*ARPU=average revenue per user

outcomes have stimulated many companies to invest in creating a database-driven CRM system (Dowling, 2002).

Some authors warn that substantial investments in CRM are not right for everyone (Gronroos, 1990, 3–11). In a small or niche business, for example, it is relatively easy to keep in touch with customers' preferences. But because of the significant increase in the amount of information that must be managed as the firm's scale and scope increase, successful CRM requires significant investments in technology, process redesign, and people. An airline or a major international hotel chain must manage substantially larger amounts of data than does a small inn to achieve a similar relationship with its customers. However, information technology (IT)—used appropriately—can help mitigate the problem. Between 1990 and today, the world has seen enormous transformations in the extent to which organizations can deploy computer power. IT allows customer data to be collected, consolidated, manipulated, and analyzed on an unprecedented scale, and IT has been identified by many authors as one of the key success factors for CRM implementation (Hall, 2001). IT allows increased reach into new markets without high incremental entry costs, and facilitates specifically tailored customer marketing and increased responsiveness (Gamble, Stone, and Woodcock, 1999).

The role of IT in CRM efforts is so important that some writers (such as Copulshy and Wolf, 1990, 16–20), and many practicing managers and vendors, associate CRM with the technology that is used to support the approach. Many use the term in the highly specific sense of database marketing, where a range of demographic, lifestyle, and purchasing activities are recorded and tracked, and subsequently used as the basis of targeting differentiated products to selected customer groups. In turn, their response to each marketing contact is tracked and used to further refine the approach. However, CRM is a broader concept than just technology. For example, CRM has been defined as "an enterprise-wide commitment to identify your named, individual customers and create a relationship between your company and these customers so long as that relationship is mutually beneficial" (Gamble *et al.,* 1999). This definition highlights several key CRM concepts—that the company will actively seek out the right customers (and, by implication, will not target those that will not do business with them), will develop a long-term, mutually beneficial relationship with each customer by starting and maintaining a two-way dialogue, will strive to satisfy customers' needs and solve customer problems, and will support customers throughout the life cycle of their interactions with the firm (Piccoli, Spalding, and Ives, 2001, 38–45).

This approach to CRM demands more than computer systems and information technology. The customer must become the focal point of the organization. All members of the organization must understand and support the shared values required for CRM, its philosophy must encompass not just marketing but the entire organization, and it must be used to manage all aspects of the customer relationship in a coordinated way.

Although limited research about the effectiveness of CRM has been published to date, most observers agree that successful CRM is predicated on the ability to effectively capture exhaustive data about existing and potential customers, profile them accurately, identify their individual needs and idiosyncratic expectations, and generate actionable customer knowledge that can be distributed for ad-hoc use at each point of contact (Newell, 2000). The objective is to achieve a comprehensive view of customers, and be able to consistently anticipate and react to their needs with targeted and effective activities at every customer touch point. CRM requires the firm to keep track of the information produced through each interaction so that it can "learn" on a continuous basis, get to know each guest better, and enrich its database of individual customer knowledge (Marsan, 2000, 91–94). Godin has likened CRM to "dating a customer," in that it is a long-term process that requires an investment of time, information, and resources by both parties (Godin, 1999). The result is an active, participatory, and interactive relationship between customer and supplier. Lastly, CRM is about customization, or the ability to consistently treat different customers differently (Newell, 2000). Relationships differ as they develop. We do not treat old friends in the same way as new friends or good friends in the same way as casual acquaintances (Gamble *et al.,* 1999). Such consistent personalized interaction requires integration and synchronization of many organizational functions, from marketing to accounting to operations and information systems. Failure to understand the scope, essence, and magnitude of CRM is likely to result in problems, rather than its promised benefits.

▶ THE POTENTIAL OF CRM IN THE LODGING INDUSTRY

Lodging-industry participants face an increasingly competitive market (Vialle, 1995). In addition, the basis of competition is changing.

Location, a key driver of business, is fixed in the short and medium term, and attracting and retaining customers based on facilities and amenities is becoming increasingly difficult as they have become increasingly standardized across competing brands. Price competition is unattractive, even more so as consumers are able to easily find and compare prices over the Internet (O'Connor, 2002, 285–293). As a consequence consumers are increasingly displaying less brand loyalty (Gamble *et al.,* 1999), and CRM is becoming increasingly attractive as a way for hotel companies to differentiate themselves from their competitors (Francese and Renaghan, 1990, 60–63).

The lodging sector is ideally suited to applying the principles of CRM. In few other industries is there such potential to build up a comprehensive and accurate picture of the client. In few other industries do customers provide the significant amount of information hotel guests divulge when making a reservation and during their hotel stay. Every interaction between the guest and the customer is an opportunity to refine knowledge about her or him and to further build a relationship. By methodically collecting, consolidating, and analyzing both guest preferences and transactional data, hotel chains have the potential to develop a deep understanding of each customer's needs and preferences, provide substantially improved service levels, individually tailor the customer experience, and generally offer more personalized service. Providing outstanding personal service is certainly not a new concept in the hotel sector. Companies such as Ritz-Carlton and the Savoy group historically maintained extensive manual guest-history systems recording guest preferences in an effort to better serve their best customers. However, when oper-

ated manually, such systems are expensive to maintain, are frequently inaccurate, and can only be used to track a limited number of clients at individual properties (Main and O'Connor, 1998, 7–15). Developments in information and communications technologies have enabled automation and efficiencies in these processes, reducing costs, increasing accuracy, and allowing comprehensive knowledge about each customer to be shared on a global basis. As a result, many companies are turning to technology to improve customer service by implementing large-scale CRM programs.

Analysis of the lodging sector shows that, driven in most cases by pressure from the marketing function, many of the dominant hotel chains are in the process of deploying (or have already deployed) the technological infrastructure to support CRM. A recent study by Arthur Andersen and New York University found that over one-third of U.S. hotel chains had a data warehouse in 2000, with another 50 percent planning to install one in the near future (*Hospitality 2000,* 8). Many chains have introduced information systems to improve the targeting of marketing and sales efforts. Such systems can help the firm to assess the value of each customer as well as their propensity to respond to various offers, and to market to them individually.

As discussed earlier, while important, such initiatives do not imply that the company has adopted CRM. In most cases, such developments focus solely on marketing objectives and lack the integration among functional areas that characterizes a CRM initiative. Only where the company reconfigures its operations to deliver a comprehensive view of the customer and to support consistent, highly personalized service at every customer touch point could it truly be regarded as CRM. Few companies in the lodging sector appear to have progressed to such an advanced stage.

Given the geographic dispersion of hotel properties and the role of brands in marketing and distribution, large-scale CRM initiatives seem most justifiable at the brand level. Implementing CRM at this level would help to increase consistency and personal service throughout the chain and at each customer touch point. However, to achieve this, consistent and comprehensive information must be captured from all properties within the brand and then consolidated, analyzed, interpreted, and subsequently disseminated to each property in time to influence the next customer interaction.

Two barriers currently prevent that from happening—a lack of standardization and IT-system integration within each franchise, and the fact that at any one time there may be up to three parties holding a stake in the operations of a particular property (owner, management company, and brand). The two issues are largely interconnected as the industry's generally reactive attitude toward IT has been exacerbated by its structural characteristics. The technical challenge is subsiding due to recent developments in technology, including the emergence of the application service provider (ASP) model. (*Note:* When software applications are delivered using an ASP model, they are not installed on the computers at the property. Rather, they are accessed by remote users via the Web. Thus, IT resources under the ASP model are not bought but acquired as a service.) A discussion of these technologies is beyond the scope of this article. Note, however, that, even assuming away technological challenges, we believe that the structure of the lodging industry creates severe obstacles to successful CRM. The remainder of the paper focuses on these challenges.

► THE LODGING INDUSTRY'S STRUCTURE

Lodging is an important component of the tourism industry, providing accommodation (and associated ancillary services) to travelers while away from home. Lodging operations are diverse, ranging from small bed-and-breakfast properties in rural locations to large hotels with several thousand rooms in major cities. Table 1.9 provides an overview of geographical dispersion, showing that the majority of the world's hotel properties are concentrated in Europe (55 percent) and North America (22 percent). The exhibit also demonstrates that the average property size in North America is larger than that in Europe (56 versus 28 rooms), with chain-affiliated properties being more common in North America. Despite controlling only a minority of room stock (approximately 30 percent of total room supply) hotel chains dominate the lodging sector (Corporate 300, 1998, 51–77) and tend to exert a disproportionate influence on industry operations and performance (Cline and Rach, 1997, 35).

In addition to generally having higher occupancy and average daily rate (Worldwide Hotel Industry Study, 1998), chain properties tend to be more profitable, delivering trading profit per room seven times more than their independent counterparts (Slattery, 1992, 90–102). As a result, the industry is expected to continue to consolidate, with an increasing number of mergers and acquisitions resulting in a small number of large companies dominating the marketplace (Corporate 300, 1998).

A differentiation must be made between hotel ownership, hotel branding, and hotel operations. Historical developments with

Table 1.9   The International Hotel Industry

	Total Revenue (10⁹) US$	Number of Hotels	Percentage of Total Hotels	Total Number of Rooms	Average Size of Hotel (Rooms)
Africa	6.3	10,769	3.5	343,347	32
Caribbean	7.9	5,290	1.7	155,253	29
Central America	1.2	1,160	0.3	41,221	35
North America	62.1	66,943	21.7	3,738,977	56
South America	9.8	14,576	4.7	487,787	33
Northeast Asia	23.7	10,192	3.3	719,480	71
Southeast Asia	12.8	13,211	4.3	453,657	34
South Asia	3.1	3,663	1.1	159,417	44
Australia and Pacific Islands	6.6	10,082	3.2	229,319	23
Middle East	9.2	4,735	1.5	162,178	34
European Economic Area	87.5	151.945	49.4	4,242,193	28
Other Europe	22.5	19,178	6.2	676,631	35
Total	*247.8*	*307,683*	*100**	*11,333,199*	*37*

Source: World Travel and Tourism Council 1995
*Total does not add up to 100 due to rounding.

Real Estate Investment Trusts (REITs) in the United States gave rise to a situation where many owners could not operate their own hotels. Instead they must use a separate management company to oversee day-to-day operations (*The International Hotel Industry,* 2001, 85), resulting in a split between hotel ownership and hotel operations. The situation is further complicated by the widespread use of both franchises and marketing agreements that provide a consumer brand and require compliance with brand standards (Singh, 1997, 89–107).

At any one time there may be up to three parties holding a stake in the operations of a particular property: (1) the owner, who holds title to the assets, is responsible for mortgage payments and provides the capital for the operation; (2) the brand, which brands the property and provides standards, distribution services, marketing, technology, and other services; and (3) the management company, which provides management talent and operates the property on a day-to-day basis. Table 1.10 demonstrates how, with the exception of Wyndham International, the major brand companies own less than one-third of their branded properties, with various management companies operating the remainder on behalf of their owners. Furthermore, as Table 1.11 shows, within each management company the brand portfolio is quite mixed, with each company operating under a variety of competing flags in different geographical markets. The data lend support to our claim that in the U.S. lodging industry there are multiple stakeholders with, at times competing, interest in the operations of the property. In the remainder of

Table 1.10 Portfolio Composition of Major U.S. Brands[1]

Parent Company	U.S. Brands	Total Properties	Company Owned	Franchised, Licensed	Management Contract
Cendant Corp.	Days Inns	1,943	0	1,943	0
	Ramada	1,005	0	1,005	0
	Super 8	1,933	0	1,933	0
	Howard Johnson	425	0	425	0
	Travelodge	475	0	475	0
	Knights Inn	226	0	226	0
	Villager Lodge	118	0	118	0
	Total	*6,125*	*0*	*6,125*	*0*
Six Continents	Holiday Inn Hotels	1,056	5	1,004	47
	Holiday Inn Express	1,083	0	1,078	5
	Crowne Plaza	77	6	51	20
	Total	*2,216*	*11*	*2,133*	*72*
			3%	*98.6%*	*1.2%*
Hilton Hotels Corp.	Hampton Inns	1,094	1	1,081	27
	Hilton Inns/Hotels	230	40	171	15
	Doubletree	153	10	49	59
	Embassy Suites	155	6	75	57
	Homewood Suites	89	14	59	16
	Total	*1,721*	*71*	*1,435*	*174*
			4.4%	*81.3%*	*9.8%*
Marriott International	Marriott Hotels	277	4	39	234
	Courtyard	493	1	236	256
	Fairfield Inn	464	0	412	52
	Residence Inn	362	0	242	116
	Renaissance	53	0	22	31
	Total	*1,649*	*5*	*951*	*689*
			.5%	*60.8%*	*38.5%*
Starwood Hotels and Resorts Worldwide	Sheraton	189	40	105	44
	Westin	57	22	10	25
	Four Points	105	6	84	15
	Total	*351*	*68*	*199*	*84*
			18.9%	*58.8%*	*16.7%*
Hyatt Hotels Corp.[2]	Hyatt Hotels and Resorts	120	18–36	4	80–98
	Total		*15–30%*	*3%*	*67–82%*
Wyndham International	Wyndham Hotels and Resorts	114	81	13	20
	Wyndham Luxury Resorts	6	3	0	3
	Summerfield Suites by Wyndham	38	27	11	0
	Total	*158*	*111*	*24*	*23*
			70.2%	*15.2%*	*14.6%*

[1]Adapted from: The Brand Report, *Lodging Hospitality,* August 2000.
[2]Hyatt Hotels Corp. is privately owned, and a precise classification of ownership is not available. Range estimates were provided directly by company representatives.

Table 1.11 Portfolio Composition of Major U.S. Management Companies

Management Company
Meristar Hospitality Corp. and Felcor Lodging Trust

Parent	U.S. Brands	Number of Properties
Six Continents	Holiday Inn and Crowne Plaza	21
Hilton	Embassy Suites	6
	Hilton Inns/Hotels	35
	Hampton Inns	6
	Doubletree	9
	Homewood Suites	6
Marriott	Courtyard	9
	Fairfield Inn	2
	Marriott Hotels	5
	Residence Inn	2
	Renaissance	0
Starwood	Sheraton	16
	Westin	3
Wyndham	Wyndham	4
Others	Multiple Brands	59
	Total	*183*

Management Company
Lodgian, Inc.

Parent	U.S. Brands	Number of Properties
Six Continents	Holiday Inn and Crowne Plaza	62
Hilton	Hilton Inns/Hotels	4
	Hampton Inns	2
	Doubletree	1
Marriott	Courtyard	8
	Fairfield Inn	5
	Marriott Hotels	1
	Residence Inn	2
Starwood	Four Points	3
Others	Multiple Brands	21
	Total	*109*

Management Company
Interstate Hotels Corp.

Parent	U.S. Brands	Number of Properties
Six Continents	Holiday Inn and Crowne Plaza	8
Hilton	Embassy Suites	1
	Hilton Inns/Hotels	4
	Hampton Inns	38
	Doubletree	0
	Homewood Suites	5
Marriott	Courtyard	10
	Fairfield Inn	6
	Marriott Hotels	14
	Residence Inn	13
	Renaissance	2
Starwood	Sheraton	2
	Westin	1
	Total	*138*

Management Company
Tharaldson Property Management, Inc.

Parent	U.S. Brands	Number of Properties
Six Continents	Holiday Inn and Crowne Plaza	16
Hilton	Hampton Inns	7
	Homewood Suites	36
Marriott	Courtyard	18
	Fairfield Inn	113
	Residence Inn	32
Others	Multiple Brands	112
	Total	*334*

Source: The Brand Report, *Lodging Hospitality,* August 2000, and the authors' independent research.

the article we demonstrate how the structure of the industry can provide significant obstacles to the success of CRM initiatives.

▶ THE DATA-OWNERSHIP DILEMMA

As was discussed earlier, CRM's success is predicated on the ability to collect, analyze, and disseminate large amounts of timely and relevant information for customer-service operatives to act on to improve the experience at each point of customer contact. Thus, a CRM initiative cannot be successful without commitment among a critical mass of properties. Hotel chains cannot provide a consistently high level of personal service unless customer data can be garnered from most, if not all, of the affiliated properties, organized and synthesized in one central location, and subsequently redistributed to each property on an as-needed basis. However, we propose that (technological constraints aside) this apparently simple theoretical proposition is difficult to realize in the lodging industry due to an inherent data-ownership conflict between the major industry stakeholders. In the following sections we present the main issues facing the brand, the management company, and the owner.

The Brand. For brands, the development of an effective CRM initiative is deemed an important competitive move as it would facilitate the development of a deep understanding of customer needs and preferences, potentially resulting in a high level of personalization, thus helping to improve service levels across the brand as a whole. As a result guests would have a strong incentive to remain loyal to the brand and patronize affili-

ated properties, thus increasing the value proposition for owners and operators through improvements in financial performance.

For the promised benefits of CRM to materialize, standardized information systems must be implemented throughout the franchise network to allow data to be obtained from all branded properties—a problem in the past, becoming less important as a result of recent technology improvements. Furthermore, the brand must be willing to share the customer knowledge generated by the consolidation of customer data chain-wide with the individuals that can take action based on it at each point of customer contact. Such data sharing presents the first dilemma. In some cases, the brand may be reticent to disseminate customer knowledge back to the property for fear that owners or operators might use it to poach high-value customers and divert them to competing brands within their own portfolios. For example, imagine a management company that operates a hotel flying one flag (Brand A) in a particular market, and a competing flag (Brand B) in others. This company might be tempted to steer high-value customers toward its Brand B hotels in markets where it does not operate Brand A hotels. Thus, Brand A is faced with a decision—either share the data it collects companywide to reap the benefits of large-scale CRM and risk the poaching of high-value customers by some of its partner management companies operating individual properties; or protect its customer knowledge from the interests of multi-flag owners and operators, thus forgoing the full benefits of CRM.

The Management Company. Management companies do not appear to have strong incentives to develop a CRM initiative for themselves. As was shown in Table 1.11, such companies tend to operate a varied portfolio of properties, each flying different flags, on behalf of different owners. By definition a CRM initiative developed across flags is unlikely to generate brand loyalty and thus is of limited interest to most management companies.

The question arises, however, as to whether management companies should actively cooperate with the collection of operational guest data by brand-level CRM initiatives. As most companies operate a varied portfolio of flags, if the management company participates in a brand-based CRM initiative, it will stand to gain only in those properties that carry that particular brand. Conversely, participation will result in a competitive disadvantage in markets where it competes against the brand. As a result, management companies have little incentive to support brand-level CRM initiatives by contributing data about customers that stay at its properties. In fact, by doing so, they would in effect be undermining their own operations in markets where the brand operating the CRM initiative is a competitor rather than an ally. Moreover, while the management company may not be interested in detailed customer data for branding purposes, it certainly finds value in customer data that allows it to create customer-value models and better target high-value prospects, particularly with respect to group business. Consequently, management companies have in effect an incentive to limit data disclosure and not cooperate with brand-level CRM initiatives.

The Owner. While owners, like operators, typically have many flags in their portfolio of properties, they have a different focus in terms of profitability. Many primarily view hotel ownership as a real-estate investment, and have a marginal interest in the question, "Who owns the data?" Where their properties fly the flag of a successful CRM initiative, they may have an advantage over other competing properties; where their properties fly competing flags, they may be at a disadvantage. Thus, the same dilemma facing the management company seems to affect the owners—whether to participate in brand-level CRM initiatives, or to refuse to cooperate with the collection and consolidation of customer data. The owners may also have interests that go beyond the use of the data strictly for operational purposes. Customer data may be used by the other entities (the brand and the management company) for marketing purposes and analyses that run counter to the owner's own interests (e.g., studying the feasibility of building new properties in the same geographical area).

► CONCLUSIONS AND IMPLICATIONS

In this paper we have drawn attention to what we term the "data-ownership dilemma"—the inherent conflict that various entities in the lodging industry face as they embrace CRM. We propose that the data-ownership dilemma represents a significant, yet often unrecognized, challenge to the success of CRM initiatives. As was discussed, CRM strategies appear most applicable at the brand level, but their success is dependent on the active cooperation of both the operator and the owner of each property. For CRM to succeed at the brand level, operators must supply the brand with in-depth customer data—a requirement with which operators in particular, and owners to a lesser extent, have little incentive to comply. Brands also face challenges in terms of maintaining control over the resulting customer knowledge and preventing its spread outside the brand network.

Because of this conflict, we believe that CRM in the lodging industry may never progress beyond its current, relatively limited, level of sophistication. While database-marketing techniques will continue to be used, we propose that few hotel companies will successfully implement large-scale, chain-wide, CRM initiatives. Only if significant change occurs in the structure or methods of operation of the sector are the full benefits of a CRM approach likely to be realized.

In closing, we speculate as to what changes will have to occur for successful implementation of CRM initiatives. We see three possible scenarios: there will be a fundamental change in the way in which hotel brands are organized; a change in the nature of franchise agreements and management contracts; or there will be more cooperation among brands to take advantage of CRM's promised benefits. These three scenarios are further developed in the remainder of this article.

The first scenario is that the need for adoption of a CRM approach will induce changes in the ownership and management structure of the lodging sector. If CRM truly provides compelling benefits, the large brands should begin to pressure the management companies and franchisees within their network to provide the data needed for successful CRM operations. Those brands that manage a relatively large number of their own hotels will be in a good position to take advantage of these initiatives quickly, should face little resistance as a result of the data-ownership dilemma, and should be able to easily reap the benefits of CRM. Wyndham International's ByRequest initiative demonstrates that highly integrated lodging brands

are moving quickly to embrace CRM (see sidebar). If these pioneers are successful in their effort and are able to attract and retain high-value customers, competing brands will have to follow suit and develop similar CRM capabilities. Such companies would have to resolve the data-ownership dilemma either by "integrating down" or by restricting the number of flags that the companies operating their hotels can fly. Integrating down implies that brands would move aggressively to take over the operational management of their branded properties. Such integrated companies should be able to standardize the IT infrastructure needed to support CRM, mandate the collection and consolidation of customer data, and provide each property with dynamic access to the central knowledge repository. Since all operations would effectively be managed by the brand, there would be no conflicts of interest and no danger of high-value customers being poached, freeing the brand to take full advantage of the CRM initiative.

Obviously, taking over operational control of their unit properties would be a dramatic and high-risk strategy. Thus, brands, particularly in the short term, may instead concentrate on restructuring their management and franchise agreements to minimize the barriers to success discussed earlier. Redevelopment should focus on two main areas—data collection and data use. While many franchise agreements require properties to feed its customer-folio data back to the central level, few specifically mention any other data collected about the guest. As CRM is dependent on building up a holistic picture of the guest's needs and behavior, this oversight may force brands to restructure contracts to force greater compliance with data needs. Such restructured contracts could spec-

A CRM EXEMPLAR: WYNDHAM INTERNATIONAL

*A*s part of our research, we investigated the CRM initiatives of large hotel chains. One such chain, Wyndham International, has made CRM a cornerstone of its brand strategy. We briefly describe the key characteristics of Wyndham's CRM approach to aid the reader in understanding the principal characteristics of large-scale CRM initiatives.

Wyndham International is one of the five largest U.S.–based hotel chains, with a portfolio of over 160 branded properties. After converting from paired-share REIT status to a C corporation in 1999, Wyndham revised its corporate strategy in an effort to become a "world-class branded hotel operating company."[1] Wyndham's differentiation strategy is nicely captured in the words of Andrew Jordan, Wyndham's senior vice president of marketing: "We said, okay, we are going to reinvent the Wyndham brand. We are going to say: We are all about personalized service. We are going to say: We are the brand who really recognizes that guests are individuals, we know you have specific needs, quirks—you tell us about them one time and we are going to remember them."[2]

The cornerstone of Wyndham's strategy is its membership-based CRM initiative: Wyndham ByRequest. When a guest joins ByRequest, he or she completes a comprehensive profile including general and contact information, room preferences (e.g., room location, needed extra items, newspaper), credit card and express check-in/check-out preferences, airline frequent-flyer preferences, personal interests (e.g., activities, music, readings, spectator sports), and complimentary beverages and snacks (e.g., preferred wine, soft drinks, juice, snacks).

The above information is compiled at Wyndham's headquarters and a pledge is made to the guest that, irrespective of which property in the Wyndham chain the guest travels to in the future, he or she can expect a consistent level of personalized service. This includes a room that is located where desired and fitted with the required amenities, a welcome snack and drink that's of the guest's liking, and information that suits the traveler's interests (e.g., reading material, information about shows or sporting events).

Key to the initiative's success is the realization that, while important, the technology underlying Wyndham ByRequest—including the website, the preferences databases, and integrated operational systems (e.g., PMS)—does not in and of itself deliver the ByRequest promise. As a result, Wyndham has designated staff members to support ByRequest and created a property-level position—the Wyndham ByRequest manager—who has responsibility over property-level execution, and Wyndham has developed integrated processes for delivering the ByRequest promise.

[1]"Letter to Shareholders," Wyndham International 2000 Annual Report, 2001.

[2]For complete information about Wyndham ByRequest, see G. Piccoli and L. Applegate, "Wyndham International: Fostering High-Touch with High-Tech," Harvard Business School Case Study, 2003; # 9-803-092.

ify that all customer data generated at the property level be extracted and loaded to the brand's central data repository. Management contracts also need to be rewritten to offer protection to the brand as it disseminates customer knowledge back to the property level. Both of these measures mean that ties between brands and operators would be strengthened, which may ultimately result in further industry consolidation as owners and operators feel pressure to fly a limited number of flags. In an extreme scenario, each operator would effectively become aligned with one brand and fly only one flag.

The final potential scenario we envision is the emergence of an industry consortium that both develops and maintains the CRM infrastructure and standardizes customer-data collection and distribution. As it has happened historically with hotel e-commerce systems such as THISCo (The Hotel Industry Switching Company), HDS (Hotel Distribution Systems) and Avendra (an e-procurement marketplace), competing brands could cooperate to develop the standards and the infrastructure necessary to capture, store, organize, and distribute customer information. Such a scenario is attractive as joint development would mean that the infrastructure could be delivered and operated at a fraction of the cost of proprietary initiatives. Thereafter, rather than being used as a basis of competition, customer data would be shared and companies would compete on the analysis, interpretation, and use of such data. For example, competing brands could use the same data to market to their chosen customer bases. Competitive advantage would come from how well they could use the data to identify, target, and build a relationship with each individual.

We believe the latter scenario to be the least likely, even though it may optimize industry-wide performance. The likelihood of an industry consortium developing and managing customer information for the benefit of the industry as a whole is small, as the industry's belief in the proprietary value of customer data, the industry's structure, privacy issues, as well as a culture that precludes trust in this domain makes the cooperation necessary unlikely. We see a change in contractual agreements and in industry structure as far more probable. In any case, given the potential proposed for lodging-industry companies, careful consideration must be given to the data-ownership dilemma to avoid failure.

1.7 SPAS AND THE LODGING INDUSTRY

Peter C. Anderson

▶ OVERVIEW

Spas are becoming such a significant component of the service menu for resorts and full-service hotels that their absence, especially in amenity-rich resort environments, is glaringly obvious. Within the leisure industries in 2003, revenues related to spas ranked number four behind golf fees and dues ($19.7 million), cruise line revenues ($14.7 million), and health club revenues ($14.1 million). At $11.2 million, spa revenues outpaced amusement park revenues ($10.3 million), box office receipts ($9.5 million), and vacation ownership sales ($5.5 million) (Thacker, 2004; Audi and Wright, 2004). In this section, we first examine trends that support a sea change in North Americans' attitude toward spa use. After evaluating spa demand demographics, we discuss the types of spas currently popular in the industry, development and operational considerations, the components of a spa experience, compensation issues, and trends in the spa industry.

► SPA DEMAND

According to the International SPA Association research, between 2002 and 2003, 11 percent of the national population over the age of 16 made one or more spa visits. This statistic shows that one in ten Americans visited a spa during that period. Additionally, of these, 41 percent were visiting spas for the first time, indicating a larger population embracing spa usage. Age demographics show that 14 percent of clients are between the ages of 16 and 24, and over 50 percent are in the 25 to 44 age bracket.

An emerging national statistic is the number of male visits to spas. Twenty-three percent of spa visits and 29 percent of spa goers were men in 2003, trending toward special gender-oriented treatments and male-only spas being opened worldwide.

Spa selection criteria are determined by a number of factors. An established and known environment—for instance, as a part of an established resort, club, or destination spa—often influences the decision, as does atmosphere, quality of treatment, and friendliness of staff. Additionally, among spa goers, nine out of ten respondents report they would return for a similar experience.

Most spa customers believe they received good value for their spa dollar. On a 10-point scale, services were given an average of 8 for value, with massage generating 8.8 on the value-for-service scale.

Spa services demonstrated the highest and heaviest demand on weekends, followed by appointments after work on weekdays. Gender demographics also play a role in spa demand, as men are more likely to go for regular weekly visits after business hours or while traveling on business. Women, however, often visit spas during regular business hours (Thacker, 2004; Audi and Wright, 2004).

The International Hotel Resort Spa Association (IHRSA) reports that branded resort spas such as Canyon Ranch are opening in the day spa market, adding new competitive pressure on the independents. Nontraditional players are also adding product supply. For example, corporations are creating in-house spa environments, hospitals are adding wellness as part of their repertoire, and medi-spas, with a primary focus on cosmetic surgery, are adding spa business as an additional profit center. Health clubs are also trying to capture a piece of the pie by adding spa practices. The rationale in this market is that time-crunched patrons can benefit from the one-stop-shopping approach to fitness and wellness, but the health club operator also uses the spa as an enticement to join the fitness center.

As the day and destination spa markets become saturated, it will become imperative for survival that each operator differentiate from the competition. The necessity for market segmentation to ensure clear communication with consumers will be a key to success in the maturing spa market. Another component of success will be a branding strategy that the consumer can immediately identify with respect to spa performance and the consumer's personal comfort level.

► HEALTH ISSUES AND SPA DEMAND

Increasingly, spa goers are looking to create prolonged wellness that integrates and renews body, mind, and spirit. To that end, Eastern and Western lifestyle issues related to medicine, philosophy, and spirituality are becoming a mainstay of many spa/wellness experiences. To best deliver this, the wellness spa (located at day, destination, or resort environments) supports guest needs by creating an experience, not just a series of treatments. All the guest amenities, facilities, treatments, and programs must be seamlessly integrated into a personally tailored guest experience. These experiences should be targeted toward couples, parents with children, and teenagers. In the early 1990s, spas were considered a natural outgrowth of fitness facilities and focused primarily on treatments related to body wellness. As market sophistication evolved, the body-mind connection attracted consumer focus. In the beginning of the twenty-first century, spas and marketers are overtly addressing body, mind, and spirit connections in order to respond to emerging market sensibilities. Among the components one might find in a modern spa are services related to:

- Complementary and alternative medicine in mainstream lifestyles
- Traditional Western medical and Eastern lifestyle/wellness practices
- A proactive approach to overall health and the quality of one's life

Body

- Action spas are attracting a greater percentage of men who are looking for a way to unwind and keep active. Because of this trend, an aggressive array of activities—including cardio-circuit courses, squash, racketball and tennis, free and fixed weights, jogging, and bike paths, hikes, and water spots—is still a basic spa/wellness requirement.
- As part of the wellness experience, medical affiliations are sometimes available to provide information and to check blood pressure, heart conditions, bone density, and so on.
- Exceptional food can be tailored to virtually any dietary restriction or request.
- When examining which body treatments to include, note that salt glows and exfoliant treatments are approximately four times more popular than any other body treatment. These items are a mainstay in successful spa services.
- Guests must be able to upgrade their experience with add-ons such as eye-firming therapies and mineral-enhanced hydrotherapy soaks. Further, it is important to sell services in several time blocks so guests can select services that fit their schedule and financial budget.

Body, Mind

- Educational programs at many levels include classes and clinics. These programs personally empower the guest, expand the wellness center's demand base, and encourage repeat visits. Health and wellness issues encompass cardiovascular health, holistic childrearing, the integration of Eastern and Western medical practices, indigenous spiritual practices, aging, intimacy, transition/death, vitality, strength training, cooking programs (macrobiotic, vegan, vegetarian, indigenous), women's issues, and so on. Traditionally, educational programs at spas have focused primarily on personal health issues.

- Mind-body techniques may include spiritual and cultural instruction. Examples include tai chi, visualization, progressive muscle relaxation and biofeedback, labyrinth walking, meditating and chanting, sweat lodges, and storytelling.

- Extensive yoga programs should include Hatha yoga for body control, Ashtanga yoga for cardio workout, Iyengar yoga for balance and alignment, and Kundalini yoga for breath work.

Body, Mind, Spirit

- Comprehensive touch/alternative manual therapies including chiropractic treatment and deep tissue massage (rolfing, myofascial release, nueromuscular massage, acupressure/shiatsu, watsu, Trager massage, etc.) are a necessary component of any wellness clinic. This modality is an extension of the basic massage offered at all spas and wellness/healing centers. Practitioners who provide manual therapies should be cross-trained in the areas of subtle energy work such as reiki, chakra balancing, and chi gung. Offering alternative touch/energy therapy as a component of traditional massage has the potential to accelerate market acceptance.

- Ayurvedic treatments are popular and provide an additional link between the East-meets-West philosophy showcased in many day spas. Elements of ayurvedic treatments can be incorporated into most touch therapies.

As far back as 1993, a well-known study by David Eisenberg revealed that one-third of all patients had visited a practitioner of alternative health care in the past year, at a cost of $13.7 billion. This indicated to the medical community that the significant out-of-pocket expenses implied not only lost revenues to traditional (allopathic) doctors but also a broad dissatisfaction with mainstream medicine. A great number of people were taking the issues of health and well-being into their own control, thus setting the stage for the popularity of proactive wellness programs.

In 1997, Eisenberg updated his study. He estimated the total number of visits to alternative medical providers at 600 million, representing an expenditure of over $27.1 billion. The number of visits to alternative care physicians in 1997 was greater than the total number of visits to traditional primary care physicians in the same year. The increasing popularity of alternative wellness modalities, the aging of the population, and the strength of the economy are all factors that support the growth of this trend. As of this writing, it appears to continue to grow.

The use of at least 1 of 16 (alternative) therapies during the previous year increased from 33.8 percent in 1990 to 42.1 percent in 1997. The fastest-growing therapies were herbal medicine, message, megavitamins, self-help groups, folk remedies, energy healing, and homeopathy. The probability of users visiting an alternative medicine practitioner increased from 36.3 percent to 46.3 percent. In both 1990 and 1997, alternative therapies were used most frequently for chronic conditions, especially back problems, anxiety, depression, and headaches. In general, it can be concluded that alternative medicine expenditure increased substantially between 1990 and 1997, and this can be attributed primarily to

Table 1.12 Most Frequently Reported Principal Medical Conditions

Ailment	Alternative Therapy	
	Primary	Secondary
Back problems	Chiropractic	Massage
Allergies	Herbal	Relaxation
Fatigue	Relaxation	Massage
Arthritis	Relaxation	Chiropractic
Headaches	Relaxation	Chiropractic
Neck problems	Chiropractic	Massage
High blood pressure	Megavitamins	Relaxation
Sprains or strains	Chiropractic	Relaxation
Insomnia	Relaxation	Herbal
Lung problems	Relaxation	Spiritual healing/herbal
Skin problems	Imagery	Energy healing
Digestive problems	Relaxation	Herbal
Depression	Relaxation	Spiritual healing
Anxiety	Relaxation	Spiritual healing

an increase in the proportion of the population seeking alternative therapies rather than increased visits per patient.

The most frequently reported principal medical conditions for which alternative therapies were sought are summarized in Table 1.12.

▶ SPA CLASSIFICATION

Spa development and its attendant popularity have deep historical roots and vast potential for the hospitality industry. The term *spa* was once reserved for European destination resorts where guests went to "take the waters" and restore a healthy and balanced life. However, the term now is used to describe many types of facilities and amenities in the U.S. lodging industry. At one end of the spa spectrum are dedicated destination resort spas aimed primarily at those seeking a specialized combination regime of health, fitness, and pampering. Modalities and treatments include massages, unique treatments, custom dietary plans, lectures, and adventures that can include, but are not limited to, an array of activities ranging from nonsurgical facelifts to helicopter skiing.

Destination resorts, such as Miraval's Life-in-Balance and Canyon Ranch, with locations in the Berkshires in Massachusetts and the Arizona desert, draw demand because of their facilities and reputation. The primary reason for going to a destination resort spa is to enjoy the spa itself and its related activities. The destination itself is a demand generator.

Closely related to a destination resort spa is the amenity spa. Amenity spas provide services to resorts and full-service hotels. The primary difference between an amenity spa and a destination spa is the scope and depth of spa services. Amenity spas, while sometimes quite extensive, *support* the resort environment, whereas destination spas are the *focus* of the resort environment. In situations where a full-service, high-end hotel is located in an urban environment and has a significantly large spa component, the spa can operate as both an amenity spa (to the hotel) and a day spa (to the local community). Later in this chapter, we study the case of the Westin Los Angeles Century City's 35,000-square-foot Spa Mystique. This spa supports the needs of the hotel's convention and individual travelers while experiencing heavy local day spa use.

Middle-market hotel properties now feel obliged to add a spa as an amenity; however, due to capital and real estate restraints, often they cannot provide a full-service location. As a result, this sector has seen an explosion in poorly conceived and executed spa additions that provide the owner the opportunity to add ". . . and spa" at the end of the business name. These are often no more than the result of subcontracting a massage therapist and converting the guest room closest to the swimming pool into an exercise room. These spas seldom surprise and delight their guests and often reflect poorly on the spa industry overall. Fortunately, the sophistication of the industry is making it harder and harder for the ". . . and spas" to succeed.

As the spa industry matures, certain development trends are emerging. In 2005, the spa industry was considered the fastest-growing segment of the travel, hospitality, and leisure market, showing 26 percent growth from 2002 to 2004. Spas are no longer considered a niche industry but rather an entity unto themselves.

The spa industry is made up of the following segments, each with its own characteristics and operational opportunities:

- Destination spas
- Resort hotel spas
- Day spas
- Medical spas
- Mineral springs
- Club spas

► Destination Spas

A destination spa is one whose sole purpose is to provide programs and facilities that support lifestyle improvements and enhance guest health. The services offered are professionally administered and include fitness, education, and lectures on lifestyle, nutrition, and disease prevention. Because of their healthful orientation, destination spas often provide programs that support postoperative conditions, address various addictions, and provide tools to cope with serious, prolonged illness.

The destination spa industry constitutes only 1.6 percent of the total spa industry, per the International Spa Association's Industry Study (Thacker, 2004). However, the growth in the development and use of destination spas reflects the market's trend toward wellness and health as a major component in spa menus.

► Resort Spas/Amenity Spas

Resort spas are located on the grounds of vacation resorts where treatments for mind, body, and spirit are offered to complement other resort activities such as golf, tennis, horseback riding, skiing, and water sports. Healthful spa cuisine is on the menu as an option, complementing traditional offerings. In the evenings, guests can enjoy resort pastimes like dancing and live entertainment. Children's programs are also offered. According to the ISPA Spa Industry Study (Thacker, 2004), the resort spa represents 14 percent of spa locations in North America but accounts for almost 41 percent of the total industry revenue, 27 percent of all spa visits, and 26 percent of the industry's employees.

A luxury resort spa has the ambience of a secluded retreat on the grounds of a first-class resort. Set in beautiful surroundings, these resorts commonly have world-class golf courses and other excellent recreational facilities. Gourmet dining and exceptional spa therapies are not only expected but demanded.

► Day Spas

Day spas are designed to provide a healing, beautifying, or pampering experience in a short period. Guests may book individual treatments that last as little as an hour or a package of treatments that take up to a whole day. Found throughout North America, day spas are freestanding or located in health clubs, hotels, and department stores. The day spa industry constitutes 72.2 percent of the total industry revenues, per the International Spa Association's 2004 Spa Industry Study. The large percentage of day spas and their growth pattern reflect spa goers' time crunch. Day spas can be owner-operated or chain-affiliated.

Preliminary data from ISPA's 2004 survey show that industry growth is still robust. As of midyear 2004, there was a total of 12,000 spas

nationally, of which 8,700 were day spas. These numbers reflect 25 percent growth in the industry in general and 20 percent growth exclusively in this market. The total number of day spa visits in 2003 was 81.2 million. However, only 13 percent of the general population had used a spa in the prior three-year period, indicating that the industry still has large growth potential.

► Medical Spas

Medical treatments in various spa environments represent a significant trend in the scope, depth, and inclusiveness of numerous spas. Medical spa treatments can range from elective, reconstructive surgery to noninvasive Eastern modalities incorporating elements of Eastern philosophy that draw on the body-mind-spirit connection to create positive, measurable changes in the client/patient. Slightly over half (51 percent) of the medical spas in North America have a partnership with a medical doctor, and 26 percent have a doctor on staff. The remaining configurations include being located in a doctor's office or having licensed staff members. Botox and microdermabrasion are the two most popular treatments, followed by chemical peels and laser hair removal.

In North America, allopathic or Western medical procedures found in medical spas often incorporate Eastern-based treatments. Day, destination, and resort/amenity spas are adding medical treatments to their spa menus. Part of this trend is directly attributed to market demand, and part is attributed to health insurance plans that reimburse for some procedures. According to the ISPA 2004 survey, medical spas are the fastest-growing spa segment with respect to number of locations. The average annual growth in medical spas by location since 1999 is approximately 45 percent. Cumulative growth from 1999 to 2004 is 205 percent and from 2002 to 2004, 109 percent. Medical spas generated an estimated 1,900,000 visits in 2003, representing 1.39 percent of the total spa visits. However, this percentage of visits accounts for approximately 2.1 percent of the total industry revenues, reflecting the lucrative nature of this segment of the industry.

► Mineral Springs Spas

Many mineral springs spas are considered to be the original spa prototype, where guests go to "take the waters." Mineral springs spas, by definition, are located at naturally occurring mineral springs, and by number of locations represent 2.8 percent of the total spa industry, or 1.3 percent of the total industry revenues, making this one of the more modest income-producing segments of the spa industry. The popularity of mineral springs spas is reflected in a cumulative growth from 1999 to 2004 of 143 percent. Growth from 2002 to 2004 represents only 15 percent, implying that the number of sites available directly affects the growth in this segment.

► Club Spas

Club spas lack a lodging component, and their primary objective is to facilitate daily fitness activities. Many club spas' services complement the primary fitness component of the club by offering sports massage (deep tissue), chiropractic services, physiotherapy, and related treatments that address issues of pain management, flexibility, and mobility. By location, club spas represent 5.8 percent of the total spa industry in North America and account for approximately 3.7 percent of the industry's revenues. Growth in the club spa portion of the spa industry is the lowest of all spa segments. Between 2002 and 2004, cumulative club spa growth was only 3 percent.

► SPA OPERATIONS

► Spas as an Operating Department

Historically, spa operations were treated by management similarly to other revenue departments, like catering and restaurants. These departments were simply perceived as an amenity needed to attract guests to the hotel. As long as the department broke even, or didn't lose too much money, their ability to increase occupancy was deemed sufficient justification for their existence. However, in the late 1990s, hotel spas followed the path of other operating departments and transformed from support facilities to profit centers. This trend is strong and continues today.

In 1999, PKF Consulting identified only 30 hotels in the United States, thousands that report data to the PKF, extensive spa facilities and analyzed the financial performance of those properties and their spa departments. Dedicated destination spa resorts were not included in the analysis due to an insufficient sample.

While spas were a relatively small source of revenues for the sample properties, spa revenues grew at a relatively strong pace. In 1999, spa revenues for the subject sample represented just 3.3 percent of total sales. However, from 1998 to 1999, spa revenues grew

16.6 percent. This compares to revenue growth rates of 5.2 percent for rooms, 12.2 percent for food, and 3.2 percent for telecommunications, and a 0.3 percent decline in revenues for the beverage department.

During 1999, the spa departments in the sample of hotels averaged a departmental profit margin of 30.7 percent. However, spa department profits did grow a strong 51.3 percent from 1998 to 1999.

Spas mirror and enhance trends in the lodging industry. Drawing heavily from residential design and the use of technology, hotel designers and operators create a spa experience that:

- Complements the lodging experience
- Drives occupancy levels
- Enhances average daily rate
- Provides a distinctive marketing advantage

North American spas are rapidly becoming more segmented, pursuing market niches well outside the traditional ladies-who-lunch demographic. Adventure spas, fitness spas, children spas, family spas, and even pet spas are part of a new generation of spa facilities, spa programs—and, most importantly, spa aficionados. Spas now attract a much wider demographic that includes men, women, couples, children, teenagers, and families.

Since the early part of the twenty-first century, spas have been redirecting their menus to include stress relief and results-oriented therapies. By focusing on the social benefits of hanging out in a safe, relaxing place, they not only address current market needs but also support the development of spa programs that can be incorporated into virtually any leisure-oriented environment or level of lodging. In particular, destination spas and full-service resorts provide platforms that have both the infrastructure and the economies of scale to support cutting-edge spa treatments, sometimes also referred to as *spa modalities*.

Spas are no longer solely about frivolous self-indulgence and luxurious pampering. They are being reevaluated and repackaged with a broader emphasis on self-care, stress relief, emotional balancing, and preventative (as opposed to reactive) wellness modalities. This trend is being embraced by aging baby boomers as an adjunct to traditional health care. Because of this trend in health care, hotels and resorts have acknowledged and embraced the need for full-service spas as part of their amenities and facilities. The inclusion of a well-integrated spa can provide additional (and lucrative) sales and marketing opportunities. Conversely, the exclusion of a spa facility may disqualify a property from consideration. Ironically, many hotel guests may dismiss a property out of hand for lacking a spa not because they require the services of a spa but rather because its absence may imply other areas of the hotel are also deficient in meeting current market expectations.

Is it logical, then, that all full-service hotels and resorts without a spa should, without hesitation, incorporate one into their property? Clearly not. Numerous factors must be considered in developing or repositioning a spa, especially in chain environments where the lodging brand is already established. Because spas are capital- and labor-intensive, they must materially enhance the property's revenue stream to be considered viable. In addition to creating spa revenue, a spa facility also must extend length of stay, drive room rates, enhance shoulder and low-season demand, augment food and beverage revenues, and capture new market segments.

Successful spa operations start with a standardized level of procedures and a prioritized sensitivity to guest needs. As it is for all departments in a lodging environment (or business models in the freestanding day and medical spa world), profitability is essential. Especially in a spa environment, a dynamic balance is essential to meet the fiscal requirements of the owners and the physical needs of the guest.

A savvy spa manager continually monitors the spa and hotel operations to ensure that everything possible is being done to enhance the synergy of the two entities. Constant monitoring also provides an early warning system to the spa operator if revenues are falling or if expenses are not in line with anticipated revenues or budgeted amounts. Spotting these trends early enables the manager to take efficient, proactive steps to ensure that positive trends are enhanced and negative ones controlled. Constant monitoring sets a standard of operations, which is an excellent way to train and motivate employees. It also puts employees on notice that the spa is a well-run business with extensive attention to detail, which should discourage any actions that might not be in the best interest of the spa's reputation and profitability.

► Customer Service Training

A spa's reputation is easily made or destroyed by its level of customer service. Guests can forgive an occasional shortcoming if the level of service is exceptional. For this reason, it is essential that all spas have an integrated quality management program that provides ongoing training to assist its employees in addressing customers' expectations. Customer service training (CST) helps ensure

that guests' expectations are exceeded. In a spa environment, expectations are usually very high, and a trusting bond can be quickly established if the spa employees are sensitive to guest needs.

The guest's arrival sequence, starting at the front desk, initiates the spa ritual that brings the spa guest to a place of trust, relaxation, and rejuvenation. CST is proactive and provides employees with the tools they need to meet or exceed guest expectations. Guest CST is a never-ending, all-inclusive process that bridges textbook training scenarios with operational realities. The traditionally high turnover of spa employees in the hospitality industry requires that CST be introduced as a part of the orientation process and reinforced regularly.

Nonproductive training time (time that does not directly produce revenue for the spa) is actually a minor expense when compared to the expenses related to employee turnover, poor service, dissatisfied customers, and, ultimately, loss of business and reputation. Budgets must include CST as a nonoptional employee expense. For long-term success, CST is vital when margins are tight, business is slow, and turnover is high. There is a strong correlation between high employee turnover and low CST. Employees should know that the training program is an investment in them.

CST gives the employee the means to understand what is expected of them as a representative of the establishment and identifies what guests expect from their visit. Seeing the process from the guest's point of view helps employees meet or exceed expectations. This minimizes the need to provide discounts or compensation in cases of service delivery problems. Discounting or "comping" goods and services is a knee-jerk response to poor service and should be reserved for the last effort in service recovery; CST should stress this.

An inclusive training program is the engine behind stellar customer service and guest loyalty. CST should be seamless; while it predominately addresses the needs of the guest, the program also includes instruction on profitability and yield management, thus addressing the needs of the owner as well. In order to meet or exceed profitability goals, customer service must be delivered in a fiscally responsible manner. Employees must understand customer service in the operational context of the property in which they are employed.

Minimizing the expense of a CST program starts with the proper selection of employees. While there is no steadfast guarantee that a potential employee will work out over the long haul, first impressions, prior work experience, references, and, above all, attitude and enthusiasm are indications of whether or not it is appropriate to hire and invest the time and money in an applicant.

Management's expectations of guest service delivery should be clearly articulated and integrated into the corporate culture and reinforced daily at all levels and in all departments. Employees, no matter what their responsibility, position, or tenure, must be treated with the same level of respect and dignity that management requires for their guests. Reinforcing the tenets of customer service within the corporate culture provides the employee with the tools to do the right thing—that is, to ask, "What do I need to do to make a spa guest happy? How do I exceed their expectations?" Sometimes the little details reap the greatest rewards.

Employee empowerment is a key component in CST. As an employee's experience and skill base develops (and as management becomes comfortable with an employee's performance), levels of empowerment should be increased proportionately. Empowerment is a vote of confidence in an employee and a way to quickly resolve problems as they arise. This situation is said by spa managers to increase job satisfaction, and the employee's ownership of his or her position.

CST also requires a strong foundation in the technical skills of how a department runs. Routine procedures, appropriate lines of oral and written communication, and what is expected of each employee in the normal course of his or her shift help minimize problems. When problems do occur, a strong foundation in technical skills makes it easier for the employee to create alternative solutions for the guest.

Training draws on employees' EQ (emotional quotient) as well as their IQ (intelligence quotient). CST requires that employees draw on their ability to empathize with the guest. This starts by training employees to suspend judgment of a situation, become attentive listeners, and know the right questions to ask. This allows them to understand what the actual problem is. Training employees in this type of customer service delivery assists them in focusing on the salient issues and creating ways to address them.

Because CST is ongoing, employees can benefit from their peers' experiences. Vehicles to exchange this type of information can be as informal as role-playing and round-table discussions, or as structured as an employee newsletter. Incentives, acknowledgments, and rewards for excellent customer service delivery are an integral part of the training program. Successful CST supports a skilled and unified staff, which translates into profitable operations. CST is an investment in property that owners can't afford not to make.

► Provide Value, Create Value

Spa aficionados are savvy. They are looking to be indulged, pampered, and nurtured, not fleeced. Setting price points with market sensitivity can create tremendous customer loyalty. Because spas are no longer a one-time indulgence but rather a lifestyle choice, it is important to price services competitively and provide incentives for customers to return regularly.

Numerous variables are involved in the development and operation of a spa as part of a hotel or resort. Doing one's homework is essential to success. When a spa is developed or repositioned correctly, it can be a lucrative and rewarding experience. When it is not developed correctly, it can be a financial liability that haunts the spa director and jeopardizes the hotel's market position.

If spas and their programming are not an integrated part of the hotel's future development, the property may lose a significant competitive opportunity. Spa-less hotels or poorly run properties have an inherent competitive market disadvantage. Not only do they find it more difficult to penetrate the market but they also often lose market share.

► HOW BIG SHOULD IT BE?

► Resort Spas

The ratio of guest rooms to treatment rooms is based on many factors, including the anticipated return on investment to the owners, the topography of the site, the scope and theme of the spa, and the competition. In a destination resort, where the reason for the spa facilities is the reason for the trip, there should be an average of 1 treatment room for every 4 to 5 guest rooms. At the other end of the spectrum, such as a casino hotel, the spa is definitely an amenity, and 1 treatment room should be built for every 50 to 100 guest rooms.

The spas at lower-end hotel properties normally are limited in scope and are often between 3,000 and 6,000 square feet, whereas luxury spas at full-service, high-end resorts average between 10,000 and 35,000 square feet. These ranges vary based on each hotel's specific circumstances, including seasonality, accessibility, meeting space, fill patterns, and local demand. Each market and each lodging product must be individually evaluated to assess the appropriate ratio of treatment rooms to guest rooms.

Another matrix that measures the viability of a resort or hotel spa is the cost to build the facility. Once again, a number of factors support various outcomes in this process, including the amount of available land, the finishes of the spa, the finishes of the hotel (these should be compatible), and the need to develop a spa either vertically or horizontally. Vertical spas are most often built in environments where land is scarce or the allocated footprint for the spa is too small for one floor. Vertical construction always raises the price per square foot, as load distribution, drainage, and the weight of equipment and water must be factored into the construction design and budget. The cost to construct a resort or destination spa can range from as low as $200 per square foot to over $450 per square foot. High land-value areas and plumbing-rich design schemes will send cost dramatically above this range.

► Day Spas

Day spas often lack the grand infrastructure associated with resort spas, and for this reason the ratio of spa revenue to treatment room space is much closer. In terms of number of square feet, day spa revenues account for 43 percent of the total spa space and provide approximately 52 percent of the total day spa revenues. The remaining 57 percent of the day spa environment is allocated to guest flow, check-in desk, retail, back-of-the-house support, and, on some occasions, food and beverage areas.

► Medical Spas

Historically, medical spas have placed less emphasis on the aesthetics of the spa experience and more on the treatment provided. Therefore, it is not surprising that 45 percent of the medical spa space provides 63 percent of all medical spa revenue. Retail sales are limited in medical spas, as outside of cosmetics and prescriptions there are limited branding opportunities. While resort spa goers are anxious to wear a sweatshirt or ball cap that announces to the world where they last vacationed, most medical spa clients do not share the same need or enthusiasm about their recent microderm abrasion or rhinoplasty. Medical spas may require the use of pharmacies to fill patient's prescriptions, which from a business model could be considered part of their treatment-related retail sales.

► Treatment Type Versus Revenue

To this point, we have evaluated the economics and use patterns of spa types. The focus of most spas dictates how the space is allocated and where the income is generated. Spas should aim to have at least 50 percent of their total space—their prime real estate—produce direct revenue. Secondary real estate is the support and public areas necessary for atmosphere and supporting functions that assist in delivering the spa services. Secondary spa real estate includes areas where people can prepare for or relax from their spa treatments. These secondary areas are an important component in the spa development plan, as they allow guests to prolong their experience, which enhances the perceived value. If guests are hurried from their massage or facial out of the spa and back onto the street, the magic that is created can be abruptly snapped and the overall spa experience is compromised. Conversely, if a guest is allowed to soak and relax for hours after a body wrap is completed, emotionally speaking, the cost of the body wrap is amortized over the entire spa experience and not just for the time the client was enjoying the body wrap in the spa's prime real estate.

Combination rooms account for about 36 percent of North American spa spaces, but because of the various treatments offered in them, a revenue percentage generated from these spaces is hard to predict. Combination spaces allow the spa to address surges in demand for specific treatments and at the same time be flexible and respond to global market changes. Massage rooms account for approximately 27 percent of the total space in North American spas but 47 percent of the spa revenue. Given these factors, an operator would need a compelling reason to not include massage on the spa menu. Facial treatment areas reflect 19 percent of the total spa space and result in about 33 percent of the spa's overall revenue. Wet rooms, often the most underutilized portions of the spa, account for 7 percent of the space and revenue. Because many spa modalities involve water therapies, many spa developers and owners believe that wet rooms are essential, even if they seem underutilized. Because wet rooms are one of the most expensive components of a spa, it is essential that they be utilized to their fullest extent. Packaging wet room treatments with other spa services is one way to better utilize the space and create value for the spa.

▶ SPA TRENDS
▶ On-Site Industry Trends

Anti-aging treatments and products are driving much of spa menu and retail development. This calls for devoting a treatment room to outpatient medical procedures. Programming and spa menu items include sun damage treatments, chemical peels for skin renewal, and other rejuvenation techniques that build on repeat procedures. Commensurately, spas are developing retail product lines that can take the spa experience home and continue the wellness regime.

Gift card sales are driving new users to spas. In the friends and family sector as well as the corporate gift-giving world, day spa certificates are creating demand that is not directly user driven. Third-party purchasing brings to spas clients who may not normally have chosen the location or treatment, creating a large but undefinable market demand.

Regional specialties that relate to indigenous and climatic influences continue to create unique spa experiences based on site-specific supply. This has excellent leverage potential for spa operators working to differentiate their product matrices in densely operated areas.

Increased stress management. It is important to position services for stress relief, especially to the male business traveler. Spa programming that requires a limited amount of special equipment and minimal changes to a property's infrastructure can do this.

Impulse appointments. "Life is uncertain, but I want a massage (reflexology appointment, yoga class, etc.) now!" This trend may result in developing adjunct programs for on-call staff resources. The as-needed portion of the program limits a hotel's payroll burden and other related fixed costs. Of course, this implies existing core programs and facilities where these programs can be developed and supported.

Shift in perspective. Self-indulgence, pampering, and luxury are being reevaluated and repackaged with a new, broader emphasis on self-care, stress relief, and emotional balancing. This is reflected in spa programming, the menu of services, food and beverage outlets, and spa-related retail. The retail positioning and spa programming components represent huge untapped revenue opportunities.

Changes in demographic use profile. Historically, the greatest segment of spa goers was women between the ages of 35 and 55. More couples and families are expected to visit the spa together as an alternative social/recreational activity. This trend has the potential to extend business-related stays, fill business hotels on the weekend, and create demand for destinations. It is important to understand this trend when evaluating ways to increase market penetration in a down market.

Medical affiliations. For some markets, an affiliation with a medical center or group in the area can be established to provide treatments such as acupuncture, nutritional assessment, laser therapies (hair removal and wrinkle reduction), Botox injections, collagen treatments, chemical peels, laser resurfacing, body contouring, microderm abrasion, and vascular procedures. When creating these types of relationships, it is essential that spa owners thoroughly investigate the legal disclosure and liability implications of being an affiliated medical service provider.

Green environments. A spa can be ecologically sensitive by incorporating environmentally friendly features into the operation. By proactively supporting programs and products that are earth friendly, the spa does something good for the environment, provides a service to the community, and creates a competitive advantage and a unique selling point that may provide significant returns, especially in a highly competitive market.

▶ Global Industry Trends

Trends in day, destination, and amenity spas influence each other. According to Susan Ellis (2004), president of Spa Finder, a spa marketing company, after the rise of the medical spa and broadening spa participation by men and teens, spa use is expected to become more popular in 2005 and beyond. Spa Finder's trends to watch for are abstracted below:

- Those personal elements that make the spa experience special will find their way into the design of personal living spaces in private homes.

- Private, gated living communities will develop around central spa facilities, much like golf and fly-in communities.

- Some spas will compete on the far outer reaches of luxury, with ever-increasing rare and proprietary products and services.

- Spas will make house calls. Legitimate spas will offer out-call services where spa technicians travel with appropriate equipment and personnel to a client's home, office, or hotel room.

- Destination spas and resorts will develop market segments focused on personal goals—everything from spiritual awareness to sexual health to detoxification.

- The spa travel segment will grow, with more clientele booking through online portals.

- Medical spas will continue to be popular and will add alternative therapies and couple traditional medical treatment with spa luxury and innovation.

- Day spas will not grow their exotic menus much more but rather focus on the traditional; destination/resort spas will be the businesses that experiment with more exotic services and products.

- Specialized cuisine developed for spa guest consumption will find its way into mainstream grocery/specialty food offerings. Restaurants may also add lines of healthy spa cuisine to their menus.

- Eco spas—those designed and operated around green principles of management—will become a growing segment of the industry.

▶ CONCLUSION

The foregoing discussion and explanation of the service and amenity potential of spas of varying types strongly suggests that they will continue to maintain a position of importance in the inventory of hotel services. Even the most modest of spa offerings can enhance a hotel guest's lodging experience. Someday basic spa services may be arranged for at even moderately priced lodging properties.

► BUSINESS PROBLEM ANALYSIS

Mitch Jucha (2004), spa director, Westin Century Plaza, Los Angeles, California

► PROBLEM

Spa Mystique, a 35,000-square-foot spa, is not turning a profit. It is a newly built, state-of-the-art spa facility located adjacent to a 728-room full-service conference center hotel. The property is located in an affluent commercial and residential area of West Los Angeles with direct access to major surface arterials and freeways.

► BACKGROUND/STATUS QUO

The Westin Century Plaza, a Commercial and Convention Property

- 728 rooms
- Occupancy level: 55–58 percent average (weekends 30–40 percent average)
- Primarily business hotel catering to large groups and transient business travelers
- The largest hotel ballroom in Los Angeles
- Breeze Restaurant
- Where U.S. presidents stay in Los Angeles since President Ford began using the hotel during his term
- Was once called the West Coast White House due to President Reagan's patronage

Facilities of Spa Mystique of the Westin Century Plaza

- 35,000 square feet
- Café Mystique, state-of-the-art fitness center, Yamaguchi Salon, boutique
- Designed by Silvia Cipieli
- 28 treatment rooms
- 4 outdoor massage cabanas
- Separate entrance for members and local guests with valet
- Tranquility lounge
- Separate locker rooms for men and women
- Signature massage, facial, and body treatments
- Spa membership available

Guest Utilization Data

- 22 percent hotel guests
- 77 percent local guests
- 6 percent group guests
- 1 percent hotel employees
- Based on the guest type distribution, marketing budget was redirected to local day spa guests.
- Additional internal marketing completed to increase in-house usage.

The Problem

- Many of the decisions herein were based on an analysis of the profit and loss statement and the general ledger.
- Allowed comparisons to industry averages.
- Examination results:
  Retail sales were below average.
  Cost of sales was too high.
  Payroll was too high.

Breakeven was roughly $150,000.

Industry average profit would not be met unless $330,000 in revenue was produced.

► SOLUTIONS

After a Sales and Marketing Evaluation

- Redirected marketing efforts to local day spa guests.
- Created departmental marketing budget.
- Placed advertisements in local papers and magazines.
- Completed renewed efforts on in-house guests.
- Increased hours.

  Increased hours of operation of Sundays to include two additional bookable hours to increase revenue and meet demand.

  More recently, extended treatment hours to 8:00 each night of the week, resulting in 50 additional services per week.

  The increased hours are expected to yield $260,000 annually.

- Pursued corporate business.

  Marketed to local corporate offices by offering midweek discounts to their employees.

  Entered into a corporate membership agreement with MGM building employees.

- Modified spa menu.

  Created 25-minute services.

  Filled 30-minutes gaps and maximized utilization.

  Catered to transient business travelers and group guests of hotel.

- Created treatment enhancements, which allowed price increases without treatment time increases.
- Added corporate spa memberships.
- Create a limited spa membership that utilized spa during low demand.

Evaluation of Competitors' Price Structure

- Performed competitive price survey.
- Survey determined that spa prices were below competition.
- Consequently, increased all spa prices by 20–25 percent.
- Implemented discounted pricing and promotions during low demand periods.
- Restructured package pricing.

Modified Staffing

- Rectified overstaffing of the locker room attendants and fitness attendants.
- Added spa group coordinator or spa sales coordinator position.
- Realigned technicians' schedules to eliminate overlapping shifts.

  Overlapping shifts created an inefficiency in utilization of treatment rooms.

  Without overlapping, treatment rooms are able to be fully utilized.

  Prior to this change, maximum utilization topped out at 70 percent.

Performed Wage Audit

- Restructured spa technicians' wages because paying the technicians an hourly rate created an inverse payroll burden during low demand.
- Removed hourly pay and created a flat-rate commissionable salary structure.

- Brought pay structure in line with spa industry standards.
- Instituted system at the top of the competitive set.
- Provided an opportunity to issue annual wage increase based on performance.

After implementation of the above tactics and strategies, Spa Mystique more than doubled revenues from the previous reporting period. The changes were considered a success, and the spa is now profitable.

REFERENCES

Audi, Lisa, and Brian Wright. 2004. *Compensation Workbook for the Spa Industry.* Chicago: Compensation Consulting Consortium, pp. 9, 11, 14, 64–77, 86–89.

Billing, M. 2002. "Another Owner Takes on Marriott." *Hotel Business* 11(18):1, 44.

Eisenberg, David M. 1997. "Advising Patients Who Seek Alternative Medical Therapies." *Annals of Internal Medicine* 127(1):61–69.

Eisenberg, David M., Ronald C. Kessler, Cindy Foster, Frances E. Norlock, David R. Calkins, and Thomas L. Delbanco. 1993. "Unconventional Medicine in the United States—Prevalence, Costs, and Patterns of Use." *New England Journal of Medicine* 328(4):246–52.

Ellis, Susan. 2004. "Top 10 Spa Trends to Watch in 2005." *Spa Finder,* December 16.

_____. 1999. *Trends in the Hotel Industry.* San Francisco: PKF Consulting, Hospitality Research Group.

Gomez.com. 2000. *State of Online Travel.* Waltham, MA: Gomez.

Hensdill, C. 1998. "Electronic Distribution: Developing Paths of Least Resistance." *Hotels* February: 41–46.

Jucha, Mitch. 2004. Private communication. Westin Century Plaza, Spa Mystique, Los Angeles.

Lewis, Robert C., and Christopher Roan. 1986. "Selling What You Promote." *Cornell Hotel and Restaurant Administration Quarterly* 27(1):13–15.

O'Connor and Horan.

PhoCusWright. 2001. *Online Travel Marketplace 2001–2003.* New York: PhoCusWright.

Preferred Research (proprietary).

PricewaterhouseCoopers, January 2000. "Forecasts and Analyses for the Hospitality Industry." In *Hospitality Directions—Europe Edition.*

Thacker, Geoff. 2004. *"Spa Industry Study: A Profile of the Spa Industry in the United States and Canada."* Toronto: Association Resource Centre, Inc., Research and Strategy Division, pp. 6–22, 23, 30, 34–50, 60–67.

Travel Industry Association of America. 2001. *Travelers' Use of the Internet.* Washington, DC: TIAA.

Travel Research International. 1999. *The European Hotel Industry.* Staff Report.

SUGGESTED READINGS

Books

Gomes, Albert J. 1985. *Hospitality in Transition.* Houston, TX: Pannell Kerr Forster.

Hilton, Conrad. 1957. *Be My Guest.* Englewood Cliffs, NJ: Prentice Hall.

Jarman, Rufus. 1952. *A Bed for the Night: The Story of the Wheeling Bell Boy: E.M. Statler and His Remarkable Hotels.* New York: Harper and Row.

Rushmore, Stephen, Dana Michael Ciraldo, and John Tarras. 2000. *Hotel Investment Handbook.* New York: West Group.

Articles

Brown, Terrence E., and Michael M. Lefever. 1990. "A 50-Year Renaissance: The Hotel Industry from 1939 to 1989." *Cornell Hotel and Restaurant Administration Quarterly* 31(1):18–38.

Greger, Kenneth R., and Glenn Witham. 1991. "The View from the Helm: Hotel Execs Examine the Industry." *Cornell Hotel and Restaurant Administration Quarterly* 32(3): 18–35.

Lee, Daniel R. 1985. "How They Started: The Growth of Four Hotel Giants." *Cornell Hotel and Restaurant Administration Quarterly* May. Vol. 26, No. 1.

Page, Gary S. 1984. "Pioneers and Leaders of the Hospitality Industry." In *Introduction to Hotel and Restaurant Management,* Robert A. Brymer (ed.). Dubuque, IA: Kendall/Hung, pp. 21–29.

Staff article. 1985. "The Evolution of the Hospitality Industry." *Cornell Hotel and Restaurant Administration Quarterly* May:36–86. Vol. 26, No. 1.

SOURCE NOTES

Chapter 1.2, "The Hotel Development Process," by John Dew.

Chapter 1.3, "How Well Does the Branded Distribution Company Allow Independent Hotels to Compete with the Chains?" by Peter Cass.

Chapter 1.4, "The Art and Science of Opening a Hotel," by Tom Dupar.

Chapter 1.5, "On-line Pricing: An Analysis of Hotel-company Practices," by Peter O'Connor, is reprinted from the February 2003 issue of *Cornell Hotel and Restaurant Administration Quarterly.* © Cornell University. Used by permission. All rights reserved.

Chapter 1.6, "Customer Relationship Management—A Driver for Change in the Structure of the U.S. Lodging Industry," by Gabriele Piccoli, Peter O'Connor, Claudio Capaccioli, and Roy Alvarez, is reprinted from the August 2003 issue of *Cornell Hotel and Restaurant Administration Quarterly.* © Cornell University. Used by permission. All rights reserved.

Chapter 1.7, "Spas and the Lodging Industry," by Peter C. Anderson.

chapter two
ORGANIZATION

2.1 INTRODUCTION

▶ CLASSIC ORGANIZATION

In hotels in the United States at the beginning of the twentieth century, the classic European hotel organization model was predominant. This structure was built around two major hotel managerial personalities: the chef and the maître d'hôtel. The chef was the chief or king of the kitchen. In many ways, he represented a feudal lord on his estate who held sway over everything that had to do with selection and preparation of food in the hotel. This structure recognized the importance of the role that food and its preparation played in the hotels of the time.

Similarly, the maître d'hôtel was the master of all service in the hotel. It was his responsibility to manage the interaction of the hotel's staff and guests such that guests were always served promptly, properly, and in line with the hotel's policy. Even the titles *chef* and *maître d'hôtel,* translated from the French as "chief" and "master of the hotel," suggest a strong European influence. That these terms are still in use today attests to a continuing influence, but the roles have changed and evolved. In several places in this book, we consider the ways in which people, organizations, and jobs have changed in the hotel industry.

For many of the same reasons cited in the Introduction as to why the management of hotels has changed, hotel organization structures have also changed. As our knowledge of our guests and the markets they represent grew and became more precise, specialization within the hotel organizational structure increased the effectiveness with which the organization managed and delivered its services.

Hotel organization structures are not immune to the influences of the economy and business cycles, so the difficulties that befall business in general during economic downturns also affect hotel organizations. *Downsizing* and *reengineering* are terms used to describe the changes hotel companies have undergone.

In the early 1990s, some hotels eliminated entire levels of management or combined managerial responsibilities to flatten the organization. In the typical functional chart, such as that depicted in Figure 2.1, the executive assistant manager was often eliminated, making division heads directly responsible to the general manager (GM). Some hotels eliminated separate managers at the division level, with all department managers reporting directly to the GM.

However the restructuring looks, organizations are still formed around principles such as those outlined by Stoner and Wankel (1986). They said that the organizing process involves balancing a company's need for both stability and change. They go on to comment on "organizing" as a multi-step process based on that proposed by Dale (1967):

- Organizing details all of the work that must be done to attain the organization's goals.

Figure 2.1   Typical Hotel Organization Chart

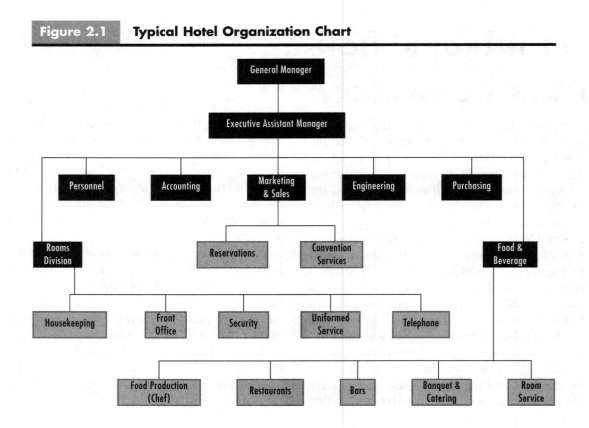

- Organizing divides the total work to be performed into groups of activities that can be performed by one person or one group of people.

- Organizing combines the work of an organization's members in some logical and efficient manner.

- Organizing sets up a mechanism to coordinate the work of the organization members such that it forms a unified, harmonious whole.

- Organizing sets up a mechanism to monitor the effectiveness of the organization's efforts to achieve its goals.

In the modern hotel organization, even a reengineered one, a linear line and staff structure has emerged to reflect this theoretical organizing process.

Figure 2.1 depicts a typical organization chart for a large hotel. Note that, with the exception of top managers, function rather than title identifies the departments. This is to indicate that job titles and associated duties vary from company to company, and, as noted, may be combined or eliminated to reflect current conditions. Looking at an organizational chart by function rather than by job title allows an industrywide perspective, for the services a hotel delivers remain the same even through financial emergencies.

Note also that in this chart the two major operating divisions are identified as *Rooms Division* and *Food and Beverage Division*. Again, on a company-by-company basis, individual functions may find homes in various divisions, but basically, hotel organizations are set up to deliver these two basic services to their guests: rooms and food and beverage.

What may differ in a given hotel company's organization is the placement of the other departments. The departments on this organization chart should be considered typical and illustrative of a generic hotel organization chart.

For purposes of illustration, the line and staff functions are defined as follows.

▶ Line Functions

Line functions are the tasks assigned to hotel employees in organizational components that bring them into regular or semi-regular contact with guests. The line operations in a hotel organization are the Rooms Division and Food and Beverage Division. Obviously, some departmental functions within each line division have more or less guest contact than others. The underlying commonalty is that most line employees are hands-on participants in the assembly and delivery of the hotel's services.

For instance, under most circumstances, members of the hotel's security staff do not have regular guest contact; housekeeping staff may have somewhat more guest contact, and housekeepers are obviously major participants in the production of the hotel's services. However, in the Rooms Division, the front office staff has the vast majority of highly visible face-to-face contact with the guest.

Similarly, in the Food and Beverage Division, the employees of the restaurants, bars, room service, and banquet departments have a tremendous amount of face-to-face guest interaction. Like the housekeeping staff, however, only under special and irregular circumstances does the food production staff under the hotel chef interact with guests. Because of their importance in the service production process, they still clearly fall under the line rubric.

▶ Staff Functions

Staff functions are generally those behind-the-scenes activities that support the line functions and, under most circumstances, have little or no guest contact, although major components of the work are to influence the quality of a guest's stay.

In this chart, for instance, engineering is included as a staff function for those reasons. The success of the engineering function heavily influences the quality of the guest's stay and, at the same time, the engineering department supports the activities of almost every other department in the hotel.

For instance, the engineering department maintains and repairs equipment that is crucial to all of the hotel's line functions, including the food production equipment in the kitchen. Engineering staff can be called on to repair the tables and chairs in the dining room, the furniture in the lobby, and the carts the bellhops use to transport guest luggage. The engineering department thus can be considered a true staff department that serves and supports at any given time any or all of the other departments in the hotel.

Other hotel organization charts place the engineering department in the Rooms Division. This may be because that is where engineering works best in the hotel's organization, or perhaps this placement is only tradition.

This situation may also be true for other departments traditionally thought of as Rooms Division functions. Security is one example. In some organizations, housekeeping has been changed to a staff function rather than strictly rooms, for housekeeping, by definition, "keeps" the entire house.

▶ ORGANIZATIONS FOR THE MODERN ERA

Organizations, of course, are more than just boxes and charts. The most modern business organization structures have not changed much in form since the Roman Catholic Church first designed the pyramidal structure as a visual depiction of organizational relationships with which we are so familiar today. If you think about it, the military, government, school systems, and nearly all businesses follow the same model.

What does affect organizations—not so much in their pictorial view but in the way they respond to external and internal stimuli—can be seen by analyzing several of the readings included here and those that are suggested at the end for further study.

At the time of his untimely death, Professor Eddystone C. Nebel III was the C.B. Smith Professor of Hotel Management at Purdue University. He had recently spent a sabbatical leave researching and observing 10 outstanding general managers and 53 key subordinates. During this research, Nebel gained critical insight into how hotel organizations function. In several chapters of his book, *Managing Hotels Effectively: Lessons from Outstanding General Managers* (1991), Nebel weaves the insights gained from the GMs with organizational theory and then incorporates the increasingly important role that committees can play in the successful organization.

Another view of the peculiar dynamics of hotel organizations is provided by Mark Conklin in his essay on how the leadership can influence a hotel's effective organization. In his position as vice president of market management for Marriott Hotels and Resorts, he is positioned to comment knowledgeably. In this instance, he proposes a radical new view—one neither the Catholic Church nor the military might be comfortable with. It does, however, appear well suited to hospitality.

While there is no lack of literature and commentary on hotel organizations, the research and opinion presented here highlight current thinking about the relationship of organizational structure, interdepartmental connections, and the organization's people. Additional insights can be gained from suggested readings.

2.2 ORGANIZATIONAL DESIGN

Eddystone C. Nebel III

This section reviews general management principles of organizational design, including the important but often neglected topic of a hotel's committee and meetings structure.

▶ THE ELEMENTS OF ORGANIZATIONAL STRUCTURE

If the efforts of people in organizations are to be channeled toward productive ends, structure must be given to their activities. Aldag and Stearns (1987) list five ways by which managers give structure to organizations:

1. work specialization
2. departmentalization
3. patterns of authority
4. spans of control
5. methods of coordination

Whenever a manager decides to make an organizational change, he or she usually must take these five elements into account.

Specialization. If there is more than one way to accomplish something, management must make a conscious decision about how to divide tasks among workers. At one extreme is the case of little or no specialization, where an individual worker is responsible for all of the tasks required to complete a job. An example is the chef in a small country restaurant who singlehandedly prepares an entire meal for 20 guests. It's rewarding to have total control over a project and motivating to see the results of one's efforts. The problem, however, is that as demand for products or services increases, it becomes more and more difficult for individuals or small groups to increase their output without changing the way they are organized.

One of management's tasks is to determine the extent to which work and jobs should be specialized. As a general rule, specialization holds out the possibility of greater worker productivity and managerial control over tasks. On the other hand, dividing complete jobs into smaller subunits tends to increase the need for coordinating the activities of numerous workers, each involved in separate, specialized tasks. Also, overspecialization can result in jobs so narrow that workers lose interest, motivation drops, error rates increase, and quality suffers.

Departmentalization. As organizations grow in size, managers are faced with the need to group certain jobs in order to ensure efficient coordination and control of activities. Most restaurants departmentalize, with food preparation and food service as separate functional departments. This is a logical and practical solution. Preparing and serving food is achieved through distinctly different kinds of work; both the process and the function of the two activities are different. Forming departments along functional lines is the most common method of organizing a business.

Authority. Every time managers restructure a job or group into different departments, they are faced with the question of how much decision-making authority to grant individual workers, managers, or departments. Organizations are never totally centralized or decentralized with regard to decision making; rather, they tend toward one direction or the other. A number of factors must be taken into account when deciding what pattern of authority is best for an organization. Managers must take into consideration the experience and personality of subordinates, the environment in which they work (Is it stable or rapidly changing?), the business strategy to be followed, and the management style with which they feel most comfortable.

Line executives have responsibility for business units that provide products or services to customers and account for the revenues of the business. In a hotel, the rooms and food and beverage departments account for most revenue. On the other hand, staff departments are set up because the principles of

work specialization and departmentalization suggest efficiencies from such an organizational design. The personnel and engineering departments of a hotel are examples of staff units. Once set up, however, staff departments sometimes cause organizational problems.

How much authority should functional staff executives have over line executives? At one extreme, line executives could be given total authority. At the other extreme, staff executives, in their specialty areas, could be granted authority over line executives. Two intermediate examples: (1) Line executives are required to consult with staff specialists before making a decision; and (2) line and staff executives are required to make joint decisions. Whatever the situation, top executives like GMs must arbitrate line-staff disputes when they develop.

Span of Control. Span of control relates to the number of subordinates reporting to a supervisor. In the past, some management scholars advocated an "ideal" span of control of exactly seven subordinates. That simplistic view is no longer held. The ideal span of control is dependent on:

- *Task similarity*—The more similar the tasks of subordinates, the wider the span of control can be.

- *Training and professionalism*—The more trained and skilled a subordinate, the less supervision required and the greater the span of control can be.

- *Task certainty*—The more routine and predictable work tasks are, the greater the span of control can be.

- *Frequency of interaction*—If relationships require frequent interaction, the span of control must be narrow.

- *Task integration*—The more a supervisor must integrate and coordinate the tasks of subordinates, the narrower the span of control must be.

- *Physical dispersion*—The more widely dispersed subordinates are, the fewer a manager can properly supervise.

Some of these factors may work in opposite directions. For example, fast food restaurants are operationally quite similar to each other, suggesting a broad span of control. However, their physical dispersion works in the (opposite) direction of limiting span of control.

Coordination of Activities. Problems arise when organizations do not properly coordinate their activities. In simple organizations of only a few people, coordination is usually not a major concern. Problems develop, however, as organizations grow in complexity. As previously discussed, work specialization and departmentalization are organizational responses to the growth of a business. As duties are subdivided, it becomes increasingly important to coordinate the activities of individuals and groups toward common goals. The kind of coordination required depends on how tasks and activities are linked. These linkages result in different kinds of interdependence between individuals and groups.

Pooled interdependence refers to activities that can be performed with little interaction between individuals or groups. Suppose a hotel has three telephone operators. Each can usually perform the required duties independently—that is, without any interaction with the others—as can room maids and cashiers at food outlets. Because these workers need not interact among themselves, coordination of their activities is best accomplished by prescribing standardized rules and procedures for each to follow, by intensive individual training, and by direct supervision. The role of coordination is to ensure that each independently performed task is carried out at the same level of efficiency and quality.

Sequential interdependence occurs when one task's output is a second task's input. This is typical of production line operations where products are progressively assembled. A hotel example is the guest check-in process. The output of a front desk becomes an input to the accounting department in the form of a guest billing record or folio. A well-planned system linking the rooms department and the accounting department is vital for this activity to go smoothly. Proper coordination is ensured through detailed planning, scheduling, and standardization. Coordination also requires identification of the linkages that exist between activities.

Still greater coordination is required in cases where the output of Unit A is input for Unit B *and* the output of Unit B is input for Unit A. Whenever there is a high level of interaction between work units, they are said to exhibit *reciprocal interdependence*. One example is the coordination needed to host a major convention. Rooming decisions made by the front desk must be coordinated with accounting, sales, housekeeping, and reservations; function room usage requires interactions among convention services, engineering, food and beverage, and accounting. Because any one department's output and activity affect numerous other departments, mutual adjustments are required. Close coordination is only possible through direct communication and joint decision making by the units involved. While standardized plans and procedures are helpful, they cannot possibly solve all of the problems resulting from such a high degree of departmental interaction. Direct communication and group meetings are needed to ensure proper coordination when activities involve reciprocal interdependence.

▶ STATIC PRINCIPLES OF ORGANIZATIONAL DESIGN

Experience has accumulated for centuries about how to organize institutions such as government bureaucracies, the military, religions, large commercial trading companies, and, since the industrial revolution, large manufacturing concerns. This experience is distilled in a number of principles that have been identified. While these principles do not hold in all circumstances, they are important and should be understood and applied where appropriate.

Chain of Command. This principle holds that everyone in an organization should have a superior to whom he or she is responsible. A hotel's organizational chart depicts the chain of command. It should be possible for any employee to trace his or her way up the organization chart's chain of command all the way to the GM. The typical pyramid shape of an organization chart is a consequence of the chain of command and the span of control concept discussed previously. Chain of command is a powerful concept. It provides structure in an organization by setting forth a system of subordinate-superior accountability for everyone.

The chain of command affects communication within organizations for both subordinates and superiors. If a GM wants to make a change in housekeeping, chain-of-command considerations mean he or she should communicate with the rooms department manager, who in turn will speak to the director of housekeeping. The traditional chain-of-command structure in a hotel has the baker responsible to the chef and the chef responsible to the food and beverage director. Accordingly, the baker should communicate with the chef and not directly with the food and beverage director.

Too strict an adherence to this principle, however, can take away the spontaneity in an organization. Experienced hotel GMs often break this principle, but in a way that is not harmful to the hotel. The immediacy of some problems in hotels sometimes requires hotel executives to issue orders directly to subordinates two or more levels down in the organization. GMs may also want to maintain personal control over some project or aspect of the hotel and choose to bypass immediate subordinates in order to do so. This does little harm as long as everyone knows what is happening and the organizational climate is otherwise healthy and trusting.

Unity of Command. This principle states that each employee is responsible to one and only one superior—that is, each person has only one boss. Unity of command is violated quite regularly in most organizations. A safety officer who reports to the personnel director might correct a food server, whose boss is the restaurant manager, for a safety violation. The server feels as if she has two bosses and, in effect, she does. This common problem occurs as organizations grow in size and task specialization takes place. Specialists in safety (or accounting, personnel, data processing, and so on) often do have authority, in their specialty area, over workers who do not report directly to them through the chain of command. Problems can develop because of conflicting orders from more than one boss. The solution is not necessarily to eliminate specialization and staff positions but rather to ensure, by closely coordinating activities, that order rather than confusion reigns. The GM plays a key role in coordination throughout the hotel.

Delegation. Young managers often find delegation a difficult task to master. A subordinate's ability to successfully carry out an assignment depends in part on the clarity of his or her superior's delegation instructions. Delegation can range from assigning a minor task to a subordinate to granting complete responsibility for a major undertaking. It's important for both superior and subordinate to understand and agree on the level of responsibility, the freedom of action, and the amount of authority that accompanies a delegated task.

Each level of delegation is useful in different circumstances. Here are examples of orders that result in different degrees of delegation:

- Gather information for my decision.
- Set out two or three alternatives; I'll then choose.
- Make a recommendation for my approval.
- Make a decision, but inform me of it before proceeding.
- Take action, but inform me of it before proceeding.
- Take action on your own; it's not necessary to communicate with me regarding this matter.

The extent to which authority is delegated depends in part on the experience of the subordinate. Young, inexperienced subordinates can expect only limited delegation until they have proven themselves. The amount of authority delegated usually increases as trust between superior and subordinate is built.

It's been said that when a person becomes a manager, he or she gives up earning an honest living. Hotel managers don't usually make beds, cook food, or provide service directly to guests. Rather, their job is to see to it that the organization they manage provides proper guest services.

▶ THE HOTEL FUNCTIONAL ORGANIZATIONAL DESIGN

Individual hotels are usually organized along functional lines, with departments grouped according to the particular work activity in which they are engaged. Figure 2.2 depicts a typical organization chart for a 500-room hotel. The hotel is divided along functional lines into five administrative departments: rooms, food and beverage, accounting, sales, and personnel. The five department heads report directly to the GM. As Figure 2.2 shows, each department is subdivided into smaller organizational units. These subdivisions represent refinements of the work performed and the knowledge and skills of the people in each subunit.

The Rooms Department. The rooms department performs the lodging function of a hotel. Reservations must be accepted, guests must be hospitably received and assigned clean rooms, the status of available and occupied rooms must be kept current, guests must receive mail and phone messages promptly, security must be maintained, public spaces such as lobbies must be kept clean, and guest questions must be answered. These are some of the important functions of the rooms department. The rooms department is divided into a number of subunits, each of which performs rather specialized tasks. In many instances, these subunits are also referred to as

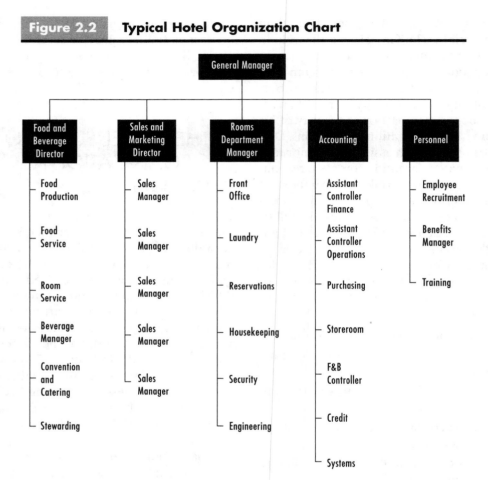

Figure 2.2   Typical Hotel Organization Chart

departments. For example, the laundry department, which in a 500-room hotel is quite large, is responsible for cleaning and pressing all the hotel's linens and employee uniforms as well as guest laundry. Its function is extremely specialized. Little of the knowledge and skills required to manage a laundry operation are transferable to other areas of hotel operations.

The front office is where guests are greeted when they arrive at the hotel, where they're registered, and where they're assigned to a room. Telephone operators and other guest communications functions usually fall under the front office department. The hotel's bell staff is also part of this department. Reservations takes and tracks hotel's future bookings. The housekeeping department is responsible for cleaning guest rooms and public spaces. Security is responsible for guest safety. Finally, the engineering department is responsible for the operation and maintenance of the hotel's entire physical plant, including electrical, mechanical, heating, air conditioning and ventilation, structure, and plumbing. It also performs minor repairs and renovations.

A great deal of interdependence exists between the subunits of the rooms department, thus calling for close coordination of activities. Linkages exist between the front office and the reservations department. Reservations must inform the front office of the number of presold rooms each day to ensure that a current inventory of rentable rooms is always available. The front office must let reservations know whenever walk-in guests (those without reservations) are registered. Linkages also exist between the front office and housekeeping. Information regarding room status must flow both ways: When a guest checks out, the front office must inform housekeeping so the room may be cleaned. Once it is cleaned, housekeeping must inform the front office so the room may be sold. These are both examples of reciprocal interdependence in which individual units provide each other with inputs. Other linkages within the rooms department are illustrative of sequential interdependence, which occurs when the output of one unit becomes the input of another. An example is housekeeping's inability to properly provision a guest room if the laundry does not supply enough clean towels or bedsheets. A less obvious example deals with the output of information from one department to another. For example, engineering cannot replace a defective light switch in a guest room if housekeeping does not report the problem. These examples illustrate the reciprocal and sequential interdependence that exists between subunits of the rooms department. Effective management under these conditions calls for standardized plans, procedures, schedules, and deadlines. Coordination between units also requires frequent direct communications between executives.

The Food and Beverage Department. The primary function of the food and beverage department is, of course, to provide food and drink to a hotel's guests. In earlier times, when an inn had only one dining room, this was a much simpler task. Today, however, providing food and drink is much more complicated. The 500-room hotel in this discussion might well have a coffee shop, a gourmet restaurant, a poolside snack bar, room service, two banquet halls, and ten separate function rooms where food and beverage may be served. It might also have a piano bar and lounge, a nightclub, and a lobby bar. This adds up to 19 food and beverage outlets, excluding room service! On a busy day (or night), it's likely that each of these outlets will be used. Often, more than one event takes place in an outlet during a 24-hour period.

There is great diversity in the activities performed by a food and beverage department and considerable variety in the skills required, so the department comprised a number of functional subunits where tasks are specialized. To begin with, there is the food production, or kitchen, department. In a 500-room hotel, this unit is headed by the executive chef, a person of great stature and authority in a first-class hotel. Under the executive chef are a variety of culinary specialists responsible for different aspects of food preparation. The service of food in a hotel's restaurants and food outlets is usually the responsibility of a separate department, which, in a large hotel, is headed by an assistant food and beverage director. The food service department contains the individual restaurant and outlet managers, maître d's, waiters, waitresses, and bus help. Because of the special problems associated with room service, many large hotels have a separate subunit responsible only for room service. The high value and profit margins associated with alcoholic beverages cause hotels to form a separate department with responsibility for the bars, lounges, service bars, and other alcoholic beverage outlets. Most full-service hotels do considerable convention and catering business. A convention uses small function rooms for separate meetings, larger rooms for general sessions, and even larger facilities for banquets. Catered events include local parties, wedding receptions, business meetings, and other affairs held by local groups. To provide for the unique needs of these customers, hotels often organize separate catering and convention departments that specialize in this kind of business. Finally, the job of cleaning the spaces of the food and beverage department, dish- and warewashing, and general food and beverage expediting is often assigned to a separate subunit known as the stewarding department.

Sales and Marketing. This department is quite small, making intradepartmental coordination fairly easy. Also, the department is removed from most day-to-day operational problems faced by other departments. Still, there is a division of work among sales managers, usually based on the type of customers a hotel is attempting to attract. Individual sales managers often specialize in corporate accounts, conventions, or tour and travel markets. Sales managers are sometimes further subdivided along geographical lines such as regional or national accounts. Still, the sales

staff, even for a 1,000-room hotel, usually does not exceed a dozen or so members. Sales managers work more or less independently in their particular market segments. Thus, problems of intradepartmental interdependence are usually not severe (Pelletier 1988).

Personnel. A hotel's personnel department is a staff organization set up to handle a specialized function. It serves no customers, books no business, and prepares no meals, yet it plays a vital role in a hotel's efficient operation. In Figure 2.2, the personnel department is subdivided into three subfunctions: employee recruitment, benefits administration, and training. The personnel director must be an expert on labor law and able to advise managers in other departments. While these three subfunctions are related, they do not present many problems of interdependence. Instead, the personnel department's major challenge occurs as it attempts to interact with other hotel departments. Personnel may recruit, interview, and screen prospective employees, but final hiring authority resides in the line departments. The same is true of promotion and disciplinary decisions, where the personnel department's input is advisory only. As a staff department, personnel's effectiveness is largely dependent on its manager's ability to form effective working relationships with other departments.

Accounting. The accounting department often combines both staff and line functions. Its traditional role is recording financial transactions, preparing and interpreting financial statements, and providing management with timely reports of operating results. Responsibilities also include payroll preparation, accounts receivable, and accounts payable. These functions are the responsibility of the assistant controller for finance. There is, however, another dimension to the accounting department that connects to operations, cost accounting, and cost control throughout the hotel. This often results in the department being called the controllers' department rather than the accounting department. The two central concerns of accounting control are rooms and food and beverage. The accounting department's front office cashier tracks all charges to guest accounts. The night auditor reconciles all guest bills with the charges from the various hotel departments. Although these employees work at the front desk and sometimes have direct guest contact, they are members of the accounting department and report to the assistant controller for operations.

The food and beverage controller, and the food and beverage cashiers, who work in the accounting department, keep track of the revenues and expenses of the food and beverage department. Food and beverage cashiers report to the assistant controller for operations, and the food and beverage controller reports directly to the hotel controller. The food and beverage department may be responsible for food preparation and service, but the accounting department is responsible for collecting revenues! The food and beverage controller verifies the accuracy and reasonableness of all food and beverage revenues. The accounting department is responsible for tracking and preparing daily reports on the costs of the food and beverage used in the hotel. In many cases, the accounting department is also responsible for purchasing and storeroom operations. Finally, the director of systems is responsible for designing the accounting and management information systems used throughout the hotel. This discussion demonstrates the accounting department's direct involvement in day-to-day operational aspects of the hotel.

We make two final points about the accounting department. First, accounting is responsible for collecting and reporting most of a hotel's operational and financial statistics. It therefore plays an important hotelwide staff role as data provider for decision-making and budget preparation. Second, the accounting department head is responsible not only to the hotel's GM but also to the hotel chain's financial vice president or to the hotel's owner. The reason for this dual reporting relationship is to provide the hotel corporation an independent verification of the accuracy of the financial and operating results of the hotel—that is, independent from the GM. Thus, unity of command is routinely violated in the case of hotel controllers.

► STRENGTHS AND WEAKNESSES OF A FUNCTIONAL ORGANIZATION

The reason for organizing a business along functional lines is to group employees who perform similar tasks or have similar skills. The strength of a hotel's functional organizational design is the resulting efficiency within individual departments or subunits. Performance of common tasks allows for work specialization, which increases overall productivity. Because functional departments perform similar tasks, workers rapidly develop specialized skills and knowledge. Training is easier because of task similarity and the many opportunities for inexperienced workers to learn from experienced workers. This helps new employees quickly learn the skills and behavioral patterns that lead to success.

A functional organization is a logical way to organize work because it fosters efficiency, teamwork, and coordination within departments. However, the functional design's most important strength is also the source of its greatest shortcoming. The success of a hotel is measured by its overall performance, not the performance of one department. A functional department's strength lies in its ability to focus on its own tasks and activities. Although this is surely important for departmental efficiency, it does not necessarily ensure the overall effectiveness of a hotel. Because they are specialized, it is sometimes difficult for functional departments to fully appreciate the relationship between their performance and the overall performance and goals of the hotel. All departments must keep hotelwide goals of customer service and profitability in mind rather than focus narrowly on their own concerns. A method must be found to coordinate the activities of individual departments and to set hotelwide strategies and goals. Left to themselves, it is unlikely that individual departments would be capable of doing this. Specialization at the department and subdepartment levels results in the need for leadership at the top of an organization. Someone above the departments must set the overall strategic course of the hotel, set hotelwide goals, coordinate activities between departments, and arbitrate interdepartmental disputes. A hotel's functional organization demands strong leadership at the top.

While functional departments produce specialists within a narrow skill category, they do not develop executives with broad hotel exposure. Consider the heads of a hotel's marketing and food and beverage departments. These two executives might only have superficial knowledge of each other's specialty. Their education and work experience are likely so different that either would be at a loss if placed in the other's department. The director of sales might have a marketing or general business degree and spend a career in sales-related work. The food and beverage director, on the other hand, could have a culinary diploma and a hospitality degree, extensive food production and service experience, and little or no sales experience. One often finds accountants running the controller's office, engineers in charge of engineering and maintenance, individuals with degrees in personnel administration heading the personnel department, and a variety of educational backgrounds among rooms managers.

Managers educated in hotel administration are capable of filling most department head slots. The longer managers stay in one department, the more narrowly specialized they become. While a manager may perform well within one department, he or she may be unprepared to address problems that require a hotelwide knowledge and perspective. Narrow specialization can result in bias, mistrust, and friction between departments unless upper management takes steps to counter this. Individual departments may pursue their own narrow interests rather than broader overall goals and objectives (Dann and Hornsey 1986). This is a particular problem for hotels because of the need for close interdepartmental cooperation in providing guest services.

► HOW MEETINGS HELP COORDINATE THE ACTIVITIES OF A HOTEL

There is plenty of potential for service breakdowns in hotels. A well-thought-out set of standard operating procedures and systems can decrease the chances of many routine mistakes. Still, because of the amount of reciprocal interdependence that exists between departments, close cooperation is a must. Nowhere is this more important than at the department-head level, where differences in functional specialties are most extreme (Dann and Hornsey, 1986). The vehicle often used to foster cooperation between functionally specialized departments is the executive operating committee (EOC).

The Executive Operating Committee. The EOC is made up of the GM and other hotel senior executives. There's no magic formula for EOC membership, but usually it's those executives who report directly to the GM. Thus, the EOC consists of the most senior members of a hotel's management staff: the heads of the functional departments who report directly to the GM and are responsible for the hotel's major budgetary units. A subgroup of these executives—the GM, rooms manager, sales and marketing director, food and beverage director, and controller—usually produce the hotel's occupancy, revenue, and profit forecasts for each year. These forecasts form the basis for the hotel's overall annual budget, and meeting annual budget goals determines executive bonuses.

The exact duties of an EOC vary from hotel to hotel. The duties and responsibilities of groups can be spelled out in detail or left ambiguous. A hotel's EOC can be loosely structured or highly structured. An important question GMs must answer is the amount of authority they wish to delegate to the EOC. Depending on the circumstances, one EOC might be structured to make certain group decisions, a second to play a strong though consultative role to the GM, and a third to have a weak or nonexistent decision-making role.

Quite apart from decision making, EOCs play an important communications role within hotels. This occurs by virtue of the fact that EOC members meet regularly to discuss hotel business. Any time meetings are held, communication takes place. Scott and Mitchell (1976) identify four functions of communication:

1. To provide information that helps executives in their decision making
2. To motivate by fostering a commitment to organizational objectives
3. To control by resolving ambiguities in the role, responsibilities, and duties of executives
4. To afford individuals the opportunity to express their feelings and emotions

It is important to note that all four of these functions of communication may take place during meetings. Meeting frequency, agenda, and the amount of decision making delegated to an EOC depend on a variety of factors. The more participative the GM's management style, the more likely the EOC is engaged in joint decision making. Authoritarian GMs find little need to foster a strong EOC. The greater the need for change within a hotel, the more likely it is that EOC meetings are frequent. The less experienced the hotel's department heads, the more helpful frequent EOC meetings are because they can serve as a learning and training vehicle for inexperienced managers.

Under the influence of a skilled GM, the EOC can play an important role. Some of the ways it may be useful are:

- To foster group problem solving and decision making
- To build a feeling of joint responsibility for overall hotel performance

- To help instill common attitudes and beliefs among top executives

- To foster top-down, bottom-up, and horizontal communication

- To assign duties, assess progress, and control activities

- To build interdepartmental cooperation

- To teach, coach, and build a responsive senior executive team

- To ensure acceptance of priorities and decisions by senior management

Other Hotel Committees and Meetings. Well-managed hotels address the need for coordination of activities through an elaborate structure of committees and meetings. Just like a hotel's organization chart, these committees and meetings constitute a formal part of a hotel's organizational structure. The GM usually prescribes a hotel's committee and meeting structure. Each group's responsibilities are spelled out (sometimes in great detail), regular meeting schedules are promulgated, and minutes are often taken and distributed to participants and to higher-level executives, including the GM. The committee and meeting structure of a hotel should be a well-thought-out part of its formal organizational structure.

The purposes of the committees and meetings in a hotel vary with the complexity of the hotel. They address a range of concerns including daily operations; intradepartmental and interdepartmental issues; hotelwide concerns; and financial, personnel, and marketing issues. Table 2.1 lists the regularly scheduled meetings of a typical large hotel. While not the meeting schedule for an actual hotel, it could be. It will pay dividends to review this list carefully. The meetings a hotel holds provide clues about what it takes to manage it.

One of the first things to note is the sheer number and diversity of meetings. Surely, one might say that if a hotel were to hold all of these meetings, there would be little time left over to do any work! In fact, the effective management of hotels requires frequent meetings. They are part of the work of the hotel. Table 2.1 shows an average of 249 scheduled meetings each year dealing with interdepartmental issues. Also, the GM attends 295 regularly scheduled meetings each year. In many hotels, this is the actual case.

There is no denying that meetings are time-consuming and sometimes unproductive. Still, there doesn't seem to be a better way to effectively manage a hotel (Conlin 1989). One often finds frustrated, dissatisfied executives in hotels where there are too few meetings. These executives complain about not being kept informed of what is going on. As elementary as it may seem, it is easy for a hotel to fail to keep its managers and employees adequately informed. This shortcoming can have disastrous consequences for the attitude and morale of a hotel's staff. A second complaint relates to service breakdowns that occur as a consequence of too few meetings. Hotels are subject to frequent, usually daily, changes. Meetings must be scheduled frequently in such an environment, or their effectiveness is lost. Too few meetings results in confusion over a hotel's goals and objectives. People need to know what is important to the hotel. What does it value most? What does it stand for? What constitutes good performance? Because hotels provide many intangible services, a constant effort must be made at all levels to provide answers to these questions. Meetings are an effective means of accomplishing this vital management function (Hosansky, 1989).

Table 2.1 Typical Meetings Structure for a Major Hotel

Meeting	Attendance	Frequency	Purpose	Meeting Length
Operations	GM, department heads, front office, manager on duty, housekeeping, security, engineering, executive chef	1 to 5 times per week	Review upcoming day's activities and previous day's results	15 to 30 minutes
Staff	GM, department heads, all subdepartment managers reporting to department heads	Weekly	Review last week's performance, this week's activities, next week's plans and special projects; present performance awards	1 to 2 hours
Executive Committee	GM, department heads	1 to 4 times per month	Performance review, policy, strategy formulation	1 to 2 hours
Sales Forecast and Marketing	GM, resident manager, front office, sales, reservations	1 to 4 times per month	Review room demand for upcoming 90 days, devise strategies to increase room-nights average rates, or both	1 to 2 hours
Department	GM as needed, department head, and all subdepartment heads, managers, and supervisors	1 to 2 times per month	Review department issues	1 hour
Subdepartment	Department head as needed, subdepartment head, all members, management, and staff	Monthly	Subdepartment, department issues	1 hour
Credit	GM, controller, sales, front office, reservations, catering and credit manager	Monthly	Review accounts receivable	1 hour
Safety	Personnel, food and beverage, housekeeping, and engineering	Monthly	Review safety program and safety record	1 hour
Energy Conservation	Chief engineer, resident manager, food and beverage, personnel, rooms, and housekeeping	Monthly	Control of energy costs	1 hour
Supervisory Staff Meeting	All management and supervisory personnel	Semi-annually	Review hotel performance, present awards, start new programs	1 hour
Annual Meeting	All hotel management and employees	Annually	Year-end review of performance and awards	1 hour
Employee Meetings	GM and selected employees from throughout the hotel	Monthly	Informal communication and discussion	1 hour
Supervisor/ Junior Manager	GM and selected first-line supervisors and junion managers	Monthly	Informal communication and discussion	1 hour

Hotels are businesses that require an extraordinary degree of interdepartmental cooperation in order to provide high-quality guest service. The functional organizational design used in most hotels fosters efficiencies within each department of a hotel but is weak with respect to coordination between departments. One of the organizing strategies employed to overcome this problem is a formal meeting structure designed to foster interdepartmental communication and cooperation. Thus, an important part of management's organizing function is to design an effective meeting structure that compensates for and complements a hotel's functionally departmentalized organization.

2.3 AS I SEE IT: HOTEL ORGANIZATION STRUCTURE

Mark Conklin

One way to represent the environment in our hotel is a chart I use at our new-hire orientation class (see Figure 2.3). I call this a *reverse organizational chart;* it is also referred to as an *organizational pyramid*—and, as you can see, the GM is on the bottom of the hierarchy.

At the top is the customer. Customers are the reason we are here. This focus on our guests creates alignment throughout the hotel. Our mission is to ensure that every guest leaves satisfied and wants to return, thus ensuring customer loyalty. One of Marriott's fundamental beliefs is: "If you take good care of your employees, the employees will take good care of your customers." This belief is at the core of who we are and what we believe in as a company.

I say that we have two types of customers: external customers—our guests—and internal customers, who are the hotel's associates. I don't use the term *employee* but have replaced it with the word *associate*. The difference is that employees work *for* you and associates work *with* you. *Associate* implies partnership and working together, which is a subtle but powerful message. *Employee* suggests a class structure wherein someone is always organizationally inferior to someone else.

It is my belief that the front line associate is the most important person in the hotel, because he or she serves the customer. The job of the supervisors, managers, and the leadership team is to:

- Support the front line and remove the barriers to doing good work.
- Lead and help people do their jobs better.

This means managers support the front line by:

- Demonstrating concern for associates (and it must be sincere).
- Solving their problems quickly and fairly.
- Above all, treating associates with dignity, kindness, and respect.

To accomplish this, leaders must develop working relationships with associates that are based on mutual trust. Quite simply, it is my

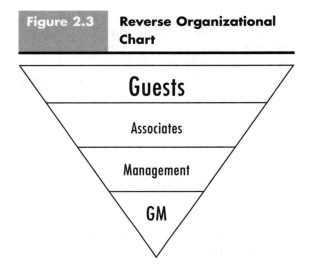

Figure 2.3 Reverse Organizational Chart

Guests

Associates

Management

GM

fundamental belief that our associates will not treat our customers any better than we treat them. This is the cornerstone of our culture, and the challenge is to keep this idea alive as the company grows.

As leaders, it is our job, then, to establish the direction and to create the environment where people focus on our customers. We set the tone for outstanding service, which requires a lot of coaching and leadership.

Putting the GM at the bottom of the pyramid shows that the leader actually works for the people who work with the leader. I view my role as doing whatever it takes to gain and keep customers. To create this environment, I've tried to capture the following key operating principles:

Select the Right People

- We work hard to select the right people using predictive screening tools. We look for people whose talents predispose them to provide great service and who have the highest potential to fit in with our culture.

- We involve our hourly associates in the selection process—after all, they have to work with the new people; therefore, line associates and managers take collective responsibility for the success of a newly hired associate.

Invest in Training

- Our emphasis on training is a reflection of Marriott's corporate culture. We invest in building the skills and knowledge of associates to give them the tools to succeed. We also provide them with an operational framework (standard operating procedures) that represents the foundation for our training.

Create Empowered Associates

- The foregoing combination of training and standards creates empowered associates who have the authority, accountability, and confidence to do their jobs. Years ago, we were challenged to operate our hotels with fewer managers. To accomplish this and to improve customer service, we had to have trained, empowered, and involved associates running the business.

- These systems and standards and this attention to detail help us deliver a consistent product and reliable service, which gives customers confidence and trust in our brand name.

Recognize and Promote

- Recognition in our organization takes place in many forms to create a positive environment. One of the greatest ways to show appreciation is by promotion. More than 50 percent of our managers started as hourly associates.

- Our associates like us, they trust us, and they act in our best interests. Recent companywide associate opinion surveys indicate that 95 percent of our associates rated Marriott as an average or above-average place to work. This is 15 points above the service industry norm.

Finally, it is my strong opinion that our managers should be hands-on. The hands-on manager is one who stays close to the customer and close to the associate—and hands-on managers never forget who is making them successful.

REFERENCES

Aldag, Ramon J., and Timothy M. Stearns. 1987. *Management.* Cincinnati: South-Western.

Conlin, Joseph. 1989. "Management Strategy: Get Control!" *Successful Meetings* 38(7):37–42.

Dale, Ernest. 1967. *Organization.* New York: American Management Association, p. 9.

Dann, D., and Timothy Hornsey. 1986. "Towards a Theory of Interdepartmental Conflict in Hotels." *International Journal of Hospitality Management* 5:23.

Hosansky, Mel. 1989. "Meetings Give You a Leg Up the Corporate Ladder." *Successful Meetings* 38(5):51–52.

Pelletier, Ray. 1988. "Overnight Success Takes Some Time." *HSMAI Marketing Review* 7(1):16–20.

Scott, W.G., and T.R. Mitchell. 1976. *Organization Theory: A Structural and Behavioral Analysis.* Homewood, IL: Richard D. Irwin.

Stoner, James A., and Charles Wankel. 1986. *Management.* Englewood Cliffs, NJ: Prentice-Hall, pp. 233–234.

SUGGESTED READINGS

Books

Nebel, Eddystone C., III. 1991. *Managing Hotels Effectively: Lessons from Outstanding General Managers.* New York: Van Nostrand Reinhold.

Articles

Pondy, L.R. 1967. "Organizational Conflict: Concepts and Models." *Administrative Science Quarterly* 12:296–320.

Schaffer, Jeffrey D. 1984. "Strategy, Organization Structure, and Success in the Lodging Industry." *International Journal of Hospitality Management* 3(4):159–165.

Schaffer, Jeffrey D. 1985. "A Dynamic Model of Organizational Performance in the Lodging Industry: The Role of Competitive Strategy and Organization Structure." *Proceedings.* CHRIE Conference, Seattle, WA, pp. 168–173.

SOURCE NOTES

Chapter 2.2, "Organizational Design," by Eddystone C. Nebel III.

Chapter 2.3, "As I See It: Hotel Organization Structure," by Mark Conklin.

chapter three

GENERAL MANAGERS: A VIEW AT THE TOP

3.1 INTRODUCTION

In most companies, someone who has attained the title of general manager (GM) or something similar heads the organization. Most of us in the hotel field consider this job the acme of one's career. In many hotel companies, the job serves as the springboard to corporate jobs or larger and more prestigious properties.

In previous editions of this book, I noted how surprising it is that so little has been written about hotel general managers. Little structured attention was paid to the development of their careers and the skills and strengths they bring to their jobs. Strangely, this is still the case.

A 1981 article by Arnaldo presented a statistical profile of hotel general managers. Arnaldo drew a demographic picture of his sample ($n = 194$) and commented that although GMs changed jobs frequently, they re-

ported a high degree of job satisfaction. He also provided an analytical framework for reporting how these GMs allocated time and importance to a number of classic managerial roles. The most important of the managerial roles ranked by the GMs were (in descending importance): leader, entrepreneur, monitor, and disseminator, with six others (figurehead, liaison, spokesman, disturbance handler, resource allocator, and negotiator) assuming less importance (see also Mintzberg, 1973).

Readers of Arnaldo's article may be struck by the similarities that echo in Nebel and Ghei's contribution here. Another useful comparison can be made by reading Arnaldo's work with that of David Ley (1980). This work, based on a small sample of seven GMs in comparable properties in one hotel company, recorded how much time the GMs allocated to the same managerial work roles

(Mintzberg, 1973). The difference here was that Ley asked for a corporate office rating of each GM's effectiveness. He compared the effectiveness ratings (highly effective, effective, and less effective) to the observed time allocations of the GMs to leadership and entrepreneurial activities. Ley concluded that in this small group, the more effective managers spent more time on entrepreneurial activities than leadership activities. In contrast, Arnaldo's much larger group of GMs devoted much more time to leadership than entrepreneurship. This should suggest to the reader some interesting questions about what sorts of activities might best prepare future GMs for that role.

This makes the Nebel and Ghei piece all the more interesting, for while still a small group, their GMs were studied intensely, and the authors propose a structural framework from which to view the job of GM. If you will, it is a hotel general manager theory that can be used to explain, predict, or control the position of GM.

A central aspect of career development among GMs is explored by Rutherford and Wigenstein (1985), which looked for the first time at the role of mentoring as it could be measured to affect the success and satisfaction of a modern hotel GM's career.

Although the demographic, salary, and operational data in that article are out of date, the focus of the research can still be useful to those who aspire to the top job in a hotel organization. Also, because the literature on hotel GMs is so sparse, the insights gained from the managers studied in this case add flesh and tone to the work of the other authors included in this section. In the mentoring research, Rutherford and Wigenstein conclude that there is ample evidence that seeking out

and developing mentoring relationships can have a positive effect on several aspects of a GM's career.

Another view of the career and personal aspects of the GM's job is discussed by Pavesic and Brymer (1990). In a number of studies in recent years, they have looked at the roles job satisfaction and stress play in managerial careers. In a review of this technical research, the authors interpret the behavioral dimensions of the GM's career, work values, and personal challenges. Hotel careers are challenging, but as these researchers point out, they do not have to be arduous.

In the research reported by Woods, Schmidgall, Sciarini, and me, we sought answers to questions regarding the importance of various operational measures, and at the same time asked GMs for suggestions about the structure of a hotel-related education. Students reading this article find solid suggestions from successful GMs, as the sample for the study was drawn from mostly upscale and luxury hotels with more than 500 rooms. Much of the financial data are out of date, but many of the conclusions are still viable.

In an interesting new article, Beth Chung-Herrera and her colleagues study the specific skills and competencies demonstrated by successful hotel leaders. The model they develop can be useful to hotel organizations, schools, and professionals crafting the structure of successful careers.

Speaking of success, the three professionals who contribute their thoughts on the job of GM have attained that level in separate areas of the country and for different types of organizations. The employment circumstances of each have also changed since the previous edition.

Previously the GM of the Rosen Centre

Hotel in Orlando, Florida, Emilio Fabico is now in the management structure of the Disney World Resort complex, also in Orlando. His perspectives from the standpoint of the GM and as a member of a management team do not necessarily change. Speaking through his writing like he was a guest in your class, Mr. Fabico shares his insights about management in this fascinating industry.

In the third edition of this book, Rob Balmer shared his experiences as the GM of a DoubleTree Club Hotel in Las Vegas. DoubleTree is part of the Hilton family of hotel products. Since then, he has managed another DoubleTree in California and was recently promoted to GM of the Hilton Burbank Airport and Convention Center Hotel, moving up in complexity and responsibility. His view from the top is instructional.

Another contributor from the last edition is Bob Peckenpaugh, who when we last read about him was operations manager at the Westin Innisbrook Resort near Tampa, Florida. He is now GM of the Rancho Bernardo Inn near San Diego. His observations about managing a relatively small but top-quality resort differ from his previous experience, but both work together to contribute to his success.

From an academic standpoint, the Nebel and Ghei contribution, coupled with the piece by Chung-Herrera et al., can be considered the overarching theory guiding the hotel GM's job. Fabico, Peckenpaugh, and Balmer provide us with the insights and views of insiders and with clear evidence that the theory actually works in practice. This is my goal for this edition of this book: to provide the reader with the opportunity to see that there should be a connection between the book learning of the classroom and what happens in the real world.

3.2 A CONCEPTUAL FRAMEWORK OF THE HOTEL GENERAL MANAGER'S JOB

Eddystone C. Nebel III and Ajay Ghei

Abstract. *This article, based on the research of one of the authors into hotel general managers' effectiveness, presents the viewpoint that the job of a hotel general manager can be better understood by analyzing the influences that shape it. The two major contextual elements that influence the job are deemed to be job demands and relationship issues. They differ depending on the time frame (short-run, intermediate-run, or long-run) under consideration. These two elements give rise to specific job functions and concomitantly suggest various managerial work roles that must be performed in each job function. Finally, the importance of the communications requirement for being effective in the job is emphasized.* Key Words: *Job demands, relationship issues, time frame, job functions, managerial work roles, communications requirement.*

Major hotels of today are diverse, multifaceted, and fast-paced businesses engaged in a wide variety of operational activities. Their organizational and operational complexity increases with size. A hotel, irrespective of whether it is an independent or part of a chain, can be managed as a separate, independent business entity. Thus, each individual hotel can, in effect, be treated as a unique profit center. While it takes more than one person to effectively manage a hotel, the executive with overall operational responsibility for this business is the general manager (GM) of the hotel. "The general manager is the key implementer of the business strategy for the property and the behavioral role model for the entire management team" (Eder and Umbreit, 1989, 333). It can thus be argued that the GM is the central management figure in the hotel business. The demands and challenges of managing hotels are reflected in the complexities of the GM's job.

This article takes a close look at the context in which GMs of major hotels work and how this context affects the nature of their job. It is based on the research of one of the authors (Nebel, 1991) into the managerial effectiveness of hotel GMs. The purpose of the research was, in part, to better understand the nature of the GM's job, and through this understanding develop a conceptual framework of it. As Dann (1990) has stated, "[T]here is now a need to . . . develop a conceptual framework for the better understanding of the actual nature of managerial work in the hospitality industry."

Ten extremely successful GMs of some of America's finest hotels agreed to participate in the study. Each of the GMs studied was an experienced, top-rated hotel executive with an average of ten years' experience in the position. One research goal was to study hotels that exhibited the fullest range of operational

and managerial complexity. Thus, the smallest participating hotel was an internationally renowned luxury property of about 400 rooms, and the largest was a great convention hotel of nearly 2,000 rooms. The author stayed as a guest at each hotel, observed each GM for three days as he proceeded through his normal workday, and recorded his every activity. The research methodology followed closely that employed by Kotter (1982). It employed a combination of participant observation of GMs at work, extensive personal interviews with both the GMs and 53 of their key division heads, background surveys, and analysis of organizational and operational information from each hotel. The personal interviews extended over a number of days and took between four and six hours with each GM, and about one hour with each of their division heads. In addition, informal interviews were conducted with at least 100 other executives and employees of the ten hotels. The field research was conducted while the author was on sabbatical leave and resulted in over 700 pages of field notes, which were subjected to extensive qualitative data analysis.

From this analysis and from an exhaustive review of the literature on managerial work in hotels (Guerrier, 1987; Guerrier and Lockwood, 1991; Koepper, 1988; Ley, 1978; Shortt, 1989; Umbreit, 1986) there has emerged a view of the hotel GM's job that is given in Figure 3.1, which presents a model of the influences that shape the job. The model incorporates ideas found in the research of Kotter (1982) and Mintzberg (1973). Kotter (1982, 10–33) showed how job demands and relationship demands affect executive behavior. Mintzberg (1973, 55–99) described ten separate work roles that managers perform. Figure 3.1 reflects how the hotel context influences the various job functions and man-

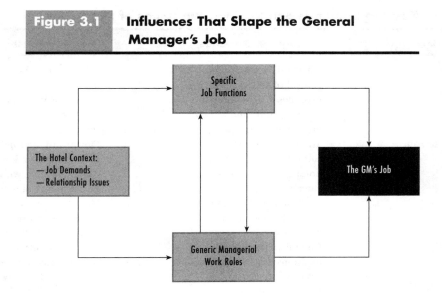

Figure 3.1   Influences That Shape the General Manager's Job

agerial work roles GMs must perform in order to be effective.

The two major contextual elements of the GM's job that affect the specific job functions and the generic managerial work roles are job demands and relationship issues. These, depending on whether they relate to the short-run, the intermediate-run, or the long-run time frame, give rise to certain specific job functions. They also suggest, in general, the various managerial work roles GMs are required to perform. It is the symbiosis of these specific GM job functions and the generic managerial work roles that actually defines the GM's job. We now proceed to discuss each of the elements described in Figure 3.1.

▶ JOB DEMANDS AND RELATIONSHIP ISSUES

Table 3.1 lists key GM job demands and relationship issues according to whether they re-

late to a hotel's short-run, intermediate-run, or long-run time frame. The structure for this table is adapted from Kotter's study of managerial behavior (Kotter, 1982, 10–33).

▶ THE SHORT RUN

The short-run demands on hotel GMs revolve around the daily, ongoing operational issues of providing high-quality guest service, controlling costs, and maximizing revenues. Hotel GMs bear direct responsibility for their properties and thus, like operational managers in charge of profit centers anywhere, are under tremendous pressure to produce short-run results. They must therefore devote a substantial amount of their time and efforts toward exercising effective operational control. An important functional characteristic of hotels is that many of their day-to-day business problems have extremely short lead times. That is to say, most service-centered problems in hotels must

Table 3.1   Key Job Demands and Relationship Issues of Hotel GMs

Time Frame	Key Job Demands	Key Relationship Issues
Short Run	Day-to-day operational control of service, costs, and revenues. Intense pressure to earn profits and render high-quality service.	Intense and frequent downward, internal verbal communication and interaction with hotel subordinates.
Intermediate Run	Train and develop subordinates. Fine-tune hotel's service strategy to changing external environment. Develop and refine the organization structure.	Downward internal communication. Lateral communication with the external environment. Upward communication with corporate superiors and staff specialists or owners.
Long Run	Capital expenditure decisions in line with hotel's strategic service vision. Develop and sustain organizational stability and vitality.	Downward internal communication to further stability and vitality. Lateral communication with the external environment. Intense upward communication with corporate office or owners.

be solved quickly or not at all. Moreover, major hotels are both organizationally and operationally complex businesses in which numerous, highly diverse activities take place constantly as well as concomitantly.

To stay on top of this complicated short lead-time business is unquestionably the single most challenging and demanding aspect of the GM's job. To be able to do so effectively and in a proactive manner so as to retain the ability to influence events, GMs must engage in intense verbal communication and interact frequently with subordinates. In discharging these responsibilities, a hotel GM can be said to be performing the job function of opera-tional controller. However, the heavy workload of short-run operational demands must not take up all the time of GMs, as they must also concentrate on intermediate-run and long-run demands and issues as well.

▶ THE INTERMEDIATE RUN

In addition to their involvement in daily operational issues, effective GMs must train and develop subordinates as well as formulate plans and programs that systematically improve their operational control over the hotel. As changes take place in the external environment, GMs must adapt and fine-tune the hotel's service strategy and organizational structure on an ongoing basis to keep abreast of these changes. These initiatives represent a proactive response to the operational demands of the business; they take time to implement and constitute the bulk of intermediate-run demands faced by a hotel GM. These intermediate-run demands, then, involve putting into place a hotel's organizational structure, systems, and people who are capable of quick and effective response to external stimuli and who can simultaneously help the hotel meet its demanding daily operational commitments. Thus, in effect, the GM is fine-tuning the hotel's service strategy and refining and realigning its operating systems to ensure a smoothly functioning business.

All these efforts require intense, downward internal communication and a high degree of interaction with subordinates. In addition, intermediate-run job demands require the GM to develop communication channels and to nurture relationships that extend beyond the specific domain of the hotel. These relationships include, first, a wide-ranging network of hospitality industry and community contacts who can help the GM better understand the hotel's external environment; and, second, the GM's corporate superiors and staff specialists, whose cooperation is needed for the successful implementation of the formulated specific plans and programs for the hotel. In carrying out these responsibilities, the job function of a hotel GM can be referred to as that of organizational developer.

▶ THE LONG RUN

Two important long-run demands of a GM's job relate to the capital needs and the organizational stability of the hotel. Capital expenditure decisions are required in order to ensure the long-run viability of the hotel, and they therefore must be consistent with the hotel's strategic service vision. The other important long-run demand on GMs is the need to develop a degree of organizational stability and vitality that is in tune with the hotel's carefully planned and clearly defined strategic service vision.

The key relationship issues for long-run capital expenditure decisions are communications upward with corporate executives or owners and laterally with an assortment of industry and community contacts as sources for intelligence concerning the hotel's competitive operating environment. Developing organizational stability depends on ongoing programs of human resources training and development and of sequential career progression. Many of the human resource programs that foster intermediate-run goals ultimately benefit long-run organizational stability and vitality.

Organizational stability enables a hotel to consistently deliver high-quality service and effectively control day-to-day operations. Organizational stability and vitality also gives the hotel the maturity and experience required for it to rethink its basic marketing and service strategies in the event of altered market or environmental conditions. Finally, stability permits the hotel to make any required transition with minimal disruption to its regular operational practices. Key relationship issues associated with organizational stability include continual monitoring of the external environment and intensive downward communication within the hotel. In fulfilling these responsibilities, the GM's job function can be described as that of business maintainer.

▶ ROLES PLAYED BY A GENERAL MANAGER

This section is organized around Mintzberg's study (1973), in which he suggested ten generic work roles for managers. Mintzberg grouped these ten work roles into three broad categories: interpersonal, informational, and decisional. Interpersonal work roles included those of figurehead, leader, and liaison; informational work roles covered those of monitor, disseminator, and spokesperson; and decisional work roles were those of disturbance handler, entrepreneur, resource alloca-

tor, and negotiator. A brief description of these generic managerial work roles is given in Table 3.2.

The influence of Mintzberg's work is reflected in the studies of hotel GMs by Arnaldo (1981) and Ley (1978) and that of restaurant managers by Ferguson and Berger (1984). The previous section explained how job demands and relationship issues had an impact on the job functions of GMs. It was from that discussion that we proposed the three specific GM job functions of operational controller, organizational developer, and business maintainer. Each of these three job functions requires GMs to perform vari-

Table 3.2 General Managerial Work Roles

Work Role	Description
Interpersonal	
Figurehead	Symbolic head of the organization. Required to perform certain legal activities and attend to social activities.
Leader	Responsible for staffing, training, direction, and motivation of subordinates.
Liaison	Develops a network outside the organization to gather information.
Informational	
Monitor	Seeks and analyzes a wide variety of outside information (from liaison role) and inside information (from leader role).
Disseminator	Transmits information received both from outside and inside the organization to other members of the organization.
Spokesperson	Transmits information about the organization to outsiders.
Decisional	
Disturbance Handler	Takes corrective action whenever organization faces unexpected, nonroutine disturbances.
Entrepreneur	Looks for ways to change the organization for the better. Seeks information externally and internally for improvement ideas. Initiates and supervises improvement projects.
Resource Allocator	Responsible for allocating all important resources of the organization, both financial and human, including how the manager schedules own time, programs work, and authorizes actions.
Negotiator	Responsible for the organization's major outside negotiations.

Table 3.3 Combining Managerial Work Roles and Job Functions in Defining the GM's Job

Time Horizon	GM Job Function	GM Managerial Roles
Short Run	Operational Controller	• Monitor and Disseminator (of internal information) • Disturbance Handler • Resource Allocator (of own time) • Leader
Intermediate Run	Organizational Developer	• Liaison • Monitor and Disseminator (of both external and internal information) • Entrepreneur • Resource Allocator (of own time, programs, and funds) • Leader
Long Run	Business Maintainer	• Liaison • Monitor and Disseminator (of external and internal information) • Resource Allocator (of programs and funds) • Entrepreneur • Leader

ous managerial work roles in order to be successful. Combining the various managerial work roles with the specific job functions helps provide a clearer understanding of the GM's job. These relationships are shown in Table 3.3.

Although the GMs studied were observed performing each of Mintzberg's ten managerial work roles, the interpersonal roles of leader and liaison, the informational roles of monitor and disseminator, and the decisional roles of disturbance handler, entrepreneur, and resource allocator were found to be of particular significance. These roles were performed regularly as GMs carried out their various job functions. We now proceed to describe the managerial work roles most often performed by GMs while discharging their three primary job functions.

► MANAGERIAL WORK ROLES AS OPERATIONAL CONTROLLER

The GM's work as operational controller is characterized by a high degree of involvement in the daily operations of the hotel. Because the activities of a hotel are both numerous and diverse, GMs must be constantly monitoring and disseminating detailed information pertaining to daily operational matters. Time and again throughout the course of the working day, GMs interact with subordinates to stay on top of the numerous operational problems that occur. GMs must also be available to effectively and quickly handle disturbances that are not covered by a hotel's routine procedures or those that subordinates perceive as being beyond their scope of authority or experience. In order to effectively play this managerial work role of disturbance handler, GMs must have rapid access to reliable internal information and, in turn, be able to quickly process and disseminate this information downward in the organization. While functioning as operational controller, the GM's work role as resource allocator revolves mostly around the allocation of his or her own time to the numerous short-run demands of the job. GMs can, of course, allocate a proportion of their hotel's financial and human resources to help solve short-run operational problems, but it is the manner in which they allocate their own scarce time that is of paramount importance when referring to the short-run operational problems of the job.

GMs perform the leader role in every contact with subordinates. Every action of a GM is analyzed and interpreted by subordinates; thus, every interaction with subordinates provides GMs with an opportunity to exercise leadership (Hales and Nightingale, 1986). That is why outstanding GMs realize they are constantly in the limelight throughout the working day. GMs also exercise leadership by deciding the operational issues on which to concentrate. Subordinates automatically look for clues regarding what GMs deem important; thus, by deciding which operational issues to focus on, GMs send an unequivocal message downward in the organization regarding what they consider important.

diate confines of the hotel. GMs must monitor information about both the community and the competitive environment, and this requires them to become a liaison between the hotel and the outside world. Further, the information GMs gather from the external environment must be analyzed and disseminated to subordinates within the hotel. GMs must process both externally and internally obtained information in order to effectively play the work role of entrepreneur, the importance of which has been stressed by Ley (1978). As entrepreneurs, GMs are the developers of specific plans and programs geared to improving the operating efficiency and service strategy of the hotel. Any new plan or program imposes additional time obligations on both the GM and on subordinates. New plans and programs often involve the allocation of financial and human resources as well. Therefore, in the course of developing and implementing these specific plans and programs for the hotel, GMs play the decisional work role of resource allocator.

Finally, GMs continue in the leader work role by virtue of, first, continuing relationships with subordinates as an integral component of the job, and, second, by choosing specific plans and programs to implement. As leaders, GMs must contend with the challenge of ensuring that subordinates fully accept the plans and programs outlined for the hotel and are committed to working toward their successful implementation. This requires that GMs pay careful attention to their work roles of monitor and disseminator of information.

► MANAGERIAL WORK ROLES AS ORGANIZATIONAL DEVELOPER

The managerial work roles of GMs as organizational developers extend beyond the imme-

► MANAGERIAL WORK ROLES AS BUSINESS MAINTAINER

The final job function of business maintainer requires the GM to see to the long-run capital requirements and organizational stability and vitality of the hotel. In seeking capital and planning a strategy for organizational stability and vitality, the GM's work roles of liaison, monitor, and disseminator of external and internal information upward to corporate executives or owners are critical, as is the work role of allocator of scarce financial resources. The resource allocator role, more often than not, requires detailed presentation of formal budget proposals that include careful financial justification. This is especially true if the GM is proposing a major directional shift in the service strategy of the hotel. As maintainer of organizational stability, the GM also plays the work role of disseminator of important information downward to subordinates. The GM must act as entrepreneur with respect to important human resource development plans and programs, and, as with all activities, continue as leader in the ongoing role of nurturing and developing managerial talent.

While GMs perform three job functions with different time horizons, it is not necessarily the case that these job functions are performed independently of each other. That is to say, it is altogether possible for GMs to perform two or even all three job functions simultaneously. It is clear from Table 3.3 that many of the Mintzbergian managerial work roles are common to more than one job function. In fact, the work roles of monitor, disseminator, resource allocator, and leader are common to all three, while those of liaison and entrepreneur are common to two of the job functions. Thus, when GMs are engaged with short-run operational concerns, they often do so in the context of longer-run considerations. For example, while responding to a short-run operational problem of slow guest check-ins—that is, functioning as operational controller—a GM may simultaneously be

monitoring and evaluating the effectiveness of a front-desk clerk training program—that is, functioning as organizational developer. The GM may also be formulating a long-run plan to purchase an advanced front-office computer system—that is, functioning as business maintainer. The actual manner in which effective GMs perform this delicate balancing act is covered later in the text.

► CONCLUSION

A hotel GM's job can be better understood by examining the contextual variables that influence and help shape it. A hotel's context presents GMs with a series of job demands and relationship issues with which they must deal effectively in order to be successful. As seen, these job demands and relationship issues differ depending on the time frame under consideration. These considerations give rise to specific job functions that GMs perform through a variety of work roles.

In the short run, the GM job function was described as that of operational controller. Here, GMs are involved with the day-to-day internal operational control of their business, requiring intense and frequent downward verbal communication within the hotel. They must be adept at the managerial work roles of monitoring and disseminating a wide variety of internal information, handling nonroutine disturbances, and allocating their own scarce time to important operational issues.

In the intermediate run, the GM job function was described as that of organizational developer. Here, GMs face the challenges of developing subordinates, formulating specific plans and programs to improve their operational control of the hotel, and fine-tuning the hotel's service strategy in the context of external environmental conditions. In addition to internal downward communication, these challenges require intense lateral communication with both the hotel industry and local community sources. This helps the GM stay abreast of market and environmental trends. The GM also maintains upward communication with corporate superiors and staff specialists to ensure their cooperation in the successful implementation of operational plans and programs. Here, GMs' work roles require them to monitor and disseminate external as well as internal information, so they act as liaison between the hotel and the outside world.

They also may initiate, as entrepreneurs would, plans and programs designed to improve the hotel's operational and organizational efficiency. This requires the allocation of their own time, as well as the financial and human resources of the hotel, to these plans and programs.

In the long run, the GM's job function was described as that of business maintainer. Here, GMs must ensure the long-term viability of the hotel through capital expenditure decisions that are consistent with the hotel's strategic service vision, and by developing a degree of organizational stability that allows the hotel to carry out its strategic plan. Intense upward communication to corporate superiors, staff specialists, and owners, as well as lateral communication with a wide variety of industry and community contacts, highlight the relationship issues of this job function. GMs are required to play the work role of liaison between the hotel and corporate office or owners as well as industry and community sources. This involves monitoring the widest variety of external and internal information and disseminating it laterally, downward, and upward. In addition, GMs play both the work roles of resource allocator of capital funds

and of entrepreneur when seeing to the organizational stability of the business. All three job functions require GMs to be leaders, a work role they play through every contact with subordinates. Finally, these job functions need not and often are not performed independently of each other.

Three important conclusions about the GM's job can be drawn from this analysis:

1. By their nature, major hotels of today provide GMs with a variety of challenges that require careful attention be paid to short-run, intermediate-run, and long-run time frame issues. Thus, GMs must be able to successfully carry out three separate and different job functions. They must be effective as operational controllers, organizational developers, and business maintainers if they are to enjoy long-term success as effective GMs.

2. To be effective at all three job functions requires that GMs perform a large variety of managerial work roles. While GMs perform all ten of Mintzberg's managerial work roles, they must be particularly effective at seven of them to be successful operational controllers, organizational developers, and business maintainers. They must develop the wide variety of skills necessary to play the work roles of leader, liaison, monitor, disseminator, disturbance handler, entrepreneur, and resource allocator.

3. The importance of communications in the hotel GM's job becomes apparent from this analysis. Every job function and every managerial work role carries with it a communications requirement. GMs must be adept at gathering, analyzing, and disseminating external and internal information, and they must be able to effectively

communicate laterally, downward, and upward. Without good communication skills, GMs cannot possibly be effective in any of their three job functions (Worsfold, 1989).

Today's major hotels are complex businesses engaged in a wide variety of activities. The demands of managing these businesses are reflected in the complexities of the GM's job. To be effective, hotel GMs must understand the key job demands and relationship issues hotels thrust upon them. They must perform three separate job functions that relate to different time frames. To do this, they must become adept at a number of managerial work roles, depending on the job function they are performing. Finally, hotel GMs must become accomplished communicators if they are to effectively meet the variety of challenges they face.

3.3 GROOMING FUTURE HOSPITALITY LEADERS: A COMPETENCIES MODEL

Beth G. Chung-Herrera, Cathy A. Enz, and Melenie J. Lankau

The ability to identify the skills and competencies required for tomorrow's industry leaders is essential for companies that hope to remain competitive. Some firms, such as Marriott International and Choice (Enz and Siguaw, 2000) have made identifying leadership competencies a priority. Identifying appropriate competencies helps senior managers in selecting, developing, and coaching future leaders, as well as mapping career paths and planning management succession. In this article we present a leadership-competency model that is industry specific and future based. Our goal in creating this model was to provide the hospitality industry with a functional-competency model that: 1) organizations can use to develop their own model for leadership development, 2) employees can use to understand the competencies they need for advancement, 3) hospitality schools can use to design curriculum, and 4) students can use to craft career paths. We first describe the nature and use of competency models and then describe our study. We examine the critical competencies that we found to be important (and those that, surprisingly, are not as important). Last, we consider the possible uses for the industry-wide model that we have developed.

► COMPETENCY MODELS

A competency model is a descriptive tool that identifies the knowledge, skills, abilities, and behavior needed to perform effectively in an organization (Lucia and Lepsinger, 1999). Designed to help an organization meet its strategic objectives through building human-resources capability, competency modeling has been in existence since the 1970s, starting with the first models created by David McClelland (Mirabile, 1997, 73–77). Such models gained popularity in the late 1980s and remain in use today.

Competency models focus on behavior rather than on personality traits, because personality traits are usually hard to measure accurately (Lucia and Lepsinger, 1999, and ACA's Competencies Research Team, 1996, 6–21). Expressing desirable traits in behavioral terms is essential for a competency model to be useful as a human-resources tool, because the model must not only define the competencies necessary for effective performance but also indicate how to tell when a particular competency is being demonstrated. Most competency models express traits and characteristics in behavioral terms on the grounds that behavior is the observable manifestation of personality traits and characteristics. Competencies are deemed critical for inclusion in a model when they distinguish superior performers from poor performers.

Competency models are less specific than is the job analysis typically performed for specific positions, and models can encompass a whole family of jobs. Choice Hotels International, for example, developed competency models for each of the top four levels of its organization (i.e., senior vice president, vice president, senior director, and director). In so doing, the company found that the competencies for success of a senior vice president were similar to those needed for the other three positions.

► USING COMPETENCY MODELS

Competency models provide a common language for discussing capabilities and performance. The development of a competency model can help provide guidance for a host of different HR practices and ensure that those practices are consistent. Specifically, competency models can be used as a foundation from which to establish criteria for a broad array of HR systems (McLagan, 1996, 60–65 and Lucia and Lepsinger, 1999). For instance, listed below are eight HR activities that can be guided or enhanced with the use of a well-developed competency model.

1. *Recruitment and selection.* Looking beyond skills to performance dimensions such as teamwork, competency models can help to establish what it takes to do well on the job. Armed with this information, companies can focus recruitment dollars on finding the greatest number of prospective employees who have the right mix of competencies for the job in question. The content of appropriate selection instruments (e.g., structured interviews, role plays) can target the key competencies—and, hence, the whole package of needed skills and abilities. Beyond their usefulness in improving selection tools, competency models also provide candidates with a clear and realistic picture of expected behavior.

2. *Training and development.* Assessing gaps between existing employee skills and those identified by a competency model can be extremely useful in devising a long-term strategic plan for leadership training and development. Identification of the skills needed to perform effectively makes it easier to ensure that the design and delivery of training are aligned with the organization's objectives. When a competency model is used as the foundation for training objectives, individual leadership gaps can be assessed and a training plan devised to address deficiencies.

3. *Performance appraisals.* Performance-management systems can be enhanced by a competency model that provides a shared set of expectations regarding what is important and what will be monitored and measured. Competency models help managers to focus performance-appraisal discussions on critical aspects of behavior, thus providing a strategic tool for consistent and meaningful evaluation.

4. *Coaching, counseling, and mentoring.* Competency models are often used as the basis for 360-degree feedback, in which a manager receives performance information from all relevant sources (including supervisor, subordinates, self, peers, and customers, if applicable). Coaches and advisers can use the information so gathered to guide the employee in designing a development plan and making critical-skill improvements. The clarity and specificity of competency models enable coaches and mentors to reinforce desired behavior and tie performance-management systems to necessary competencies.

5. *Reward systems.* A tremendous percentage of a hospitality organization's operating expenses is devoted to employee compensation. To attract, retain, and motivate employees, reward systems must be equitable and linked to desired behavior. Competency models can be extremely useful for defining the behavior that will be rewarded.

6. *Career development.* For employees who aspire to reach the next level on a career path, a competency model serves as a map. Competency models make employees aware of the behavior and skills needed to advance and achieve success, allowing them to prepare accordingly.

7. *Succession planning.* Competency models can be used to identify possible successors for critical jobs by clarifying the requirements for the job and providing a method for assessing a particular candidate's readiness. Without a clear understanding of the competencies needed by future leaders, it is difficult for a firm to measure its "bench strength"—that is, to determine whether the organization has people with those capabilities and, if it does, who they are.

8. *Change management.* Organizations can work toward an uncertain future by creating models that are based on competencies that may be necessary for future leaders, as well as competencies needed for current operations.

Competency models confer several advantages on a company. First, a competency model is useful for building an integrated framework for developing a company's human-resources system. Used consistently, such a model should lead to improved and consistent performance standards. More important, the model can be a critical guide during periods of instability and change. Moreover, making HR decisions on the basis of carefully developed competency models reduces legal challenges to those decisions. (*Note:* Include specific competencies in the job description to reduce legal liability, especially if the competencies will be used for performance appraisals.) Finally, well-developed competency models enhance a company's ability to communicate with its employees regarding the behavior connected with success, thereby increasing the firm's ability to achieve its business objectives (ACA's Competencies Research Team, 1996).

► LEADER COMPETENCIES FOR THE LODGING INDUSTRY

With point number eight in mind, we sought to devise a future-oriented leadership-competency model for the lodging industry. We consider this endeavor to be important given the absence of an industry-focused model that works across many organizations. (Our research found no current models for hospitality leadership.) Having an industry-wide model is important because it can inform students and employees alike about the expectations for future leaders as identified by senior-level managers. Furthermore, an industry-wide model helps to paint a comprehensive picture of the critical skills needed by the entire industry, thereby assisting senior managers in hotel organizations as they devise and implement their recruitment, selection, and development systems.

Looking ahead. We focused our competency model on managerial behavior that industry executives anticipated would be needed ten years from now. We wanted a model that could be used as a prototype to

Table 3.4   Self-Management: Dimensions of a Competency Factor

Factor	Self-Management			
Dimensions	**Ethics and Integrity**	**Time Management**	**Self-Development**	**Flexibility and Adaptability**
Characteristics	• Acts in an ethical manner. • Treats people fairly. • Treats people with respect. • Displays consistency between words and actions. • Considers ethical implications prior to taking action. • Protects confidential information.	• Effectively handles multiple demands and competing priorities. • Manages time to ensure productivity. • Spends time on the most important issues, not just the most urgent ones.	• Deals constructively with own failures and setbacks. • Seeks feedback from others. • Adjusts behavior in response to feedback and experience. • Pursues continual learning and self-development. • Demonstrates awareness of own strengths and weaknesses.	• Adapts to changing circumstances. • Works constructively under stress and pressure. • Works effectively in ambiguous situations. • Views problems as opportunities and mistakes as progress.

guide people's aspirations in the coming years and to create future leaders. Asking leaders to focus on the future is a common approach when building competency models, although the resulting model may not identify all necessary competencies (given that one cannot see the future). (*Note:* Firms including PDI, DDI, and Hay Management employ forecasting techniques. We used the linkage systems method, asking participants to forecast future important behaviors; see Linkage, 1997.) The essential limitation in asking current leaders to project future competencies is that they may be unable or unwilling to define the future differently from the present. However, many thoughtful executives are able to envision and plan for a future that is not simply a reflection of the present, highlighting behavior that they see as increasingly important.

Using a number of different competency studies (Mirabile, 1985; Evarts, 1988; Zingheim, Ledford, and Shuster, 1996; Blancero, Boroski, and Dyer, 1996) as a starting point, we constructed a provisional behavioral-competency model that captured the most important dimensions of leaders' behavior across several industries. Using this preliminary model, we refined the components through hospitality managers' feedback, developing the competency model by means of the customized generic model method (Dubois, 1993). We collected managers' comments by surveying individuals from around the globe who participated in senior-level executive-education programs at Cornell University. In our pilot survey, respondents could add other competencies that they felt were becoming increasingly important and eliminate those items that they deemed inappropriate.

Based on the feedback from the pilot study, we modified the competency model to reflect hospitality-specific behavior. In this fashion, we arrived at a final competency model consisting of 8 overarching factors, 28 dimensions, and 99 specific behavioral competencies. The factors and dimensions were derived from the literature on competency models and through hospitality managers' feedback. The eight overarching factors are communication, critical thinking, implementation, industry knowledge, interpersonal skills, leadership, self-management, and strategic positioning. Each of those factors comprised up to six dimensions that captured various aspects of that factor. Leadership, for example, is composed of the following six dimensions: developing others, embracing change, fortitude, fostering motivation, leadership versatility, and teamwork orientation. As another example, Table 3.4 shows the behavioral items and dimensions for the self-management factor.

We listed the 99 hospitality competencies (Table 3.5) in a survey that was faxed worldwide to 735 senior-level industry executives at various hotel companies. Using a five-point Likert-type scale ranging from 1 (not at all important) to 5 (extremely important), respondents were asked to rate the importance of each of the 99 competencies or skills for a senior-level manager ten years from now (see the accompanying list). A total of 137 industry leaders responded either online or via return fax, yielding a response rate of 18.6 percent. Participants' positions ranged from director to CEO or chair of international hotel chains and corporations. Response rates for executive-level employees are notoriously low, and our response rate for this sample was typical for this population (Agle, Mitchell, and Sonnenfeld, 1999).

Table 3.5   99 Lodging Competencies

(1) Anticipates obstacles and develops contingency plans.

(2) Adapts to changing circumstances.

(3) Manages time to ensure productivity.

(4) Monitors progress of others and redirects efforts when necessary.

(5) Works effectively in ambiguous situations.

(6) Prepares people to understand changes.

(7) Seeks feedback from others.

(8) Works toward win-win solutions with others whenever possible.

(9) Steers conflicts away from personalities and toward issues.

(10) Provides employees access to information.

(11) Takes a stand when resolving important issues.

(12) Integrates planning efforts across work groups or functional units.

(13) Displays consistency between words and actions.

(14) Identifies measurable action steps that support the hotel's strategy and mission.

(15) Works constructively under stress and pressure.

(16) Acts in an ethical manner.

(17) Presents ideas in a convincing manner.

(18) Expresses disagreement in a tactful and sensitive manner.

(19) Treats people with respect.

(20) Considers a broad range of factors (internal, external, and trends) when solving problems and making decisions.

(21) Translates business strategies into clear objectives and tactics.

(22) Brings together different perspectives and approaches and combines them in creative ways.

(23) Summarizes and clarifies what people say to ensure understanding.

(24) Coaches others in skill development.

(25) Challenges others to make tough choices.

(26) Works to understand why others resist change instead of forcing others to accept change.

(27) Accurately identifies strengths and weaknesses in others.

(28) Stays informed about industry practices and new developments.

(29) Examines and monitors trends in the hotel business.

(30) Understands the agendas and perspectives of owners, staff members, managers, and other parties.

(31) Clarifies expectations to staff members about assignments, roles, and responsibilities.

(32) Selects leadership style most appropriate for the situation.

(33) Provides challenging assignments to facilitate development.

(34) Applies cross-functional knowledge to understand and solve problems.

(35) Expresses confidence in people's competence to do their jobs.

(36) Addresses and works through conflict.

(37) Interacts with people in a direct and open manner.

(38) Views problems as opportunities and mistakes as progress.

(39) Works to establish strong relationships with owners.

(40) Understands and harnesses individual differences to create a competitive advantage.

(41) Develops action plans to meet customer needs.

(42) Reduces redundancies in processes and procedures.

(43) Gives specific, timely, and constructive feedback.

(44) Adjusts behavior in response to feedback and experience.

(45) Models the changes expected of others.

(46) Considers alternatives before making decisions.

(47) Listens to people without interrupting.

(48) Protects confidential information.

(49) Encourages employees to use their initiative to remedy problems when they first occur.

(50) Takes calculated risks when appropriate.

(51) Builds networks with people inside and outside the hotel.

(52) Spends time on the most important issues, not just the most urgent.

(53) Commits organizational resources for community events.

(54) Considers pros and cons of proposed solutions to problems.

Table 3.5 *(Continued)*

(55) Develops new systems or processes for increased efficiency.

(56) Encourages others to express their views, even contrary ones.

(57) Listens carefully to input and concerns expressed by others.

(58) Deals constructively with own failures and mistakes.

(59) Handles multiple demands and competing priorities.

(60) Knows the strengths and weaknesses of competitors.

(61) Defines and sets up quality standards for employees.

(62) Gives others the authority necessary to accomplish their objectives.

(63) Adjusts leadership approach to fit other individuals.

(64) Involves others in critical decisions that affect them.

(65) Understands complex concepts and relationships.

(66) Delegates enough of own work to others.

(67) Identifies and defines problems.

(68) Determines which of many problems may become crises.

(69) Defines priorities for the staff.

(70) Confronts problems early before they become unmanageable.

(71) Works as a member of a team.

(72) Considers ethical implications prior to taking action.

(73) Gets others interested and involved in the change process.

(74) Creates needed systems and procedures to support changes.

(75) Keeps others updated with information.

(76) Considers customer needs when making decisions.

(77) Considers the effects of decisions on community well-being.

(78) Champions new ideas and initiatives.

(79) Focuses on important information without being distracted by unnecessary details.

(80) Employs a team approach to solve problems when appropriate.

(81) Understands owners' and stakeholders' values and how they perceive issues.

(82) Influences and shapes owners' and stakeholders' decisions.

(83) Recognizes and seizes strategic opportunities in the environment.

(84) Promotes respect and appreciation for diversity and individual differences.

(85) Treats people fairly.

(86) Allows others to lead under the appropriate circumstances.

(87) Pursues continual learning and self-development.

(88) Promotes quality initiatives.

(89) Deliberately allows direct reports to use their own methods for completing tasks.

(90) Demonstrates awareness of own strengths and weaknesses.

(91) Understands organizational strengths and weaknesses.

(92) Writes in an effective manner.

(93) Actively and frequently listens directly to customers.

(94) Sees how things fit in the big picture.

(95) Promotes teamwork among groups; discourages us-versus-them thinking.

(96) Inspires and motivates others.

(97) Makes sound decisions under time pressure and with limited resources.

(98) Speaks clearly and articulately in a variety of situations.

(99) Builds partnerships and alliances with community organizations.

► KEY COMPETENCIES IDENTIFIED

Competency in self-management is the over-arching factor that was rated highest by our respondents, followed by knowledge of strategic positioning, implementation skill, and critical thinking. (Table 3.6 summarizes the ratings.) The self-management factor achieved a mean importance score of 4.32 out of 5. This factor consists of four behavioral dimensions, namely: (1) ethics and integrity, (2) time management, (3) flexibility and adaptability, and (4) self-development. Looking at the behavioral dimensions within each competency factor, we found that the behavior of acting ethically or with integrity was the most important to the responding senior leaders. *Post-hoc* Scheffe tests from an analysis of variance revealed that this behavioral dimension of self-management was rated significantly higher than the other three dimensions. The ethics-integrity dimension contains six specific behavioral competencies, such as "Treats people with respect," "Displays consistency between words and actions," and "Considers ethical implications prior to taking action" (see Table 3.4). The overriding importance of ethical behavior is consistent with previous competency models devised by managers outside the lodging industry. (See competency research reports by consulting firms such as Personnel Decisions International (www.personaldecisions.com) and Center for Creative Leadership (www.ccl.org).) The other specific competencies that fall under the self-management factor are "Works constructively under stress and pressure," "Seeks feedback from others," and "Spends time on the most important issues, not just the most urgent." Overall, self-management skills encompass actions related to the personal characteristics of the leader and how she or he handles himself or herself.

Competency in strategic positioning was the overarching factor considered to be second in importance for future leaders. This factor comprises the following four dimensions: (1) awareness of customer needs, (2) commitment to quality, (3) managing stakeholders, and (4) concern for community. Examples of behaviors that fall under these dimensions include "Influences and shapes owners' and stakeholders' decisions," "Promotes quality initiatives," and "Considers customer needs when making decisions." This factor clearly captures the hospitality industry's service orientation. The senior managers whom we surveyed suggested that future lodging-industry leaders need to be vigilant in their commitment to both quality and the needs of a variety of different stakeholders, including owners, Wall Street, employees, and customers.

Implementation, critical thinking, and communication skills were also deemed "extremely important" by senior managers. Leaders of the future will need to possess a strategic orientation and approach to decision-making that permits them to both plan and redesign their organizations. In addition, communicating persuasively, listening, and enabling others will be essential skills for managers hoping to reach senior leadership positions.

Industry knowledge, leadership, and interpersonal skill were factors that, while important, were ranked lower than the others by our respondents. The relatively low score for industry knowledge seems to suggest that the importance for leaders of industry-specific

Table 3.6 Leadership Competency Model for the Lodging Industry

Factor	Mean	Dimension	Mean
Self-management	4.32	Ethics and integrity	4.58[a]
		Time management	4.28
		Flexibility and adaptability	4.22
		Self-development	4.12
Strategic positioning	4.17	Awareness of customer needs	4.39
		Commitment to quality	4.26
		Managing stakeholders	4.21
		Concern for community	3.67[b]
Implementation	4.16	Planning	4.23[c]
		Directing others	4.15
		Reengineering	4.02
Critical thinking	4.15	Strategic orientation	4.24[d]
		Decision making	4.18
		Analysis	4.17
		Risk taking and innovation	4.03
Communication	4.12	Speaking with impact	4.27
		Facilitating open communication	4.14
		Active listening	4.06
		Written communication	4.06
Interpersonal	4.09	Building networks	4.20[e]
		Managing conflict	4.07
		Embracing diversity	4.01
Leadership	4.09	Teamwork orientation	4.25[f]
		Fostering motivation	4.19
		Fortitude	4.14
		Developing others	4.02
		Embracing change	3.98
		Leadership versatility	3.97
Industry knowledge	4.09	Business and industry expertise	4.09

a. "Ethics and integrity" scored significantly higher than the other three dimensions in this factor ($p < .01$).

b. "Concern for community" scored significantly lower than the other three dimensions in this factor ($p < .01$).

c. "Planning" scored significantly higher than "Re-engineering" ($p < .05$).

d. "Strategic orientation" scored significantly higher than "Risk taking and innovation" ($p < .05$).

e. "Building networks" is significantly higher than "Embracing diversity" ($p < .05$).

f. "Teamwork orientation" scored significantly higher than did "Developing others" ($p < .05$), "Embracing change" ($p < .01$), and "Leadership versatility" ($p < .01$).

expertise is decreasing as time goes on. One reason for this is that industry expertise can be acquired by an adept leader, while the capacity for flexibility in a changing business environment can be hard to learn and often is inherent in an individual's personality and skill set. Interpersonal and leadership skills also scored lower than did other factors. We found it particularly interesting that the dimensions of developing others, embracing diversity and change, and leadership versatility were viewed as some of the least essential skills for the future.

Concern for community was a particularly low-rated dimension of strategic positioning. Scheffe *post-hoc* tests revealed that this dimension was rated significantly lower than the other three strategic-positioning dimensions. Although this dimension is not typically included in competency-modeling research, we (incorrectly) thought that it might be important to hospitality leaders because of their extensive connections with local community events and activities. This dimension consisted of three items: "Commits organizational resources for community events," "Considers the impact of decisions on community well-being," and "Builds partnerships and alliances with community organizations." Contrary to our thinking, the results revealed that those three were among the lowest-rated of all 99 items presented on the survey. When compared to other activities, a concern for and relationship with the local community in which the company operates does not seem to be a core competency needed for future hospitality leaders. On the other hand, competencies that appear to be the likely core attributes of future leaders are ethics, awareness of customer needs, time management, speaking with impact, commitment to quality, and team orientation.

► USING INDUSTRY-WIDE COMPETENCY MODELS

We believe that competency models can be important in building an effective human-resources system. They can also help in educating future generations of leaders by guiding university faculties in designing curricula to meet the industry's future needs. An increasing number of university programs are focusing on competency building in an effort to prepare students for a specific industry (see *Journal of Management Education* 25(2)). For example, the master of management in hospitality (MMH) program at Cornell University assesses entering students against three core competencies that are deemed necessary for graduation. These competencies are leadership skills, teamwork and group-process skills, and written and oral communication skills. Students are evaluated through an assessment center as they enter the MMH program and are given feedback at the end of the assessment center, as well as after each subsequent semester. If they have weaknesses in any of the three competencies, the students must make plans to improve their skills. Students' competency development is further supported by special modules offered by faculty members to enhance key skill areas. These modules contain both lecture and experiential components.

Industry-specific competency models can also help students seek out employment and career tracks that will give them ample opportunity to develop needed skills. The model presented here provides a comprehensive framework to inform future managers about what will be needed or expected to lead future lodging firms. A good competency model serves as both a roadmap and a prototype for achieving success.

Employees in lodging organizations may find this model useful as a general guide for self-development. In the absence of an institutional program to help develop a promising manager, a competency model can be used by an individual to design and plan her or his own career choices.

Last, individual lodging organizations can use this industry-wide model to build their own specific model. Once an organization has tailored the model to its specific needs, that firm can use the model in a variety of ways. For example, Choice Hotels International now uses its competency database to perform annual readiness assessments to determine managers' leadership capability. The competencies in Choice's model are the basis for the company's selection, promotion, and succession planning. Marriott employs a system-wide leadership-development initiative, called the Benchstrength Management System, which is used by current senior managers to build leadership capacity. Using the tools and measurements from this system, Marriott's senior managers are responsible for identifying potential leaders and ensuring that those individuals develop the skills and competencies needed to carry the company forward. Targeted development plans are created to assist senior managers in filling critical positions that are "stretch" assignments for high-potential managers. The Benchstrength Management System provides Marriott with a consistent approach to evaluating its leadership potential and ensures that the company focuses on core capabilities that are key to future success.

3.4 AS I SEE IT: WHAT I DO

Emilio Fabico

In reflecting upon what it is I do as a manager in the hospitality industry, it's clear that there are the tasks that I must complete, and then there is all the other stuff. Throughout our careers, there are always plenty of duties that we're responsible for completing and that are important to our business. These processes are typically mandated by operational need, fiduciary responsibility, or regulatory requirement. The manner in which virtually all of these tasks are completed is typically inflexible and requires little or no creativity. It's unlikely that one's professional success will come from one's ability to perform these duties successfully.

► THE OTHER STUFF

The swirled, chocolaty surface of a 3 Musketeers bar is not unlike that of any other candy bar; it's the fluffy stuff inside that makes it unique. We're not sure exactly what it is, but it sure is good and differentiates it from the others. That's the other stuff. That's what I spend most of my time focusing on and constantly working to improve. That other stuff is leadership. There's a world of people smarter than me who have written books on this subject, so I certainly don't profess to have any of the answers. What I can share with you is what the zigs and zags of my career path have taught me.

▶ IF IT WEREN'T HARD, EVERYONE WOULD DO IT

It's called *leadership,* not *maintainership.* Leadership is about leading. It's being proactive rather than reactive. It's being out ahead of challenges, as opposed to chasing them. It's about truly being engaged in and passionate about your work. It's about wanting to be and working toward being the best. As I walk the resort and interact with our employees and guests, I attempt to be aware of the challenges that each of the operations is facing. What are they proud of that they should be recognized for? What barriers are preventing them from continuing to improvement? What might be around the corner that we're not aware of yet? What's important to our guests? What can we do, for our guests and employees, to make us better than our competition? How can we meet our employees' developmental needs? Woven into all of these questions and what should always be factored into the answers are *people*—individuals with diverse backgrounds, varying opinions, and different needs. As a leader, I must be able to recognize those differences and respond appropriately to each of them. Being skilled at listening is just as important as leading. How can one answer without knowing the questions? In a 24/7 industry like ours, this interaction and these questions never stop.

Early in my career, when I was a shift manager, a clear line divided work time and off time. After my ten-hour day, the hotel and I went our separate ways until I was back for my next shift. In more senior leadership roles, this line is no longer as clear. Especially in the age of the Blackberry, that line can completely disappear. Here's the part where I make a pitch for balance. That, too, is a valuable leadership skill. Without question, it's possible to be a great leader and still have balance. This is important not only to the leader, but also to those he or she leads, as they often feel compelled to follow the leader's example. This should remain a priority throughout one's career.

▶ SIX DEGREES OF SEPARATION

I have found that many of the successes or failures I face every day can be traced to one source: respect. I must respect the fact that I work for a public company and must ensure that growth and the success of the business remain at the forefront of the decisions I make and the actions I take. I must respect the talents of my direct reports. I must work to inspire, influence, and support them toward their goals. I must not micromanage them. I must also strive to identify their accomplishments and celebrate their successes. I must respect that people enjoyed feeling fulfilled, so I must work to provide the tools and environment that will allow them to be successful. I must respect that our guests have choices when selecting their hotel. They have decided to entrust us with their money, time, and away-from-home experience. We have an obligation to provide them with an experience that will leave them with a lasting positive memory and influence them to return time after time. I must lead knowing that all of us want to be treated fairly and respectfully. When employees are asked why they leave their employment, the answer generally centers on lack of respect or being valued.

► "WHAT MAKES THE MUSKRAT GUARD HIS MUSK? COURAGE!"

Well said by the Wizard of Oz's Cowardly Lion. Although courage is not always easy to find, my role requires me to have it. I must have the courage to give honest, timely, and constructive feedback to my direct reports and my peers. I must have the courage to speak up when what I have to say may not be popular or may cause others pain. I must have the courage to take risks, if the calculated outcome will benefit our operation.

► JUST SAY NO

On a personal level, I must be true to myself. I can recall in school knowing exactly what my professional values were and never doubting that I would always remain true to them. As the years passed, the titles got fancier and the paychecks got bigger. I found myself separating from my beliefs. After losing a job a few years ago (I didn't truly lose it; I know where it is, but someone else now has it), I came to the realization that my paycheck was like a drug. I was thinking in terms of what I could do to get more of it. I had lost sight of how fun and exciting our industry is. Don't be afraid of the zigzagging career path. I found that it often leads where you never planned to go and teaches you what you could have never planned to learn.

And that's as I see it: what I do.

3.5 A DAY IN THE LIFE OF A HILTON HOTEL GENERAL MANAGER

Robert O. Balmer, CHA

I often have heard that professionals in the hotel business enjoy it because every day is different. While I find this to be a huge understatement, I, too, enjoy this business for the same reason.

My day begins with a large cup of coffee. I like to arrive at work early so I can walk the property and greet the early-morning team members and check on the daily banquet functions.

Every morning at 8:30 we have our daily operations meeting. This meeting is attended by our top lieutenants who run the day-to-day operations. The directors of sales, front office, housekeeping, and property operations are there, along with my executive assistant. At this meeting, we cover in detail our daily arrivals. With Hilton Hotel Corporation's advanced technology, we have the capability of ascertaining which guests are new to the hotel, which are returning guests and how many times they have been here, which are new to any Hilton brand, and which have experienced problems in the past. We also know if guests have special preferences or requests. Our focus is to exceed guest expectations and increase customer loyalty.

During this morning briefing, we also discuss our banquet events, arriving VIPs, and any and all comment cards from the night prior. It is a great way to jump-start the morning. The team members briefly describe their day and are sent off with their marching orders. I do enjoy helping every team member be their best.

By this time, my email box is reaching capacity. What did we ever do before email, I wonder? I attempt to sift through and prioritize the messages.

The majority of my day is spent at various times strategizing and communicating with our director of sales and marketing and director of revenue management. Revenue is our lifeblood and of course cures most woes!

Between meetings with department or division heads, I can expect numerous interruptions coming from any direction. The director of finance requests assistance in reviewing a report that must be submitted quickly to our ownership group. The director of human resources needs to brief me on a new hire or recalcitrant team member. The executive chef and director of catering would like to review the banquet event order for the upcoming Mayor's State of the City luncheon.

I usually have lunch with clients, local dignitaries, guests, or of course team members in our four-star team dining room! Increasingly, the job of general manager has an outward focus, projecting the image of the hotel to the surrounding community.

After lunch, it is time to check more emails and to catch up on daily correspondence. Typically, I've got a corporate report due and phone calls to make and return. I spend a great deal of the afternoon reviewing forecasts and working on and updating action plans.

Running a large hotel is essentially the same as being the CEO of a small company. It is essential to have a strong executive committee so each department can run independently. This is the key to success. Success breeds success.

Funny things happen every day. One day during a staff meeting attended by corporate vice presidents, I was interrupted by our director of safety and security. The safety of our team members and guests was in jeopardy. The authorities had arrived at the hotel regarding a guest involved with drug trafficking. When the authorities attempted to apprehend the guest, he ran through the hotel waving a weapon. I arrived at the front entrance of the hotel to witness the guest face down on the ground being handcuffed while the authorities surrounded him with their guns drawn. I didn't want the VPs to be alarmed and leave the meeting room. Before I knew it, the guest had been arrested and business was back to usual. As I was returning to my meeting, a guest approached me and asked if someone was filming a movie. I responded, "Welcome to the media capital of the world! I'm glad you enjoyed the show." There are days I feel like the ringmaster of a three-ring circus. I think this is what keeps each day fresh and exciting.

I often giggle at the old hotel industry phrase, "If it weren't for those darn guests and team members, my day would be much more productive!" However, if it weren't for them, this job would not be different every day.

3.6 A DAY IN THE GENERAL MANAGER'S LIFE

Bob Peckenpaugh

You've made it! It is officially your turn. This is what you have worked for your entire career, the golden carrot, the title of general manager. So what is so different?

No matter what position(s) prepared you for this goal, it is all yours now. Total responsibility for the profit and loss statement and the success of the entire operation is in your hands. This is your opportunity to lead the senior management team in achieving the desires of the ownership, the management company, or both. You are now setting the tone for the operation and providing the results to the next level up.

Results are what your game plan is built around. Whether you work for an independent or a corporation, someone is going to want answers. What do they expect? Is it all about bottom-line profits, five-star services, or a happy medium? What elements of performance are most important to the company? Ask these questions and you are well on your way to developing your goals, the outline for your future success.

Set your goals, document them, and begin measuring your results. Obvious categories are guest and employee satisfaction, great communications, and positive financial results. Remember, you are now the general manager with a supporting cast of managers who each love specific talents and knowledge. Utilize these skills by communicating your goals and ask your team to outline their goals to support what you have set forth.

Sounds simple right? Here is where your day begins. You are now leading those who were your peers yesterday. How are you going to set the tone for your team and create an atmosphere that will support your expectations?

Create the image. A mission statement is a good starting point. What were the expectations given to you? How do you want the team to function? At the Rancho Bernardo Inn, we developed the following mission statement: "To be the finest family-owned destination resort, exemplifying comfortable elegance and service of unmatched warmth and sincerity. We will treat all of our guests and each other as lifetime friends. The way the world is supposed to be." The mood is set, the expectation is laid out, and we are all going to be friends in a world that's the way we want it to be, the one we are creating.

Give direction. How are you going to support the mission statement? Get the team involved; you will be amazed at how easy this is. We have developed a set of core values to show how we want to operate and what our roadmap looks like:

1. Anticipate and exceed guest expectations with genuine sincerity.

2. Maintain a professional staff at the highest standards through continuous training and development.

3. Treat each guest and employee as a member of our family, with respect, honesty, appreciation, and concern.

4. Protect and further our financial well-being.

5. Perform all duties safely, legally, and ethically.

6. Continuously strive for product improvement.

7. Respect and care for the property and its aesthetic image.

8. Communicate positively about the resort, on and off property.

Set the stage. Now focus on the experience. How will you conduct yourself with your staff, and how do you expect your staff to treat the guests? Each time you come on duty, you are stepping on stage. Describe the performance everyone is expected to give. We do this through a set of service expectations:

1. Anyone who receives a guest request owns it. Accommodate all special needs in a positive and timely fashion, and follow up with the guest.

2. Anyone who receives a guest problem owns it. Show genuine concern, apologize graciously, resolve the issue, and follow up with the guest.

3. Acknowledge every guest within 10 feet with eye contact, good posture, and a smile. Provide a positive and friendly greeting within 5 feet. Always be the first person to speak.

4. Ensure that guests are escorted to their destination.

5. Always acknowledge guest needs first by opening doors, offering the right of way, and ceasing personal conversations when a guest approaches.

6. Seek to identify the guest's name and use it at every opportunity, whether in person or on the phone.

7. Answer phones within three rings, saying "[Department name], this is [employee name]." Ask permission before putting the caller on hold and announce transfer calls. Always offer voicemail as an option.

8. Ensure that uniforms and personal appearance are immaculate. Nametags are part of the uniform.

9. Take responsibility for order and cleanliness of the facility. Pick up litter, reposition furniture, and prevent damage.

10. Always use appropriate professional language. Avoid using slang and hotel jargon.

Remember, the team needs direction, and they need it daily; you set the tone, and they create the atmosphere you want by following your example. Don't underestimate the value of each team member watching your actions. Treat others as you want to be treated!

Now take your creation on the road. Get the word out. It is like a campaign; infuse it into every communication: general meetings for all staff members, staff meetings for managers, departmental meetings for more intimate settings, and daily line-up meetings for repetition. Make it known what the expectation is and hold everyone equally accountable.

In a typical day as a general manager you will have contracts to sign, new managers to guide, senior managers to focus, vendors to negotiate with, forecasting to accomplish, guests to intrigue, and controls to monitor. Interruptions are commonplace. The chief engineer may call you to discuss the effects on your guests of the chiller going down. The director of human resources is on the line because a manager just overstepped his bounds with an employee. As you are comparing notes from the individuals involved, your cell phone rings; it's the golf course superintendent, who is on the twelfth hole in the rain watching the river that runs through your property flood the course and the neighbors' houses. Now you have to find time to coordinate the insurance adjusters, geologists, and canal clearing teams to determine liabilities, flow patterns, and potential problem solving for the future. Now it is lunchtime. Have you kept your head about you? Are you following the philosophies noted above?

General management is about using your brain, not your brawn. As you can see, your day can consume you. Don't let it. Surround yourself with the best talent possible and set the level of expectation high. You can spend the day involving yourself with every detail you can dig up, or you can find and nurture talent that can help free your time. Take pride in helping *others* learn to handle situations so you have time to focus the direction you have set.

Educate yourself. Read trade journals and newspapers. Keep up with community issues. Seek the latest trends in food and drink. Is your room product better than the competition? Being on the front end of a trend could mean free press for your hotel. Let your passion show through.

Get the word out. Employ a public relations company to ensure you get your fair share of accolades in the places your target guests will see them. Use your marketing team to research advertising opportunities, direct mail, and Internet options. Make yourself available to the sales team. The general manager's influence during a decision-maker's site inspection can make a profound difference. Be available, active, and involved. The phrase "Build it and they will come" only works in the movies. The team must be energized to sell. They need to believe in your direction and vision as much as you do.

Special assignments can be rewarding. You may be called on to determine the direction of the development of the property. Your analytical skills may be tested in explaining to the ownership how a new ballroom will make them more money. You may be called on to sell the idea to community planning leaders to ensure the permitting process is successful. Your speaking skills may be further challenged in a town hall forum, with tough questions coming directly at you with no time to prepare an answer. You can do it; just translate the skills you learned from guest interactions. Remember your vision.

Community involvement can be vital. Keep up with the economic indicators in your region. Serve on a board for the Hotel and Lodging Association or the Convention and Visitor Bureau. You must be involved with politicians when transient occupancy taxes are a topic of city fund-raising. Will community involvement benefit your hotel or company? The current mayoral race may set the tone for many decisions that will affect the hospitality business in the next four years; your influence and support for right candidate may be needed. The property you run will develop a reputation that will be your signature. You will be setting a tone throughout the community in everything you do at your hotel.

Remember that you represent your hotel. Its ultimate success will be your success, so don't get too distracted. Keep focused and have fun. You have earned it!

3.7 MINI CASE: SUNSET HOTELS AND SUITES

Shortly before the end of 2001, Mr. Andre Johnson, President of Sunset Hotels and Suites, Inc., heard through the company grapevine that several department and operational managers at the company's hotels in northern California were unhappy with their promotion prospects. Unwilling to risk losing these young managers, Johnson was contemplating how to help these men and women manage their careers, at the same time making staying with Sunset attractive and challenging.

Sunset Hotels and Suites is a growing West Coast chain with nine properties in southern California, six in the San Francisco Bay area (northern California), and five in the Seattle-Portland region. The hotels in the Bay area were the most recent acquisitions, and although fewer in number than the southern California region, boasted 20 percent more rooms and were more recently built. They also included the youngest management staff, many of who were retained from the staffs of the acquired hotels. Sunset is a privately owned company, operated as an S-corporation, with all of the corporate officers and hotel GMs holding shares of the company's stock.

Several of the unhappy managers had talked with their GMs and human resource officers about their frustrations. These included:

- Many of the GMs were young, in their thirties and forties, successful, and tending to not move.

- There are no regional managers, as Johnson prefers to run a fairly flat corporate organization.

- Several felt locked into narrow specialties (convention services, catering sales, housekeeping management, and front office) without clear prospects for cross-training to add breadth to their career.

- They were not particularly unhappy with salaries and the usual benefits, but some grumbled about the valuable stock options the GMs get, largely based on the performance of the operating managers' departments.

Johnson called a meeting of the Bay area managers at the Mark Hopkins Hotel in San Francisco (*not* a Sunset property) and invited all department managers from Sunset to be his guests for a two-day conference. Similar meetings were announced and planned in the Pacific Northwest and southern California.

REFERENCES

ACA's Competencies Research Team. 1996. "The Role of Competencies in an Integrated HR Strategy." *ACA Journal* Summer:6–21.

Agle, B.R., R.K. Mitchell, and J.A. Sonnenfeld. 1999. "Who Matters to CEOs? An Investigation of Stakeholder Attributes and Salience,

Corporate Performance, and CEO Values. *Academy of Management Journal* 42:507–525.

Arnaldo, M.J. 1981. "Hotel General Managers: A Profile." *Cornell Hotel and Restaurant Administration Quarterly* 22(3):53–56.

Blancero, D., J. Boroski, and L. Dyer. 1996. "Key Competencies for a Transformed Human Resources Organization: Results of a Field Study." *Human Resource Management* 35(3): 383–403.

Dann, D. 1990. "The Nature of Managerial Work in the Hospitality Industry." *International Journal of Hospitality Management* 9(4):319–334.

Dubois, D. 1993. *Competency-based Performance Improvement: A Strategy for Organizational Change.* Amherst, MA: HRD.

Eder, R.W., and W.T. Umbreit. 1989. "Measures of Managerial Effectiveness in the Hotel Industry." *Hospitality Research and Education Journal* 13(3):333–341.

Enz, Cathy A., and Judy Siguaw. 2000. "Best Practices in Human Resources." *Cornell Hotel and Restaurant Administration Quarterly* 41(1):48–61.

Evarts, H.F. 1988. "The Competency Programme of the American Management Association. *Journal of Management Development* 7(6):48–56.

Ferguson, D.H., and F. Berger. 1984. "Restaurant Managers: What Do They Actually Do?" *Cornell Hotel and Restaurant Administration Quarterly* 25(1):27–37.

Guerrier, Y. 1987. "Hotel Managers' Careers and Their Impact on Hotels in Britain." *International Journal of Hospitality Management* 6(3):121–130.

Guerrier, Y., and A. Lockwood. 1991. "Managers in Hospitality: A Review of Current Research." In *Progress in Tourism, Recreation, and Hospitality Management,* C.P. Cooper (ed.), 2:151–167. London: Bellhaven.

Hales, C., and M. Nightingale. 1986. "What Are Unit Managers Supposed to Do? A Contingent Methodology for Investigating Managerial Role Requirements." *International Journal of Hospitality Management* 5(1):3–11.

Koepper, K. 1988. "Management Effectiveness: A Hotel Industry Appraisal." *Lodging* 14(4):53–57.

Kotter, J.P. 1982. *The General Managers.* New York: Free Press.

Ley, D.A. 1978. "An Empirical Examination of Selected Work Activity Correlates of Managerial Effectiveness in the Hotel Industry Using a Structured Observation Approach." Unpublished Ph.D. dissertation, Michigan State University, East Lansing, Michigan.

Linkage, Inc. 1997. *Introduction to Competency Modeling.* Lexington, MA: Linkage.

Lucia, A.D., and R. Lepsinger. 1999. *The Art and Science of Competency Models.* San Francisco: Jossey-Bass.

McLagan, P. 1996. "Great Ideas Revisited: Competency Models." *Training and Development* 50(1):60–65.

Mintzberg, H. 1973. *The Nature of Managerial Work.* New York: Harper and Row.

Mirabile, R.J. 1985. "A Model for Competency-based Career Development." *Personnel* April:30–38.

———. 1997. "Everything You Wanted to Know about Competency Modeling." *Training and Development* 51(8):73–77.

Nebel, E.C., III. 1991. *Managing Hotels Effectively: Lessons from Outstanding Hotel Managers.* New York: Van Nostrand Reinhold.

Shortt, G. 1989. "Work Activities of Hotel Managers in Northern Ireland: A Mintzbergian Analysis." *International Journal of Hospitality Management* 8(2):121–130.

Umbreit, W.T. 1986. "Developing Behaviorally-anchored Scales for Evaluating Job Performance of Hotel Managers." *International Journal of Hospitality Management* 5(2):55–61.

Worsfold, P. 1989. "A Personality Profile of the Hotel Manager." *International Journal of Hospitality Management* 8(1):51–62.

Zingheim, P.K., G.E. Ledford, and J.R. Shuster. 1996. "Competencies and Competency Models: Does One Size Fit All?" *ACA Journal* Spring:56–65.

SUGGESTED READINGS

Books

Nebel, E.C., III. 1991. *Managing Hotels Effectively: Lessons from Outstanding Hotel Managers.* New York: Van Nostrand Reinhold.

Powers, Tom. 1999. *Introduction to Management in the Hospitality Industry,* 6th ed. New York: John Wiley and Sons.

Woods, Robert H., and Judy Z. King. 1996. *Quality Leadership and Management in the Hospitality Industry.* East Lansing, MI: Educational Institute of the American Hotel and Motel Association.

Articles

Ley, D.A. 1978. "An Empirical Examination of Selected Work Activity Correlates of Managerial Effectiveness in the Hotel Industry Using a Structured Observation Approach." Unpublished Ph.D. dissertation, Michigan State University, East Lansing, Michigan.

Ley, David. 1980. "The Effective GM: Leader or Entrepreneur?" *Cornell Hotel and Restaurant Administration Quarterly* 22(3):53–56.

Morey, Richard C., and David A. Dittman. 1995. "Evaluating a Hotel GM's Performance: A Case Study in Benchmarking." *Cornell Hotel and Restaurant Administration Quarterly* 36(3):30–35.

Nebel, Eddystone C., Ju-Soon Lee, and B. Vudajivuc. 1995. "Hotel General Manager Career Paths in the United States." *International Journal of Hospitality Management* 14(34):252–256.

Pavesic, David V., and Robert A. Brymer. 1990. "Why Young Managers Are Quitting." *Cornell Hotel and Restaurant Administration Quarterly* 30(4):90–96.

Rutherford, Denney G., and Jane Wiegenstein. 1985. "The Mentoring Process in Hotel General Managers' Careers." *Cornell Hotel and Restaurant Administration Quarterly* 25(4):16–23.

Sparrowe, Raymond T., and Pamela A. Popielarz. 1995. "Getting Ahead in the Hospitality Industry: An Event Analysis of Promotions Among Hotel and Restaurant Employees." *Hospitality Research Journal* 19(3):99–117.

Woods, Robert H., Denney G. Rutherford, Raymond A. Schmidgall, and Michael Sciarini. 1998. "Hotel General Managers: Focused on the Core Business." *Cornell Hotel and Restaurant Administration Quarterly* 39(6).

SOURCE NOTES

Chapter 3.2, "A Conceptual Framework of the Hotel General Manager's Job," by Eddystone C. Nebel III and Ajay Ghei.

Chapter 3.3, "Grooming Future Hospitality Leaders: A Competencies Model," by Beth G. Chung-Herrera, Cathy A. Enz, and Melenie J. Lankau, is reprinted from the June 2003 issue of *Cornell Hotel and Restaurant Administration Quarterly.* © Cornell University. Used by permission. All rights reserved.

Chapter 3.4, "As I See It: What I Do," by Emilio Fabico.

Chapter 3.5, "A Day in the Life of a Hilton Hotel General Manager," by Robert O. Balmer, CHA.

Chapter 3.6, "A Day in the General Manager's Life," by Bob Peckenpaugh.

chapter four

OPERATIONS: ROOMS

4.1 INTRODUCTION

The student of hospitality management will find the hotel's front office referred to as the *hub,* the *nerve center,* the *brain,* or some other name suggesting centrality. As H. E. Heldenbrand stated in his classic 1944 book *Front Office Psychology,* "To the guest, the manager is largely represented by the front office, and the unseen head will be judged favorably or otherwise by the guest treatment there" (Introduction). The observations, opinions, and research presented in this section are chosen to illustrate the centrality of the front office in the modern hotel.

A theme that recurs throughout many of the readings in this section is that of communications. In an increasingly communications-oriented society and world, information—its storage, retrieval, dissemination, and evaluation—can mean a competitive edge and, to a certain extent, power. Technology has given

us the Internet, cellular phones, electronic mail (e-mail), telephone- and computer-transmitted facsimiles (faxes), overnight delivery of letters and packages, and personal data assistants (PDAs). These all combine to generate an expectation of clear and nearly instantaneous communication and, by logical extension, fast and efficient services based on communications. This, in turn, has increased the complexity of the hotel's front office and at the same time delivered increased opportunities to serve the hotel's guests. It has, therefore, significantly changed the role of the front office and the front office manager from that described by Heldenbrand.

In 1985, Rutherford studied a national sample of front office managers (FOMs) and concluded that communication had emerged as a central issue. FOMs had added to the predictable role of department manager responsibilities as facilitator and broker of communication in its various forms among the other hotel departments, the front office, and the hotel guests. The model that emerged from this analysis carries with it the powerful message that the FOM's job clearly revolves around communications. A major conclusion of this study was that hotel firms should consider communication skills an important criterion in considering candidates for the position of FOM.

When communication is coupled with the aforementioned complexity and guest expectations of instant availability of information and data, it is easy to see why the front office and its staff operate under considerable stress. Being the hub or nerve center of a modern hotel has as one of its positive aspects the fact that front office staff can be keenly aware of what is happening at virtually every level of the hotel's organizational structure. One of the negative aspects is that the front office serves as a lightning rod for guest complaints. Dealing with complaints can be one of the most difficult tasks for the front office staff to learn, especially given the frequency and sometimes the intensity of guest complaints and expectations.

Successful FOMs ideally possess demonstrated competencies in both oral and written communications to deal with these complexities and challenges. The FOM, therefore, is not only a manager and a communicator among the front office staff, the hotel departments, and the guests but also a communicator in yet another way—that of teacher and trainer.

This contextual theme of communications is carried forward in the essay contributed by James Bardi. Bardi discusses the job of FOM, providing insights about the complexities of the job relative not only to communication but also to elements of an FOM job analysis, intrahotel relations, and the emerging and popular concept of employee empowerment.

To see how this all fits together, walk a few miles in the shoes of FOM Garry Dickover. At the time this was written, Dickover was the FOM of two hotels: Marriott's River Center and Riverwalk Hotels in San Antonio, Texas. Currently general manager of the Courtyard Convention Center in Las Vegas, Dickover invites you to see the inside of the FOM's job and how he practices the theory of managing the front office.

In 1993, Glenn Withiam researched and wrote "American Concierges Set Service Standards," an essay used in the second and third editions of *Hotel Management and Operations*. Withiam also wrote an earlier piece, "Keepers of the Keys: Concierges in American Hotels" (1983). The "keys" references the practice in European hotels of hotel guests leaving their room keys with the concierge upon leaving the floor of their room. The concierge therefore "kept the keys" for the guest. The job today has evolved to use *keys* as a metaphor for the processes of gatekeeping access to hotel and community services on behalf of the guest. Concierges have a professional society, Les Clefs d'Or, which uses crossed keys as an identifying device. The concierges who are members and so certified are said to be keyed.

For this fourth-edition article on concierges, Dr. Mario Arnaldo of Hawaii Pacific University acknowledges Withiam's work as the heritage and underpinning of his current research, which led to this chapter. Herein, Arnaldo presents an overview of research he did on the post–9/11 American hotel concierge and guest service staff. The strict application of the title *concierge* indicates a hotel employee working at a concierge-designated desk in a hotel property. To accurately assess the contributions of these hotel professionals, Arnaldo contacted dozens of contemporary concierges and guest service staff members, who generously provided examples of their concierge experiences. The author reviews in an accessible, conversational manner the following questions: What's up with concierges these days? Who does the office work? What are the organizational departments they work in? What kind of interactions do they have with other hotel departments? What is their greatest wish?

The theme of active communications is carried through the piece contributed by Bill Quain and Steve LeBruto. If hotels are going to actively find the best pieces of business, then there must be good communications channels among all the organizational components that guide the guest to a purchase decision. Whether this is at the front desk, through the reservations system, or through a travel agent, it is important to recognize the most attractive pieces of business and what potential bookings may be logically refused. Yes, refusing business is a central component of successful yield management, but not always. In their words: "Yield management is usually thought of in the context of turning away undesirable business during excess demand periods. However, the real art of yield management is in learning how to turn undesirable booking requests into desirable ones."

Their article helps the reader, in an interesting and entertaining way, learn to make these management decisions.

Yield and revenue management are also treated in the marketing section of this book with other, in some ways contrasting, views by Chappelle. The reader who wants additional insights into these concepts is directed to the contributions by that author.

The articles and essays presented here for your consideration represent only a fraction of the potential range of issues attendant on any modern hotel front office. The duties, obligations, and responsibilities of front office personnel change from hotel company to hotel company based on such variables as market segmentation, organizational structure, corporate philosophy, and individual leadership. A large amount of management literature exists that is not specific to the front office but nonetheless pertains to the various issues and challenges that face FOMs. The articles chosen for inclusion in this section are as specific as possible to functional aspects of front office management. Other pertinent managerial insights may be applied from other contexts once the reader has a good functional grasp of front office activities. Included in the suggested readings are textbooks that treat in great depth the functional and technical aspects of front office operations. What has been attempted here is an overview of pervasive managerial issues typical of those currently facing FOMs.

4.2 THE ELECTRIFYING JOB OF THE FRONT OFFICE MANAGER

James A. Bardi

The exciting atmosphere of a hotel lobby often intrigues students of hotel management. People from all walks of life and corners of the world cross paths to discuss and share ideas, greet family and friends on special occasions, attend conferences to debate issues, or discuss business deals. Questions concerning arrivals, meeting times, rates, food and beverage services, directions, transportation services, or whereabouts of the management staff and guests create a commotion that seems overwhelming at times. Is someone in charge here? The preprofessional who sets as his or her career objective being the general manager of a hotel and hopes the required tenure as a front office manager (FOM) proceeds with haste will find the role challenging. If you begin your career in hotel management as a front desk clerk, bellperson, or cashier, you have a vast opportunity to explore just who is in charge.

In a 1985 study, Rutherford discussed the important dimensions of the FOM's job, including communications, facilitation, and organizational interface and technical minutia. Selected job functions reported in the research findings included communications with guests and employees; facilitating medical emergencies, selling up, power failure procedures, walking guests due to overbooking, and design of computer systems for the front office; and organizational interface with the director of marketing, controller, food and beverage manager, and catering manager. These job skills and interactions require a person to prioritize and to resolve many issues, to make quick decisions based on sound

corporate management concepts, to empower employees, and to refine exemplary communication techniques.

Bardi (1990, 345–349) stated, "[T]he front office manager must take an active role in gathering information of interest to guests and in developing procedures for the front office to use in disbursing this information." This information is also needed by various departments to assist in delivering and organizing hospitality. This is a tall order for the FOM to fulfill, especially considering the total realm of potential information guests may require and from what departments. Those hotel departmental areas and their sources of guest information are included below:

Interdepartmental Communication

Department	Information Needed from Front Office
Marketing and Sales	Guest history, reservations, first impressions, relay messages, and guest function information
Housekeeping	Room status, potential house count, security concerns, and requests for amenities and supplies
Food and Beverage	Relaying messages, accurate voucher information, posting of charges to guest accounts, predicted house counts, and paid-outs

Banquet	Information on scheduled events, process of payment of guest charges for scheduled events, preparation of daily function board and marquee, and a public communication post
Controller	Daily summary of financial transactions, financial data for billing, and credit card ledgers
Maintenance	Room status and guest requests for maintenance service
Security	Fire safety, emergency communication information, and investigation of guest security concerns
Human Resources	Initial point of contact and screening for potential employees

Thus the FOM must embrace the charge of becoming a proactive communicator and facilitator. This hotel executive must analyze and seek the pieces of information guests will probably need and figure out which departments must interact to fulfill these needs.

Further inquiry into the role of the FOM can be accomplished by reviewing the elements of a job analysis of this position. Bardi (1990, 49–50) presents a job analysis of an FOM's duties on a typical day.

- Reviews night audit report.
- Reviews incoming reservations for the day.
- Communicates information to employees on all shifts concerning reservations, room assignments, and room inventory.
- Communicates information to other departments—housekeeping, marketing and sales, banquets, food and beverage, plant engineering, and security.
- Resolves guest billing discrepancies and other complaints.
- Prepares budget with general manager and controller.
- Prepares forecasting sheet.
- Conducts business meetings to promote room sales.
- Assists in check-in, check-out, reservation confirmations, updating reservation system.
- Interviews potential front office employees.
- Communicates with night auditor.
- Maintains front office equipment.

Although this list shows only a few of the many duties performed in any one day in the life of an FOM, it provides the aspiring hospitality professional with an idea of the range of managerial activities. The FOM must stay in control of all activities that affect the delivery of hospitality to the guest—a major function of a hotel's financial success.

If delivering hospitality to the guest is a major responsibility of the FOM, what are the components of this subsystem of the hotel operation? How does the front office and, subsequently, the FOM fit in? An answer to this question can be derived from reviewing the guest service cycle in a hotel (adapted from Albrecht and Zemke, 1985). If the FOM analyzes the various guest-departmental contacts, he or she can move toward understanding how the front office fits into the efficient delivery of the hotel's hospitality services. The potential departmental contacts in the cycle are:

- **Marketing**—Preparing and administering customer surveys with concern for guest satisfaction, advertising methods, and incentive promotions.

- **Reservations**—Developing and monitoring a reservation system with respect to ease of access to toll-free numbers, fax, national reservation system, and telephone manner of personnel handling reservations, cancellations, accommodation availability, complimentary services and products, and general information.

- **Registration**—Developing and monitoring a registration system with respect to concern for managing a guest transportation shuttle system, ensuring a first-contact greeting; providing assistance with luggage; organizing an efficient check-in procedure; maintaining a room status system; processing credit cards; operating a guest information system that centralizes all communication between the guest and the hotel about housekeeping, food and beverage, maintenance, and other hotel departments.

- **Guest stay**—Coordinating guest communications with all departments in the hotel to ensure guest satisfaction in restaurants, lounges, room service, gift shops, housekeeping services, security, wake-up calls, telephone system, and guest folio availability.

- **Check-out**—Developing and providing an efficient check-out system with respect to coordinating flexible check-out times, providing assistance with luggage, maintaining in-room video check-out option, monitoring guest wait-time in line, and providing folio accuracy and printout.

This list of components in a guest service cycle suggests the vast array of duties the FOM encounters in managing the delivery of hospitality services. However, one piece of "electrifying magic" is still required to make front office hospitality relevant to modern service delivery realities: employee empowerment.

Sternberg (1992) discusses the concept of empowerment as a granting of authority to employees to make everyday decisions within guidelines. For example, many guests of a hotel feel they are in the middle of a bureaucracy when they want to have a charge adjusted on their account folio. "Step aside and I'll call my supervisor" is too often the response to a guest's inquiry about a charge adjustment. The cashier is only doing what he or she was trained to do. However, the guest doesn't care what the training was; he just knows the system isn't user-friendly. As Sternberg emphasizes, if guidelines are established and communicated, the cashier should know what to do. Here is the manager's chance to provide that first electrifying jolt of empowerment.

Charges within a specified dollar amount that are debated can be credited or adjusted without the supervisor's approval. A corresponding control system can be implemented that will reveal the extent of the credit granted per cashier.

Another example of providing empowerment opportunities for front office staff is provided by Allin and Halpine (1988) in describing quality assurance training at the Waldorf-Astoria:

> While there can be many reasons to combine the positions of registration clerk and cashier, and many aspects were considered at the Waldorf-Astoria, the decision was driven by a desire to improve guest service where its impact is most obvious—at the front desk. Cross-trained employees speed the check-in and checkout process by performing both functions, as the traffic at the desk dictates. Registration

clerks can cash checks and cashiers can issue duplicate room keys, in many cases eliminating the necessity of having the guest wait in two lines.

Other opportunities to provide employee empowerment can be identified through careful analysis by the FOM of the progress of the guest through the guest service cycle.

The potential opportunities to serve or mis-serve the guest can be appreciated when viewed in the context of guests times service contacts. If 12 million guests pass through a hotel company's entire system in a year and each has an average of 12 contacts with hotel staff—guest service staff, housekeepers, front office clerks, and others—that's 144 million chances for the chain to give a good or bad impression (Bardi, 1990, 233). As the gatekeeper of many, if not most, of these potential contacts, the FOM is in a unique position to help his or her staff enhance the guest experience. Empowerment is another powerful tool in the FOM's managerial arsenal.

The role of the FOM demands a mastery of communication, operational details, and, increasingly, empowerment. The challenging and attractive nature of this role allows the new hospitality professional to try various ways to apply interpersonal skills that will yield a profit for the hotel. It is a challenge that will last a lifetime.

4.3 A DAY IN THE LIFE OF THE FRONT OFFICE MANAGER

Garry Dickover

It's 6:00 on a Saturday morning. The alarm clock is blaring its normal "beep, beep, beep, beep." The sun is peering through the window. Time to start another day as front office manager. It is going to be a busy day featuring 800 arrivals and 750 departures. Plus, the hotel is 50 rooms oversold. It is going to be a fun one.

It's 7:00 A.M. The drive to work is an easy one this Saturday morning. It gives me a chance to think about one thing in particular that is on tap for today. There is a 9:00 A.M. pre-convention meeting for the group that is arriving today. There is the regular morning pre-shift meeting. Today I also have to review hospitality standards with the front desk staff. You would think that it would be easy to have people smile and greet the guest, use a guest's name, add a value statement about the hotel or city, and thank the guest for his or her business. I don't ask for much, but to train people to do those four things can be a challenge.

Pre-shift meetings are an important start to the day, but it can be a hassle getting everyone together. There are a lot of reasons why an associate can't make a pre-shift meeting, but attendance is important to the success of my department. It is the time I have everyone together, let them know what is going on for the day, and get a chance to share with them the standards we have set and how they can apply them to the customer. At 1:00 P.M. today I have a Safety Committee meeting, and at

4:00 I have my weekly rap session with the telephone department. Yeah, I think to myself, it is going to be a full day.

As I arrive to work, I can see that the check-outs have already started. It is nice to see the bellmen taking care of our guests. As I scan the grounds, I make sure there is no trash on the ground, the bell carts are clean, and the valet parking staff is hustling to retrieve guest cars. I look at the windows of the entryway to the hotel to check for cleanliness. The front drive is the first and last thing a guest sees, so it has to be looking good. Today, all looks good.

It is better for me to spot-check the area before the general manager comes by and sees any problems. As the FOM, I learned the GM's route when he arrives at work, so I make sure the area is clean. (This is something they did not teach me in college, along with how to repair printers and copy machines—some things you gotta learn by doing.) This morning, things look good.

It's 7:50 A.M. I make my way to the back of the front office. My desk managers are busy getting information ready for the pre-shift meeting. As I walk through the area, I always make it a point to greet people as I pass and wish them a good morning. I know how important it is to give each and every associate a cheerful good morning. It sets the stage for the day. And you know, it really does make people feel good. A good department head recognizes his or her associates. The first words that come out of your mouth should be pleasant. The front office team takes the brunt of all the complaints. They don't need me to harp on them.

The pre-shift meeting goes smoothly. The desk managers prep the team for the day, I review the hospitality standards, and we are set. As we are about to finish, I notice some tension on the staff's faces. They know they are in for a tough day—remember, 50 rooms oversold. It is important that I don't let the team see any stress I may feel on my face. The team knows how important it is to sell out the hotel. They know that once a room is empty overnight, you never get a chance to sell that room again. They also know you have to oversell the hotel. This is the time I can reassure them that the revenue department has calculated all of the slip percentages for the big group checking in. A slip percentage is the expected variation from stated arrival and rooms pick-up percentages the group's meeting planner promised. It is important for me to develop a good relationship with the revenue department. The FOM must be active in the forecast meetings to ensure the hotel is not "sold up the river," meaning overcommitted by the sales staff.

Relationship building is an important job for the FOM. It is where trust is established—trust between you and the other departments. It is not me versus them; it's *us* trying to maximize revenue and occupancy and to continue to build loyalty. This is the time to reassure the team that if we do our jobs as we have been trained, all will be fine. We do a little cheer, and out to the desk they go! Now for a cup of coffee.

I review the plans with the desk managers for the sold-out night. This is also the time I check availability at other hotels, check the stayover requests and no-show percentages, and check for duplicated reservations. It looks like they have it under control. I double-check the staffing during the peak periods and remind the managers to get everyone to lunch. (As simple as this sounds, sometimes we forget.) I check my watch; 30 minutes to the pre-con. Better pull out the group resume, which is our profile of the group that includes, among many other things, a historical profile of the group's room pick-ups, occupancies, and food and beverage revenues.

At 8:45 A.M., I'm off to the pre-con. I head by the desk to wave to the staff, and I stop by the telephone system, bellstand, and the concierge desk. All seems to be going smoothly. At the pre-con, we all do our formal introductions and meet the group's representatives, usually the meeting planner and members of the group's leadership. We each discuss our individual departments and the relationship we will have with the group. This is our time to sell them on how well we will do for their group. It is a successful pre-con; all the parties seem happy. I spend just a couple of minutes with the group convention manager, giving an update on the oversold situation. If we have to walk guests, it is important to let the group convention manager know about the situation. Today I said we might, but we should be in good shape. She thanks me for the update.

As I make my way back to the front office, I end up walking with the resident manager (RM). He asks me how things went last night and how our hotel is for tonight. As an FOM, it is important to know what your boss is going to ask you. Bosses are all different, but they always seem to ask the same questions. It is important to review the daily sales and occupancy report from the previous day so you know what is going on and can share this information with the RM. I gave the RM the information he wants, always emphasizing the positives.

When I get back to my office, I have a couple of associates wanting to talk to me. They are bothered by the new schedule. They wanted some specific days off and, because of the business, they did not get them. This is a delicate situation. You want to be fair to the team, but you also have to respect why your managers did what they did. The best thing to do is to listen to what your associates say and then review the situation. I have found that 80 percent of the time there is an alternative. You want to create win-win solutions. By spending time with your associates, you demonstrate to them you care about their situation; this helps build loyalty. *Remember that they don't care how much you know until they know how much you care.* Another situation solved.

The next couple of hours I spend reviewing the previous day's information and getting caught up on email, memos, and other communications. Generally, this is the time I get a couple of phone calls from upset guests. This could be for a variety of reasons. Before check-out, some people always want to let the manager know how things went. It is important to listen to customers when they complain. It is a great way to find out what deficiencies you may have in the hotel's service processes. Most complaints are caused by a breakdown in the process. Sometimes people get upset over the smallest things. Sometimes they have a right to be upset. One example from past experience was the room being so cold that when the guest lifted the toilet seat, the water had a small sheet of ice on it. Ensuring customer satisfaction is a large part of the FOM's job. You have to own hospitality. Your team sets the stage for a guest's entire stay. It better be good!

By now it is 12:15 P.M. and time for lunch. I grab the information I need for the 1:00 P.M. safety meeting. I will go directly to that meeting after lunch. As I make my way, I check on the desk and the house count. We are now only 29 oversold. We have had some canceled reservations, and we also had 18 early departures. Things are looking good.

At 1:00 P.M. I walk into the safety meeting. This is never an exciting meeting, but it is always important. Accidents are costly to the hotel. It is important to keep accident prevention a priority for all associates. Today we talk about the most current accidents, how they could have been prevented, and the next steps. We also discuss the implications of safety and security interests for our guests. This is important to avoid lawsuits and provide guests with a safe and secure environment. The meeting wraps up at 2:30 P.M.

As I come down the escalator, I see the check-ins are starting to arrive. I head to the bellstand to see if the bell captain is caught up. All is well. Because lines are forming, I go behind the front desk to handle a few check-ins. I always like this part of the job. It also gets a smile from the desk clerks. Before you know it, you have helped move the line. Because the desk is staying busy, it is time for me to move out and manage from the lobby. This is a great way to watch what is happening. You can view your whole front office team by being in the lobby. (You can also ensure the cleanliness of the area. This helps our friends in housekeeping.) A big part of the job in the lobby is just answering questions and giving directions. Every guest I help means one guest who did not have to go to the front desk and one more guest who did not have to stand in line. This is the fun part of the job!

At 3:50 P.M., my pager goes off. It is a reminder about my 4:00 P.M. rap sessions. I can't believe 90 minutes passed while I was in the lobby. It is a good day.

Meeting with associates allows me to take the pulse of their work situation. I do it in small groups or as a one-on-one rap. It helps build a relationship within the team and also helps identify challenges I was unaware of. I ask leading questions so the session does not become a bitch session; this helps me control the meeting. During this meeting, I discover some equipment that is needed and that we need more uniforms for the team. It would be great to buy them all new uniforms, but I have to stay within my budget. Sometimes that is hard to do. I take notes on their comments and will pass them on to the other managers. It is important for all of the managers to be in the loop. I always keep the raps to about an hour.

By now it is 5:00 P.M., our peak check-in time. I go back out to the lobby to see how things are going. On a busy day like today, I typically spend the next couple of hours helping out in the lobby. At 5:30 P.M., the night manager on duty (MOD) comes out to meet with me. We usually work the lobby together while I tell him about the day. He tells me about the previous night. Of course, the first thing he shows me is the house count: 24 rooms oversold and 352 arrivals expected. We are in good shape. It is important to track the number of no-shows. This helps you make better decisions to maximize your revenue. The MOD is a little nervous. I tell him not to worry, we will be fine. We review the sold-out night so we don't miss anything. He tells me he already has the walk letters (expressing our regret and outlining our promises to a guest who is walked to another hotel) out on the desk. This brings a good laugh. We have done this plenty of times, so I trust that the hotel is in good hands.

It's 7:00 P.M., and things seem to be in good shape. Time to go home. I make one more trip around to the departments in the front office to see how they are doing and wish them a good evening. Another good day!

The day described above is a typical day as a front office manager. Some days have different meetings, some days have more upset guests, some days have more upset associates, and some days are just better than others are. The thing I have learned over the years is that the job of the FOM is the same. Take care of the associates, who take care of the customers, who take care of the business. It's the same job, just different players, and I love it.

4.4 YIELD MANAGEMENT: CHOOSING THE MOST PROFITABLE RESERVATIONS

William J. Quain and Stephen M. LeBruto

▶ INTRODUCTION

Yield management, as a term, is not very exciting. However, the *results* of a well-run yield management program are certainly exciting! Properly implemented, it means that a business can make more money. The keys are to sell more and to sell more profitable items.

The first step in a yield management program is to determine who is the best customer. The best customer is the one who can spend the most money at your property purchasing profitable items. The products and services you provide are the best fit for their needs. The best customers for the property are the ones who receive the greatest benefit from your services. They are willing to pay more, buy more frequently, and remain more loyal because you are satisfying their needs.

Many operations do not know who the best customers are. However, the answer is in a property's data collection system. Guest histories, food and beverage checks, cash register receipts, and the records of strategically allied business partners contain most of the information any property needs to determine the ideal customer base. In order to properly implement a yield management project, the property must be viewed as a collection of profit centers. A profit center is a place where value is created and exchanged.

One of the techniques of yield management is to let the guest in on the secrets of the establishment. Give him or her all the information necessary to truly enjoy the experience. As part of the yield management plan, management must be willing to make experts of the guests by sharing information on how they can utilize all of the profit centers.

An important part of analyzing the potential of each profit center is to identify all the possible sources of revenue. This means analyzing both the revenue-producing outlets and the people who spend the money. Every establishment has a wide variety of revenue outlets. They can range from the sale of rooms to valet service, flower delivery, specialty drinks, cigars, and creative take-out services.

Strategic alliances with car rental agencies, cooperative advertising, couponing, and packaging of all sorts will vastly change the number of channels the guest can use to spend money in the profit centers of the enterprise.

Restaurants can increase revenues by serving take-out food, catering private parties off-premises, adjusting the menu mix, and developing reward systems for servers. Especially during hours of peak demand, restaurants can design product/price combinations that offer incentives to customers to change their demand patterns. Why accept any reservation at any time? Instead, select the most profitable reservations and use incentives to move the other reservations to non-peak or shoulder times.

Profits are the only true measure of business success. The following groups all benefit from enhanced profits:

1. **Guests**—They are one of the primary beneficiaries of increased revenues and profits. If revenues are on the rise, it can mean only one thing: You are serving the guest better. Guests are happier, more loyal, and eager to tell others about the great experience they had.

2. **Employees**—In order to achieve long-term success, employees must be involved in the profit making *and* the profit taking. Let them earn as much money as they possibly can by making more money for the property.

3. **Management**—Structured reward systems are necessary for management. These systems reflect their need for income and achievement and further the profits of the property.

4. **Shareholders and investors**—Return on investment, dependable growth, share prices, and so on are all outcomes of increased revenue. Money attracts money, and the investors will relish the long-term growth potential of their investments.

Managers face six major obstacles in their efforts to implement a yield management system. These impediments are:

1. **Lack of creativity**—Does your company do things the way they have always been done? There is a need for standardization in recipes and operating procedures; however, this sometimes spills over into other areas. Training sessions in most organizations do not stress the creative side of customer satisfaction.

2. **Lack of attention**—It is difficult to stay in focus all the time. The minute you stop paying attention, things go wrong.

3. **Monitoring the wrong signals**—We tend to monitor the easy things to measure, such as food cost and inventory. We should be looking for opportunities, not statistics.

4. **Conflict between sales and service**—When profits depend on a mutual delivery of both the sale and the service, conflict can arise. Front-of-the-house and back-of-the-house employees must work together for the common cause of serving and satisfying guests.

5. **Targeting the wrong customers**—The right customers are those who will purchase the most of your products and services. Look for the customers with the money to spend to give you a reasonable profit. Use the marketing mix variables of product price, promotions, and distribution to attract and hold the right customers.

6. **Rewarding the wrong behavior**—Many sales management policies are designed to encourage occupancy and average daily rate. Restaurants, by allowing customers to reward the waitstaff, may encourage promotion of higher-priced items. In either case, the sale may not reflect the best interests of the property. Yield management is designed to increase profit, not just gross sales.

► BASIC CONCEPTS OF YIELD MANAGEMENT

Yield management requires knowledge of guests' expected behavior, plus an understanding of which business is most beneficial to a hotel—but it does not necessarily require high-power computers. Three main revenue management concepts allow hotels to pick up relatively easy money, or low-hanging fruit. The three concepts are simplifying the yield management system to make it manageable; examining the rate controls to make certain they allow acceptance of the business that yields the strongest revenue return; and using length-of-stay controls to shift demand from sold-out periods to slack periods.

Group business, as it relates to the above three points, is a special case. The change needed, if any, is to think in terms of which business is best for the property on a given date. By implementing the concepts discussed here, the property should see revenue gains in the next several months.

► AN OLD PROFESSION

One may think of yield management as a relatively recent practice, but the lodging industry has applied yield management principles for many years. In one early instance, Marriott Corporation used yield management principles long before it installed its current sophisticated system. Back when young J. W. "Bill" Marriott was working at the family's first hotel, the Twin Bridges in Washington, D.C., the property sold rooms from a drive-up window. As Bill tells the story, the property had a flat single rate and charged extra for each additional person staying in the room.

When availability got tight on some nights, Bill recalls leaning out the drive-up window to assess the cars waiting in line. If some of the cars were filled with passengers, Bill would turn away the vehicles with just a single passenger to sell his last rooms to fuller cars. That technique demonstrates the core concept of yield management.

From that simple start, yield management mechanisms have become complicated—so complicated that some managers whom we have met seem to think they cannot improve revenue unless they have access to the most sophisticated tools. Worse, the hotel manager may have created an overly complex system of discounts and packages. If the manager then insists on managing every rate or package individually, the result is a sense that the property has too many programs to track and control, and it probably does. For this reason, the first suggestion for a straightforward approach to yield management is to cluster rates into a few groupings of similar programs and then work on controlling these clusters or rate categories.

The goal of yield management is to select which business to accept and which business to turn away (when demand exceeds supply), based on the relative value of each booking. Most properties do not need more than four to six rate buckets for their transient bookings. As an example, the following gives transient rate categories that combine programs of similar value:

Level 1   Rack (no discount)
Level 2   10 to 20 percent discount
Level 3   25 to 35 percent discount
Level 4   40 to 50 percent discount
Level 5   greater than a 50 percent discount

Each level or bucket in the above hypothetical structure might comprise several room rates. Given such a structure, a manager need not agonize over whether to restrict rooms offered at a rate of $150 in hopes of getting a rate of $155. While it is given that those $5 bills would pile up, the complexity is not worth it, especially when one might be working so hard on the $5 difference that one overlooks the opportunity to earn, say, $50 more by selling at rack rate.

If a given set of discounts isn't working, the hotel should change the categories. For instance, if a hotel's business fell entirely in Level 1 and Level 2, with virtually no business in Level 3, a manager should rearrange the rate buckets. The three rate buckets could be discounts from rack rate of 10 to 15 percent, 20 to 40 percent, and greater than 40 percent—or any other arrangement that makes a meaningful division among rate categories.

The following principles apply to setting up categories to manage rates at a hotel:

1. Segment programs based on clusters of discounts representing similar values. Yield management requires risk and reward management. Rate categories are designed to enable turning down one booking request in favor of a higher-value booking projected to come later. However, risking $150 in certain revenue in hopes of achieving a $155 booking seems to make little sense if the latter is not a sure thing.

2. In deciding whether to accept a particular customer's business, take into account both the cost of opening rooms and the offsetting ancillary spending that occurs when a room is sold. To take an extreme example, the most valuable guest for a casino-hotel—the high-stakes gambler—might be paying the lowest room rate.

3. Limit the total number of transient rate categories to no more than six or so, particularly if there is no automated yield management system. The chief reason for that limit is that yield management requires forecasting demand for each rate category. Not only is it time-consuming to forecast numerous categories (with diminishing returns as the number of categories increases), but the more categories are created, the less accurate the forecasts are for each.

4. Each rate category should have a reasonable volume of activity to allow monitoring of traffic in that category. If it is found that one of the categories is rarely used, consider redistributing the rate hierarchy.

5. Group business should have a separate hierarchy of buckets to allow the operator to track pick-ups of room blocks. In addition, mixing group activity with individual booking activity clouds the historical information as you trend data by which rate categories are collected.

► RATE CATEGORY CONTROLS

The point of yield management is to use demand forecasts to determine how much to charge for rooms on a given day. When the hotel sells out, the ability to determine which reservations to accept or deny is lost, because all requests for the sold-out date (including those for multiple-night stays that involve the sold-out date) must be rejected. A property's yield management objective should be to sell out the hotel as close to the arrival date as possible, because the further in advance the hotel is sold out with discounted (or short-stay) business, the greater is the likelihood that high-value bookings will be turned away. This forecasting regime requires a continual process of comparing remaining demand for high-rate stays (and multiple-night stays) against remaining available inventory. Rate category controls help ensure available inventory to accommodate the projected high-rate demand.

Table 4.1 demonstrates how rate categories are controlled to increase total room revenue. The table assumes a 500-room hotel (or a hotel with 500 rooms remaining to be sold). The objective is to hold rooms open for high-rate demand without leaving a large number of rooms unsold. In this example, although the hotel would prefer to sell all 500 rooms at rack rate, the hotel's managers project that they can sell 380 (or more) rooms at rack rate. Their inventory plan is set up to maintain room availability for this forecasted high-rate demand. The managers would like to sell the remaining 120 rooms in the next rate category down (Bucket 1), but their demand forecast projects they will not be able to sell all 120 in that rate category. Based on current trends, however, even though they have a total of 500 rooms to sell, they won't be selling any rooms in the deep-discount category because there is sufficient demand at higher rates.

When evaluating how well a property is managing its inventory, there are two basic indicators: (1) On dates the property is selling out, it should be observed how far in advance that sellout occurs; (2) if the property is not selling out, it must be determined whether the property ever turned away business as a result of discount controls or because the property had committed too many rooms to groups—that is, if a group does not pick up its room block, did the hotel, as a result, refuse reservations from transient guests?

Full-occupancy dates frequently receive less attention from property managers than one might expect, given the revenue potential of a sellout. One reason is that some properties are too slow in closing out discounts to restrict room availability to expected high-rate business. Hotels do close the discounts, but not always soon enough. A common practice is to set threshold levels at which discounts are closed at a predetermined level (90 percent occupancy, for example). While this approach is well meant, all it succeeds in doing is preserving the last 10 percent of the hotel's inventory for high-value guests, when a proactive approach might shut down discounts earlier and gain the hotel even more high-paying guests (and revenue).

Another reason hotels often don't focus

Table 4.1 Hypothetical Room Rate Structure

Rate Buckets	Discount Off Rack Rate	Available Rooms (estimated)	Demand Forecast
Rack (General)	None	500	380
Bucket 1	10%–20%	120	63
Bucket 2	25%–35%	57	75
Bucket 3	40%–50%	0	140

on sold-out dates is that the persons responsible for managing the hotel's inventory are also usually responsible for high-profile tasks, including forecasting daily occupancy. Thus, a revenue manager may spend more time determining whether a particular date will run an occupancy of 65 percent or 75 percent than determining how to make the most out of excess demand on a projected 100 percent occupancy date. The process of forecasting a date's occupancy is important, but so is determining how to gain the most revenue from a sold-out date.

For all the time spent in month-end analysis of occupancy levels, average rates, and market comparisons, rarely is conclusive evidence found that properties perform as well as they could. Moreover, the more often those two questions are asked (i.e., did we fill too early? and did we turn away business on days we didn't fill?), the more employees work to give the desired revenue results. As occurs in many cases, you get what you inspect, not what you expect.

► LENGTH-OF-STAY CONTROLS

Implementing length-of-stay controls takes the rate management decision a step further. The essence of rate category control is having one room left to sell and deciding whether to sell it to one guest for $100 today or to wait and sell it to another guest for $150. The essence of length-of-stay controls, on the other hand, is having one room left to sell at $150 and deciding whether to sell it for one night or to wait, with the prospect of selling it to another guest for four nights. In the rate

category decision, the hotel can net an additional $50, while the length-of-stay decision can generate as much as $450 in additional revenue.

Managing stay lengths is complex, but mastering length-of-stay patterns may be the most rewarding of yield management functions. The most sophisticated inventory management controls requests down to granular levels of detail: by program or rate category, by length of stay, or by day. This level of control really requires an automated system. As is the case with managing rate discounts, however, measurable revenue improvements connected to length of stay can be achieved without sophisticated automated systems, as long as the application of controls is kept fairly simple.

Just as setting rate control categories requires an understanding of demand by rate category, length-of-stay management requires an understanding of demand by various length-of-stay intervals. To make the call in the above example, the manager needs to know the level of demand for four-night stays before he or she turns away (or accepts) the request for a one-night stay.

The most common length-of-stay statistic used in the hospitality industry is average length of stay, which describes the average duration of a guest's hotel stay over a range of dates. One needs more effective statistics than simple average length of stay to manage stay patterns. What the revenue manager needs to know is the total number of arrivals on a given date for one night, two nights, three nights, four nights, five nights, and so forth. To illustrate the difference between those two statistics, imagine that a manager was determining whether to apply minimum-stay restrictions on a peak night. The manager could know that the average length of stay is 3.6 nights, or the manager could have specific length-of-stay information (e.g., 10 percent of the arrivals on a given date are for one-night stays, 25 percent are for two-night stays, and so on). Naturally, the manager wants to know how much of the demand will be affected if he or she were to reject all one-, two-, and three-night stays with the expectation that the hotel can be filled with people staying four or more nights. Table 4.2 shows an example of a chart with this type of information.

Most central reservation and property management systems developed in the last few years facilitate stay pattern controls, although at varying levels of sophistication. The ideal system enables a property's managers to set controls for each arrival date by discrete lengths of stay. Such a system enables the property to close availability to one-, four-, five-, and eight-night stays, for instance, but allow stays of two, three, six, seven, or nine nights (or longer). Most new systems at least allow minimum-stay controls by rate category.

Caution: One aspect of yield management systems' stay controls can become overused. Most systems allow managers to place a closed-to-arrival restriction on selected dates. This restriction enables a property to sell through stays arriving before the given date—that is, multiple-night stays for which the closed date is a second or subsequent night—but rejects all requests to arrive on that date. The problem hotels create for themselves by using this approach is that they end up saving space for two- and three-night stay-throughs while rejecting multiple-night stays by guests proposing to arrive on the closed night.

Obviously, the hotel does not want to lose revenue from stay-through guests to those staying for just the closed night, but having the system forbid a multiple-night stay that begins on the peak night may actually be worse than having no controls at all. In such a case, some form of minimum or other discrete length-of-stay controls is appropriate. Any property still using a flat closed-to-arrival restriction should reconsider in light of this problem.

Table 4.2 Hypothetical Stay-Length Forecast

Day	Occupancy	Arrivals	Arrivals per Day Length of Stay (Days)				
			1	2	3	4	5+
Wednesday	76%	117	7	9	21	41	39
Thursday	82%	103	8	17	21	24	33
Friday	90%	118	10	24	12	26	46
Saturday	100%	138	28	23	22	28	37
Sunday	83%	111	19	13	16	22	41
Monday	78%	86	12	13	18	21	22

► GROUPS: RATES, DATES, AND SPACE

Yield management is usually thought of in the context of turning away undesirable business during excess demand periods. However, the real art of yield management is learning how to turn undesirable booking requests into desirable ones. Thus, an important element of yield management is teaching all employees the art of saying yes.

The art of saying yes is particularly important in negotiating group business, which generally involves decisions about rates, dates, and space. *Rates* are how much the group is going to pay; *dates* are when the group is going to be staying; and *space* is how many rooms the group will use. Turning an undesirable proposal into a desirable contract involves varying these components until both the hotel's sales associate and the meeting planners have what they consider a worthwhile package. Too often, hoteliers either deny a group's request outright or focus on adjusting the group's proposed room rate to make the request appealing to the hotel. At times, the better response is to give the group the rate it requests but to change the dates of the proposed business to a time when the hotel's forecast is for empty rooms. Even less obvious is the option to ask the group to change the number of rooms it proposes to block. Committing to more rooms (and thus more overall revenue) or fewer rooms (reducing displacement) leaves the opportunity to sell to a second group interested in your property.

Applying revenue management principles to group business involves more than changing a group's proposal from undesirable to acceptable. Perhaps even more important is the ability to make a proposal that is merely acceptable into a contract that represents a great piece of business. Working within a hotel's normal acceptable boundaries, one thing that typically makes a proposed piece of business undesirable is the hotel's ability to sell that space to others at a better profit margin. That's why the most common response to an unacceptable proposal is to ask for a higher price.

Turning a mediocre proposal into an excellent piece of business might work as in the following example. Say that one group requests 200 rooms at a 350-room hotel for $80 per room, which is a $16,000 piece of business that was really not expected. The forecast shows that the total revenue without the group for that date would have been $29,000 with 290 rooms booked at an average rate of $100. The group's business will bring the hotel to 100 percent occupancy and generate a total of $31,000 in revenue (having displaced some of the forecasted transient arrivals). The revenue on the 60 extra rooms gives the hotel more than enough incentive to accept this group, with a $2,000 increase in total revenue. (Assume per-room ancillary spending offsets the variable costs on the extra rooms.)

Any good sales director is going to feel good about the $16,000 in business he or she helped bring to the hotel. Even if someone points out that the business really brought only $2,000 in additional revenue to the hotel, there still is reason to feel good about this arrangement. Another way to look at this group, however, is that it represents $16,000 in unanticipated room revenue from which the hotel is extracting only an additional $2,000 in revenue because the group has displaced higher-rate business. By manipulating the other variables and, in this case, moving this group to a date that will displace little other business, the hotel can extract maximum value from this group. Even if the hotel needed to reduce the room rate to $60 to entice the group to move to other dates, the added value would be $12,000 instead of $2,000, because the group would be displacing less (anticipated) higher-rate business. Note that the calculations for this example are for only one night, but a group would typically stay for multiple nights, thus amplifying both the benefit of moving the group and the penalty for accepting the proposal as offered.

The hotel could also propose that the group's room block be smaller—for example, in a situation where the group is attending a convention for which the dates are already fixed. This proposal is less effective from both the hotel's point of view and that of the group, but it still increases the value of the group. Because the forecast is that the group would displace 140 rooms that would have sold to transients at $100 each, the hotel gains back $20 in displaced revenue for every room sold to transients instead of to the group. Cutting the group's room block in half, for instance, actually nets the hotel another $2,000 in revenue. While the group has little incentive to reduce its request for rooms (unless the market is otherwise sold out), the hotel could insist that the group block fewer rooms if the group's original offer did not make up for revenues the hotel would have obtained from transients.

► CONCLUSION

Whether a hotel is just getting started or is ready to take the next logical step toward more sophisticated inventory controls, systems are available to support its efforts.

The concept of volume discount does not always apply in an environment where the supply is limited, as in the case of a hotel that is near to selling out. Sometimes less is more. This is a particularly important message for meeting planners who inflate their numbers, assuming this will make their business more appealing to the hotel.

Unfortunately, forces may work against taking the types of revenue-enhancing actions discussed here. One is the tendency to accept the first option that clears the hotel's minimum standards, or to accept the business but negotiate on the rate. Current sales-incentive plans are possibly another hindrance to these opportunities. Even the more progressive incentive plans that reward sales activities based on revenues rather than just room-nights can discourage behavior that benefits the hotel. This is done by encouraging the salesperson to book business that may not develop the highest revenue for the hotel, as in the example of the group that proposed to book 200 rooms.

► CASE STUDY: THE POWER OF INFORMATION

This case study explains how Disney uses simple information about hotel guests' stay patterns to increase revenues at their Orlando resort hotels (Quain et al., 1998). One of the highest-demand weeks of the entire year in Central Florida is the holiday week between Christmas and New Year's Day. Ironically, this strong week is followed by one of the lowest-occupancy weeks of the entire year, the first week of January. Disney's Orlando resorts typically sell out the Christmas to New Year's dates by the end of September, if not sooner. But the first week in January has been a challenge for Walt Disney World's marketers, who have developed programs and events to fill the void caused by the exit of the holiday crowd. Although Florida residents can be tempted with deep discounts to boost the occupancy for the month of January, the resorts cannot develop enough demand to fill their rooms one week following one of the biggest holidays of the year.

Disney took many creative measures to boost the resorts' occupancy that week. For example, the Walt Disney World Marathon, which was originally held during the three-day Martin Luther King Jr. holiday weekend to help ensure the race's success, was moved to the first weekend of January. The move was a win for both the race and the hotels. The Martin Luther King holiday weekend maintained its strong occupancy levels without the marathon, and the end of the first week of January received a much-needed occupancy boost from the marathoners and their families. The good news for racers, moreover, was that more of them could find a room at the Walt Disney World resorts because they no longer had to compete with vacationers for limited rooms over the King holiday weekend. Despite the marathon's success, Walt Disney World's marketers knew this was not the complete answer, and they continued to look for ways to increase hotel occupancy immediately following the holidays.

As part of the effort to increase occupancy during the first week of January, the revenue management department at Disney began studying ways to use minimum-stay controls in conjunction with New Year's Eve to preserve rooms for guests who wanted to stay beyond New Year's Day. This was in the early days of yield management, when length-of-stay controls were relatively uncommon and a new corporate culture had to be developed. Such a seemingly extreme concept drew skepticism and concern within the company. Senior managers had to be reassured that this new form of controlling inventory would not end up causing them to carry empty rooms during their busy season.

In another demonstration of how knowledge is power, the revenue management department had recently developed a report that summarized arrivals by length of stay (a concept discussed by Cross, 1997). This report demonstrated two things: First, they did indeed have demand for guests arriving late in the holiday week and staying through several days into January; second, over 35 percent of arrivals during the holidays were guests staying three or fewer nights. Disney's estimates of unconstrained demand over the holidays indicated it could easily afford to accept stays of four nights or longer only and still sell out its peak nights.

Taking a deep breath, Disney's revenue managers set a minimum-stay restriction for arrivals during the holiday week accepting reservations for four nights or longer only. This calculated decision was intended to improve revenue during the first week of January while presenting minimal risk to the normal strong revenues during the preceding holiday week. The experiment attracted attention throughout the company. When late September came and the resorts were not sold out, some people were concerned the holiday might not fill. However, the forecast predicted the resorts would not be sold out by the usual late September date under the four-night minimum stay restraint. Because of the limitation, Disney was turning away shorter-stay requests that in previous years would have been accepted (and sold out the holiday week by September), with the forecasted expectation that the resorts could book longer stays to guests calling in October, November, and even early December. Trend reports helped affirm the resorts were still on a pace that would sell out the hotels, which eased some minds in the revenue management department. (It is worth noting that guests desiring a short stay could be offered almost their pick of rooms the week after New Year's Day.)

The final results were well worth the effort and nail-biting. The hotels filled to capacity over the holidays, having sold out in late October. Occupancy for the first week of January rose 10 percentage points, almost entirely driven by guests arriving prior to New Year's Day and staying the minimum four nights. The room revenue contribution alone was worth over $1.5 million.

Disney's success in this example highlights a simple principle that many hotels miss. Disney was not paralyzed by the fact that it did not have perfect information or that it was not in a position to maximize revenue with optimal inventory controls. Instead, Disney's revenue managers made use of the information available to them to achieve a measured improvement in revenue while minimizing their risk.

▶ THE REVENUE MANAGEMENT GAME

The following game (accessible at www.goconcierge.net/gotconcierge/gotconcierge.pdf), developed by Dennis Quinn, has been used by guest speakers at Cornell University's School of Hospitality Administration to initiate discussions on the objectives of yield management. It is not an exercise in identifying who is proficient at yield management decisions. Rather, it is intended to demonstrate how capacity controls can affect a hotel's revenues and to develop an appreciation for the process throughout the organization.

▶ Objective

Maximize room revenue for a five-room hotel.

▶ Rules

As each reservation request is announced (use Table 4.3), participants decide whether they wish to accept the request at the time it is made. Accepted reservations are recorded on the chart with the room rate written in each date block (Table 4.4). Once a day is sold out, subsequent requests that include that day must be rejected. At the end of the game, participants add up the total revenue they generated for that week.

Hints

- Participants cannot go back and add a prior reservation once the next call is announced. The prior guest has hung up and booked with the competitor.

- No, overbooking is not an option.

- The host should fill in a booking grid on a first-come, first-served basis, denying requests only when days are sold out. This will serve as the no-control method.

- You can let the audience know they will receive a maximum of 18 calls, if you want to help out.

- Remember, this is not a game of skill. It is a game for demonstration and discussion. The hotel's next revenue manager will not

Table 4.3 Reservation Requests

Call Number	Room Rate	Arrival Day	Stay Length	Comments
1	$ 80	Thurs	3	
2	$ 80	Tues	2	
3	$120	Fri	2	
4	$ 40	Mon	1	$40 is below your average rate goal for the week. Should you take it anyway if Monday is going to run vacant? We've seen incremental groups turned away because management warned sales to meet the monthly average rate goal. Be careful of what you ask for.
5	$120	Tues	1	
6	$ 60	Thurs	3	First, tell audience this is AAA discount (instead of telling them the rate). Point out the value of tracking rates versus source of business when managing inventory.
7	$120	Sat	1	
8	$ 60	Tues	5	
9	$ 60	Thurs	3	This is a package that includes dinner shows, meals, and recreation, which adds $110 in value to the hotel each night. Discussion: room revenue goals versus total profitability. Assign programs to rate buckets based on total value, not just room rate.
10	$ 40	Tues	5	
11	$ 80	Tues	5	
12	$120	Sat	1	
13	$100	Mon	2	
14	$ 60	Fri	2	
15	$100	Fri	2	
16	$100	Sun	7	What does it cost for you to lose this business?
17	$ 40	Sun	3	
18	$ 60	Sun	4	

be selected based on the results of this game!

► Game Discussion Points

Each participant should compare the difference between optimal revenue and the actual revenue achieved. (Optimal revenue in the above game is $2,360.) Divide the difference into actual revenue to show the percentage of potential improvement. For example, if a participant earned $2,000, the potential for improvement is 18 percent—that is, (2,360 − 2,000) + 2,000 = 18.

How much is that percentage improvement in annual room revenue worth to the hotel? How about half that improvement? How much revenue might management be leaving on the table at the hotel? For exam-

Table 4.4 Booking Grid for Five-Room Hotel

Fill in the room rate for each accepted reservation for the appropriate number of days.							
	Sun.	**Mon.**	**Tues.**	**Wed.**	**Thurs.**	**Fri.**	**Sat.**	**Total**
Room 1								
Room 2								
Room 3								
Room 4								
Room 5								
Total								

ple, what would be the hotel's annual room revenue multiplied by 118 percent? How about by 109 percent?

What is the percentage occupancy of the hotel in the no-control environment? How does that make participants feel about low-occupancy months?

Did anyone score below the no-control level? What does this tell you about the need to make responsible decisions when accepting reservations?

4.5 CONCIERGE (CONE-SEE-AIR-J)

Mario Arnaldo

I vividly remember my first and last contacts with a concierge.

First contact. Not knowing the correct term, I would simply have called him "the Supe," or building superintendent. We had just moved to France after enjoying a year in Somalia, East Africa. My dad used to work for the United Nations, so we literally moved to different countries and continents every two or three years. This time our home was an apartment on the seventh floor of a well-used building in the immediate outskirts of Paris. We have our own concierge? Wow! And his name is Monsieur Guy de Roquefort? I was only 14 years old, so it was easy to get impressed, or disappointed. Well, Monsieur de Roquefort's scent certainly reminded me of the cheese with his namesake. He was unshaven and less than tidy. His uniform *du jour* was an undershirt, a stick of Gauloises

(French cigarettes) in one hand and a glass of cheap beaujolais in the other. But Guy had a good heart, engaged me in titillating conversations about "cherchez les femmes" (much more rewarding than the four-hour French lessons I had in school), always fixed the toilets that wouldn't flush, and delighted in announcing every single piece of mail we received. He probably would not get within 50 feet of an employment agency. However, if I could give him a shower and a shirt, I would hire him in a heartbeat. Monsieur Guy de Roquefort's *soul* was in the right place. I still remember him, see? That was in 1964.

I fondly remember my most recent contact with a concierge.

Last contact. This article was written in 2004. Forty years later is a long stretch of time after my first contact with a concierge. Thanks to my dad's international assignments, I've used up seven passports. Thanks to my two international airline jobs, I've filled up my last passport with immigration stamps from 32 cities in five continents. I have enjoyed a privileged opportunity to meet and work with a multitude of professionals, but one, in particular, in Seattle stays in my memory.

She was punctual. Polite. Charming. Endearing. Never forgot the slightest detail. Never overbearing or invasive. Made my socks roll up and down with legendary service. Went *way* beyond the call of duty in answering the simplest of requests. "Where can we get great fresh oysters? Where is . . .? How do we . . .?" It was as if my engagement and honeymoon to come were made in heaven. This was in 1997. Since then, she has faithfully written us every year during the holiday season with neat, short, handwritten, personal notes. Her envelopes are also written by hand. She does not use insensitive, computer-generated labels. She always hopes we will

come back to visit her again and enjoy Seattle. She has *never* asked questions like, "Can we book a room for you?" We correspond regularly about hospitality concepts to bring reality to my hospitality students, or ideas she can bring to her in-house training programs. On two occasions, Mr. Robert Thurston, managing general partner, enthusiastically gave us permission to study his hotel as a class project, long-distance from Honolulu!

That's Annie Delucchi, former concierge at the Inn at The Market, a great boutique hotel in Seattle, literally a shout away from Pike Place Market. Eight months prior to our arrival at the IATM, my fiancée and I had never met Annie. All our interactions were via email. Not even a phone call. Annie has since been promoted to executive liaison at the IATM. Know what? If my wife and I were given complimentary reservations at another Seattle property, we would still go to Annie's property and pay for our rooms. You see, I'm not just a reservation record on the IATM database. I can be me, someone who has a preference for fresh oysters! My wife is not "the Mrs." She, too, can be herself. She can spend the whole day walking back and forth to Pike Place Market to select just the right bouquet of fresh flowers or just the right jewelry accessories. Annie Delucchi's *soul* is in the right place.

Wassup? During the fall 2003 semester, I was designing interactive games for my international students to enjoy as part of our weekly class discussions. One of these games was the Concierge Game. This game is the basis for the research I did on concierges for this article.

So I reviewed the Withiam concierge articles, used Google to point me to a few hundred pages of articles, scoured dozens of concierge-related websites, emailed and talked to dozens of hospitality professionals, and finally interviewed concierges in Honolulu, Hawaii, to highlight six significant findings about the modern concierge. The six findings concern passion, titles, technology, Les Clefs d'Or, stars, and Aloha!

Finding #1: Passion. The concierges and guest service staff I talked to, whether they had their keys or not, are, without exception, passionate about what they do. They all have what some have called *gotta-wanna,* an almost insatiable desire to exceed customer expectations with minor regard for themselves or the time clock.

Finding #2: Titles. Got concierge? Job titles I compiled included concierge, head concierge, chef concierge, concierge supervisor, lobby concierge, guest service agent, guest services manager or supervisor, activity agent, and the more recent compcierge and technocierge, for those who assist road warriors with laptops and other electronic paraphernalia. However, whether or not properties enjoy a keyed concierge, management must openly recognize and support the need to provide concierge services. Anecdotally, seasoned concierges, no matter what they are titled, will tell you, as do Nargil, Kahn, and Peterson (2003) that "one doesn't have to be at an upscale property to provide the kind of service that will keep guests coming back." Presence of a concierge, keyed or not, is a plus when it comes to four-star and five-star ratings (*Mobil Travel Guide*) or four-diamond and five-diamond ratings (AAA). The concierges and guest service staff I met are part of front desk operations, with a designated area close to—but distinct from—the check-in area. When I visited some Honolulu hotels, the front desk areas appeared to have lulls in operation during midmorning hours, after check-out rush time, and before afternoon check-in times. In contrast, the concierge area appeared to be continuously busy whether midmorning, noon, afternoon, or early evening.

More and more organizations are answering "Yes!" to the question "Got concierge?"

A fall 2003 television series, *Life of Luxury,* with Robin Leach, featured one of the more exclusive U.K. concierge services, Quintessentially. Quintessentially, a membership organization affiliated with luxury facilities worldwide, essentially provides the same services the lobby-based concierge would without the restrictions of being in a facility. According to their website (www.quintessentially.com/home.php):

> Quintessentially aims to satisfy practically any last-minute whim our members may have, from front row seats at a fashion show and spur of the moment chartered yachts, to impossible dinner reservations at some of the world's most exclusive restaurants and last-minute theatre tickets, and with 24/7 member telephone and email assistance our experts are always on hand to save you time, hassle and money. Fantastic offshoots of the Quintessentially brand include the Quintessentially magazine and the exclusive Quintessentially 'Beyond Black' credit card. Quintessentially members are also continuously kept up to date with what's hot and what's not through our weekly newsletter, offering indispensable advice on the essential art and cultural events of the moment, as well as invitations to charity affairs, gala balls, shopping evenings, film premieres and exclusive after-event parties.

In the middle of finalizing this article in December 2003, my own university, Hawaii Pacific University, advertised its latest service. Guess what it was? Yep! A concierge desk to help students and other stakeholders access and utilize the services of the university.

Finding #3: Technology and the Concierge. I predict that no amount of technology will ever replace the concierge or guest service staff. Inger Boudouris and the other concierges I interviewed or emailed agreed with this prediction. However, there is room to enjoy and take advantage of what the current technology has to offer. You don't have to look far. Check out the extensive usage of PDAs in last fall's TV series *Las Vegas* and *The Threat Matrix.* At one end of the technology spectrum, the Westin Santa Clara uses Sony's Contact-ME for remote video conferencing from the concierge's home (a three-hour round-trip commute) directly to the hotel lobby's monitor, some 80 miles away. After some weeks of emailing, I obtained permission from the Westin Santa Clara general manager and support from Clifford Planning, LLC, a premier Hawaii-based architectural firm, to conduct a one-hour videoconference between Anna Morris and my hotel and resort management students. We had a terrific experience; this is a perfect example of the application of technology to enhance a traditional service rather than replace it.

At another level of technology, interactive software programs such as GoConcierge (GC) [http://www.goconcierge.net/home/] allows a user to manage and provide guests with information and services in a consistently impressive manner. Adam Isrow, who designed and developed this interactive web-based program, provided me a username and password and gave me an opportunity to validate and confirm for myself how user-friendly GC was. I predict the concierge's uniform will include a wireless PDA, a camera-video cell phone, a software program similar to GoConcierge, and other electronic gadgetry. Isrow said in an interview:

I think you appropriately summarize the commonality of the concierge position with passion! These people (generally speaking) love what they do, love people, and are therefore great people to be around. I enjoyed your prediction—video cell phone and a PDA—I don't think you are too far off!

And then there's Mike Doi, a guest services coordinator, sitting in the Outrigger lobby on Waikiki Beach, with his uncanny memory for names, places, phone numbers and his reliable Rolodex. He does have a computer monitor at his desk, but like many concierges, prefers not to use it while interacting with a guest. Mike also shifts from speaking English to Japanese to pidgin and back without blinking an eyelash, on the phone and with walk-ins who step up to his desk.

Others exemplified by Dave Nishi and Sally Yates agree it would be wonderful for their properties to enjoy state-of-the-art technology, more computers, more staff, and more space. From my conversations with them, I found that both Dave and Sally are equally adamant about not letting the gadgetry come between the guest and the service provider. Know what? Dave, guest services manager at the Ohana Maile Sky Court, can't even spell *Les Clefs d'Or,* but he has over 25 years of customer service under his belt. Dave also has many years of information technology (IT) experience, but given the choice, says, "I always prefer to deal with the guests face to face. Sometimes you just can't trust your computer or PDA." Sally is one of only a handful of Les Clefs d'Or concierges in Hawaii, and she has enjoyed her position as senior concierge at the Halekulani Hotel for over 10 years. She says, "We enjoy working with our guests on a personal one-on-one basis at the desk, and sometimes the computer work takes us away from that service." One concern we discussed was maximizing eye contact with the guest, or avoiding interactions that take your eyes away from the guest.

I found these statements enjoyably revealing because (a) they were self-initiated, (b) Dave works in a three-star property and Sally in a four-star property, and (c) Dave and Sally have never met.

Finding #4: Les Clefs d'Or (LCD) USA. In the original Withiam article on concierges (1983), there were about 40 members in LCD USA. Back then, many travelers didn't know whether a concierge was Mozart's second movement in D flat or the alternate entrée. In 1993, there were 200 U.S. concierges in the LCD membership, and the savvy traveler started looking for the concierge. Even in fiction, 007 (James Bond) had his hotel contacts—concierges! In 2003, there were 450 concierge members in LCD USA representing over 100,000 rooms in 250 four- and five-star properties.

Over 3,400 international members from 37 countries make up the LCD worldwide. The LCD headquarters in Paris is called the Union International des Concierges d'Hôtels. Although the concierge position is predominantly male in Europe and other countries, 53 percent of U.S. concierges are female.

Concierges continuously network with one another and the communities in which they work. Concierge associations are found in many cities throughout the United States. Some only admit hotel concierges as members (LCD as well as non-LCD concierges); others include local vendors and employees from car rental agencies, tour companies, tour guides, restaurants, art galleries, and so on (maybe even university concierges! Who knows?).

Many concierge country sections also have community-based organizations. In the United States, for example, Les Clefs d'Or Foundation of the Americas (United States, Canada, Mexico, and Brazil) provides financial support and in-kind donations of goods and was founded to respond to the suffering of concierges and/or their families and significant others affected by catastrophic or life-threatening illnesses.

Charles Holzer, director of media for LCD USA and chef concierge at the River-Place Hotel in Portland, Oregon, explained to me:

> Each [LCD local chapter] is different in its composition, yet each association's purpose is the same: to positively enhance the guest experience through knowledge, education, mentoring, networking, and friendship. In general, local meetings consist of an educational element, whether that is speakers from local organizations, vendors, or attractions. This could also entail bringing in members from the hospitality industry to discuss strengthening the concierge desk, enhancing revenue, or working in a more supportive manner with management.

After I interviewed Inger Boudouris by phone, we spoke and corresponded many times. In one of our discussions, this is what Inger told me about concierges:

> You know, being a concierge is being a "concierge for all seasons," because you must be able to turn around on a dime, multitasking and at the same time making important decisions while talking on the phone, et cetera! I love being a concierge because of what I call the unpredictable challenges, and it makes one's life very exciting—no day, no hour, no minute is the same. There is no time for stress because you are always in the midst of happenings.

Today, it's snowing. We have a wedding ceremony in our lobby this afternoon. Afternoon tea will be served in the pub today, wedding receptions everywhere, and in the middle of all this, guests will be checking in and out—I love it!

A brief but supremely informative phone interview with Shujaat Khan, vice president of LCD USA and chef concierge at the Capitol Hilton in Washington, D.C., revealed these weathered and tested beliefs:

- Time management of your skills is extremely important when you have only limited resources!

- How much do you really love people? The professional in you needs to come out, especially when you're being challenged with the unruly customer, the overdemanding VIP, or the jealous significant other!

- The successful concierge operation is always a major business revenue generator.

- How do you fix the dissatisfied? The process usually ends up being more important than the end product.

- Of paramount importance to the future concierge: exercising the best balance of ethics and the highest code of conduct.

Finding #5: Got stars? Not? Don Massagli (2002) wrote an article that at first glance appears to be a straightforward commentary applauding the assurance, confidence, and customer relations packaged in your hotel concierge. The reader should know that Massagli brings an uncommon perspective, as he is the senior vice president of Park Ridge, Illinois-based *Mobil Travel Guide* (http://www.mobiltravelguide.com/). The *Mobil Travel Guide* inspects and rates thousands of hotels and restaurants and publishes the travel guide and other travel publications. Coincidentally, I had an opportunity to interview Massagli in person; he repeated to me that concierges add a touch of distinction to any property, regardless of its star status. I predict that hotel management will pay increasingly more attention to their concierge and concierge services, whether the property has two stars or five. Jameson (Witham, 1993) sums it up best: "[G]uests are going to ask the kind of questions that concierges routinely answer, regardless of whether the hotel has a concierge desk."

Finding #6: Aloha. (In Hawaii, *Aloha* means more than just "hello" or "goodbye." It also refers to a spirit that encompasses welcoming, friendly accommodation that embodies giving the gift of friendship. —Editor)

Silverman (Witham, 1993) hit the nail on the head: "Does management create the environment to make exceeding expectations possible?" Probably not all the time. Whatever the number of stars the property has, management must continuously maintain a dynamic environment enabling all employees, whether or not they work in guest services, to exceed guest expectations. So what is the energy source of all the legendary stories of Houdini-like concierges? My interaction with concierges in Hawaii, the "Land of Aloha," tells me that concierges are loyal and have a built-in desire to please and satisfy within legal and moral limits. The concierge in Hawaii makes it happen by practicing "service through Aloha." And when he or she doesn't have that particular desired resource (the dinner reservation, a hard-to-find gift for the significant other), he or she knows how to network out the solution through Aloha with fellow concierges.

At the time of this writing, there was no

Les Clefs d'Or section in Hawaii, but there are several Les Clefs d'Or concierges on Oahu, Kapolei, and the other popular resort areas of the state. According to Pam Davis, publisher of the *Oahu Concierge* newsletter:

> Our goal is to disseminate pertinent information to the hospitality industry as a whole, focusing on the latest happenings, keeping them informed on recent changes and improvements at places they might very well recommend, as well as including industry changes and promotions. As we are the only industry publication on Oahu located in one of the few cities without an official [Les Clefs d'Or] organization, we have an additional burden to try to fill that void by holding regular gatherings where industry professionals can mingle and share information, but unfortunately they are not monthly, and they rarely (due to travel complications) include those from the outer islands.

▶ LAST THOUGHTS

My research revealed Holly Stiel has probably written more about concierges than anyone else anywhere in the English-speaking and -writing world. I urge students, educators, and professionals in all service industries to browse through her website (http://www.thankyouverymuchinc.com/index.html). Any one topic she writes about could be a customer service seminar or workshop. During an interview with Holly, I was reminded of one of the quotes from her website:

> The reality is that there is no sign above the [hotel] entrance telling customers how to behave, and sometimes they behave badly. So the responsibility for appropriate behavior falls on the service provider.

And, I would argue by extrapolation, this responsibility falls specifically to guest services employees such as the concierge.

The modern concierge serves as the knowledgeable, sensitive, and efficient interface between the guest and the array of hotel and community services available to travelers. It is this exciting profession I have attempted to overview in this article.

4.6 AS I SEE IT: MANAGEMENT OF THE FRONT OFFICE

Oliver Meinzer

The following article is not based on extensive research but rather on my experience working in front office operations, either as an associate or a manager. It looks at the operation from my point of view. In this article, I write about the setup of key areas of the front office operation, namely the bell stand, the front desk, and the guest relations department. I provide some ideas about the physical setup as well as ideas about hiring the right associates and the training tools. I also provide insights into the daily tasks in all areas, what I look for as a manager, and the reasons behind certain processes and actions in the day-to-day operation.

This article should give the reader an idea about what the front office operation incorporates and what it takes to run such a department. The information can be used by the reader to understand processes better and get a good idea if working in this area is something he or she might be interested in. At the end of the chapter, I provide a timetable of a regular workday in the life of a front office manager.

► BELL STAND

The bell stand and its associates are important because they are usually the first and last encounter the guest has with the hotel and its staff. Traditionally, the bell staff was considered concierge as well, as they usually had the best insider knowledge about the location and attractions, and they always had a friend or relative working there as well to get the guest a special deal. This is still the case in hotels where the bell staff has been with the property for many years. In newer properties, it is primarily the concierge who has this kind of connection. The basic duties of a bell person include but are not limited to handling incoming and outgoing guest luggage, greeting arriving and departing guests as they enter or leave the hotel lobby, storage of luggage for guests, and being present in the lobby area to answer questions or assist the guests with any requests they might have. Specific tasks differ from property to property.

Depending on a property's check-in and check-out procedures, the bell staff may spend a significant amount of time with the guest, accompanying him or her to the room and explaining the features of the hotel and its surroundings. This is a key encounter for the hotel, as the bell staff has a lot of influence on the guest, enabling the staff to steer the guest toward the hotel's outlets and amenities. This, of course, is only possible and effective if the associates are trained properly and have the necessary knowledge about the hotel offerings. The bell staff gets a lot of information from guests about their stay, experience, and encounters, and about the guests themselves. This kind of information is invaluable for the hotel. If proper reporting channels are in place, the hotel can be proactive in addressing an incident before the guest considers it a problem. This information also helps the hotel recognize special occasions like birthdays and anniversaries. The bell staff is the hotel's eyes and ears, the ambassadors for the property. It is important to understand their significance and the influence they have on the hotel and front office operation.

The bell stand is usually located in the main entrance area, easily accessible by both guests and staff. It is usually close to a storage room where luggage and other guest items can be stored. The bell stand should have a telephone with an outside line to enable the staff to make reservations, inquire about hours of operations, and so on. A computer with access to the Internet and the property management system (PMS) allows the bell staff not only to provide the latest online information but also access guest information like room numbers and contact information or to leave messages on guest accounts. Maps and informational material about attractions in the surrounding area help the bell staff point guests in the right direction after making recommendations about leisure activities. If no printer is attached to the computer, preprinted driving directions to popular destinations (e.g., airport, train station, landmarks) can be handed out to guests.

Luggage tags are used to label guest luggage for storage. There are usually two parts to the ticket, one for the bag/item and the second for the guest to claim the stored items later. The storage room should be big enough to handle the storage demands for the property. The shelving should be arranged and labeled to reflect the numbers or letters on the luggage tags. This makes it easier for the bell staff to store and retrieve items, and it keeps the storage room organized and clean. The bell stand should also be equipped with plenty of luggage carts. Those carts should match the decor and category of the hotel (you probably do not want to use a wooden dolly in a five-star property). The bell staff must ensure that the carts are kept in good condition. This includes polishing the metal or brass parts as well as maintaining the carpeted area and wheels to ensure proper functionality.

Another important item for the bell stand is a so-called trip log, a simple spreadsheet where the staff marks the room numbers of check-ins and check-outs they performed. This log is a great help if you have to retrace a luggage delivery or pickup or simply as a tool to communicate which room is next. Sometimes luggage gets delivered to the wrong room, but the trip log helps the staff rectify the situation immediately.

The bell stand is a front-of-the-house area with direct guest contact. It is important that this area is kept clean and organized. The bell staff must ensure that they are wearing the proper uniform and that the uniform is in top condition. In order for the staff to attend to all guest requests and questions, it is imperative for them to have all the necessary knowledge before they start their shift. Helpful

tools that ensure daily information is communicated to the front-of-the-house staff include a pre-shift meeting, where the important details for the day are being discussed, a white board with information on it, or a daily newsletter in everybody's mailbox. However, it is the front office manager's responsibility that the associate either attend the pre-shift meeting or read the information provided on the whiteboard or newsletter to get the necessary information for their shift (as a front office manager, you can make this part of the shift, and therefore the property's attendance policy applies).

The bell staff itself should be trained like any other front-of-the-house staff. First of all, it is important to hire the right candidates. As a front office manager, you look for applicants who are outgoing, comfortable with working in public, well groomed, and articulate, and who have a good understanding of service and a positive attitude. It is always better to interview more candidates to make sure you find the right person for the job than to go with the first decent applicant. Never compromise when it comes to hiring great staff!

Once a new bell person is hired, proper training is key. A possible training rotation should include housekeeping (great insight into the room setup, the different room types, and locations), front desk (basic check-in and check-out procedures and basic knowledge about the property management system), the outlets (knowledge about the restaurant menu, spa offerings, etc.), loss prevention (first aid, security, and emergency procedures), as well as basic training to cover the phones—and, of course, guest contact etiquette.

Once the staff member completes the required training and is working regular shifts, regular performance checks should be implemented to ensure knowledge stays up to date. It is the front office manager's responsibility to supply the bell staff with the appropriate tools and information to perform their duties. Therefore, regular meetings are necessary to communicate any changes or additions and to collect feedback from the staff. The bell staff is at the front of the line. Their input is invaluable for the front office operation. It is important to stop everything, listen, and use their information to adjust and improve the front office operation and, ultimately, the guest experience. It has proven helpful in my workplace to cross-train other associates at the bell stand as well. Associates in loss prevention, room service, the front desk, or any other department are then able to help out at the bell stand if necessary. Sometimes, check-ins come in waves, and the current bell staff might not be able to get bags to guest rooms in a timely manner. Having the flexibility of calling associates from other departments to help out ensures guest satisfaction and is a nice change for the other associates.

Because in many cases the bell stand is located in a high-traffic area and is the first area the guest sees and interacts with, the hotel must make sure that the guest's first and last impressions are positive.

▶ FRONT DESK

The front desk or reception area is where staff-guest interaction is probably most intense. The front desk manages the room inventory as well as the check-in and check-out process and the account activities for each guest in house. The front desk assigns rooms to the arriving guests according to their preferences and requests (many properties have a staff person, called the rooms controller, who is in charge of assigning rooms to incoming individual guests and groups). This is the department with the most traffic in the front office area. The agents deal with the check-in/check-out procedures, handle cash, resolve conflicts, address reservation/billing inquiries, and perform guest services. They have to be jacks-of-all-trades because the front desk is the most important access point for information, complaints, and requests at the hotel.

The front desk is usually located in the lobby area (sometimes, in high-rise properties, the front desk is located on a higher floor), easily accessible from the main entrance door and the guest room elevators. In some properties, front desks take the form of individual islands instead of a long counter. The advantage is that the agent can access the lobby area much more quickly to greet or assist the guest. The desk is divided into several equally equipped workstations. The number of workstations depends on the size of the hotel. A good rule of thumb is 1 workstation per 100 guest rooms. Each workstation has (this again varies from property to property) a computer or PMS terminal with a credit card swiper and printer, room key encoder, telephone, reference guide with information about room location, outlet location, currency exchange, market codes, rate codes, technical support information, cash, credit card and check handling instructions, emergency procedures, and other property-related information. It is vital that this folder—an important front-desk tool—is in order and up to date at all times. Other necessities for each workstation include paper and pens, area maps, key cards, key sleeves, and scissors. As with the bell stand, it is important to keep workstations clean and organized at all times, as they are all in direct view for the guest and reflect on the hotel's operation.

The primary tasks for a front desk associate are the check-in and check-out of guests. During the check-in process, the agent should verify specific information related to the guest's reservation. The information includes but is not limited to duration of stay, requested room type or room preference, room rate (it is important for the front desk agent to verify the guest's eligibility for discounted rates by checking membership cards [e.g., AAA or AARP], company IDs, government credit cards), special requests or arrangements, method of payment, and any frequent-stay membership/airline affiliation. The verification of this information is important to avoid discrepancies in the billing process and adjustments during check-out, and to ensure accuracy in room availability.

Discrepancies in the billing process can be time-consuming and therefore a significant inconvenience to the guest. It is important to verify the room rate during the check-in process (especially if a guest's room rate changes during the stay); otherwise, the front desk must adjust revenue during the check-out process, which takes extra time and affects the room revenue figures negatively. Billing discrepancies are the most common reason for guest complaints.

The verification of length of stay helps the front desk manage room inventory more accurately. Especially in a sold-out situation, the hotel depends on all guests who are supposed to check out, according to the property management system, to actually check out, as their rooms have been sold to other guests for the night. If a guest's departure date is incorrect and he or she needs to be extended, the hotel may find itself in an oversold situation. This causes a chain reaction of additional problems and costs. If a guest's actual length of stay is shorter than the property management system shows (because it was not verified during check-in) and the guest checks out

earlier than expected, the hotel might have lost an opportunity to sell the room. Accuracy is thus very important to maximizing hotel revenue. However, there will be occasions where guests depart before the confirmed departure date. It is up to the individual property or chain if an early departure fee (usually one night-room and tax) is charged.

The correct room type and location can be essential to guest satisfaction. Selection is a matter of training and experience, as there are several aspects to consider when allocating rooms to reservations. The order of importance of the criteria may depend on local or corporate standard operating procedures.

- **Rate:** This selection criterion is pretty much self-explanatory. If there are two guests with the same room type request, you may want to assign the nicer room to the guest who pays the higher rate.

- **Length of stay:** A guest who checks in late and stays only one night might not be too concerned about the view or location of the room as long as he or she gets a good night's sleep. On the other hand, a guest staying with family or a spouse for several days will certainly have expectations regarding view and room location (the concept of proper segmentation applies here).

- **Loyalty to the hotel and company/ frequent-stay program membership level:** With competition fiercer than ever, loyalty is becoming more and more important. Almost every hotel chain has a frequent-stay program that offers various membership levels based in number of room-nights spent with the company. These membership levels have a great impact on room allocation. The hotel must ensure the most loyal customers to the brand or chain are recognized for their repeating business. Benefits of higher membership level benefits (usually platinum or gold level) include room type and upgrade guarantees. Some programs even penalize the individual property if those guarantees are not met. This shows the importance companies place on these frequent guests and the money they spend with the chain. In addition, many hotels have developed local repeat guest programs to acknowledge and reward guests who frequently stay with one specific property. These guests are not necessarily members of the hotel company's reward program.

• **Reservation guarantees:** Many corporations have introduced the concept of reservation guarantees. Examples include room type, bed type, smoking preference, or connecting rooms, guaranteed when the reservation is made and based on availability. Many companies offer monetary compensation to their guests (penalties for the hotel, as mentioned above) if the guarantees are not met at check-in.

• **VIP levels:** Hotels have individual VIP levels indicating the importance of the guest checking in—for example, a group VIP, meeting planner, corporate executive, celebrity, political figure. The VIP levels might include specific room assignments and check-in procedures (such as the manager on duty or general manager escorting the guest to the room) or the type of amenity for the guest.

In addition, special requests on the reservation might include information about allergies, rollaway and baby crib requests, high floor/low floor, request for a universally accessible room, and so on. Property management systems have codes that identify such requests. This helps when printing reports and

when the front desk associate, during the check-in process, verifies that the requests and guarantees are met.

A method of payment must be secured either prior to check-in (e.g., for a prepaid reservation) or during the check-in process. Payment can be made in cash or by valid credit card or check; some properties also accept money orders. In most cases, a credit card imprint is made during check-in, either electronically or manually. The total amount of room and tax and an incidental amount (for phone calls, movies, room service, etc.) are authorized on the credit card to secure payment. The incidental amount varies from property to property, depending on guest room amenities and services. If a guest wishes to use cash, an equivalent amount should be collected and deposited on the guest account. Each property management system checks regularly to see if the authorized amount has been exceeded and, if so, authorizes additional funds on the guest's credit card. Any guest account without sufficient authorization appears on a credit limit exceed report, which the front desk runs regularly. Local standard operating procedures determine the next steps the front desk associate takes. Usually, the front desk tries to contact the guest via phone or text message. However, if the guest does not respond to any of the messages, the front desk might go as far as locking the guest out of his or her room. This requires the guest to stop by the front desk to get a new key issued—a good time to inquire about an alternative method of payment or to ask for an additional cash deposit.

It is important for the front desk associate to know that when guests use a debit card during check-in, the amount authorized will not be available for the guest to withdraw from the checking account until he or she checks out of the hotel and the hold is released. It should be part of the check-in procedure to inform the guest about this before taking an electronic imprint of a debit card. However, if necessary, the front desk can release holds on credit card and checking accounts immediately by contacting the appropriate bank directly. The number for the institution can be found on the back of the credit/debit card. Most front desks are equipped with a check verification system (similar to grocery stores). If a guest decides to pay by check, the front desk associate can get immediate clearance to secure payment and avoid bounced checks.

Throughout the day, the front desk associate spends a significant amount of time providing guest services including directions, restaurant and activity recommendation, reservations, and rate inquiries. Therefore, it is important that all front desk associates receive detailed training in these areas. It is helpful for all new front desk associates to spend a few days in other departments (housekeeping, concierge, maybe even the restaurant) to learn about them and their mode of operation.

Working in housekeeping gives the front desk associate great knowledge about room setup, location, amenities, and views, but also an appreciation for the work the housekeeping staff does. Working with the concierge helps the front desk associate learn about the area and its attractions and activity options for the guests. With all this knowledge, the front desk associate can handle the majority of guest requests and questions, and the check-in process is faster, as the associate knows everything about the room type and location. It is helpful for the associate to visit a guest room once in a while to get refamiliarized with the room types and locations and learn about any changes made to the setup or amenity offering. Training is definitely an on-going process. In addition, the associate should be familiar with the in-room technology, like high-speed Internet access and movie systems. This, of course, not only includes knowing how to connect to the Internet and how to order a movie but also what movies are currently showing on the hotel channel.

Most hotels these days provide an express check-out option. A copy of the guest's folio is delivered to the guest room the morning of check-out. The guest may use this as the receipt and need not have to stop by the front desk to check out (only if the billing is accurate, of course). Many in-room entertainment systems also feature a video check-out option, which allows the guest to check out through the TV screen. However, this works only if sufficient funds are secured in advance to cover the balance on the account. To this day, though, many companies require their associates to present a zero balance receipt for their expense report. Therefore, there is still significant check-out traffic at the front desk.

During this process, the front desk associate verifies that all charges are correct and confirms the method of payment on the account. The guest still has the option of changing to a different method at this point. During check-out, the associate should also verify that the guest has a frequent-stay membership number on file, and if not, inquire about the guest's membership to ensure proper credit. At the end of the check-out process, the front desk associate should offer assistance with luggage and transportation and, of course, thank the guest for staying at the hotel. This is the last opportunity for the front desk to get feedback from the guest. If the guest experienced any problems during the stay, the hotel may lose the chance to rectify the situation and compensate the guest. Therefore, it is useful to inquire about the guest's experience while processing the check-out request.

The initial training of newly hired front desk associates is crucial to guest and associate satisfaction. Unless the front office manager provides the associates with the right tools from the beginning, the service encounter can become a frustrating experience for the associate and guest. Initial training should include a rotation so the associate can experience other departments, see how departments interact, and become familiar with the property, its features, and its offerings. However, training should be ongoing. It can be in the form of on-the-job training (new processes and procedures, revisiting associate actions to discuss alternative solutions for the future), a daily 15 minutes of learning, where a new topic is discussed every day, or specific job-related training classes (problem resolution, service recovery models, public speaking, interpersonal skills). Secret shoppers, organized by the front office manager, can be helpful in identifying opportunities for improvement. Using friends and family for this purpose gives them a fun night out and provides the department with valuable information about the team's performance.

Again, success starts with a good hiring process. You should look for certain characteristics when interviewing applicants for the front desk. Candidates should be very comfortable with working in the public arena. They must be able to multitask in a fast-paced environment and able to handle stressful conflict situation without losing their cool. As with all front-of-the-house jobs, candidates should be well polished and groomed and should possess a service-oriented personality—the willingness to go the extra mile for guests and fellow associates.

The front desk is the front-of-the-house nerve center of the hotel. You want to be sure the best associates are represented here. Selecting and training these associates is one of the main responsibilities of the front office manager. Providing them with the right tools to do their job well is key to success and guest satisfaction.

▶ GUEST RELATIONS

Guest relations are getting more and more attention these days. This attention helped many companies to develop new guest relation models focusing on the one-stop-shop guest experience—for example, the Whatever Whenever Department at Starwood's W Hotels, Marriott's At Your Service, and Westin's Service Express. Guests can conveniently make any request or order room service by dialing a single extension; the associate who answers takes care of everything. Many companies have also implemented a customer retention database where every request is logged to better learn about guests' habits, preferences, and problems during their stay. This is invaluable information for hotels that want to anticipate guest needs and develop a clear idea about trends that might lead to potential problems. These data can be used in many ways and should be shared with every department.

▶ Specific Customer Preferences

If all requests are logged properly, the hotel has an enormous amount of information about each guest. With reference to this information, the staff can place certain items the guest usually requests in the room when he or she returns. Most systems allow the hotel to print repeat guest reports for each day that show the preferences of repeat customers, as well as incidents and requests from prior stays.

For example, the data may show that a specific guest called for extra pillows during her previous two stays at the hotel. If you tell the guest at check-in that extra pillows have already been placed in her room, you have won a customer for life. Anticipating the needs of the guests before they have to ask sets the hotel apart from the competition. The company that manages to set up a centralized database of this data for the entire chain has a significant advantage over competing brands. Consistency, though, is the key to success. Once a hotel has started this process, it must ensure consistent delivery. Otherwise it might lose its credibility and no longer stand out in the mind of the guest.

► Requests and Incidents

The other important use for such a system is the analysis of the data logged through the guest's requests. It is important that all requests and issues are logged in order to make this process work. It is up to the hotel—or, more specifically, the front office manager or guest relations manager—to extract information from the system and learn from it.

Requests: Reports show the requests (e.g., towels, in-room coffee) made from which guest rooms. This information can be helpful in several ways. Towels and coffee are basic room amenities and should always be there. An increase in the number of these requests should catch the manager's eye. Reports can be narrowed by floor or even by housekeeping section to see if the performance of a particular housekeeper is the reason for those increased requests (i.e., items are not replenished when the room is cleaned). On the other hand, if the requests do not show a clear pattern, one might want

to consider other reasons. For example, during the summer, people take towels to the pool, so you might experience requests for clean towels when guests get back to the room. This finding might lead the hotel to increase the number of towels in the rooms in summer. This will reduce the number of calls from the guests, reduce the time spent delivering towels, and thus free up time to take care of other guest requests faster. Similarly, an increased number of requests for mouthwash might cause the hotel to add mouthwash to the basic bathroom amenity set.

Incidents: Reports show any problems guests experience during their stay (only, of course, if the guests report them). These data help the hotel identify topics for retraining (in case of service issues) as well as engineering-related opportunities. Again, with the reports these systems allow the hotel to produce, you can narrow the problem to specific associates (in cross-referencing with department schedules), specific rooms, or mechanical equipment such as a malfunctioning plumbing riser, hot water pump, or electrical appliances. For example, an increased amount of calls for a burned-out light bulb in a specific room might be an indicator for a broken—or dangerous—light fixture; several calls from a room indicating that the HVAC system is not working might signal a clogged filter.

If a hotel has such a reporting and tracking system in place, it is essential that every staff member is behind it and reports every issue or problem so it can be entered into the database. (The concept of "garbage in, garbage out" is relevant here.) The support for this initiative must start at the top: The general manager must give full support. This is the only way to convince everybody else to work with the system as well. This is the only way to make these systems produce accurate results that could save hotels a lot of money.

To reiterate, training the associates in the guest relations department is critical and probably more intense than other departments. The associates must be familiar with literally *everything,* as they must respond to every request and complaint. The hiring process should be similar to that at the front desk, as the characteristics of a potential guest relations associate are the same. Training should likewise include a rotation through every department to develop the insight and product knowledge that will help the staff member make the right decision. Service recovery and problem resolution training is key as well and should be a constant part in the associate development. Computer training is important too. Working with the different systems is a big part of associates' responsibilities, and the more comfortable they are with the systems, the faster they will be able to work with them. The associates in the guest relations area are the hotel's eyes and ears, but all staff and management must be aware of the importance of this area.

Working in the hospitality industry, with its crazy hours, stressful and challenging situations, weekend and holiday obligations, and so on, requires passion. If you love what you do, the rewards will come. I would not want to work in any other industry. For me, it is the greatest reward when a guest or associate thanks me for what I do.

► A DAY IN MY LIFE AS A FRONT OFFICE MANAGER

This is a typical schedule as I have experienced it during my time as front office manager. Of course, days are never the same in this business. However, this timetable should give the reader a sense of the challenging job of a front office manager:

7:00 A.M.	Arrive in the office.
7:00– 8:00 A.M.	I walk all my areas and welcome my staff. Managing by walking around is a powerful tool. As a department manager, you want to be visible and accessible to your associates while you are on property (or even if you are off property). Communicating with your staff helps build team spirit and trust. It is important the staff sees that you are always willing to do what you expect them to do. Talking to your staff shows them you are interested in their lives and you value their feedback. This is also a good opportunity to get information about problems from the previous evening and night you need to follow up with.
8:00– 9:00 A.M.	Checking emails and voice mails and trying to return them in a timely manner (*very* challenging).
8:20 A.M.	Mr. X is at the desk complaining about his room service breakfast and wants to talk to a manager. I meet with Mr. X and take care of the issue. After the conversation, I follow up with the room

service staff and the food and beverage manager to ensure the issue has been addressed. I double-check that the incident is entered into our guest relation database so Mr. X does not experience it again when he returns.

9:00–9:15 A.M. Morning meeting with all the managers. This is the daily meeting where we discuss the previous day, the current day's events, VIPs, special guests, repeat customers, and any announcements pertaining to the overall operation (scheduled site tours, media appearances, managers out of the office, etc.).

9:15 A.M.–noon Work in the lobby with the associates. Meet and greet our regular guests and help out at the bell stand. This is what we call being the lobby ambassador. I also cover the breaks for the front desk associates to ensure proper staffing at all times. Ensuring your associates take breaks is important—and the law.

10:00–10:15 A.M. Mr. Y, a repeat customer, calls inquiring about his next stay. His usual rate is not available and he does not want to pay the available rate, which is significantly higher. I negotiate with Mr. Y, and we agree on the regular rate (important if your company has a best rate guarantee); in addition I guarantee him an upgrade for his upcoming stay.

Noon–12:30 P.M. Lunch (this is not a regular occurrence).

12:30–2:00 P.M. Catching up with emails and voice mails (between other things).

12:40–1:00 P.M. Associate X calls off for the evening shift. It will be a busy evening, so I need to find a replacement soon. Associate Y offers to stay a little longer. I call the night auditor, and he agrees to come in early. The shift is covered.

1:00–1:30 P.M. Meeting with Associate Z to go over her performance review. Regular feedback is important. You want to make sure your associates are aware of their performance. This helps them identify areas of opportunity and makes them grow. It is the responsibility of the front office manager to provide such feedback either in official reviews or in-the-moment coaching.

1:30–2:00 P.M. I am paying my invoices. Accounting and finance knowledge is important to department managers. The department budget is your responsibility, and you have to be able to

	read and interpret financial statements to control your budget and secure your contribution to the bottom line.
2:00– 3:00 P.M.	Operations meeting. We critique the events of the past week and discuss details about the events for the coming week. This is an important way to collect information regarding check-in and check-out times, group VIPs and contacts, arrival patterns, room preferences, meeting schedules and locations, etc. Such information is crucial to scheduling as well as preparations such as pre-keying guest rooms, setting up remote check-ins, etc.
3:00– 3:30 P.M.	Interview with an applicant for the front desk.
3:30– 4:00 P.M.	I walk all my areas and meet and greet the associates of the evening shift. I want to make sure everybody is okay and has the tools to do their job right. I also want to make sure to hear about issues (guest or associate) early before they become serious problems.
4:00– 4:15 P.M.	Mrs. Y wants to talk to a manager because we do not have an upgraded room available for her. I talk to Mrs. Y and explain the sold-out situation. I compensate her with access to our VIP lounge. She is satisfied and checks into her room. A lot of times guests who are complaining and want to speak to a manager just want to be heard. Good listening skills and demeanor are important to show credibility to the guest.
4:30– 5:00 P.M.	Meeting with the director of room operations to discuss the sports team check-in for the next day. Proper preparation is key to success and a smooth operation.
5:00– 6:30 P.M.	I am in the lobby, helping my staff during the peak check-in time. Here I also have the opportunity to interact with our guests, welcome our repeat customers, and assist wherever necessary. Being in the lobby makes you accessible to your guests; talking to them, listening to them gives you a lot of information and feedback. I cannot stress enough the importance of this feedback for your operation; it is a great learning source for everybody. It also helps cover the front desk while the P.M. shift takes their breaks.
6:30– 7:00 P.M.	I walk all my areas one last time before I leave to make sure everything is

going well and everybody is happy. I make sure all my associates know how to contact me if necessary. I stop by my office to check for emails and voice mails one last time, and then I leave for the day.

4.7 MINI CASE: THE NEW FOM

After being transferred and promoted to front office manager of a 600-room resort hotel in Miami from a smaller property of the same chain, Jennifer Waters spent the first five or six months familiarizing herself with the hotel's markets, the area, and the resort's facilities and amenities. She also spent a significant amount of time learning the job of front office manager and concluded that it is significantly different from that of assistant front office manager in a smaller property.

The front office staff are young, mostly students, who are in South Florida for the weather and the social amenities. Many want to become actors and are active in dinner theaters and small theater companies in the greater Miami area. For the most part, they are bright and attractive people, but they lack the professionalism that comes from a solid core of knowledge and training. Among the things that concern Jennifer as FOM are the following:

- Several members of a national association board of directors complained of rude treatment while checking out of the hotel.

- Several times a week, after guests have checked in, they are escorted to rooms that are out of order, not clean, or already occupied.

- Four times over the last six weeks, cruel and demeaning practical jokes have been played on the front office assistant manager and the manager on duty during the evening.

- Guest complaints, either in person or by letter, about the hotel, its services, and its staff have more than doubled over previous years and are outpacing complimentary letters and comments by a ratio of two to one.

Jennifer believes her relations with her staff are pretty good. Her relationships, however, with other managers in the hotel are strained, particularly with housekeeping and sales.

As Jennifer seeks to understand the complexities of these problems, she decides to compile a list of their possible causes. What items might be on this list? What form could their potential solutions take?

Be sure to include rationales for the solutions and a plan that will allow her to demonstrate to top management that the analysis and solutions are likely to result in resolutions of these difficulties.

4.8 TO CHANGE OR NOT TO CHANGE: A CASE STUDY AT THE FRONT DESK

Nancy Swanger

Morgan Black has been described by the corporate office as the Miracle Worker because of the troubled properties that were turned around under Morgan's leadership. It is hoped the story at the Coug Inn will have the same happy ending; however, the Coug Inn is in a remote location, hundreds of miles from any other corporate properties.

The Coug Inn is a 150-room full-service property with several medium-sized conference rooms; it caters mostly to business travelers and visitors affiliated with the local university. The bulk of the revenue is generated between August and May, with periods when classes are not in session being extremely slow. The hotel is at full occupancy only during football weekends and commencement. Occupancy has been declining for the last year or so, with last month's RevPAR at a record low. Since arriving at the Coug Inn, Morgan has made several observations about the hotel's situation. It seems that most of the problems involve the front desk. After analyzing several previous months' comment cards and informally chatting with guests at the hotel, Morgan has sensed real dissatisfaction with the check-in process. Several common themes have emerged: The process seems to take forever, the paperwork at check-in is perceived as lengthy and hard to fill out, the front desk clerks always appear to be running around "like chickens with their heads cut off," and guests have been checked into rooms that were not clean.

After discussing the problems with the front desk manager, Morgan is in a quandary about how best to move toward a solution. The front desk manager complains that the reservations staff does not always submit the day's reservations to the front desk in a timely manner. Thus, guests arrive, and the desk clerks have no idea what rate was quoted or the room preference of the guest. This results in the guest having to refurnish information that was previously given when making the reservation. Many times, clerks are forced to leave the guest at the counter while they attempt to retrieve missing information from the reservations. Further, with over 65 percent of the housekeeping staff speaking a first language other than English, communication is difficult at best, and room status is often mistaken. The front desk manager suggests that the hotel advertise its check-in time to be from "say around 1:00 P.M. or 2:00 P.M. to 7:00 P.M." to reduce the crunch time and allow front desk clerks more time to work with each guest's check-in needs. The front desk manager further states that the new hotel in town, the Suite to Sleep Inn, has an earlier check-in time and "it seems to work okay for them!" Morgan asks the front desk manager how the staff might respond to moving to a fully automated property management system. The response was not favorable; the front desk manager mumbled something about "old dogs and new tricks" and that the corporate office had not put any money into the place in years. What would make Morgan think they would put out the cash now?

In an attempt to reach a compromise, Morgan considers changing the check-in time in exchange for the front desk manager's support of the conversion to an automated system.

1. What must Morgan take into consideration before final decisions are made to adjust check-in time and install a fully automated property management system?

2. How should Morgan proceed in resolving the communication issue?

3. Who needs to be involved in the final decisions? Why?

4. How might Morgan present the case to the corporate office?

REFERENCES

Albrecht, Carl, and Ron Zemke. 1985. *Service America!* New York: Dow Jones–Irwin, pp. 37–38.

Allin, Nancy J., and Kelly Halpine. 1988. "From Clerk and Cashier to Guest Agent." *Florida International University Hospitality Review* 6(1):42.

Bardi, James A. 1990. *Hotel Front Office Management.* New York: Van Nostrand Reinhold.

Cross, Robert G. 1997. "Launching the Revenue Rocket: How Revenue Management Can Work for Your Business." *Cornell Hotel and Restaurant Administration Quarterly* April:38(2): 32–43.

Massagle, Don J. 2002. "Multitasking Concierges Provide Added Value to Properties." *Hotel and Motel Management* (August 1).

Nargil, J., S. Khan, and Mark Peterson. 2003. "Professional Concierges Offer Tips to Improve Guest Services." *Hotel and Motel Management* (January 13).

Quain, William J., Michael Sansbury, and Stephen LeBruto. 1998. "Revenue Enhancement, Part 1: A Straightforward Approach for Making More Money." *Cornell Hotel and Restaurant Administration Quarterly* 39(5):44–45.

Quain, B., M. Sansbury, and D. Quinn. 1999. "Revenue Enhancement, Part 3: Picking Low-hanging Fruit—A Simple Approach to Yield Management." *Cornell Hotel and Restaurant Administration Quarterly* (40)2:76–83.

Rutherford, Denney G. 1985. "The Front Office Manager: Key to Hotel Communications." *Florida International University Hospitality Review* 3(2):38–48.

Sternberg, Lawrence E. 1992. "Empowerment: Trust vs. Control." *Cornell Hotel and Restaurant Administration Quarterly* 33(1):69–72.

Stiel, Holly. (no date). *Ultimate Service: A Complete Handbook to the World of the Concierge.* Englewood Cliffs, NJ: Prentice-Hall.

Withiam, Glenn. 1983. "Keeper of the Keys: Concierges in American Hotels." *Cornell Hotel and Restaurant Administration Quarterly* 24(3):40–48.

———. 1993. "American Concierges Set Service Standards." *Cornell Hotel and Restaurant Administration Quarterly* 34(4).

SUGGESTED READINGS

Books

Bardi, James A. 1996. *Hotel Front Office Management,* 2nd ed. New York: Van Nostrand Reinhold.

Bryson, McDowell, and Adele Ziminski. 1992. *The Concierge: Key to Hospitality.* New York: John Wiley and Sons.

Deveau, Linsley T., Patricia M. Deveau, Nestor de J. Portocarrero, and Marcel Escoffier. 1996. *Front Office Management and Operations.* Upper Saddle River, NJ: Prentice-Hall.

Ford, Robert. 2000. *Managing the Guest Experience in Hospitality.* Albany, NY: Delmar.

Heldenbrand, H.V. 1944. *Front Office Psychology.* Chicago: American Hotel Register Company. (*Editor's note:* This little volume is out of print but generally is carried in hotel school libraries and some faculty offices. Many of Heldenbrand's observations are as valid today as they were in 1944.)

Vallen, Gary K., and Jerome J. Vallen. 1996. *Check-In Check-Out.* Chicago: Richard D. Irwin.

Articles

Brownell, Judi. 1990. "Grab Hold of the Grapevine." *Cornell Hotel and Restaurant Administration Quarterly* 31(2):78–83.

Brymer, Robert. 1991. "Employee Empowerment: A Guest-driven Leadership Strategy." *Cornell Hotel and Restaurant Administration Quarterly* 32(1):58–68.

Kasavana, Michael L. 1993. "Front Office Operations." In *VNR's Encyclopedia of Hospitality and Tourism,* Mahmood Kahn, Michael Olsen, and Turgut Var (eds.). New York: Van Nostrand Reinhold.

Lewis, Robert C. 1983. "When Guests Complain." *Cornell Hotel and Restaurant Administration Quarterly* 24(2):23–32.

Lieberman, Warren H. 1993. "Debunking the Myths of Yield Management." *Cornell Hotel and Restaurant Administration Quarterly* 34(1):34–41.

Murthy, Bvsan, and Chekitan S. Dev. 1993. "Average Daily Rate." In *VNR's Encyclopedia of Hospitality and Tourism,* Mahmood Kahn, Michael Olsen, and Turgut Var (eds.). New York: Van Nostrand Reinhold.

Rutherford, Denney G. 1985. "The Front Office Manager: Key to Hotel Communications." *Florida International University Hospitality Review* 3(2):38–48.

Van Dyke, Tom. 1993. "Guest Registration." In *VNR's Encyclopedia of Hospitality and Tourism,* Mahmood Kahn, Michael Olsen, and Turgut Var (eds.). New York: Van Nostrand Reinhold.

Vallen, Gary K. 1993a. "Organizational Climate and Burnout." *Cornell Hotel and Restaurant Administration Quarterly* 34(1):54–59.

———. 1993b. "A Comparison of Hospitality Burnout with Other 'High-Burnout' Industries." *Hospitality and Tourism Educator* 5(2):31–36.

SOURCE NOTES

Chapter 4.2, "The Electrifying Job of the Front Office Manager," by James A. Bardi, adapted from *Hotel Front Office Management,* 2nd ed., by James A. Bardi, Copyright © 1996 by John Wiley & Sons, Inc. Adapted by permission of John Wiley & Sons, Inc.

Chapter 4.3, "A Day in the Life of the Front Office Manager," by Garry Dickover.

Chapter 4.4, "Yield Management: Choosing the Most Profitable Reservations," by William J. Quain and Stephen M. LeBruto, is adapted from the following two articles:

Quain, B., M. Sansbury, and S. LeBruto. 1998. "Revenue Enhancement, Part 1: A Straightforward Approach to Making More Money." *Cornell Hotel and Restaurant Administration Quarterly* 39(5):42–48.

Quain, B., M. Sansbury, and D. Quinn. 1999. "Revenue Enhancement, Part 3: Picking Low-hanging Fruit—A Simple Approach to Yield Management." *Cornell Hotel and Restaurant Administration Quarterly* 40(2):76–83.

Chapter 4.5, "Concierge (cone-see-air-j)," by Mario Arnaldo.

Chapter 4.6, "As I See It: Management of the Front Office," by Oliver Meinzer.

OPERATIONS: HOUSEKEEPING, ENGINEERING, AND SECURITY

5.1 INTRODUCTION

► HOUSEKEEPING

A while back, I was talking with a large group of housekeeping directors representing most of the major metropolitan hotels in a large northeastern city. I asked the following question: How many of you, as part of your career plan, initially considered housekeeping as a managerial role that had any attraction to you? The answer, not surprisingly, was none!

This points up a major dilemma facing modern hotel management structures. One of the most important, most labor-intensive, and largest cost centers in the hotel is neither universally understood nor respected by the bulk of the hotel's department managers, their employees, and, to a large extent, the hotel's guests and clients. Some encouraging signs indicate that this situation is in a state of change. Some hotel companies are experi-

menting with taking housekeeping out of the rooms division and making it a staff function, with the director of housekeeping reporting directly to the general manager. Others are combining housekeeping and other property management functions such as maintenance and engineering. At one firm's resorts, housekeeping directors are titled Director of Services and have responsibility for all non-golf recreation in addition to traditional housekeeping.

Historically, however, information on housekeeping administration for hotels has been organized around models set forth in textbooks that date to the 1951 treatment of hospital housekeeping by LaBelle and Barton. Brigham (1955) focused her analysis of the structure of the housekeeping functions and responsibilities on the small hotel. Tucker and Schneider (1982), Schneider and Tucker

(1989), and Martin and Jones (1992) provided a comprehensive inventory of the theoretical constructs, responsibilities, relationships, and techniques important to the modern housekeeper in a range of operational situations. (See the Jones contribution elsewhere in this section that updates those authors.)

Generally speaking, these works present information in a traditional structure that says the housekeeper administers four major areas of responsibility:

1. Management of people, equipment, and supplies
2. Preservation of building finishes, fabrics, and furnishings
3. Cost control
4. Recordkeeping

(Tucker and Schneider 1982, 38)

In analyzing the differences between the folklore and fact of the manager's job, Mintzberg (1975) concluded that substantial differences existed between the popular or academic notion of managers' jobs and their actual work.

In the last study of its type, Rutherford and Schill (1984) studied housekeepers in a similar fashion. They addressed this question: What is the relationship between what has been written about housekeeping and what housekeeping directors themselves deem important?

A survey was sent to a national sample of housekeeping executives asking them to rate on a scale of 1 to 5 the importance of 100 theoretical constructs common to the housekeeping literature. Statistical procedures (factor analysis) grouped the housekeepers' responses into eight groupings. While the traditional responsibilities of records, costs, supplies, and furnishings were still important, the issues central to the management of people

were of overwhelming importance. Specifically highlighted were the following:

- Leadership
- Communication
- Strategic planning
- Hotel organizational interactions
- Departmental management
- Training

The authors concluded that new arrangements of traditional knowledge, constructs, and tactics such as those explored in their model may present future managers with windows of operational, educational, or marketing opportunity that improve competitive position or streamline the transfer of knowledge. The dissemination of this knowledge in the most efficient and effective manner is also important, for, as Mintzberg (1975) points out, "[T]he manager is challenged to find systematic ways to share his privileged knowledge."

Since 1985, very little, if any, analytic empirical research has been done on operational aspects of housekeeping and other labor-intensive hotel departments. Until there is, there will be little forward movement in the theory of housekeeping. Inspired practical experimentation on the part of housekeeping managers, however, is not lacking.

When he started his career in hotel management, Kurt Englund, like the housekeepers referenced at the start of this section, never expected that housekeeping would be a major stop on his career journey. It was, however, and he feels the many tasks involved in keeping the house for a major asset like a Four Seasons property prepared him well to be the resort manager at the Four Seasons Resort Costa Rica at Peninsula Papagayo. He was previously the director of rooms for the luxury hotel, Regent Beverly Wilshire. In this view of a day in his life, it is important to note that housekeeping is still one of his important responsibilities.

Professor Tom Jones of the University of Nevada, Las Vegas, describes how housekeeping departments are organized and staffed. He provides an overview and organizational perspective of the department, paying particular attention to the responsibilities of the various personnel within the modern housekeeping department. Professor Jones brings deep knowledge of executive housekeeping management to his writing and structures his description of the organization with a real-world, tell-it-like-it-is narrative.

As John Lagazo states in the introduction to his description of being an executive housekeeper, most people are surprised to learn that housekeeping is an important career stop for hotel managers. Now the director of operations at the luxurious Madison Hotel in Washington, D.C., Lagazo still deals with housekeeping every day, although it is now one of his direct reports. John wrote this piece for the third edition, but it holds up so well, I am including it here because he captures the essence of the job of managing this complex organizational element.

In most cases, the management of the housekeeping function is no longer the province of the lead maid type. Increasingly, the expense of running the department coupled with the large numbers of employees on its staff mandates that the head of this department be well versed in all managerial skills and a sophisticated and creative leader.

▶ ENGINEERING

In a way, housekeeping, engineering, and security can all be considered guest services. In most hotels, guest services (see previous section) is a visible component that can include concierge, uniformed service, garage, and specialized recreational and leisure activities. Housekeeping, security for the hotel and its guests, and the maintenance of the hotel's engineering systems are under the best of circumstances behind the scenes and neither noticed nor experienced by guests in any but an abstract sense. They are, nonetheless, services that are critical to a safe, comfortable—and, by extrapolation, successful—guest stay at your hotel.

As stated in the first of the two articles included here on the engineering function, in the past, the chief engineer and his or her department have been metaphorically relegated to roughly the same position in the hotel's organization that they physically occupy—usually the basement or otherwise out of sight. These two articles explore the numerous indications that the importance of the engineering function can no longer be ignored or treated with less respect than any other aspect of management.

It is important that the reader recognize that the first of these articles overviews the department, explores some of the issues that affect hotel engineering, and outlines typical job functions. Part of the thrust of this article is that unlike in the past, the chief engineer is responsible for major components of the asset and the physical comfort of the guest. This argues for consideration of the chief engineer as no different than any other hotel department head.

The DeFranco and Sheridan article on how chief engineers (CEs) use financial information illustrates that idea. As their research demonstrates, computer technology and the use of financial information in the engineering department are vital in maintaining an efficient operation. This was not widely true even ten years ago. This research contributes to the argument that, like that of the executive housekeeper, the position of CE in the modern hotel organization mandates a leader who is more manager/leader than technician. At the same time, the CE still must manage a diverse collection of talents and skills among the engineering staff. In a fashion, this raises the question of what type of manager such a person is. Structured research is still sparse on this topic.

The number of employees for which the CE is responsible varies widely, mainly with the size of the hotel. A 1986 study (Fisher) set the ratio for an engineering staff at 3.9 for each 100 rooms, but a lot has changed since then. Other factors that can influence the diversity of human-related management for the engineering manager are market niche, sophis-tication of the building's design and equipment, and corporate philosophy. Therefore, if a 1,000-room hotel has 40 or more people on the engineering staff, each of them presumably highly trained, qualified, and skilled technical people, the CE's job takes on aspects of management that strongly suggest a need for refined people-related skills.

When Wasmuth and Davis studied the management of employee turnover, they found it to be relatively low in engineering departments in the majority of the hotels studied. They also found that quality of supervision was a key element in maintaining low turnover rates among these engineering departments. The most successful supervisory style had as a critical element the talent that "allowed and encouraged (the engineers) to work autonomously" (1983, 68).

Allowing the engineering staff to work autonomously pays tribute to both the nature of their jobs and concern for the human side of management. It also suggests that while some supervisory or management styles may be appropriate in engineering departments, others may not. Managerial style refers to the way managers manage, control, motivate, and otherwise direct subordinates. It is through managerial style that employees may or may not be encouraged and allowed to work on their own. The extent to which an atmosphere is fostered by the manager significantly affects the range with a manager's human-related challenges, of which turnover is a prime example.

An unpublished, proprietary study of 49 hotel CEs with one hotel company sought to determine their managerial styles. They were asked to take a standardized managerial-style inventory and fill out a short demographic questionnaire in order to determine what managerial style predominates among the self-described successful chief engineers in a major international hotel corporation.

This inventory instrument judges primary managerial style to be in one of six categories (see below), with a secondary or backup style that is one or a combination of the others.

Managerial Styles

- **Coercive:** The "do-it-the-way-I-tell-you" manager closely controls subordinates and motivates by threats and discipline.

- **Authoritative:** The "firm but fair" manager gives subordinates clear direction and motivates by persuasion and feedback on task performance.

- **Affiliative:** The "people first, task second" manager emphasizes good personal relationships among subordinates and motivates by trying to keep people happy with fringe benefits, security, and social activities.

- **Democratic:** The "participative" manager encourages subordinate input in decision making and motivates by rewarding team effort.

- **Pacesetting:** The "do it myself" manager performs many tasks personally, expects subordinates to follow his or her example, and motivates by setting high standards and letting subordinates work on their own.

- **Coaching:** The "developmental" manager helps and encourages subordinates to improve their performance and motivates by providing opportunities for professional development. (McBer, no date)

A managerial style profile reflects both primary and backup styles. *Primary* is the managerial behavior one uses most often, is most comfortable with, and is the style to which one normally turns under stress. *Backup* refers to an alternative way of managing one uses when the primary style is ineffective. Some individuals have more than one primary style, and some utilize multiple backups.

The comparisons showed that each group of CEs is primarily affiliative in style, a trait that flies in the face of their reputation as crusty curmudgeons.

With affiliative as the primary style of this group of engineers, it was somewhat surprising that the backup style was democratic. Combining the democratic backup style with the predominant affiliative style would certainly produce an organizational atmosphere where the employees would feel encouraged to be independent and autonomous.

The data developed through application of this instrument to this sample of CEs tends to support the theory that successful CEs and their departments favor management styles that put people first. At least at this juncture, it appears that the affiliative style works best in the milieu with people and tasks managed by the CE. This was, however, a small study of a single company and as such can only be suggestive. The data in this study do, though, provide us with a broader view of the facets of management of the modern hotel engineering function.

▶ SECURITY

It is an unfortunate fact of modern hotel management that the days of simply providing comfort, high-quality food, beverage and lodging services, and a home-away-from-home atmosphere are severely affected by the inventory of problems presented by the predatory elements of modern society. At the same time, hotel security departments are responsible for protecting the hotel's assets from loss.

Hotels are usually fairly close-mouthed about their security and its functions, duties, and personnel. On an individual basis, a good overview of security can be found in publications of the Educational Institute of the American Hotel and Motel Association (http://www.ei-ahla.org/). Typically, however, the modern hotel security department is organized as a staff function, with the director of security reporting directly to top management. We have little data or insight about the manager of the hotel security function, as little, if any, research has been done on the subject. Anecdotally, from the editor's experience, most of the managers recently hired to fulfill this function have a security background in the military or a law enforcement career with civil authorities.

Typically, the director of security has a staff in keeping with the nature and size of the threats to a particular hotel, the size of the hotel, its location, and its managerial strategy. A director of security administers the functions of his or her department against two broad and general classifications of threats: external and internal.

External threats are generally those that present risk for the hotel and its guests due to the actions of outsiders. Internal security is a functional area that generally is concerned with reducing the threat of loss of assets; in most cases, this refers to control of highly attractive and popular consumer goods such as wine, expensive foodstuffs, furnishings, and, of course, the hotel's cash.

The responsibilities of the security manager in contending with the above threats include the following:

- Providing physical security at the perimeter of the hotel

- Adapting policies and procedures to the building design and location

- Utilizing electronics, modern telecommunications devices, proximity alarms, motion detectors, and closed-circuit TV to enhance the hotel's ability to eliminate threats

Security directors participate in certain levels of administrative or operational activities that deal with policies, training, education, and human resources to avoid hiring what has become known as the high-risk employee. This is due primarily to the increasing risk hotels and other employers face from negligent hiring.

Having policies and procedures in place to deal with the management of emergencies is also a fundamental aspect of the hotel security director's job. These emergencies can take a number of forms; in recent years they have been known to include fires, hurricanes, floods, earthquakes, blackouts, robberies, bombs or bomb threats, medical and dental emergencies, and some forms of terrorism. It is a fact of modern life that the properly managed hotel, from a security standpoint must have contingency plans in place and training programs to help its employees deal with these potential threats.

A further responsibility of the security director is liaison with civil authorities. Increasingly, as the article included here points out, hotels are being held accountable for what they either knew or should have known about potential threats. The best way to keep up on this is by cultivating a good relationship with the local police.

Finally, the major responsibility of a modern hotel security director is to assist in policy development. Hotels must have policies that guide the implementation of procedures, training, and inspection to meet the inventory of potential risk. Hotels also must gather data to make sure they are aware of all facets of the risk environment. The security function must also assist the hotel in formalizing a structure that links all pertinent parts of the hotel's organization to the concept of total security for the organization, its employees, and its guests.

In the legal analysis contributed to this edition, Melissa Dallas outlines and discusses the major families of risk facing hotel managers. She also includes in her analysis current examples of how the law affects the management of hotels in the modern era. This comprehensive and detailed article has a conversational and engaging style unusual in legal treatises.

In the article included here by Abbott and Fried, the authors explore in some depth one of the trickiest risk environments that (literally) surround many hospitality operations: the parking lot. Because parking lots can be remote, poorly lighted, or not patrolled, they are increasingly sources of risk. Courts are increasingly finding that landlords have liability for third-party criminal activity, so operators are advised to be aware of this potential liability.

As if that were not enough to give one pause, the article by Beattie and Gau serves notice that there is yet another realm of risk that now affects our ability to manage hotels safely. Workplace violence—including homicide—is a growing problem for hospitality operations. The authors explore telling examples and discuss a structural theory to guide further research and the establishment of policies.

► SUMMARY

Housekeeping, engineering, and security, while not, typically, obvious functions, are nonetheless critically important to the management of any hotel. All of them are and have been evolving for the past several years into professionally managed departments responding to internal and external stimuli that can critically affect their interactive relationships with other hotel departments and, ultimately, in the delivery of hotel guest services.

A number of books dealing with these departments are listed as suggested readings. The reader seeking more in-depth information can find it in these books.

5.2 A DAY IN THE LIFE OF A DIRECTOR OF ROOMS

Kurt Englund

A day in the life with Four Seasons Hotels and Resorts focuses on people, both guests and employees. One of the first things I do in the morning is walk around the departments that are my responsibility: front desk, concierge, communications, valet parking, door attendants, bell desk, health spa, housekeeping, laundry, and valet. It is important to be visible with the staff we depend on to provide a superior level of service to all of our guests. Knowing who they are and what they are facing each day makes a big difference in how they carry out their job.

Every morning, we have an operational meeting to review how we are going to take care of our guests, the other key component in hospitality. This meeting is attended by a wide range of managers: the general manager, hotel manager, all of the planning committee (including the director of human resources), housekeeping, conferences services, sales managers, and catering managers. The entire day is laid out, reviewing the expected arrivals for the day from the VIPs to return guests, guests with pets, guests with special dietary requirements or mattress firmness. We discuss these to ensure the requirements are met in advance. We also include in the discussion all catering functions and any other movement of individuals en masse.

In our effort to provide a high-quality experience, we also discuss any glitch or poor experience any of our guests may have experienced. Our concern is not whose fault the glitch was but rather how can we make the stay better for our guest and prevent it from happening to any of our other guests. If the city decides to jack hammer at 8:30 in the morning on a Saturday, it may not be directly our fault, but it is certainly our guests who have been inconvenienced. We will do a follow-up with the guest to explain what we know, offer a new room if appropriate, and ascertain their overall happiness with their visit.

We have a number of other meetings to keep the communication going. Our weekly meetings include planning committee, group resume, and rooms division. Every other week we hold a department head meeting.

As mentioned, we hold the care of our employees to be as important as taking care of our guests. One of the ways we do this is by being prepared to work alongside them when business levels suddenly peak. We do our best to staff at appropriate levels, but sometimes everything hits at once. We call these *crunches* and respond with an all-page for assistance to the area in need. The management response is incredible; from our general manager on down, we get the assistance we need to help in valet parking, bell desk, front desk, room service, and so on. This is an excellent example of the teamwork at our hotel making an impact on the morale of the staff.

Walking around the hotel and checking in with staff is an important communication tool. Employees develop a comfort level for raising concerns about their jobs. It is equivalent to bringing the open-door policy to employees in their work area. Issues have been brought to my attention in this format such as conflicts with coworkers, questions about paychecks, suggestions to improve a work procedure, and requests for assistance in following up with maintenance concerns.

Hiring new staff is another crucial role in day-to-day activities. Our interviewing process involves a screening by HR, an interview with the department head, an interview with the division head, and final approval from a meeting with the hotel manager or general manager. We attempt to be as flexible as possible when it comes to making time to interview these candidates. If the right candidate comes through the door, we make every effort to free our schedule so we can keep the interview process moving.

Balancing the needs of our guests and employees requires flexibility. There is no typical day in our business, which is one of the reasons I enjoy my job. I face a new challenge every day.

5.3 HOUSEKEEPING ORGANIZATIONS: THEIR HISTORY, PURPOSE, STRUCTURES, AND PERSONNEL

Thomas Jones

▶ ORIGINS OF HOSPITALITY AND HOUSEKEEPING

By definition, *hospitality* is the cordial and generous reception and entertainment of guests or strangers, either socially or commercially. From this definition we get the feeling of the open house and the host with open arms, of a place where people are cared for. Regardless of the reasons people go to a home away from home, the presumption is that they need to be cared for there. They need a clean and comfortable place to rest or sleep, food service, an area for socializing and meeting other people, access to stores and shops, and a secure surrounding.

Americans have often been described as a people on the move, a mobile society. Even as our country expanded, we required bed and board. Travelers in the early 1700s found hospitality similar to that in their countries of origin, even though these new accommodations might have been in roadhouses, missions, or private homes, and the housekeeping might have included no more than a bed of straw, changed weekly.

Facilities in all parts of young America were commensurate with the demand of the traveling public, and early records indicate that a choice was usually available; travelers based the decision on where they expected to find good food, overnight protection, and clean facilities. Even though the inns were crude, they were gathering places where anyone could learn the news of the day, socialize, learn the business of the area, and rest.

The business of innkeeping has become the hotel industry of today, but the main tenets remain: a clean, comfortable room, access to food and entertainment facilities, and a courteous and concerned staff who mean it when they ask, "May we be of service?"

Housekeeping departments play a vital role in today's lodging industry. People involved in housekeeping operations service guest rooms, maintain and service public and special areas, and, in many instances, operate laundries and recreational and health facilities. The people of housekeeping are also a part of the overall team of hosts and hostesses who welcome the hotel's guests. They show concern and care when something goes wrong with the guest's visit, and they are quick to initiate action that will make things right again.

Major hotel companies have been quick to recognize the value of housekeeping and other service industry workers. Good hotel management does not see housekeeping work as demeaning or menial. To the contrary, all high-quality hotel operational management personnel have, at one time or another, performed housekeeping functions; as a result, they understand the worth and value of the people who perform such functions regularly.

Students of the service industry should remember the statement made proudly by one of America's most prestigious resorts, The Greenbriar of White Sulfur Springs, West Virginia. This statement appears on a sign that is visible as one enters the resort: "Ladies and Gentlemen Being Served by Ladies and Gentlemen."

▶ THE ROOMS DEPARTMENT

▶ Front Desk and Housekeeping

The rooms department of a lodging establishment is directly and solely involved with all aspects of the sale, occupancy, and servicing of guest rooms. The department manager is usually called the resident manager, although the title is somewhat misleading in its implication that this manager lives on the premises; most do not. Synonymous titles include rooms manager, rooms director, director of rooms operations, and, simply, hotel manager (not to be confused with the general manager).

The rooms department is usually a combination of two principal operating departments: the front office and the housekeeping department. The manager in charge of the front office oversees several subdepartments: reservations, front desk, bell staff, PBX, transportation, possibly concierge, and any other form of guest reception function.

The manager in charge of housekeeping functions is most commonly known as the executive housekeeper. Depending on the size of the hotel, subdepartments within the housekeeping sphere of operations (e.g., in-house laundry, recreation department), and, in some cases, corporate policy, the person in charge of housekeeping may have any one of

a number of titles, all considered synonymous with executive housekeeper. A few such titles are:

- Housekeeper
- Housekeeping manager
- Director of services
- Director of internal services
- Director of housekeeping operations

For the purposes of this article we refer to this manager as the *executive housekeeper*.

There was a time when most executive housekeepers worked under the direction of the front office manager. They were, in fact, not executives but people who had worked their way up from a maid's position, with little or no managerial training. Today, however, the size, cost, and complexity of housekeeping operations have put the executive housekeeper on an equal footing with other department managers. As a result, executive housekeepers are now seen as sharing equally in responsibility under the resident manager for the operation of rooms departments.

The hotel industry is a highly labor-intensive hospitality business. More total employees may be involved in food and beverage (F&B) operations than in any other department. Because of the diversity of F&B operations (restaurants, lounges, banquet services, and kitchen), there are plenty of managers to control the total operation. In housekeeping, however, a single department head (the executive housekeeper) is responsible for the largest staff, operating cost center, and physical area of the property.

Today's modern executive housekeeper must be a trained manager skilled in planning, organizing, staffing, directing, and controlling operations. He or she must also be skilled in employee and human relations, have a superior understanding of cost controls, and have a strong technical background in purchasing, decorating, and renovation. Last but not least, the executive housekeeper must be an able delegator. Without strong expertise and the inclination to pass tasks to others, convey the necessary power to act, and, finally, hold others accountable for their actions, the executive housekeeper must personally perform all working functions. This writer has never yet found the person who could make 3,000 beds in one day.

► ORGANIZATION

Housekeeping organizations are as varied as types and sizes of hotel. Except for bed-and-breakfast operations, the trend today is away from the small, 80-room mom-and-pop hotel. It is therefore appropriate to discuss hotels of a size that might be considered a model appropriate to the greatest variation—say, 200 or more rooms. Most hotels would have identical functions, but size might dictate that one person perform several functions in a small hotel. Obviously, the larger the facility, the greater the need for a large staff with enough individuals to fill each unique function. Consider then, the following hotel:

- A modern suburban corporate transient hotel
- 350 rooms
- Two restaurants (one 24-hour and one dinner house)
- Banquet area with 15,000 square feet of meeting space
- Room service
- Kitchen to support all food services
- Main lounge with nightly entertainment

- Banquet beverage service and service bar outlets for both restaurants and room service
- Outdoor pool and winter indoor pool with health club facilities, sauna, and steam room
- Game room (video games, pool, and table tennis)
- In-house laundry for rooms department and banquet linen
- Two company-owned gift shops.
- Front desk fully computerized with a property management system

► Hotel Organization

Prior to investigating the housekeeping department organization, it is appropriate to visualize an organization for the entire hotel. The organization diagram in Figure 5.1 could easily be that of the model hotel just described.

Note the position of the executive housekeeper within the organization. Executive housekeepers may occupy greater or lesser positions in any organization. Some executive housekeepers report directly to the general manager; others even hold corporate executive positions. Others report to the chief of maintenance. In this case, however, the executive housekeeper is a middle manager—a full department head, equal to the front office manager and other principal department heads within the staff. Two junior managers report to the executive housekeeper, the housekeeping manager, and the laundry manager. Both the executive housekeeper and the front office manager report to the resident manager, who is a member of the property executive committee. This committee is the top

| Figure 5.1 | Hotel Organization (Through Department Head) |

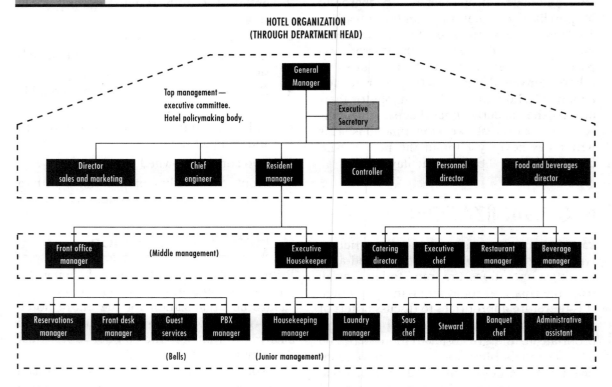

policymaking body for the property under the general manager.

▶ The Housekeeping Organization

Figure 5.2 describes a typical housekeeping department organization, suitable for the model hotel.

Note the utilization of the two principal assistants. The housekeeping manager is the first assistant to the executive housekeeper and is in direct charge of all guest rooms in the hotel. This emphasizes the delegation that has taken place in that the housekeeping manager is not just an assistant to the executive housekeeper but a junior manager with a functional responsibility. This part of the organization can be managed in several ways. Each individual room attendant can be scheduled independently, or attendants may be grouped into schedule teams, with the same hours on and the same time off. In this illustration, team staffing and scheduling are presented because this approach is more efficient for daily scheduling.

The laundry is another specific function

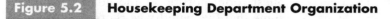

Figure 5.2   Housekeeping Department Organization

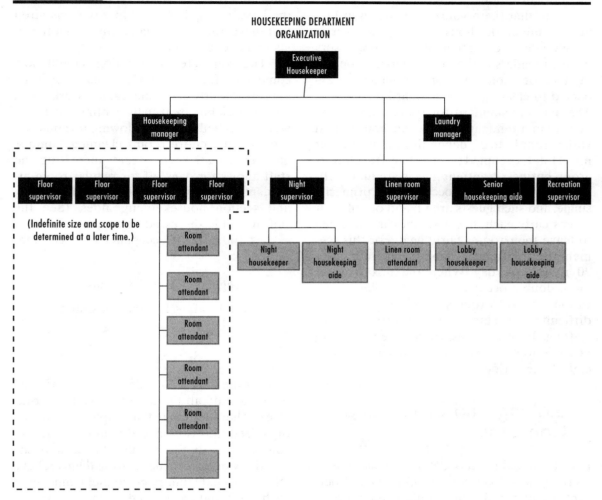

to which a junior manager is assigned. In this case, the required technical expertise is more specific. It includes knowledge of commercial laundry machinery and equipment, knowledge of piecework production, the utilization of chemicals, and their effects on an expensive inventory of linen.

Both junior managers and the executive housekeeper have line supervisors who report directly to them. (Below the management level, we recognize an hourly structure for employees who are paid by the hour at a given wage rate as opposed to being on salary.) Each supervisor has one or more hourly workers who round out the department organization.

Note that the organization shown in Figure 5.2 under the housekeeping manager is incomplete. The number of floor supervisors or team leaders and workers depends on the number of rooms a room attendant is expected to clean in a given eight-hour period. The national standard for rooms cleaned by one room attendant in one eight-hour period varies from 13 to 20, depending on the market mix. Hotels occupied primarily by traveling or group business transient guests are more efficient to clean because occupancy is primarily single, and such guests are up and out of their rooms early each day. Also, they are inclined to leave their rooms fairly neat. For this segment, room attendants can clean from 18 to 20 rooms per day. When the mix features more double occupancy with families on vacation, access to rooms for cleaning is more difficult and cuts into the efficiency of staffing. In such cases, room attendants are not able to clean as many rooms in the same eight-hour period.

▶ Staffing and Scheduling Concerns

For our model hotel of 350 rooms, assume an 18-room workload per day. On any 100 percent occupancy day we would need approximately 20 room attendants to clean all guest rooms. Placing these room attendants in teams of five, each working under one floor supervisor, creates a need for four supervisors. Also assume that one section housekeeping aide is assigned to each team to handle corridor cleaning, provide certain services to room attendants during the day, and to care for other public areas within the guest room portion of the hotel. Finally, assume that five laundry workers are needed in the laundry regularly, and that persons hired to relieve room attendants on days off can also relieve in the laundry.

The complete organization should now come into focus, except for one remaining concern. Hourly personnel cannot work seven days a week but are usually confined to a five-workday schedule. The following formula can establish the entire rooms cleaning, laundry, and relief staff requirement; increasing the staff allows for days off for regular room attendants, laundry workers, floor supervisors, and section housekeeping aides. (See the staffing guide, discussed below.)

At 100 percent occupancy on a continuous basis:

$$\text{regular staff} \times \text{seven days} =$$
$$\text{total staff} \times \text{five day maximum}$$
$$S_1 \times 7 = S_2 \times 5$$
$$S_2 = S_1 \times 7 \div 5$$

For the model, $S_2 = 25 \times 7 \div 5 = 35$ total working staff, all limited to a five-day workweek. The additional ten employees can be organized into two special teams identical in composition to the regular teams and the laundry workforce. These swing teams relieve all regular and laundry personnel teams twice each week and have two days off themselves. This portion of the organization can now be scheduled to work by team units rather than as individual workers, which greatly simplifies personnel scheduling. (For further information on scheduling techniques, the reader is encouraged to read the basic text from which this article is drawn.)

The balance of the housekeeping organization is noted in the functions to be per-

Table 5.1 Department Staffing Guide

Position No.	Title	Name Assigned
	Management Team	
1	Executive housekeeper	_____
2	Housekeeping manager	_____
3	Laundry manager	_____
	Fixed Team	
4	Linen room supervisor	_____
5	Linen room attendant	_____
6	Senior housekeeping aide (public area supervisor)	_____
7	Public area housekeeper 1 (male)	_____
8	Public area housekeeper 2 (female)	_____
9	Public area housekeeper (relief)	_____
	Evening Team	
10	Night supervisor	_____
11	Night section housekeeper	_____
12	Night housekeeping	_____
13	Night (public area) housekeeper 1 (male)	_____
14	Night (public area) housekeeper 2 (female)	_____
15	Night (public area) housekeeper (relief)	_____
	Regular Rooms Cleaning Teams:	
	Red Team	
16	Senior housekeeper (supervisor)	_____
17	Section housekeeping aide	_____
18	Section housekeeper 1	_____
19	Section housekeeper 2	_____
20	Section housekeeper 3	_____
21	Section housekeeper 4	_____
22	Section housekeeper 5	_____
	Yellow Team	
23	Senior housekeeper (supervisor)	_____
24	Section housekeeping aide	_____
25	Section housekeeper 6	_____
26	Section housekeeper 7	_____
27	Section housekeeper 8	_____
28	Section housekeeper 9	_____
29	Section housekeeper 10	_____

Table 5.1 *(Continued)*

Position No.	Title	Name Assigned
	Brown Team	
30	Senior housekeeper (supervisor)	_____
31	Section housekeeping aide	_____
32	Section housekeeper 11	_____
33	Section housekeeper 12	_____
34	Section housekeeper 13	_____
35	Section housekeeper 14	_____
36	Section housekeeper 15	_____
	Green Team	
37	Senior housekeeper (supervisor)	_____
38	Section housekeeping aide	_____
39	Section housekeeper 16	_____
40	Section housekeeper 17	_____
41	Section housekeeper 18	_____
42	Section housekeeper 19	_____
43	Section housekeeper 20	_____
	Laundry	
44	Laundry supervisor (washman)	_____
45	Laundry helper/sorter	_____
46	Laundry attendant (ironer)	_____
47	Laundry attendant (ironer)	_____
48	Laundry attendant (folder/stacker)	_____
49	Laundry attendant (folder/stacker)	_____
50	Laundry attendant (folder/stacker)	_____
	Swing Team 1	
51	Senior housekeeper (swing supervisor)	_____
52	Section housekeeping aide (ST-A)	_____
53	Section housekeeper A-1	_____
54	Section housekeeper A-2	_____
55	Section housekeeper A-3	_____
56	Section housekeeper A-4	_____
57	Section housekeeper A-5	_____
	Swing Team 2	
58	Senior housekeeper (swing supervisor)	_____
59	Section housekeeping aide (ST-B)	_____
60	Section housekeeper B-1	_____
61	Section housekeeper B-2	_____
62	Section housekeeper B-3	_____
63	Section housekeeper B-4	_____
64	Section housekeeper B-5	_____

formed, and for purposes of illustration must be scheduled individually. Specifically, personnel required for the second shift, persons required to staff the linen room housekeeping communications central, and personnel organized under the senior housekeeping aide for public area cleaning and maintenance round out the total department staff.

The entire housekeeping department staff might then take on the appearance provided in the staffing guide outlined in Table 5.1.

The staffing guide is created to accurately document the need for total personnel. Every position within the department is listed and can be used to fill vacancies when they occur. Note teams identified by color.

This identification system shows which teams are regular teams, the one that works in the laundry, and which ones are considered swing teams. This particular staffing guide presumes that a 100 percent staff has been hired to support an occupancy averaging 85 percent or more for an extended period. Should occupancies be forecast as a lesser amount, a 100 percent staff need not be hired, and staff vacancies can be distributed over the entire team network. Fluctuations in daily occupancy are dealt with by scheduling down within each team on a fair and equitable basis. This task can be delegated to the floor supervisor, but controls must be in place that guarantee fairness to all who must be cut out of a day's work due to low occupancy.

▶ PERSONNEL AND JOBS IN THE HOUSEKEEPING DEPARTMENT

What follows is a listing of the jobs one might find in a hotel housekeeping depart-

ment. The basic function and scope of responsibility are indicated for managerial positions, and for hourly jobs, titles and responsibilities are listed. Where several names or titles apply to the same function in the hourly structure, each name is noted.

▶ The Executive Housekeeper

The executive housekeeper usually assumes complete direction, operational control, and supervision of the housekeeping, laundry, and recreation departments.

The scope of responsibility is normally broad to ensure that the incumbent has the freedom necessary to do the job. This position is now recognized as a career-enhancing step. The executive housekeeper operates the departments under his or her control in the most efficient manner possible through effective application and enforcement of company policies, the use of methods described in standard operating procedures, and the use of sound management principles. He or she is primarily responsible for the cleanliness of guest rooms and public areas assigned to the housekeeping department. He or she accomplishes tasks through proper training, motivation, and supervision of all personnel assigned to the housekeeping, laundry and recreation departments.

▶ The Housekeeping Manager

In the model organization, the housekeeping manager assumes primary responsibility for guest room cleaning and servicing and acts as the primary assistant to the executive housekeeper.

Under the direction of the executive housekeeper, the housekeeping manager is responsible for the efficient and orderly management of guest room cleaning, servicing, and the reporting of rooms status.

He or she represents employees directly involved in rooms cleaning and is directly involved in their work schedules. He or she must react to occupancy in scheduling to keep costs under control.

▶ The Laundry Manager

The laundry manager normally assumes primary responsibility for operation of the hotel's in-house commercial laundry. He or she also acts as second assistant to the executive housekeeper.

Under direction of the executive housekeeper, the laundry manager is responsible for the efficient and orderly management and operation of the hotel laundry. Through the proper use of assigned personnel, he or she provides clean linen to the house and to the banquet department according to plans and budgets.

▶ HOURLY EMPLOYEES

▶ The Guest Room Attendant (also known as the GRA, maid, or section housekeeper)

The guest room attendant is primarily responsible for guest room cleaning and servicing. He or she is usually assigned a section of rooms each day, constituting a workload of a designated number of rooms to be cleaned. In general, the room attendant performs the same functions in each room assigned. The room attendant also conducts rooms checks at set times to assist in determining the reporting condition of the house: rooms occupied, rooms ready (vacant and ready to rent), and rooms on change (vacant but not yet serviced; also known as check-outs).

The room attendant also participates in general cleaning of one or more rooms each day as it is serviced in order to keep quality standards high.

Most room attendants work in compliance with standard operating procedures (SOPs) that may specify as many as 60 items that must meet a given standard in each guest room. This is not as daunting as it may sound, but the SOP system guarantees coverage where necessary.

Finally, the room attendant reloads his or her own linen cart at the end of each workday.

If so organized, the room attendant is one of several members of a housekeeping team under a floor supervisor.

▶ The Section Housekeeping Aide (previously Section Houseman)

The section housekeeping aide works in the guest room portion of the hotel, attending to the regular and daily cleaning of corridors, elevator cabs and landings, stairwells, service areas, floor linen rooms, vending areas, and other public spaces in the vicinity of guest rooms. The aide also helps room attendants with general cleaning, if necessary. He or she also removes soiled linen and rubbish from room attendants' carts on a regular schedule and brings supplies from storerooms to floor linen rooms when needed. The section housekeeping aide works at the direction of the floor supervisor and, when so organized, as a member of a housekeeping team.

► The Floor Supervisor (also known as Senior Housekeeper or "Inspectress")

Floor supervisors are team leaders to whom several room attendants and a section housekeeping aide report. They are assigned to specific divisions of the rooms section of a property and are responsible for the quality of work performed in the several rooms sections to which their room attendants are assigned. They also are responsible for the public sectors assigned to their section housekeeping aides. They make inspections and reports and are, in all respects, supervisors of the persons assigned to their teams. They also assist in the personnel administration of the people assigned to them.

The floor supervisor is sometimes called *inspectress,* but this may be outdated. [*Editor:* It *is* now outdated, for the term was coined to indicate a female inspector. Most operations now simply call this job *inspector,* regardless of gender.] Many floor supervisors are inspectresses just because they inspect rooms. Other inspectresses do nothing but inspect rooms and report directly to the manager on what they observe, but they have no responsibility to correct identified discrepancies because no other staff is assigned to them for work purposes. [This writer is of the opinion that persons who do nothing but inspect guest rooms, then have no employees or authority with which to take corrective action, are a superfluous use of manpower.]

► The Senior Housekeeping Aide (in the past known as Head Houseman)

The senior housekeeping aide is a major supervisor in the housekeeping department. He or she is usually in charge of all public areas not directly associated with guest rooms: lobbies, major public corridors, public rest rooms, offices, and other areas specifically negotiated as part of the overall housekeeping responsibility. The senior housekeeping aide is usually responsible for basic training of section housekeeping aides and for supervision of utility housekeeping aides who might perform tasks such as shampooing carpets, washing windows, or project work. The senior housekeeping aide is usually responsible for the storage and accountability of cleaning and guest supply inventories. He or she normally works as a supervisory assistant to the executive housekeeper and performs other tasks as the executive housekeeper directs.

► The Night Supervisor

The existence of a night supervisor presumes a second shift to which no management is regularly assigned. This situation, of course, can vary with the size and complexity of night operations. Other than as intermittently visited by housekeeping management, the night supervisor assumes total control of the department after the major rooms and hotel cleaning evolution for each day is concluded. Overseeing one or two night room attendants, a night section housekeeping aide, and several night lobby or public area personnel, the night supervisor is accountable for the balance of services performed by the housekeeping department. He or she ensures that all rooms are left cleaned and ready to rent and that guest requests for service or equipment such as cribs, bedboards, and extra linen are fulfilled. The night supervisor works closely with the hotel night manager, is usually on beeper, and makes routine inspections throughout the hotel until the department is secured each evening at the designated time. The night supervisor, like the senior housekeeping aide, is a major supervisor within the department.

► The Linen Rooms Supervisor

The main linen room, a service area of the hotel, is the hub of housekeeping communication and activity. It might be better described as housekeeping central. The linen room supervisor, under the executive housekeeper, is the supervisor in charge of main linen room operations. His or her primary responsibility is maintaining and operating the communication link to the front desk, engineering, and each guest in need of housekeeping attention. In addition, the linen room supervisor is sometimes referred to as the chief status operator for housekeeping. Keeping up with, changing as necessary, and reporting the status of each guest room throughout the day is another major function of the linen room supervisor. He or she is the prime guest contact representative. Also, he or she oversees the activities of one or more linen room attendants who perform supply and distribution functions for items such as bedspreads, blankets, bed pads, and curtains. On the second shift, the night supervisor assumes the responsibilities of the linen room supervisor.

► The Laundry Supervisor

Working as a principal assistant to the laundry manager, the laundry supervisor, as the title indicates, supervises the activities of laundry attendants. Normally the laundry supervisor works as the head washperson and is in charge of all major wash equipment and chemicals. He or she also supervises the workload process and production. In our model hotel, when the laundry supervisor and team of laundry attendants is scheduled off, a swing team supervisor assumes the responsibilities of the laundry supervisor and brings his or her swing team into the laundry. Because there are two swing teams, each works in the laundry one day each week, providing the entire department with maximum flexibility and training.

► The Recreation Supervisor

In our model hotel, the recreation supervisor, under the direct supervision of the executive housekeeper, assumes responsibility for all recreation areas of the hotel. All swimming pool attendants work for the recreation supervisor and are fully Red Cross or water safety instructor qualified. (Swimming pools are properly signed to indicate "No lifeguard on duty. Swimmers enter at their own risk." This prevents the guest from abdicating responsibility for their own and their children's safety. However, all pool attendants are fully qualified to save a life.) Pool attendants, under direction of the recreation supervisor, also work in the health club, sauna, and game room, providing service to guests and maintaining cleanliness and order.

▶ Other Employees

Other employees may be found in the department, their titles indicating their activities and who they might work for. All such positions have titles appropriate to either male or female employees and are therefore nonsexist. Such titles are as follows:

- Utility housekeeping aide
- Linen room attendant
- Lobby housekeeping aide
- Laundry attendant
- Housekeeping trainer (a secondary job sometimes carried by a room attendant to ensure standardization of training)

▶ NEW HORIZONS IN HOUSEKEEPING

The National Executive Housekeeper's Association (NEHA) has long recognized the similarity in responsibilities of persons performing housekeeping functions in hospitals, hotels, and nursing homes. The association therefore draws its membership not only from hotels, retirement centers, and contract cleaning establishments but also from hospitals and nursing homes. The movement of management personnel between venues is well documented. When asked how difficult it is for a manager to make the transition in either direction, a member in hospital service once remarked, "The main function of housekeeping in both areas is to clean rooms and public areas, and to dispose of trash and rubbish. There

is only one major difference, however, and that is in hospitals, we know exactly what we are walking into, and in hotels, we don't know what we may be dealing with." That was true—until the advent of the AIDS crisis.

On December 2, 1991, new rules issued by the Occupational Safety and Health Administration (OSHA) made it mandatory that employers provide to all employees who might, as a result of their job classification, come in contact with human blood or other bodily fluids, information, training, and compliance with federal precautions designed to maintain a safe workplace with regard to bloodborne pathogens (microorganisms that can cause disease in humans), especially the HIV virus and the HBV (Hepatitis B) virus.

Specifically, department managers must establish control plans to combat the threat and provide access for employees to read and understand the OSHA compliance standard. Employees such as housekeeping and laundry personnel, who as a part of their regular daily assigned duties come in contact with bodily fluids such as blood, semen, sputum, and vomit and with spent needles (sharps) discarded by diabetics or drug users, must be advised of the potential dangers. Furthermore, they must be trained and tested in how to handle such risks when they occur, and they must be offered the opportunity to be inoculated against the HBV virus at company expense. Records must be kept of all training conducted and of all exposures that occur.

▶ CONCLUSION

Housekeeping operations is no longer the exclusive territory of women, nor is it considered menial or less important than any other function in the hospitality organization. Anyone who thinks otherwise should try to imagine hotel operations without housekeeping; the picture might have general managers and presidents cleaning rooms.

Because of the large staffs involved, housekeeping operations provide junior managers outstanding opportunities to develop leadership and supervisory skills, an opportunity not always available in other departments.

This writer recalls a moment of truth several years ago when a general manager was overheard commenting to a utility aide who at the time, happened to be mopping a men's room at 1:00 A.M. The general manager said, "You know, what you are doing is just as vital and necessary as what I do every day. We just do different things and work at different skill levels. When the company thinks they can do without either one of us, they'll abolish our jobs. I don't think they will, so until they do, don't forget: Your job is just as important around here as mine is!"

5.4 ON BEING AN EXECUTIVE HOUSEKEEPER

John Lagazo

Ah yes, those were the days, sitting in our university classes, wondering where our education and futures would take us. I thought it would be quite easy—go through the management training program, become an assistant department head for a little while, move to department and then division head, then presto—general manager!

After going through the management training in my first company, I decided I wanted to stay in the rooms division—more specifically front office, so the path was laid out: hotel assistant manager, then front office manager, brief exposure in either housekeeping or reservations, then so on and so on. Never did I think I would be the executive housekeeper in arguably what are some of the finest hotels and resorts not only in the United States but even the world.

Why housekeeping? When my friends ask what I do and I say, "I'm an executive housekeeper," the first response is, "Oh, so you clean rooms?" Depending on who is asking, I either agree or say it is much, much, more. Over the years, I have had trainees or first-time assistant managers who say that housekeeping was never their initial choice, but by the time they were done, they had a different appreciation for the department.

So what is housekeeping? Is managing housekeeping just making sure the room attendants clean all the rooms every day? It is actually just a little more than that.

It is managing what usually is the largest regular staff in the hotel and the budget to pay them. It is managing supplies—whatever is in the room for the guests to use and whatever is used to clean anything and everything in the hotel, from the sidewalks to the staff areas (e.g., locker rooms, cafeteria, offices), from meeting spaces to food and beverage outlets—not to mention the guest rooms themselves.

It is managing teamwork and coordinating with all other departments in the hotel—to make sure the rooms are ready for the guests when they arrive. It is making sure that all instructions and requests from sales are carried out. Accounting must be satisfied that we are in control of dollars. It is making sure the food and beverage outlets are as clean as the guest rooms. It is making sure all of the human resource reporting requirements are met.

For the hotels that have a full-service laundry, it is managing that too—and if the hotel utilizes an off-property service (for laundry, overnight cleaning of the kitchens and public areas, uniform and guest clothes cleaning), the executive housekeeper must manage that operation as well! Even though off-property services are their own business, they represent the hotel; if they do not clean the linens well or are not efficient, it costs the hotel money.

Executive housekeepers must be detail-oriented and organized. Housekeeping is a 24/7 department, and it can get out of control very quickly. This means phone calls at home at 11:00 P.M. saying that your staff has not shown up or that because the boilers are down, there is no steam for the laundry. The wildest calls I received (not too often, thank goodness) were when I worked in Hawaii. Because of the staffing challenges, I had room attendants and housepersons ferried over from a neighboring island. If the weather was bad or the boat had a mechanical problem, the phone rang around 4:00 A.M. to tell me so. I then had to figure out Plan B for cleaning rooms and the rest of the hotel that day.

Getting away from the technical side of things, being an executive housekeeper taught me a lot about managing people; I was "diversity managing" well before it became politically correct and one of the new management buzzwords. The staff is usually the most ethnically diverse, with an accompanying challenge being the level of English competency and overall education. These staff members are asked to work with hazardous chemicals in an environment with a high accident potential; they push and pull heavy weights, are exposed to bacteria, and work with dangerous equipment such as sheet and towel folders and garbage and cardboard compactors.

These people have one of the most detail-oriented jobs—a room checklist can have as many as 150 items that must be completed to proper standard.

Contrary to popular belief, this staff should also have high guest contact skills. Just because room attendants and other housekeeping staff members do not interact with guests every time they perform their duties, this does not mean they should not be skilled in guest contact. One of my former room attendants consistently told me the travel plans of one of the regular CEOs that stayed with us. She wrote down his travel dates and let us know if his wife would be with him. Because he was such a regular, we rarely had problems in accommodating him even if we were sold out, and he always had the same room with the same room attendant.

In many of the hotels, the challenge was to pull the ethnic groups together to work as a team. Housekeeping gave me a great chance to learn about different cultures—I probably would still not know what a quincinera is (a Sweet 15 birthday/debut in Latin American countries). I have eaten foods that I probably would not have otherwise and have picked up smatterings of many languages (Spanish, Creole, Tongan, Polish, Cantonese, Filipino)—which, depending on the situation, can either get me in serious trouble or give everyone a good laugh.

I learned about management styles and group dynamics, and I advise all of you who read this to learn as much about these subjects as possible. I learned about identifying the informal leaders of groups and how to influence them. I learned about individual personality styles, how to manage them, and how to get them to work together to get things done. From the people of different cultures I have worked with, I learned about the ones who avoid eye contact when you speak with them, I learned about the ones that had Old Country traditions—for instance, not respecting a female or young boss—and how to turn them around.

Housekeeping taught me how to adapt—which, on the outside, should not have been an issue because I was the boss and the staff should do as I say (traditional management). Managing people continues to change and evolve—first there was Total Quality Management, then Generation X management, and now whatever new theories are out there. To me, the bottom line is that to be a success, you must manage not only yourself but also groups of people. Manage and lead the environment (department), and you will be successful in your endeavors. Get exposure to different environments—work in city and remote resort locations—and know and understand that everywhere you go, the guest and staff makeup is different. If you are adaptable, you will also be successful.

There are some other interesting things too—for example, when I shop for home cleaning items, I know way more than I need to. Don't bother listening to commercials; send me an email or work in housekeeping and you will know why I will not buy "window cleaner with ammonia." Having managed

laundry operations, I shop for clothes not only for style but for materials used and construction of the item. If you buy an item with lots of extra frills, beads, decoration, metallic buttons, and bring it to my dry cleaning store, don't be surprised if I charge you extra for what it takes to properly clean it. I may even turn you down and say I won't clean it unless you sign a damage waiver. I now know that the dry cleaning and laundry processes are murder on fabrics.

I have many great memories from housekeeping over the years:

- Using a bullhorn to conduct a morning meeting with 70 room attendants.

- Proving a Mobil inspector wrong (I had been in his room during the incident in question).

- Being the executive housekeeper at the host hotel for the Mobil five-star winners award ceremony—imagine having every room checked with a magnifying glass and white gloves!

- Having a local TV station doing a *60 Minutes*–style report on hotel cleanliness—we passed with flying colors!

- Having my rooms director keep checking on me to make sure I did not get food poisoning because of food my staff would give me—I was adventurous enough to eat whatever was placed on my desk and yes, jellyfish does have an interesting texture.

I have encountered other situations too. After a suicide in a hotel room, I could only get new staff members to go into the room because of the strong superstitious beliefs of some attendants. I have managed through both strikes and decertifications in union hotels. The celebrity stories—those alone could take up a whole book. Perhaps I could get rich from writing it!

I am glad my career path has taken me through housekeeping. At the end of the day, it really is the memories of the people I have met and friends made over the years that have made the difference. I think I would have learned the technical aspects one way or the other, but the people skills have been even more valuable. Yes, I did hold the positions of hotel assistant manager, front office assistant manager, and front office manager at various points in my career, in addition to spending time in all housekeeping management positions, including laundry/valet manager.

Where did I get all of these memories and experiences? Since leaving my alma mater in the mid-1980s, I have been at:

- Hyatt Hotels in California and Louisiana
- A Wyndham Hotel in California

- Ritz-Carlton Hotels/Resorts in California, Boston, Florida, Hawaii, and Puerto Rico (when I worked in these hotels, they were all five-star and/or five-diamond, except for Puerto Rico, which was still too new)
- Four Seasons Hotels in Boston and Chicago (both five-star, five-diamond properties)
- Short stints in St. Louis and Florida with Adams Mark and an independent four-star resort

From my current perspective as director of operations of the Madison Hotel in Washington, D.C., can I say my housekeeping experience helped me? You bet! The varied experience with people, places, and management styles has prepared me for *anything* in this great hospitality business.

5.5 THE HOTEL ENGINEERING FUNCTION: ORGANIZATION, PEOPLE, AND ISSUES IN THE MODERN ERA

Denney G. Rutherford

▶ INTRODUCTION TO THE ENGINEERING DEPARTMENT

▶ History of Department

Historically, the functions and duties of the chief engineer, his staff, and the engineering department have been relegated to the sub-conscious of hotel management and certainly of the hotel guests. Their place in the organization was roughly analogous to their place in the building structure: toward the bottom and basically out of sight. The only time the functions of the engineering department became noticeable was on those unhappy occasions when something went wrong with one of the building systems and guests and/or management were inconvenienced.

Consequently, in the past, "out of sight, out of mind" treatment evolved for the engineering department, and as a result its relative importance was diminished. Also, the personnel of the engineering department were craftspeople and semiskilled workers, usually managed by one of their number who through longevity and perseverance worked their way up through the ranks to supervisory status.

▶ Evolutionary Stimuli

There is now clear evidence that this department is changing in many of the same ways that other departments of a modern hotel have had to change. The reasons for these changes are many, but four can be highlighted here. Several of them, of course, are closely connected.

Competition. As more and more hotel organizations seek the business of ever more carefully segmented markets, many of the mechanisms of competition manifest themselves first in features of the physical plant. These can range from building design, landscaping, elevators, and in-room amenities and facilities to the latest in traditional fixtures and building systems such as plumbing, kitchen equipment, elevators, heating, ventilating and air conditioning (HVAC), and the other behind-the-scenes paraphernalia that make up the domain of the chief engineer.

Sophistication. Many building systems in today's hotels are interconnected, managed in conjunction with other departmental systems, and monitored by computerized facilities. This increased sophistication has mandated more sophisticated and knowledgeable man-

agement in all departments, but perhaps the most drastic and substantive changes will be (and are) occurring in engineering.

Return on Investment. Many modern hotel plants are the result of plans and investments by a wide range of participants, including (but not necessarily always) the management firm that operates the hotel. These investors expect a certain return on their investment and subsequently expect the hotel company will not only keep the hotel filled with guests but keep the property in such a state that the guests will continue to want to come there. This also mandates new dimensions of the engineer's job. The combination of increased competition and sophisticated systems makes for more than a traditional repair-and-maintenance approach to providing engineering support in all areas of the hotel. To keep the hotel positively contributing to the investors' return on their money, the engineering staff must be considered a major role player in the financial health of the organization.

Energy. The cost, use, management, and conservation of energy have added a new and singular dimension to the job of the chief engineer—one that did not exist in pre-1973 operations, simply because energy was so cheap. Since the OPEC oil embargo of 1973, energy prices have undergone many changes, none of them making it any cheaper. Prior to that, buildings were neither engineered nor managed to save energy.

Since then, most hotels and most modern hotel companies have come to recognize energy as one building expense in which significant savings can be made. If accomplished with care, engineering can provide for delivery of hotel services without adverse or negative effects on the guest. We want to avoid, for instance, the extreme step of requesting guests to take short showers while at the same time asking them to pay $180 a night for their room.

The residual effects of the embargo are twofold. Hotels built prior to 1973 were not constructed to be particularly energy efficient. Engineers in those hotels have a more difficult job with respect to managing energy.

On the other hand, hotels that were designed and built after 1973–1974 exhibit increasingly more sophisticated systems for managing and conserving energy without adversely affecting guests.

The first instance presents the managerial problem of making do for the engineering manager; the second presents the dilemma of expanding one's knowledge in a rapidly changing technological environment. It should be noted that energy remains a significant management issue for the engineer in the year 2005, and will for the foreseeable future.

In no business system as complex as a hotel is a mechanical or electronic system the only answer. A tremendous amount of attention must be given to training personnel to overcome wasteful habits where energy is concerned. A classic example is that of kitchen employees who turn on every appliance in the kitchen at 6:00 A.M. when maybe only 20 percent of them are used for the preparation of breakfast and most of the rest are not needed until close to lunch. This is representative of the sort of wasteful habit that is out of the engineer's control but that he or she is obligated to point out to other department heads. Clearly, the engineer now must have an active presence as a full member of the management staff and must be adept at interacting with other department managers.

► PERSONNEL

► Manager of Engineering Function

Variously referred to as the chief engineer, director of building operations, building superintendent, or some combination of those terms, this is the individual responsible for the management of the building's systems and its maintenance, repair, and upkeep (Figure 5.3).

As stated earlier, in the past, chief engineers typically were people who had worked their way up through the ranks from either one of the crafts or as an engineering employee specializing in one of the building systems. They may have been in hotels all of their professional career or may have come to a hotel company from engineering positions in organizations as diverse as shipping lines, manufacturing companies, office buildings, university settings, and hospitals.

Research evidence, however, suggests this trend may be changing (Rutherford 1987). Chief engineers responding to this survey describe themselves collectively according to the data set forth in Table 5.2. Over 25 percent of those responding to this nationwide survey indicated they have a university degree. Three-quarters of those degrees were in some area of engineering. This suggests that the sophistication of modern hotel building operations may be mandating management by those whose formal education is more extensive than that required in the past.

In this study, the typical engineer was 44.5 years old and had been in the hospitality business about 11 years. This suggests that this "typical engineer" probably had significant on-the-job experience or training in his field

| Figure 5.3 | Engineering Department Organization |

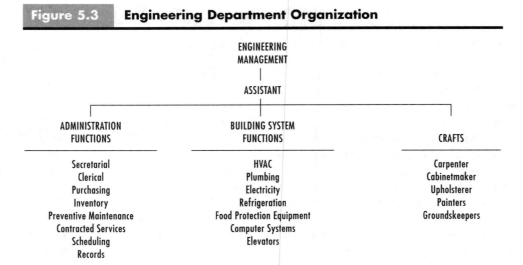

in other industries and only recently came into the hospitality industry. After entering the hospitality industry, however, it appears they moved rapidly into management and were fairly stable in their careers, as evidenced by the congruence of average years in present position and average years at present hotel.

Commenting on these data, one chief engineer said that, in his experience, more and

Table 5.2 Chief Engineer Demographics

		(Raw Number, if Applicable)
Average age	44.5	
Percent male	100.0%	
Percent Caucasian	92.9%	
Median salary	$35,000	
Percent university degree	27.0%	(20)
Percent of degrees in engineering	75.0%	(15)
Percent of degrees in hotel/business	25.0%	(5)
Average years in hospitality industry	10.9	
Average years at present hotel	6.3	
Average years in present position	6.15	

74 respondents

more industry engineering managers in the larger or international hotel firms are being recruited from among those people who have had at least some college education, if not actually holding a college or university degree in engineering. He suggested that in his company this does not necessarily reflect a preference for academic training over practical experience but rather recognizes the realities of doing business in today's competitive environment. Having completed college study also suggests that the candidate will understand and be able to manage the sophisticated building systems that the company anticipates installing and being developed for new hotels into the next century.

In that comment lies one key to understanding the future of the chief engineer's job. The most successful engineers of the future will very likely be those whose training and education prepares them to think strategically, to recognize trends, and do their part to help the hotel and its owners meet and deal with the evolutionary issues discussed earlier.

▶ Other Departmental Management Staff

Refer again to Figure 5.3. Depending, of course, on the size of the hotel and the extent and sophistication of its engineering functions, the chief engineer may enjoy the services of a staff of administrators, including assistant managers. These people help carry out the administrative details of operating an increasingly complicated hotel department. Related tasks include secretarial support, which may be combined with a clerical function.

Among the most important administrative functions of the engineering department are:

- Helping other department heads make purchasing decisions.
- Keeping an inventory of spare parts and building equipment.
- Arranging for the performance of preventive maintenance on all building systems.
- Administering contract services such as pest control, window washing, landscaping, swimming pool maintenance, groundskeeping, and construction projects.

As the department grows in size and scope, a major administrative function involves scheduling equipment and personnel to accomplish the tasks of the department. While scheduling may benefit greatly from technological advances such as microcomputers or the hotel's mainframe computer system, in a building whose systems are as complicated and interrelated as those of a hotel, part of the engineering function must be the ability to react to nonscheduled events ranging from overflowing toilets to stuck elevators, gas leaks, and so forth.

A final administrative function is setting the groundwork and maintaining the basis for managerial and administrative decisions that affect the long-term operation of the engineering department and, by extrapolation, the hotel itself. This involves keeping accurate and up-to-date records regarding the various building systems and the installation of capital equipment for which the engineer is responsible.

These sorts of administrative details complicate the job of any manager but may be particularly troubling to the engineer. One of the main reasons is that while the engineering department is responsible for the maintenance and repair of sophisticated and complicated building systems, under most circumstances these systems, or their components, are often operated by (and perhaps misused by) non-engineering employees and guests. Particularly in the case of guests, the engineer has little or no control over the way in which they treat guest room equipment and fixtures for which the engineer is responsible. Engineers who have the luxury of a well-developed administrative staff find their job in managing the building and its systems and the attendant problems much easier if complete, accurate, and up-to-date records are available to formulate the basis for planning, purchasing, budgeting, and control.

▶ Technical Specialists

Typical building functions, which are the responsibility of the engineering department, are listed in Figure 5.3. Each has its own place in providing for the comfort of the guest and participating in the delivery of the hotel's services to the guests. Each has attendant complications that provide challenges for the management and staff of the engineering department.

Heating, ventilating, and air conditioning (collectively known as HVAC) is concerned with supplying the production, public, and guest room areas of the hotel with a clean, controlled, and comfortable indoor environment. Modern building HVAC systems provide for heating or cooling the air, adding or deleting moisture from the air to adjust for optimum relative humidity, filtering or cleaning the air, and moving the air from place to place within the hotel to provide for a number of complete changes of air in a room per hour, depending on local codes and activities within that particular area of the hotel.

Among the complicating factors here that challenge the engineering department are that different areas of the hotel have different requirements for air. It is easy to see that kitchens and guest rooms place different demands on the HVAC system. Lobbies have different requirements than do other public areas such as bars, restaurants, and housekeeping laundry facilities. Engineers call this job of meeting diverse air needs "providing the system with balance," and it is a major function of the individuals in charge of the HVAC to deliver the optimum environment to each area of the hotel.

The plumbing system in a modern hotel must also perform a number of balancing functions. First and foremost in the mind of management, of course, is the delivery of high-quality water service to guest room areas. Guests want high-quality water that is free from visual defects such as dirt and rust, does not carry odors, and tastes clean and fresh. Guests also want water that is hot enough to shave, bathe, and wash in without the danger of scalding themselves, and they also want that water in generous supply. Nothing is more frustrating to a hotel guest who is paying over $200 a night for a room to find that the hotel has run out of hot water in the middle of a morning shave or shower. At the same time, the engineering department is expected to deliver production hot and cold water to the kitchen areas, the housekeeping and laundry areas, and the food service areas. Providing for the delivery of high-quality water service to the various user groups in the hotel is a major part of the engineering function—one that, of course, is noticed only when the system is malfunctioning.

A similar case may be made for the delivery of electricity. The electrical systems of the hotel, like the plumbing systems, must be designed and maintained to serve various user groups. Again, like plumbing, there is no substitute for electricity. The engineering staff must provide the hotel with electrical service that meets the needs of individual departments and the needs of guests.

Refrigeration, food production equipment, and computer systems are examples of other building system functions for which the engineering department may be responsible for repairing, maintaining, replacing, or managing. While the maintenance of many of these systems may be contracted to outside agencies such as the supplier, the engineering department nonetheless is the first line of defense in keeping them operating efficiently.

In most modern hotels, the installation and service of elevator systems are generally the province of the elevator manufacturer, and hotels typically have extended maintenance agreements for the elevators. Most engineering departments, however, closely monitor the operation of the elevator systems. In modern high-rise hotels with high-speed elevator service, the slightest problem with that service should be quickly and easily identified and reported to the contractors. It is generally the responsibility of the engineering department to monitor these services and their contracts closely and carefully.

The crafts represented in Figure 5.3 illustrate the sorts of specialized skills required by most hotel engineering departments. Depending on the size of the hotel and complexity of its services, an engineering department may employ on a full-time basis one or more carpenters and cabinetmakers to maintain, repair, and build fixtures and furniture for the hotel's guests and staff. Similarly, if the service is not contracted out, hotels may employ an upholsterer whose major task is to maintain the high-quality appearance of the vast collection of furniture in a typical hotel.

Painting, upkeep of the hotel's grounds, and landscaping are additional ongoing functions that require constant attention. These services may be contracted to outside agencies or suppliers but are included here to suggest the range of functions for which the engineering department is responsible.

▶ ISSUES

In the Rutherford study (1987), the engineers surveyed were asked to judge the relative importance of the items on a list of 58 statements relating to the operation of a modern hotel engineering department. A statistical procedure was applied to rank-order the statements in terms of their rated importance. The ten most important facets of an engineer's job, as derived from this list, are reproduced in Table 5.3 and serve as the basis for suggesting the most pressing issues facing hotel engineering managers at this time. While these data are 20 years old, they still represent important concerns of the modern maintenance chief. An informal telephone survey of 15 CEs, utilizing the same items found little change in the hierarchy. "Knowledge of maintenance of equipment" became secondary to energy-related items and "relations with top mangement," but they were all bunched closely at the top.

▶ Departmental Management

Items #4, 6, 7, and 8 of Table 5.3 suggest that modern hotel engineers deem activities relating to management of their departments of high importance to success. Communicating with employees; providing a safe environment;

Table 5.3 Importance of This Item to Operation of My Department

Rank	Item	Mean	SD	N
1	Knowledge of maintenance of equipment	4.760	.633	75
2	Energy conservation	4.655	.804	74
3	Energy management	4.589	.761	73
4	Responsibility for communication with employees	4.587	.680	75
5	Relations with top management	4.520	.811	73
6	Responsibility for leadership	4.514	.726	74
7	Responsibility for safety	4.486	.904	72
8	Responsibilities of an effective organizational ability	4.453	.810	75
9	Energy costs	4.444	.854	72
10	Knowledge of the types of equipment	4.370	.791	73

Scale: 1 = not at all important
     5 = of vital importance

being able to organize the tasks, activities, and personnel in the department; and providing leadership all suggest that the foremost issues facing the chief engineer today call for managerial skills rather than the traditional technical skills.

▶ Energy

The fact that three energy-related items were rated in the top ten by all responding engineers suggests that the realm of issues relating to energy has not yet been addressed satisfactorily by the majority of these professionals. It also suggests that energy will continue to be an issue in the foreseeable future.

▶ Relations with Top Management

Another major dimension of the engineer's job can be seen by the importance attached to relations with top management. Of the other departments that the engineers were asked to rank their relationships with, only two, housekeeping and purchasing, ranked within the top 50 percent of the 58 survey items. Many of the chief engineers contacted for comment agreed with this ranking with top management. They said it is becoming an increasingly important part of their job not only to report to top management but also to educate top management about the importance of the engineering function.

▶ Equipment

It should be noted that the technical aspects of the chief engineer's job are not ignored in the collective rankings assigned to these operational statements. That knowledge of equipment maintenance ranked clearly first among the statements and that knowledge of types of equipment made it into the top ten suggests that while the job of the chief engineer may in fact be evolving toward one of a more managerial nature, its traditional technical aspects still play a major role in the daily discharge of an engineer's responsibility.

▶ FUTURE AND CONCLUSION

▶ Data from Empirical Research

Interpretation of the data gathered in a survey of a broad cross section of chief engineers and subsequent follow-up conversations with selected engineers suggests that the job of the chief engineer is, in fact, evolving, as suggested at the outset of this chapter.

The engineers describe many more incidents involving issues and problems related to people and departmental action and interaction than in the past, when most issues and problems involved equipment and systems.

It also appears that in the future, chief engineers are going to have to be more adept at inter- and intradepartmental organizational politics. To provide the hotel and its guests with high-quality services relative to the physical and environmental systems of the building, the chief engineer must compete with other department heads for scarce resources related to personnel, technology, and operating elbow room.

Summing up, the engineering department, its management, and, to a certain extent, its staff and technical experts represent an organizational function of the modern hotel that is in the process of evolutionary change. This change is driven by a number of factors. The future of successful hotel organizations will hinge, to a great extent, on the ability of hotel management to recognize the importance of the contributions of the engineering department to the delivery of guest services and maintaining a high return on investment for the owners of the property.

5.6 THE ENGINEERING DEPARTMENT AND FINANCIAL INFORMATION

Agnes Lee DeFranco and Susan B. Sheridan

The engineering department is a vital part of a hotel. Energy cost alone runs anywhere from 4 to 6 percent of a property's total operation budget. Savings in energy cost can be accomplished by instituting simple steps such as modifying staff members' behavior (Dale and Kluga, 1992). How can financial data be used to continuously improve the performance of the engineering department? To an-

swer this question, a survey was performed to collect data from hotel engineers to determine their use of financial information. It is postulated that if financial information is analyzed correctly, the engineering department can serve its profit centers better, which in turn will assist these profit centers in reducing both their cycle time and errors.

A number of studies have been done on

the use of financial information by managers in profit centers of hotels, but not many were performed specifically to collect information regarding the engineering department. Malk and Schmidgall (1995) discuss the use of financial statements and information in the food and beverage department of a hotel, particularly in an effort to contain costs and maintain a profit. Turkel (1993) also advocates the development of profit and loss statements and allocating costs properly to ascertain the profitability of a food and beverage department. Malk and Schmidgall (1994) also investigate the cost percentages in the rooms division to help rooms division managers with cost containment. Quain (1992) explores the use of profit analysis by the customer segment in addition to yield management, and the topic of menu engineering to improve profits in food and beverage establishments has also been discussed (Bayou and Bennett, 1992; Dougan, 1994). However, few, if any, studies can be quoted for the engineering department.

► THE SURVEY

The purpose of the study was to investigate the use of financial information by hotel engineers. Therefore, questions asked included the types of financial information used, the frequency at which this information was generated, the methods used to generate the data, and the type of hardware and software used in the department. Hotel engineers were also interviewed to see how their use of financial information could improve quality in their departments by reducing cycle time and eliminating errors.

The population for this study consisted of directors of engineering in U.S. hotels that were listed in the *Hotel and Travel Index*, Spring 1994 edition. The sample was randomly selected from this index, and the selection criteria were based on the number of rooms in the property. The sample hotels all had 200 or more rooms. It was believed that hotels of this size would probably have an engineering department. The sample size was 400 hotels, and the sample hotels were located throughout the 50 states.

For the first mail-out, a cover letter and a questionnaire were sent to the general manager of each sample hotel. It was felt that if the surveys were addressed to the general managers by name, they would be more likely to read the surveys and pass them along to the directors of engineering. The initial response rate, however, was only 15 percent. In order to improve the response rate, three weeks after the initial mail-out, a second mail-out was sent. The second mail-out was addressed specifically to the director of engineering. Follow-up letters and questionnaires were sent to the entire sample. A total of 97 of the 400 questionnaires were eventually returned for a response rate of 24.25 percent.

► THE TYPICAL CHIEF ENGINEER

Of the sample, 38 percent of the respondents reported that *chief engineer* was their official title, while 36 percent held the title *director of engineering* and 7 percent *director of property operations*. The majority of the respondents (52 percent) had less than 6 years of experience with their present company and less than 3 years with their specific property (51 percent). However, when asked their years of experience within the hospitality industry, most

Table 5.4 Profile of Respondents

	n	%
Job Title		
Chief engineer	33	38
Director of engineering	32	36
Director of property operations	6	7
Facilities manager	3	3
Others: Eleven different titles	14	16
Number of Years with Company		
0–3	31	32
3.1–6	19	20
6.1–9	11	11
9.1–12	11	11
12.1–15	13	14
15 and over	12	12
Number of Years with Property		
0–3	49	51
3.1–6	17	18
6.1–9	10	10
9.1–12	12	12
12 and over	9	9
Number of Years in the Industry		
0–3	5	5
3.1–6	9	10
6.1–9	12	13
9.1–12	23	24
12.1–15	18	19
15 and over	28	29
Number of Years with Engineering Department		
0–9	15	16
10–18	37	39
19–27	31	32
28 and over	12	13
Number of Rooms in Property		
200–300	29	31
301–400	28	29
401–500	16	17
501 and over	22	23
Average Daily Rate		
Less than $50	2	2
$51–$100	48	56
$101–$150	26	31
$151 and over	9	11
Number of Employees in Department		
3–6	16	17
7–9	31	32
10–12	13	14
13-15	11	11
16 and over	25	26

of them (56 percent) had 6 to 15 years of experience.

The respondents also reported having substantial experience in engineering and property operations and maintenance departments. The highest response category was 9 to 18 years (39 percent), followed by 18 to 27 years (22 percent) and 0 to 9 years (16 percent).

The majority of the respondents (60 percent) worked in hotels that had 200–400 rooms, and these hotels had an average daily rate of $95.60. The largest group of respondents (32 percent) employed 7 to 9 engineering employees. Overall, the work performed was primarily done in-house and by outside contractors. Table 5.4 provides a summary of the characteristics of the respondents.

department, the respondents were asked to rate ten criteria. A Likert rating scale of one to five was used, with 1 being not important and 5 being very important. Table 5.5 ranks these ten criteria as perceived by the directors of engineers.

The area that received the highest mean score of 4.70/5.00 was "control costs more effectively," with 80 percent of respondents rating the criterion at 5 and 14 percent at 4. This was followed very closely by "evaluate the performance of the department" and "plan ahead more effectively," both rated at 4.49. The criterion that received the lowest rating (3.55) was "improving communications with the department staff." Therefore, the majority of these managers were aware that financial information was an essential and integral part of the operations of the department.

► HOW IMPORTANT IS FINANCIAL INFORMATION?

In order to assess how financial information can affect the performance of the engineering

► THE COMPILATION PROCESS

These data show overwhelming agreement that financial information can enable man-

Table 5.5 Usefulness of Financial Information

Criterion	Ranking	Mean Score	Standard Deviation
Control cost more effectively	1	4.70	0.09
Evaluate the performance of my department	2	4.49	0.14
Plan ahead more accurately	2	4.49	0.15
Be a better manager	4	4.47	0.16
Have information for evaluation purposes	5	4.33	0.16
Be more flexible financially	6	4.00	0.19
Be more innovative	7	3.99	0.19
Staff accordingly	8	3.93	0.22
Improve communication with my staff	9	3.63	0.22
Improve motivation of my staff	10	3.55	0.23

agers of the engineering department to control costs more effectively. The respondents were then asked about the compilation process. They were asked to specify the types of financial reports that are generated, the frequency at which they are generated, the number of people involved in the process, and the methods used to compile these reports.

All respondents used budgets or cost tracking in their property. Variance analysis, comparing the budgeted and actual figures, was done by 95 percent of the respondents, and 60 percent stated that a departmental income statement was prepared.

The frequency at which these reports were generated was quite varied. The respondents were asked to indicate whether the above-mentioned statements were generated on a daily, weekly, biweekly, monthly, or annual basis, and to check all that applied. For the departmental income statements, monthly reporting was the norm (51 percent). This was also true for the budgeted income statement (50 percent), cost tracking on individual accounts (40 percent), variance analysis (49 percent), and flexible budget (55 percent).

In addition to preparing these statements monthly, 22 percent of the respondents prepared daily department income statements, and 31 percent did daily cost tracking. Although budgeted income statements and variance analysis were not done daily, they were compiled weekly.

The number of people involved in preparing these statements ranged from one to ten. The responsibility, however, was generally shared between the engineering department itself and the accounting department. Half of the respondents reported that cost tracking was done by their own department and by the accounting department. Cost tracking was the analysis the engineering department performed on their own more often than they did any of the other four analyses. The accounting department, on the average, performed 62 percent of the engineering department's financial work.

The majority of the respondents used computers to prepare these statements. Approximately 60 percent of the respondents used computers to compile all of the five statements. A combination of manual methods and computers was the second most commonly used method (40 percent), and no respondents reported that financial information was compiled manually only.

► COMPUTER TECHNOLOGY AND FINANCIAL INFORMATION

Because computers were used in compiling information, the respondents were also asked to describe the types of hardware and software used in this endeavor. Among the directors of engineering who used a computer, the IBM PC configuration was most widely used. Overall, they reported that they used custom software. For spreadsheet applications, they reported using Lotus 1-2-3 and Excel.

► COMMENTS FROM THE FIELD

In addition to completing the surveys, a number of engineers in a large metropolitan area in the southwestern United States were interviewed in an effort to determine, in greater depth, how they used financial information.

One of the engineers stated that he used financial information now more than he used to. His role as an engineer has changed over the years, and he is currently much more of a financial planner than he used to be. He reviews all of the financial statements that relate to his department with his supervisory employees in an effort to help contain costs. This process was found to help empower employees because they could see how their performance was directly linked to the results of these statements.

Budgets were critical to all of these engineers, and they generally felt it was important to properly allocate their costs. This information was also useful because it showed if their costs (particularly repairs, maintenance, and utilities) were in line with their projections. One engineer was particularly adamant about properly accounting for his costs. In his hotel, bonuses were given on overall profitability of the hotel, and he wanted to make sure, as much as he could, that everyone received a bonus. Another engineer stated that he used financial information to help conserve and cut down on waste. He also used his financial information to be proactive in dealing with costs. The engineers believed financial information could help them in eliminating errors such as problems in ordering inventories, or to just make sure their departments were operating as efficiently as possible, thereby reducing cycle time.

► CONCLUSIONS AND IMPLICATIONS

It was apparent that managers of engineering departments recognized the importance of financial information. They worked together with the accounting department to compile budgets, actual statements, and variance analyses, which were then used to evaluate the performance and success of the engineering department. Computer technology was common in their operations.

However, improvements can always be made to achieve zero defects, reduce cycle time, and enhance employee empowerment. As noted, "improve motivation of my staff" and "improve communication with my staff" were rated as the bottom two of the ten criteria given. In addition, two was the average number of people involved in the preparation of these reports. If it is not practical to have more employees share in the compilation process, the least an engineering department can do is to have more employees participate in the analysis process. When more employees are involved, motivation and communication tend to increase. This positive attitude may be passed along to other employees and guests.

Asking employees to be involved does not mean they must *do* the accounting work. Rather, those who compile the information can share with other staff members the importance of cost control and how cost savings in the engineering area can affect the bottom line, which may ultimately affect their job performance and bonuses. These discussions can be in the form of employee meetings where employees may make suggestions for improvements. Because employees encounter day-to-day problems and situations that managers may not be aware of, they may be able to offer comments and suggestions that address concerns such as staffing, cost control, and physical plant improvements. This process may help the entire department become more innovative and further empower engineering employees, reduce cycle time, and, possibly, eliminate errors.

The majority of respondents (60 percent) used computers to compile financial information. The rest used a combination of computers and manual methods. Engineering departments that do not use a computer may find that working with one may help improve their overall efficiency.

As this study has shown, computer technology and the use of financial information in engineering department are vital in maintaining an efficient operation. According to the National Restaurant Association's 1994 Restaurant Industry Operations survey, utility expenses for restaurants increased 6.9 percent from 1992 to 1993, while repairs and maintenance increased 5.8 percent in the same period (Riehle, 1994). If not watched, these costs will probably continue to eat away the profits. It is up to the engineering department to use restaurant financial information to help contain these costs.

5.7 THE LEGAL ENVIRONMENT OF LODGING OPERATIONS

Melissa Dallas

Hotels, like other business entities, are subject to a large and continually changing body of law. However, because lodging facilities are complicated systems, the laws affecting them are more numerous and complex than those affecting most other types of businesses. Because not complying with laws can result in fines, lawsuits, and even imprisonment, it is important that managers be familiar with the many legal dangers to which hotels are subject. This does not mean they have to be lawyers, but managers should have enough legal knowledge to be aware of strategies that minimize the property's exposure to potential litigation and to train employees to minimize risks in their departments.

This chapter is a brief introduction to the legal environment in which hotels operate. We begin with a discussion of where our laws come from and how they are classified. This should give you a fundamental understanding of the legal content. Then we look at the laws and regulations that are specific to typical hotel departments. Notice the significant number of detailed references and footnotes. These are included to provide further detail for specific discussion points and to provide a source for reference.

► HOW LAW WORKS

The following section briefly introduces you to the law—where it comes from and how it is classified. This will help you when we turn our attention to the specifics of the law and how it applies to the lodging industry.

► Sources of Law

Law comes from four sources: (1) judge-made common law (also called *case law* and *stare decisis*); (2) the Constitution; (3) legislative statutes and ordinances; and (4) administrative agencies. Each of these is discussed below.

Common law originated in England and, although decisions issued by courts in the United States have added considerably to this body of law, some decisions made several hundreds of years ago still influence present-day judicial decisions. The primary purpose of common law is to provide stability and predictability as judges rule on cases. Judges use past decisions as a precedent for deciding current cases. This decision becomes binding for lower courts in that jurisdiction and can even be used as persuasive authority for courts in other jurisdictions faced with cases having a similar pattern of facts.

Constitutional law, of course, is derived from the U.S. Constitution, which protects individuals from government excesses. When the Supreme Court, made up of nine justices, grants a *writ of certiorari,* it agrees to hear a case and then renders a decision that subsequently becomes the law of the land. On the other hand, if the Court refuses to issue a *writ,* the law stands as decided by a lower court.

Statutory law is made by local, state, or federal legislatures or other governing bodies. Federal and state laws are called *statutes,* and local laws are called *ordinances.* Legislatures can choose to modify or change common law by enacting statutes that codify, or spell out, a new law.

Finally, administrative law consists of regulations passed by agencies such as the Food and Drug Administration and the Occupational Safety and Health Administration. Congress approves the agencies, then authorizes them to make regulations that affect businesses as well as individuals.

▶ Classifications of Law

Laws generally fall into one of three major classifications: civil, criminal, or international. Most complaints filed against hotels are civil suits in which an individual has been wronged by another individual or by a corporation (which, incidentally, is a legal individual). The injured party—the plaintiff—files a lawsuit that describes the facts of the situation and asks for damages. These damages may be compensatory or punitive or both. Compensatory damages are meant to restore people to their original condition and include monetary judgments for actual damages such as back and future wages, medical costs, pain and suffering, and breach of contract. Punitive damages, on the other hand, are awarded to punish the wrongdoer. Because punitive damages in civil suits are awarded only in the case of violence, malice, or fraud, they are relatively uncommon.

Most civil cases filed against hotels involve claims of negligence. In order for plaintiffs to be successful, they must prove four elements. First, they must prove the hotel had a duty to them. Next, they must prove the hotel breached that duty. Third, they must show the breach was the reason for the incident occurring in the first place, and the hotel should have been able to foresee injuries. Finally, they must have been injured in some way so they can collect damages. The theory of negligence requires a hotel to act reasonably to prevent foreseeable injuries to guests and visitors. To illustrate this theory, assume a front office employee did not require identification when issuing duplicate keys. A person was issued a room key by this employee, then used the key to enter a guest room and injured a guest. Here, the hotel would likely be found negligent because it breached its duty to keep guests safe by not practicing proper key control. The intrusion and resulting injury would not have happened but for the employee issuing a duplicate key without requesting identification, and this omission resulted in injuries to the guest.

In order for someone to be criminally prosecuted, on the other hand, he or she must be charged with committing a wrong against society as a whole. Crimes require intent on the part of the defendant; if found guilty, the defendant may be charged a fine, imprisoned, or both. Crimes most often affecting hotel operations include theft, assault, and battery. Theft, of course, can relate to goods, services, or both. Assault is defined as the imminent threat of bodily harm, and battery is the actual harmful physical contact. An example of an assault is a bouncer in a nightclub wrongfully threatening a patron and running toward the patron with his arms raised. Battery is the bouncer picking up the patron and wrongfully throwing him down the steps and out the door of the club.

Although the hotel industry is becoming increasingly global, international law that is actually enforceable against an individual or a hotel company is rare. Most international laws are in the form of treaties, while others are customary laws followed by nations over time. The primary international laws applied to hotel companies are treaties that govern intellectual property such as trademarks and copyrights. The Paris Convention of 1883 affords its signatories (meaning citizens of the countries that signed the treaty) the right to file for trademark protection in any country that also signed the treaty.

Suppose, for example, a hotel chain named Paradise Lodges opened in the United States. Under the Paris Convention, the owners could file for trademark protection in other countries, thereby globally protecting the identity of Paradise Lodges. The Berne Convention of 1886 gives its signatories the right to file for copyright protection of any original literary or artistic material. Here, suppose a hotel wanted to prevent other hotel chains from using its unique jingle or song that is integral to its marketing efforts. Under the Berne Convention, the hotel could safeguard its song and prevent others from using it in their advertising campaigns.

► LAW AND THE LODGING INDUSTRY

Now that you have a basic understanding of how law works, we get more hotel-specific. The only way to protect a hotel company from lawsuits is to practice preventive law. This requires management to know the common legal dangers for each department and to follow the law as closely as possible.

We must first review one other concept. *Respondeat superior* is a Latin term that literally means "let the master answer." Under the theory of *respondeat superior,* employers are liable for acts of their employees if the employees are at fault and were doing work for the employer at the time of the accident or incident. The financial implication of *respondeat superior* for a hotel is obvious—the hotel pays!

► Food and Beverage

Potential costly legal situations are present in all restaurants and bars. The most commonly litigated areas involve food safety and alcohol service.

Food Safety. Many laws governing food safety are administrative laws established by the Food and Drug Administration (FDA).[1] The FDA regulates everything from food processing[2] and labeling[3] to packaging.[4] Food and beverage sales are controlled by the Uniform Commercial Code (UCC), which lays out rules governing the sale of goods and, specifically, requires all food and beverages to be merchantable, or fit for human consumption.[5] This warranty applies whenever and wherever food or beverages are sold.[6]

In order to be protected from lawsuits, the food preparation area should be inspected regularly to ensure that no hazards exist. For example, employees should make certain that no light bulbs or food shields are broken, as glass could easily get into the food. If a server breaks a glass in an ice bin, the bin must be emptied and carefully cleaned out before it is refilled with fresh ice.

Additionally, food must be properly handled to ensure its safety. *E. coli,* bacteria often present in undercooked hamburger, can be dangerous or even deadly.[7] This threat has prompted some restaurants to cook all their hamburgers to 160 degrees to kill the bacteria.

Salmonella, bacteria that can result in severe diarrhea, fever, and abdominal cramping, is most often found in undercooked eggs, beef, and poultry, and can also be found in milk and vegetables. Cooking meats until all juices run clear and training employees to practice good handwashing techniques are imperative. Eggs pose a more difficult problem, however. In order to be perfectly safe, a restaurant would warn patrons about the possibility of salmonella before serving poached, over-easy, or over-medium eggs, hollandaise sauce, Caesar salad dressing, mayonnaise, and tiramisu. The practicality of this practice is doubtful, but perhaps a general warning on the menu would suffice.

Food and beverages must be served at safe temperatures as well. In an often discussed case involving McDonald's,[8] a 79-year-old woman, Stella Liebeck, was seriously burned when coffee spilled on her lap. After her grandson gave her the coffee he purchased from the drive-through window, he stopped so Liebeck could add cream and sugar to her drink. The entire contents of the Styrofoam cup spilled on her lap, and she received third-degree burns on over 6 percent of her body. The temperature of the coffee was initially believed to have been between 180 and 190 degrees Fahrenheit. A McDonald's quality assurance manager testified that this was the standard serving temperature range for the company's coffee. For the sake of comparison, the temperature of most home-brewed coffee usually reaches between 135 to 140 degrees.

The jury initially awarded Liebeck $200,000 in compensatory damages (reduced to $160,000 as Liebeck was found to be 20 percent at fault), and $2.7 million in punitive damages. An investigation following this verdict revealed that the actual serving temperature of the coffee was 158 degrees Fahrenheit, so the court reduced the punitive award to $480,000, or three times compensatory damages. McDonald's and Liebeck then agreed to an undisclosed settlement to close the case.[9]

The point here is that hotels need to serve safe food and beverages and to serve food and beverages safely. At the very least, customers should be advised of any known risks so they can decide for themselves whether to eat the food or drink the beverage. Food and beverage do not need to taste good under the UCC, but they must be safe![10]

Alcohol Service. Establishments that serve alcohol open themselves to a different type of legal danger. Dram shop laws are state statutes that permit an injured third party to sue the establishment that unlawfully served the alcohol. For example, let's say a bartender at the XYZ Hotel overserved a patron. The patron then got into his car to drive home. On the way home, the intoxicated patron lost control of his car and severely injured a bicyclist. Dram shop laws permit the injured cyclist to sue the XYZ Hotel for damages. Some states that have not enacted dram shop laws permit third-party suits under their common-law theories of negligence.

Increased attention to alcohol problems has caused an increasing number of states to require their managers, servers, and bartenders to be trained in responsible alcohol service.[11] Although training does not completely protect an establishment from alcohol-related suits, it may lower punitive damages.

▶ Housekeeping and Maintenance

Inspection and Repair. The primary legal dangers in both housekeeping and maintenance are related to negligence and involve lack of inspection and repair. Broken furniture, loose carpeting, slippery floor surfaces, potholes in parking lots, unmarked changes in elevation, snow- and ice-covered walkways, and faulty electrical cords can easily injure guests and visitors alike. In fact, injuries sustained from slips and falls are the most common type of lawsuit hotels encounter. Failure to regularly inspect rooms and public spaces for dangers may be grounds for a successful suit. Recovery for a plaintiff is even more likely if the

hotel knew about a danger and did not address it.

Probably the most tragic maintenance-related cases involve injuries or even death to children. The attractive nuisance doctrine holds a property owner liable for any injuries resulting from "a potentially harmful object so inviting or interesting to a child that it would lure the child onto the property to investigate."[12] It recognizes that children, because of their age, cannot fully appreciate danger.

Lodging facilities with more than one level and those who have swimming pools must be especially diligent. Children should not be able to open windows more than a few inches, and all balconies must have railings that are close together to prevent accidental falls. Swimming pools must be maintained properly and accessible only with a room key. Signage around the pool area should be large and clearly written and require adults to accompany children at all times. Children should be entirely banned from Jacuzzis and saunas.

The best way to prevent suits in these areas is to be attentive. Both housekeepers and maintenance workers should be required to follow a regular preventive maintenance schedule. Professionals can be hired to complete periodic safety audits of hotels.

Lost and Stolen Guest Property. The housekeeping staff in hotels collects an amazing array of items left behind in guest rooms. Potential privacy problems arise if a hotel contacts guests to notify them of articles they left behind. The better way to handle this is to transfer the items to a secured area, then hold them until the guest contacts the hotel. Many states have laws that govern the finding of lost property. Generally, if the owner cannot be found in a certain period, the property may be sold in accordance with the state statute.

Stolen items pose an entirely different set of challenges. All hotels are required to provide safes for guest use. Many hotels now have in-room safes that must be programmed by the guest and are reset when the guest checks out. If guests choose not to use the safe and find some valuables missing from their room, the hotel is generally not liable.[13]

All states have enacted limiting liability statues that limit a hotel's liability for guests' property losses. These statutes vary from state to state, but in all cases, a hotel must strictly comply with the requirements to be protected.[14] Common requirements include posting the availability of the safe as well as stating the maximum amount for which the hotel is liable in case of theft.

▶ Front Office

Reservations and Overbooking. Every time someone phones a hotel for a reservation, he or she forms a contract with the hotel for a room. What if the hotel overbooked or if a guest stayed over and a room was not available for a guest with a reservation? Technically, the hotel breached the contract. To avoid liability, front desk agents should check area hotels for availability if they know that overbooking is likely. In the case of a civil suit for breach of contract, the would-be guest could recover compensatory damages including payment for travel to a different hotel, the additional cost of lodging, if any, and other costs associated with the inconvenience.[15]

Due to the potential legal liability and the damage to their reputation and goodwill, some large hotel chains have completely eliminated the practice of intentional overbooking. Others continue to take the risk to ensure their hotel is completely full.

Key Control. Poor key control practices are dangerous, potentially expensive, and mostly preventable. Too often, hotel guests have been injured or even killed when a stranger entered their room using a key given to him by a front office staff member. Jury awards have been staggering, especially if the guest was raped or killed due to employee negligence and if the hotel had been put on warning for a similar event.

Good key control practices include:

- Requiring identification when issuing a replacement or additional key.
- Installing a key card system.
- Changing locks when a room key is missing (assuming the hotel does not have a key card system in place).
- Limiting the number of master keys issued to employees.
- Installing elevators that require a key to activate.
- Not having room numbers displayed anywhere on the key.
- Writing, not announcing, the assigned room number when a guest checks in.
- Not orally confirming a name and room number by telephone within earshot of a non-employee.
- Refusing to give out room information—period. The front desk agent should always phone guests to verify visitors or inquiries.
- Placing key drop boxes behind the counter on the front desk, not on top of the counter.
- Regularly inspecting room locks for damage and wear.

Although a hotel is not a complete ensurer of guest safety, it must show diligence in its duty to provide a safe environment. Employee negligence has often been the cause of violent crimes against guests, but proper training and reinforcement of acceptable key control practices can drastically reduce, if not eliminate, this type of tragedy and this type of lawsuit.

▶ Sales

Writing sales contracts is a regular part of any salesperson's job. Contracts are written for catered events, wedding receptions, conventions, meetings, and many other purposes. If one party does not honor the contract, the other party can sue for breach, so it is essential that all sales staff receive careful and thorough training in contract writing.

Everything agreed to by the hotel and the client should be written in the contract. This practice ensures that the contract is enforceable in court and leaves no doubt as to the agreement. All the contract terms must be clear and unambiguous. It is important to note that contracts are always interpreted against the drafter, so in the case of a breach, the contract would be interpreted in favor of the client rather than the hotel.

A good rule of thumb for sales staff members to follow: The more complex the event, the more detailed the contract. No detail is too small to put in writing!

▶ Human Resources

Wrongful discharge, discrimination, and Federal Labor Standards Act claims are becoming more and more commonplace. The human resource staff handles the resolution of these types of claims and many more.

Wrongful Discharge. Even in states that follow an employment-at-will doctrine, which permits an employer to terminate an employee at any time, without cause or reason, wrongful discharge suits are relatively common. Wrongful discharge claims arise when an employee is fired for reasons that are not legitimate. These wrongful discharge cases are one of two types: traditional or constructive.

Traditional wrongful discharge claims arise when an employee is unlawfully fired. An example is firing an employee for filing a workers' compensation claim, assuming the state had a statute making this discharge unlawful. Another example is firing an employee for whistle-blowing (reporting a company's illegal activities to an official).[16]

Constructive discharge occurs when an employer's actions, such as continual or severe harassment, force an employee to quit. If the hotel company is found liable, the plaintiff can receive both compensatory and punitive damages.

The wisest strategy for hotels is to develop a formal policy manual that details the possible reasons for discharge and disciplinary procedures. Employees should be thoroughly advised of these policies, and all supervisors and managers should follow the policies as closely and systematically as possible. Finally, management should document, document, and document some more!

Discrimination. Discrimination in the workplace has not always been unlawful. In fact, not until 1964 was a federal statute enacted that addressed discrimination. Since that time, other important federal statutes have been passed dealing with pregnancy, age, and disabilities. Sexual harassment suits have become commonplace recently, and they are, in effect, based on gender discrimination.

Title VII of the Civil Rights Act of 1964[17] made it illegal to discriminate against applicants or employees based on race, religion, color, national origin, or gender. The Act applies to employers with 20 or more employees, and it created the Equal Employment Opportunity Commission (EEOC) as its enforcement arm.[18]

Only in the case of business necessity or bona fide occupational qualification (BFOQ) can a hotel legally discriminate.[19] Note that the courts interpret these exceptions quite strictly, often resulting in rulings for the plaintiffs.

The Pregnancy Discrimination Act of 1978[20] made it illegal to discriminate against pregnant women unless the discrimination is a business necessity or not being pregnant is a BFOQ for the job. For example, a hotel could probably refuse to hire a woman who is seven months pregnant as a lifeguard because the pregnancy could affect her ability to act quickly to save lives.

The Age Discrimination Act of 1967 was amended in 1986[21] to make it illegal to discriminate against an applicant or an employee who is 40 years old or older. Although portraying a youthful and energetic image is important to many hotels, it is simply illegal to discriminate against an employee who is at least 40 years old as long as that employee can perform the job better than a younger employee.

The American with Disabilities Act (ADA) of 1990[22] forbids discrimination against otherwise qualified individuals on the basis of a physical or mental disability. Title I of the ADA bans discrimination in employment and applies to applicants or employees who are otherwise qualified for the position. This means the applicant or employee must be able to perform the essential elements of the job regardless of the disability. Title III bans discrimination in public accommodations (lodging facilities, for one) and commercial facilities. The ADA requires all accommodations to be reasonable[23] and to create no undue burden[24] for the business. The courts, on a case-by-case basis, determine what constitutes an undue burden.

Finally, the Civil Rights Act of 1991[25] gave plaintiffs claiming discrimination the right to a jury trial as well as possible punitive damages. The possibility of larger awards for plaintiffs has caused more employers to adopt stricter and clearer policies for selection, promotion, layoffs, and termination.

By now, most people are familiar with the plethora of sexual harassment claims that have been filed in courts. The nature of the hotel industry leaves hotels vulnerable to more claims than business in most other industries—the late and long hours of work, the privacy of hotel rooms, and the alcohol service.

Courts recognize two types of sexual harassment. The first, *quid pro quo,* literally means "this for that." *Quid pro quo*[26] claims occur when one person threatens action against another unless he or she agrees to perform a sexual act. Hostile work environment[27] claims are much more common. Here, the behavior must be sufficiently severe or pervasive, unwelcome, and not voluntary, and must affect a term, condition, or privilege of employment. Workplace behaviors found to create a hostile work environment are repeatedly sending sexually suggestive letters and notes,[28] sending risqué emails,[29] and prominently displaying nude pictures (when combined with other lewd behaviors).[30]

The best tactic for management to employ is to adopt a no-tolerance policy. This policy should be included in the employee handbook and posted conspicuously throughout the hotel. Also, employees must feel free to speak with more than one person in the event of a sexual harassment complaint, because their supervisor might be the person who is doing the harassing.

It is important to note that states and localities can adopt even stricter laws than the federal statutes. For example, some areas prohibit discrimination based on sexual orientation.[31] Others disallow discrimination based on marital status.

Federal Labor Standards Act. The Federal Labor Standards Act[32] (FLSA) mandates minimum wages, overtime pay, and equal pay for equal work, and restricts child labor.

The rate of minimum pay is established by Congress and applies to virtually all employers with annual sales of $500,000 more.[33] The FLSA, however, includes certain exceptions such as training wages[34] and tip credits.[35] Training wages at 85 percent of the minimum wage may be paid for the first 90 days to employees who are between the ages of 16 and 19 and entering the workforce for the first time. Tip credits permit employers to pay regularly tipped employees, such as servers, at a rate of pay equal to one-half of the current minimum wage. However, the combination of tips and actual wages must equal at least the current minimum wage rate. For example, if the minimum wage is $6.00 and a server receives tips averaging $3.00 per hour, the hotel could pay the employee at a rate of $3.00 per hour. If a server made only $2.00 per hour in tips, the hotel would be required to pay the server at a rate of $4.00 per hour to raise the hourly wages to the minimum $6.00 required by law. Some states or localities require a minimum wage rate higher than the federal mandate.

Overtime wages must be paid to nonexempt employees, meaning those who must be paid at least minimum wage, who work over 40 hours in one week. These wages are mandated at a rate equal to 1.5 times the regular hourly wage rate.[36] On the other hand, overtime rates need not be paid to exempt employees. The FLSA defines exempt employees as those who spend 40 percent or more of their time performing management functions or work for a seasonal amusement or recreational establishment.[37]

It is important to understand that the FLSA uses a weekly pay period to determine overtime. This is especially important to hotels who pay employees biweekly. For example, if an employee works 30 hours during the first week of the pay cycle and 50 hours during the second, the hotel must pay 10 hours of overtime for the extra hours worked during the second week of the cycle, even though the total hours worked during the pay period equaled 80.

The equal-pay-for-equal-work requirement of the FLSA requires that employers pay employees at the same rate if they perform substantially similar work that requires equal skill, effort, and responsibility.[38] Human resources must identify the core or essential elements of each position, as the courts look at these elements when comparing jobs.

Child labor laws affect many hotels, as many of the employees are young, especially during the summer season. The FLSA requires all employees to be at least 14 years old. Further, the Act restricts the number of hours that teenagers under the age of 18 can work during a one-week period. During school days, 14- and 15-year-olds cannot work more than 18 hours per week and no more than 3 hours per day.[39] Some state laws are even stricter than the federal ones, further restricting work hours for teenagers.

Violations of the FLSA are reported to the U.S. or state department of labor and can be costly for hotels. If the violations are found to be intentional, employers may be fined up to $10,000 per offense. A second offense may result in imprisonment for up to six months.[40] Many states have even stricter penalties for noncompliance.

▶ Security

While larger hotels often hire their own security personnel, smaller properties usually either outsource this function or rely on local law enforcement officials in the case of a problem. Regardless, every employee is responsible for the security of the hotel's guests. Most jurisdictions require that lodging facilities exercise reasonable care to protect guests and patrons from reasonably foreseeable crime risks.

When deciding what preventive actions are reasonable, courts look at certain factors to determine if the hotel was put on notice. Courts consider factors such as the frequency and severity of past crimes, a recent increase in the area crime rate, and security problems posed by the facility's design. Courts also look at training and personnel activities and design modifications the hotel has undertaken in the effort to keep its guests safe.

The most common areas in which crimes are committed against guests are guest rooms and immediately outside of the property. While proper key control is vital to guest room safety, so is the regular inspection of hotel room doors and locks. In a highly publicized case, singer Connie Francis was raped at gunpoint by a man who entered her room through a sliding glass door that was easily unlocked from the outside. Francis recovered $2.5 million.[41]

Crimes can also occur in hotel parking lots. Low lighting levels support an ideal environment for crimes. If the hotel is put on warning of criminal activity, meaning it is aware of crimes that occurred on the property or in the immediate neighborhood, it should take further security precautions. These precautions might include hiring additional personnel, installing more lights, constructing a fence around the parking lot, adding a guarded gate, and adding more security monitors.

Again, all hotel employees are responsible for keeping the property as safe as possible. Employees must report any suspicious activity or person to management. Guests, too, can do their part. Placards should be conspicuously placed in guest rooms warning guests to keep their doors locked, not divulge their room number, and report any concerns to the front desk.

▶ SUMMARY

Many laws at the federal, state, and local levels affect hotel operations. It is the responsibility of management to be well informed of these laws and to take preventive measures to protect its employees, guests, and owners. Because laws often change and, in the case of a jury trial, damage awards can be quite high, it is important for management to keep abreast of the constantly evolving interpretation and application of all relevant laws. The best ways to keep current are to be active in professional associations, read trade journals regularly, and utilize the resources of legal counsel.

CHAPTER 5 ■ ENDNOTES

1. Pure Food and Drug Act of 1906, 21 U.S.C. Sections 1–5, 7–15, as amended by the Federal Food, Drug, and Cosmetic Act of 1938, 21 U.S.C. Section 301.
2. See Food Safety and Inspection Service, Department of Agriculture, 9 C.F.R. Chapter III, establishing HACCP and other controls.
3. Nutrition Labeling and Education Act of 1990, 21 U.S.C. Section 343.
4. Fair Packaging and Labeling Act of 1966, 21 U.S.C. Sections 1451–1461.
5. U.C.C. 2–314.
6. See, for example, *Webster v. Blue Ship Tea Room,* 198 N.E.2d 309 (1964), in which the court held that the fish chowder was merchantable because bones are a natural part of fish and should be reasonably expected. See also *Evart v. Suli,* 211 Cal.App.3d 605, Cal.Rptr. 535 (1989), in which the court held that a jury could find that hamburger containing a large bone might not be merchantable. Finally, see *Kilpatrick v. Superior Court,* 8 Cal.App.4th 1717, 11 Cal.Rtpr.2d 323 (1992), in which the court decided that bacteria in oysters were "foreign" to oysters and, thus, made the food unmerchantable.
7. In 1993, more than 600 people in Washington got sick from eating Jack in the Box hamburgers contaminated with *E. coli* bacteria. Foodmaker, the parent company of Jack in the Box, set aside $100 million to cover lawsuit settlements. The largest single-case settlement was $15.6 million to the family of Brianne Kiner, who lapsed into a coma for 42 days after eating a tainted burger. The *Seattle Times,* October 30, 1997. The full text of the article is at http://seattletimes.nwsource.com/extra/browse/html97/jack_103097.html.
8. *Liebeck v. McDonald's Restaurants, P.T.S., Inc.,* No. CV-93-02419, 1995 WL 360309 (N.M. Dist., 1994).
9. Miller, Norman & Associates, Ltd. *Electronic Newsletter,* 1(1), April 3, 1996. Can be found at http://rrnet.com/mna/newsltr1.html.
10. The Educational Foundation of the National Restaurant Association offers both ServSafe and HACCP certification.
11. The Educational Institute of the American Hotel and Motel Association offers Controlling Alcohol Risks Effectively (CARE) certification. The Educational Foundation of the National Restaurant Association offers Bar Code certification. Also widely used is Training for Intervention Procedures (TIPS) certification. For the current laws of individual states, go to http://www.gettips.com/.
12. From 'Lectric Law Library, at http://www.lectlaw.com/def/a090.htm.
13. See, for example, *Gooden v. Day's Inn,* 395 S.E.2d 876 (Ga. App. 1990), in which an innkeeper was not liable for the theft of a bag of money from a guest's room. The court recognized that the hotel provided a safe for guests' valuables, and the guest assumed the risk of theft by failing to lock up the money.
14. See, for example, *Searcy v. La Quinta Motor Inns, Inc.,* 676 So. 2d 1137 (La. App. 1996), in which the motel was liable for $4,938.95 for property stolen from a guest's room despite a state statute limiting the motel's liability to $500. Although the motel posted notices of the statute in guest rooms, it failed to do so in the registration area as the statute required.
15. See *Vern Wells et al. v. Holiday Inns,* 522 F.Supp. 1023 (Mo., 1981), in which Vernon Wells and Robert Hughes had reservations with a Holiday Inn in San Francisco. The hotel could not honor the reservations because it was overbooked. The plaintiffs paid less to stay at another hotel but were awarded reimbursement for their cab fares to the other hotel.
16. A number of states have enacted whistleblowing statutes for both the public and

private employment sectors: California, Connecticut, Florida, Hawaii, Illinois, Iowa, Louisiana, Maine, Michigan, Minnesota, New Hampshire, New Jersey, New York, North Carolina, North Dakota, Ohio, Rhode Island, and Tennessee.

17. Title VII of the Civil Rights Act of 1964, as amended, 42 U.S.C.A. Sections 2000e-2000e-17.

18. Title VII of the Civil Rights Act of 1964, as amended, 42 U.S.C.A. Sections 2000e et seq., Section 705.

19. See *Wilson v. Southwest Airlines Company,* 517 F. Supp. 292 (N.D. Tex. Dallas Div. 1981), in which the court held that being female was not a BFOQ for flight attendants.

20. 42 U.S.C. 2000e(k).

21. 29 U.S.C. Sections 621–634.

22. 42 U.S.C. Sections 12102–12118.

23. 42 U.S.C. Section 12111(8). See, for example, *Martin v. PGA Tour, Inc.,* No. 9835309 (9th Cir. 2000), in which the court held that it was reasonable to permit professional golfer Casey Martin, who has a congenital disability, to drive a cart during golf competitions, as doing so would not alter the nature of the sport.

24. 42 U.S.C. Section 12112(b)5(A). See, for example, *Rascon v. U.S. West,* in which a U.S. West network technician suffered from post-traumatic stress disorder as a result of his service in Vietnam. The court required U.S. West to grant Rascon's leave for treatment, as doing so would be a reasonable accommodation and would place no undue burden on U.S. West.

25. 42 U.S.C.A. Sections 2000e et seq. Section 105(b).

26. The first case decided under the quid pro quo theory was *Barnes v. Costle* (D.C. Cir. 1977).

27. The first sexual harassment case to reach the Supreme Court was *Mentor Savings Bank v. Vinson,* 477 U.S. 57 (1986), in which the Court defined a hostile workplace environment.

28. *Ellison v. Brady,* 924 F.2d 872 (9th Cir. 1991).

29. See, e.g., *M.V. v. Gulf Ridge Council Boy Scouts of America, Inc.,* 1988 WL 85195 (Fla. D. Ct. App. 1988), which holds that an employer can be liable if the employer knew or should have known that a supervisor was harassing an employee and failed to take any action or even investigate the claim. More recently, in *Faragher v. City of Boca Raton,* 524 U.S. 775 (1998) a court tightened the standard and held that employers would be liable only if they knew that the harassing activities were occurring. The "should have known" was eliminated. Therefore, if employers know of harassing emails or jokes being sent to employees, they would likely still be held liable.

30. *Andrews v. City of Philadelphia,* 895 F.2d 1469 (3d Cir. 1990).

31. Currently, at least 14 states have executive orders, at least 71 cities or counties have civil rights ordinances, and at least 41 cities or counties have council or mayoral proclamations banning sexual orientation discrimination in public employment.

32. Fair Labor Standards Act of 1938, as amended, 29 U.S.C. 201 et seq.

33. 29 U.S.C. 201, Section 3(s)(1)(A)(ii). 29 U.S.C. 201, Section 6(a)(1) sets the minimum wage.

34. 29 U.S.C. 201, Section 6(d)(2)(g) and Section 14(b)(1)(A).

35. 29 U.S.C. 201, Section 3(m)(1) and (2) and Section 3(t).

36. 29 U.S.C. 201, Section 7(a)(1) and Section 7(e).

37. 29 U.S.C. 201, Section 13(1) and (3).

38. 29 U.S.C. 201, Section 6(d)(1) and 29 U.S.C.A. Section 206(d).

39. 29 U.S.C. 201, Section 3(l).

40. 29 U.S.C. 201, Section 16(a).

41. *Garzelli v. Howard Johnson's Motor Lodges, Inc.,* 419 F. Supp. 1210 (N.Y. 1976).

5.8 ASPHALT JUNGLE

Je'anna Abbott and Gil Fried

Because criminal activity can occur near major public facilities, developing risk-management solutions for parking facilities is now a focus of concern. Due to courts' findings of landowner liability for third-party criminal acts, eliminating or at least reducing the risk of any criminal activities must be an important component of any property's risk-management plan. Ensuring public safety within the facility itself is, of course, essential. Parking lots and adjacent areas, however, are equally important and should not be overlooked. This article discusses the landowner's potential liability for the criminal acts of third parties and describes some crime-abatement actions that can be accomplished through facility design. Of course, landowners should seek their own counsel for specific remedies that might fit their particular circumstances. For the purposes of this article, the term "landowner" will include owners, managers, tenants, and lessors.

► PARKING FACILITIES AND CRIME

Little in-depth analysis is available concerning criminal acts occurring in parking garages or parking lots. Crime statistics, however, clearly indicate that parking facilities are the location of much criminal behavior. A Crime Control Institute study in Minneapolis showed that many of the police departments' chronic-call locations were businesses with parking lots (Berlonghi, 1990, 259). In 1993 over six million simple assaults were reported throughout the United States, and a large percentage of those incidents occurred in parking facilities (Maguire and Pastore, 1995, 249). In 1994 parking lots and garages represented the second-most-frequent location for attempts to take property without injury and the most-frequent location for motor-vehicle thefts (Maguire and Pastore, 1996, 230). Furthermore, the same report showed 8 percent of all violent crimes, 7 percent of all rapes and sexual assaults, and 7 percent of total assaults in 1994 occurred in parking lots or garages.

Despite the risks, parking lots and garages clearly are critical to the success of major public facilities. In terms of sports events, only 5 percent of fans attending games use public transportation, while a similar number arrive on leased buses (Baim, 1994, 200). Considering the large number of professional-sports venues (both indoor and out) as well as managed college stadiums and arenas, and adding to those the number of hotels, convention centers, and similar public-access facilities, one can easily imagine that there are several million parking spaces in use by major facilities in the United States.

Security Risk. Parking facilities generally cover large areas and are open to the public. While there is plenty of activity inside a shopping mall, office building, stadium, or convention center, there is relatively little or, at times, no activity at all in the parking lot. Additionally, to make the best use of space, cars are parked fairly close together, resulting in tight, shadowy spaces between parked cars that generally are excellent hiding places for criminals. Moreover, due to the cost and availability of land, many venues rely on multi-level parking garages. Parking garages typically have poor sight lines and numerous dark corners and stairwells, making them a potential harbor for criminal activity. Patrons walking through a parking lot or a parking garage may be inattentive to such hiding places or to other individuals in the lot.

As we've just described, then, parking facilities present a significant opportunity for criminal activity. Hospitality-industry professionals, however, often rank parking lots and related facilities near the bottom of their list of risk-management concerns. For example, a 1991 survey of approximately 600 sports- and special-event professionals evaluated a variety of risk concerns (Berlonghi, 1996, 13). Few of those surveyed felt that parking-lot security was a concern. Indeed, only one in ten felt that "no parking lot security" was a problem at all (when offered that choice among a list of security issues). In other words, parking-lot security was rated lower by these events professionals than were other risk concerns such as weather conditions, insufficient budgets, one-of-a-kind or first-time events, and slippery surfaces. We wonder, however, whether those survey results indicate that parking-lot-related crimes are simply under-reported. Outside security firms or police often handle those crimes and may not report specific events to facility managers. It's also possible that landowners misunderstand and underestimate the magnitude of potential problems, perceiving crimes perpetrated in parking areas to be low risk. On the other hand, when specifically asked about just parking lots, "lack of security" represented the highest-rated concern by those same survey respondents.

► CIVIL LIABILITY

Victims of criminal misconduct are increasingly seeking compensation from the owner or manager of the property on which the criminal activity occurred (Gordon and Brill, 1996, 1–6). Such claims fall under the rules of premises liability and, typically, Gordon and Brill point out, allege a problem with the property's security system. Premise liability is founded on negligence principles. In a negligence claim, a plaintiff must prove (1) the defendant owed the plaintiff a particular standard of care, (2) the defendant deviated from that standard, and (3) the deviation caused the plaintiff's injury.

In the case of a person's injury or loss while using a parking facility, the critical question is whether the landowner had a duty to protect that individual while she was using the parking facility. A landowner normally does not have a duty to protect individuals from the criminal acts of third parties unless the acts are foreseeable. Yet if crimes on the property are likely, then a landowner has some duty to warn customers, guests, and others who may seek access to the property. A landowner incurs varying degrees of duty toward three types of people: "business invitees," licensees, and trespassers. The scope of this article is limited to the first category of individuals.

The duty owed to someone who is on the premises for a business purpose or who is providing some benefit to the landowner (i.e., a business invitee) is a high duty. The court requires a landowner to protect this person from any hidden dangers the landowner knew about, or should have known about. With respect to parking facilities, the fact that such areas may be remote does not alleviate a landowner's duty to warn a business invitee of all possible risks and, of course, to keep the facility well maintained and in good repair (see Ammon, 1993, and Maloy, 1993).

Burden of Proof. Premises liability can arise from such seemingly innocent activities as a drunk committing an unintentional battery. In one case, for example, a female spectator was walking across a parking lot after a college football game when an intoxicated man fell on her, breaking her leg [*Bearman v. University of Notre Dame, 453 N.E.2d 1196 (1983)*]. The court in this case considered whether the university had notice of the potential harm and, once the university had notice, whether it had a duty to protect its patrons. The court concluded that the university not only had notice but also owed the spectator, a business invitee, a duty of safe ingress and egress from the facility.

Another pertinent case involving a parking lot and foreseeable conduct is *Bishop v. Fair Lanes Georgia Bowling, (803 F.2d 1548, 1986)*. A group of bowlers complained to the bowling alley's management of harassing behavior by the bowlers on an adjacent lane. The management took no action and, moreover, continued to serve alcohol to the harassing group despite their obvious intoxication. At 2:30 A.M. the two parties were the last to leave the facility, at which opportunity the intoxicated group attacked the other bowlers in the alley's parking lot. The *Bishop* court concluded that a jury could reasonably find that the bowling alley's managers knew or should have known of the potential for a dangerous altercation between the patrons before the altercation occurred and would, therefore, be negligent for taking no action and failing to make its premises safe for invitees.

Thus, the key point of analysis is the existence of information that puts a landowner on notice that an assault or accident is foreseeable (Miller, 1993; van der Smissen, 1990, 3). Attaching foreseeability to seemingly random accidents further expands the specter of liability should serious criminal acts occur. In other words, don't be in denial about potential liability.

The Premonition. Notice is the key requirement for proving foreseeability. For instance, in a suit stemming from a brawl during a 1980 AC/DC rock concert, the concert promoters claimed they did not have notice because "no unruly behavior had taken place in the arena, no fights had broken out, and no drinking had been observed" (McCarthy, 1995, 7). Even though the arena had no prior problems, the court nevertheless concluded that the promoter was on notice because a police officer had investigated prior AC/DC tour stops and had knowledge of various problems at other venues, which he reported to the concert promoters. The officer also knew that when the band appeared at the arena the previous year, the band had attracted a rowdy, drunk, drug-using crowd even though apparently no specific incidents of inappropriate behavior had officially been reported [*Comastro v. Village of Rosemont, 461 N.E. 2d 616 (1984)*]. Other cases have also stressed the need for landowners to act assertively to deter criminal conduct when they have information that indicates the possibility of such conduct (see, for example: *McNeal v. Days Inn of America, Inc., 498 S.E.2d 294 (Ga. 1998);* and *Whataburger, Inc., v. Rockwell, 706 So.2d 1226 (Ala. 1997)*.

Mean Streets. If a facility's location is in an area with a significant history of assaults, muggings, and robberies, landowners may be liable if they take no steps to protect patrons from known potential dangers. That is, foreseeability issues can extend even to criminal activity in surrounding neighborhoods (Clery, 1995, 5). A classic example of such a case is *Banks v. Hyatt Corporation* [*Banks v. Hyatt Corporation, 722 F. 2d 214 (5th Circuit, 1984)*]. Hotel guest Dr. Robert Banks was robbed and shot to death as he approached the New Orleans Hyatt Hotel's front entrance. His widow and family brought a lawsuit against Hyatt, asserting that, although Banks was not actually on the hotel's property at the time of the robbery and shooting, reasonable precautions had not been taken by the hotel to protect him, and the hotel had a duty to do so. Hyatt argued that it had taken reasonable precautions to protect its guests and could not be expected to protect guests who were off the premises. Besides, the hotel contended, "Dr. Banks was guilty of contributory negligence or had at least assumed the risk by going out" (Rutherford and McConnell, 1987, 60). The jury heard testimony from both sides, including evidence that Hyatt managers were aware of numerous robberies and shootings that had previously occurred in and around the same area where Banks lost his life. Further, Hyatt employees had logged incidents, many involving weapons, in other areas around the hotel. The jury looked at the evidence of prevalent crime in the area and determined that the security precautions provided by the hotel were simply not sufficient; that the hotel did have a duty to "take reasonable care for the safety of its guests, and that the duty [extended] to adjacent areas where guests [were] likely to go and where the hotel could effectively maintain control of safety" (Rutherford and McConnell, 1987, 62). The jury awarded the Banks family $975,000.

Back to the Future. To a degree, the frequency of prior acts represents the probability that a certain risk or injury might occur (Nilson and Edington, 1982, 34–37). Yet even in the absence of prior criminal activity, landowners must take precautions to prevent reasonably foreseeable crimes. Rather than examining just the frequency of prior acts, courts are examining all the circumstances that together indicate whether a landowner should have reasonably foreseen a harm. In making this determination, the court considers the following factors (Berlonghi, 1996, 13; Gordon and Brill, 1996, 5–6):

1. The nature of the facility,
2. The facility's surrounding locale,
3. Whether the facility's records are adequately maintained,
4. The experience of the facility manager,
5. Whether the manager was aware of the criminal activity levels at the facility,
6. Security personnel's compliance with assigned patrols, and
7. The lack of customary security precautions.

Therefore, it is vital for landowners to work on the implementation of a comprehensive crime-prevention program, addressing all reasonably foreseeable criminal actions. This means that landowners should include parking-area security as a critical concern in their risk-management plans (Ammon, 1993, 117; Berlonghi, 1990, 10–11). While it is impossible to eliminate all potential suits, risk-management plans can help identify, document, and eliminate potential risks, and may reduce the prospect of being sued (van der Smissen, 1990, 3).

To determine liability, courts determine whether a property's security precautions were sufficient to prevent the criminal activity and whether patrons were warned of impending risks (allowing for the impossibility of predicting all dangerous incidents or violent behavior). When reviewing specific precautionary measures, landowners should ask the following (Clery, 1995, 5):

1. Are statistics maintained on the frequency and type of criminal activity occurring at the parking facility, and in the surrounding neighborhood (within a quarter mile)?

2. What is being done to prevent criminal behavior?

3. Do both security and non-security personnel understand and use proper security measures?

4. Is there a program in place to inform patrons and employees about security concerns?

5. Have security policies been reviewed, revised or updated, and implemented? Does such a review take place at least once a year?

6. Are there any long-range plans for enhancing security and crime-prevention initiatives?

7. What is the cost-benefit analysis of adding security measures in light of the possible harm or injury sustained by a guest, or in light of a potential jury award to a victimized patron or visitor?

Later in this paper we address common yet critical approaches to risk management (e.g., security patrols, alcohol management, crowd control). First, we discuss design factors that are often overlooked and yet can substantially affect the safety and protection that a facility can offer its guests.

► ENVIRONMENTAL DESIGN

Environmental design refers to the process of building or renovating facilities so that their physical characteristics serve aesthetic and practical functions, including crime abatement or prevention. The use of architectural details to enhance patrons' security is spreading throughout the world (Sheard, 1995, 26–28). Litigants claiming negligent facility supervision are starting to argue that an approach such as Crime Prevention through Environmental Design (CPTED), first addressed by Jeffery (1971), could have reduced criminal activities or, had a CPTED-like system been used, it would have uncovered foreseeable hazards (Gordon and Brill, 1996, 1–6).

CPTED principles. CPTED is a relatively easy and economical way to augment security efforts if incorporated at the time of facility construction. It is possible, although somewhat more complicated to implement CPTED after the fact. The general principles of CPTED include natural surveillance, access control, and controlling the environment, all of which can be used effectively to discourage violence in parking facilities.

CPTED involves carefully selecting building features, materials, and systems to meet established passive-security and active-security requirements. Passive security refers to the physical design, such as lighting, while active security refers to the human element, such as uniformed guards, intercoms, and closed-circuit cameras.

Even though CPTED has been around for almost 30 years, many parking facilities have been designed with little or no attention to security. There are several reasons for this oversight. For one thing, little time is devoted to parking-facility design in architecture curricula and the principles of CPTED are thus not widely recognized by developers and architects. Further, since the parking lot's design is often looked at as basic if not routine, that task is generally left to the newest and least experienced person on the architectural team.

Lack of planning, therefore, means that active security methods are later needed to correct problems that could have been avoided if the architectural team had incorporated CPTED principles from the start.

► CPTED Concepts

With respect to parking facilities, CPTED includes the following areas: lighting, natural surveillance, stair towers and elevator access controls, and restrooms.

The Light Ahead. Lighting is generally considered to be the most important security feature in parking facilities. It is a well-established fact that good lighting deters criminal activity and increases the public's perception that the facility is safe (which may increase patronage). Installing a parking-lot lighting system reduces the need for active security and reduces or eliminates car break-ins.

The basic principles of lighting design include illumination, uniformity, and glare. Illumination is simply the intensity of light falling on a surface. Uniformity refers to the ability to achieve a consistent level of lighting throughout the parking facility. (Consistent lighting can allow both patrons and security personnel to see into the far edges of parking stalls, as compared to seeing only the driving lanes well.) Glare reduces the contrast of an object against its background, making it difficult for the eye to perceive depth accurately. This condition is especially dangerous for individuals with weak or impaired vision. Glare can be minimized by the careful selection and positioning of fixtures in the parking facility. (For example, many light manufacturers design lights with glare shields, and those lights can be located above the parked cars rather than in the driving lanes to further reduce glare.)

One approach to achieving the desired quality of lighting is the Level of Service (LOS) approach developed by Mary S. Smith (1996, 2–9). Each level is represented by a grade, and this approach should be as familiar to parking-facility owners, city officials, and architects as it is to traffic engineers. The highest grade is LOS A, which denotes superior design; LOS B is above average; LOS C is average; and LOS D is the Illuminating Engineering Society of North America's minimum standard.

In addition to meeting industry standards and providing glare-free lighting, lights must be: reliable, easy to maintain, able to withstand the elements, and vandal proof.

Where good lighting is not available due to design or expense, concrete staining may be an alternative. Concrete staining is the process of dyeing walls, ceilings, and beam soffits white to increase brightness. This cost-effective method has been shown in some designs to increase the LOS by an entire grade. A top-quality concrete stain will last about ten years. A good white paint will have the same effect but requires constant maintenance. (One problem with white stain or paint, however, is that it may encourage graffiti. Fortunately, there are anti-graffiti stains that accommodate easy cleanup.)

Vision Quest. The second most critical security-design issue is natural surveillance, or the ability of individuals to observe their surroundings. Natural surveillance is easiest to achieve in open parking facilities; however, it is not impossible to achieve in parking garages. The most difficult garages in which to use natural-surveillance concepts are those garages that have numerous sloped parking areas. So today's designers are shying away from extensive ramps. Moreover, because openness increases natural surveillance, high ceilings and open exterior facades are now preferred as well. Clearly, an underground parking garage cannot allow for open facades. Yet there are underground-design schemes that incorporate natural light and ventilation, and that make it easy to hear a person in distress.

Natural surveillance also includes the manner in which employees direct people and vehicles within the parking facility. For example, it is best to direct pedestrians to designated areas where other people are likely to be walking (and criminals absent), rather than to let those guests wander through the parking facility. Likewise, concentrating entrances and exits makes supervision of those areas easier.

The Glass Tower. Since stairs, lobbies, and elevators are high-risk areas for personal injury, CPTED addresses such areas with an eye toward open design. One of the basic precepts of CPTED is to plan stairways and elevator lobbies as openly as the building codes will permit. The more visibility one has the better, including using exterior and open-air spaces. Where that option is not available due to weather or code constraints, glass may be a compromise, allowing both protection and visibility.

A Safe Place. If the facility is in a low-risk area, access control may seem unnecessary at first. Nevertheless, it is prudent to consider access control in the design stage, as the risk level may change with time. Screens and gates can be used to discourage unauthorized people from entering the parking area. If possible, the parking facility's design should guide vehicular traffic through gated pathways. Even if there is no charge for parking, an individual receiving a ticket and interacting with an attendant is given the impression of security. Moreover, measures such as those discourage criminal activity.

Location of security personnel is a critical CPTED component. Some landowners don't wish to "advertise" potential security concerns, and therefore locate their security personnel and parking-attendant booths to the rear of the facility. That thinking is backward; according to CPTED principles, landowners should locate security personnel or attendant booths at the front of the parking area, next to the primary entrance. Besides giving security employees a clear view of the property, it's a way for the owner to make a public statement about the importance of security and guests' safety.

The Hiding Place. Landowners should not include restrooms in parking-facility designs, especially in underground garages. Such restrooms present special security problems because they make excellent hiding spots for criminals. Many patrons recognize the potential danger and avoid using such facilities themselves, resulting in minimal traffic and thereby presenting a potentially dangerous condition for the patron who happens to use the restroom. Within the confines of the shopping mall, convention center, or office building is a much more appropriate place for public restrooms.

Secret Weapons. While CPTED generally encompasses passive design concepts, a few active ones are notable. Active design concepts include panic buttons, emergency phones, intercoms, sound surveillance, closed-circuit cameras, and trained guards. Parking facilities that failed to incorporate CPTED during the planning stage often find it necessary to use active techniques later. Although all of those features have obvious advantages, by themselves they are not an alternative to CPTED. Further, they tend to be expensive, and some are prone to abuse by pranksters and vandals.

ALCOHOL MANAGEMENT

For certain types of events, alcohol management is a key component of a risk management plan. Arrests or evictions at sports events often revolve around alcohol abuse.[1] Alcohol management policies can be enforced in several ways, including by preventing patrons from bringing their own alcoholic beverages into the facility. Also, in many venues, the sale of alcoholic beverages is terminated after a certain period in the competition (e.g., after the seventh inning or at the end of the third quarter).

Additional risk management strategies designed to reduce alcohol-related injuries and incidents include controlling tailgate parties and creating a designated driver program.[2] Finally, designating certain areas within the stadium or facility as alcohol-free zones may make events more attractive to families and other users[3] and reduce the likelihood that under-the-influence fans will disrupt or interfere with sober patrons.

[1] B. Gilbert and L. Twyman, "Violence: Out of Hand in the Stands," *Sports Illustrated,* January 31, 1983, pp. 62–72.
[2] R.E. Ammon Jr., "Alcohol and Event Management," *Crowd Management* 1, no. 4 (1995):16–19.
[3] R.E. Ammon Jr., "Risk and Game Management Practices in Selected Municipal Football Facilities," unpublished doctoral dissertation, University of Northern Colorado (Greeley, CO), 1993.

▶ OTHER RISK-MANAGEMENT STRATEGIES

In addition to CPTED methods, there are other critical aspects to risk management that are well known but sometimes overlooked. We address a few of those here.

Watch It. In a recent survey of municipal football stadiums, 86 percent of the respondents "always" had security personnel located in the parking lot before and after the game (Ammon, 1993, 117). According to that study, only 3 percent of the respondents did not offer any security protection in parking lots. In 63 percent of the stadiums, law-enforcement authorities provided protection. Private security firms, facility employees, or a blend of employees, private security, and law-enforcement agencies provided the remaining security. There is no consensus on the number of on-duty security personnel required for given situations or even about the best security measures. Risk-management professionals agree, however, that providing adequate security is an ongoing, evolutionary process that requires consistent and detailed monitoring (Ammon, 1993, 117–120; Christiansen, 1986, 46–52; Miller, 1989, 419–437; Ross, 1985, 22–29; van der Smissen, 1990, section 23, 3).

One common measure is the use of roving security patrols. In many parking lots, such as those of malls, hotels, schools, and large stores, roving patrols can be effective and useful. Wal-Mart, for example, now employs uniformed security personnel on golf carts in some regions. Wal-Mart conducted a study on store crime and discovered that 80 percent of non-shoplifting crimes occurred outside the store. A Wal-Mart in Tampa, Florida, in particular, had been the scene of 226 car thefts, 25 purse snatchings, 32 burglaries, and 14 armed robberies prior to its implementing the golf-cart idea. Once the golf-cart program was in place, however, crime outside the Tampa store was reduced to zero (Lee, 1997, E1). Although a guard with a vehicle of some sort and the necessary security equipment (e.g., two-way radio, flashing lights) can cost about $45,000 a year, there is a strong possibility that such an investment can reduce actual risk and therefore help the store avoid costly lawsuits (or, at least, give the store's security efforts some credibility once in court). Wal-Mart, for example was ordered to pay 75 percent of a $1.5-million award to a man shot in the head in a Wal-Mart parking lot (Lee, 1997, E1). With that in mind, $45,000 a year is a small price to pay to achieve better security and a reputation within the neighborhood and among customers as a safe place to shop.

The Crowd. Another risk-management technique used to protect patrons when entering and exiting a facility involves the use of crowd-management personnel (Ammon, Jr., 1995, 16–19). Traditionally, those individuals were used to inspect patrons' belongings for alcoholic beverages at the entrance to events (e.g., a football game or a concert). Today, those same workers are as likely to assist individuals (e.g., the elderly or disabled) as required and to direct visibly intoxicated individuals to a secure waiting room. Crowd-management personnel are now used for all sorts of public events, whether it be a rock concert, an exposition at a conference center, or a farmers' market at a shopping mall. In all cases, some training for the job is desirable. The number of security staff needed can vary based on the following factors (Berlonghi, 1996, 13):

1. The type of facility or event,
2. The number of entrances and exits,
3. The number of limited- and restricted-access areas,
4. The number of parking levels (or areas) in the facility,
5. The facility's capacity,
6. The facility's history of unruly behavior or dangerous conditions,
7. The time and length of the event (and, in some cases, the expected weather),
8. The number of spectators,
9. The demographic profile of the expected crowd,
10. Whether admission was free or paid,
11. Whether alcohol consumption is allowed or expected (see box),
12. The types of security personnel on duty (including municipal law-enforcement officers) and the level of supervisory expertise,
13. The presence and location of electronic protection devices, and
14. Specific requirements imposed by insurance carriers.

Sign of the Times. Signs are an important consideration in a risk-management and safety plan. In the parking facility itself, signs should assist patrons in moving quickly through the lot or garage to their destinations. Lost and confused guests—whether arriving or leaving—make easy targets for criminals.

Landowners therefore should strive to provide clear, visible signs that are both understandable and memorable so those guests can safely move to and from their vehicles. Furthermore, signs can be used to deter criminals by announcing that regular security patrols and electronic-monitoring systems are in place.

Contract. Risk-management planning should, of course, reduce potential fiscal losses arising from the misconduct of others. Appropriate contractual provisions help to protect against such losses—in this case, when dealing with parking-security personnel retained from outside firms. Contracts with independent security vendors should contain a clause promising indemnity and setting forth what specific risk-management steps are to be taken to secure the parking areas. The contract should specify the number of security personnel to be deployed, when those workers will change shifts, what quality-control measures are to be used (e.g., spot inspections), how security personnel will handle intoxicated persons, what specific actions to take should a criminal act or personal-injury event occur, and what follow-up reporting procedures are appropriate after an injury or crime.

► THE SECURITY AUDIT

The design of a parking facility and the level of security needed depend on many factors. Because there is no "one size fits all" solution, a security audit is a good way to determine exactly what security a particular facility needs.

The security audit is actually quite simple. A facility might exist that originally incorporated CPTED but that has undergone many physical changes over the years. For example, imagine a convention center that started out as a simple rectangular structure. Now, picture how various asymmetrical additions could be built into the parking lots over time. Such additions now make it impossible to view large sections of the parking lot at the same time from the same vantage point. A facility such as this should undergo a security audit to identify the security lapses caused by the building expansions. Additionally, if the facility has not changed its exterior lighting system, the older system will almost certainly be insufficient to meet the current needs of the reconfigured parking areas, including being unable to light some corners at all (Gordon and Brill, 1996, 6). A security audit will show what actions need to be taken to return the level of security to where it once was.

Witness for the Defense. One aspect of crime prevention is that the sight lines of potential witnesses (patrons, employees, security personnel, and passersby) not be obstructed or hindered. For example, there should always be a clear view into and out of any cashier's cubicle. If the windows of the cubicle are covered with posters, handbills, or other advertising or personal effects, a cashier would be unlikely to witness a nearby crime, should it occur. By the same token, the posters would also hinder a potential witness's view of an attack on the cashier (Gordon and Brill, 1996, 6).

► HESITATE, THEN LITIGATE

Protecting facility visitors and lowering the risk of liability exposure is a primary concern of landowners. To avoid liability, many landowners are not waiting for criminal activity to occur, but are implementing risk-management plans, including for their parking-facility operations. Security patrols, crowd control, signs, alcohol management, and concise agreements with independent security providers are just some of the ways a landowner can make the parking facility safer. Using CPTED concepts is another effective method of reducing crime and liability. Today, with litigation so frequent, it seems absolutely mandatory for a landowner to take all precautions possible.

5.9 WORKPLACE VIOLENCE IN HOTELS

Mark Beattie and Jacinta Gau

Violence is the leading cause of workplace fatalities in the hospitality industry (U.S. Department of Labor, 2002). Preparation for dealing with a crisis situation is vital to management and employee training. There are two categories of workplace violence: explicit and implicit. Explicit violence is specifically directed at a hospitality employee, while implicit violence occurs in a hospitality establishment but is not directed at an employee. Managers and employees need training tools to effectively manage violence prevention, crisis management, and the aftermath of traumatic incidents. Consider the following case:

Bruce Larson, Jr., was fatally shot in his room at the Orchard Inn in Wenatchee, Washington. Larson, his brother, and several friends had rented rooms at the Inn during Wenatchee's 1998 Apple Blossom Festival. The group threw a party. A friend of Larson's invited a young man named Jeremy Read to the party at the Inn. At three o'clock that morning, an altercation ensued, and Read pulled out a gun and shot Larson in the chest (*Larson v. MOA Hospitality, Inc.,* 2003).

Larson's estate subsequently filed suit against MOA Hospitality, Inc. (the corporation that owned the Orchard Inn), for breaching its legal duty to protect guests from harm. The estate alleged that the Inn should have known that criminal activity increases during the Apple Blossom Festival, should have taken greater steps to ensure guests' safety, and should have prevented Read from entering the property. The Washington Court of Appeals, citing its holding in *Wilbert v. Metro Park Dist. of Tacoma* (1998, 10), reasoned that "[W]hen there is no evidence that a business owner knew of the dangerous propensities of the individual responsible for the crime and there is no history of such crimes on the premises, criminal conduct is unforeseeable as a matter of law." The court entered summary judgment in favor of respondent MOA Hospitality because the record failed to establish that Orchard Inn recognized—or reasonably should have recognized—that Read posed a foreseeable threat to Larson's safety.

The linchpin of the Larson decision was foreseeability: An innkeeper has a duty to protect guests who are within a zone of foreseeable danger. Had the record indicated that the Orchard Inn knew or should have known that Read was dangerous, summary judgment would have been denied, and the case would have been put before a jury.

Would you have been ready for this situation? How well trained are you to deal with a violent situation on your property? Have your employees been adequately prepared to deal with such situations? Is your night auditor trained to be alert for potentially dangerous situations? Do your housekeepers have a procedure to follow if they discover weapons or other dangerous items in a room? Does your human resources manager know what to do for employees who are victims of domestic abuse or stalkers?

Workplace violence exists globally in all segments of industry. The European Commission defines *workplace violence* as "Incidents where persons are abused, threatened or assaulted in circumstances related to their work, involving an explicit or implicit challenge to their safety, well-being or health" (Wynn, Clarkin, Cox, and Griffiths, 1997). Violence is noted in reports from the European Agency for Safety and Health, the United States National Institute of Occupational Safety and Health (NIOSH), and the United States Department of Labor. The hospitality industry is among the top five most dangerous industries in which to work, ranking higher than police in prevalence of violence (Hoel and Einarsen, 2003).

According to Isaacs (2004, 13), there are four categories of perpetrator–victim relationships:

- Acts by persons who have no connection to the workplace
- Violence directed at employees by customers
- Violence against coworkers
- Violence committed in the workplace by a nonworker with a connection

Due to the constant and sometimes intense face-to-face contact in service encounters in the hotel and hospitality businesses, physical and psychological stressors are often intertwined in the conditions contributing to a violent situation (Hoel and Einarsen, 2003).

▶ MANAGING THE CRISES

Crisis management theory combines three views of workplace violence—psychological, social-political, and technical-structural—and pragmatic planning for an emergency situation is important. From each of these viewpoints, crisis situations can be assessed by examining the causes, consequences, cautions, and coping mechanisms of impending situations (Pearson and Clair, 1998). Tools for crisis management planning can then be provided in the curricula of management training programs, and hospitality employees will subsequently be prepared to deal with the aftermath of a violent situation.

The most extreme form of workplace violence is homicide. Homicide within the service sector accounted for 52 percent of all 347 workplace fatalities in that sector in 2002 (U.S. Dept. of Labor, 2004). Retail trade workers under the age of 18 were the second highest grouping of workplace fatalities between 1992 and 2000; 63 percent of those deaths were attributed to violent acts (NIOSH, 2003). Homicide is the leading cause of occupational death for women and occurs predominately in eating and drinking establishments (Levin, Hewitt, and Misner, 1996). Because statistical tracking is generalized and inconsistent, the available data are limited in scope (Hoel and Einarsen, 2003), and the limited empirical research available indicates a lack of effective training tools.

Workplace violence can devastate businesses financially, especially when litigation results from an incident. Statistics provided by Jury Verdict Research show that, "[A]ccording to the reviews of more than 3,000 verdicts rendered since 1993, the median compensation awarded by juries against hotels for [sic] assaults [was] $275,000" (Donohue, 2000, 12). A study by the Liberty Mutual Research Center for Safety and Health placed the costs of nonfatal workplace violence at $84 million between 1993 and 1996 (Hashemi and Webster, 1998).

Again, training is important; many violent situations are preventable before they escalate. The Equal Employment Opportunity Commission (EEOC) enunciated these guidelines in 1965: Establish company policies, train employees, support employees' legal rights, implement investigative procedures, and punish the wrongdoer, not the victim (Donohue, 2004). These guidelines enable the hospitality manager to spot and prevent a situation before it becomes a problem. There will, however, continue to be unforeseeable events, such as those that transpired in the *Larson* case.

► RESEARCH FOR TRAINING PROGRAM

Data collection is central to the success of a preventive training program and vital to prevention of workplace violence. The data pro-gram logs incidents occurring within some discrete reporting period, as are the data complied by the Bureau of Labor Statistics. These incidents are coded as explicit or implicit, then narrowed into "categories of interest" to facilitate incident analysis (Rossman and Rallis, 2003, 321). These categories of interest reflect the four types of perpetrator–victim relationships described in Table 5.6.

Taxonomizing workplace violence in this manner provides the foundation for a series of category-specific case studies. These case studies focus on identifying the training tools that exist to enable the hospitality employee to identify and manage a crisis situation effectively. Case study methods are based on developing a participatory relationship between the researcher and the participants through interviews and compilation of material culture such as press coverage and police reports (Shank, 2002). A series of case studies ultimately results in what Shank (2002, 55) describes as a "cumulative case study, a single topic examined through the perspectives of many different case samplings. A single complex case is built by ordering of individual cases." Information from these case studies is coded according to standardized organizational schemes for cross-case displays. The displays are conceptually ordered to highlight the three focus areas: prevention, crisis management, and aftermath. These displays are analyzed using a case-ordered effects matrix

Table 5.6 Categories of Interest by Incident Type

Relationship	Implicit	Explicit
Criminal intent (no prior relationship)	C-I	C-E
Customer/Employee	CE-I	CE-E
Coworker	CW-I	CW-E
Nonworker Connection	NW-I	NW-E

to explain different effects that each emergent theme may have (Shank, 2002). The emergent themes point out critical areas for hospitality curricula. To explain and justify the identified emergent themes and their relevance to practice, researchers rely on "assertorial" logic, which "draws on supportive evidence to convince the reader that conditions in the new circumstances are sufficiently similar to the original research conditions for generalization to be appropriate" (Rossman and Rallis, 2003, 105). Replication of this research model in other settings adds to the reliability and generalizability of the findings. Trustworthiness is maintained through methodological rigor in the interview and fieldwork procedures.

Further research focuses on the recognition of stressors that can catalyze violent situations, as well as problems such as posttraumatic stress disorder (PTSD) that victims and witnesses may develop in the aftermath of an incident. Models used in emergency responder curricula—such as the Assaulted Staff Action Program (ASAP), used with police officers, firefighters, and emergency medical technicians—may offer useful templates to develop this curriculum component (Flannery, 1998). The hospitality industry has an obligation to provide a safe and healthy environment for its guests and employees. Huntley (2004, 1) asserts, "A workplace shooting that claims the lives of an employee and a customer would be a nightmare for any company. For a retailer dependent on public perception, it's a crisis that demands careful handling." The time has come to develop curricula that enable managers to better prepare for an incident of violence and more competently address the aftermath and ramifications. Only then will the hospitality industry be in a better situation to manage a crisis such as the following before, during, and after the event.

> November 10, 2004, *Chicago Tribune:* At 2:30 A.M., Gregg P. Phillips, clad in a bulletproof vest, used an Uzi 9mm assault rifle to fatally shoot his girlfriend, Sandra Wisniewski, at the Comfort Suites Hotel in Oak Ridge, Wisconsin. A German businessman staying in the next room was also killed, and two other people were injured. Phillips took a hostage, whom he ultimately released unharmed. Police called the rampage a "domestic violence situation." Upon surrender, Phillips asked, "How many people did I kill?" (Black, 2004).

5.10 CASE STUDY: HOUSEKEEPING, ENGINEERING, AND SECURITY

► INTERDISCIPLINARY SECURITY PLAN

In 2001, as a regional manager for a hotel chain that operated three urban core hotels in a large eastern city, Denise Tomes was becoming concerned that the hotels for which she was responsible were increasingly vulnerable to threats of physical harm or financial loss to guests from a variety of criminals. She knew through news and media reports that the streets of the city her hotels operate in were becoming increasingly unsafe due to aggressive panhandling, street crime, muggings, physical and sexual assaults, and automobile-related felonies.

Because her hotels total in excess of 1,500 rooms and cater mainly to convention, corporate, and free independent traveler (FIT) markets, Tomes knew that at any given time a large number of her guests were on the streets of the city and that, additionally, due to the public nature of hotels in general, it was likely that criminals could enter the hotel properties seeking victims.

These hotels were built during the late early 1980s and, although regularly redecorated and remodeled to continue to appeal to the upscale market, they still reflected the architectural and security consciousness of their era in operational terms. This meant that guest room door locks were still of the standard keyed variety; elevators, fire stairs, out-side hotel entrances and exits, parking structures were relatively obscure and unmonitored; and housekeeping, engineering, and guest services staff training had not, as yet, reflected the security concerns of the twenty-first century.

To help her deal with the potential problems presented by the current situation, Denise Tomes called a meeting of the heads of security, housekeeping, and engineering. She challenged them to come up with a plan to increase security for the hotels and their guests without building armed fortresses. The first task of the directors of security, housekeeping, and engineering was to set forth for Tomes an analysis of the potential risks. The second is to produce a range of alternative suggestions about how those risks might be managed through the efforts of their departments and respective staffs, combined with specific recommendations for equipment and facility upgrades.

REFERENCES

Ammon, R.E., Jr. 1993. *Risk and Game Management Practices in Selected Municipal Football Facilities.* Unpublished doctoral dissertation, University of Northern Colorado, Greeley, CO.

Ammon, R.E. Jr. 1995. "Alcohol and Event Management." *Crowd Management* 1(4):16–19.

Baim, Dean V. 1994. *The Sports Stadium as a Municipal Investment.* Westport, CT: Greenwood, p. 200.

Bayou, M. E., and L.B. Bennett. 1992. "Profitability Analysis for Table Service Restaurants." *Cornell Hotel and Restaurant Administration Quarterly* 33(3):49–55.

Berlonghi, A. 1990. *Special Event Risk Management Manual.* Dana Point, CA: Event Risk Management, p. 259.

———. 1996. *Special Event Security Management, Loss Prevention, and Emergency Services.* Dana Point, CA: Event Risk Management, p. 13.

Black, L. 2004. "$1 Million Bail Set for Suspect in Hotel Killings." *Chicago Tribune,* North Final Edition, November 10, page 2, section C.

Brigham, G.H. 1955. *Housekeeping for Hotels, Motels, Hospitals, Clubs, Schools.* New York: Ahrens.

Christiansen, M.L. 1986. "How to Avoid Negligence Suits: Reducing Hazards to Prevent Injuries." *Journal of Physical Education, Recreation, and Dance* 57(2):46–52.

Clery, B. 1995. "Commercial Insurance Carriers Write Disclaimer for Crime." *Campus Watch* (1)1:5.

Dale, J. C., and T. Kluga. 1992. "Energy Conservation: More Than a Good Idea." *Cornell Hotel and Restaurant Administration Quarterly* 33(6):30–35.

Donohue, Chris Hiley (ed.). 2004. "Prevent Workplace Harassment and Discrimination." *Hospitality Law* (October):12.

———. 2000. "Study Reviews Seven Years of Hospitality Litigation." *Hospitality Law* (August):12.

Dougan, J. 1994. "Menu Engineering with Electronic Spreadsheets." *Bottomline* 8(6):15–17.

Fisher, Reed Allen. 1986. "A Documentation of Factors Which Determine Staffing Levels for the Engineering Department of a Hotel Property." *MPS Monograph*. Ithaca, NY: Cornell University School of Hotel Administration.

Flannery, R. 1998. *The Assaulted Staff Action Program: Coping with the Psychological Aftermath of Violence.* Ellicott City, MD: Chevron.

Gordon, C.L., and W. Brill. 1996 "The Expanding Role of Crime Prevention through Environmental Design in Premises Liability." *NCJ Publication No. 157-309.* Washington, DC: U.S. Department of Justice, pp. 1–6.

Hashemi, L., and B. Webster. 1998. "Non-fatal Workplace Violence Workers' Compensation Claims (1993–1996)." *Journal of Occupational and Environmental Medicine* 40(6):561–567.

Hoel, H., and S. Einarsen. 2003. *Violence at Work in Hotels, Catering, and Tourism.* Geneva, International Labor Office, Sectoral Activities Programme, WP.211.

Huntley, H. 2004. "Business Hit by Violence Must Act Quickly to Address Its Workers' Concerns." (Washington) *Tribune Business News,* November 20, p. 1.

Issacs, A. 2004. *Workplace Violence: Issues in Response.* E. Rugula, E. (ed.). Quantico, VA: Federal Bureau of Investigation, FBI Academy.

Jeffery, C. Ray. 1971. *Crime Prevention Through Environmental Design.* Beverly Hills, CA: Sage.

LaBelle, A.M., and J. Barton. 1951. *Administrative Housekeeping.* New York: G.P. Putnam's Sons.

Larson v. MOA Hospitality, Inc., 2003 Wash. App. LEXIS 1872, 2003.

Lee, L. 1997. "Parking Lots Open to Crime." *Houston Chronicle,* April 27, p. E1.

Levin, P.F., J.B. Hewitt, and S.T. Misner. 1996. "Workplace Violence: Female Occupational Homicides in Metropolitan Chicago." *AAOHN Journal* 44(7):326–331.

Maguire, K., and A.L. Pastore (eds.). 1995. *Bureau of Justice Statistics: Sourcebook of Criminal Justice Statistics—1994.* Albany, NY: Hindelang Criminal Justice Research Center, p. 249.

———. 1996. *Bureau of Justice Statistics: Sourcebook of Criminal Justice Statistics—1995.* Albany, NY: Hindelang Criminal Justice Research Center, p. 230.

Malk, M., and R.S. Schmidgall. 1994. "Financial Analysis of the Rooms Division." *Bottomline* 8(6):18–21.

———. 1995. "Analyzing Food Operations." *Bottomline* 10(3):23–27.

Maloy, B.P. 1993. "Legal Obligations Related to Facilities." *Journal of Physical Education, Recreation, and Dance* (64)2:28–30, 64.

McBer and Company. (no date). *Managerial Style Questionnaire.*

McCarthy, P. 1995. "Lessons in the Law: To What Extent Must a Venue Owner Be Held Responsible for Injuries On-site?" *Crowd Management* 1(4):7.

Miller, A.W. 1989. "Risk Management." In *Law for Physical Educators and Coaches,* G. Nygaard and T. Boone (eds.). Columbus, OH: Publishing Horizons, pp. 419–437.

Miller, L.K. 1993. "Crowd Control." *Journal of Physical Education, Recreation, and Dance* 64(2):1–32, 64–65.

Mintzberg, H. 1975. "The Manager's Job: Folklore and Fact." *Harvard Business Review* (July–August):49–61.

National Institute for Occupational Safety and Health. July 2003. "Preventing Deaths, Injuries, and Illnesses of Young Workers." Retrieved August 10, 2004, from http://www.cdc.gov/niosh.

Nilson, R.A., and C.R. Edington, 1982. "Risk Management: A Tool for Park and Recreation Administrators." *Park and Recreation* (August): 34–37.

Quain, W.J. 1992. "Analyzing Sales Mix Profitability." *Cornell Hotel and Restaurant Administration Quarterly* 33(2):57–62.

Pearson, C., and J. Clair. 1998. "Reframing Crisis Management." *Academy of Management Review* 23(1):59–76.

Riehle, H. 1994. "Table Service Restaurants Post Sales Gain in 1993." *Restaurants USA* 14(9): 43–44.

Ross, C. 1985. "Managing Risk." *Athletic Business* (June):22–29.

Rossman, G., and S. Rallis. 2003. *Learning in the Field: An Introduction to Qualitative Research,* 2nd ed. Thousand Oaks, CA: Sage.

Rutherford, D.G. 1987. "The Evolution of the Hotel Engineer's Job." *Cornell Hotel and Restaurant Administration Quarterly* 27(4):72–78.

Rutherford, Denney G., and Jon P. McConnell. 1987. "Understanding and Managing Your Liability for Guest Safety." *Cornell Hotel and Restaurant Administration Quarterly* 27(4): 58–63.

Rutherford, D.G., and William J. Schill. 1984. "Theoretical Constructs in Practice: Managers Rate Their Importance." *International Journal of Hospitality Management* 3(3):101–106.

Saied, Jamelia. 1990. "Approaches to Risk Management." *Cornell Hotel and Restaurant Administration Quarterly* 31(2):45–55.

Schneider, Madelin, and Georgina Tucker. 1989. *The Professional Housekeeper,* 3rd ed. New York: Van Nostrand Reinhold.

Shank, G. 2002. *Qualitative Research: A Personal Skills Approach.* Columbus, OH: Merrill Prentice-Hall.

Sheard, R. 1995. "Architectural Influences in Crowd Management in the U.K." *Crowd Management* (2)2:4–7, 26–28.

Smith, M.S. 1996. "Crime Prevention through Environmental Design in Parking Facilities." *Research in Brief.* Washington, DC: U.S. Department of Justice, NCJ Publication No. 157–310, pp. 2–9.

Tucker, G., and M. Schneider. 1982. *Professional Housekeeping.* Boston: CBI.

Turkel, S. 1993. "Deflating F&B Results." *Bottom Line* 8(2):8–10.

U.S. Department of Labor, Bureau of Labor Statistics. 2004. *Census of Fatal Occupational Injuries, 2002.* Retrieved August 13, 2004, from http://www.dol.gov.

van der Smissen, B. 1990. *Legal Liability and Risk Management for Public and Private Entities.* Cincinnati, OH: Anderson, p. 3.

Wasmuth, William J., and Stanley W. Davis. 1983. "Strategies for Managing Employee Turnover." *Cornell Hotel and Restaurant Administration Quarterly* 24(2):65–75.

Whataburger, Inc. v. Rockwell, 706 So.2d 1226 (Ala. 1997).

Wilbert v. Metro Park Dist. of Tacoma, 90 Wn. App. 304, 309; 950 P.2d 522 (1998).

Wynn, R., N. Clarkin, T. Cox, and A. Griffiths. 1997. *Guidance on the Prevention of Violence at Work.* Brussels, European Commission, DG-V, Ref. CE/VI-4/97.

SUGGESTED READINGS

Books

Berlonghi, A. 1990. *Special Event Risk Management Manual.* Dana Point, CA: Event Risk Management.

Cournoyer, Norman G., Anthony G. Marshall, and Karen L. Morris. 1999. *Hotel, Restaurant, and Travel Law: A Preventive Approach.* Albany, NY: Delmar.

Marshall, Anthony G. 1995. *Don't Lose Your Hotel by Accident.* Cleveland, OH: Advansta Marketing Services.

Martin, Robert J. 1998. *Professional Management of Housekeeping Operations.* New York: John Wiley and Sons.

Newland, Loren E. 1997. *Hotel Protection Management: The Innkeeper's Guide to Guest Protection and Reasonable Care.* Spokane, WA: TNZ.

Prestia, Kenneth Lane. 1993. *Chocolates for the Pillows, Nightmares for the Guests.* Silver Spring, MD: Bartleby.

Schneider, Madelin, Georgina Tucker, and Mary Scoviak. 1999. *The Professional Housekeeper.* New York: John Wiley and Sons.

Smith, Harry. 1993. *Hotel Security.* Springfield, IL: Charles C. Thomas.

Articles

Bean, Nelson R. 1992. "Planning for Catastrophe: The Fast Track to Recovery." *Cornell Hotel and Restaurant Administration Quarterly* 33(2):64–69.

Dale, J. C., and Theodore Kluga. 1992. "Energy Conservation: More Than a Good Idea." *Cornell Hotel and Restaurant Administration Quarterly* 33(6):30–35.

Malk, M., and R.S. Schmidgall. 1994. "Financial Analysis of the Rooms Division." *Bottomline* 8(6):18–21.

———. 1995. "Analyzing Food Operations." *Bottomline* 10(3):23–27.

SOURCE NOTES

Chapter 5.2, "A Day in the Life of a Director of Rooms," by Kurt Englund.

Chapter 5.3, "Housekeeping Organizations: Their History, Purpose, Structures, and Personnel," by Thomas Jones, adapted from *Housekeeping Operations,* 2nd ed., edited by Robert Martin, Copyright © 1992. Adapted by permission of John Wiley & Sons, Inc.

Chapter 5.4, "On Being an Executive Housekeeper," by John Lagazo.

Chapter 5.5, "The Hotel Engineering Function: Organization, People, and Issues in the Modern Era," by Denney G. Rutherford.

Chapter 5.6, "The Engineering Department and Financial Information," by Agnes Lee De-Franco and Susan B. Sheridan.

Chapter 5.7, "The Legal Environment of Lodging Operations," by Melissa Dallas.

Chapter 5.8, "Asphalt Jungle," by Je'anna Abbott and Gil Fried, is reprinted from the April 1999 issue of *Cornell Hotel and Restaurant Administration Quarterly.* © Cornell University. Used by permission. All rights reserved.

Chapter 5.9, "Workplace Violence in Hotels," by Mark Beattie and Jacinta Gau.

chapter six

FOOD AND BEVERAGE DIVISION

6.1 INTRODUCTION

In discussing the ways that hotel organizations have changed, we pointed out that in earlier times food played a significant role in the organizational structure and product/ service mix of hotels. It has been speculated that the preeminent role played by hotel foodservice in society became significantly diminished with the onset of Prohibition and during the 1920s. People stopped going to foodservice establishments where they couldn't "get a drink." Prohibition gave rise to competition from street restaurants that operated sub rosa as speakeasies. These restaurants were not constricted by the visible, public nature of hotel dining rooms. This diminished role was compounded in many ways by the depression years of the 1930s and the war years of the 1940s.

In general, it was difficult for most hotels' foodservice to recover from the effects of recognition lost during Prohibition. Recovery was further delayed by the Depression and the uncertainty and reordered national priorities that accompanied World War II.

In 1945, at the conclusion of World War II, well-documented major shifts in population and economic emphasis began to occur. Free-standing restaurants continued to compete effectively with hotel foodservice. Movement was away from downtown and central business district hotels. Motels and motor hotels were built on highway and freeway interchanges to take advantage of the mobility of the American family. Fast-food restaurants, too, affected the away-from-home eating habits of Americans. Consequently, many hotel companies saw as too great the cost of providing high-quality competition in the face of these forces. The net effect was that many hotel guests and operators came to believe that hotel foodservice was little more than a necessary evil. For many operations, this became a self-fulfilling prophecy, and hotel foodservice floundered for many years.

This situation has been reversed in recent years. Of the many factors mentioned earlier that forced organizational change (market segmentation, return on investment, demographic shifts, and so forth), it seems that return on investment has played a dominant role in this turnaround. The double-whammy issues of construction cost and return on investment expectations of people outside the hospitality industry strongly suggest that space devoted to foodservice should contribute at least its share to the profit structure of the modern hotel service system.

As a result, hotels seem to be willing to try anything to capture additional revenue, prestige, and competitive advantage. Among the tactics addressed in several of the articles and essays included in this section are partnering with restaurant companies, outsourcing a hotel's foodservice, new catering and beverage management strategies, celebrity chefs, and rethinking the entire role of hotel food and beverage.

▶ FOOD

Over 35 years ago, Allen Hubsch (1966) suggested a number of ways to revitalize hotel food and beverage service that have proved eerily prescient. Among his suggestions were:

- Hotel food and beverage facilities must become profit centers—no more a necessary evil!
- Food and beverage management calls for new and increased professionalism and less reliance on the old chef–maître d' model.

- Food and beverage outlets must become amenities that produce room-nights.
- Hotel food and beverage units must adopt street restaurant philosophies; merchandising, advertising, decor/ambience, menu, and service must compete with local competition.
- Food and beverage can be used to fill marginally profitable space in rentals, storage, or production areas.
- New food and beverage outlets can leverage existing facilities like storage and kitchens by spreading fixed costs over a wider sales base.

Hubsch's article, now considered a classic, is among the suggested readings for this section.

Robert H. Bosselman is the director of the Dedman School of Hospitality and Dedman Distinguished Professor of Hospitality at Florida State University. From his perspective, looking ahead to the future state of hotel food and beverage operations, Bosselman provides an in-depth analysis of the way the hotel food and beverage organization has changed over the last eight to ten years and offers tantalizing clues and examples that echo the prescriptions proposed by Hubsch. He also addresses the structure of the organization, interactions of food and beverage elements within the lodging operation, operating ratios, and potential trends in this major—and expensive—operational component.

Dominic Provenzano is director of operations of the Downtown Marriott at Key Center in Cleveland, Ohio. From the perspective of a previous position as director of food and beverage, he provides front-line detail of how Bosselman's theory of food and beverage plays out for the food and beverage director.

In a major research effort that began in 1998, Laurette Dubé, Cathy Enz, Leo Renaghan, and Judy Siguaw of the Center for Hospitality Research at Cornell University studied the best practices of hotels in the U.S. lodging industry. In their words, "The goal of this research was to surface and summarize practices of use and value to the entire lodging industry" (Dubé et al., 1999, 7). Siguaw and Enz summarize several of the practices from that study that have been developed by hotels to achieve the "strategic charge of profitably meeting customer needs" (1999, 50). The authors describe how top hotels integrate the ideas of restaurant design and conceptualization with all of the variables that affect the quality of the food and the experience for the guest.

The concept of outsourcing was mentioned earlier in the context of how some hotel companies are rethinking the role of hotel food and beverage and how to maximize investments in facilities, furnishings, and equipment for foodservice outlets. According to Strate and Rappole (1997), because hotel restaurants have often been managed as a secondary function, owners and operators are questioning the conventional wisdom about how hotel food and beverage is conceived and managed. They state that this new focus on hotel foodservice results in innovative concepts and strategic alliances with well-known restaurant brands. In their article, they analyze this trend outlining historic antecedents of the practice and use the Texas firm Bristol Hotel Company as a case study.

Few would argue that should a hotel choose to do its own foodservice, a first-class executive chef is essential to allow a hotel organization to compete effectively for food and beverage business in today's market. It is, however, fairly clear that chefs today do not have the dominant role they had a century ago. Given the importance of the food and beverage function, as established by the foregoing articles, the chef is nevertheless an integral part of the competitive strategy and a full-fledged department leader. He or she is no longer purely a technician. This individual must have developed a significant range of managerial skills to complement the technical and artistic training we have come to expect from an executive chef. The appearance of ultra-high-profile celebrity chefs adds another interesting variable to the food and beverage director's mix of challenges. If a hotel commits much of its food and beverage strategy to the talents of one famous person, it can enjoy a significant competitive advantage but also become hostage to that person's whims and personality. Many high-profile hotels in Las Vegas have "name" chef programs, and in many major population centers, top chefs have made their hotels destination venues due to their fame in the kitchen.

Patti Shock and her colleague John Stefanelli highlight the importance of the banquet and catering functions of hotel food and beverage in their piece, updated for this edition. With the increased national attention and focus on the importance of conferences, conventions, meetings, and events of all kinds, foodservice professionals who specialize in planning and serving meals and beverages to large groups of people are increasingly important. The authors note, "Although on-premise catering is generally the second-largest source of revenue for most hotels, following sleeping rooms" and "often the highest visibility the hotel has on a local level," banquets and catering are still too often ignored by hotel school curricula. In this article, we partially address this lack.

Catered affairs represent a significant contribution to the profit picture of hotel food and beverage service. The efficacy of a hotel's efforts in selling and servicing the group business market may very well be the difference between profitability of the food and beverage function and some less desirable outcome. Shock and Stefanelli explore the organization, personnel, and processes of the catering department and give the reader an in-depth view of catering executives and banquet organizations. The article includes Internet addresses for additional information.

It is the revenue and visibility importance of the catering function that makes the energetic essay by Rich Benninger so intriguing. From rising at 6:00 A.M. or so, thinking today is the day he will "get everything done" in the catering and convention services office of a 5,000-room resort hotel casino in Las Vegas, to hitting the sack after midnight, Benninger gives the reader an insider's view of life in the fast lane of Vegas catering and convention services. As executive director of catering and convention services at the Caesar's Palace Resort Hotel and Casino, Benninger is uniquely positioned to provide these insights.

▶ BEVERAGE

In any hotel that has more than one formal bar, there is usually a separate function within the food and beverage department called *bar* or *beverage management*. Ideally, that office coordinates all matters that concern liquors, beers, and wines. The beverage manager is responsibile for purchasing, receiving, storing, and issuing liquor, wine and beer inventory, and quite obviously has the managerial responsibility to control that inventory.

Additionally, the beverage manager:

- Hires, trains, schedules, and controls all beverage and bar personnel.
- Promotes the various beverage department services.

- Coordinates the requests of other departments that require beverage services—for instance, banquet and catering, room service, chefs, management.
- Assures that his or her department is in compliance with federal, state, and local laws and regulations.

The beverage manager administers or manages up to four types of bars.

The front or public bar is that in which the guest can, if he or she so desires, interact with the bartender and other service personnel. There are provisions for guest seating at the bar itself, which may be part of a restaurant or a separate room or area. Separate tables and stand-up areas may also be available for beverage service. A front bar may or may not incorporate entertainment.

A service bar is a hidden bar designed for use by the hotel's food and beverage service staff only. It may serve one or more foodservice areas and/or room service, and it is designed specifically for efficiency and economy of service. In most cases, speed is considered the essential ingredient in service bars. Service bars typically are centrally located in the back of the house, out of guest view.

Portable bars are designed for maximum flexibility and can be used in conjunction with beverage sales associated with guest activities anywhere in the hotel or on its grounds. This may be extended in resort areas to include recreational areas.

A new facility popular in many hotels is that of the in-room bar, mini-bar, or honor bar. While sometimes the responsibility for inventory of these bars rests with room service, the beverage manager in most cases is also deeply involved in their design, marketing, and control.

In many ways, the beverage manager's job can be compared, in terms of historical stereotype, to that of the housekeeper. Often the beverage manager has worked his or her way up through the ranks of beverage server and preparer and through experience, longevity, and interest becomes the beverage or bar manager. There is reason to believe that in many ways this pattern is changing. Like many other areas of hotel management, the beverage management function now faces a range of issues that are more sophisticated and complicated than traditional beverage management problems of the past. It may be that the beverage managers of the future will have to bring to their job a level of managerial, organizational, and administrative sophistication that was previously unnecessary.

The issues, responsibilities, and structural management of the hotel's beverage function are analyzed and discussed by Valentino Lu-ciani, professor of beverage management at the University of Nevada, Las Vegas. Luciani's essay, reprised here from the third edition, draws on his industry experience, research, and teaching beverage management and provides a view of how the modern beverage manager has evolved from his or her historical counterparts.

The planning, preparation, service, and management of food and beverage in modern hotels have changed significantly since the first edition of this book was written. The essays, research, and commentary presented here are chosen to illustrate the breadth and depth of this process of change. The reader who is interested in hotel food and beverage should be able to synthesize an accurate vision of the practices and realities of this major operational division of modern hotels.

6.2 MANAGING FOOD AND BEVERAGE OPERATIONS IN LODGING ORGANIZATIONS

Robert H. Bosselman

Like the lodging industry in general, foodservice in the hotel market has improved its position over the last few years. A typical characteristic is a market posting steady but not significant growth and emphasizing cost containment and innovation. As lodging foodservice competes with the multitude of commercial foodservice operations for the consumer dollar, value remains the focus of both operators and consumers. A number of studies have identified food and beverage services as a primary contributor of value to a customer's lodging experience.

This introductory essay discusses the mission and goals of food and beverage departments in lodging operations, the organizational structure of such departments, interactions of food and beverage elements within the lodging operation, operating ratios, and potential trends in the area.

▶ MISSION AND GOALS

"The goal of our food service operations is to provide the highest quality of food and service in a sophisticated, comfortable ambience, by friendly and professional staff, ensuring that every patron returns," states the Four Seasons Hotel in Las Vegas. This statement, succinct and focused, exemplifies what lodging operations nationwide are seeking. Most lodging executives identify food and beverage operations as one of the more complex areas to manage in the entire lodging arena. Lodging foodservice not only involves the traditional difficulties associated with both producing and serving food and beverages but also the performance of these functions every day, often 24 hours a day. The resulting labor costs and operational expenses prove burdensome for many lodging establishments. In order for these food and beverage operations to survive and thrive, they must draw not only guests of the lodging facility but also consumers from the external market of the lodging property. Hoteliers are analyzing their operations to identify ways of increasing the percentage of guests who stay to dine onsite, known as the *capture rate*.

In fact, the more profitable lodging food and beverage operations obtain more than 50 percent of their business from non-guests of the property. The hotel or motel guest is not a captive diner; he or she has many other opportunities for dining. Yet, in order for a hotel property to be profitable, a significant percentage of sales must be produced by food and beverage operations. To accomplish this, lodging facilities must successfully compete with the numerous chains and independent restaurants that offer a variety of services. One advantage for full-service hotels is the banquet business, which can be a major revenue producer and operate at a high profit margin. It becomes critical for lodging operators to research tourists' specific food needs and wants, and how their specific operation

can better serve these tourists. In addition, a clear, objective analysis of local competition is necessary to determine the segment and genre in which the hotel can compete and succeed.

If the hotel is competing with an established local competitor, then the hotel food-service operation must outdeliver on all levels of quality, service, and ambience. In a large hotel, it is also necessary not to compete directly with another unit in the same hotel. Units must be diverse to give different segments of the market a choice; the ideal outcome is that hotel and local guests choose to dine in one of the hotel's offerings. A strong food and beverage program that delivers a high-quality product and experience can be used as a competitive advantage as well as a sales tool for the lodging facility.

Many hoteliers choose not to compete in this environment. Instead, their strategy is to eliminate food and beverage operations altogether, or to lease food and beverage operations to outside companies, either chain-operated or an independent restaurant (see the article by Strate and Rappole elsewhere in this section). In particular, food and beverage sales in motels and motor-hotel restaurants continue to decline as a percentage of overall sales when compared to full-service hotels, primarily as a result of an increasing number of lower-priced lodging operations offering free breakfast and no other meal service. However, that free breakfast has become a competitive positioning statement for the property. Guests now expect it, and they expect quality, yet such lodging facilities must maintain their cost structure.

While the reader may start to think that hotel food services are not major players in the overall foodservice market, 2005 projected sales were estimated at $25 billion, according to the National Restaurant Association. There are five major hotel chains whose foodservice sales per hotel average more than $2.3 million. At the top lies Sheraton Hotels, whose properties average well over $4.6 million in foodservice sales. It should be noted that a number of convention/resort hotels could do well over $30 million in annual food and beverage sales. Clearly, foodservice professionals have as much or more opportunity for success as in other segments of the foodservice industry. With potential sales like those noted, lodging food services remain a critical partner with respect to both the revenue and profit of the property. A smart, resourceful manager makes the foodservice operation unique, thus attracting additional patrons to the lodging establishment. Thus, foodservice can be looked on as a means of gaining competitive advantage over other lodging operations.

The field of lodging has a long history of serving people food and drink during their travels. From the earliest days of the Roman Empire, when people traveled on foot, on animal, or in vehicles drawn by animals, to the modern age of air, rail, and car transportation, hotels and inns provided for their needs. In fact, early hotels were usually the center of community activity and often the only place one could eat away from home. The glamour years of the late nineteenth and early twentieth centuries produced grander hotel properties, the so-designated palaces of the people, which solidified this perception of hotels as centers of public entertainment and as sources of food and drink for guests. This reputation continued well into the twentieth century, as hotels became the logical place to meet for entertainment and business discussion. Foodservice operations independent of hotels were rare even in the larger urban centers. It was not until the post–World War II era that independent restaurants and restaurant chains grew in both number and influence over the customer. As we enter the twenty-first century, lodging foodservice accounts for approximately 7 percent of the total foodservice market. From total domination of the market to its role as a secondary player today, lodging foodservice has undergone dramatic change. As properties struggle to decide whether or not to offer foodservice and, if so, the number of foodservice units and the level of service to offer, future managers must recall what the goals and mission of the foodservice operation should be:

1. To provide the appropriate level and degree of food and beverage service to the property's guests.

2. To support the overall goal(s) of the property.

3. To assist the property in gaining a competitive advantage over other lodging establishments.

4. To function efficiently and effectively in order to produce a profit.

► ORGANIZATIONAL CONSIDERATIONS

The organization of foodservice departments within lodging establishments varies depending on the type of facility and, in the case of chain operations, corporate policies. Due to this degree of variety, categorizing lodging properties can be difficult. For example, a property located in a resort environment may also have extensive convention space. A property known primarily as a convention hotel has room enough to accommodate large groups. Foodservice outlets likely include restaurant(s), lounge(s), banquet facilities, and room service. A resort property provides all the amenities that focus on guest entertainment and relaxation, with emphasis on specialty restaurant(s) and room service. Unique problems may face resort managers with respect to seasonality of operations, location, and layout. The latter points are important because the property itself, as well as individual food and beverage outlets, may be located in hard-to-access areas, which affects operational expenses.

An example of a resort is the Renaissance Sea World Resort in Orlando, Florida. David McKeever, director of restaurant operations, is responsible for three full-service restaurants as well as banquet and conference services. David notes that his facilities aim for an upscale perspective, highlighted by regional and contemporary menu influences and characterized by upscale wine sales. He identifies the property clientele as wanting a relaxed environment in food and beverage services.

Lloyd Wentzell, vice president of food and beverage, provides a slightly different view of these services at the Riviera Hotel and Casino in Las Vegas. He notes that the food and beverage operation there is an amenity. The buffet and coffee shop are for in-house guests, and the (three) gourmet rooms are for guests including those who come to the shows at the hotel's four entertainment venues. The snack bar in Nickel Town is used to bring visitors from nearby properties. Room service is a necessary loss leader used to maintain resort hotel status.

Airport properties have grown with the increase in air travel. Quite often, travelers choose these properties based on the convenience factor. While occupancy rates are high during weekdays, weekend business tends to drag. There does not appear to be an emphasis on food and beverage operations in such facilities.

Economy properties are coming off a period of significant growth. This is the segment that often rejects offering foodservice operations. Midscale brands such as Ramada Inn and Hampton Inn are noted for their aggressive growth in building new properties with little or no food services. Additionally, significant growth is expected in the lower-tier extended-stay market. However, some properties are attempting to redefine the concept of value to the customers. An example is Courtyard by Marriott, which combines comfortable lodging with downsized foodservice operations. All-suite properties remain one of the hottest concepts in the lodging field. While some units contain kitchen facilities, many offer complimentary food and beverage services—particularly at breakfast—for the busy traveler.

The Four Seasons Hotel in Boston demonstrates one example of how a hotel food and beverage operation can be organized. The food and beverage division has four departments; food preparation, catering sales, stewarding, and sales outlets. The latter has five operations: private bars, room service, a full-service lounge, a fine dining restaurant, and banquet facilities. Each department has line employees who report to assistant managers who, in turn, report to department heads, who then report to a director of restaurants and bars, who, in turn, reports to the director of food and beverages. Regardless of the size of the lodging facility, food and beverages must be produced and served. However, the increased size and complexity of some operations makes it critical that managers communicate well with all levels of employees. The trend may be toward flatter organizational structures as well as to completely separating out certain functions of the food and beverage area.

► FOODSERVICE PERSONNEL

Who are the key people in the organization of lodging foodservice? Our attention here is on the operational players, those individuals most often responsible for the work of pleasing the guest while holding the line on costs.

In most kitchen operations, an executive chef is responsible for management related to production activities. Depending on the size and complexity of the operation, the executive chef may actually perform little in the line of food production. In a small operation, the chef may also be a part owner and perform most of the food-related functions. One of the exciting trends today is the use of big-name chefs in hotel food services, often allowing them to create a signature room in the lodging property. The proper positioning of the restaurant in a niche market can also have a residual positive effect on average rate and occupancy. Marketing a celebrity chef as a primary component of a hotel may yield a competitive advantage among that specific hotel's competitive set.

With the trend toward downsizing operations, it would be the rare organization in lodging foodservice that employed numerous back-of-the-house employees engaged in a single function. Some examples of the past might include the sous-chef, the executive chef's assistant and often the staff supervisor; the saucier, or sauce cook; the garde-manger, the cook in charge of all cold food preparation; the chef pâtissier, or pastry chef; and the banquet chef in charge of catering. Each of these positions would have had assistants. In addition, other jobs were steward, purchasing manager, storeroom clerk, and several janitorial staff.

Some examples of how lodging foodservice is organized today have been reported in studies of best practices. The Boulders, located in Arizona, created a food forager position to improve quality of products. Menus are designed around foods actually located, which saves time spent trying to find ingredients to fit a menu while providing guests with a unique dining experience. The Greenbrier, in West Virginia, designed a formal three-year culinary apprentice program. This allows the resort to attract a continuous supply of talented chefs as well as create a cooking school for guests (thus adding value to the guest experience). The Pierre in New York City utilizes an independent consultant to manage purchasing. This frees the chef to focus on food production and has led to reduced food and labor costs.

The dining room can have an equal degree of complexity, depending on the operation. There may or may not be a supervisor, often called a host or hostess, or a maître d'. This individual greets guests and supervises the waitstaff. At the actual service level are the captains, servers, bussers, and cashiers. If a lounge operation is present, so are bartenders and cocktail servers. As one can readily imagine, working as a team is imperative.

In today's cost control environment, food and beverage operations are trimming payrolls and consolidating job responsibilities to cut operational expenses. This cross-training of staff allows an individual to take on multiple responsibilities. The Breakers Hotel in Palm Beach, Florida, utilizes a cross-training program that allows the property to completely reorganize its staff annually, facilitating mobility of staff as well as improved service to guests. In the past, it was not uncommon for the food and beverage operation to employ workers around the clock, as most items were made from scratch. With modern equipment and the use of more convenience food items, such as preportioned meats, it is now rare to find butcher shops or pastry shops in hotels. Again, hotel operations are concentrating on quality, value, and cost. If the property can find a product on the market, the trend is to purchase rather than make from scratch.

There has been increased attention on the education level of chefs in lodging operations. In recent years, traditional culinary arts programs have expanded from two-year to four-year education programs, while traditional four-year hospitality institutions have expanded their curricula into culinary arts. Under the direction of the author (when he served there as department chair), the Department of Food and Beverage Management in the Harrah College of Hotel Administration at the University of Nevada, Las Vegas, was the first four-year hotel administration degree program to offer a bachelor of science (B.S.) in culinary arts management. People who earn this degree can command rewarding pay, but much is expected of them as well. They must be able to produce high-quality products utilizing minimal resources. They must also direct all activities in the back of the house, including the training and supervision of employees. Their responsibility is the means by which a food and beverage unit produces profit for its parent institution, the lodging facility.

▶ OPERATIONAL INTERACTIONS

Hotels are complex institutions divided into separate operational areas, among them rooms, engineering, administrative, accounting, human resources, and sales, in addition to food and beverage. These divisions interact in every imaginable way 24 hours a day to produce the guest experience. It is necessary that the strategy or mission of the operation as a whole be communicated to all levels of the organization to ensure a consistent guest experience. In order to maintain continuity within the organization, all strategic moves must be consistent with the mission of the operation and build toward the long-term goals of profit, quality, guest satisfaction/loyalty, and employee retention and growth.

Perhaps the best way to describe this interaction is to characterize food and beverage and other departments as mutually dependent. Direct interaction can be observed between food and beverage and the front desk with respect to specific guest service issues. Direct interaction can also be observed with the sales department and the convention/banquet department. Indirect interaction between departments comes from areas such as rooms, in the form of overnight cleaning; engineering, in the form of maintenance and repair; and accounting, in the form of financial analysis. For example, food and beverage team members must communicate their reservation needs or restrictions to concierge and bell staffs. One example is announcing a new menu that has been initiated, or that a special activity will occur. Likewise, food and beverage depends on information submitted to them regarding occupancy, VIP guests, or demanding guests.

No matter the type of lodging property, it is critical for management and staff to meet regularly to discuss department interaction and better ways to service the guests. Another example with a special case to consider is a casino resort hotel. Historically, food and beverage has been perceived as an amenity for players. The casino and slot departments are continually in contact with food and beverage units, particularly room service, to request special arrangements for their clients. These requests might range from amenities being delivered and set up in the guest room to supplying the gaming area with special foods and drinks.

The type of client sleeping in the guest rooms significantly affects the revenue-generation potential of a lodging food and beverage operation. Because a majority of food and beverage customers may be hotel guests, it is important to book the right type of people into the hotel. The sales mix of the hotel is a delicate balancing act. Sales staff must make sure they are contracting groups that maximize hotel revenue per available room (Revpar). Do you know the utilization rate of the food and beverage outlets for the various market segments? Do business travelers eat more or drink more than the leisure/pleasure market? Which convention uses the food and beverage outlets more than others? The ballroom space must be managed closely to ensure that the best business opportunities are maximized from the rooms and food and beverage perspectives. Groups with high demand for banquet space must meet room-night obligations at a given rate and provide the necessary revenue in catering. Local niche opportunities must be explored when there is an opportunity to sell the ballroom when hotel guests are not utilizing it. It is possible that local catering sales can be a larger portion of the total catering dollars, particularly when the rooms mix changes to a larger proportion of transient guests. Your management and sales staff must know the answers to these types of questions. Sales personnel cannot just be concerned with achieving room-night quotas or generating revenue; they must know the impact of their decisions throughout the

hotel and how they affect its profitability. When developing annual budgets, the team must take into consideration seasonality, group business and its particular needs, transient guests, and regional events that may affect guest occupancy and mix.

The food and beverage manager must know who the customers are and how many patrons to expect. Information about hotel guests such as house counts, market mix reports, group commitment reports, and rival/departure patterns assists the food and beverage team in making decisions on scheduling, food ordering, and whether or not to close a particular outlet.

Every hotel employee is a sales agent for the property's food and beverage outlets. The staff must be trained to refer and recommend hotel services to guests. It is clear that the quality of food and beverage operations can affect overall hotel operations and profitability. Quality is particularly important for convention hotels and resort hotel properties. Guests come to such properties for specific purposes. Therefore, a reputation as a high-quality food and beverage operation will attract customers. These operations generate word-of-mouth advertising from travel agents, corporate meeting planners, cab drivers, airline companies, and tourism offices. While this reputation can attract guests, it is the responsibility of management to plan effectively for their needs.

Imagine you run a hotel restaurant, operate room service, provide food and beverages for employees, and now are also catering several types of meals/functions for different groups. Recall that the goal of the hotel property is to service its clientele. Therefore, each area of the hotel must complement the other in providing the service. Managers, particularly in food and beverage, must communicate effectively and train constantly in order to maximize the goals of the lodging operation.

▶ OPERATING RATIOS

Many operating ratios are utilized by the food and beverage department. Controlling operational expenses is perhaps the biggest challenge facing food and beverage managers. Managers at every level must be controllers. In addition, it is the duty of every food and beverage manager to maximize the revenue and profit potential of his or her specific unit. An empty seat cannot be resold later. If a restaurant has a significant drop in sales on a given day or time of year, a strategy must be developed and implemented to fill that void and thus provide a new revenue source. Most hotels' food and beverage operations have a minimum fixed cost that must be maintained in order to meet the needs of the hotel.

It is increasingly difficult to make a profit and provide high-quality service when revenue does not support the labor necessary for even minimum levels. The challenge is to maintain a strong revenue flow so that efficiencies of scale take place. The kitchen is the highest cost producer of any part of the food and beverage operation. The challenge of the kitchen manager or chef is to deliver a high-quality product, yet maintain close controls on food and labor costs.

The key for success in this area is to have a clear understanding of production management so as to reduce waste and spoilage, create dynamic menus that drive business, and continue to build an ongoing training program to instill the best practices into line associates. In very large establishments, the kitchen manager or chef may find himself or herself using a computer more than a knife.

A number of club managers the author recently spoke with noted that operating ratios are important to keep expenses in check, as well as to monitor improvements or income contributions from one area of the property to another. They identified food cost and labor cost percentages as most important. A casino hotel controller from Las Vegas utilizes operating ratios such as cost per cover, percentage of sales, cost per employee, utilization rate (number of covers/number of guests), revenue per occupied room, sales per hotel guest, average check, sales per employee, table turnover, inventory turnover, revenue per square foot, revenue per seat, cost per square foot, return on investment, covers per employee, average covers per day, and average sales per day. Industry professionals note that ratios are only tools and that it is more important to have a clear idea of what needs to be measured and the impact of each variable on the overall operation.

What we can observe is that food and beverage managers utilize ratios to determine whether or not they have been successful in generating revenues and minimizing expenses. Such ratios can then be compared with figures from prior accounting periods of that operation. Let us examine some of the more common ratios.

Food and Beverage Sales per Available Room

$$\frac{\text{Total Food and Beverage Sales}}{\text{Number of Available Rooms}} = \$$$

Food and Beverage Occupancy

$$\frac{\text{Number of Covers}}{\text{Number of Seats}} = \text{Turns}$$

Sales per Available Seats

$$\frac{\text{Food and Beverage Sales}}{\text{Number of Available Seats}} = \$$$

Average Check

$$\frac{\text{Food and Beverage Sales}}{\text{Number of Covers}} = \$$$

Ratio of Beverage Sales to Food Sales

$$\frac{\text{Beverage Sales}}{\text{Food Sales}} \times 100 = \%$$

Food Cost Percentage

$$\frac{\text{Food Cost}}{\text{Food Sales}} \times 100 = \%$$

Labor Cost Percentage

$$\frac{\text{Food and Beverage Labor Cost}}{\text{Food and Beverage Sales}} \times 100 = \%$$

Note that costs are usually stated as a percentage of sales. These percentages can then be compared with those of previous time frames. While the dollar values for costs are necessary to determine the percentages, it is difficult to compare dollars to dollars expended per time period. Measures of revenue often tell management how much effort food and beverage staff have expended for the benefit of the operation. Those ratios combining food and beverages can be broken down by category. Note from the comments provided earlier that ratios utilized vary depending on the operation. Your goal as manager is to gain the best information available to assist you in making decisions.

Individual units, such as catering, room service, coffee shop, and sit-down restaurants, have different as well as similar factors. For example, average check is common to all, while a measure of seat turnover applies only to the coffee shop or the sit-down restaurant. The accumulation of information should be as easy as possible for management. The use of point-of-sale technology enhances this process. Technology can also be applied to storeroom management, including inventory controls and purchasing. Labor management technology has contributed to attaining optimal staffing guidelines based on forecasts, group needs, and position qualifications. Use of the Internet is now a standard tool in marketing strategy, where the guest may book a reservation directly online. Managers should not spend all their time determining what the ratios are or what they mean. Management should be able to quickly ascertain what has occurred in the operation and take corrective action, if necessary.

► TRENDS IN LODGING FOODSERVICE

In presenting trends, we must exercise caution, as what works in one food and beverage operation may not in another. Recall that the goal of lodging food and beverage operations is to meet hotel guests' desires, with attention paid to price, value, quality, service, and atmosphere. Food and beverage managers are wise to study similar hotel operations as well as restaurant operations. Guest surveys are also essential to determining customer desires. Your objective should be to discover what customers want and need in terms of food and beverage products and delivery, and how your operation can better serve them.

Hilton Hotels has added to its Vacation Station program. It provides children a canvas bag with an insulated compartment to hold lunch or snacks, with a mesh-net drink holder on the side. Parents can order from a variety of Snack Pack selections via room service for pickup later. Radisson Hotels and Resorts teamed with a culinary school and supplier to create a low-carbohydrate menu. Sheraton Hotels has also introduced a Lo-Carb Lifestyle program in its restaurants, banquets, room service, lounges, and to-go snacks.

Holiday Inn Hotels and Resorts is testing use of a wireless electronic menu that allows a customer to view a list of options updated in real time. The consumer can find related nutritional information while searching for information about the hotel itself. Also in an experimental phase is their new prototype restaurant, Kem's Café, named for founder Kemmons Wilson. Guests can use the e-menu to order from a choice of comfort food.

Back at the Breakers Hotel in Palm Beach, management renovated their existing formal dining and casual dining restaurants, developing single-theme outlets to give guests choice of cuisine rather than choice dictated by guest attire. This has led to stronger hotel restaurant identities and an increased capture rate. Peacock Alley in New York's Waldorf-Astoria Hotel replaced appetizers and main courses with a variety of dishes of in-between portion sizes and added more wines by the glass and half-bottle to complement the expanded possibilities of the new menu. This version of a tasting menu was developed in response to diners, who kept substituting dishes from the regular menu.

The concept of branding has also affected hotel food and beverage operations. For example, Country Inns and Suites has co-branded with established restaurant concepts (see Chapter 6.5 by Strate and Rappole). The restaurants average approximately 20 percent of their business from hotel guests, and this cooperative arrangement eliminates the capital cost of building a restaurant on site. Westin has teamed with established steakhouse chain operators The Palm and Shula's Steak House in its properties. Doubletree also developed specialty steakhouses, but with their own proprietary concept, Spencer's.

Another example of branding your own concept comes from the Riviera Hotel and Casino. They created Hound Doggies as an outlet that targets the walking traffic on Las Vegas Boulevard (the Strip). The location is only a few steps off the sidewalk and has been successful in drawing nonstaying guests into the property. They implemented this concept only after studies identified walking traffic as a potential market. The goal for the outlet was quite basic: Bring people in the door. Through the use of a 1950s theme, high-quality food, and low prices, the Riviera has exceeded its expectation of nonstaying guests. As the unit was not created specifically as a revenue-generating center, success is measured by its impact in other areas, such as increased slot play.

Some Four Seasons Hotels and Regent Hotels and Resorts are promoting the strategic use of a single food and beverage outlet coordinated with the concept of cuisine choices. This strategy has resulted in a more focused approach. In properties where it is implemented, the strategy has resulted in significant capture rates as well as increasing local traffic (nonstaying guests).

One of the more exciting trends in lodging foodservice operations is in hotel beverage operations, specifically hotel bars. In many large-city properties, hotel operators have found such facilities to be considerable moneymakers—as much as 50 percent bar profit margin. These bar operations are clearly driven by the youth and vitality of the new Internet, or millennial, generation. The bars are seen as lively gathering places where business and personal time merge. Lodging chains are taking notice of such activity. Starwood purchased a stake in a company that initiated a popular bar chain. Even the names of the bar operations reflect a youthful vitality associated with the location: Whiskey Blue, Skybar, and Whiskey Rocks. One concern associated with these bar operations can be their impact on traditional hotel guests. Many outsourced bar operations do not extend traditional amenities to lodging guests, such as billing to room, preferred seating, and even reservations. In fact, the clientele of the bar may be quite different from the hotel guest.

In order for your lodging food and beverage operation to succeed, sound marketing and keen observation of what people want must accompany high-quality food and service. While consumers choose your hotel for specific reasons, such as price or service, they seek more creativity in a food and beverage operation. If you cannot attract the hotel guest, you will find that attracting clientele from the local area is also difficult. Quite likely, each hotel has its own character that suggests a variation of food and beverage operations in different markets. Management is wise to remember that a food and beverage unit in a hotel serves the interests of the hotel as well as its own.

While some limited-service lodging operations have entered into cooperative relationships with foodservice companies, the concept holds significant potential for the appropriate market. One example is where the hotel's foodservice operation is marginal at best. The lodging property can concentrate its resources on rooms and lease the food and beverage service to an identifiable brand. Hotels should be aware, though, that restaurant com-

panies, for example, might not be familiar with room service or catering. In an extreme case of moving away from foodservice, some lodging properties limit services to in-room minibars and microwaves, with limited food items available for sale in the gift shop. The gift shop may even be transformed into a convenience store.

We have observed that some properties sense a rebirth of simplicity in food and beverage operations. A good example is a coffee shop. Over the last ten years, the coffee shop concept has been abandoned in favor of higher-priced dining. But in letting a coffee shop be a coffee shop, you tap into the consumer's consciousness of value as well as menu variety and fast service. While some find the concept boring, consumers often seek the comfort of knowing they can get a good meal at a good price day after day in your operation.

Room service is also seeing significant changes. In some properties, the concept of room service has been eliminated, while in others it has been revived. For example, menus are limited to particular concepts, such as pizza or Asian food. Food items are packaged to appear as though they came from a freestanding restaurant. In some cases, the lodging property has an agreement with a local restaurant to provide the room service. Some lodging properties even list the room service phone number under the name of the food item (for example, pizza). The key, again, is to know your clientele. But the move to simpler menus, accompanied by lower prices, could bring room service back as a major contributor to overall operations. Some larger hotel operations are focusing on a tighter menu and faster service through room service. For example, one property has converted a freight elevator into a mobile kitchen unit, thereby allowing service delivery within minutes of an order. While this option may not be possible for all hotels, it again points out knowing what to offer your specific clientele. Room service has seen a resurgence in certain lodging properties, primarily as a result of guest lifestyle. With more adults working and engaged in active lifestyles, convenience and accessibility become paramount. Room service fits the criteria of convenience and accessibility.

▶ CONCLUSION

As you can see from the foregoing discussion, it can be difficult to pinpoint which trends may be most important to any individual hotel. What we *can* say is some lodging properties, notably chain properties and large-size properties, seem to be differentiating themselves to provide excitement for their food and beverage clientele. These operations are essentially reinventing themselves in order to keep fresh and provide creative food and beverage opportunities for staff and guests. These operations view foodservice as integral to the overall success of the lodging operation.

On the other hand, we can also see a trend toward reduced or even nonexistent foodservice, primarily in smaller properties and the lower-end chain lodging properties. These operations view their business as strictly lodging and leave foodservice to someone else, now often a well-known national brand restaurant.

It should be obvious from reading this overview that an emphasis on cost control is likely a key strategy for lodging foodservices. With increased competition from other foodservice operations, hotels are finding it more difficult to generate revenues and increase customer counts. Attention to value and service is of significant concern to consumers. Managers of lodging foodservice must utilize better control tools, such as sound forecasting techniques and menu analysis. Banquets, catering, and room service hold the most potential for profit generation in lodging foodservice. These functions allow management the best opportunity for accurate forecasting and staffing. Beverage areas, such as lounges, continue to be profitable despite a trend toward less alcohol consumption throughout the population.

The probability of producing profit in hotel restaurants depends on their type and size. There is no reason why a hotel cannot do well, but attention to detail is often lacking in some operations. It is clear that lodging foodservice offers managers unique challenges in the dynamic world of foodservice management. Food and beverage operations may not be the major focus in a lodging property. However, they may have significant impact on the customer's perception of the quality of the entire property. Therefore, food and beverage operations in lodging properties can serve to differentiate top performers in the crowded lodging market and enhance guest loyalty for the specific property.

6.3 AS I SEE IT: HOTEL DIRECTOR OF FOOD AND BEVERAGE

Dominic Provenzano

A food and beverage director in a major lodging property must be ready for a variety of tasks each and every day. In one sense, this position requires two different individuals to keep the operation moving forward. One is the leader, or strategic visionary, looking ahead to the future of the operation (that may be just one or three months, or it could be one full year out). The other is the day-to-day manager, constantly moving through the organization to be sure all events are proceeding according to plan and guests are treated beyond their expectations.

In this position, I have the responsibility of overseeing several departments: culinary, banquets, room service, specialty and theme restaurants, and all private bars. While an ideal day is spent on planning, more often than not I find myself in discussion with staff or guests. Regular meetings include the following examples:

- (Daily) *Banquet Event Orders (BEO) Meeting.* Purpose: To go over BEO for the day.

- (Weekly) *Food and Beverage Meeting.* Purpose: Review operations with department managers.

- (Weekly) *Executive Meeting.* Purpose: Overview operations with all executive committee members and the general manager of the hotel.

- (Weekly) *One-on-One Meetings.* Purpose: Meet with individual food and beverage departmental managers to establish goals and cover issues specific to each department.

- (Monthly) *Staff Meeting.* Purpose: Review operations by all department managers and general manager of the hotel.

- (Monthly) *Employee Recognition Meeting.* Purpose: Honor employees of the month at a luncheon.

To gain a better appreciation of the job of a director of food and beverage, we should look at an actual job description. Again, recognize that all job descriptions are written as an ideal, and every day brings deviations from that ideal, given the unique daily circumstances found in any dynamic lodging property.

▶ Position: Director of Food and Beverage

Reports to: General Manager

Objectives:

1. Meet and exceed guests' needs and expectations by ensuring proper service standards, providing quality food and beverages, and managing all aspects of operations, resulting in an increasing guest satisfaction index (GSI) and decreasing guest complaints.

2. Provide all guests with the highest quality food and beverage experience by working as a team with all food and beverage

outlets ensuring prompt, courteous, and professional services, resulting in increasing employee morale, decreasing employee turnover rates, and lowering employee service times.

3. Seek profitability in the food and beverage department by decreasing all costs, maximizing sales in all outlets, achieving budget and profit guidelines, creating promotions, and meeting and/or exceeding long and short range goals.

Specific Operations Functions:

• Provide the highest quality in food, beverage, and service in all food and beverage outlets. Includes at least one daily walk-through of all food and beverage areas.

• Maintain existing programs and develop new programs ensuring the highest quality of food and service. Consists of daily talks with all staff and managers, reviewing plate-ups in different outlets.

• Maintain a high-quality hotel image through effective housekeeping and sanitation in the F&B operation.

• Maintain physical security for all F&B property and inventories.

• Maintain knowledge of local competition and current industry trends. Includes changing menus based on seasonality, product availability, and input from staff.

Specific Management Functions:

• Direct and coordinate the activities of all assigned personnel and departmental responsibilities. Examples are daily contacts with staff and performance reviews.

• Maximize sales potential through aggressive marketing of each F&B unit. Includes ongoing monitoring of business levels and review of daily performance.

• Achieve budgeted sales and maximum profitability.

• Maintain an appropriate level of community public affairs involvement.

• Maintain fair wage and salary administration in the department in accordance with division policy.

▶ Guest Relations

A major part of my job involves maintaining warm, hospitable guest relations in all guest contacts and positive employee relations in a supportive environment. I also try to increase guest satisfaction index scores (our feedback mechanism) and to lower guest complaints by ensuring prompt, courteous, and proper service and surveying guest comment cards to correct negative situations immediately.

It is also important to ensure that my division is operating in compliance with all local, state, and federal laws and government regulations. To assure that our guests have a quality stay, I am also responsible for communicating effectively within and between departments, ensuring good safety practices of employees and performing special projects as requested.

In trying to achieve or exceed budgeted sales goals, our division management team constantly seeks ways to operate within budgeted guidelines by maintaining effective controls. This includes developing and forecasting accurate and aggressive long- and short-range financial objectives and monitoring them through daily, weekly, monthly, quarterly, and annual reviews of our performance.

► General Functions

I am expected to perform special projects as requested and to maintain a high level of professional appearance, demeanor, ethics, and image of subordinates and myself. Part of our culture in this hotel concerns professional development of staff associates, and it is among my responsibilities to find ways to provide for this.

As you can see, the job of a hotel food and beverage director requires a high-energy person who loves working with people in a variety of dynamic situations. The ability to lead a group of employees in pursuit of operational goals is paramount. Students should actively seek experiences in their college career that provide opportunity to learn the skills mentioned in this article.

6.4 BEST PRACTICES IN FOOD AND BEVERAGE MANAGEMENT

Judy A. Siguaw and Cathy A. Enz

One critical attribute of successful hotel food and beverage outlets is their ability to appropriately respond to the changing needs of the market while maintaining a profitable operation. Yet few hotel food and beverage outlets excel at this fundamental strategy. Instead, generic restaurants that provide undistinguished menu items and offer guests a poor value-for-money proposition frequently characterize hotel food service. Such hotel restaurants fail to provide menu choices, ambience, or service desired by the dining-out market (let alone their guests), and therefore they frequently operate at a loss. Indeed, some analysts have declared that hotel restaurants by their nature will lose money (Hanson, 1984).

Recently, as part of a large, comprehensive study on best practices in the United States lodging industry conducted by Cornell University's School of Hotel Administration (Dubé et al., 1999), we identified a group of best-practice food and beverage champions that had developed practices to successfully

accomplish the strategic charge of profitably meeting customer needs. The champions selected via an intense screening process are The Boulders, The Breakers, Country Inns & Suites, Four Seasons & Regent Hotels & Resorts, The Greenbrier, Hyatt Arlington Hotel, The Pierre, Walt Disney World Resorts and Theme Parks, The Waldorf-Astoria, and Wyndham Hotels and Resorts (see Table 6.1). Through their best practices, this select group demonstrates the capability of executing the strategic mandate of making money while responding to the needs of their target markets through revitalized food and beverage operations.

In the following pages we first present the several practices that have been used by our food and beverage champions to provide their outlets with a competitive advantage. We then examine the measures of success and report the advice our champions give others on how to prosper with hotel food and beverage service.

Table 6.1   Overview of Food and Beverage Best-Practice Champions

F&B Champions	Practice Initiated, Developed	Measure of Success
The Boulders	Food forager to improve quality of restaurant offerings	Increased food quality, decreased food cost, decreased waitstaff turnover, and increased prices, profits, and waitstaff gratuities
The Breakers	Single-theme restaurant concepts	Increased revenues
Country Inns & Suites	Cobranding of hotel and brand-name restaurant	Increased customer satisfaction, reduced hotel capital cost (from not building a hotel restaurant), increased lunch and dinner business
Four Seasons & Regent Hotels & Resorts	Single dining venue with broad cuisine choices (and two dining rooms)	Boosted capture rate of hotel guests; increased local patronage, labor cost savings
The Greenbrier	Establishing resort as a center for culinary excellence, including a culinary-apprentice program	Maintained occupancy and reputation, retained skilled kitchen staff, increased off-season business
Hyatt Arlington Hotel	Reconceptualization and redesign of dated dining room, sports bar, and lobby lounge	Doubled revenues and cover counts, received rave reviews
The Pierre	Independent consultant made responsible for food purchases (with preferred-vendor program)	Decreased food and kitchen labor costs, reduced number of vendors
The Waldorf-Astoria	Applying revenue-management practices in all F&B outlets (plus staff training)	Doubled cover counts, increased effectiveness of F&B marketing, improved customer satisfaction
Walt Disney World Resorts and Theme Parks	Restaurants designed to provide a touchable experience	Achieved high customer satisfaction and return rate
Wyndham Hotels and Resorts	Upgrade of organization's food and beverage culture	Achieved higher average checks, increased staff earnings and retention, increased total sales, wine sales, and profits

► THE BEST PRACTICES

The best practices adopted by our champions can be broadly categorized into three areas. One group stresses providing a high-quality F&B product to their guests (comprising practices by The Boulders, Country Inns & Suites, Four Seasons & Regent Hotels & Resorts, The Greenbrier, and Wyndham Hotels and Resorts). A second group emphasizes the elements of restaurant concept and design in their best practices (namely, The Breakers Hotel, Hyatt Arlington Hotel, and Walt Disney World Resorts and Theme Parks). Finally, The Pierre's and The Waldorf-Astoria's best practices focused primarily on controlling costs and generating additional revenue (see Table 6.2).

Table 6.2   Food and Beverage Best-Practices Cases, Descriptions, Implementation, Contact People

F&B Champion, Title of Case	Description of Case	Method of Implementation	Contact Person
The Boulders *Food Forager to Improve Quality in F&B*	Created position of food forager to obtain the best fresh products, allowing creativity in the kitchen.	Forager first focused on buying the highest-quality produce only within the state of Arizona, where the resort is located. Later, the forager broadened the search and expanded the number of items sought. Forager hotline keeps all F&B outlets apprised of incoming supplies. Menus are restructured around the products the forager finds.	Gray Ferguson, *food and beverage director* 602-488-9009 Fax: 602-595-4664
The Breakers *Annual Food and Beverage Staff Reorganization and Single-theme Restaurant Concepts*	Replaced formal dining and casual dining restaurants and bars with single-theme outlets to give the guest the choice of the cuisine desired rather that the choice dictated by guest attire.	Transformed old-fashioned formal dining room into a modern, Florentine restaurant; casual restaurant into a top-caliber steak-house; main bar into an oceanside restaurant; and a Victorian restaurant into a southern Italian pasta house; plus opened a French Riviera–style restaurant.	Joanne Schultz, *director of food and beverage* 561-659-8434 Fax: 561-659-8452
Country Inns and Suites *Successful Cobranding with Established Restaurant Concepts*	Developed cobranding strategy to locate Country Inns and Suites adjacent to (co-owned) T.G.I. Friday's or Italiani's.	Seeks an "A" location that provides visibility, convenience, high traffic count, and proximity to dense residential areas for the restaurant. Positions restaurant at forefront of property.	Paul Kirwin, *president* 612-212-1326 Fax: 612-212-1338

Table 6.2 *(Continued)*

F&B Champion, Title of Case	Description of Case	Method of Implementation	Contact Person
Four Seasons and Regent *Informal Dining Venue and Alternative Cuisine*	Uses only one F&B outlet with two dining rooms. Provides cuisine choices of Alternative Cuisine, homestyle, and vegetarian options.	Single outlet allows for a focused approach for improving food quality and presentation, grasp of small details, and delivering of higher service levels due to small, qualified staff. Alternative cuisine was developed in response to a need for healthier items, homestyle cuisine was added for frequent travelers who were tired of traditional restaurant food, and vegetarian was added due to increased trend of vegetarianism among guests.	Alfons Konrad, *senior vice president, food and beverage* 416-441-4306 Fax: 416-441-4381
The Greenbrier *Programs Establishing the Resort as a Center for Culinary Excellence*	Instituting a formal culinary apprentice program, a culinary school for guests, conferences and seminars with food critics and writers, and a high school culinary-training program. Also publishes *The Greenbrier Cookbook* and sends newsletters to 600,000 guests.	Established relationships with principal culinary schools in the United States. Opened formal three-year apprentice program to graduates of two-year culinary schools or individuals with equivalent experience. Successful applicants work in all areas of the hotel's kitchens and attend formal classes. Promises permanent employment to applicants from local high school.	Rod Stoner, *vice president of food and beverage* 304-536-1110 Fax: 304-536-7860
Hyatt Arlington Hotel *Redesigning and Revitalizing a Food and Beverage Outlet*	Dated dining room, sports bar, and lobby lounge were reconceptualized into Mediterranean cuisine restaurant.	Comprehensive research and analysis indicated likely success of a fusion of contemporary and Mediterranean themes. Floor-to-ceiling windows replaced one side of building, and martini bar complemented redesigned restaurant.	George Vizer, *general manager* 703-525-1234 Fax: 703-875-3298

Table 6.2   *(Continued)*

F&B Champion, Title of Case	Description of Case	Method of Implementation	Contact Person
The Pierre *F&B Cost-Plus Purchasing Agreements*	Has given financial responsibility for food purchasing to an independent consultant.	The consultant and . executive chef write specifications for food products; consultant negotiates contracts with a single vendor in each food category on a percentage markup basis. Consultant audits the vendors' books annually.	Franz Klampfer, *executive chef* 212-838-2000 Fax: 212-826-0319
The Waldorf-Astoria *Revenue Maximization for the Food and Beverage Department*	Instituted revenue management for all food and beverage outlets, scheduled staff more efficiently, and repositioned outlets to attract non-hotel markets.	Each unit developed a plan to increase revenue and profitability, with a focus on reducing labor costs. Matched staffing levels with expected volume of business. Trained line staff to ensure the highest level of service.	Christophe Le Chatton, *director of food and beverage* 212-355-3000, ext. 4804 Fax: 212-872-7272
Walt Disney World *Providing a Touchable Dining Experience*	A touchable dining experience is provided via the atmosphere and the food to transport guests to another setting, another country, or another culture while they dine.	Theme restaurants are designed to be as authentic as possible in the decor, menu, beverages, and service. Line-level employees are empowered to make decisions with respect to service recovery.	Dieter Hannig, *vice president of food and beverage* 407-566-5800 Fax: 407-560-9131
Wyndham *An Integrated Approach to Food and Beverage*	Created "Best of Class" program to upgrade the food and beverage culture.	Reengineered menus and recipes; reconceptualized restaurants; modified dining rooms and introduced exhibition kitchens; upgraded tabletops and uniforms, and china, glass, silver, and specialty merchandise; developed seasonal F&B festivals and promotions; promoted F&B	Patrick Colombo, *vice president of food and beverage concepts* 214-863-1000 Fax: 214-863-1665

Table 6.2 *(Continued)*

F&B Champion, Title of Case	Description of Case	Method of Implementation	Contact Person
		products within the hotels; recruited culinary talent; obtained unique product from vendors; implemented wine-by-the-glass program; developed server-training program emphasizing product knowledge and upselling; implemented waitstaff incentive programs; and reinvented room service standard operating procedures.	

Note: The case titles correspond to the cases written on each champion in: Laurette Dubé, Cathy A. Enz, Leo M. Renaghan, and Judy A. Siguaw, *American Lodging Excellence: The Key to Best Practices in the U.S. Lodging Industry* (Washington, D.C.: American Express and the American Hotel Foundation, 1999).

► FOCUS ON PRODUCT QUALITY

The problem for The Boulders was that the variety and quality of the produce it was obtaining were not up to the resort's high standards. As a result, the food and beverage department's culinary passion seemed to be declining along with the quality of the food ingredients. The resort's management responded by creating the position of food forager, who initially focused on buying high-quality produce locally (i.e., in Arizona). Later, though, the forager traveled farther afield and took on the additional responsibil-ities of purchasing spices, shellfish, cheeses, and meats. To keep the kitchen apprised of what items are coming, the forager uses a hotline to report expected delivery dates and expenditures. The Boulders' chefs then adjust menus based on the incoming items. Consequently, the food ingredients are of the highest quality, and the chefs have the chance to experiment with a continuously changing menu.

Also seeking to instill a passion for food and beverage, Wyndham Hotels and Resorts designed its "Best of Class" program, with the overall objective of making Wyndham a leader in food and beverage innovation, quality, and service. The Best of Class was a wide-ranging effort that involved both sides of the house. The chain:

1. Reengineered menus and recipes.

2. Reconceptualized its restaurants.

3. Modified dining rooms and introduced display kitchens.

4. Upgraded tabletops, waitstaff uniforms, china, glass, silver, and specialty merchandising pieces.

5. Developed seasonal food festivals and beverage promotions.

6. Promoted F&B products within the hotels.

7. Recruited outstanding culinary talent.

8. Collaborated with food vendors to obtain distinctive products and with wine vendors to upgrade wine lists and conduct tastings.

9. Implemented a wine-by-the-glass program using premium varietals with high brand awareness.

10. Developed a server training program that emphasizes product knowledge and upselling techniques.

11. Implemented incentive programs designed to motivate servers to become better educated about food and wines being served.

12. Reinvented room service procedures by providing training in proper service etiquette, modifying training videos and manuals, and upgrading equipment.

13. Revised in-house marketing materials, such as menus and in-room directories.

To deliver high-quality food and beverage products to its guests, Country Inns & Suites chose to develop a cobranding strategy with restaurant brands that are co-owned by Carlson but freestanding, primarily T.G.I. Friday's or Italiani's. This practice ensures the guest access to a high-quality, brand-name restaurant on site, but it eliminates the capital cost of building a generic restaurant in the hotel. While the core concept of locating a limited-service hotel adjacent to a restaurant is not new, Carlson's approach to the strategy is innovative, since it owns all the brands (another brand that expressly pursued a strategy of locating next to restaurants in the 1980s was Days Inns). To implement this cobranding strategy, Carlson seeks a large, "A" location that will support the restaurant, which is built at the forefront of the property for visibility. Both the restaurant and hotel benefit from this arrangement.

The goal of Four Seasons hotels is to be rated as having one of a given city's top three restaurants. To achieve this goal the chain offers a single restaurant in its hotels—but that restaurant has two dining rooms, one more formal and one less formal. Thus, with a single F&B outlet the hotel can offer two dining rooms that differ in design, but that share the same menu, chefs, line cooks, and kitchens. Compared to having multiple outlets, this approach allows its F&B staff members to provide greater attention to food quality and presentation, to focus on small details, and to deliver higher service levels via a small, highly qualified staff. In response to guests' stated desire for alternatives to a heavy, meat-based cuisine, Four Seasons has broadened its menu choices to include its trademark Alternative Cuisine, comprising a nutritionally balanced menu of alternative meals, vegetarian dishes, and homestyle preparations. Alternative Cuisine items are low in fat, cholesterol, sodium, and calories to correspond with guests' greater interest in health and fitness. Similarly, vegetarian recipes have been added to the menu in response to an increased trend of vegetarianism among guests. Homestyle recipes, on the other hand, are just what the name implies: they have been developed from the chefs' favorite family recipes. The latter cuisine choice suits travel-weary guests who wish for a homecooked meal.

The Greenbrier has instituted several practices to establish itself as a center for culinary excellence. The resort had to address two major problems, both of which stemmed from its remote location. First, for a time the resort was having difficulty attracting and retaining experienced culinary personnel. To end a constant cycle of recruiting and training workers and to improve the food product being offered to guests, The Greenbrier established a three-year culinary-apprenticeship program. The resort recruits candidates from principal culinary schools in the United States to complete an apprenticeship in all areas of the kitchens, as well as attend classes. Because the program runs for three years, the apprenticeship has helped to stabilize the kitchen staff. Further stability comes from an agreement with the local high school by which the resort will provide permanent employment to interested students. The second problem is attracting guests during shoulder and off-season times. Continuing with its theme of culinary education, The Greenbrier established cooking classes for guests and promoted symposiums conducted by food critics and writers. The Greenbrier issues a quarterly newsletter to 600,000 guests and has published *The Greenbrier Cookbook* to further identify the resort as a culinary center—and to remain in contact with potential guests.

▶ RESTAURANT DESIGN AND CONCEPTUALIZATION

The common thread of the following cases that feature restaurant redesign is that the existing restaurants were operated in a functionally competent fashion. They had lost their competitive spark, however (or stood in danger of doing so), because of changes in guests' preferences. In response, operators took a lead from freestanding restaurants and focused tightly on customers' current wishes for theme-based casual dining.

The Breakers recognized that the public has long had an aversion to hotel restaurants, which stems from the days when hotel restaurants tried to have some of every variety of food they thought a guest might desire—none of it particularly distinguished and all of it seemingly overpriced. In response to guests' negative feelings about hotel restaurants, many hotels have dropped food service entirely, but this option is not open to a five-star hotel or resort. Instead, The Breakers chose to create its own strong restaurant identities through single-theme outlets that replaced the resort's existing formal- and casual-dining restaurants and bars. The practice not only helped The Breakers change the public perception of hotel restaurants, but it allowed guests to choose their cuisine according to what they wanted to eat, rather than what they wanted to wear. Thus, the resort's old-fashioned formal dining room became a modern, Florentine-style gourmet restaurant. The owners converted the former casual dining room to a top-caliber steak house—with ambience to match. Perhaps most strikingly, the resort converted its main bar and lounge, which had virtually no business during the day, to a beautiful ocean-side seafood restaurant. The former Victorian restaurant became a Southern Italian–style pasta house, and the Beach Club was converted to a French Riviera–style restaurant. Thus, the resort now has five restaurants that feature their own distinctive decor and ambience, without a loss in food quality.

The food and beverage outlets of the Hyatt Arlington Hotel similarly had lost their customer appeal because of their dated concept and design. After the hotel undertook a comprehensive market-research study, the hotel's managers selected a restaurant theme that blends contemporary (postmodern) and Mediterranean concepts. In developing the new theme, the hotel replaced the restaurant's outer wall with floor-to-ceiling windows to transform the previously dark and unimaginative restaurant into a sun-drenched venue splashed with the Mediterranean's vivid colors. To complement the new restaurant, the hotel installed a quintessential martini bar.

Walt Disney World Resorts and Theme Parks has long recognized the value of themes to a guest's experience—not only in its parks, but also in its many restaurants. Consequently, WDW set out to create a "touchable" foodservice experience for the guest that combines design, decor, ambience, food, service, and entertainment in such a way as to stimulate all of the senses, not just the palate. The idea is to "offer a personal experience which is highly customized, memorable, and judged by our guests to be worth the price," remarked Dieter Hannig, vice president of F&B.

With more than 500 theme food-and-beverage outlets, WDW's managers realized that a restaurant's design is crucial to providing the "touchable" experience for the guest. Each restaurant is designed to be as thematically authentic as possible so that all elements of the physical facility and operations combine to transport the guest to another setting, country, or culture. The dining adventure is intended to produce the feelings, tastes, sounds, and excitement the guest would experience at the actual locale being replicated. Access to the restaurants is designed to be easy and uncomplicated. Accordingly, many restaurants are freestanding so that guests do not have to walk into hotel lobbies or down corridors. Further, line-level employees are empowered to make decisions to improve service recovery and ensure a great dining experience for the guest.

▶ CONTROLLING COSTS

Our last two champions focused on costs and revenues in the food and beverage arena. The Pierre focused on upgrading its restaurant's purchasing function—that is, setting specifications, selecting vendors, obtaining best prices, and monitoring receiving. However, The Pierre's management was concerned that controlling purchasing activities would divert the executive chef's attention from the kitchen's culinary creations. To allow the executive chef to focus on the menu the hotel delegated financial responsibility for food purchasing to an independent consultant, who worked with the chefs to develop specifications for all food products. The consultant analyzes available foodstuffs and may recommend changing specifications if a less expensive item can be substituted without comprising quality or when off-site preparation would be equally good but less expensive than preparing the food item on site. The consultant also trained kitchen employees to adhere to strict receiving standards. Most important to cost control, the consultant negotiated contracts with each vendor specifying that the vendor would earn a given percentage profit over its cost. (Some existing vendors may have blanched at this proposal, but most signed on to keep the hotel's business.) To ensure that costs are in line and that vendors are fulfilling their agreements, the consultant regularly audits inventory and cost lists from each vendor and annually audits the vendors' books to verify that the vendors are accurately stating the cost of each item.

The Waldorf-Astoria's management also believed that the revenue potential of the hotel's foodservice operations was not being achieved, but they looked beyond cost controls. Instead, the hotel took several steps to boost F&B revenue—instituting a revenue management program, implementing cost-cutting measures, training chefs to schedule employees more efficiently, and repositioning F&B outlets to attract guests from outside the hotel. The hotel created a marketing position to coordinate the marketing efforts of all food and beverage units and to help implement revenue-maximization efforts. Service recovery systems were improved. The hotel trained line employees on wines to improve their efforts in selling and serving wines. A new restaurant reservations system was introduced to improve dining-room use, cut telephone use in restaurants, and improve communication with guests. Lastly, a dining-out program, which allowed servers and kitchen employees to dine in various Waldorf-Astoria restaurants, generated many ideas for improvement and created an increased awareness of food and service quality.

► SUCCESS OF THE PRACTICES

The success of these practices can be gauged by various indices, depending on the practice. The food forager program at The Boulders, for instance, improved the quality of the food and lowered food costs. With new and interesting foodstuffs, the chefs have developed distinctive menus that allowed price increases—boosting average checks and profits. As a result of the increased average check, waitstaff gratuities are higher and employee turnover has been reduced. The resort also implemented menu meetings in which chefs explain their creations to servers. Chefs are once again passionate about their creations, and the meetings have created a greater rapport between the front and back of the house.

Wyndham's "Best of Class" program also reenergized the chain's F&B culture—resulting in a 15 percent increase in total sales and a 40 percent increase in wine sales. Since costs were controlled as part of the program, the hotels enjoy a 55 percent profit flow-through on the newly generated revenue. As at The Boulders, Wyndham's higher average checks have increased staff earnings and improved retention. In addition, the promotion of high-quality food has upgraded the chain's overall image.

At The Breakers the new theme restaurants have increased F&B revenue by 70 percent over the last four years, with much of the growth being fueled by the substantial amount of local business attracted by the new outlets. Likewise, the Hyatt Arlington Hotel has doubled cover counts and revenues since its restaurant renovation, and the restaurant receives rave reviews.

WALT DISNEY WORLD'S F&B AWARDS: A SAMPLING

*S*ince 1989, Walt Disney World properties have earned more than 100 food and beverage awards. Listed below is a representative sample of those honors.

- "Award of Excellence" (1999), from *Wine Spectator* magazine, awarded to Victoria & Albert's.

- "Best Wine and Spirits Restaurant of the Year" (1999), from *Santé* magazine, awarded to California Grill.

- One of the "Top Ten Sports Bars in the Country" (1998), from *USA Today,* and one of the "Top Five Sports Bars in the Country" (1998), from *Men's Health,* both honors awarded to ESPN Club.

- "Best Kid's Menu" (1998, Readers' Choice Foodie Awards), from *Orlando Sentinel,* awarded to Chef Mickey's.

- Among the "Best New Restaurants" (1998), from *Esquire,* awarded to Citricos.

- "Best Cover" (1998), from *Restaurant Forum,* awarded to Flying Fish Cafe.

- "Restaurant Wine Award" (1995), from *Wine Enthusiast,* awarded to Artist Point.

- "Most Imaginative" (1993), from the National Restaurant Association, awarded to Grand Floridian Café.

- "America's Best Bar Menu" (1993), from *Cheers* magazine, awarded to Crew's Cup Lounge.

- "Top of the Table" (1991, first place), from *Restaurant Hospitality* magazine, one each awarded to Beaches and Cream Soda Shop and the Yacht Club Galley.

One of many reasons that guests choose to stay at The Greenbrier is its excellent culinary reputation. Thus, its reputation as a center for culinary excellence plays an important role in maintaining guestroom occupancy. The ability of Walt Disney World Resorts and Theme Parks restaurants to provide a "touchable" dining experience contributes significantly to WDW's profitability. Furthermore, both the number of return guests and percentage of satisfied customers are high—and several WDW restaurants have won awards in recent years (see sidebar).

The Country Inns & Suites cobranding strategy has been a winning situation both for the hotels and for guests. For guests, having a popular brand-name restaurant adjacent to the hotel ensures that their dining needs will be satisfied. For the restaurant, the hotel guests account for 15 to 20 percent of its business. For the hotel, the proximity of a name-brand restaurant is an amenity that can encourage guests to book a room.

By using an independent consultant to negotiate with vendors and to monitor the F&B purchasing function, The Pierre was able to reduce food costs by approximately 5 percent and kitchen labor costs by 2 percent. In addition, the number of vendors used has decreased, resulting in greater efficiency for the hotel. Finally, The Waldorf-Astoria's revenue maximization strategy improved cover counts by a staggering 100 percent, while increasing wine sales and guest satisfaction.

▶ INSIGHTS

Our food and beverage champions offer the following advice and observations to managers seeking to implement similar programs:

1. The foundation for successful implementation is meeting challenges with enthusiasm and passion.

2. Some practices, such as food purchasing by an independent consultant, may not be warmly received by staff or vendors, but the commitment of upper management and a demonstration of benefits will help gain acceptance.

3. Those practices that require constant adaptation (like the food forager) will not work in a rigidly structured organization.

4. Cobranding strategies are suitable only when the hotels are partnered with restaurants that are targeting the same market segment.

5. Hotel F&B outlets' development must incorporate the guest's total experience (and focus on competing with freestanding restaurants).

6. Resources must be focused on a relentless commitment to food and beverage consistency, even when business is slow.

▶ PROFITABLE AND VITAL

Contrary to much conventional wisdom, the experience of these F&B champions shows that hotel restaurants can not only turn a profit but can contribute greatly to the hotel's overall competitive position. We note, however, that virtually all the F&B champions are operating in the upscale, deluxe, and resort segments of the lodging industry. While many hotel restaurants at all levels struggle to turn a profit, the actions of our champions indicate that focusing on guests' needs can radically reverse the downward trend of hotel restaurants. As Rod Stoner, vice president of food and beverage at The Greenbrier, pointed out, managers must stay abreast of industry trends, study the programs of other properties, and seek distinctive ideas for adaptation to their own hotels. This overview of best practices in food and beverage champions provides a starting point for what Stoner suggests. We hope that those managers seeking to revitalize or maximize the revenue potentials of their F&B operations will carefully examine the practices discussed here and will continue their progress by also investigating the practices of other properties and other industries. As a result, forward-thinking managers will be able to identify those best practices that will serve as the catalyst for improving customer satisfaction and financial performance.

6.5 STRATEGIC ALLIANCES BETWEEN HOTELS AND RESTAURANTS

Robert W. Strate and Clinton L. Rappole

Over the years hotel restaurants have often been managed as a secondary function of the hotel—that is, as a costly amenity rather than a revenue center. In part because of the high cost structure of hotel restaurants, which means high prices relative to other restaurants, they developed among potential customers a reputation for being a poor value, offering indifferent service and inferior food. Today, however, many hotel companies are rethinking how to integrate food and beverage services into lodging facilities. In the process of doing so, hotel owners and operators are asking at least four key questions about their property-level F&B service.

- What are the hotel customers' food and beverage needs and expectations?
- Which food and beverage concept best aligns with the positioning of the hotel?
- Would converting the hotel's restaurant to a brand-name restaurant concept improve the property's overall bottom line?
- Would turning to a brand-name F&B operation give the property a competitive edge?

Two results of owners' and operators' new focus on hotel food service are that (1) innovative hotel F&B concepts are being created, and (2) strategic alliances are being established between well-known brand-name hotel and restaurant companies.

The primary focus of this article is to answer the four questions stated above and provide the basic decision-making framework for matching the correct F&B concept to the target market for which the hotel has been positioned. We will identify key criteria for establishing a seamless partnership between the hotel and the restaurant. The results of such a marriage should be an improved property image overall, enhanced customer value, increased revenues, and a competitive edge. The following four main topics will be addressed:

- The value of a brand-name partner
- Existing hotel-and-restaurant alliances
- A description of Bristol Hotel Company's alliance with Good Eats Grill (including critical-decision elements)
- Future trends

▶ ALLIANCES

Developing alliances between brand-name hotel and restaurant companies is not a new business strategy, but it does seem that this approach is currently being used more frequently than ever to help companies maximize their profit potential (*Lodging*, September 1995). There are at least five reasons for this. An alliance may:

1. Create financial benefits.
2. Provide customers with greater value.
3. Improve a property's overall image.
4. Strengthen an operation's competitive position.
5. Create operational advantages.

One of the first branded restaurant concepts to operate in hotels was probably Trader Vic's, founded by Victor Bergen in 1937. By 1949 Western Hotels (which became Westin) integrated Trader Vic's into 13 hotel-based restaurants in nine countries (Withiam, 1995a, 14). Other chains also hosted the restaurants and today, 60 years later, Trader Vic's still operates in such hotels as the Beverly Hilton, the Palmer House (Chicago), the Marriott Royal Garden Riverside (Bangkok), and the New Otani properties in Tokyo and Singapore. Ruth's Chris Steakhouse is another example of a popular restaurant brand operating successfully in unison with hotels, including properties operated by Hilton, Marriott, Holiday Inn, and Westin.

Despite the evidence of successful alliances between brand-name hotel and restaurant companies, most hotel companies manage their own food and beverage services, including those that also host Trader Vic's. In part that approach reflects the long industry tradition of offering travelers both food and lodging. The Marriott Corporation is a good example of a hotel company that has used this strategy of going it alone. John Randall, Marriott senior director of food and beverage concepts, states that it is Marriott's primary strategy to "completely manage our own F&B services to provide food, service, and quality consistency from property to property" (Hensdill, 1996).

The strategy of developing their own F&B concepts has not been successful for all hotel companies. This is evident from the fre-

Table 6.3   Hotel and Restaurant Company Strategic Alliances

Hotel Companies	Restaurant Companies
Holiday Inn Worldwide	Damon's, Denny's, Ruth's Chris Steakhouse, T.G.I. Friday's, Convenience Courts (Mrs. Fields, Little Caesars, Blimpies, Taco John's, Sara Lee)
Doubletree Hotel Corporation	New York Restaurant Group (Park Avenue Café, Mrs. Parks Café)
Marriott Hotels	Ruth's Chris Steakhouse, Studebakers, Benihana, Trader Vic's, Pizza Hut
Hilton Hotels	Trader Vic's, Benihana, Ruth's Chris Steakhouse, Damon's
Four Seasons	Bice Ristorante
Choice Hotels	Picks Food Courts, Pizza Hut
Promus Corporation	Grace Services, T.G.I. Friday's, Olive Garden, Pizza Hut
Radisson Hospitality Worldwide*	Carlson Hospitality* (T.G.I. Friday's, Country Kitchen), Damon's

*The relationship between Radisson Hospitality Worldwide and Carlson Hospitality is not an alliance per se but rather an example of a hotel company that owns and has vertically integrated both its lodging and foodservice products into one corporation.

Sources: See "Restaurant Chains Partner with Hotels to Satisfy Different Needs, Tastes," *Lodging,* September 1995, pp. 1, 8–9; "Holiday Inn Offers Assorted Food Options with New Quick Food Concept," *Hotel Business,* June 1996, p. 9; "Holiday Inn Offers Convenience Court Concept," *Nation's Restaurant News,* May 1996, p. 208; Frank H. Andorka, "High Recognition Restaurants," *Hotel & Motel Management,* November 1995, pp. 43–44; Cherie Hensdill, "Partnerships in Dining," *Hotels,* February 1996, pp. 57–60; Judy Liberson, "A Working Marriage," *Lodging,* February 1996, pp. 63–66; and Madelin Wexler, "Partnerships That Pay Off," *Hotels,* May 1995, pp. 47–50.

quent "reconcepting" found among hotel restaurants. A hotel might run a lounge one year, convert it into a brasserie the next year, and later decide to make it a grill. The end result is inconsistency in F&B service and quality, and therefore low sales and profits (Parseghian, 1996). Several factors may contribute to a general manager's believing that she or he can operate the hotel's restaurant services better than a branded restaurant company, not the least of which may be a sense of self-assurance. Some hotel general managers want to prove that they can provide a fine-dining experience whether or not a market actually exists. Others say it is because some hotel F&B operations continue to try to be all things to all people rather than providing a product that is affordable and matches customer expectations (Wolff, 1995, 24). Moreover, hotel restaurants in general have a high cost structure relative to the freestanding F&B operation down the street. Hotel restaurants have to contribute to the overall property's expenses while the restaurant next door has little capital expense and is probably just leasing square footage.

A current trend among hotels that have reevaluated their F&B operations is to replace the formal fine-dining, white-tablecloth concept with a more casual and relaxed dining experience (Allen, 1996; Liberson, 1996). Another trend indicates that more and more hotel companies are looking to establish strategic alliances with brand-name restaurant companies. Doing this has allowed hotel companies to focus on managing the hotel itself. Listed in Table 6.3 are examples of strategic alliances between hotel and restaurant companies. These examples illustrate that some of the largest hotel companies have already established strategic alliances with major restaurant chains.

▶ BRISTOL AND GOOD EATS GRILL

To comprehend fully the rationale and advantages of a hotel's decision to turn to a brand-name restaurant for the hotel's foodservice, we analyzed the Bristol Hotel Company's decision to match two of their hotels with Good Eats Grill (Withiam, 1995b, 13). Before creating the alliance with Good Eats Grill, the Bristol Hotel Company's primary F&B strategy was to use its own internally developed restaurant brands. This is a strategy that has worked well for Bristol—for example, eight outlets produced 32.4 percent F&B profit margins in 1995, and 20 out of 22 Bristol hotel-restaurants continue to use their own internally developed restaurant brands.

Despite the success of Bristol's own F&B operations, the firm decided to link two of its properties (Holiday Inns in Jackson, Mississippi, and Houston, Texas) with a franchised restaurant brand called Good Eats Grill—a concept developed by Gene Street, who also developed the Black Eyed Pea and Dixie House restaurant brands. We wondered why Bristol deviated from its successful formula, and so we decided to investigate why the Bristol Hotel Company elected to team with Good Eats Grill. We narrowed our focus and analysis even further by evaluating just the Houston property using interviews of the principals involved.

We asked executives from both Bristol and Good Eats Grill 70 questions in all, conducted site visits, and found additional research information in various hospitality periodicals. Additionally, Mike Feldott, of HRC Consultants, L.C., was a key adviser on restaurant brands and operations for hotels.

PRODUCT BRANDING

Product branding refers to establishing a well-known name for a given product or service whereby the particular product or service and its attributes are highly recognizable and easily recalled by consumers. The basic concept behind such so-called branding is to establish a standard on which consumers may rely to predict value (e.g., price, quality, convenience). Within the hotel industry a multitiered branding strategy has evolved among lodging companies. The following table illustrates how some hotel brands have become associated with different tiers. Note that some companies have developed products for more than one tier.

Economy, Limited Service	Middle Market	Luxury, First Class	All Suites
• Motel 6	• Holiday Inn	• Four Seasons	• Marriott Suites
• Days Inn	• Ramada Inn	• Ritz-Carlton	• Embassy Suites
• La Quinta	• Sheraton	• Marriott Marquis	• Residence Inns
• Hampton Inn	• Hilton	• Beverly Hilton	• Homewood Suites
• Travelodge	• Courtyard by Marriott	• Hyatt	• Bristol Suites
• Sleep Inn	• Radisson	• Westin	• Clarion Suites
			• Guest Quarters

Source: Ron N. Nykiel, "Corporate Strategy within the Hospitality Industry," in *The Complete Travel Marketing Handbook,* ed. Andrew Vladimir (Lincolnwood, IL: NTC Business Books, 1988).

An example of the multiple-branding strategy can be illustrated by examining the different hotel brands of the Marriott Corporation. Marriott has developed Marriott Hotels, Marriott Resorts, Marriott Marquis, Courtyard by Marriott, Marriott Suites, Residence Inns, and Embassy Suites.

A somewhat similar branding strategy also exists in the restaurant industry, as shown in the following chart.

Bristol Hotel Company. The Bristol Hotel Company is a 39-property chain with corporate headquarters in Dallas, Texas. In January 1995 Bristol acquired a Memphis-based hotel company, United Inns, Inc., that had 26 hotels based in six states. By the end of 1995 Bristol Hotel Company had grown from 8 to 38 properties with more than 10,000 rooms, which generated $192 million in total revenues. (Many of the properties acquired in 1995 required renovation, and many of these rooms were out of order, which negatively affected year-end 1995 financial numbers.) The revenues predicted for 1996 are around $250 million. The following key indices summarize Bristol Hotel Company's performance in 1995:

Quick Service	Casual, Family	Upscale	Theme
• McDonald's	• Red Lobster	• Ruth's Chris Steakhouse	• Planet Hollywood
• Taco Bell	• T.G.I. Friday's	• Trader Vic's	• Hard Rock Café
• Pizza Hut	• Damon's	• Del Frisco's	• Benihana
• Domino's	• Good Eats Grill	• Bice Ristorante	• Lettuce Entertain You
• KFC	• Chili's	• Palm Restaurant	• Front Row Sports Grille
• Church's	• Olive Garden	• NY Restaurant Group (Mrs. Parks)	• Country Kitchen

The Country Hospitality Partnership, a subsidiary of Carlson Hospitality Worldwide, is an example of a restaurant company with a multitier branding strategy. The Country Hospitality Partnership restaurants include Country Kitchen (252 restaurants), T.G.I. Friday's (365 restaurants), Italiani's (14 restaurants), and Front Row Sports Grille (3 restaurants). Additionally, Carlson provides a good example of a hotel company that owns and has vertically integrated both the hotel and the restaurant product into one corporation. Carlson Companies, Inc., owns both Radisson Hotels Worldwide and Country Hospitality Partnership. The T.G.I. Friday's concept is being integrated into many Radisson Hotels (see: Laura Koss-Feder, "Radisson Seeks Marketing Advantages," *Hotel & Motel Mangement*, pp. 3, 43; Ron Ruggles, "T.G.I. Friday's Cruises into Summer," *Nation's Restaurant News*, June 1996, pp. 14, 43; and Lawrence White, "Growth Meister," *Lodging*, September 1996, pp. 52–58).

The Marriott Corporation is another example of a hospitality company that owns and integrated its own restaurant brands into its hotels. The key point is that the brand is recognizable, and this recognition equates to reliable value from the customer's perspective. This enhanced customer perception can be used by a firm to gain a competitive edge and, in turn, increase revenues and profits for the company.

Average occupancy	64.10%
Average daily room rate	$62.67
RevPAR	$40.20
Gross operating margin	29.62%
Rooms margin	71.61%
Food, beverage margin	24.84%

Bristol primarily uses an owner-operator strategy versus management contracts in managing its hotels. As of the time of our study it owned 36 of its properties (93 percent) and managed the other three properties. Bristol's primary focus was in the full-service segment, with 35 full-service properties (89 percent) and only four limited-service properties.

Its primary target market is the mid- to upper-level corporate traveler (the source of 90 percent of the company's revenues). It also does substantial group-meeting business. Bristol is anticipating that full-service hotels will play an important role in meeting the future lodging and business demand of those two market segments. John Beckert, the chief operating officer of Bristol, considers the "full-service segment as a segment that has been somewhat abandoned, but Bristol considers the segment to be 'solid' as far as demand (anticipate 6 to 10 percent increase in demand) and a segment that allows for greater pricing power."

Bristol's overall strategy is to provide customers with a first-class-hotel experience—but without being stuffy—and extraordinary overall value (price and quality). While those goals are not unusual among hotel companies, Bristol has distinguished itself in several ways. First, it has an excellent track record, established in part by achieving strong operating and financial results during the industry's recent recession.

Second, it maintains a distinct corporate culture and management style that translates into low executive-management turnover.

Third, its centralized management structure allows managers to focus on the quality of a guest's stay as the number-one priority.

The company's primary operating strategies are listed in Table 6.4.

Throughout our discussion we will analyze Bristol's six operating strategies. However, our emphasis will be on understanding why Bristol Hotel Company aligns its F&B services within their hotels in a certain fashion and how it reaches the decision to do so one way instead of another.

Among its 39 hotels Bristol has 22 hotel restaurant outlets and uses three internally developed restaurant brands in 20 of those properties, as shown in Table 6.5.

Table 6.4 Bristol Hotel Company Operating Strategies

Strategies	Implementation
Unique management culture	Entrepreneurial and team-oriented
Control over hotel operations	Owner-operator focus
Assets in select geographic markets	28 properties located in Atlanta, Dallas, and Houston (fast-growing markets)
Direct sales and marketing	Focus on local market
Flexible use of brand names	*Operate under its own brand names:* Harvey Hotels, Bristol Suites, Harvey Suites *Operate under national franchise brands:* Holiday Inn, Marriott, Promus properties, Hospitality Franchise Systems brands
Emphasis on food and beverage services	Bristol's F&B profit margins (32 percent original eight and 25 percent overall) are above December 1994 national industry levels of 17.1 percent.

Source: Bristol Hotel Company 1995 Annual Report

Table 6.5   Bristol's Own Restaurant Brands

Brand	Concept
Scoops Diner (4 units)	• Theme restaurant with a 1950s concept
	• Comfortable and casual
Remmington's (4 units)	• Eclectic
	• More upscale than a Scoops
	• Nice hotel coffee shop
Bristol Bar and Grill (12 units)	• Designed as a hotel restaurant
	• Flexible in handling fluctuations in sales volume
	• Self-serve
	• Friendly and fast

In addition to Bristol's own restaurant concepts and the two franchised Good Eats Grills previously mentioned, Bristol executives are considering leasing space to a branded restaurant in two of their limited-service properties.

Good Eats Grill. The Good Eats Grill Company is a privately held firm that currently has 17 restaurant outlets, of which 16 are located in Texas and another in Mississippi. Four of the 17 restaurant outlets are franchised, while the others are owned and operated by the company founder, owner, and president, Gene Street. Bristol Hotel Company is the only hotel company that is currently allied with Good Eats Grill. In 1995 Good Eats Grill's annual revenues were $23 million. Good Eats Grill is a casual, family restaurant stressing food quality and low price. A Good Eats Grill can seat 150 to 200 diners, serves lunch and dinner, has a comfortable decor and casual atmosphere, and offers excellent food quality at an affordable price. Good Eats Grill's best-selling entrees are its chicken-fried steak and vegetable plate. The approximate square footage required for a Good Eats Grill is 4,000 to 6,500 square feet (includes both front and back of the house).

The following key indices summarize Good Eats Grill's 1995 performance:

Total revenues	$23 million
Food-revenue percentage	94%
Beverage-revenue percentage	6%
Overall F&B cost percentage	28.5%
Food-cost percentage	29%
Beverage-cost percentage	22%
Average check	$8.12
Covers/year (approx.)	2.8 million

Table 6.6 summarizes the Good Eats Grill menu.

At the time of this writing, Good Eats Grill was doing business with no other hotel company besides the Bristol Hotel Company. We wondered why, and asked key people within the Good Eats Grill management why they had agreed to team with Bristol Hotels. The key factors from the perspective of those managers were:

- The companies share similar proactive, team-oriented management styles.
- The firms' corporate cultures blend well.
- The projects were financially feasible.
- Bristol was looking for exactly the product that Good Eats Grill could deliver (i.e., customer value in terms of quality and price).
- Both companies wanted the deal to happen.

Good Eats Grill executives believe more hotel-and-restaurant alliances are imminent and such deals represent a trend that is here to stay. Good Eats Grill's management expects to do more restaurant-franchise deals with hotel companies as doing so offers a viable option for expanding quickly without intensive capital requirements.

Property location. For our study we selected the Holiday Inn Intercontinental, a Bristol Hotel Company property located near the Houston Intercontinental Airport. From the outside, the Good Eats Grill appears as if it is a freestanding restaurant, but in reality the restaurant is as much a part of the hotel as the lobby.

This particular Holiday Inn, a 400-room property opened in 1971, recently underwent $11.5 million in renovations (of which some $1.5 million was for the conversion of the previous restaurant into a Good Eats Grill). This hotel generates approximately $7.5 million in room revenues, operates at an 85-percent occupancy level, and has an average daily rate of $60 and RevPAR of $48. Restaurant revenues are targeted to be approximately $1.5 million; food profit, 25 percent; beverage profit, 55 to 60 percent; food cost, 28 to 29 percent; and beverage cost, 20 to 22 percent.

Property selection. During 1995, the year Bristol acquired the United Inns properties, Bristol Hotel Company executives evaluated all of their hotel-restaurant outlets and made decisions as to which restaurant concept best supported the targeted positioning of each individual hotel. Among Bristol's development strategies was a decision to use the Good Eats Grill concept in two of its properties. Just as

Table 6.6   Good Eats Grill Menu

	Menu Items	Price Range	Comments
Appetizers	6	$1.99–$4.99	
Soups and salads	5	$2.19–$5.79	
Burgers and sandwiches	7	$5.29–$6.29	
Entrées	20	$5.99–$8.99	Steaks, pork chops, chicken, pasta, grilled fish Served with garden-fresh vegetables Add salad for 99 cents
Desserts	5	$2.49–$2.99	
Beverages (alcoholic and nonalcoholic)			Full service

Source: "Ride the Branding Wave," *Lodging,* September 1996, pp. 62–73.

we asked the Good Eats Grill executives, "Why Bristol?" we asked Bristol executives, "Why the decision to go with Good Eats Grill versus going with proven internally developed restaurant brands or renovating the existing restaurant?" The key element in Bristol's selection of Good Eats Grill for two new locations was in Bristol's overall assessment of which restaurant concept would be the best match for the repositioning strategies for those specific hotels.

At the Houston Holiday Inn Intercontinental, the existing restaurant, the Grand Cargo Cafe, was a typical hotel restaurant with a coffee-shop feel. The Grand Cargo Cafe had average food quality and service, low profit margins (5 percent), low sales volume, high employee turnover, little name recognition, and a below-average reputation among those customers familiar with the operation. In short, the Grand Cargo Cafe was a costly amenity for the hotel's previous owners and Bristol executives quickly determined that a change was required.

Bristol first looked at the possibility of replacing the Grand Cargo Cafe with one of Bristol's own internally developed F&B concepts (i.e., Bristol Bar & Grill, Scoops Diner, or Remmington's). After some consideration it was determined that Bristol's own concepts did not adequately complement the property's repositioning strategy. The Bristol Bar & Grill is a quick-and-friendly self-serve concept that is primarily focused on serving hotel guests (i.e., banquet guests). Such a foodservice arrangement would be inappropriate for the repositioned Holiday Inn Intercontinental, which has a large sales-volume potential comprising both walk-in diners (85 percent of the lunch trade and 40 percent for dinner) and overnight guests (15 percent at lunch and 60 percent at dinner).

Another objective in replacing the Grand Cargo Cafe was to change dramatically the perceived atmosphere of the outlet from that of a coffee shop to a substantial restaurant. Bristol's Remmington's concept, also reminiscent of a coffee shop but more upscale than Grand Cargo Cafe in price and quality, was not considered sufficiently different to achieve that goal. Moreover, Remmington's did not completely match the "casual and comfortable" atmosphere desired to complement the overall hotel repositioning strategy.

Bristol's Scoops Diner concept offered a close match to Bristol's goal of providing the customer with good overall value in a casual and comfortable atmosphere. Scoops' 1950s-theme concept, however, was developed primarily for walk-in diners rather than a hotel's overnight and meeting guests. Like Remmington's, then, the Scoops concept did not exactly fit the needs of the property's new target markets.

While hotel guests were to be a prime customer base for the Intercontinental's restaurant, the property was seen to also offer great opportunity for walk-in business. (Here are some of the key site-specific characteristics of the Holiday Inn Intercontinental that indicated a freestanding restaurant could generate substantial walk-in business: (1) the physical layout of the property—parking, entrance, signs, and size—was considered excellent; (2) the property is located close to Houston International Airport on a major highway; and (3) there was limited restaurant competition in the area despite the potential for customers from local businesses and surrounding hotels, some of which are limited-service properties.) With that in mind, Bristol executives realized that the Scoops and Remmington's concepts did not have sufficient preexisting customer brand awareness in

Houston to generate substantial walk-in traffic. In the final assessment, then, Bristol purchased the franchise rights to operate a Good Eats Grill in Houston (and at one other location).

A good match. Bristol management considers Good Eats Grill to be a competitive concept that offers a quality product, a casual environment that customers enjoy, a respected and recognizable restaurant name in the Houston area, and proven sales volume. Another key factor mentioned by Bristol executives was that the two organizations clicked, meaning that the corporate culture of each was well matched with the other. Both have an entrepreneurial base, both are flexible, and both have high-quality standards for a midlevel product at an affordable price. Shown on the next page is a table that compares the hotel, restaurant, and combined marketing strategies of the two companies (Table 6.7).

Key positioning criteria. We found that a critical factor in the selection process of a hotel's F&B brand or concept is to determine the customer perception that you want to create at the property and then select a restaurant theme that complements the overall property's image. Bristol COO Beckert illustrated this by saying, "At Bristol we try to identify uniqueness in our F&B concepts, which then become selling points for the property. The restaurant then goes on a short list that our sales staff use to sell rooms."

The "right" match between the hotel and the restaurant can vary from property to property. At Bristol, all 39 properties were evaluated to determine which F&B concept best fit each property, and only two locations were selected for a Good Eats Grill franchise. As we will point out later, several key factors such as conversion costs and nearby competition must be taken into consideration prior to making the final decision.

Turn up the volume. Another element related to positioning is to determine the volume and customer mix expected. For example, let's review Bristol's existing company-owned restaurant brands: Scoops, Remmington's, and Bristol Bar & Grill. Bristol management will locate a Scoops or a Remmington's in those properties that have above-average hotel volume, and where restaurant-customer volume comprises primarily walk-in diners who are not using the hotel's other services. A Bristol Bar & Grill concept is used when the F&B

Table 6.7 Operating Strategies

Hotel	Restaurant	Combined
• Primary market 　—Corporate business travelers 　—Mid- to upper-range travelers • Secondary market 　—Family travelers • Brand recognition • First-class hotel, but not stuffy • Physically competitive	• Family-style restaurant • Excellent food quality 　—Fresh • Value • Brand recognition • Casual, comfortable decor	• Appeal to corporate and family travelers • Mid- to upper-market value • Casual and comfortable • Best overall value 　—Price and quality

market is primarily hotel guests and banquet business. The Bristol Bar & Grill is targeted specifically to serve hotel patrons with a quick-serve breakfast, convenient lunch, and buffet-style dinner. The Good Eats Grill concept, on the other hand, generally operates as a freestanding restaurant, has a proven sales volume ($1.5 to 2 million per year), offers consumer value, and has a comfortable decor that's attractive to both walk-in diners and hotel guests.

During Bristol's examination of its hotel restaurants, it was determined that a Good Eats Grill should be used when (1) it is necessary to reposition the hotel, (2) a great restaurant-volume potential exists, (3) the physical layout and location of the property can sustain a freestanding restaurant, and (4) the market mix comprises both hotel guests and walk-in customers.

Why Houston? Bristol's management felt that the Houston Holiday Inn Intercontinental needed repositioning and a recognized restaurant brand like Good Eats Grill was essential for any repositioning strategy to work. Good Eats Grill already had two successful freestanding restaurants in the Houston region. Additionally, Good Eats Grill maintained an ongoing investment in local advertising. By contrast, a Remmington's, a Scoops, or even the Grand Cargo Cafe did not have anywhere near the same level of local brand awareness and consumer acceptance.

The following list summarizes the key factors that Bristol's executives considered when selecting Houston as a location for a franchised Good Eats Grill.

- The property was being repositioned.
- Financial feasibility was evident.
- The property's existing hotel restaurants were producing low revenues.

- The physical layout of the property allowed for conversion.
- Parking, entrances, and signs would be relatively easy to provide.
- The local labor market could support the concept.
- The high-traffic location of the property (in a commercial area near the airport).
- Since there was only one freestanding restaurant within a two-mile radius, the potential for non-hotel-guest business was great.

▶ SELECTION PROCESS

A summary of the key advantages and disadvantages to consider when going with a franchised restaurant brand in your hotel are listed below (*Lodging*, 1995), while illustrated on the next page is a flow chart of the basic steps to take when evaluating and choosing which franchise restaurant company to use (Figure 6.1).

Advantages

- Integral part of repositioning the hotel
- Potentially increases revenues, occupancy, profits
- Restaurant franchiser is continually assessing the menu, whereas a hotel's tendency is not to change the menu
- Franchiser is knowledgeable about the restaurant business

Disadvantages

- Franchise fee
- Requires a certain level of volume to warrant utilizing a franchise brand
- High initial investment

Figure 6.1 Selection-process Flow Chart

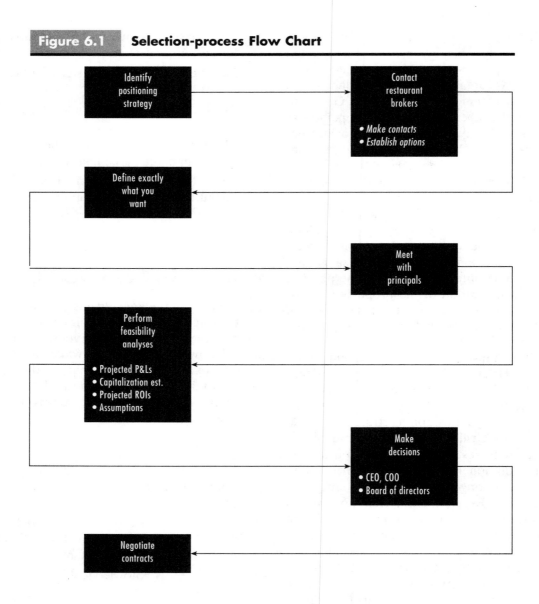

- Brand can lose reputation and recognition or quality levels could drop during the term of the franchise agreement
- Room service and banquet service could still require a separate kitchen operation

As previously noted, Bristol chose the Good Eats Grill concept over other restaurant companies because the Good Eats management was (1) flexible and (2) determined to minimize the bureaucracy to make the deal

CRITICAL ELEMENTS TO CONSIDER

*S*ummarized below are critical elements to consider when assessing which restaurant brand concepts will best match a particular hotel property.

1. Determine the desired hotel market position and customer perception you want to create for each property. This includes knowing all about the property's competition, environment, and customers, and involves creating a unique image for your property.

2. Make sure that you objectively assess the revenue and expense potential of each operational option when examining your financial trade-offs. Such options include running your hotel company's own brand, buying and operating a franchised brand, and leasing space to a brand-name restaurant company.

3. Select a restaurant company that has a corporate culture that mirrors your hotel's corporate culture and also shares the same basic operational goals.

4. Evaluate each property on a stand-alone basis using all available facts and data. Avoid making generalizations about what will work for all properties.

5. The key criteria in identifying which properties could benefit most from a brand-name franchise-restaurant concept are:

- Desired positioning of the hotel
- Financial trade-offs and feasibility analyses
- Competitive marketing analysis
- Physical layout of the facility (parking, entrances, signs, location of kitchen)
- The site location
- The local labor market

6. The key criteria in selecting a particular restaurant company are:

- Similar business goals and corporate culture
- Initial investment cost
- The menu offered
- Ongoing new menu development
- New recipes on a regular basis
- Cooking specifications
- Franchise fee
- Restaurant decor
- Training support
- Management support
- The ability to handle room service and banquets

7. View the hotel's restaurant outlet as a selling point that can enhance rooms sales and as a profit center that can be held accountable for achieving established profit.

happen. In today's competitive market, business decisions must be made quickly and accurately or else the window of opportunity may be lost. In this particular example the basic deal was struck after two executive meetings (however, it did take the lawyers a little longer). The rest of the steps in the process caught up with the decisions that were made after those two executive meetings. Such a quick decision was possible because the two companies have similar proactive management styles, the project made financial sense for both companies, the corporate cultures blended well, and the decision-makers went with their instinct.

► CONTRACT RELATIONSHIPS

There are four basic types of operational options that can be established between the hotel and the F&B outlet in a hotel. Those four options are (1) internally developed restaurant brand, (2) franchised restaurant brand, (3) straight lease, and (4) management contract. Bristol's first choice (used for 20 of its 22 restaurant outlets) is to use its own internally developed restaurant brands. Bristol believes it has a proven track record in managing F&B operations profitably (*Hotel Business*, 1996).

When Bristol introduced Good Eats Grill into two of its 22 hotels with food service, it showed a willingness to purchase a franchised brand, provided Bristol could maintain full control of restaurant operations and products (as long as all franchise agreements were maintained). Currently Bristol is also assessing a leasing arrangement with yet another restaurant company for a couple of Bristol's

Fairfield Inn properties. In those cases Bristol managers seem to be indicating that it would be more profitable for them to lease out square footage in the hotels versus operating the F&B outlet themselves.

Key franchise elements. Bristol has purchased the franchise rights for its two Good Eats Grill operations. The key elements of the franchise agreement are the menu, recipes, cooking specifications, franchise fee, restaurant decor, music package, training support, and negotiated special provisions (e.g., use of Good Eats Grill recipes for banquets). Basically, Bristol purchased a turnkey operation from Good Eats Grill. Moreover, Good Eats Grill provides pre- and post-opening training support, new and updated menu development, and such regional management support as consulting, auditing, and trouble-shooting.

In exchange for the franchise and its management services Good Eats Grill receives 3.5 percent of lunch and dinner revenues as a franchise fee.

► MARKETING

We have already mentioned how the Bristol sales office uses the company's restaurants as a selling point to assist in booking rooms, meetings, and banquets. In addition there are three other marketing concerns that need to be considered: (1) the competition, (2) customer expectations, and (3) advertising.

Competition. The primary hotel competitors for Bristol's Houston Holiday Inn Intercontinental are a Marriott hotel (569 rooms), a Hyatt hotel (315 rooms), and a Sheraton hotel (450 rooms). As for nearby foodservice competition, Marriott uses internally developed restaurant brands (Allie's American

Grill and CK's) along with a Pizza Hut kiosk, while the Hyatt and Sheraton offer typical hotel restaurants. Additionally, there are some limited-service hotel properties in the area that factor into the secondary market competitive analysis.

The freestanding restaurant competition in the area is negligible. There is a Kettle Restaurant nearby, but it does not pose a strong business threat to Good Eats Grill as it has a different target market. There is a Bennigan's and T.G.I. Friday's within three miles of the Holiday Inn, but there is no other notable restaurant competition within a two-mile radius of the hotel. As it turns out, the Holiday Inn's Good Eats Grill is popular with Marriott's, Hyatt's, and Sheraton's hotel guests, and also with those hotel guests that are staying at the surrounding limited-service properties. It can be expected, then, that a guest who stays at a hotel other than the Holiday Inn, yet eats at the Good Eats Grill, may decide to stay at the Holiday Inn on return trips to Houston. The value of the strategic alliance between the hotel and the restaurant is that it establishes a unique identity for this property that sets it apart from its competition and provides a marketing edge.

Customer expectations. A primary mission-statement goal of both companies is to exceed customer expectations. With the alliance of the Holiday Inn Intercontinental and Good Eats Grill, Bristol management believes the customer is pleasantly surprised with the overall product and services that the property provides. Even though the hotel and restaurant renovations were completed just recently, in July 1996, the perceived overall value of this property to the customer is already generating new corporate accounts. Bristol management believes the hotel repositioning strategy in combination with the ad-

dition of the Good Eats Grill is a major reason it is landing those new accounts.

Advertising. Bristol Hotel Company believes in a direct sales-and-marketing approach. The company therefore relies less on national promotion activities than many other firms. The Holiday Inn Intercontinental is no different in this regard. The hotel does some limited local advertising, but it relies primarily on a direct-sales approach along with making personal local contacts. Other than the signs around the property, there is no joint advertising or promotion done between the hotel and the restaurant. Good Eats Grill has four lighted signs on the property, and Bristol purchases no billboard ads for this property. There are two other Good Eats Grill restaurants located in Houston, and Good Eats Grill does do some radio promotion and rents billboards for those two restaurants.

▶ OPERATIONS

As a franchisee Bristol maintains total operational control of the restaurant, but Good Eats Grill recipes must be followed exactly. Unlike other Bristol properties, the restaurant has its own general manager. Bristol determined quickly that this particular property needed to establish the restaurant as a priority, but did not want the hotel general manager to get distracted from managing the rest of the hotel. Bristol therefore elevated the restaurant-manager position to that of restaurant general manager at this property. The restaurant GM reports to the hotel GM, and the result is that the property receives maximum management focus for all of its key operations.

Another distinguishing operational element at this property is the way room service and banquets are handled. The Good Eats Grill kitchen serves them. There is no separate kitchen or menu to handle room service. Bristol also uses the Good Eats Grill kitchen for banquets, and has the final say in establishing banquet menus and costs. Moreover, Bristol has the option of using Good Eats Grill menu items and recipes in preparing the banquet meals (provided that the recipes are followed exactly).

► FINANCE

We have shown how the correct match between a restaurant company and a hotel operator can help to reposition a hotel, increase occupancy, and increase F&B profit. We can investigate other potential financial gains by comparing a summary of the actual 1995 profit-loss statement of the Holiday Inn's original (pre-Bristol) foodservice concept (Grand Cargo Cafe) with a conservatively estimated profit-loss statement of the Good Eats Grill for 1997 (its first year of full operation; see Table 6.8).

A quick comparison of those profit-loss figures shows how establishing a strategic alliance between a hotel and restaurant can improve the overall profitability of the property. Other expenses such as franchise initiation fee ($40,000–$50,000), cost of renovation ($750,000), cost of signs ($5,000), and other miscellaneous marketing costs (grand opening, flyers), must also be factored into assessing the feasibility of converting or opening an

Table 6.8   Profit–loss Comparison

| Grand Cargo Cafe | | | Good Eats Grill | |
Actual 1995	%	Item description	%	Projected 1997
831,519	70.5	Outlet revenues[1]	59.8	1,269,455
199,920	16.9	Banquet revenues	28.4	601,000
148,072	12.6	Other revenues[2]	11.8	251,430
1,179,511	100.0	Total revenues	100.0	2,121,885
405,354	34.4	Food cost	26.4	561,137
525,634	44.5	Payroll[3]	43.2	917,621
43,561	3.7	Other expenses	7.1	148,532
974,555	82.6	Total expenses	76.7	1,627,289
204,956		Profit in dollars		494,596
	17.4	Profit percentage	23.3	

[1]Outlet revenues include restaurant revenues and room service.
[2]Other revenues include banquet-room rental, house portion of the gratuity, and miscellaneous banquet fees.
[3]Including employee benefits and payroll taxes.
Source: Bristol Hotel Company.

Table 6.9 Key Property Performance Indicators

	1996	Projected 1997
Hotel occupancy	72%	85%
ADR	$49	$60
Food profit	5%	25%
Beverage profit	50%	60%

operation prior to proceeding with a project like the one between Holiday Inn Intercontinental and Good Eats Grill.

Final analysis. Throughout this case study analysis, we emphasized how important the repositioning strategy was in turning around the Houston Holiday Inn Intercontinental. A quick look at key property performance indicators (Table 6.9) demonstrates the success of that repositioning strategy.

Moreover, we focused primarily on only one part of the hotel's repositioning strategy, that is, its strategic alignment with a particular restaurant concept. Other factors also contributed to the property's improved performance, including new ownership and management, an influx of cash for renovations, and its new market position. Nevertheless, the alliance between Bristol and Good Eats Grill is seen as key to the property's turnaround. The property's previous restaurant, the Grand Cargo Cafe, was being operated as a hotel amenity rather than as a profit center. To capitalize on the restaurant's po-

tential, the Bristol management team recognized that a new restaurant concept was needed. After objectively evaluating their options, including their own F&B concepts, the team determined that a Good Eats Grill franchise matched Bristol's restaurant needs for this particular property. The Bristol experience demonstrates the importance of evaluating each property on an individual basis rather than making generalizations about what will work for all hotel properties.

In conclusion, from our perspective there is no question that now and in the future we will see more hotel and restaurant companies establishing strategic alliances. It is no longer financially feasible for a hotel restaurant to be operated as just a support function to the hotel's lodging operations. The hotel restaurant must now be viewed as a selling point to generate increased room and restaurant revenues. The hotel restaurant must be managed as its own profit center where the goal is to maximize overall property profits. For the entire property to be profitable, the restaurant concept and the hotel's market position must complement each other. Put another way, in today's competitive business environment the hotel restaurant cannot—and should not try to—be all things to all people. To achieve a competitive edge, hotel companies must consider operating a franchised restaurant brand or leasing space within the hotel to a restaurant company. Doing so may improve customer perception and value, and as a result increase the overall profitability of the property.

6.6 CONTEMPORARY HOTEL CATERING

Patti J. Shock and John Stefanelli

Although on-premise catering is generally the second largest source of revenue for most hotels, following sleeping rooms, the on-premise catering area has been virtually ignored in the hotel school curriculum. The colleges that do offer a course in catering usually focus on hands-on classes consisting of planning, cooking, and serving a meal, which is good background, but is not the role of the hotel catering department.

Catering is often the highest visibility the hotel has on a local level. Catering can create an image for the hotel, both locally and nationally.

▶ DEPARTMENT ORGANIZATION

In most hotels the Director of Catering reports to the Director of Food and Beverage, with Banquet Managers and Banquet Set-Up Managers reporting to Catering. In other hotels you may find a Director of Catering and Convention Service reporting to the Director of Marketing, with the Banquet positions reporting to Food and Beverage. In the latter arrangement, Convention Service usually handles food and beverage functions for groups with 20 or more sleeping rooms with Catering selling and servicing the local social and business markets. Convention Service then does not sell; the room sales department handles that aspect. Convention Service in most hotels, however, handles all of the non-food related logistics, including room set-up,

audio-visual requirements, etc. In hotels where conventions are not an important market segment, Convention Service may not exist, in which case Catering would handle all food and non-food logistics.

The Director of Catering assigns and oversees all functions; oversees catering sales managers; oversees all marketing efforts; interacts with clients and catering managers; coordinates with the hotel sales director; and works with the chef to update and create menus.

Under the Director of Catering there may be an Assistant Catering Director who helps with marketing, oversees Catering Sales Managers, and services one or more accounts. There may be several Catering Sales Managers, depending on the size of the hotel. Catering Sales Managers maintain client contacts and service accounts. Their role is to sell and service functions. They must seek and consult with clients, plan menus, themes, room set-up and decor; negotiate prices; and coordinate with inside departments and outside vendors. There are several excellent graphic room-setup software packages available on the market.

The Catering Department may also employ Catering Sales Representatives who are usually involved only with selling, leaving the servicing to others.

The Banquet Manager implements the Director of Catering's requests; oversees room captains; supervises functions in progress; staffs and schedules servers and bartenders; and coordinates all support departments. He or she is the operations director, as opposed to catering executives, who primarily sell and work with clients to plan events.

The Assistant Banquet Manager reports to the Banquet Manager and supervises table settings and decor. There may be two (or more) assistants; for example, a hotel may have one for the day and one for the evening shift.

The Banquet Set-up Manager supervises the banquet set-up crew; orders tables, chairs, portable bars, and other room equipment from storage; and supervises the tear-down of the room after the event has concluded.

The Scheduler, often referred to as the Diary Clerk, enters bookings in the Master Log (now usually computerized); oversees the timing of all functions and provides adequate turnover time between functions; is responsible for scheduling meeting rooms, reception areas, pool-side areas, meal functions, beverage functions, other functions, and equipment requirements; keeps appropriate records to ensure against overbooking and double booking of space; and is responsible for communicating this information to relevant departments.

The Maître d'Hôtel is the floor manager. He or she is in charge of all service personnel and oversees all aspects of guest service during meal and beverage functions in the various function rooms on the floor.

The Captain is the room manager and is in charge of service at meal functions in a specific room. Captains typically oversee all activity in the entire function room or, depending on the size of the room, in a portion of it. They also supervise the Servers in their room or section of the room.

There are two types of Servers, Food Servers and Beverage Servers. Food Servers deliver foods, alcoholic and non-alcoholic beverages, and utensils to the table; clear tables; and attend to guest needs. Beverage Servers serve alcoholic beverages, usually at receptions. Bus persons, whose primary responsibilities are to clear tables, restock side stands, and serve ice water, rolls, butter and condiments, sometimes back up servers.

The Bartender concentrates on alcoholic beverage production and service. Bartenders are often assisted by Bar Backs, whose primary responsibility is to initially stock and replenish the bars with liquor, ice, glassware and other necessary supplies.

Housemen (sometimes referred to as porters) set up function rooms with risers, hardware, tables, chairs and other necessary equipment. They report to the Banquet Set-up Manager.

Attendants "refresh" meeting rooms during breaks by emptying ashtrays when smoking is permitted, refilling water pitchers, and removing trash. Some catered functions also require Coat-Check Attendants or Restroom Attendants.

The Clerk (or Secretary) handles routine correspondence, types contracts and banquet event orders (BEOs), handles and routes telephone messages, and distributes documents to relevant staff members and other hotel departments.

The Engineering Department provides necessary utilities service, such as air conditioning/heating, setting up electrical panels for major exhibits, hanging banners, and setting up audio visual displays.

Other miscellaneous positions include the following. A Sommelier (or Wine Steward) is used only at fancy, upscale events. The Cashier sells drink tickets to guests at cash bars. A Ticket Taker may be required to collect tickets from guests at the door to the function. Finally, most catering departments employ Stewards to deliver the proper amount of china, glassware, and silver to function rooms.

Whatever the organizational structure, catering's favorable impact on hotel profitability is primarily due to the fact that catering has more control over the variable expenses than does the manager of a typical restaurant. In a restaurant, labor must be scheduled, heat/air conditioning must be on, and food must be kept in inventory, whether or not any guests are present in the facility. In catering, a function must be booked before these items are scheduled or purchased. So there are more variable costs in catering, and more fixed costs in restaurant foodservice.

► THE SALES AND SERVICE PROCESS

Selling is a vital part of catering (see Figure 6.2). To sell a catering event, potential markets must be identified and cultivated. Target markets must be established. Potential markets include association meetings (local monthly meetings as well as the national annual conventions); corporate meetings, including training sessions and incentive banquets; weddings and anniversaries; bar mitzvahs; proms; garden clubs; holiday parties; reunions, both school and military; and fraternal organizations, such as Rotary and Lions. The list is endless.

A marketing plan should be developed that clearly defines the desirable target markets; defines the demand; describes competing caterers; sets financial goals; considers other potential income that catering can generate for the hotel; and describes standardized procedures that must be used to canvass for new clients, qualify leads, make sales calls,

develop contracts, and provide required products and services.

The initial contact for a function can come from the client or the catering department. In many cases, the potential client makes the first inquiry. He or she may contact you by phone, by letter, fax, email, or in person.

If the contact is by phone, be sure the person answering the phone can answer questions, or that someone knowledgeable is always available. Too often a low-paid, untrained person in the office answers the phone, and this can hamper the selling effort. The phone should always be answered within three rings. Always secure the name and phone number of the caller.

If the initial contact is by letter, email, or fax, try to answer with a phone call. Copies of the letter were most likely sent to several caterers and it is best to be the first to respond. More information is often needed, such as the budget the client has for the event or the objective of the function. This initial contact also provides the opportunity to invite the potential client to the property for lunch and a tour. Every effort should be made to get the potential client into the hotel, on your home turf.

Sometimes a letter will include a Request for Proposal (RFP), which is a written prospectus from professional meeting planners. An RFP usually indicates that the potential client is very knowledgeable about catering and is usually a sophisticated negotiator.

If potential clients stop by in person without an appointment, have someone see them as soon as possible. Offer some light refreshments to keep them occupied until someone is available. Give an accurate estimate of how long they will have to wait. Have the recep-

Figure 6.2   Steps in Selling and Servicing a Catering Event

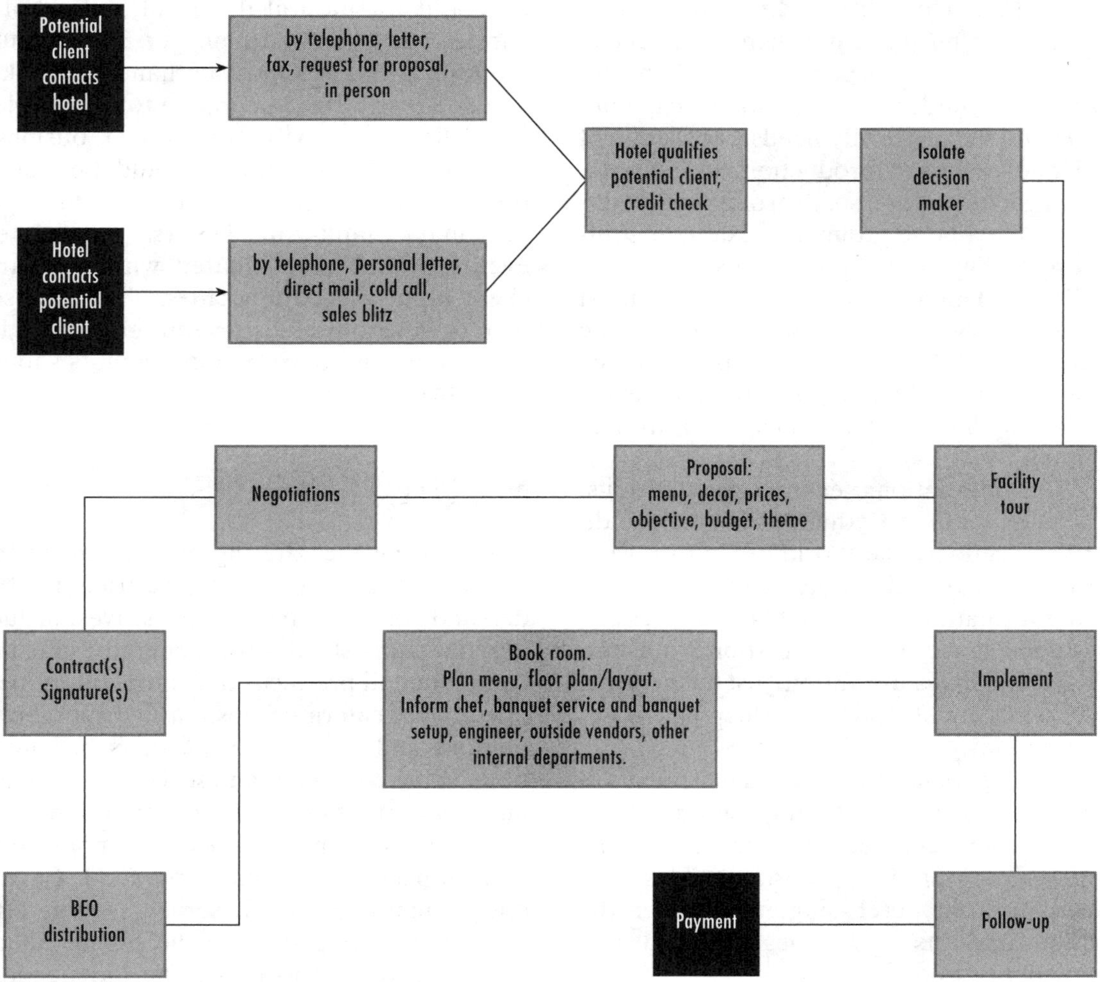

```
Potential          by telephone, letter,
client             fax, request for proposal,
contacts           in person
hotel                                              Hotel qualifies         Isolate
                                                   potential client;       decision
                                                   credit check            maker
Hotel              by telephone, personal letter,
contacts           direct mail, cold call,
potential          sales blitz
client

                                        Proposal:
            Negotiations            menu, decor, prices,          Facility
                                    objective, budget, theme      tour

                                    Book room.
Contract(s)                    Plan menu, floor plan/layout.
Signature(s)              Inform chef, banquet service and banquet    Implement
                          setup, engineer, outside vendors, other
                                  internal departments.

BEO                                                          Payment    Follow-up
distribution
```

tionist obtain preliminary information, such as their desired date(s) and type of function, to get them involved in the planning process right away. Also, keep a binder handy for browsing that contains testimonial letters from happy clients and photos of previous events.

A Group History File should be created whenever initial contact is made. The file should include all facets of the business relationship, from initial contact to final disposition. Standardized information includes name of contact, name of decision maker, titles, organization, types of events held, number of events held, when events are held, attendance figures, all correspondence, notes from phone conversations, contracts, credit history, potential for future business, and client preferences.

The manager responding to client inquiries must understand the hotel's capabilities. He or she especially needs knowledge of food and beverage production and service. Planning a menu for a small group is quite different from a large group. For example, soufflé for 1,000 would be quite impossible.

When planning a menu, the caterer must first know the occasion or reason for the event. The style of service also depends on the occasion. It would be inappropriate to have a deli sandwich buffet for an auspicious awards banquet.

With international events, protocol must be considered in everything from decor to dietary restrictions. The World of Culture website (http://www.webofculture.com/) provides good information on a variety of cultures.

Public space or function rooms must be forecast for space utilization, just as the hotel sales department forecasts sleeping rooms requirements.

Working well with inside departments is critical. Linens have to be requisitioned from the linen room; engineers must insure that the room temperature is appropriate; tables must be set up; and purchasing must order the correct amounts and types of food and beverages.

Outside vendors, such as decorators, audio-visual companies, florists, printers, and photographers may be needed by the client to ensure a successful event.

Performing well is the next step. Here the emphasis shifts from sales to service. Guests must be treated with care; service must be punctual; foods, presentations, cleanliness, and ambiance must meet desired quality standards; professional attention must be paid to all details; the function host should be made to feel like a guest at the event, instead of a harassed and worried manager. Last minute requests and crises must be handled quickly and efficiently. It is imperative to be flexible.

Follow-up is vital for repeat business. Standardized procedures should be developed for thank-you calls and individualized, personal thank-you letters. Completed events should be evaluated with staff and client input. Referral business should be solicited. Appropriate souvenir gifts may be presented. And outstanding accounts should be settled.

▶ FUTURE ISSUES

Issues facing the catering department in the future include new alcohol restrictions; the demand for more menu alternatives, including low-fat, pesticide-free, generally safe, uncontaminated products; the competition from off-premise catering firms; waste disposal regulations and recycling; consumers becoming more value conscious; and service becoming a more important point of differentiation.

Subcontracting will become more common, especially for labor and food. Calling one company to provide servers is more efficient than having staff on the phone calling individual on-call workers. The independent labor contractor trains staff and does all of the payroll and paperwork.

Caterers can't afford to have all types of expertise on their staffs. With a Japanese theme, a sushi restaurant may be subcontracted. Or a local barbecue specialist, oyster roaster, or coffee service company can handle unique events. The hotel would add about 20 percent markup to the subcontractor's bill, and then add the cost of the rest of the meal prepared in-house.

In the past, menus rarely changed. Today, many menus are changed with the season. In the future it will be important to be able to distinguish between a fad and a trend. Fads, such as Nouvelle Cuisine, are short-lived. Trends, such as the demand for fresh foods and more nutritious food, are more permanent.

Probably the biggest challenge is the perception among guests that all caterers are exactly alike. Buyers may feel that there is always another caterer able to provide similar service. It is imperative for the successful caterer to differentiate their food and service from their competition. The price/value rela-tionship will become more important as caterers attempt to rise above the competition.

There are a multitude of resources available on the web, including, for example, Room Calculator (http://www.mmaweb.com/meetings/Workshop/roomcalc.html), which will determine how many guests you can fit into a room in various configurations. Many caterers have their menus online which are interesting to see. Special Events Magazine (http://www.specialevents.com/magazine/) and Event Solutions (http://www.event-solutions.com/) have timely articles that are archived online and are searchable.

A large collection of useful catering web links can be found at: http://www.unlv.edu/Tourism/Catering_and_Special_Events.html.

6.7 A DAY IN THE LIFE OF AN EXECUTIVE DIRECTOR OF CATERING SALES AND CONVENTION SERVICES

Rich Benninger

Each day I wake up saying, "Today is the day I will get everything done." It is my optimist side taking control before my realist side has a chance to ruin my day. Because I ply my trade at a 5,034-room hotel with over 380,000 square feet of banquet space, it is usually around 8:00 A.M. when my realist side kicks in. By this time I have been at work for an hour or more and start taking victories as soon as they come. The day is half over for the dedicated line cast members who started working at 4:00 A.M. so our thousands of guests can enjoy their morning breakfast. These employees are the backbone of catering. Their workday here will end in four more hours, and many will go to a second job.

The day will not end for the catering director until a few things are completed. The director has just one job, sort of, and is the front person for the operation. Now, please allow me to take you on a journey through a typical day in the life of a catering director. But first I must make coffee. Nobody else in the office notices that 1 ounce of coffee left in a pot does not mean "There's coffee in the pot." The following describes what I did today.

▶ BOOKING BUSINESS

Customers are the number-one component of a successful catering operation. Without customers, the grandest ballrooms, the most spectacular cuisine, and the best service are all moot points. So, every day you must work to fill the pipeline with customers. The rooms sales managers are really doing a great job. They are booking over quota and getting contracts with great food and beverage minimums. For just a moment, I fantasize that this will never end and life will always be good.

Oh no! We have just been asked why the week between Christmas and New Year's does not have any events. Transient room sales are strong, but they do not use function space. It's up to catering sales to fill in the hole. My team tells me that had sales not already done so they could easily fill space a week before or a week later, but that holiday week is going to be tough to fill. I know this is true, but the senior vice president does not care that something is tough. He wants to know what we are doing to get business. And by the way, not discount business. We start out looking for full-paying customers and if that does not work, *then* we will look at discounting.

I am excited to meet a customer for a site visit at 7:30 A.M. I am the first property she is looking at for a 2,500-guest reception and concert. I just talked to her yesterday for the very first time. All our meeting space is booked but I'm in luck; we have space in our arena. I work with the arena for about an hour to get the space and brainstorm on things we can do to book this business. The arena operations guys are great to work with. They enjoy coming to the catering office for cappuccino. I smile when I think how cheap cappuccino is and how many favors it buys from operations cast members.

We spend an hour walking our customer through her event. Her company sells very large industrial trucks, and when we tell her we can put a concrete mixer right in the middle of her reception she is all smiles. I make note to get the dimensions of the roll-up doors. We are going to be more expensive than the competition, but we provide more value. We can make this a one-stop shopping experience. I make a note to call transportation companies and gather quotes. I know the other properties will not get involved in dealing with all the outside vendors, and I use this as a selling advantage. I make a note to list this as a tentative piece of business worth $165,000 or more.

Next I make a hasty trip across property to check on a breakfast we are doing on the stage of our production show. We are lucky to have an incentive house tour our property, and we have pulled out all the stops to let this VIP group know we value their business. I am pleased with the spectacular stage sets and the look of the breakfast. I laugh with the sales manager when he apologizes for only giving us 36 hours notice on the breakfast. I assure him the financial rewards of getting large incentive bookings will more than make up for the short notice. I make a note to send each guest a thank-you note for taking the time to tour our property.

▶ FINALIZING PROGRAMS

The only time a program is truly finalized is once the customers are gone and the final bill is paid. And then just the physical stuff is over. Conversations about the really good stuff and the sometimes bad stuff can go on for years. Repeat customers are usually the best ones to have, but they tend to remember that five years ago the potato salad did not have a spoon in it when the company president went to the buffet 15 minutes before it was scheduled to open. "Let's not let that happen this year."

You spend months working to get everything planned at least three weeks in advance. Then you give all the information to the operating departments two weeks out. For some groups this works really well, and once you work out the details they only make minor changes. Other groups are not quite so tidy in their planning.

Today I had a group arrive on site, and we reviewed their banquet event orders. It would be easier to say we redid their banquet event orders (BEOs). At 9:00 A.M. we started reviewing 45 meal function BEOs. By 2:15 P.M. we had made major changes to 42 of them. I wonder aloud if they would like to change the other three just for good measure. The chefs are circling the catering office like sharks. All the food ordering is on hold until the revised BEOs are signed off on. While I'm working with the clients to refinalize, the chefs and purchasing agents are on the phone undoing all the ordering they did days ago. Purveyors are all on standby to rush product to us. I am thankful we have excellent relationships with these wonderful people, who will now pull off miracles to get us product over the weekend.

My assistant is ready to shoot someone. Making the changes once is enough of a challenge, but now we are changing things for a second and third time in one day. I smile as I say, "Yes, I'm sure I can get you a completely new set of BEOs by 5:00 P.M." Just as I tell myself we must be done with changes, my contact calls and changes two of the remaining original three BEOs. I get no comfort from the fact that the one lone original BEO is for an event that does not happen until five days from now. I do, however, get great comfort from the knowledge that my clients will spend over $800,000 in the next eight days.

► CREATING MENUS

I promise a major corporate client that I will write three custom menu options for their opening reception. I tell them I will do it on Saturday and I'll fax the menus so they have them for a Monday meeting. I promise myself I will not commit to doing any more projects on Saturday. It is going to be my catch-up day, and I've been filling the day with new projects. I may have to work a few hours on Sunday to get on track for next week. The great thing about writing custom menus is every time I do one I add it to my hot menu file and just keep reusing it. I do make a notation of whom I send each one to. I would hate to send someone the same custom menu twice.

In this world of ever more sophisticated customers, the quest for new menus has taken on a life all its own. The unfortunate side of this sophisticated customer often comes with fond memories of a gourmet dinner for two at some exotic trendy restaurant. Other favorite sources of wonderful ideas are glossy cooking magazines and TV cooking shows. Now the simple task of any caterer is to figure out how to make these menus, designed to serve eight, work for hundreds or thousands. Of course, you are not alone in this situation. The culinary staff is right there with you. Please don't take it personally that many of them think you are crazy.

► WORKING EVENTS

Luckily for my catering department, we work at a property where we are cast in the role of salespeople. Another team of professionals handles operations. Still, I can't resist taking 10 minutes and going down to see how setup is going for a poolside reception. Somehow

I spend 45 minutes at the pool, and now I'm going to have to rush to a pre-con meeting. The clients who spent the day making changes are very big customers, and the pre-con will be a big production. We have all our top executives coming by to say hello. I am anxious to see how the eight cheerleaders will do with the dance number they are performing in the center of the hollow square. I am very pleased to see the banquet and entertainment departments have everything in perfect order.

► LEADING AN OFFICE

One of my catering managers comes into my office and asks to talk. In two days she will renew her wedding vows and she is very nervous. I go into father mode and we make a list of things she has to do. I laugh when I ask her why she is nervous about having a party for 30 people when every day she books parties for hundreds of guests. I try to ease her burden of preparing some of the food herself. I suggest she just bring in the bowls she wants to use and I'll have the kitchen fill them up with whatever she wants. I smile when she says, "No, thank you, I make really good salads myself." I wonder, does that mean our salads are not really good?

Throughout the day, my staff gives me encouragement while I am working to get all the changes made on my group. They all offer to help, and I notice the number of things I am asked to look at is very low today. I am proud of my staff and make a note to have a special breakfast at our catering meeting next week. It has been almost two months since we started a new format for our catering meetings, and I must say they are much better and everyone seems happier with them.

► BUDGETS

Yesterday we had our review for next year's budget. I must start working on a really aggressive marketing plan to make the revenue number we are after. For today, I'll just start by having a binder made so I feel like I'm making progress. I ask my assistant to run some reports so I can take them home and look at them. I know I'll never look at them while I'm home, but if I find spare time I'll have them, just in case.

► MENTORING AND INDUSTRY INVOLVEMENT

I call two new interns from the university to confirm their Saturday appointments with me. I need to meet with them to determine their interests and what program they are going to follow for the eight months they will spend with us. I hope they will want to work on the marketing plan and be active in the National Association of Catering Executives (NACE). I also have a protégé from the university, and it would be nice if all three can work together on projects. I feel pressure to provide these students with an overwhelmingly positive experience. Last year I was voted Outstanding Mentor of the Year, and now I feel a higher level of expectation.

Unfortunately, I have to cancel my NACE Board of Directors meeting scheduled for today. I am the president of our chapter, and I have not had time to work on the things I need for the meeting. I do not want to waste the board's time. I make a note to call our NACE intern and schedule a meeting to see what tasks I can have her handle for the Board. Involvement in NACE is rewarding, but it is like a part-time job. What was I thinking when we agreed to do a fund-raising dinner for 1,000 in February? I'm sure it was the same thing I thought when I said I would love to teach an extension class at the University. It all seems so far away when I say yes. Somehow it all works out.

▶ ENTERTAINING

It's 5:00 P.M. and I need to leave for a cocktail party at a sister property across the street. I am joining the vice president of sales and the executive director of convention services to entertain clients. We have a cocktail party and then a 7:30 P.M. dinner and a 10:00 P.M. show. The evening is wonderful. Our clients really enjoy the special attention we give them. When 10:00 P.M. comes, I wonder if I'll stay awake at the show. My fears are unjustified. The comedian is so funny my sides hurt from laughing. I think, what a great career. I get to have fun while I work. As the evening ends at 11:30 P.M. I confirm that I'll play golf in two weeks—just another sacrifice for my clients.

▶ PERSONAL LIFE

My four golden retrievers are really happy to see me. I know they have had dinner and were well cared for while I was gone, but I feed them again. It is the most wonderful thing I do each day. I take my suit off and get into sweats. It's time to go for a walk and tell them all about my day. They agree that making so many changes is just not right. We devise a plan to keep others from making my day so stressed. Then we talk about the three-day trip we are taking to Utah the day my in-house group ends. It will be our first motor home trip, and we are all excited. It seems my golden retrievers are tired of camping in a tent. Additionally, I plan to spend time working on my online masters degree, and a motor home will be a good place to work. I try not to think too hard about my degree. It makes it hard to sleep when I think of working on my final project.

Now it's 12:30 A.M. and I need to get in bed. As I lie down, I resolve that tomorrow will be "the day I get everything done."

6.8 THE ORGANIZATION AND MANAGEMENT OF HOTEL BEVERAGE OPERATIONS

Valentino Luciani

▶ BRIEF HISTORY OF BEVERAGES

A beverage such as a glass of wine, a beer, or a cocktail has the magic power of bringing people together. Beverages have always made an impact on the evolution of humankind. Thanks to modern technology and more advanced carbon-dating techniques, archeologists have now established with certainty that our species has been around for several hundred thousand years—a lot longer than was estimated 50 years ago. In accepting the fact that alcohol is as old as we are, it would be of great interest to discover what type of beverages were consumed over such a span of time. We can only assume that the earliest beverages were fermented cider-type concoctions made from various kinds of fruit, or brews made from grain, seeds, and anything else nature had to offer. These drinks were perhaps enriched with spices, herbs, and probably more exotic flavoring agents, some of which have been forgotten or lost over the centuries.

What is known for certain is included in recorded history, and it is relatively recent when compared to the newly found lifespan of *Homo sapiens erectus*. In recent excavations, some of the first evidence of eating food and consuming a beverage in a communal fashion is found in the Orkney Islands, close to Denmark. It was a custom then to build dwellings around a common dispenser where foods and drinks were prepared.

Egyptologists have recently published photos of wall paintings found in pharaohs' tombs. In these remarkably preserved works of art one can clearly see Egyptian workers harvesting grapes and preparing them for winemaking. The (presumably filled) wine vessels were then placed in an orderly fashion next to the tomb. The Egyptian nobles believed that these beverages made the best companions for the pharaoh's eternal travel.

Greek and Roman historians report that wine and other alcoholic beverages played a vital role in their societies. The fun-loving Romans went as far as worshiping a beverage deity: Bacchus, the god of wine. Wine and brew shops, which are thought to have been introduced approximately 6,000 years ago, could be found at every street corner of ancient Rome. In the United States, the first person on record to own a tavern and sell alcoholic beverages to patrons was Samuel Cole. His beverage business was already prospering by 1634.

Beer, which presently accounts for 51 percent of alcoholic beverage sales, carries on a fine tradition in our country. According to the diary of the *Mayflower*'s captain, the ship was not scheduled to dock on Plymouth Rock but was made to stop there mainly because it had run out of beer.

Nonalcoholic beverages such as coffee, tea, fruit juices, and, later, carbonated beverages have also made a considerable impact on our evolution and lifestyle. During the past five decades, Coca-Cola has taken the world by storm. Of the hot beverages, coffee and tea are the uncontested kings. One has to only observe the proliferation of specialty coffee shops and kiosks to begin to understand the impact of this beverage.

► OVERVIEW

The beverage industry grows in popularity every year. *Restaurant U.S.A.*, the official publication of the National Restaurant Association, reported in 1995 that total sales for bars and taverns neared the $11 billion mark. For the year 2005, total sales for bars and taverns are expected to exceed the threshold of $15 billion in sales. Hotels, restaurants, and resorts have for some time regarded the beverage sector as a profitable one. In a medium to large-size hotel, a typical beverage department can produce a profit of over 50 percent of sales. In comparison, a food department shows, at best, a profit of between 15 and 18 percent of sales. Beverage is also gradually gaining a larger share of sales. Hotel operators report that while two decades ago the sales ratio was

85–15 (85 percent food sales, 15 percent beverage sales), today the average is closer to 80–20.

Before World War II, in a small to medium-sized hotel and restaurant operation, the person in charge of the beverage department was the restaurant manager. In many properties, a lead bartender or the wine steward was given the responsibility to run the department.

Today, in a medium to large-size hotel operation, the beverage department has a distinct place in the organization chart, and the beverage manager is the person in charge of running and supervising all of the department activities. The organization chart is a diagram that shows the operation's working positions and how they interconnect. The beverage manager usually reports to the food and beverage director. In a very large hotel operation (over 2,000), the F&B director reports to the vice president of food and beverage.

During the last decade, some properties have adopted a different strategy where there are separate food and beverage directors. In these properties the executive chef, who in most cases acts more as a food director than a hands-on chef, is placed in charge of the food

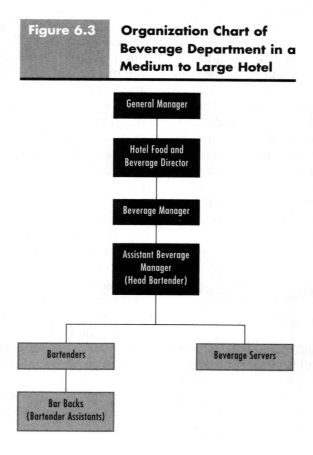

Figure 6.3   **Organization Chart of Beverage Department in a Medium to Large Hotel**

- General Manager
- Hotel Food and Beverage Director
- Beverage Manager
- Assistant Beverage Manager (Head Bartender)
- Bartenders
- Beverage Servers
- Bar Backs (Bartender Assistants)

department. He or she enjoys a higher degree of independence and reports directly to the general manager, vice president of operations, or, in some instances, directly to the hotel president. The same is true of the beverage director.

Both of these directors are considered equal in the organization chart. They strive to work together effectively and to communicate daily. They are interdependent in many ways but also aware of the need for communication. In addition, each must establish a sound working rapport with department heads of other hotel sectors. These include front desk supervisors, executive housekeepers, human resource directors, and so forth. Typical of this case, the food manager and the beverage manager, particularly, come together at the end of the month, when the results of their efforts are included in the same profit and loss statement.

Although larger properties find this organization chart modification beneficial to the operation, the majority of hotel properties retain the traditional hierarchy, structuring the chain of command in the same fashion as for the past six or seven decades. A typical example of a classic organization chart for a beverage operation in a large hotel is shown in Figure 6.3.

► SHOP TALK AND THE ACTIVE MANAGER

The bar manager or beverage director is the person who makes it all happen in relation to hotel beverages. Although specific responsibilities may vary from one hotel to another, the fundamental role of the manager is to make certain that the five basic functions of management are applied effectively. As in many other business sectors, these are planning, organizing, directing, staffing, and controlling. The wise and competent bar manager applies and adapts the fundamental principles of each of these functions to the specific needs of the operation. All five functions are determining factors in meeting the operation's ultimate objective: profitability.

It all begins with planning and continues in directing and organizing so that the staff on a daily basis diligently adheres to the established standards. Examples: checking bartenders' opening and closing duties, standardizing drink recipes, verifying that the bar par stock (established amount of beverage product) is at the proper level, scheduling, forecasting, frequently communicating with other fellow managers (in particular the catering manager and the executive steward), and so forth.

The competent bar manager always finds sufficient time to inspect the underbars (the working area behind and underneath the bar counter), the jockey boxes (the small compartment next to the ice bin), and the speed racks (where the inexpensive, or well, bottles and the more popular brand-name liquor are placed).

The above are also the areas where managers cannot place enough emphasis on how vital it is to the operation to continuously apply sanitary standards and practice the utmost cleanliness. Glassware must not only be cleaned but sanitized as well.

An important organizational and training function is the sequencing of beverage stock. This is the order in which spirits and cordials are placed on the shelves or speed rack. It also refers to the order by which the drinks are called to the bartender by the serving staff, and it must always be the same. Supervising the beverage staff and ensuring that control methods are foolproof are crucial and demanding tasks; sequencing provides part of the structural mix that helps assure consistency of product and service.

► MARKETING AND MERCHANDISING

Throughout the competitive hotel industry, beverage managers consider smart marketing and effective merchandising the keys to success. The marketing of the overall operation and the merchandising of the beverage product require time, experience, and commitment. To make the beverage operation attractive to different types of patrons and to convey a message of value in the service of beverages, bar managers and directors regularly brainstorm. More trendy cocktails are being created daily. Light and refreshing blush wines and sparkling wines are introduced in the preparation of new drinks. Promotional programs and attractive entertainment are featured to keep lounges full and patrons eager to return.

Conscientious beverage managers never rest on their laurels—they are always on the lookout for profitable ways to stay ahead of the competition. As the beverage sector grows and patrons' expectations increase, there are always new and challenging tasks to deal with. The following is a list of managerial tasks with which beverage managers are occupied on an ongoing basis:

- Introducing control systems that are more effective in monitoring the operation—for example, upgrading forms for properly storing and issuing beverage products and for inventory purposes.

- Establishing ongoing training sessions.
- Evaluating beverage staffs' work performance.
- Checking city and county ordinances regarding the service of alcohol and reviewing state and federal laws on handling liquor responsibly.
- Preventing bartenders from committing fraud and attempting illegal practices.
- Ensuring proper sanitary standards are applied throughout the bar outlets and the storage and the service areas.
- Making certain everyone in the department adheres to proper safety standards.
- Writing, rewriting, and updating bar working manuals and handbooks according to need.
- Evaluating the bar menu offerings and, whenever possible, substituting slow-selling liquor brands with more attractive and trendy ones.
- In particular, renewing beverage product selection of specialty beers (e.g., by featuring microbrewed products), brandies, and cordials.
- Tracking trends. For example, a current trend is apparent in cordials or liqueurs. Beverage operators are finding that light, sweet, and pleasant-tasting cordials such as Godiva White Chocolate, Nocello, Grand Marnier, Frangelico, Drambuie, and Bailey's Irish Cream are enjoying newfound popularity. They are also seeing lots of movement in attractive new products such as Remy Red and the fabulous premium tequilas and Polish vodkas.
- Last but not least, assuring the consistency and quality of the service provided to the bar and lounge patron.

► HUMAN RESOURCES

Outstanding service is the result of a sound organization and diligent recruiting. Bartenders and beverage servers can be talented and willing, but if they are not provided with the necessary resources, total management support, encouragement, and guidance, their efforts will be in vain. A situation may arise where the deciding factor in the delivery of fine and consistent service depends less on personnel skills and attitude than on the role played by management.

Service is the backbone of the hospitality industry. According to Kotschevar and Luciani (1996), "with the new millennium passing by, customers' expectations are on the rise." An effective leader finds the proper ways and means to provide the employees with the tools they need to meet these expectations.

Progressive beverage managers now also use the empowerment concept. Empowerment is a management decision by which an employee is given authority to take steps outside the spectrum of regular duties and make certain decisions that are normally in management's domain. According to many new beverage managers, the progressive coach approach seems to yield positive results among beverage staffs. The old disciplinarian management style is increasingly out of place in today's beverage business world.

► THE FUTURE OF BEVERAGE OPERATIONS

In medium to larger hotel properties, like all department managers, beverage managers are required to prepare a business forecast based on historical data, hotel occupancy, and special event bookings for the forecasting period. An accurate forecast helps the manager prepare for clientele volume so that potential revenue can be maximized. It also helps greatly in effectively managing beverage stock, payroll, staff scheduling, and other expenses.

Many hotel executives agree that the first decade of the twenty-first century will be significant for the beverage industry. One peculiar prediction is that, although total hotel revenues are expected to grow considerably, the ratio of beverage sales to room sales will remain the same or decrease slightly. Because of the terrorist attacks in 2001 and the ongoing wars in the Middle East, hotel revenues have not met expectations. Beverage sales, though, have seen an increase in revenue growth. Much of this is due to vigorous promotion and merchandising, particularly of new cocktails and ambitious—even spectacular—wine sales programs. Independent bar and lounge operators also feel confident that, unless more unpredictable events take place, the rest of the decade will be challenging but prosperous.

Beverage distributing firms are also optimistic. They foresee a wider availability of beverage products not only for the hospitality industry but also in areas such as convenience stores, supermarkets, and beverage-specific retail outlets. Beverages that are expected to substantially increase in sales volume are bottled waters, bottled specialty teas, single-malt Scotch whiskys, Cognacs, aged bourbons, premium tequilas, and grappas. There is a general consensus among vendors that beer sales will remain static and that wine will experience a marginal but steady growth, particularly from new areas of production, both nationally and internationally.

It is expected that federal and state liquor laws will remain substantially unchanged, with minor exceptions. It also appears that the states will maintain the basic structure of belonging either to control or license categories. Many beverage managers are concerned about government-imposed taxes on liquor and hope they will not be increased.

Beverage managers are concerned about the continuing lowering of the blood alcohol threshold for driving under the influence (DUI) of alcohol or drugs. The lower the threshold—say, 0.08—the more careful in hiring, training, and supervising managers have to be. Over-service of alcohol is an industry-wide problem that presents managers with a variety of challenges. It is important to have policies under which the manager and operation work that minimize the risk to the business and to the public while legally selling and serving beverages.

Education in beverage management is expected to extend to new horizons. Sonoma State University offers a bachelor of science degree in wine management. Through a well-planned university extension program, the University of California, Davis, is expanding on specialized short courses associated with their degree programs in enology and viticulture. The William F. Harrah College of Hotel Administration at the University of Nevada, Las Vegas, started a beverage management major commencing in the fall semester of 2001. Cornell University's School of Hotel Administration, among others, is considering expanding their professional development courses and adding courses on handling and serving alcoholic beverages with care.

▶ AS I SEE IT

While reviewing the industry's projections, it would be difficult to leave out hotel executives' most recent comments on labor issues and concerns. During the past decade, it has been frequently reported that staffing or finding the person most suitable for a particular job is becoming a tougher management function. Many managers agree that staffing responsibilities are requiring more time and effort than ever before. Part of this is attributed to labor trends. The pool of steady and loyal workers is decreasing in size. In addition, the hospitality industry is experiencing unprecedented employee turnover. A major restaurant company has recently reported to me employee turnover of nearly 200 percent for hourly employees, 60 percent for clerical and secretarial staff, and 25 percent for managerial staff. The turnover ratio of bartenders and cocktail servers was reported to be almost the same as that of typical dining room staff such as food servers and bus persons (Lattin, 1998). One can imagine the frustration of a beverage manager who, after spending considerable effort, time, and company money in coaching and training a new bartender, finds out she is planning to quit the following week.

What can be done to deal effectively with this concern? Rewards as motivators provide some positive results. Other means of providing monetary incentives so the operation can retain employees longer may also be effective.

It is strongly recommended here that the best measure management can undertake for this purpose is to provide the employee with a comfortable working environment, promote teamwork and camaraderie, and foster healthy working relationships. In short, the beverage manager is challenged to become the employer of choice for beverage professionals.

In general, the beverage future looks brighter than most other sectors of the hospitality industry. However, the managers and directors who truly will make a difference will be those who step out, participate, and make things happen. The aggressive new manager always finds ways to establish a good rapport with community leaders and is tireless in devising and developing new means of attracting additional clientele. Whenever possible, he or she makes the effort to attend beverage conventions and trade shows; uses the hotel website to reinforce marketing strate-gies and list bar special drinks, promotions, and happy hour times; and never rests on his or her laurels.

The modern beverage manager is no longer just the head bartender. This professional is responsible for millions of dollars of the hotel's assets and operates in a high-energy, fast-paced, and challenging environment. It's a lot of fun, though, and rewarding, too. It is a managerial position with a solid future.

6.9 CASE STUDY: CRISIS IN THE FOOD COURT

Nancy Swanger

Morgan Black is the director of operations of an on-property food court made up of five branded quick-service restaurant concepts and one full-service casual dining outlet. The resort hotel, of which the food court is a part, attracts affluent guests who are traveling with their families. The food court is located in a common area not far from some of the resort's most popular, kid friendly recreational activities. It also attracts local guests who are not staying at the resort, but just visiting.

One Sunday afternoon, when the hotel's 2,500 rooms and suites were nearly at full occupancy, an incident occurred at the branded sandwich shop that was both bizarre and frightening to those involved.

As was typical of the property, lunchtime in the common restaurant area was busy and extended well into the afternoon as families arrived for weeklong stays. A father and son approached the counter of the sandwich shop to order a bite to eat. They were nearing the register to pay for their meal when the son suddenly collapsed and fell to the floor, hitting his head on the glass window separating the customers from the sandwich preparation area. The boy, who was wearing short pants, fell into a puddle of his own bloody feces as he hit the floor. As it all happened so suddenly, those who were witnesses said it was like the boy must have voided as he was collapsing, as there were no signs of any problem prior to the actual fall.

As one might expect, the scene caused quite a stir among guests in the area. One of the shop's employees promptly called 911 for an ambulance. Within a very short period, paramedics arrived to care for the boy. It was several minutes before he was stable enough to transport, as they could not get the bleeding to stop. Morgan, who was on property, arrived just as the boy was being transported to the local hospital for treatment.

Of course, a crowd had gathered, and talk

of the tragedy was spreading rapidly throughout the property. The store was immediately closed and the area around the sandwich shop cordoned off. In trying to assess the situation, Morgan discovered the following:

1. When the young boy hit the floor, the puddle of bloody excrement splattered everywhere—even hitting other guests who were in line.

2. One of the employees, who probably reacted without thinking, began to clean up the mess with her bare hands.

3. The identities of the father and son were not known.

4. A reporter from the local newspaper was a guest at the food court that day and wanted comments on what happened.

Suggest a plan for Morgan's handling of the situation.

Points to Consider

- Involvement of the health department?
- Notification of the brand's corporate office?
- Condition of the boy?
- Clean-up process?
- Treatment of contaminated items?
- Handling affected guests and employees?
- Methods to reassure resort guests?
- When to reopen and resume business as usual?
- Implications of what happened—short and long term?
- Role of the resort's crisis team?
- Training gaps?

6.10 CASE STUDY: OUTSIDE THE BOX IN THE FOOD AND BEVERAGE DIVISION

The Corporate Food and Beverage Committee, through its executive director, has ordered each hotel in the SunRise Hospitality chain (11 medium-size, full-service hotels situated in the Southeast, South, and Southwest) to submit a plan to completely rethink one restaurant in each hotel. SunRise Hospitality specializes in catering to the upscale business traveler and, increasingly, the high-tech companies that are now moving to the South from California, the Seattle region, and the Northeast. Their average room rates are consistently in the top 15 percent of all hotels in their market areas. Historically, though, this has been a fairly conservative and risk-averse hotel company.

The corporate office wants to change this and, in the process, to involve each hotel in decision making. The executive director of F&B wants to evaluate plans from each hotel's food and beverage director that "think outside the box." Among the ideas floating around the company on the F&B directors' grapevine are the following:

- Feature menus that emphasize local or regional cuisine. The idea here is to utilize fresh ingredients and local meat, produce, and seafood, and to feature the ethnic and cultural diversity of each hotel's local market area. One goal of this plan is to make the hotel restaurant appeal to local clientele in addition to its guests.

- Outsource one restaurant to a well-established regional independent operator.
- Outsource one restaurant to a national chain.
- Hire a celebrity chef to bring prestige and favorable publicity to the hotel.

These are only a few of the possibilities. As food and beverage director, you have brought this plan to a meeting of your staff for purposes of general background discussion and ideas about how to proceed. Included in this meeting are the executive chef and chief steward, the manager and assistant manager of your formal French-service dining room, the wine steward, and the director of purchasing.

After presenting the corporate plan, you ask for ideas and comments. The chef, who is French, is absolutely devastated and seems to be treating the corporate directive as a personal insult. He walks out in a huff, threatening to pack up his knives and recipes and go back to France. The restaurant manager is interested in the corporate idea but says she has just spent the last five months hiring and training about half of her restaurant staff in tableside preparation and service of the French menu. She is worried that switching menus this fast may cause her operation to suffer, at least in the short term.

The wine steward considers the challenge somewhat ambiguous because, depending on what eventually is decided, he will have to choose a complementary wine list to enhance the new concept or lose his job to an outsider.

The director of purchasing is intrigued by the idea of exploring new local markets. However, he too worries that some of the options may diminish his responsibilities.

Your job as director of food and beverage is to help each department head to develop a plan that will satisfy his or her concerns while following the dictates of corporate policy.

(*Note:* Additional insights into potential solutions to this case may be gained by reading the essay by C. Lee Evans later in this book.)

REFERENCES

Allen, Robin Lee. 1996. "Hotel Chains 'Taking It to the Street' in Quests for Mainstream Dining Appeal." *Nation's Restaurant News* 30(17).

Dubé, L., C.A. Enz, L.M. Renaghan, and J.A. Siguaw. 1999. *The Key to Best Practices in the U.S. Lodging Industry.* Ithaca, NY: Cornell University, Center for Hospitality Research.

Hanson, Bjorn. 1984. "Hotel Foodservice: Where's the Profit?" *Cornell Hotel and Restaurant Administration Quarterly* 25(2):92–96.

Hensdill, Cherie. 1996. "Partnerships in Dining." *Hotels* 30(2):57–60.

Hubsch, Allen W. 1966. "Hotel Food and Beverage Management." *Cornell Hotel and Restaurant Administration Quarterly* 7(3):9–11, 18–19.

Kotschevar, L., and V. Luciani. 1996. *Presenting Service.* Chicago: Education Foundation of the National Restaurant Association.

Lattin, Gerald. 1998. *The Lodging and Foodservice Industry.* East Lansing, MI: Educational

Institute of the American Hotel and Motel Association.

Liberson, Judy. 1995. "Restaurant Chains Partner with Hotels to Satisfy Different Needs, Tastes." *Lodging* (September):1, 8–9.

———. 1996a. "The Global Dinner Plate." *Lodging* 22(1):85–88.

———. 1996b. "Holiday Inn Offers Assorted Food Options with New Quick Food Concept." *Hotel Business* (June):9.

Parseghian, Pamela. 1996. "Branding Offers Hotels Opportunities to Increase Food Sales." *Nation's Restaurant News* 30(23):96.

Siguaw, Judy A., and Cathy A. Enz. 1999. "Best Practices in Food and Beverage Management." *Cornell Hotel and Restaurant Administration Quarterly* 40(5):50–57.

Strate, Robert W., and Clinton L. Rappole. 1997. "Strategic Alliances Between Hotels and Restaurants." *Cornell Hotel and Restaurant Administration Quarterly* 37(3):50–61.

Witham, Glenn. 1995a. "Trader Vic's Wraps Up 60th Birthday Bash." *Cornell Hotel and Restaurant Administration Quarterly* 36(3):14.

———. 1995b. "Harvey: Expansion and Conversion." *Cornell Hotel and Restaurant Administration Quarterly* 36(4):13.

Wolff, Carlo. 1995. "Hyatt Regency Columbus Blazes F&B Trails." *Lodging Hospitality* 51(9):24.

SUGGESTED READINGS

Books

Birchfield, John C., and Raymond T. Sparrowe. 2002. *Design and Layout of Foodservice Facilities,* 2nd ed. New York: John Wiley and Sons.

Foster, Dennis L. 1992. *Food and Beverage: Operations, Methods, and Cost Controls.* Lake Forest, IL: MacMillan/McGraw-Hill, Glencoe Division.

Katsigris, Costas, Mary Porter, and Chris Thomas. 2002. *The Bar and Beverage Book,* 3rd ed. New York: John Wiley and Sons.

Khan, Mahmood A. 1990. *Concepts of Foodservice Operations and Management,* 2nd ed. New York: John Wiley and Sons.

Pavesic, David V. 1999. *Restaurant Manager Handbook Series: Menu Pricing and Menu Design.* New York: Lebhar-Friedman.

Shock, Patti J., and John M. Stefanelli. 1999. *Hotel Catering: A Handbook for Sales and Operations.* New York: John Wiley and Sons.

Articles

Allen, Robin Lee. 1996. "Hotel Chains 'Taking It to the Street' in Quests for Mainstream Dining Appeal." *Nation's Restaurant News* 30(17):124–128.

Hanson, Bjorn. August 1984. "Hotel Foodservice: Where's the Profit?" *Cornell Hotel and Restaurant Administration Quarterly* 25(2): 92–96.

Hensdill, Cherie. 1996. "Partnerships in Dining." *Hotels* 30(2):57–60.

Hubsch, Allen W. 1966. "Hotel Food and Beverage Management." *Cornell Hotel and Restaurant Administration Quarterly* 7(3):9–11, 18–19.

Parseghian, Pamela. 1996. "Branding Offers Hotels Opportunities to Increase Food Sales." *Nation's Restaurant News* 30(23).

———. 1996. "Holiday Inn Offers Assorted Food Options with New Quick Food Concept." *Hotel Business* (June).

Witham, Glenn. 1995. "Harvey: Expansion and Conversion." *Cornell Hotel and Restaurant Administration Quarterly* 36(4).

SOURCE NOTES

Chapter 6.2, "Managing Food and Beverage Operations in Lodging Organizations," by Robert H. Bosselman.

Chapter 6.3, "As I See It: Hotel Director of Food and Beverage," by Dominic Provenzano.

Chapter 6.4, "Best Practices in Food and Beverage Management," by Judy A. Siguaw and Cathy A. Enz, is reprinted from the October 1999 issue of *Cornell Hotel and Restaurant Administration Quarterly.* © Cornell University. Used by permission. All rights reserved.

Chapter 6.5, "Strategic Alliances Between Hotels and Restaurants," by Robert W. Strate and Clinton L. Rappole, is reprinted from the June 1997 issue of *Cornell Hotel and Restaurant Administration Quarterly.* © Cornell University. Used by permission. All rights reserved.

Chapter 6.6, "Contemporary Hotel Catering," by Patti J. Shock and John Stefanelli, adapted from *Hotel Catering,* by Patti J. Shock and John Stefanelli, Copyright © (year and owner). Reprinted by permission of John Wiley & Sons, Inc.

Chapter 6.7, "A Day in the Life of an Executive Director of Catering Sales and Convention Services," by Rich Benninger.

Chapter 6.8, "The Organization and Management of Hotel Beverage Operations," by Valentino Luciani.

Chapter 6.9, "Case Study: Crisis in the Food Court," by Nancy Swanger.

chapter seven

MARKETING AND ASSOCIATED ACTIVITIES

7.1 INTRODUCTION

For most hotel companies, it was only during the 1980s that the word *marketing* was anything more than a euphemism for sales. Indeed, in the competitive landscape of the not too distant past, an aggressive and knowledgeable sales staff could accomplish most activities that related to putting guests in rooms. In the competitive environment of the present time, this has become impossible. Hotel companies that design and market a sophisticated inventory of hospitality services need a similarly sophisticated scheme for letting potential clientele know about their services.

For most hotel companies in the twenty-first century, true marketing has evolved to reflect this sophistication. This development also acknowledges increased sophistication on the part of guests and potential clientele. Business travelers, travel agents, and meeting planners who represent and book group and convention business are educated and informed consumers. To serve this clientele, hotels have had to develop marketing efforts and product segmentation, first to interest the market, and second to allow people representing that market to make intelligent choices among competitors. Increasingly, individual consumers and small businesses are becoming more sophisticated in arranging their own travel plans over the Internet. This represents yet another challenge to hotel marketers: How do we market most efficiently to all groups? Good question.

Marketing has become an umbrella term that covers a number of strategic and tactical activities designed to tell the clientele the story of the hotel's services and to encourage that clientele to make choices based on how one hotel's marketing message matches their needs better than the available alternatives. In any given hotel or hotel company, marketing includes a range of sales activities, public relations, advertising in all media, design of symbols and images, and (increasingly) the departments of convention services, reservations, revenue management, and, perhaps, catering.

It should be noted that research plays a major role in designing marketing strategies and tactics. The monograph presented in this edition by Bianca Grohmann and Eric Spangenberg has a research orientation at its core. It is designed to assist managers in choosing and generating data that are useful to staying successfully competitive. It is important that managers understand the range within which this data may be interpreted and applied. Successful managers and high-quality organizations are always seeking information and data that allow them to make accurate decisions and design effective marketing and managerial efforts.

These data can take a number of forms but, for the most part, deal with the characteristics of the hotel's target market segment that affect their choice of hotels. In this case, the research seeks to understand how consumers make choices among hotels based on the value of their various attributes.

Among other data that hotels find mechanisms to accumulate and interpret are these kinds:

- *Geographic:* what sorts of communities are represented; what parts of the country or world; how far people travel

- *Demographic:* age, sex, occupation, income, ethnicity, family, education

- *Psychographic:* client's self-image, social or peer group, lifestyle, personality traits

- *Behavioral:* whether the hotel choice is a routine or special occasion; what guest

seeks in terms of quality, service, economy; user status (nonuser, ex-user, potential user, regular user, first-time user); usage rate (light, medium, heavy); loyalty (none, medium, strong, absolute)

While many of the specific details or programs implied under the marketing umbrella may be farmed out to agencies that specialize in advertising or public relations, the genesis of the hotel's strategic marketing plan must be within the hotel organization itself.

The article contributed to this section by Fletch Waller provides a strong argument for broadening the definition of *marketing* to include all operational aspects of the hotel. This article is an excellent overview of the marketing process. Waller illustrates the relationship between marketing and operations as a "continuing process" without which hotels probably cannot remain competitive.

Yield management, long a practice of the airline industry, has found total acceptance by hotel marketing and reservations systems. Indeed, it has become an industry standard. The article in this section by Paul Chappelle can be read in conjunction with that by Quain and LeBruto in Section 4 for a comprehensive primer on yield management. Together, these articles explore various aspects of that practice from the viewpoint of Chappelle, current practitioner. Chappelle lives the theory of yield and revenue management on a daily basis and provides insights about how it works in practice. As the revenue manager for over 30 hotels, Chappelle has the experience to back up the theory.

New for this edition, the Sinclair essay on hotel pricing should be read in the context of the issues and suggestions raised by the contributions on yield management. But it goes beyond that. Drawing on Sinclair's deep experience in hotel operations, particularly sales, this contemporary work on pricing is up to date and useful not only from a conceptual standpoint but a practical one.

Shaw and Morris bring their collaborative talents in academe and industry to the essay on the organization of the sales function in hotels. Because, as noted elsewhere in this text many times, the potential markets for a hotel's services and the types of hotel are so numerous, sales efforts can be complicated. Shaw and Morris present this complex departmental function in a clear, straightforward fashion that is both theoretically relevant and operationally practical.

Traditionally, the function of public relations for any organization, particularly hotels, was oriented toward the generation of favorable—usually free—publicity and the suppression or management of bad news. Louis Richmond proposes the different and expanded but not necessarily contrary position that public relations activities can positively enhance the hotel's sales and marketing efforts. He discusses his experiences in the case of the Seattle Sheraton Hotel and Towers. Using that example, he argues that through creative cooperative efforts with local charity,

cultural, and volunteer organizations, hotels can serve the activities of those groups' fund-raising efforts and simultaneously position themselves to show the arbiters of potential business how well the hotel can perform. His examples are instructive. Richmond, who is president of his own very successful public relations firm in Seattle, retains the Sheraton and other hospitality concerns as clients.

All in all, the strategies, tactics, activities, personnel, and concepts described in articles and essays in this section provide an overview that only hints at everything important to effective management of the marketing function. Marketing is perhaps the most written-about topic in hospitality literature. Because of the great diversity of opinion, it can be argued that there is no one "right" way to market, nor is any single piece of literature generally considered seminal to hotel marketing. The reader is urged to consider the references cited by contributing authors, the suggested readings, and active perusal of recent hospitality journals to achieve greater understanding of this fascinating process—and, by extension, its management.

7.2 BUILDING MARKET LEADERSHIP: MARKETING AS PROCESS

Fletch Waller

The hotel business has changed enormously over the last 30 years, embracing special niche forms of lodging (e.g., extended stay), new ways of segmenting markets (e.g., W's "fashionables"), brand proliferation and consolidation, new tools for acquiring customers (e.g., email), distribution innovations (e.g., Expedia), and globalization. These changes in mar-

kets and in ways hotels relate to and capitalize on them have put new demands on marketing.

Marketing, as addressed herein is not the sales and marketing department; I mean marketing in its broadest sense of how hotels respond to and seize on market opportunities. Definition? Marketing is a process of creating and sustaining productive relationships with desirable customers. Its goal? To produce such relationships more effectively than competitors do.

Let's examine the definition and its implications. Marketing is . . .

- **. . . a process . . .** A process, a series of functions and actions for approaching and dealing with opportunities. *Marketing,* as used herein, is not a job but a way of proceeding to create and operate a hotel focused on customers and competitors, a way that incorporates all members of the hotel staff and its support.

- **. . . of creating . . .** The essence of marketing is creation: imagination, insight, willingness to change and evolve, and, yes, discard.

- **. . . and sustaining . . .** Loyalty over time and repeat customers are the key to productivity and optimal contribution margins.

- **. . . productive relationships . . .** A relationship must be two-sided, with benefits for both partners in the relationship. In the case of customers, the benefits are wants and needs consistently fulfilled and full value received; in the case of staff, professional satisfaction and operating profits sufficient to fund improvements provide attractive compensation, and provide returns on investors' or owners' capital.

*I*n the late 1990s, rising costs of acquiring customers in U.S. hotels were masked by strong increases in the average daily rate (ADR). In 1995, marketing costs per occupied room (franchise and marketing fees, commissions, reservation costs, and property marketing and sales expenses) in full-service hotels averaged 15.3 percent of ADR. By 2000, it had risen to 15.6 percent; that three-tenths of a point increase over four years hardly alarmed people. But consider, of the expenses that make up the costs of acquiring customers, only commissions vary directly with rate; most of the expenses are personnel compensation and benefits and purchases— of ads, brochures, sales calls, websites, global distribution system (GDS) delivery services, telephone time, and so on. These expenses grow over time, but not as a function of the price for which a room is sold. If marketing were truly productive, we should have been seeing costs per unit dropping.

In dollar terms, full-service hotels saw marketing costs per occupied room balloon 38 percent in just five years, to $17.96 in 2000 from $12.99 per room-night in 1995! In higher-rated full-service hotels, acquisition costs rose to $22.71 from $15.86, a 43 percent increase. Resorts suffered a 27 percent increase, to $22.96 from $18.07 just five years earlier. By 2002, as rates and occupancies softened, marketing costs per occupied room in full-service hotels had begun to be reined in, at $17.02, but now accounted for 16.4 percent of ADR (PKF's Trend Reports, 1996, 1998, 2001, 2003.) The main culprit is distribution costs. Whatever the cause, marketing productivity must be improved.

- **. . . with desirable customers.** Not all customers are equally desirable; we want those who are willing to pay, growing in numbers, making multiple purchases, and whose needs we are able to fully satisfy.

And the goal?

- **. . . To produce such relationships . . .** *Production* implies inputs, outputs, and the measurement of productivity. Marketing productivity has been lagging for the last decade; the rising costs of acquiring customers must be reined in. (*Note:* If marketing efforts are a cause of customer decisions to purchase, then marketing productivity is the cost of stimulating that purchase decision relative to the value of that decision. Productivity is best measured by the cost of acquiring a customer not only as a percent of sales but also as dollars per *unit* of sale—for example, dollars per occupied room, dollars per group contract, dollars per cover.)

- **. . . more effectively than competitors do.** Marketing success is judged in relative terms, using competitors and similar hotels as benchmarks. As a creative process, especially in a field like hospitality wherein innovations are unprotected and easily copied, the benchmarks and goals are always moving targets. Besting the competition is the constant challenge.

By the end of this chapter, it will be clear that successful marketing of a hotel requires the orchestration of a wide variety of talents and skills, of which sales and marketing personnel are only a part. Chain hotels approach the process one way; independents must do so another. But in either case, market success depends on an effective integration of marketing and operations at the property level under the direction and leadership of a market-driven general manager.

▶ THE MARKETING PROCESS

Peter Drucker (1974) says the purpose of operating a business is to create a customer and keep him (or her). Investors in a hotel may have return on investment as their purpose, but for us operators, it is useful to conceive our purpose as being to create and keep customers. If we do this successfully, profits and capital returns flow. Our marketing process is our way of creating and keeping customers.

Every business has a marketing process, a way it "goes to market." It is the way management decides what they are going to do and offer, with whom they will compete, how they will attract the customers, and how they will satisfy and keep them. Most businesses, many hotels among them, do not reflect on and carefully articulate their marketing process; they just do their thing by habit and by tradition. Other businesses make concerted efforts to regularly plan and review their "going to market."

A hotel is a 24/7 business, running without stop. Typically, because of the pressure just to keep up, we do what we've done in the past, repeating our marketing process by habit. This is risky, for customers and competitors are always changing. Does a hotel need a planned and regular review of its marketing process? Considering our high fixed costs and the large leverage on profits from small changes in revenues, yes—hotels *should* take concerted and disciplined care of their marketing process. For a hotel to remain effective, it should formally review its marketing process at least once a year to be sure it is still suited to its market; if it is not, revise it to fit changing customer and competitor patterns. Further, the hotel must measure the cost of acquiring its customers so as to steadily

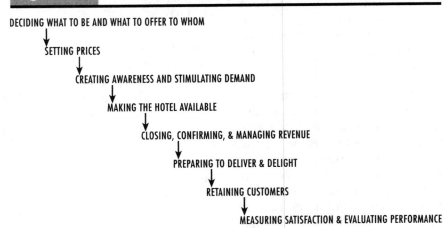

Figure 7.1   **The Hotel Marketing Process**

DECIDING WHAT TO BE AND WHAT TO OFFER TO WHOM
↓
SETTING PRICES
↓
CREATING AWARENESS AND STIMULATING DEMAND
↓
MAKING THE HOTEL AVAILABLE
↓
CLOSING, CONFIRMING, & MANAGING REVENUE
↓
PREPARING TO DELIVER & DELIGHT
↓
RETAINING CUSTOMERS
↓
MEASURING SATISFACTION & EVALUATING PERFORMANCE

increase the productivity of its marketing process.

A hotel marketing process (Figure 7.1) starts with *deciding what to be and what to offer to whom*. This is not just for new hotels in pre-opening; existing hotels must adjust and fine-tune their offerings as market conditions change. The next step is to *set the price structure*. These first two steps establish the hotel's value proposition.

Next, *create awareness and stimulate demand* among the people you hope to make your customers. Then you must *make the hotel available* to them, and close the sale—that is, *commit, confirm, and manage revenue*. Flexible rate management within the pricing structure and response to short-term swings in demand and supply are necessary to create customers and optimize revenue per available room.

Now begins the transition to operations, but this is no less a part of the marketing process. In fact, this is the critical part of the process. You must *prepare the hotel staff* to meet and fully satisfy the wants and expecta-

tion of these customers you have attracted. Then you have to work to *retain those customers* and turn them into repeat loyalists. Lastly, you must *measure their satisfaction* and evaluate your performance.

Let's examine these steps and, along the way, comment on ways of improving their effectiveness and productivity.

► DECIDING WHAT TO BE AND WHAT TO OFFER TO WHOM

In an existing hotel, the developer and architect already may have decided many of the things it is—high-rise or resort, in the business center or on the edge of town, large rooms and baths or smallish, one restaurant or several, wood or marble, with ballroom or not, and so on. Even so, the management team must still consciously examine what they intend the hotel to be and offer to whom. The type of customer originally in mind may not be available now in enough numbers to support the hotel. Perhaps a competitor has come in and taken away a piece of the market. Perhaps the business center has shifted to another part of the city. Perhaps new customers from Korea or California have replaced the original ones from Europe and the East Coast. Even though the owner has provided a basic envelope within which to operate, there still are options—many things the hotel team can control, many choices to be made on what to offer and to emphasize to various market segments. Is the hotel the place to be seen or the place that guards privacy? Is it better to stress family style or crisp, professional business style? Should the hotel add services, like a Japanese breakfast, to meet the needs of one particular group? Should the team put in meetings express and add more small meeting spaces to tap the short-lead-time corporate meetings market? Should it drop some services the market no longer wants to support?

The answers to what to be and offer are found by studying the *marketing situation,* which comprises three parts: (1) strengths and weaknesses, (2) the kinds and numbers of customers available in the marketplace, and (3) the other hotels with whom this hotel competes for these customers. Careful analysis yields a picture of which segments the hotel is best able to attract and serve. These become the *target markets*—the "to whoms"—and their needs and wants become the "what to be's." The key to successfully deciding what to be and offer to whom is a matter of strategic selection of, focus on, and commitment to a well-defined set of markets for whom the hotel is best suited to compete. Trying to be all things to all potential customers is a guarantee of ineffectiveness.

A good example of focus and targeting is Starwood's W. At risk of turning off a sizeable portion of the business and leisure travel market and leaving families well behind, Starwood focuses tightly on a lifestyle segment of professional and business people, with remarkable success.

The talents required to assess the marketing situation, create a data model of the market's segments, calculate a feasible share of each, and select the targets on which to focus are comfort with data, the ability to observe and infer, creativity, patience with detail, comfort with the hypothetical, and an analytic curiosity. Usually, such analyses are uncomfortably foreign to people with backgrounds in sales, and often to operators as well. It is essential that we teach, motivate, and reward curious, careful, insightful analysis of history and market information—skills that are not natural to those typically attracted to hospitality management.

IMPROVEMENT TIPS

- Send prospective general managers and directors of marketing to a marketing course, one with examples or cases in market analysis.

- Assign analytic exercises to a prospective director of marketing, like coming up with three options for cutting into the small business meetings of a competitor or increasing sales of the gift shop.

► SETTING PRICES

Having decided what to be and offer and to whom, the next most important decision is price. Pricing is a critical decision because it determines, first, whether or not the intended customers will purchase, and second, whether they will be satisfied with the value offered and, thus, be willing to return. Third, it determines whether the hotel will be financially healthy enough to maintain itself and reward its employees so customers can once again be satisfied when they do return.

Three factors must come into consideration in pricing—the Three Cs of pricing, if you will: costs, competition, and customers' comfort zones. In F&B, costs drive pricing of menu items and beverages. Drucker (1999, 115–6) says American industry has too much cost-driven pricing, and that it needs more price-driven costing. Doesn't F&B have the opportunity to build and test menus to discover where price points should be set, and is not the chef challenged to manage ingredients and portion size to deliver the cost and margin structure desired? Yet the cost-driven practice continues.

In rooms, competition is most often the dominant factor. Costs play a role, but changes in variable cost of an occupied room are generally small and rooms' contribution margins are large, typically 65 percent or better. Moreover, hotel accounting does not measure discounts from a standard price, as do almost all other industries. So there is no visible cost in reducing price to meet competitors. Remember: Any damn fool can cut his price, and some damn fool always will. Must everyone follow? No. The key is to get in the head of the customer. The truly controlling factor is customer comfort zones, and all too often hotel management leave money on the table because they don't know what those comfort zones are. At what price does the offer attract and deliver value? That is the key question in setting prices.

Price setting requires talent and skill in data gathering and analysis, accounting and building pro formas, interpreting and drawing inferences, and decision making. Do not let salespeople set prices; do not let controllers set prices. Only one person—the GM—can pull together the inputs of sales, control, operations, reservations, and the rest, and make this crucial judgment call. Also, build at least three price scenarios and have the controller and marketing director agree on occupancy impacts. Then run a GOP pro forma on each. Out of that exercise will come a sense of the best pricing approach to take. Setting prices is the one task the GM cannot delegate, for he or she must live with and be accountable for all that results from this critical decision.

PRICING TIP

*I*nclude staffers in contact with customers in pricing discussions. *A ski resort owner-operator asked me to review his proposed price schedules. I asked to have included in our meeting a senior reservation agent, a bellman, a bartender, and a front desk agent. After probing them on what they heard from customers about value, we increased four of the seven proposed room type prices, to the owner-operator's delight.*

POSITIONING IN FIVE QUESTIONS

1. Who are the prospects; what do they like; how do we find them?

2. What do they now know or believe about us?

3. What, specifically, do we want them to do?

4. What do they need to come to believe so they will do that?

5. What reasons can we offer them to hold this new belief?

► CREATING AWARENESS AND STIMULATING DEMAND

Herein are the typical roles of the marketing department: using sales, communications, and promotions to attract the target markets. But creating awareness is not only marketing's job. Everything the public sees and hears about the hotel—its name or brand, its signs, its restaurants, the public activities of its managers, its charitable support and festivals—all create a meaning, a picture of what this hotel means and offers.

Starwood's W again offers an example: Every element of their presentation expresses the "to whom" they target. In decor, uniforms (costumes?), tone, and attitude, they focus and send a coherent message. It is critical that every department understands the target markets and agrees on the idea, the meaning the hotel intends to have for each of the target customer groups. This is called *positioning;* it's something done not to the product but to the mind of the prospect.

The team should prepare written positioning statements, including a compatible but individual positioning statement for each market segment they intend to target. These statements are the blueprint against which each ad, promotion, and sales call is tested to assure consistent messages are being sent. And those statements should be shared with all employees. When all parts of the hotel are sending a coherent and consistent message of what the name or brand means and what underlying promise is being made, the hotel establishes a clear position in the mind of the prospects—ideally, one that is attractively distinctive from competitors.

Marketers can use a variety of tools to create awareness and stimulate demand—for example, sales blitzes, telemarketing, newspaper ads, Internet sites and ads, partnership alliances, radio ads, and price promotions. The marketing mix is the range and balance of tools selected and resources devoted to each to achieve the hotel's marketing goals.

In most hotels, direct selling is still the primary marketing tool used to create awareness and stimulate demand. There are two parts of effective direct selling: sales skills and sales management. Consider one the weapon, the other the shooter.

Sales skills are not natural; enthusiasm may be natural, liking to meet people may be natural, but selling is a process that anyone

SALES PRODUCTIVITY TIPS

- Track competitors' group commitments so that a market's uncommitted meeting spaces for future dates are foreseen, guiding pricing.

- Don't "be fair" by treating everyone the same; motivate each salesperson individually with incentives and attention suitable to his or her own style and need.

- Focus on team members who are below average, constantly improving the bottom and driving average production up.

- Don't just focus on room-nights. Calculate the number of contracts needed (using your average size of group) to fill the annual room block and set goals for weekly contract production as well. This will balance the sense of importance among salespeople, whether assigned to large or small group segments.

- Don't waste sales talent on cold calling. Use a prospecting service to qualify leads; focus your selling power on prospects.

- Clean out files at least annually. Salespeople tend to hold on to prospects long after the likelihood of a booking has dwindled.

- Automate. Customer and booking management systems pay.

can learn and that must be practiced. Make sure your salespeople are taught how to research their prospect, to listen for needs and purposes, to acknowledge that they have heard the prospect, to transform relevant features into benefits and to sell the customer's success, to anticipate objections and prepare responses, to negotiate, to ask for the order, and to thank the customer and facilitate delivery.

Sales management is quite another thing; often (usually?) the top salesperson does not make the best sales manager. The sales manager must be able to select salespeople; reinforce their training; coach, counsel and motivate them; assign them to prospects and market segments; set goals, manage compensation, review performance; and troubleshoot. He or she must also be the gatekeeper on contracts and rates, making sure that inventory of group space is optimally committed.

Compensation of salespeople need not be complicated. *First principle:* Tie compensation to goals set in terms of what you want them to do—that is, produce contracts and room-nights. Don't just set room-night goals; add measures of relationship or share of a specific customer's business. Have salespeople suggest their own goals for the coming year; participation builds commitment. *Second:* Provide them near-term reward and reinforcement, not postponed rewards. Pay out bonuses quarterly. *Third:* Build teamwork so that one salesperson supports and encourages another. Add a team bonus multiplier to personal performance measures. *Last:* Separate performance bonuses from overall job appraisal. No one attends to suggestions for performance improvement if he or she has just received a big check for exceeding goal.

Many full-service hotels are over-resourced in group sales and under-weighted in transient market tools. Sales efforts should be balanced with other parts of the marketing mix—advertising, publicity, and promotions.

The range of communication options increases geometrically with proliferation of new media—cable television, news magazines and national papers, the Internet, and direct mail and telemarketing. But the eyeballs are not growing apace, meaning the audience for any one medium is steadily shrinking, putting increasing demand on measures of productivity, care in allocating resources, and creativity to get through the clutter. As audiences of prospects become increasingly expensive to reach through advertising, the tools of publicity, the Internet, and direct marketing are increasingly the media of choice.

The Internet is a demanding medium for communication; use professional help to design, maintain, and market the hotel's website as though it were, itself, a product for which awareness must be created and demand stimulated. To draw audience to the site and manage its visibility in search engines are skills beyond the property team. Set specific goals for the site: They might be to attract qualified prospects, to sell services, to provide customer service. Don't just have a site. And measure the experts against those goals. A passive, unmanaged, and undermarketed site is a waste of money.

Promotions can powerfully stimulate demand, but too often, price promotions are resorted to as a last-minute attempt to prop up a weak demand period. Promotions should be planned, justified on a breakeven basis, and used sparingly. Not all promotions need be price promotions; customers invest energy and time in transactions, too: value-added promotions that offer nonmonetary savings can be used to avoid habituating consumers to buying only on sale or shopping only on price. Well-forged alliances for copromotion can increase both productivity and absolute sales volume.

The skills and talents necessary in a comprehensive effort to create awareness and stimulate demand include:

- *In sales:* Initiative; being goal-directed; listening with empathy and imagination; time management; self-confidence.

- *In sales management:* Coaching and counseling; quantitative skills (for setting

COMMUNICATION AND PROMOTION TIPS

- Run breakeven analyses on each ad or promotion, asking what percentage increase over normal unit sales it will take to return these dollars, using contribution margins, not revenues. Is that a reasonable expectation?

- Assign individual toll-free numbers to each ad and medium so response to each can be tracked.

- Don't ask if your GM likes an ad; ask if the intended prospect is likely to respond to it.

- Make sure the message the audience will take away is consistent with your basic positioning: what you intend to mean and offer to that market.

booking goals and recordkeeping); priority setting, time management, and sense of urgency; leadership and problem solving; ability to manage incentive programs.

- *In communications:* Ability to write clearly; ability to select, engage, and manage professional creative talents; ability to evaluate and allocate resources among options; comfort with and appreciation of the Internet and the Web.

- *In promotion:* Ability to analyze breakevens; creativity; anticipation; conceiving and selling partnerships and alliances.

▶ MAKING THE HOTEL AVAILABLE

Once a person in one of your target markets is interested in buying, how does he or she reach you? Your hotel's reservations office, the central reservation system, airline global distribution systems, corporate sales offices, and your property sales office are all parts of a distribution network. Travel agents, corporate travel managers and secretaries, meeting planners, and travelers themselves reach your hotel through this network.

Travel industry distribution channels are in chaos by virtue of the shift of travel agencies from commission to fee-for-service models, the rise of the Internet as a consumer's direct booking channel, and online third-party intermediaries like Expedia and Travelocity. Increasingly, the Internet will become your key distribution channel, but in the meantime, you must manage two parallel systems, the traditional central reservation and travel agency channels and the new electronic channels. Are the rooms you want to offer available in both systems, with helpful and up-to-date information? Are your prices sensible in each outlet? Making the hotel available is no longer a passive stance but an active part of your marketing.

In other industries, distribution channel revolutions have brought efficiencies that benefit both consumers and suppliers. In the travel distribution revolution now underway, the consumer has benefited, but costs to hotels—the suppliers—have skyrocketed. Since 1993, full-service hotel costs of distribution (commissions, Global Distribution System fees, and reservation expenses) more than doubled, to $1,377 per occupied room per year in 2002 (PKF, 2003).

Along with these new channels and third-party room merchants has come pressure on prices. In the downturn of 2001–2003, this was devastating. Price comparisons are quick and easy for the consumer. Packagers and auction sites, like Priceline.com, unconsciously cultivate the destructive idea that a hotel room is a commodity, as is an airline seat. But hotels are not commodities; each differs in location, features, and benefits. A hotel team must resist the idea that a room is a room is a room, must emphasize their hotel's distinctive positioning, and must resist the urge to simply match the lowest price offered.

For the foreseeable future, both the traditional and Internet-based distribution systems will coexist and have to be managed. This raises a new question: What channels do you want to encourage, and what ones discourage? Conventional wisdom, in recent years, has been to make the hotel's inventory and rates available via as many channels as possible so as to capture from anywhere in the world the last drop of demand for arrival on a given day. Given their sharply differing costs, however, and the difficulty of managing

TIPS FOR DISTRIBUTION PRODUCTIVITY

• Bid all groups on net price basis; do not commission meeting planning agencies.

• Analyze and understand the contribution margins achieved through each chan-

nel, not just the revenues and average rates. Consider differential prices by channel to equalize contribution margins after variable distribution costs.

coordinated presence in these new and overlapping channels, the time may be coming for a new strategy. One possibility is to starve undesirable channels with limited information and access while being fully open and transparent to others. Another approach might be to price differentially among channels to reflect their different costs. A large Hawaiian resort group is already doing that by explaining to consumers what comparative options and costs are. Other chains advertise a guarantee that the lowest price will be found on their own website, which is a low-cost channel for them.

Reservations, revenue, and channel management constitute the fastest-changing part of hotel management today. Channel management requires a comfort with and interest in technology and systems, and a knack for problem solving, anticipating, and risk taking (to shut down past patterns and undertake new initiatives).

► CLOSING, CONFIRMING, AND MANAGING REVENUE

How one commits space—a room, meeting space, ballroom, or even a restaurant table—and at what price—determines the revenues

and financial health of the hotel and determines the customer's expectation of value. Revenues must be managed to optimize financial returns and customer satisfaction—that is, the customer's willingness to return.

No one department controls the tools of revenue management. They are shared among salespeople, catering and banqueting managers, front desk agents, reservation agents, and so on. To manage properly requires frequent and open conversation between managers, good forecasting, skillful selling by customer contact people, and an appreciation of each week's goals and targets for the hotel. Poor forecasting, inflexible inventory policies, and conflicting approaches by different departments with whom the customer deals can undo all the best advertising, selling, and promotion.

Through the same forecasting disciplines, hotel teams manage their revenues to maximize the productivity of the hotel and assure its financial health. Revenue management tools and increasingly affordable yield systems can have a major and salutory effect on the financial health of the hotel.

Another part of revenue management is incentives for reservations upselling, conversion of callers, and average rate increases, and for front desk agents upselling. In the same way, F&B staff should be viewed as salespeople and given training on suggestive selling.

PRODUCTIVITY TIPS

• Eschew seasonal price schedules and adopt pricing tiers based on forecast occupancy for the dates in question.

• Saturday has become the highest demand day of the week; make sure you are not leaving discounts on the table out of habit.

• Teach reservation agents that stay-through restrictions are not mistreating guests. A three-night stay room is a different inventory unit than a one-night stay room, and is to be rationed.

Inventory policies for tier price quotes by forecast levels of occupancy, for stay-through restrictions, for same-rate substitutions and upgrading to clear demand inventory categories—all these are tools through which reservation and revenue managers optimize the RevPAR performance of the hotel.

It is in the area of revenue management that chains, especially multibrand management companies, have achieved significant advantage over independent hotels and franchisees that do not participate in cluster or regional revenue management. Decisions on pricing are still the domain of the property GM, but with a centralized expert staff collecting data and forecasting, the advice and guidance available has brought yield and RevPAR premiums to the chain member properties.

Revenue management requires attention to detail and analytic and forecasting skills; tolerance for ambiguity and comfort with change; and managing, training, leading, and motivating reservations agents. This is one of the most critical and dynamic areas of hotel management, one with which every aspiring general manager or director of sales and marketing should take pains to become familiar.

► PREPARING TO DELIVER AND DELIGHT

A marketer of a product can count on the factory quality-control system to deliver a consistent product for sale. When the sale is closed, the customer takes the product away and uses it. In a service business, however, the product is human behavior, and the customer uses the product in the hotel. Because we are humans, both customers and employees, our interactions are never the same one time to the next. The job of the marketer is to help employees understand what the customer will want, need, and expect, and to sell employees on doing their job with enthusiasm.

In a full-service hotel, the conference services department embodies this preparing idea as its primary function. Conference service managers are the essential group business brokers between sales and operations. Conference services people can create loyal and repeat meeting planners; the job requires empathy, attention to detail, willingness to work unusual hours, action orientation, internal relationship building, and persuasiveness.

Preparing the hotel to fully satisfy and regularly make customers happy is as much a marketing task as attracting customers in the first place. What makes marketing hospitality services harder than marketing a tangible product is that for every market segment there must be two marketing programs, one directed externally to customers, the other internally to employees.

► RETAINING CUSTOMERS

The key to both financial health and market leadership is retaining a higher proportion of customers than do any of your competitors. Retain more customers than others do, and over time your costs drop—because of efficiency, lower advertising and selling costs, better forecasting—and your occupancy and rates rise. Numerous studies validate the high correlation between profit leadership and customer retention.

Frequent-stay rewards are often mistaken for retention programs. They are not. Rewards can motivate returns only as long as the customer values the points or airline miles or whatever. But they do not create loyalty. They are valuable only insofar as they give employees the opportunity to come to recognize and satisfy the guest, and insofar as they give the marketing department information on who the customer is and where he or she is coming from.

Retaining customers takes more than just doing the job well. Guests and customers must come to know they are valued. Management must build relationships—the tie that binds regardless of a new hotel opening in the market or a hot promotional offer from across the street. Relationships are built on

recognition and familiarity, on trust, and on appreciation. Thus, guest and customer retention must be a planned and creative activity that involves both sides of the relationship—the customers and the employees. It takes more than just smiling and trying hard. Among the talents and skills needed are analytic skills, curiosity, direct marketing planning, and management of data retrieval and direct marketing service providers.

► MEASURING SATISFACTION AND EVALUATING PERFORMANCE

If the purpose of the business is, in part, to keep customers, does a financial statement of rate, occupancy, revenue, expense, and profit give enough information? No. Also needed is a scorecard of customer satisfaction, of how likely customers are to return or tell others about your good hotel. That scorecard is the guest satisfaction survey. Accounting statements tell of the hotel's financial health; a guest satisfaction scorecard tells of its reputation's health. The scorecard also helps management spot changes in expectations. Customers are not the same from one visit to the next. Experience with a new hotel, perhaps even in another city, may raise a customer's standards. To measure satisfaction, one needs quantitative skills for tracking, analyzing, and reporting data, and the ability to manage the logistics of repetitive distribution, collection, and processing.

(*Note:* Many hotels rely on comment cards for tracking guest satisfaction. That may work in some situations, but if your property has a high rate of repeat customers and/or frequent business travelers, comment card data are unreliable. It is the infrequent traveler who bothers to fill out comment cards—unless there is a gripe to be expressed. Develop and use a continuing survey to get a reliable measure of guest satisfaction levels.)

The information helps management figure out what the hotel needs to be and to offer next in order to remain competitive and keep customers. Note, now, the return to the first step of the marketing process.

continuous circle around which management must go again and again as competition improves and as the customer segments in the market change. Only by reviewing and renewing the marketing process will a hotel get ahead and continue to be the leading hotel in its market. This model of the marketing process applies to both the whole hotel and to any revenue or profit center within it. Use it like a checklist when thinking through improving the revenue and competitiveness of any operation.

► THE CIRCULAR MARKETING PROCESS

In other words, the marketing process isn't the straight-line, step-by-step process shown in Figure 7.1 but rather, as shown in Figure 7.2, a

► THE MEASURES OF MARKETING

The health of the marketing process should be measured over a longer time than a month or quarter or fiscal year, and it should

Figure 7.2 **The Hotel Marketing Process**

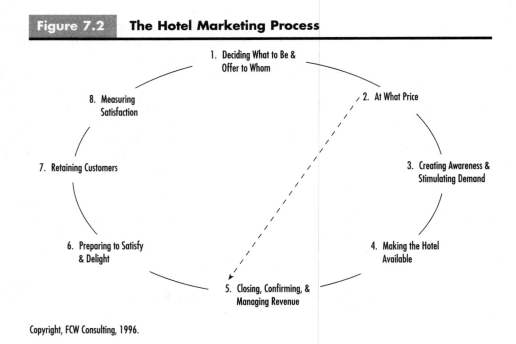

1. Deciding What to Be & Offer to Whom
2. At What Price
3. Creating Awareness & Stimulating Demand
4. Making the Hotel Available
5. Closing, Confirming, & Managing Revenue
6. Preparing to Satisfy & Delight
7. Retaining Customers
8. Measuring Satisfaction

Copyright, FCW Consulting, 1996.

be measured by more than just profit and loss data. A healthy marketing process results in:

- Rising room revenues per available room and rising F&B revenues per available seat and catering space.

- Rising market share to a share index over 100—that is, a larger share of a competitive set's occupied rooms than the hotel's share of the set's available rooms, which is its "fair share."

- Falling costs of acquiring customers, not on a percentage-of-revenue basis but as dollars per unit of sale—for example, dollars per occupied room, dollars per cover, and so on. What is the acquisition cost? The total of the advertising and business promotion budget (more often now called the marketing and sales expense), plus commissions, reservation costs, franchise fees, and marketing fees. These costs in times of inflation may not actually decline but at least should grow more slowly than do gross operating revenues.

- Rising customer satisfaction ratings.

- Increasing retention rates measured by the percentage of business from repeat customers.

- Growing top-of-mind awareness among target customer segments and, if the hotel can afford to measure it, preference by segment rising to number one among your competitive sets.

Management and owners should ask for an annual report card on the health of the marketing process—of the hotel, of a chain, of a franchise group.

► MANAGEMENT OF THE PROPERTY'S MARKETING PROCESS

As should by now be clear, the marketing process is larger than any one individual's job. Further, no hotel can afford the myriad talents and skills that must be orchestrated to create and sustain a healthy marketing process; a single hotel is simply not a large enough business to afford having all those talents on staff.

Franchise companies and managed chains have the mass to employ a large proportion of those talents at headquarters, but even they must call on outside services in design, database management, advertising, direct marketing, and so on. But the chains' ability to invest in new tools and hire diverse talents has led branded chains, both management companies and franchisers, to collect increasing numbers of hotels under their umbrellas. The trend toward centralizing marketing functions to serve several hotels in a region, often even hotels of different brands, is accelerating, especially with the advent of Internet-driven information sharing. The advantages are the ability to integrate multiple sources of information, to hire experts that a single hotel might not be able to afford, to share the cost of sophisticated systems for forecasting, revenue management and customer relationships, and to reduce the expense of marketing to individual properties.

Independents must counter such attractions with cooperative activities and aggressive local marketing. The Internet has leveled the playing field somewhat, allowing independents to be found and reviewed by consumers and travel agents in a way not possible when GDS systems were the only means of access.

▶ PROPERTY RESPONSIBILITY FOR ITS OWN MARKETING

To optimize performance, a property can neither abdicate its marketing to a chain or franchise group nor passively rely on location and presence to bring customers to the door. Each property, whether flagged or independent, must be responsible for creating and managing a marketing process tailored to its particular marketing situation—that is, its available customers; its inherent strengths, weaknesses, and employees; and its competitors. Each marketing situation is unique, even among cookie-cutter chain properties. Each has its own location, competitor, and customer dynamics.

So, given the wide range of talents and skills that must be orchestrated to create an effective marketing process, who is to lead it? Directors of sales and marketing cannot, for the process is much larger than the marketing department. Only the general manager can lead his or her marketing process; only he or she can integrate chain supports, operating departments, human resources (HR), the controller, and—yes, marketing and sales.

▶ THE GM AS LEADER OF THE MARKETING PROCESS

General managers must come to see themselves as the leader of their marketing process and be comfortable in the role. This does not mean becoming expert in all tools and disciplines; it does mean seeing the whole and appreciating when to bring in what talents, when to apply what tools, and how to judge the effectiveness of the process. It means using the marketing process as an organizing concept for creating the management team and a unified viewpoint of mission and challenge.

When a hotel is led by a general manager who sees herself or himself as leader of the marketing process, when that process is thoughtfully conceived and well executed, when all employees see themselves as joint operators/marketers, that hotel becomes customer-centered, competitive, and a leader in its markets.

Few GMs are trained to do this. Many come to appreciate that location and flag are not enough; many intuitively pick up a smattering of sales, distribution, advertising, and customer retention. But it is the rare GM who weaves these parts into a coherent whole and thinks through the challenge of creating and leading the marketing process. As marketing continues to develop more complex tools and as marketing productivity becomes a more pressing matter, owners, universities, and chains must address this issue of how to develop GM candidates who are comfortable with and capable of leading a comprehensive marketing process.

▶ THE MARKETING PROCESS MODEL AS A PROBLEM-SOLVING TOOL

One last word: The circular model of the marketing process is presented here mainly in terms of rooms marketing. But the model can be applied to every revenue department—to food and beverage outlets, catering, the health club, the business center, and even the laundry. The model can be used for planning, for business reviews, for presentations to lenders and owners, for troubleshooting, and as a checklist when preparing proposals for new services or facilities.

Use the model, make it part of your bag of management tools, and get your team to see their role in terms of this holistic and never-ending marketing process. If you achieve that, you will have gone far to create a customer- and competitor-focused organiza-tion, one in which employees see themselves as operators/marketers rather than just "in operations" or "in marketing" or "in HR." The few hotels that achieve and nurture a well-tuned marketing process and whose em-ployees see themselves as integral parts of it become leaders—in market share, in cus-tomer and employee loyalty, and in financial returns to owners.

7.3 CONSUMER DECISION RULES AND IMPLICATIONS FOR HOTEL CHOICE

Bianca Grohmann and Eric Spangenberg

Consumers' choices are influenced by the goals they attempt to achieve. Once a person has recognized a need, such as the need for ac-commodation when traveling for business or pleasure, he or she engages in an information search to identify alternatives from which to choose. Understanding how consumers evalu-ate competing alternatives in their purchase decision processes enables marketers in the hospitality industry to design better advertis-ing and promotional campaigns leading to a more favorable evaluation of their offerings in travelers' eyes. This is an important step in in-creasing the likelihood that consumers will choose their offering as opposed to that of competitors. Given that most travelers' desti-nations offer several hotels, how do people choose among them? The answer to this ques-tion lies, in part, in research on consumers' attitudes and their relation to purchase inten-tions and subsequent purchase behavior. This chapter describes several methods consumers may use to make choices based on the evalua-tion of identified alternatives.

Attitude is the tendency to respond in a consistently favorable or unfavorable manner toward a target (e.g., brand or product). Im-portant to marketers is that, if measured ac-curately, attitudes are predictive of behavioral intentions and relatively stable over time. Simply put, consumers generally form inten-tions to choose a hotel brand toward which they hold positive attitudes. Behavioral inten-tions, however, do not always translate into corresponding behavior. For example, al-though some consumers have preferences and therefore form intentions to stay at Fair-field Inn when traveling across the country, they might end up choosing other forms of ac-commodation from time to time. Why would they act inconsistently with their intentions? Traveling with friends who have different at-titudes and preferences, temporary price re-ductions of competitors, or the fact that a

Fairfield Inn is not readily available in a specific area might be reasons for inconsistencies between behavioral intentions to stay at a Fairfield Inn and actual choice behavior.

Despite situational factors sometimes influencing travelers' choices, attitudes are ultimately useful in predicting actual behavior; changing or strengthening the basis of consumer attitudes may therefore increase the likelihood of consumers engaging in desired behaviors. In order to change attitudes and subsequent related behavior, marketers must understand a few basic decision rules associated with consumer attitudes. Below we introduce decision rules likely to be implemented by different segments of consumers under varying market conditions.

▶ DECISION RULES

Decision rules are strategies consumers use to choose among alternatives. Several factors can influence what decision rule consumers ultimately apply in a specific situation. Typically, the more important and less frequent a purchase decision is, the more time and effort consumers are willing to expend making that decision. Choosing a resort at which to spend a twenty-fifth wedding anniversary, for example, is a decision most consumers face only once and therefore are likely to take a relatively long time to make, and they are likely to be careful and thorough in evaluating alternatives. On the other hand, a salesperson traveling frequently in a familiar territory likely chooses a hotel using a routine process where far less time and consideration are given to alternatives. Further, brand-loyal customers might choose to stay with the same hotel chain whenever possible, thereby avoiding a situation where they are forced to

choose among alternatives. In general, the stronger a consumer is motivated to search and the greater the risk associated with a choice, the greater the complexity of the decision rule he or she implements.

Another important characteristic of modeling decisions is the fact that (counterintuitively and often counterattitudinally) people often do not attempt to optimize choice. If a person's goal is optimal choice, considerably more time and effort is typically required to identify and evaluate alternatives. Therefore, consumers often choose a satisfactory (as opposed to optimal) alternative (as opposed to the best alternative possible) in order to save time and effort. The use of decision rules in these instances enables people to take shortcuts in making decisions in the face of the apparently unlimited or overwhelming amounts of information available regarding all possible alternatives. Consumers usually work with a consideration set (i.e., a subset of alternatives from the entire universe of choices) so they do not have to work as hard cognitively when required to make a decision in a given product category. They then make a final decision from this reduced set of alternatives. Such decision rules are referred to as *heuristics* or rules of thumb. Employing heuristics, people save time and limit complex information processing while still making reasonable or satisfactory choices based on the few brand attributes or characteristics most important to them at the time of choice. In the context of hotel choice, brand attributes are things like location, room rates, and availability of a swimming pool, restaurant, and so forth.

Although the number of consumer decision rules is almost infinite and likely varies by consumer, basic categories and a few specific examples serve as useful tools in modeling and predicting traveler decisions. Two general categories of decision rules are (1) compensatory and (2) noncompensatory. Below we discuss how travelers make decisions using these two types of rules.

▶ Compensatory Decision Rules

Compensatory decision rules model consumers as deriving an overall brand evaluation such that alternatives performing poorly on one attribute can *compensate* for their respective shortcomings by positive evaluations of other attributes. For example, a high-priced hotel might not be perceived positively on the dimension of room rates by some travelers; however, these same travelers might be willing to spend more money knowing they will receive better service or that the hotel is conveniently located—that is, in this example, service and location compensate for the perceived disadvantage of high room rates. The multi-attribute attitude model described in the next section is perhaps the most popular compensatory decision rule.

Multi-attribute Attitude Model. The multi-attribute attitude model we describe herein is also referred to as a *weighted additive model* or the *Fishbein* (1975) *linear compensatory model*. In this model, people not only assess the value of each salient (or important) attribute of brand but also consider the extent to which a given alternative possesses the attributes. (*Note:* In this context, it is important to note salience is essentially equivalent to importance. Further, the attributes salient to one market segment may be very different from those of another segment. For example, business travelers may not care at all about a spa, an airport shuttle, and room service breakfast quality, while to another

market segment, these property attributes may be very important.) The evaluations of salient attributes and the beliefs that brands possess the salient attributes are included as weights in an equation determining overall brand attitude. The model is represented as:

$$A_{\text{brand A}} = \sum_{i=1}^{n} e_i b_i$$

where $A_{\text{brand A}}$ is the overall attitude toward hotel brand A, e_i is the evaluative weight associated with attribute i, b_i is the extent to which the consumer believes brand A possesses attribute i (i.e., strength of belief that i is present in brand A), and n is the number of salient attributes in consideration.

Operators and marketers typically measure importance weights and strengths of beliefs using questionnaires. First, survey respondents are asked to provide evaluative weights associated with each of the attributes salient to their decision; these numbers represent each attribute's relative positive or negative associations in consumers' minds. Although scale endpoints may vary by researcher preference, our demonstration of this model assumes use of a 7-point scale on which -3 is the lowest importance rating possible, $+3$ is the highest, and a neutral importance rating is zero. An attribute that is evaluated entirely negatively by survey respondents (e.g., the availability of guest laundry) would be assigned a value of -3, whereas an attribute that is highly positive in a consumer segment's evaluation (e.g., low room rates) might be assigned a value of $+3$.

Once consumer attribute evaluations are determined, survey respondents state the extent in which they believe a brand possesses respective attributes. Again, for simplicity of demonstration, we assume that the belief strength regarding any of the attributes to be evaluated ranges between -3 (i.e., the brand definitely does not possess the attribute) and $+3$ (the brand definitely possesses the attribute). For example, if a traveler believes that Hotel X is a relatively high-priced establishment, the consumer might assign a belief value of -2 to this hotel on the attribute "low room rates," thereby indicating that Hotel X does not possess the attribute "low price" to a great extent. In other words, Hotel X performs poorly on the traveler's low room rate criterion. The hotel offering the absolute lowest price—say, Hotel Q—may be assigned a value of $+3$ on the attribute "low room rates," thereby indicating the traveler strongly believes that Hotel Q does indeed offer low room rates.

The next step in the model is multiplication of attribute evaluation (e_i) and belief strength (b_i) for each of the salient attributes. If the traveler evaluated low room rates very positively ($e_{\text{room rate}} = +3$), and Hotel X received a belief score of $b_{\text{room rate}} = -2$, we calculate Hotel X's contribution to overall attitude score relative to the attribute "low room rate" by multiplying evaluation and belief scores $e_{\text{room rate}} \times b_{\text{room rate}} = (+3) \times (-2) = -6$. Evaluation of Hotel Q on the low room rate attribute will be more favorable—specifically, $e_{\text{room rate}} \times b_{\text{room rate}} = (+3) \times (+3) = 9$. This procedure is followed for each salient attribute for all brands in a consideration set. Other attributes, for example, could include location near the airport, availability of room service, or complementary breakfast, and the $e_{\text{attribute}} \times b_{\text{attribute}}$ products calculated for each brand and attribute.

Finally, the products of $e_i \times b_i$ for each salient attribute are summed for each brand. The resulting scores represent the relative overall attitudes held for each brand. This weighted additive model is applied to all the brands included in the survey as the consideration set, and the brand associated with the highest overall attitude score is selected as the preferred alternative.

A few considerations should be kept in mind that are important to implementation of this model. First is the notion that the model is relative in nature—that is, an overall attitude score of $+21$ for a single hotel means nothing unless it is compared to the overall attitude scores of its competitors as evaluated by survey respondents in a relevant market segment. Further, it is important to include all relevant competitors in the model. As a relative model, it may be that the market segment considers only one of five low-budget properties when traveling to a particular locale. If so, include only those five; it is not helpful to have comparisons made (explicitly or implicitly) in respondents' minds if they are not realistic (e.g., it is likely that inclusion of the Four Seasons in the consideration sets of Quality Inn customers is inappropriate). By the same token, leaving out alternatives that respondents in the market segment may truly consider can introduce error; the result may be a finding that the property has the highest attitude score among those included on the survey, yet the model is not predictive because the survey omitted a strong competitor. Also of paramount importance is the selection of appropriate salient attribute sets. If critical, differentiating attributes are left out of the model, summated scores are not predictive of behavioral likelihood; consumers using a compensatory model in actuality are implicitly calculating scores using attributes that may have been missed by survey administrators. Thus, it is critical to select the appropriate salient attributes for inclusion in the model. Note that *appropriate* does not mean *all* attributes. Surveyors often ask about things that do not really matter to respondents. Once primed, however, respondents provide a score on attributes they may never have thought of on their own, thereby contributing falsely (positively or negatively) to overall attitude scores.

We now provide an example of the linear compensatory model, necessarily simplified with regard to number of brands under consideration and salient attributes included. Consider Charlie and Elsa Brown, a wealthy New York couple looking for a hotel to stay at while spending a weekend skiing in Vermont; the Browns represent a market segment that regularly visits this area for this purpose. Based on a discussion with friends who know the area well, the Browns identified four hotels (associated with four different brands) in the area they plan to visit. Table 7.1 shows four salient attributes the Browns consider, the importance of each attribute (e_i ranging from -3 to $+3$) and the beliefs (b_i ranging from $+3$ to -3) regarding the extent to which each of the properties possesses attribute i. (Note that there could be more or fewer salient attributes depending on the product or service in consideration and the attributes salient to the perspective market segment.)

Using the above scores derived from survey responses, we derive an overall attitude score for each of the hotels in the Browns' consideration by computing the sums of the products of importance (e_i) multiplied by belief strength (b_i) for each attribute for each brand. For example, for Brand E:

$$\text{Attitude}_{\text{Brand E}} = \sum_{i=1}^{n} e_i b_i$$

$$= (e_{\text{proximity to skiing area}})$$
$$\times (b_{\text{proximity to skiing area E}}) + (e_{\text{low rates}})$$
$$\times (b_{\text{low rates E}}) + (e_{\text{fine restaurant}})$$
$$\times (b_{\text{fine restaurant E}})$$
$$+ (e_{\text{indoor pool}}) \times (b_{\text{indoor pool E}})$$

Note that the evaluation weights (e_i) assigned to attributes remain constant across brands, while belief strength may differ from brand to brand (indeed, *should* differ, unless brands are identical). The overall attitude toward hotels E, F, G, and H can therefore be calculated as follows:

$$A_{\text{Hotel E}} = (+3)(-1) + (-2)(-1)$$
$$+ (+1)(+3) + (+2)(0)$$
$$= -3 + 2 + 3 + 0 = 2$$

$$A_{\text{Hotel F}} = (+3)(+2) + (-2)(-2)$$
$$+ (+1)(+3) + (+2)(+2)$$
$$= 6 + 4 + 3 + 4 = 17$$

$$A_{\text{Hotel G}} = (+3)(+3) + (-2)(+1)$$
$$+ (+1)(-2) + (+2)(+3)$$
$$= 9 - 2 - 2 + 6 = 11$$

$$A_{\text{Hotel H}} = (+3)(+1) + (-2)(+2)$$
$$+ (+1)(+1) + (+2)(+3)$$
$$= 3 - 4 + 1 + 6 = 6$$

Thus, assuming an optimized score being sought in this instance, Hotel F, scoring highest in overall brand attitude (17), is most likely to be chosen. Hotel E, on the other hand, scored lowest on overall brand attitude (2), and is unlikely to be selected.

► Noncompensatory Decision Rules

Although many factors (e.g., high involvement, high physical, social, or economic risk) associated with a decision may lead consumers to use a compensatory decision rule, the effort is relatively complicated and often too time- and effort-intensive for people to

Table 7.1 Four Salient Attributes K Considers

Attribute	e_i	Hotel E b_{iE}	Hotel F b_{iF}	Hotel G b_{iG}	Hotel H b_{iH}
Proximity to skiing area	+3	−1	+2	+3	+1
Low rates	−2	−1	−2	+1	+2
Fine restaurant	+1	+3	+3	−2	+1
Indoor pool	+2	0	+2	+3	+3

employ for many day-to-day decisions. As suggested above, consumers may use a compensatory decision rule if they spend a lot of time on the road, for a special vacation, or for an extended stay abroad. However, they are unlikely to use such an elaborate rule when purchasing a beverage at a gas station or when they need to find inexpensive lodging in the middle of a long drive to visit friends. Thus, many decisions are made using much simpler rules. Noncompensatory decision rules tend to simplify decision making; they may lead to less than optimized results but are often employed when consumers *satisfice,* or seek an outcome that is good enough rather than optimal.

When noncompensatory decision rules are used, a brand or product cannot compensate for weak performance on one attribute by performing well on other attributes when competing alternatives are compared. For example, if consumers choose a hotel based on the single criterion attribute of low room rates, a hotel offering higher-priced accommodations with better service would not be chosen (unless rooms are not available at the hotel offering lower rates). In this case, consumers do not trade off room rates and service quality but make their decision guided solely by a property's rates.

The most commonly used noncompensatory decision rules are the *lexicographic decision rule,* the *elimination-by-aspects decision rule,* and the *conjunctive decision rule.* To demonstrate consumers' use of noncompensatory decision rules, we can use the same survey data as the compensatory decision model regarding salient attribute evaluations and brand beliefs regarding those attributes. The data, however, are used differently, as described below. For the noncompensatory rules defined below, we again consider the evaluations and beliefs regarding Hotels E, F, G, and H introduced in Table 7.1.

Lexicographic Decision Rule. When using a lexicographic decision rule, consumers select a brand according to the alternative that scores highest on a single attribute deemed most important. This is probably the way we make a lot of decisions. What is cheapest? What is most convenient? What is the best-looking alternative?

Consider the values in Table 7.1 as results of a different survey for consumers from a different market segment: Four brands of hotels are evaluated on the four attributes of proximity to skiing area, low rates, fine restaurant, and indoor pool. The importance of each of these attributes is given by e_i. Importance ratings are proximity to skiing area (+3), low rates (-2), fine restaurant ($+1$) and indoor pool ($+2$). Proximity to skiing area is the most important attribute in this case of hotel choice, followed by indoor pool, fine restaurant, and low rates, respectively. According to the lexicographic decision rule, proximity to skiing area is the attribute determining consumer choice in this case. Consumers have reason to believe that Hotel G is closer to the slopes ($b_{\text{proximity to skiing G}} = +3$) than are the other hotels in the consideration set, and therefore Hotel G is chosen.

Elimination by Aspects. When an elimination-by-aspects decision rule is used, attributes are again ranked according to their importance. Unlike choosing the hotel brand that performs best on a single most important attribute as with the lexicographic rule, however, elimination by aspects involves the use of cutoff values. A cutoff value is a minimal performance score a brand must have to stay in the consumer's consideration set. A consumer first looks at performance scores of brands regarding the most important attribute and eliminates all brands that do not exceed the predetermined cutoff value. We often do this with multiple attributes: "I won't pay more than $110 a night in city X, so I don't even look at properties more expensive than that, but my choice also has to have a pool." We essentially eliminate by the aspect of price first and then by whether or not the hotel has a pool.

In the example shown in Table 7.1, proximity to skiing area is the most important attribute, with an importance rating of $+3$. Let us assume the consumer's cutoff value is $+2$. That means that all of the hotel brands that have a score of at least $+2$ on the proximity to skiing area attribute are retained in the consideration set, while brands that do not meet this cutoff criterion are dropped from the

consumer's consideration set. For this example, only Hotel F ($b_{\text{proximity to skiing area F}} = +2$) and Hotel G ($b_{\text{proximity to skiing area}} = +3$) meet the cutoff criterion ($+2$). Hotel E ($b_{\text{proximity to skiing area E}} = -1$) and Hotel H ($b_{\text{proximity to skiing area H}} = +1$) are not close enough to the skiing area to make the cut.

When implementing the elimination-by-aspects decision rule, the consumer replicates these steps: He or she now considers the performance of the remaining brands with respect to the attribute ranked second-highest in importance. In our example, the consumer next looks at the availability of an indoor pool at Hotels F and G. Assuming the cutoff value to be employed is $+2$, both brands remain in the consumer's consideration set, as the scores for indoor pool Hotel F ($b_{\text{indoor pool F}} = +2$) and Hotel G ($b_{\text{indoor pool G}} = +3$) both meet this criterion. At this point, the consumer has not yet found the best offering according to the elimination-by-aspects rule.

Consequently, the consumer applies the same procedure to the attribute ranked third—that is, the availability of a fine restaurant. Assuming the consumer still uses a cutoff criterion of $+2$, Hotel G ($b_{\text{fine restaurant G}} = -1$) is eliminated from the consideration set. Hotel F ($b_{\text{fine restaurant F}} = +3$), on the other hand, exceeds the cutoff criterion, is now the only brand left in the consumer's consideration set, and is therefore selected.

Note that using the same data set, the elimination-by-aspects decision rule leads to a different choice than the lexicographic decision rule. From a strategic standpoint, the fact that some consumers use an elimination-by-aspects decision rule should encourage hotels to improve their performance on several attributes important in consumer choice. It is not enough to be situated close to a skiing area. Other aspects of the offering might also be important in consumers' hotel selections, and performance in these areas should be monitored and, if necessary, improved. You can see, however, that it is crucial to improve services that are valued by consumers—in other words, aspects of a hotel's offering that have high importance ratings. Shortcomings in aspects that are valued highly by consumers, such as cleanliness and employee friendliness, cannot be compensated for by strong performance in areas to which consumers attach no importance (e.g., internal cost-control systems).

Conjunctive Decision Rule. When a conjunctive decision rule is employed, consumers process information by brand, as opposed to attribute by attribute, as with the lexicographic and the elimination-by-aspects decision rules. With this rule, consumers establish a cutoff criterion that must be met by alternatives in the consideration set on all salient attributes for brands to remain in consideration.

Let us assume that a consumer desires that the chosen hotel should have a score of at least +1 on all of the attributes he or she considers important. In our example, then, proximity to a skiing area, low rates, fine restaurant, and indoor pool must all rate a +1 on each of these dimensions to remain in the consideration set. First, the consumer evaluates Hotel E on each of these attributes. While Hotel E meets the cutoff criterion of +1 on fine restaurant, it falls short of the consumer's cut-off rule when it comes to proximity to skiing area, low rates, and indoor pool, and therefore is eliminated from consideration. The consumer then turns to evaluation of Hotel F, which meets the cutoff value of +1 on three out of four relevant attributes. It is eliminated from choice consideration, however, due to its failure to deliver on low rates. The consumer's assessment of Hotel G also

leads to elimination from choice consideration because it does not meet the cutoff criterion of +1 on the attribute "fine restaurant." Hotel H, on the other hand, exceeds the cutoff criterion of +1 on all of the criteria. Thus, using a conjunctive decision rule, Hotel H is selected.

Accounting for Ties. Note that ties can frequently occur using compensatory or noncompensatory decision rules; this usually results in consumers moving to a new rule in order to break the tie. For example, if compensatory values were equal for two competitors (not shown in the examples above), a consumer might implement a lexicographic decision rule with proximity to a skiing area as the most important attribute used to pick a hotel. Or, if the conjunctive cutoff value were −1 for all attributes, both Hotels E and H in our example would stay in consideration; the consumer may then use a lexicographic decision rule based on availability of an indoor pool, resulting in Hotel H being chosen as it is rated higher on this attribute than Hotel E.

▶ MARKETING IMPLICATIONS

Once consumer evaluations of salient attributes (e.g., availability of room service, conference facilities, wheelchair accessibility, children's programs) are determined and their beliefs regarding a hotel brand's offerings are known, managers can use this information to improve their hotel's competitive positioning in the market. The goal of any marketing strategy is to increase positive attitude toward the offering or to encourage the use of certain decision rules, thereby increasing the likelihood of being chosen by consumers.

As we have seen, when consumers use a compensatory decision rule, the overall attitude toward a hotel is determined by the sum of the products of evaluations multiplied by beliefs regarding salient attributes associated with the offering. Consequently, travelers' overall attitudes toward a hotel can be rendered more positive by strategies targeted at increasing the evaluation of an attribute in consumers' decision making, or by changing consumers' beliefs about a hotel's offerings.

Travelers' attribute evaluations can be influenced by stressing the attribute in advertising (e.g., less money spent on accommodation can be used to have more fun with the whole family by spending the savings on other activities, the availability of a business center enables business customers to save time). This strategy of influencing attribute evaluations is effective in attitude change and also relatively easy to pursue. It is, however, not a strategy always recommended for changing consumers' attitudes when they are using a compensatory model. The potential problem associated with this approach is that attribute evaluations are constant across brands in a consideration set. In our example above, travelers evaluating importance of the availability of an indoor pool (+2) is the same for all hotel brands, E, F, G, and H. If Hotel H were successful in a marketing message in increasing the evaluation of an indoor pool with a segment of consumers, say to a rating of +3, it would increase consumers' overall attitude toward its brand. At the same time, however, consumers' overall evaluation of Hotel G would increase by the same amount, as both brands do not differ with respect to consumers' beliefs about their having a great indoor pool (i.e., both have a belief rating of +3). In the end, the attempt to increase consumers' overall attitude to-

ward Hotel H would also benefit some of its competitors.

Thus, sometimes a more effective strategy for improving consumers' overall attitude toward a hotel's offerings is to improve consumers' brand-specific belief ratings. For example, Hotel F could strive to improve consumer belief that it offers a pleasant indoor pool by providing a picture of the pool on its website, or by stressing the availability of the indoor pool in advertisements. While consumer brand-specific beliefs are then likely to increase, Hotel F's competitors will not benefit from its strategy, and Hotel F thereby improves its competitive position.

Assuming that Hotel E cannot do anything to increase consumers' belief that it is not located in proximity of a skiing area (i.e., its location is indeed far from a skiing resort), a strategy it may employ to increase consumers' overall attitude toward the property is to add a salient attribute to the set of attributes consumers consider when making hotel choices. For example, Hotel E could provide free accommodation for children staying with their parents. It is likely that parents would consider this option important when choosing a hotel. As long as other competitors do not offer this service, Hotel E enjoys some advantage in the choices made by its target market. It is essential that when adding a new attribute, marketers consider the following: First, the attribute added must be important enough to the hotel's target market to be included in consumers' subsequent decision making (i.e., is it indeed salient?). Second, the belief that a particular hotel possesses this attribute must be stronger than the belief that any of its competitors do. This marketing strategy, often referred to as a *strategy of differentiation,* is likely to be successful when these conditions are met.

Differentiation, however, is unlikely to be sustainable—that is, over time, competitors identify what added attributes successfully attract customers and copy them, thereby creating consumer belief regarding their own properties. Thus, the hotel that introduced the new salient attribute often can expect to lose its differential advantage over time unless it maintains a unique characteristic like a special location (e.g., "there is only one view property on this section of coastline") or a fabulous chef in the kitchen.

Increasing belief strength for a hotel's attributes is not always a successful strategy, assuming a compensatory model is being used. For example, consumers may find it relatively unimportant whether the hotel offers low room rates or not. In the example data in Table 7.1, the importance rating for low room rates is -2—that is, consumers in this particular target segment evaluate low room rates negatively, perhaps because they associate low rates with low quality or with small, underfurnished rooms. In this case, stressing that a particular hotel offers low rates, thereby increasing the strength of consumers' beliefs, may adversely affect consumers' overall evaluation of a property. If you compare Hotels F and H, you will see that the strong belief that Hotel H offers low rates ($b_{\text{low rates H}} = +2$) negatively affects its overall evaluation, as ($e_{\text{low rates}} \times b_{\text{low rates H}}) = (-2)(+2) = -4$. Hotel F, on the other hand, benefits from consumers not being aware of low rates, such that ($e_{\text{low rates}} \times b_{\text{low rates F}}) = (-2)(-2) = +4$.

It is important to note that importance weights associated with attributes vary across market segments. For example, while business travelers on corporate expense accounts or consumers on a once-in-a-lifetime vacation, such as a honeymoon, may attach less importance to low rates, more price-sensitive market segments usually weigh low rates more heavily in their hotel choice. It is therefore important for marketers to carefully define the targeted market segment(s) prior to conducting their research and applying evaluation weights and beliefs to similarly disposed consumers.

In general, it is crucial to find out what attributes targeted consumers feel are most salient to their decisions and, in response, increase performance (or perceived performance) regarding these attributes and commensurately inform market segments of this stronger position. The resultant positive attitude toward the offering should then increase the likelihood of the hotel being chosen by travelers using a compensatory decision-making model. Alternatively, as a strategic move, particularly for special niche properties, marketers may want to encourage consumers to abandon the linear compensatory model. Niche market segments may exist or may be created through marketing communications; these target markets might be better served by hotels focusing on one or more of the noncompensatory decision rules presented. For example, a segment of highly price-sensitive customers predominantly using a lexicographic decision rule with low rates as the most important attribute may constitute the primary target market for a property. In this case, travelers can be targeted by offering low prices and/or frequent-stay loyalty programs. At the same time, services deemed unnecessary or unimportant by this customer segment can be eliminated or minimized. The fact that some customer segments expect a minimal level of performance on several attributes (e.g., cleanliness, convenience, and friendly service) when they use an elimination-by-aspect or conjunctive decision rule, however, implies that focusing performance and/or marketing on a single attribute may be inadequate for some segments of travelers. A hotel would then benefit from creating a level of "at least acceptable" attributes in addition to providing stronger packages of the same attributes offered by competitors targeting the same market segment. Overall, knowing how consumers make decisions should help hotel managers to design better properties, packages, and services, and help them market those offerings to their respective target segment(s), thereby improving competitive position.

► COMPREHENSIVE EXERCISE

Understanding consumer decision-making rules enables you to make strategic and marketing decisions, thereby effectively targeting segments with varying goals, using multiple criteria, and following different decision rules when choosing hotel venues. This exercise gives you an opportunity to review the consumer decision-making rules discussed in this chapter and demonstrate the strategic implications of these rules for marketers in the hospitality industry.

Shannon Clarke is a chocolatier operating a small chocolate store in Knowlton, Quebec. This year, she is planning to attend the Sixth Annual Chocolate Show in New York City. Shannon has carefully considered various transportation options and decided to travel by car. She is now considering a number of accommodation alternatives. Shannon knows very well what characteristics are salient to her regarding hotel choice. For example, low rates are significant, as Shannon has a limited budget for traveling expenses. It is also imperative that the hotel offer free parking and be located not too far from the Metropolitan Pavilion on Eighteenth Street, where the Annual Chocolate Show will take place. To keep in touch with her business while staying in New York, Shannon would also like Internet access from her room. On the other hand, she does not require the hotel to offer a nice restaurant, as she will go out on the town each night to have dinner with fellow chocolatiers. Other attributes considered in the hotel choice of small business owners attending trade shows and conventions in New York are noted in Table 7.2.

Shannon identified four hotels in an online search. The information provided online makes it easy to determine what services are offered at what rates for each of the

Table 7.2 Shannon's Salient Attributes

Attribute	e_i	Hotel Park b_{iP}	Hotel Union b_{iU}	Hotel Chelsea b_{iC}	Hotel Lion b_{iL}
Low rates	+3	+2	+2	+3	−1
Location	+3	+2	+3	+2	−1
Free parking	+2	+3	+2	+1	+2
Internet access	+1	−1	+2	+1	+3
Fitness facilities	0	−1	+1	−2	+3
Nice restaurant	−1	+1	0	−2	+2

properties. Shannon now must decide which of the four hotels she should choose. Table 7.2 shows relevant attributes, evaluation ratings, and belief ratings to be taken into consideration in Shannon's decision-making process.

Use the information provided above to answer the following questions:

1. Calculate the overall brand attitudes for all of the brands using the weighted additive/linear compensatory model.

2. According to beliefs and evaluations shown in the table above, which hotel is in the best competitive position? Which hotel is in the worst competitive position?

3. Describe three strategies the hotel with the lowest overall attitude rating could use to improve consumer attitudes.

4. Which hotel would be chosen using a lexicographic decision rule if Shannon Clarke considers low rates most important?

5. Which hotel would be chosen using the conjunctive decision rule with a cutoff value of 0?

6. Given the lexicographic decision rule with "nice restaurant" as the most important attribute, what should Hotel Chelsea do? What should Hotel Lion do?

7. List salient attributes not included in the table that could be considered for hotels catering to small business owners attending conferences and trade shows in the New York area.

8. Using the elimination-by-aspects rule, which hotel would be chosen given a cutoff value of +2?

Answers to Practice Questions

1. The overall brand attitudes are calculated using the formula $\sum_{i=1}^{n} e_i b_i$.

$$A_{Hotel\ Park} = (+3)(+2) + (+3)(+2)$$
$$+ (+2)(+3) + (+1)(-1) + (0)(-1)$$
$$+ (-1)(+1) = 6 + 6 + 6 - 1$$
$$+ 0 - 1 = 16$$

$$A_{Hotel\ Union} = (+3)(+2) + (+3)(+3)$$
$$+ (+2)(+2) + (+1)(+2) + (0)(+1)$$
$$+ (-1)(0) = 6 + 9 + 4 + 2 + 0$$
$$+ 0 = 21$$

$$A_{Hotel\ Chelsea} = (+3)(+3) + (+3)(+2)$$
$$+ (+2)(+1) + (+1)(+1) + (0)(-2)$$
$$+ (-1)(-2) = 9 + 6 + 2 + 1$$
$$+ 0 + 2 = 20$$

$$A_{Hotel\ Lion} = (+3)(-1) + (+3)(-1)$$
$$+ (+2)(+2) + (+1)(+3) + (0)(+3)$$
$$+ (-1)(+2) = -3 - 3 + 4 + 3$$
$$+ 0 - 2 = -1$$

2. If the weighted additive/linear compensatory model is used, Hotel Union is in the best competitive position because its overall attitude rating (+21) is higher than its competitors'. Hotel Lion is in the worst competitive position because its overall attitude rating (−1) is lower than its competitors'.

3. **Strategy 1:** Hotel Lion could attempt to change the perceived relevance of some of the attributes. It could stress the importance of a good restaurant and excellent fitness facilities for a hotel in which businesspeople stay while attending a trade show or conference. The drawback of this strategy is that some of its competitors could also benefit from it. **Strategy 2:** Hotel Lion could improve its performance on some of the attributes considered important by consumers in this target segment, thereby increasing the strength of consumers' belief that it possesses these attributes. More specifi-

cally, Hotel Lion could lower rates if financially feasible, or provide better free parking. **Strategy 3:** Hotel Lion could encourage consumers to consider other relevant attributes when choosing accommodation for trade show visits or conference attendance. These attributes should be associated with a strong performance by Hotel Lion and a weaker performance by other competitors. For example, Hotel Lion might introduce a shuttle service to important conference and trade show locations to make it convenient for business travelers and conference participants to reach their destination; they could also offer a coffee shop for short breaks and breakfast suited for their target segments' busy schedules, and/or introduce secretarial or other business services for travelers.

4. If a lexicographic decision rule were used, with low rates as the most important attribute, Hotel Chelsea would be chosen. It scores highest on this attribute ($b_{\text{low rate C}}$ = +3).

5. Hotel Union would be chosen because it is the only hotel in the consideration set meeting the cutoff value of 0 on all salient attributes.

6. Assuming that a lexicographic rule in this instance is looking for positive belief ratings on nice restaurant (i.e., evaluation score is now positive), Hotel Chelsea must improve its restaurant offering in terms of food, beverage, and service. These changes must be fairly substantial in order to affect consumers' impressions of the restaurant. It is thus likely that a considerable amount of time and money will have to be spent to rethink the restaurant concept and offerings. Hotel Lion should maintain its high level of restaurant quality; it would also be possible to strengthen consumers' belief that Hotel Lion offers an excellent restaurant by increasing marketing communications. It is important to note here that understanding the consumer decision-making process is crucial in devising a successful marketing strategy: Only if a substantial (in terms of number of customers and/or profit potential) market segment is using the lexicographic decision rule based on positive evaluations of a nice restaurant in choosing a hotel does it pay to improve the restaurant (for Hotel Chelsea) or to maintain a nice restaurant offering (for Hotel Lion). If the targeted segments rely primarily on a compensatory decision rule using importance weights described in Table 7.2 above, then establishing or maintaining a nice restaurant may be counterproductive, as these consumers do not positively value that attribute ($e_i = -1$). In this case, creating a strong belief that a nice restaurant is offered decreases overall evaluations of the hotel—*and* is operationally expensive and time-consuming—that is, when targeting customers like Shannon, offering a great restaurant will not increase Hotel Lion's likelihood of being chosen. The hotel could, however, benefit from its strong performance on attributes like "nice restaurant" or "fitness facilities" not valued by the current market segment through changing its target marketing strategy. A property could, for example, target business travelers for whom exercise and fine dining are more important than low room rates or central location.

7. The following is a (nonexhaustive) list of additional attributes hotels might

consider that might be salient for entrepreneurs attending trade shows and conventions: access to fax and copy machines, secretarial services, complementary breakfast, cable TV, including channels covering business topics, complementary newspaper, and shuttle service to train station or airport.

8. Using elimination by aspects (cutoff value = +2), we initially eliminate Hotel Lion and see that hotels Park, Union, and Chelsea stay in consideration based on beliefs about those brands regarding the equally important attributes of low rates and location. The next most important attribute is free parking, and we are left with hotels Park and Union in consideration after eliminating Hotel Chelsea. Finally, we eliminate Hotel Park and select Hotel Union based on the Internet access attribute (lowering the cutoff value to +1).

7.4 HOTEL PRICING

Marta Sinclair and Carl R. Sinclair

▶ TRADITIONAL APPROACH

The single most important criterion of success in any business, including hotels, is profit. The purpose of this article is to discuss the importance of hotel pricing and its influence on yield or revenue management, especially in terms of profit generation, and because of inherent dangers to the industry worldwide, integrity of the established pricing structure. Historically, price has been determined by the triangular relationship of cost and demand in the context of competition (see Figure 7.3). The actual pricing structure is developed with one of these three components as the deciding factor while the other two play supplementary roles.

The traditional pricing strategy was largely cost-driven. Many hotel operators tended to favor the rule-of-thumb method. This approach, also called the $1 per $1,000 rule, states that hotels should charge approximately $1 per night for every $1,000 of room cost, based on an average 70 percent occupancy. Although popular in its day, the calculation of cost was commonly misunderstood (see Hanson, 1995). Another widely used quantitative method was the Hubbart Formula, developed in the late 1940s as a guideline issued by the American Hotel Association. It focused on computing an average room rate that would cover operational costs

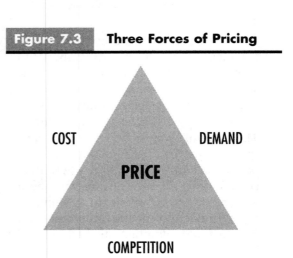

Figure 7.3 **Three Forces of Pricing**

COST

DEMAND

PRICE

COMPETITION

and yield a reasonable return on investment (ROI). These quantitative methods are fairly static and therefore suited for a stable economic environment. Qualitative pricing approaches, such as percentage increase of previous-year rates adjusted for inflation, payroll increases, and new cost of supplies, reflect more realistically the projected cost.

Other qualitative techniques are less ex-act but, by being competition-oriented, they offer more flexibility. The Pied Piper or Follow-the-Leader method uses competition as the basis for rate setting, while the Gouge 'Em approach tries to lure business away from other properties by undercutting their prices. If there is no competition to speak of, Hit or Miss fluctuation of rates tied to profitable occupancy levels could be employed.

Table 7.3 Traditional Room Rate-Setting Methods

Quantitative Methods		Qualitative Methods	
$1 Per $1,000	• Determine the cost of the property (building, furnishings and equipment). • Divide the total by number of rooms. • Divide the calculated cost per room by $1,000. • Estimate at 70% average occupancy.	Gouge 'Em	• When demand is low, set rates below the market level. • When demand is high, set rates at a premium.
Hubbart Formula	• Calculate operating expenses. • Add taxes and insurance. • Add expenses for asset depreciation. • Deduct income from sources other than room revenue. • Divide the total by number of rooms in the hotel. • Adjust the calculated room rate for estimated occupancy.	Hit or Miss	• Record occupancy at each pricing level. • Analyze the collected information periodically to determine which level was most profitable. • Set the rate at the most profitable level.
		Percentage Increase	• List the rates that were charged in the previous year. • Calculate rate of inflation, payroll increase, the new cost of supplies. • Convert the increased cost into percentage increase. • Increase previous year rates by the calculated percentage increase.
		Pied Piper	• Set rates according to what other hotels in the area are asking for comparable accommodation.

Source: DeVeau, L.T., P.M. DeVeau, N.J. Portocarrero and M. Escoffier. 1996. *Front Office Management and Operations,* pp. 83–91.

The drawback of competition-driven pricing is its sole focus on rate comparison, ignoring differences in operating expenses and customer-perceived value. An effective approach, therefore, calls for a mix of methods adjusted for different situations (see Table 7.3). The fundamental question remains: What should be the driving force in formulating a sound pricing strategy? In today's dynamic business environment, which discards the traditional view that market demand for room rates is largely inelastic, demand orientation seems to provide the best fit.

► CURRENT PRICING CRITERIA

"**O**ur pricing is market-driven, not cost-based," says Scott Farrell, corporate director of distribution with Fairmont Hotels and Resorts, a Toronto-based chain of luxury properties. When the chain is setting its prices, it starts with comprehensive market research. Based on the data, the correct price for each marketplace is determined. If there is a major shift in a market, then the prices will adjust for that. However, if there is a major shift in a demand curve, then a shift of price may have no effect. It may actually leave more money on the table. For example, if the airlines go on strike, a significant shift in the demand curve would result. Under such conditions, decreasing the rate by $50, for example, would only result in a $50 loss. If there is an opportunity to go after a new targeted market with a specific offer, enabling the chain to capture a greater market share, then lowering the rate serves its purpose. Generally, however, lowering rates across the board is not the preferred pricing strategy.

► PRICING: WHO IS IN CHARGE?

While independently owned properties make their own pricing decisions, in case of a chain it is usually corporate headquarters (HQ) that sets pricing guidelines. Often, individual properties are still responsible for the actual pricing. Because they are held accountable, they must balance corporate guidelines with their autonomy to set their prices. Caroline Shin, member of the revenue management team at Starwood Hotels and Resorts Worldwide, which operates a number of upscale brands, such as Sheraton and W Hotels, stresses the cooperative nature of this relationship. Successful pricing strategies arise from an ongoing interaction of both sides. Corporate HQ provides sophisticated tools and in-depth market analysis that would be beyond reach of individual properties. Property managers, on the other hand, offer their experience and knowledge of regional specifics that may have gone unnoticed by the corporate team. "The people who have been in the property understand the dynamics of that market, and they have developed pricing intuition," explains Shin. Some experts view intuition as a valuable part of the pricing mechanism, and even managers who are technically savvy check the numbers against their gut feeling.

► PRICING: SCIENCE, ART, AND INTUITION

Pricing distribution and revenue management techniques are a mix of science and art. Recent research shows that two-thirds of managers making strategic decisions under pressure and time constraints use a combination of analysis and intuition (Sinclair, 2003). The advent of modern technology, such as yield management software packages, has further strengthened this link. "Even the most sophisticated analytical model for forecasting, may it be for hotel pricing or for thermal dynamics of a nuclear plant, still needs variables based upon assumptions," says Shin, who used to work as a nuclear engineer. The more business-savvy hotel management becomes and the more they understand the hotel dynamics and the market, the more can be gained from training them how to define their experience-based intuition and put it into numbers. In this respect, an interaction between the corporate revenue management team and individual hotels is paramount. "Every time I go out to a property, I learn something new. It only helps me when I build my analytical models to almost translate what they know into numbers," confirms Shin. The better hotels can do that, the better models they can develop. Nonetheless, inaccurate historical data remains a major limitation.

No model is ever going to be perfect, though. What seems to work best is to teach hotel managers how to use the model and to understand the direction of the pricing decisions they need to make. That is the scientific part. The art piece comes into play when they infuse the model with their knowledge and intuition. Staff training is an important part of this process. "We can't just have Ph.D.s sitting in one room coming with all these models and we just roll it out. At the same time, we can't just have people with intuitions run around and set prices," says Shin.

Revenue management teams must make sure that hotels understand how to employ the models in their daily pricing decisions. When science is applied, the revenue team can go to their experts, ask probing questions, and get solid results. Even though intuition is a part of this process, it is based only on a hypothesis that could have been triggered by a discussion with a customer, knowledge of what is happening in the marketplace, or historic trends. That is why pure intuition is not sufficient. "Managers must have reliable data to support their hunches," cautions Scott Farrell.

▶ CUSTOMER NEEDS

Customer satisfaction is a crucial part of marketing, pricing, and yield management. Any pricing strategy established by the hotel management must attract customers willing to pay the specified rate. While price is a determinator of the customer profile the hotel is looking for, it is also an indicator of the quality of services and the market segment the hotel is competing in. Therefore, yield management uses information about targeted customers' purchasing behavior and product sales to develop pricing strategy together with inventory control that delivers products that are better matched to customer needs, create greater demand, and, on that account, produce greater revenues. Lieberman (1993) states that yield management is the process of maximizing profits from the sale of perishable assets, such as hotel rooms, by controlling price and inventory and improving service through systemization. An exact definition of the target market is essential. There is a definite and firm perception in the psyche of the customer, who views the price as the value forthcoming. Therefore, the eventual satisfaction of the customer is the paramount task of the pricing mechanism. This is the make-or-break factor of the entire hotel, especially if the value expected does not match the price.

▶ ROLE OF TECHNOLOGY

While the approach to hotel pricing is still ruled by supply and demand, speed and sophistication of room-rate yield or revenue maximization is now much increased due to two technological factors: yield management software and Internet bookings.

Yield management software packages enable hotels to use a higher number of room-rate levels, or buckets, and to control inventory for rate availability in real time. Each level may consist of several room rates open under given conditions to yield a maximum profit. Traditionally, hotels used between three and five rate levels; otherwise, the adjustment became too complex for the human brain to work with. The introduction of software removed this barrier, and some hotel chains now use up to ten rate levels. This allows implementation of much narrower ranges for each bucket, thus optimizing price elasticity. This further means the software model recognizes the point at which the same number of bookings can be achieved at a higher rate.

Online monitoring of room inventory in real time facilitates the timing of the adjustment. So far, the biggest limitation is the reliability of historical data. Even in its imperfect form, the system has made a difference. However, hotel managers are fully aware that it takes years to develop brand recognition and quality but just a push of a button to damage or even destroy it, if the pricing is not set up knowledgeably. As the technology becomes more sophisticated, it will eliminate such questionable practices as overbooking, which aims at compensating for last-minute cancellations by taking in more than 100 percent reservations. Besides the question of whether overbooking is ethical and, in some countries, even illegal, better technology would definitely improve the quality of service provided by properties that engage in this practice.

Another area where technological advancement had a great impact on hotel pricing is the Internet. Its use as a booking tool has created a new level of pricing transparency and tiered competition. It also penetrated the negotiation of corporate rates. Many hotels see the effect of the Internet as both good and bad. The good side is that website bookings are growing every day. As more customers become familiar with their favorite hotel websites, hotel companies have started investing heavily in website development and upkeep, which gives them several advantages. First, the cost of online bookings is lower than for bookings made through other distribution channels. Companies do not have to pay commission because the booking is direct, circumventing all intermediaries. Online booking also provides an opportunity to monitor inventory in real time without reliance on a distributor willing to share and regularly supply data. Last but not least, it generates loyal customers by making them eligible for bonus points, which they cannot earn if they use an Internet intermediary.

That is exactly where the flip side of the Internet lies. The intermediaries are getting more powerful and growing significantly in volume. Because most of them show all hotel rates on their website, they make the information accessible to any computer user. One way to meet the challenge of more powerful intermediaries, especially if hotels need to move inventory, is to utilize auctions where the name of the hotel is not disclosed to the customer until the transaction is finalized. Such action, however, calls for extreme caution so that it does not damage a hotel's reputation or threaten its strategic partnerships. As intermediaries become bigger, rate transparency will increase to the point where it will drive the market, especially when computer literacy and Internet access become the norm.

Moreover, the Internet allows nonbranded hotels to compete more heavily with the branded hotels because they can now be displayed just as readily. Without significant advertising expense, they can compete on price. For some markets this does not matter, especially when the brand is powerful enough to charge the premium and get the business. In highly competitive markets, however, the competition creates an additional strain for the individual property. Many branded hotels must now compete with other brands through the traditional distribution channels and with nonbranded hotels on the Internet, which, in principle, lowers hotel rates. A frequently adopted strategy is to invest heavily in website development and customer loyalty programs, assuring excellent website functionality and that customers are rewarded for booking directly through the hotel website rather than through the website of a third-party intermediary. Both Fairmont and Starwood, for example, utilize their high-quality loyalty programs in this way.

Internet booking also changed the way corporate accounts are negotiated. Because many companies now require that their employees make business travel arrangements via the corporate website, the placement of a hotel or a brand on this booking tool is of strategic importance. Being listed first in the accommodation section, for example, may bring in a higher volume of business and thus substantiate a lower negotiated rate.

► LONG-TERM STRATEGY FOR THE INTERNET

Because hotels cannot expect that Internet distributors will go out of business, they smartly conclude that a partnership with the devil is better than a fight with him. Besides using their own websites, hotel companies are also making sure that the cost of their transactions goes down continuously so they can compete even at lower rates—while maintaining a good relationship with their carefully selected online intermediaries.

There is a large number of distributors to choose from. On one end of the spectrum is, for example, Expedia, which allows participating hotels to control their rates, meaning a hotel can change its rates any time it wants. At the other end are companies, such as Hotel Reservation Network (HRN), that bind hotels contractually to a locked rate that cannot be changed. Some hotel chains do not want to partner with these distributors because they like pricing flexibility and want to make sure their rates yield as much as possible.

Adaptation to new technology has been the biggest component of change for intermediaries as well. Companies that do not have the most current technology working in real time or allowing hotels to yield rates in real time are usually not considered a suitable distribution partner for some chains. On the other hand, companies that invest in real-time technology to yield rates are ideal partners because, as the industry sees it, they work with, not against the industry by permitting hotels to raise or lower rates in real time. "They work with us," says Caroline Shin. "They give data to us very frequently so that we understand the travel pattern bookings on their website. Then we compare it with what is happening on our website and also what we are getting outside the Internet to make sure that our market mix is set appropriately." Pricing flexibility, compatibility with the desired hotel image, and protection of its strategic partnerships, together with cost, play important roles in selecting an intermediary.

► THE ROLE OF CREATIVITY IN PRICING

Creativity, either of an individual or a team, can and often does lead to innovative pricing ideas. However, its application must be specific, not just directional. It is not enough to state, "We have to do something about our occupancy level." A pricing campaign must target a number of sold rooms or generated revenue that is required in order to break even or to do better. This specific approach injects efficiency into allocating marketing money to areas where it is most effective and in periods when it is desired. If there is no task direction or overall pricing leadership, the most creative idea may book only ten room-nights instead of one hundred. It may generate more customer loyalty, but that is something the hotel may not need at the moment, although it could be an acceptable outcome in a low-season month. Pricing leadership helps team members understand the hotel's current situation and direct money and creativity to do exactly what is needed. Creativity comes up with the idea, which serves as a vehicle, but spending marketing money the smart way is a matter of experience in innovation, which turns the idea into a successful product. Creativity also plays a large part in employee satisfaction, and it lowers turnover.

In a sluggish economy, some hotels start paying attention not only to profit as the bottom line but also to revenue. This means they monitor closely the accrued cost as well as the generated revenue, thus achieving the maximum yield. Interestingly, contemporary price leadership may take different forms. It could mean, for example, elimination of smoking rooms throughout the property. Many U.S. motels are revamping rooms, ripping off cigarette-damaged furniture and carpets, and designating them as nonsmoking. This saves on maintenance and adds to overall packaging flexibility when the business is hurt by lackluster demand. This tactic means drapes, carpets, bedding, and other furnishings must be replaced less frequently; it also mitigates fire risk and enhances cleanliness and overall safety.

► THE ROLE OF HUMAN RESOURCES IN PRICING

Some large chains recognize that pricing is a complex issue and that they need to get better at it. There is a new focus on analyzing the culture of pricing (how it is being done) and how it can be improved. This approach is reflected even in the kinds of people chains are hiring.

Although the majority of staff involved in strategic pricing are in the hotel industry and have a background in revenue management, others are in the airline industry and have in-depth travel revenue management experience. Some chains have sought access to this experience by hiring from outside the hotel industry. This is to encourage diversification of thinking and new ways of thought—completely out of the box, as the traditional team members are joined by researchers doing a different kind of optimization analysis. The goal could be as radical as trying to manage risk or optimize toward the railroad industry and its scheduling. On the surface, these tactics have nothing to do with revenue management per se. A lot of experience in optimizing difficult travel, however, can only be gained by bringing in people with different backgrounds in consulting or with in-depth Internet experience. In order to move pricing and revenue management to a different level of thought, a new mix of people is necessary. For this approach to work, adequate training must be in place.

In this respect, basic HR functions, such as hiring and training, have an impact on pricing. What is necessary is not only to train personnel in quantitative core skills but also in strategic thinking. For example, when a hotel does not want to take a specific piece of business, it must ask such questions as: What is the revenue? What is the rate? What am I displacing by this decision? Where do I think this will go? How does it help my RevPAR?

Hotel managers must become more analytical so they can use all the new tools now available. When reports are created, team members must be taught how to use them. A lot of training must be provided for corporate executives, general managers, and regional revenue directors as well. They all must be trained to think more strategically and to understand analysis and the reports so they can help their individual properties.

► DIVERSIFICATION: THE IMPROVEMENT OF THE PRICING PROCESS

As noted, exclusive hotel industry experience may lead to ossification due to one-sided judgment and the inability to see beyond the familiar. From this perspective, experience is

both an asset and a liability. It is human nature to take for granted the way things are done after being in the same environment for a while. Therefore, hotel chains are continuously creating and refining pricing strategies to accommodate not only different market segments but also different situations a hotel may face based on occupancy levels.

Corporate HQ tries to identify these different situations and associated variables. "It is almost like a bag of goods, a bag of pricing strategies that should be tested," says Caroline Shin. Hotels are given the full menu and encouraged to try a certain strategy if they are in a specific situation. Depending on the region, an individual property may use one set of strategies more than another. In a weak economy, however, the chains have to work harder and be more flexible because the market is overflowing with demand. Adapting step by step, a hotel may apply a different strategy every week. The problem for the corporate office is to identify situations a hotel might be in and seek remedy. For example, if group bookings are low this week but competitors are full, how can the property make up the difference with transient or leisure business? The general manager may ask the corporate team, "What pricing strategies can I use in order to fill my house?" Then he or she may ask, "What else worked before for other hotels, and what may work for me based on my market specifics and market characteristics?" That way he or she can test each strategy using the provided tool and personal experience.

► PRICING: SUPPORT AND PROTECT

The corporate pricing structure is also in place to support and protect members of the chain in a number of areas including pricing and partnerships. The corporate office sets guidelines for hotels in terms of pricing structure and the market segments they deal with. Fairmont Hotels and Resorts, for example, focuses on four segments: transient leisure travel, group travel, business travel, and wholesale. The corporate structure provides guidelines about how the segments fit with each other, how they cross over, and where they reside in the overall pricing structure. This information is necessary because every segment acts differently. Most market segments are dynamic and require frequent rate adjustments. One exception is the wholesale market, where pricing is still largely done the traditional way: A wholesaler provides a net rate, marks it up, and sells it to the general population. There may be a hidden cost, however, if the distribution chain includes an operator acting as a middleman between the wholesaler and the supplier.

When setting up the overall pricing structure, one starts with the retail rate, which is a bucket of premium or best available rates (BAR) charged on the open market. They usually do not carry any restrictions, such as cancellation fees, and they are fully billable. Depending on the level of occupancy, one of these rates is available on any given day when the hotel is not fully booked. It is up to the yield management system to identify which BAR to offer. All other rate types, such as discount rates and prenegotiated rates, are determined in relation to the retail rate. For instance, a corporate rate for a high-volume client will be probably set lower than the BAR rate that is estimated to sell most during the period when the contract is in place. This way the rates are nested within each other in a manner that makes economic sense.

The corporate pricing guidelines follow two main criteria: to maximize revenue and to protect key partnerships. While the hotel sales force negotiates contracts with key partners, such as longstanding corporate accounts or wholesale volume accounts, they make sure to protect these partnerships and provide them value. At the same time, they take every opportunity to maximize revenue. One cannot survive without the other, reiterates Scott Farrell. However, it is up to the hotels themselves, with guidance and additional research, to determine in their marketplace what their pricing structure should look like.

A diversified corporate team, with a mix of people with a hotel industry background and others skilled in optimization modeling, fulfills an additional function. It acts as a risk prevention mechanism, a necessary prerequisite for managing the risk inherent in pricing. Any chain with a wide variety of hotels must make sure the properties are covered in all kinds of situations. One risk containment scenario might be that the chain, in response to a changing demand curve, acquires a type of business that the brand has not catered to traditionally. Caroline Shin explains, "Sheraton did not take on airline crew business because we did not want crew members lingering in the lobby; it affected our brand image. But we thought maybe we could start taking that when our RevPAR index or occupancy slips to a certain point. So we are trying to change the standards of different market segments we are willing to take."

On the international scale, another risk management plan would be analyzing operational cost and determining whether to close down part of the hotel if market research shows occupancy will not be high enough. When PESTEL (political, economic, sociocultural, technological, environmental, legal) analysis indicates demand will drop precipitously for an extended period (due to political unrest, economic crisis, or health scare, for example), instead of hoping for the best and running a full house with a full staff, the hotel may decide to shut down floors or restaurants and save cost until the market picks up again. Selection of the appropriate strategy will depend on the market specifics and protection of the image. A property may opt to close down several floors over the weekend if it caters mostly to business clientele staying during the week. It would not, however, suspend room service, although unprofitable, if that is considered an integral part of the offered product. In a worst-case scenario, the chain may decide to sell properties in global risk areas when it determines the external circumstances make it difficult to raise occupancy on an ongoing basis.

site it does not mean a chain can use it and advertise a lower rate, which would undermine a partnership of many years. In terms of cost, the chain must review its pricing strategy not only by market segment but also by distribution channel. "Several years ago, we would not consider the cost of distribution in our ROI. Today we do," concedes Scott Farrell.

Another challenge is to keep up with new Internet sites. The chains must reevaluate constantly and prioritize their yield so as to choose which channels to keep or drop. Fairmont Hotels and Resorts, for example, applies the 80–20 rule. They focus on the 20 percent of the online wholesalers that capture more than 80 percent of the business. As Scott Farrell puts it, "Why would I play with the other 10–12 percent? I only have so many hours in a day to manage. I may as well work with the lion's share."

► BETTER UTILIZE YOUR DISTRIBUTION CHANNELS

The Internet creates a new level of transparency as it allows the opportunity to maximize profitability. There is now a multitude of channels to choose from. Understanding the cost of each channel in relation to the value of provided service has an impact on the quality of pricing decisions. Therefore, it is necessary to determine how much revenue bookings through an Internet intermediary generate and whether or not they justify the accrued cost. There is also a tremendous risk involved. As discussed earlier, one of key guidelines of corporate marketing is that partners are protected. Just because there is a new Internet

► QUALITY ABOVE ALL?

Criteria for selecting an online distribution partner vary by price levels as well. Budget and economy properties are driven mostly by financial considerations, while upscale and luxury hotels are more concerned with compatibility. As for chains, they ask two basic questions: (1) How can the partnership increase our brand recognition or a brand reach, and (2) How much is it going to bring us in terms of revenue or profitability? Their choice has to match the brand first, and then it has to drive the revenue. If the brand is equaled with quality, online providers that project a connotation of cheapness will not be considered at all. The quality image refers not only to the hotel asset itself but also to how and where this asset is sold.

Fairmont Hotels and Resorts, as a quality brand on the luxury side, cannot compete on price. The quality of their product and the offering of the experience must be considered by the customer at the price being offered. When their hotels play with price, the corporate office watches closely. Scott Farrell explains, "If our property wanted to shift their rate by $50, I would ask why? Give me the case behind it and tell me what you are going to do to make up the additional $50 you are going to lose. If they come back to me and say they are moving their rate from $300 to $250 while driving a certain volume, I would make them go through the process of determining what incremental volume they will need to make up for the $50 in loss." In other words, pricing decisions must be driven by ROI, not only a feeling. Feelings and experience may be involved, but properties must present a strong case based on the estimated ROI and what they plan to get out of the proposed strategy. It allows them to go into the pricing change with their eyes open. They also must consider how the competition will respond. A carelessly lowered rate may lead to a price war.

▶ SPEED AND STRATEGY

The speed and immediacy of exposure via the Internet have reshaped how marketing campaigns are conducted. Having eliminated the delay of exposure to marketing collateral material, such as brochures or newspaper advertisements, hotels can conduct targeted discount mini-campaigns on their own websites when the yield management system indicates a drop in occupancy for specific dates. In a similar manner, brand recognition can be enhanced by a carefully orchestrated online auction. The South African hospitality group Protea (2000) was among the first in the industry using this method by offering their prospective guests the opportunity to bid on a limited number of weekend getaways in their properties that needed to boost occupancy. By setting a minimum bidding price, the integrity of the hotel image was protected. Similar auction systems, used to encourage room-night sales during slow periods, are nowadays available in the United States and Canada via several Internet intermediaries.

For chains in particular, a long-term strategy in distribution pricing is paramount. It stipulates the criteria and accepts or rejects short-term adjustments depending on what is happening in the industry, what is new in the technology, and who the new players are. In terms of corporate hierarchy, pricing is formulated and executed on three levels: (1) strategy, (2) tactics and execution, and (3) measurement. Strategy comes first, followed by tactics meant to support that strategy and their execution. Finally, the achieved outcome is measured against the set benchmarks. If the strategy is sound, it will last longer than the other two steps. Frequently, new tactics must be implemented; these drive the execution and the measurement. This requires a development of proprietary criteria for measurement and their continuous adjustment to changing conditions.

▶ PRICE ELASTICITY

Contrary to the traditional view that hotel rates are, in the long-term, generally inelastic, price elasticity is receiving a lot of attention nowadays thanks to yield management. Its goal is to take advantage of and to cover the entire spectrum of the customers' ability to purchase. Price elasticity allows hotels to capture customers who do not mind paying the high rate as well as those who are more price-conscious. This can be done in a number of ways. By using different room categories, a luxury hotel can have on the same day suites available at $500 and entry-level rooms at $200. Every room rate category has a different value proposition associated with the incremental revenue. If the variance between a standard room and a deluxe room is $75, the latter should provide an adequately greater value to the customer. The result is a clear product differentiation, which can be also achieved by stay restrictions or by the use of fencing. Examples of physical differences, or fences, are room type, view, amenities, and location. Nonphysical fences may mean different customers, transactions, or consumption characteristics. These bear many similarities with airline pricing strategies, which differentiate the product by, for example, cancellation restrictions or last-minute availability of a prenegotiated corporate rate. The result is nested pricing, allowing properties to have a very high rate available on the same day as a rate that is more attractive to the lower-end customer.

► NEW AREAS OF PRICING AND YIELD MANAGEMENT

Hotel pricing strategies traditionally have been limited to setting and adjusting room rates and other ongoing activities. In order to survive in the current dynamic, competitive, and even dangerous global environment, hotels and resorts are taking on other types of business, some of which are one-time projects. Organizing shows, festivals, and conferences or undergoing renovations requires a new type of core competency. Therefore, in addition to mastering current pricing strategies, hotel practitioners must acquire project management skills, such as those that are taught and practiced by Project Management Institute (*pmi.org*). Mastering these skills will make hotel team members capable of maximizing yield from project-type functions the same way as they optimize revenue from room rates.

7.5 A DAY IN THE LIFE OF A REGIONAL REVENUE MANAGER

Paul Chappelle

As the sun rises, so does the stack of reports on my desk. Every morning I am greeted with the accomplishments of the day, week, month, and year before, all in the form of paper-and-ink reports roughly 2 inches thick. Each report attempts to explain the basic numbers pertinent to the smooth function and revenue generation of a hotel. Although I enjoy the development and success of the latest revenue management systems, I still prefer to do things the old-fashioned way. These reports are my comfort food for revenue management.

The first meeting of the day is the revenue maximization meeting, or revmax for short. The meeting consists of the hotel's revenue manager, general manager, director of rooms, and the entire sales and catering staff. We discuss what happened the day and night before, and we evaluate sales leads from the previous day. As a group, we decide what our approach is to each lead. We evaluate whether we will pursue the lead or refer it to a nearby hotel within the company. The revenue manager upholds any decisions made regarding the rate strategy for that day and for the next few days, which are set at that time. Any changes that need to be made are communicated throughout the day.

The next meeting of the day is the revenue management meeting. This meeting, facilitated by the revenue manager, happens once a week and is attended by the general manager, controller, director of sales and marketing, director of rooms, reservations manager, and most operations managers. In this meeting, similar to the daily revmax meeting with the sales team, we go over the numbers in much greater detail and for a much longer time. We look at the number of room-nights and rates generated through the different revenue channels, trends both good and bad, upcoming marketing strategies, and the results of past marketing strategies, and we talk about anything and everything that may affect the number of room-nights and the rate the rooms are sold at the hotel for the past year and as far out as one year.

After the leadership team has identified our opportunities, we discuss a plan for how we are going to exploit these opportunities and how we are going to measure whether what the team decided was an effective strategy. Each of these meetings is repeated in some form or another in person or over the phone for all the hotels I oversee.

► RESPONSIBILITIES

The daily, weekly, monthly, and yearly forecasts are the most important responsibility of a revenue manager. I am responsible for forecasting the number of rooms and the rate at which the guest will pay for a given period. I generate these forecasts based on many critical factors and some less critical. History is always a good indicator of what the future will hold for hotels. The correlation between what happened last year on this day in this month to what happens today can be between 60 percent and 80 percent.

What is going on in the area can have a huge impact on the occupancy and rate of a hotel. Local events such as festivals, races, and tournaments can all affect the number of additional persons in the city who need hotel rooms. The competition can negatively affect your hotel by running a special promotion. On the other side of the coin, the competition can and will create a positive situation for your hotel when they have abysmal service or a ramshackle product.

Other factors that may contribute to a forecast are additions to the supply of hotel rooms in the area, weather, seasonality, pickup and departure patterns of conventions, and the ever-changing local and regional economies. However, when it comes down to it, a forecast is exactly that—it is a guess of what we think may happen or what we really want to happen.

Once the forecasts are completed, they are used to project the amount of variable costs associated with running a hotel—for example, labor, or how many housekeepers, front desk clerks, and hash slingers we are going to need for a given period. Goals are set for sales and catering managers based on the forecast. The quarterly and annual forecasts are reported to the corporate offices for the purpose of forecasting the entire company's projected revenues and expenses. In turn, that information is put out to the stockholders and others with a financial stake in the company.

Forecasts and tracking of how we did compared to the forecast take up 75 percent of my time. The other 25 percent is spent exploring new opportunities for revenue growth, maintaining the various revenue channels into the hotel, managing the reservations department, acting as the liaison between the sales department and operations, and having fun.

Additional duties include exploring new revenue channels for the hotel. I have been known to visit the local competitor on a particularly busy day and offer a shuttle to our hotel and a no-line guarantee—this as the line behind the front desk stretches out the front door and halfway to the street. I am responsible for researching the demographics of the travelers coming to the area. Why are they coming? Are they traveling because of business, conventions, leisure, or are they part of a contract piece of business? How often do they come? How long do they stay? How much do they spend when they come? Where are they coming from?

The most important thing I do as a revenue manager is to ensure the different revenue channels are set up and functioning properly. These channels include the hotel brand's generic toll-free vanity number and central reservations office, the convention and visitors bureau, the local hotel's reservation and front desk, the Internet, and the global distribution system (GDS). The most critical of these channels is the Internet, which includes the brand website. Only a few years ago

it was GDS that was the most critical. In our chains, in 2004, Internet channels generated almost twice the volume of the GDS. However, the GDS is still crucial for the survival of almost every hotel. It is the system that travel agents and some of the Internet sites use to make reservations at my hotels. It contains information about rates and availability at a hotel. It must be checked daily and routinely maintained. The scary thing about the GDS is that most hotels don't know they have a problem until several months down the road. As technology grows and more and more people stop calling and start booking through their travel agents and directly over the Internet, so does the need to understand the GDS and exactly how it affects the hotel. When one of our competitors initiated a cleanup of their GDS, it resulted in several million dollars in additional revenue in six months.

Managing the reservations departments is the easy part of my job. Interacting with people is always easier than trying to interact with numbers and reports. The staff must be kept up to date on changes in strategic goals of the hotel and changes in marketing the discount and frequent-stayer programs. I am responsible for ensuring that the training of the reservations staff and anyone else who takes reservations is consistent and current, complete with ongoing positive feedback.

It is key that a revenue manager be skilled in the art of diplomacy. As the liaison between the operations and sales departments (see Waller, 7.2), I sometimes must mediate any challenges that may occur. Part of the diplomacy is understanding each department's strategic goals and how both departments depend on each other for their own survival. The easiest and simplest approach to serving as a liaison between the two departments is facilitating frequent, open, and honest communication between all parties.

Having fun is one of my key goals in working at a hotel and in a regional capacity. It is important to maintain a balanced approach to work in a hotel. It is easy to get burned out trying to do too much. The nature of the hotel is that it is open 24 hours a day and 365 days a year. Anything that can happen to a person on any given day can happen at a hotel as well.

7.6 HOTEL SALES ORGANIZATION AND OPERATIONS

Margaret Shaw and Susan V. Morris

► SALES AND MARKETING

Sales and marketing are related concepts, and each is an art and a science. Sales flow from marketing. Marketing, well stated by Lewis et al. (1995), "is communicating to and giving target market customers what they want, when they want it, where they want it, and at a price they are willing and able to pay." The primary focus of sales is on the communication aspect of marketing. It involves direct personal selling to potential customers that you and your organization have the right product, in the right place, at the right time, and at the right price—be it a hotel, a restaurant, a casino, or contract food services.

Marketing is getting and keeping a customer, a macro approach to managing a successful business. In a broad sense, marketing is the development and delivery of a successful product, that is, the development and delivery of a satisfied customer. Hotel sales comprises finding that customer and matching his or her specific needs with the right product offering, a micro or one-on-one approach to customer satisfaction. For example, a meeting planner from Texas Instruments (TI) is planning an annual sales meeting to be held in Dallas. From a macro perspective, this planner has selected the city and is searching for full-service lodging accommodations for 200 TI sales representatives for a five-day conference. From a micro perspective, he or she visits several hotel alternatives and meets with the hotel sales representatives to find the best "fit." Various aspects of the meeting being planned are discussed including dates, rates, guest room accommodations, function room requirements, food and beverage services, and so forth. It is the job of the hotel sales manager to learn the specific needs and wants of the planner and "create" the right product, place, time, and price for a successful conference.

A successful conference is what the planner is really buying, not bricks and mortar. Thus, successful selling is understanding the real needs of the buyer, communicating how your product and service can best respond to those needs, and then delivering it. In another context, McDonald's Golden Arches markets fun, simplicity, good service, and a good price. McDonald's sells friendly service, good value for price paid, convenient locations, and those delicious golden chicken nuggets on which many of us grew up. Ronald McDonald is an ancillary product, a public relations endeavor, which augments and supports the idea or concept of kids and why they are special.

Public relations, advertising, and special promotions often support the selling effort. Advertisements for the Ritz-Carlton Hotel Company are directed to their business traveler clientele. Such advertisements incorporate both the selling and marketing aspects of this upscale hotel chain. The company is simultaneously selling hotel rooms to busy business executives and marketing a hotel that "remembers your needs," and is hallmarked by the vision implicit in their slogan "ladies and gentlemen serving ladies and gentlemen." A travel agent, a corporate travel manager, or a secretary, however, may have handled the actual purchase of the hotel room. Thus, the Ritz-Carlton advertisements support the sale, but they do not actually make the sale happen.

► SALES AND OPERATIONS

Sales is the critical link between marketing and operations. While hospitality professionals may espouse marketing, all too often it becomes ignored in the daily hustle and bustle of operations. It is the role of sales to help bridge this gap and find ways for the key customer-contact members of the hotel to keep the promise of marketing.

Selling starts by the professional sales managers prospecting, making contacts, establishing relationships with clients, uncovering their specific needs and wants. But it doesn't end there. Sales is also the host or hostess greeting restaurant patrons. Sales is the front desk clerk welcoming a guest at the local Holiday Inn or at the Waldorf-Astoria in New York City. Sales is the housekeeping staff delivering the extra set of towels requested by a guest. Sales is the sommelier in a gourmet restaurant recommending wines to complement an entrée choice. Sales is the front office cashier saying, "Thank you for staying with us. We hope you enjoyed your stay." It is amazing how a simple thank-you can express appreciation for a customer's patronage and bring them back.

All client-contact personnel of a hospitality organization perform personal selling either consciously or unconsciously. This includes staff who does not regularly have guest contact, such as the credit manager. One of the authors nearly lost a $100,000 annual account when a poorly trained credit manager called the client to collect a payment that had not yet been billed. A well-trained and motivated employee who understands how a hotel works is key to successful selling. This is accomplished through the hiring and training process, and although the many facets of human resources are beyond the scope of this chapter, its importance to guest satisfaction cannot be overstated.

In this particular context, however, the hotel's human resources department can perform services on behalf of the sales department by recruiting sales associates who understand the nature of the hotel industry and its place in the broader category of the services segment of business. Services are different from products and require specialized knowledge and training to be competitive.

Because hospitality is very much a part of the services industry, it is useful to understand how services differ from products. Those characteristics that are unique to the services industry product include perishability, simultaneity, heterogeneity, and intangibility.

Perishability refers to the short shelf life of the hospitality product. If it is not sold today, the potential revenue from the sales of that product is gone. A hotel room has a 24-hour shelf life. A restaurant seat has a two-hour shelf life. Manufactured goods have a much longer period of durability. If a television set is not sold today, it can be sold tomorrow or next week. The potential revenue from the sale of that product is not lost. But a Tuesday-night hotel room cannot be resold on Wednesday. Tuesday has come and gone. If the hotel guest room goes unsold Tuesday, the potential revenue lost from that vacant room cannot be recouped.

Simultaneity means that production and consumption occur at the same time. How can you produce a guest experience without the guest? Our customers, in a sense, are part of the assembly line. They need to be present for final production of the product offering. A vacant guest room produces nothing. Yes, the carpeting is installed; the bed is made, the bathroom plumbing works. But it all just exists until a guest arrives to use it. Simultaneous production and consumption is a unique challenge for successful operations in hospitality management. The guest needs to be present, because many of the facets of the service involve performances by hotel staff.

A related service characteristic in hospitality is *heterogeneity*. Heterogeneity refers to the variability of service delivery. Guest service agents have their moods. Customers have their moods. All have personalities of varying shapes and sizes. Hospitality is a very people-oriented business. Service personnel change from shift to shift, typically on an 8-hour schedule. Though operational manuals exist in most hospitality establishments, rarely are policies and procedures followed in an exact manner. Guests' "personalities," too, can change throughout their stay, and it may have nothing to do with how they were treated by service personnel. Dealing with heterogeneity

in service operations is dealing with reality. Mistakes will happen. But more importantly, mistakes can be addressed. Often a simple apology can win back a customer regardless of who was at fault when a mistake happens.

Intangibility is a fourth major characteristic of service businesses. Some consider it the most important component to recognize. Intangibility refers to the highly intangible nature of the service product offering. Intangibility is a feeling; it is having a sense about something that one cannot fully articulate. The intangible nature of the service product cannot be prejudged. Consumers cannot really see, touch, smell, hear, or taste a service product prior to consumption. They can only anticipate. One can test-drive a car before an automobile purchase is made to see what it feels like to drive. But a hospitality customer cannot test-drive a hotel weekend package or a restaurant meal prior to consumption. The intangibility aspect of hospitality emphasizes that service delivery is critical to customer satisfaction. Most customers have an idea of what to expect. But, in the end, they are really not sure of what they are buying until the hospitality experience actually takes place. Finally, after the service has been consumed, the guest has only the memory of the performance.

The foregoing unique characteristics represent the foundational challenge to the hotel's sales staff: they must find a way to promise performance and experience in such a way that the hotel's operations departments can deliver on the promise. If the essence of marketing is finding and keeping a customer, then the sales promise is fundamental to that effort. Operations' most important role is the keeping of that promise to the customer—having that customer walk away with a positive and memorable experience and want to return again.

▶ MANAGEMENT OF THE SALES PROCESS

Sales management is effectively directing the personal selling efforts of a hospitality establishment. It involves managing the sales process from both an individual and team perspective. In other words, sales management addresses the logistics of sales solicitation and the development of sales account executives to enhance their sales productivity. Sales account executives need to manage their day-to-day activity, sales teams need to coordinate their efforts, and customers need to feel that they are working with a professional and well-managed organization.

There are several components to hospitality sales management. These include sales organization, sales account management, recruitment, training and development, goal setting, and performance appraisals. Sales organization refers to departmental and individual organizational issues and inventory management. The following section focuses on the sales organization aspect of hospitality sales management.

▶ SALES ORGANIZATION

Sales organization can be viewed from three perspectives. These include departmental organization, individual planning of sales activity, and inventory management. A sales department needs to be organized, and sales managers within that organizational setup need to coordinate their efforts. Sales managers need to plan or organize their individual activities on a daily, weekly, and monthly basis. Allocating the sale of inventory to various customer segments needs to be managed, as

well. These are important issues in hospitality sales management, and following is a more detailed discussion of each.

▶ Departmental Organization

Organizing a sales department means determining who is going to do what. Sales solicitation needs to take place, administrative tasks need to be completed, and managerial decisions need to be made on a regular basis. In medium- to large-size hospitality establishments, a director of sales and/or a director of marketing coordinates these efforts. In smaller operations, it is not unusual to have one individual responsible for all of the above. For most bed and breakfast operations in the United States and Canada and the small boutique hotels in Europe, for example, the owner and/or manager of the establishment typically handles sales activities.

Figure 7.4 is a sample sales organizational setup for a midsize urban hotel targeting business clientele. The sales managers in this example are organized by target market and by geographic territory. Sales manager 1 is responsible for corporate accounts located in the immediate downtown and surrounding area. Sales manager 2 is responsible for national corporate accounts. This refers to companies based in other areas that conduct business or have the potential to conduct business at the hotel. Both of these sales managers solicit group and transient business from their account base.

Sales manager 3 targets meetings and convention business from national association accounts. This business may include executive board meetings, committee meetings, regional conferences, and annual conventions.

Figure 7.4   **Organization of an Urban Hotel Sales Department**

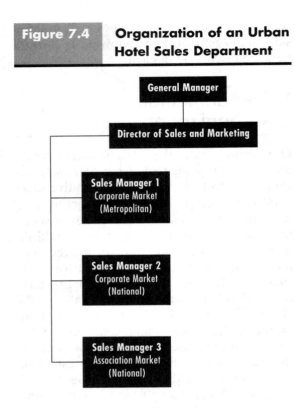

In this example, once group events have been booked they are turned over to the conference services department for service delivery. Both the sales managers and director of conference services report to the director of sales and marketing. The sales team meets weekly to discuss issues pertinent to achieving the department's sales objectives.

Weekly sales meetings are very much a part of a sales department's organizational structure, be it a sales force of two or twelve sales account executives. They are critical for effective communication within the department. At these meetings, each team member highlights his or her weekly activity with regard to new prospects uncovered, tentative bookings, verbal definites, cancellations, etc. (Verbal definites are bookings where clients have verbally committed their meeting or function to the facility but a signed contract is not yet in hand.) In other words, sales managers share with each other progress reports on various accounts they are currently working on. Thus, each team member gets an up-to-date informal report on the status of all current sales activity.

For example, one sales manager may be working on a tentative booking but considers it weak because of strong competition for this particular account. Call this Group A. Another sales manager may have a new prospect with similar space requirements interested in the same dates. Call this Group B. Assume, however, that the property has the capability of booking only Group A or Group B over the same dates because of space limitations. When these types of issues surface at sales meetings (which they frequently do), discussion will occur raising the following types of questions:

- What is the likelihood that either group will eventually book its business at the property?
- What is the estimated profitability and/or contribution margin for each group?
- Is either group a regular client?
- What is the likelihood of repeat business from either group? In other words, what is the long-term profitability for each?
- Can either group consider alternative dates? (A *very* important question.) What would incite them to move dates?
- Do convention history reports match their current space allocation requests?

These are just a sampling of questions that need to be raised and answered. It is a never-ending process in hospitality sales management to search for the best fit for both the buyer and seller.

▶ CONCLUSION

The organization of sales management is the process of directing the personal selling efforts of a hospitality establishment. It involves effectively managing the sales process from both an individual and team perspective. Sales or account managers need to manage their day-to-day activity; sales teams need to coordinate their efforts. Sales account management involves developing, maintaining, and enhancing customer relationships. Sales managers develop expertise for specific market segments, industry segments, and/or customer accounts, and common traits among successful sales account executives include self-confidence, high energy, empathy, enthusiasm, and a sense of self-worth.

This chapter introduces the foundation for hospitality sales and marketing. First and foremost, sales flow from marketing. If management doesn't have a marketing mindset, then sales efforts will be all for naught.

Marketing is giving the targeted customers what they want, when they want it, where they want it, at a price they are willing and able to pay. Sales is direct communication with potential customers letting them know we have what they want. In many respects, sales is the link between marketing and operations. Operations is essentially the delivery component of marketing and the final determination of a happy (or unhappy) customer.

Marketing begins, transcends, and ends with the consumer. Sales makes sure it happens.

7.7 PUTTING THE PUBLIC IN PUBLIC RELATIONS: THE CASE OF THE SEATTLE SHERATON HOTEL AND TOWERS

Louis B. Richmond

The powerful world of nonprofit organizations can make or break a hotel. This is a very strong statement when you consider our public relations firm, Richmond Public Relations, represents the Seattle Sheraton Hotel and Towers, a hotel that has potential revenues of $80 million to $100 million a year in rooms, food, and beverage and employs more than 600 people. Although the fortune of large convention hotels usually rests on the approval of large associations, meeting planners, Mobil and AAA awards, and myriad corporate decisions, nonprofit organizations definitely play a role in a hotel's financial success. The time and effort that hotels allot to public relations and nonprofits can profoundly influence destination decisions of meeting planners and major associations.

▶ DONATIONS, DONATIONS

Every day the Sheraton receives three or four letters from local organizations soliciting donations of cash, rooms, and meals for benefits, auctions, and raffles. These seemingly simple requests add up to approximately 1,000 requests every year. All of these organizations have nonprofit status and are doing valuable work in the community. They range from the symphony, opera, and ballet to large hospitals and universities. The smallest of preschools and local grassroots citizen activist organizations are also regular solicitors. Each of these organizations has a mission and purpose, that, if realized, could make the community a better place in which to live. Because mostly every request is valid, how does the hotel or public relations firm go about deciding which organizations to support? Each decision must be based on a benefit to the hotel.

Let me give an example of how working with the community has, indeed, benefited the hotel. One such request was a handwritten note from an elementary school student requesting a complimentary room for her school raffle. We were promised in the letter that the hotel would be mentioned in the raffle and given as much publicity as possible. This school was located 20 miles from the hotel in a small town that, on the surface, did not seem it could provide a lot of return benefit to the hotel. Due to the sincerity of the request, we decided to donate a room package. About four months after the donation was made, our firm received a call from someone who worked for a very large company in Seattle wanting to make room reservations. He called me rather than the hotel because he wanted me to know he was booking the Sheraton be-

cause of its donation to his child's school. Because we were the only hotel to donate a room to his child's school auction, he felt an obligation to have his guests stay at the Sheraton. Therefore, his company was moving from another hotel to ours because of a donation that in actuality cost about $35. The potential revenue from his account was valued in the thousands of dollars. Additionally, his company is a member of trade associations that hold numerous regional and national conventions that can also influence business to the Sheraton.

Other benefits linked to this donation were that the Sheraton's name was seen in print on more than 1,000 raffle tickets, and people who attended the drawing were made aware of the Sheraton's contribution. The return on investment from this one donation was enormous in direct revenue alone and also generated an excellent amount of goodwill in the local community. All of this revenue and potential revenue was due to one small donation!

▶ ASSOCIATIONS, NATIONAL MEETINGS

When large associations choose Seattle as the host city for their national conferences, the individual hotels bid on being the host hotel. The host hotel is in a favorable situation concerning room rate and food and beverage functions. A well-thought-out public relations program can play an important role in an association deciding which hotel to use. Working with the sales staff, the public relations firm can obtain as much information about the association as possible and decide how they can influence the association to use the Sheraton.

A major southwestern association was in the process of deciding which hotel to use for its Seattle conference. With research, we found that this particular organization supported a major national charity that was also supported by the Sheraton. We contacted the director of the local charity organization, who, in turn, phoned his counterpart in the southwestern city. He was informed of the Sheraton's sponsorship of his nonprofit and that one of his large corporate sponsors was looking for a hotel to use in Seattle. The director of the southwestern nonprofit called his contact in the corporation and apparently did a good job of convincing him to use the Sheraton. Whether or not the decision was made directly because of this call or the combination of other sales efforts, most of the sales and marketing staff concurred that the hotel's support of the local nonprofit organization was instrumental in securing a major piece of association business. We have found that the nonprofit world will go all out to help corporations that help them. In addition, nonprofit organizations can effectively utilize this win-win model of partnership between business and nonprofits to solicit help from other companies and businesses.

▶ SOCIAL EVENTS AND FUND-RAISERS

The social catering business is fiercely competitive. Nonprofit organizations are always seeking the lowest possible rates and prices, but because of their standing in the community, they sponsor important events at hotels. The more prestigious the organization, the higher the ticket price and the more potential that the attendees can generate revenue for

the hotel in the future by booking rooms for other events. Most members of the boards of directors of nonprofit organizations are leaders in the community and business world. Their recommendation can go a long way toward securing a favorable image for the hotel in the local market.

In dealing with social catering events for nonprofit groups, we always inform organizations that the hotel staff will work closely with them to ensure the success of their event. However, the nonprofit must clearly understand that the hotel is a *for-profit* business. We have to strike a deal that is good for the organization and, at the same time, good for the hotel. The organization is helped to understand that the more profitable the hotel, the more support can be provided for the nonprofit organization. If the hotel does not make a profit, it cannot continue to offer its support. By offering the organization special services rather than lowering the price to the point where the hotel will not make any profit, we ultimately help the organization raise even more money for their event. We have come up with many creative contributions to nonprofit organizations that not only increase their potential for raising money but also favorably highlight the services of the hotel.

One of the hotel's most popular donations to nonprofit organization auctions is a series of cooking classes for ten people that includes a kitchen tour and lunch. This item, usually set at a minimum bid of $500 to $700, enables a group of people to combine their financial resources for a potentially higher bid. The cooking classes also enable the hotel to highlight one of its chefs and give people a back-of-the-house view of the kitchen. We have tracked the success of these cooking classes and found that almost every one of the participants has booked reservations in the hotel restaurants. What is given away as a donation comes back many times over in increased business and greatly enhances the perception of the hotel's goodwill in the community.

Another innovative donation was a tour with the hotel's curator of the corporate art collection. The Sheraton, well known for its art collection, employs a professional curator. Most of the major social service organizations and nonprofit organizations show an interest in the arts, and this type of donation stands out from the overnight accommodations typically offered by other hotels.

The hotel's limousine can also play a part in the donation program. The use of the limousine always adds a prestigious quality to a gift and raises more money for the organization while costing the hotel only a minimal labor and operating cost.

Making a major donation to social catering fund-raisers that are booked in the hotel helps ensure the event will be rebooked the following year (assuming the food and service are high quality). The ability to predict annual bookings provides savings in sales staff time and marketing efforts.

When major social catering events are held in other hotels, the Sheraton also makes significant donations to show organizations it is interested in supporting their cause no matter where their event is held. Of course, the hotel remains interested in having the group book their event at the Sheraton next season. However, our agency always encourages the Sheraton to purchase a table when events are hosted in another hotel, for several reasons: to show support for the organization; to let the staff see how the event is managed at another facility; and to compare quality of service and food.

▶ HOLIDAY CARD PROGRAM

Another significant community contribution we make is our annual holiday card. Each year we select a different organization to be the beneficiary of this program. We print the Sheraton corporate holiday card and then provide the organization with an extra 10,000 cards for its own fund-raising campaign. These cards are printed at no charge to the organization as long as they provide us with original artwork. The organization that is chosen is always selected so there is a return to the hotel. The organization chosen in 1987 had previously held a major event at another hotel. We informed them that if they switched to the Sheraton, they would be the beneficiaries of the 1988 holiday card campaign.

▶ CONTROL

The hotel has certain prerequisites in making donations to nonprofit organizations.

1. The organization must be a 501(c)3 organization recognized by the Internal Revenue Service.

2. A request must be received in writing on the organization's stationery.

3. The organization must return to the hotel written notification of the donation through a raffle advertisement, program book, or announcement.

4. The donation must be in a live and not a silent auction whenever possible.

5. All responses are filed, and when a request for next year's gift arrives, we check to see if we received the recognition we required.

Different levels of donations are awarded based on the event and the amount of recognition received. The Sheraton has donated gift certificates to the dessert buffet and a dinner for 100 people in Fullers, the hotel's award-winning restaurant.

Our commitment to the community is based on the belief that each member of the organizations we support can act as a public relations spokesperson for the hotel. When businesses help organizations, their members and volunteers usually develop a loyalty to the giver. Our goal is to infiltrate the community aggressively as a good corporate citizen. At the same time, we want the community to know that we need their business. The more business they give us, the more help we can return to the community.

▶ CLASSIFICATION OF ORGANIZATIONS

The nonprofit world can be divided into six general areas, as set out below. For each classification, major examples of the many possible representative organizations are listed.

Cultural Organizations

Most of these organizations have a large and prestigious board of directors. There is a tremendous amount of potential room business and catering functions from the organizations and their board members.

- Symphony orchestras, opera companies, ballet companies, chamber music organizations, and presenting organizations, as well as campus cultural organizations
- Art museums, museums of history and industry, science museums, and craft and folk art museums

- Major, alternative, and community theater companies

Health Organizations
- Hospitals
- Medical schools
- Research centers

Educational Organizations
- Alumni associations
- University and college fund-raising campaigns
- High school and PTA organizations
- Preschool and private school fund-raisers

Religious Organizations
- Churches
- Synagogues
- Religious schools and camps
- Adult religious community organizations

Social Service Agencies
- United Way
- Community charity groups
- Neighborhood grassroots organizations
- Charities such as Easter Seals and March of Dimes
- Food banks
- Cystic Fibrosis Foundation
- Juvenile Diabetes Foundation
- Boy Scouts of America

Social and Fraternal Organizations
- Rotary
- Kiwanis
- Elks
- Shriners

► MARKETING APPROACHES

Before you approach an organization, you need to have a plan that puts you on the offensive rather than the defensive. Many times hotels find themselves responding to people asking for money rather than actually going to the organization to tell them they are there to help them. The more creative you can be, the easier it will be for the organization to work with you. Your plan should include researching the following items:

- The members of the board of directors and their company affiliations
- The needs of the organization
- Their budget—easy to do because they are a tax-exempt organization
- Past catering functions—where they were held, prices, and number of attendees
- Housing needs of the organization and how you can help

Read newspapers about the organization and totally familiarize yourself with their goals. Make sure you meet with a major staff member and a board member. To meet with just one or the other simply means you will have to hold another meeting to review what you discussed at the last meeting. The most important overall consideration is to understand the nonprofit organization's needs and to work together with their representatives for a win-win solution.

Make sure you work out before the event how the hotel will be credited and recognized. Recognition of the hotel's contribution is often assumed, forgotten, or left to chance. The hotel can be recognized in many ways. A complimentary ad in a season's program or newsletter will go a long way in justifying your investment. If you are trying to attract the organization, it must have an audience that is part of your marketing mix. Calculate what it would cost to advertise in their program book throughout the season. Bargain with the organization for a complimentary ad for the amount of the donation you are making. Other possible returns for your donation include:

- Having the organization give the hotel complimentary tickets that can be used by the staff for entertaining clients. This strategy can be effective if concerts are sold out and your hotel is in possession of the only tickets.
- Asking the organization to give you access to their mailing list. This strategy can be crucial in trying to publicize a new weekend program or the opening of a new food and beverage outlet.
- Requesting the organization to commit to a two-year contract. This strategy not only makes it easier for the organization to plan ahead but helps the hotel in projecting revenues.
- Donating meeting rooms to the organization for seminars and retreats if food and beverages are ordered. Most organizations have to pay for meeting facilities.

One of the most important aspects of any donation is the follow-up. Make sure you are aware of the news created by the organization you are helping and make them feel they are part of *your* organization. If major events take place, have the hotel's general manager send a congratulatory letter. If someone has a birthday, have your pastry chef send over a birthday cake. If you can help them publicize their events in your newsletter, work with them and inform them you are giving them complimentary publicity. Work together all the time so that each organization receives something from each other, if possible, on a fairly regular basis.

▶ CASE STUDY

Our firm approached the board of directors of the Seattle Symphony in hopes that they would move a major luncheon to the Sheraton. We told them we would be happy to offer complimentary room accommodations for the conductor and his wife for the duration of the symphony season if they would help influence their women's organization to use the Sheraton for their luncheon. By hosting the conductor and his wife in the best available room, we not only built up a good relationship with the conductor but also showed the board of directors we were very interested in supporting the symphony.

By proactively informing the board of directors that the Sheraton was committed to the symphony, we, at the same time, helped them understand our need for their board members' business so we could continue our support for them. Donating to significant cultural institutions is often a sound business decision because most members who serve on boards of large cultural organizations are the community's business leaders. They know the wisdom of a sound decision, and, indeed, continue to offer ongoing support to the Sheraton. As a result of the Sheraton donating a room to the conductor and his wife, the symphony moved the luncheon to the hotel. The hotel maintains a strong relationship with the conductor, and the symphony continues to use the Sheraton for their room, food, and beverage business. In a classic example of a

win-win situation, the symphony supporters, their board of directors, and their musicians act as public relations spokespeople for the Sheraton. In many ways, the results of this strategy have ensured several hundred people working on our behalf.

▶ PRESS AND MEDIA

It is important to remember that the people in the press are also part of the community. Ultimately, donations to nonprofits will touch many press and other media people in personal ways by helping their local organizations, such as schools, hospitals, and social service and cultural organizations. They will be especially interested in publicizing events with personal impact. It is also important to realize that hotels with many events create a buzz that generates more local press activity. Organizations like to be involved in active and exciting hotels. If a certain number of events are in one hotel and twice that amount are in another hotel, the more active hotel is bound to have more requests for events.

▶ COSPONSORSHIP

Another effective way to maximize public relations in the area of nonprofit donations or charities is to cosponsor events with radio stations or newspapers. The exposure that can be provided through this medium not only places your property with other responsible companies but helps spread the word of your company's involvement automatically through the media.

Take advantage of your local and regional radio stations to develop joint promotions. Work with the promotion director to find out how the hotel can help the station's favorite charity. Donate the ballroom or smaller meeting rooms for dances, parties, etc., with a guarantee of a no-host bar. The radio station acts as a free advertising service to draw people to the event. It is in their best interest for their advertisers to draw large audiences. Have the nonprofit organization receive an admission charge to the event so that it is up to the nonprofit organization to also try to draw a large audience. By working with the radio station and the charity, the hotel not only maximizes its exposure but also increases its potential revenue.

▶ REGIONAL ORGANIZATIONS

Identify major nonprofit organizations in feeder markets and work with them in their major fund-raising events. This will help increase weekend business and act as a reinforcer to advertising placed in those markets. The impact of regional organizations can be just as strong as your local organizations. If your property has a strong regional weekend market, this program can be an effective way to increase room business.

Identify corporations that have branches in feeder cities with ties to major nonprofit organizations. Any time your property can get its name across to the public in a major feeder market, you reinforce advertising dollars or actually save them. Remember, the return on investment, if carefully monitored, can be significant.

▶ CONCLUSION

The more times your hotel property is written and talked about, the more people automatically identify it with positive community activity. It is eventually in the best interest of a community to ensure the business success of your hotel when it knows you will help its favorite charities or organizations. In order to work with the community, you must educate the community to work for and with you. The best recommendation is that made by the public, and only when public relations truly works with the public can the property benefit. By putting the public in public relations, the public speaks for you and your property and results in profits through public relations.

7.8 MINI CASE: REVAMPING THE MARKETING RESEARCH DEPARTMENT

You're the new director of marketing research for the Mississippi Region Affiliated Resorts (MRAS), located along the length of the Mississippi River from Minneapolis to Memphis. This branded distribution company of 38 independently owned and operated hotels has become a major player in its regional competitive marketplace. As part of the company's strategic plan, however, it has been determined that the structure of the market is changing, and the general future direction of the hotels will be toward more sales and service to the conventions and meetings market that has become increasingly important because of the central location of the chain.

To become more competitive in this burgeoning market, the company has undertaken and encouraged an ambitious remodeling program among its members that has upgraded the furnishings, fixtures, and equipment of the hotels. The hotels are also committing to a minimum of the following capital investments:

- 60,000-square-foot ballroom
- 30,000 square feet of meeting and break-out rooms
- 15,000-square-foot registration and pre-function areas

With these upgraded facilities, the company feels it can compete effectively for the lucrative conventions and meetings market with the hard-flagged chains.

This strategy and capital investment requires a consequential change in research paradigms. As the director of marketing research, you've been requested by the company president to propose a completely revamped research department that will reflect this new strategy and be designed to help the independent member hotels market their new facilities most effectively.

Propose a model marketing research department for your firm that will produce the sorts of data that hotels in the chain can use to help compete with the national chains. Include in your proposal what new sorts of data would be most useful, where those may be found, and how they might be specifically useful to reflect the new mission.

REFERENCES

DeVeau, Linsley T., Patricia M. DeVeau, Nestor J. Portocarrero, and Marcel Escoffier. 1996. *Front Office Management and Operations.* Upper Saddle River, NJ: Prentice-Hall.

Drucker, Peter F. 1974. *The Practice of Management.* New York: Harper and Row.

Drucker, Peter F. 1999. *Management Challenges for the 21st Century.* New York: Harper Collins, pp. 115–116.

Fishbein, Martin, and Icek Ajzen. 1975. *Belief, Attitude, Intention, and Behavior: An Introduction to Theory and Research.* Reading, MA: Addison-Wesley.

Hanson, Bjorn. 1995. "The $1 per $1,000 Rule." *Cornell Hotel and Management Administration Quarterly* 36(4):7.

Lewis, R.C., R.E. Chambers, and H.E. Chacko. 1995. *Marketing Leadership in Hospitality: Foundations and Practices,* 2nd ed. New York: Van Nostrand Reinhold p.3.

Lieberman, Warren H. 1993. "Debunking the Myths of Yield Management," *Cornell Hotel and Restaurant Administration Quarterly* 34(1):34–41.

———. 2003. *PKF Trends Reports.* Dublin, Ireland: Pannell, Kerr Forster.

Protea Hotels Partners with SalesBid. 2000. Press Release. June 8.

Sinclair, Marta. 2003. "The Use of Intuition in Managerial Decision-Making: Determinants and Affective Moderators." Ph.D. dissertation. University of Queensland [Australia] Business School.

SUGGESTED READINGS

Books

Astroff, Milton T. and James R. Abbey. 1998. *Convention Sales and Service,* 5th ed. Cranbury, NJ: Waterbury.

Ismail, Ahmed. 1999a. *Catering Sales and Convention Services.* Albany, NY: Delmar.

————. 1999b. *Hotel Sales and Operations.* Albany, NY: Delmar.

Kotler, Phillip, John T. Bowen, and James C. Makens. 1996. *Marketing for Hospitality and Tourism.* Upper Saddle River, NJ: Prentice-Hall.

Kudrle, Albert E., and Melvin Sandler. 1995. *Public Relations for Hospitality Managers: Communicating for Greater Profits.* New York: John Wiley and Sons.

Lewis, Robert C. 1989. *Cases in Hospitality Marketing and Management.* New York: John Wiley and Sons.

Lovelock, Christopher, and Lauren Wright. 1999. *Principles of Service Marketing and Management.* Upper Saddle River, NJ: Prentice-Hall.

Lovelock, Christopher. 2001. *Services Marketing: People, Technology, Strategy.* Upper Saddle River, NJ: Prentice-Hall.

Shaw, Margaret, and Susan V. Morris. 2000. *Hospitality Sales: A Marketing Approach.* New York: John Wiley and Sons.

Articles

Cunningham, Mark W., and Chekitan S. Dev. 1992. "Strategic Marketing: A Lodging 'End Run.' " *Cornell Hotel and Restaurant Administration Quarterly* 33(4):36–43.

Jarvis, Lance P., and Edward J. Mayo. 1986. "Winning the Market Share Game." *Cornell Hotel and Restaurant Administration Quarterly* 27(3):73–79.

Levitt, Theodore. 1981. "Marketing Intangible Products and Product Intangibles." *Cornell Hotel and Restaurant Administration Quarterly* (August):37–44.

Lieberman, Warren H. 1993. "Debunking the Myths of Yield Management." *Cornell Hotel and Restaurant Administration Quarterly* 34(1):34–41.

McCleary, Ken. 1993. "Marketing Management." In *VNR's Encyclopedia of Hospitality and Tourism,* Mahmood Kahn, Michael Olsen, and Turgut Var (eds.). New York: Van Nostrand Reinhold.

Morgan, Michael S. 1991. "Travelers' Choice: The Effects of Advertising and Prior Stay." *Cornell Hotel and Restaurant Administration Quarterly* 32(4):41–49.

Nordling, Christopher W., and Sharon K. Wheeler. 1992. "Building a Market Segment Model to Improve Profits." *Cornell Hotel and Restaurant Administration Quarterly* 33(3):29–36.

SOURCE NOTES

Chapter 7.2, "Building Market Leadership: Marketing as Process," by Fletch Waller.

Chapter 7.3, "Consumer Decision Rules and Implications for Hotel Choice," by Bianca Grohmann and Eric Spangenberg.

Chapter 7.4, "Hotel Pricing," by Marta Sinclair and Carl R. Sinclair.

Chapter 7.5, "A Day in the Life of a Regional Revenue Manager," by Paul Chappelle.

Chapter 7.6, "Hotel Sales Organization and Operations," by Margaret Shaw and Susan V. Morris, adapted from *Hospitality Sales: A Marketing Approach,* by Margaret Shaw and Susan V. Morris, Copyright © 2000 by John Wiley & Sons, Inc. Reprinted by permission of John Wiley & Sons, Inc.

Chapter 7.7, "Putting the Public in Public Relations: The Case of the Seattle Sheraton Hotel and Towers," by Louis B. Richmond.

chapter eight

FINANCIAL CONTROL AND INFORMATION MANAGEMENT

8.1 INTRODUCTION

This section on financial control and information management was substantially reconfigured for the third edition. At the suggestion of reviewers and textbook users, articles were chosen to illustrate the relationships among and between the activities that contribute to the hotel's profitability and operational success through the managerial responsibility for operational control. That philosophy is continued in this fourth edition.

As a department, financial management in a hotel—called many things, but usually *controller*—is far more important to the success of that hotel than the few readings included here would suggest. In most major hotel firms, the chief financial officer or controller ranks among the top two or three decision makers in the hotel's hierarchy. The importance of this job can be established by the observation that many traditional hotel

departments have been reorganized so that major portions of their functions are now responsible to the controller's office. The prime example of this is in the front office, where in the past the front office manager supervised the activities of the night audit staff, cashiers, and other front desk clerks. Increasingly, hotel firms are transferring the responsibility for night audits and cashiers to the accounting office, with the ultimate responsibility for these information-gathering and controlling functions resting with the hotel controller.

It should also be noted that an increasingly important department in hotels is the one responsible for the swiftly changing world of information management, or information technology (IT). In many instances, IT is now also the responsibility of the hotel controller. This recognizes the training and the ability of hotel controllers to provide for the structured accumulation, storage, and reporting of data in forms that are most useful to the operating departments and other executives of the hotel.

In his lead article on the hotel chief financial executive, longtime contributor to this series of books Professor Ray Schmidgall, Hilton Professor with the School of Hospitality Business at Michigan State University, reviews recent research on the hotel controller and compares findings over time. This review presents a good view of the job and responsibilities of this key hotel executive. Schmidgall finds interesting differences in the groups studied over the years and provides a wider window for viewing the hotel controller as a career path in management of a modern hotel operation. In the past, students were merely instructed in the process of accounting and auditing and, for the most part, were unaware of the sort of career that can result from a flair for management, leadership, and number-crunching.

In Schmidgall's companion piece written with Agnes DeFranco, the critical practices of budgeting and forecasting are examined. While this is only a sampler of the critical duties of the hotel's financial function and its leadership, in today's business environment the accuracy of forecasting and budgeting may indeed be the difference between profit and loss.

If the Schmidgall and DeFranco pieces represent the academic side of examination of the hotel's financial leadership, Mike Draeger is the chief financial executive who lives the theory on a daily basis. After a significant career with Four Seasons Hotels and Resorts and the Cal-Neva Lodge, he now serves as the controller for a company operating a number of casinos in Nevada. Join Mike

for a look at the chief financial executive's job in his "As I See It" essay. Pay particular attention to his war story about the budgeting process—and, yes, the lessons from the embezzler.

No discussion of financial and operational control in a hotel would be complete without attention paid to the extremely important function of purchasing.

In the past, when the bulk of a hotel's purchasing revolved around food and beverage items, the executive chef, chief steward, and other department managers usually developed their own sources for the goods and services needed to effectively and efficiently run their department. In the modern context, however, with the vast and diverse needs of hotel operating and staff departments, this practice is no longer advisable. Neither is it a good idea from a control standpoint. Most hotel companies have established a professional purchasing function. If purchasing is not a whole department, it is the responsibility of at least one highly experienced individual.

The purchasing director or manager typically is a person who knows a great deal about departmental operations in every phase of the hotel. He or she is able to discuss and analyze intelligently the needs of all department managers. This individual is expert in the markets where hotels purchase goods and products essential to accomplishing the department and hotel missions. The purchasing director is familiar with variety, quality standards, style, and methods of packaging. Such arcane technical details as chemical composition, fabric and furnishing lifetimes, and other details too numerous to mention here are also the responsibility of the purchasing manager.

Lee Evans, who held corporate executive positions in purchasing with Station Casinos,

Westin Hotels and Resorts, and at the hotel level, offers the reader real-world insights into the duties, responsibilities, and interactions of the hotel purchasing director. His essay provides rich detail and examples of how a hotel's purchasing director fulfills the purchasing requests of numerous hotel departments. Evans is currently director of purchasing for the Oasis Resort, Casa Blanca Spa and Golf Resort, and the Virgin River Hotel and Casino in Nevada.

Few people in this day and age would disagree that the management of data and information in all its forms is critical to business success. As recently as 1995, the year the second edition of this book was published, the Internet and World Wide Web were still pretty much off the radar screens of most businesses. Well . . . now it seems that the pace of technology and the means and necessity to manage huge volumes of information are as common as any other aspect of business in the twenty-first century. In other words, "What did we ever do without it?"

That's why I am hesitant to include too many readings here about IT and information management—it will be old news in a couple of years, or maybe even a couple of months. I bought a new PDA last summer (2004), and it is already out of date!

The success of any hotel firm in the modern era will depend on how well it manages, controls, and utilizes the available information. This is true for current operations, but as managers develop new—unheard-of now—sources of information in the lodging business environment, the information will have to be managed like any other asset or product component. In the last edition of this book, I included an article about data warehousing. In the words of the author (Griffin, 1998), "data warehousing" represents a "central information storehouse designed to answer business questions." This usually involves a company-wide database system designed to provide information to all corporate components. In a way, information has become a commodity, and data warehouses are designed to most efficiently manage this new commodity. Well, maybe. According to the "Data Mining. . ." article included here by Magnini and his coauthors, identifying important variables in these warehouses can be a daunting task; hence the need for data mining. Their article discusses this new development.

Because this area is so volatile and developments in IT happen so swiftly, it is probably best for the student to develop broad, general outlines of what is possible rather than, in the context of this textbook, to focus on details of current technology. As we've seen, progress in even our desktop computers has been so rapid that any current writing will probably be outdated by the time this book reaches print.

The articles included in this section are designed to help the reader gain knowledge about and appreciation for the range and realm of activities, largely behind the scenes, that contribute to the financial and operational health of the hotel. These activities are often overlooked by those of us who focus our attention on the more public aspects of hotel management, but they are, nonetheless, critical to any hotel's success.

8.2 THE LODGING CHIEF FINANCIAL EXECUTIVE

Raymond S. Schmidgall

Chief financial executives of lodging operations are given various titles including controller, chief accounting officer, vice president–accounting, and chief financial officer. The most common title, at the property level, is *controller*. Who are these people? What are their skills? What responsibilities do they have? Answers to these questions and many others are provided in this chapter.

The lodging financial executive historically was viewed as a mere bookkeeper—that is, he or she prepared financial statements. Research shows that the lodging controller has evolved into a full-fledged member of the management team of a lodging property.

Considerable research has been conducted over the past 20 years of the membership of the Hospitality Financial and Technology Professionals (HFTP), formerly known as the International Association of Hospitality Accountants. The results of this research form the basis for this chapter. The HFTP was founded in 1953 for the purpose of advancing the accounting profession. Its chief publication, *The Bottomline,* is published eight times annually (bi-monthly and two special editions). The HFTP currently has over 4,300 members in over 50 countries. The HFTP in 1981 established the Certified Hospitality Accountant Executive (CHAE). Since that time, more than 840 hospitality accountants have earned their CHAE. In 1994, the HFTP established the Certified Hospitality Technology Professional (CHTP), and in the past six years over 100 technology professionals have earned their CHTP. These two certifications bring immediate recognition to these professionals in the hospitality industry.

▶ PAST RESEARCH

Over the past 20 years, several studies have been made of HFTP members. Geller and Schmidgall conducted one of the first studies in 1984. They surveyed 1,000 HFTP members, and 311 lodging financial executives completed questionnaires covering education, skills, authority, responsibilities, salaries, and involvement with committees of their properties.

Geller, Ilvento, and Schmidgall replicated this study in 1990, mailing the questionnaire to 750 members of the HFTP associated with the lodging industry.

The DeVeaus surveyed the 291 CHAEs in 1988. Their survey covered the usual demographics of age, gender, title, compensation, and education. They also addressed marital status, hours worked, and community/industry participation. This study included all CHAEs, not only those in the lodging segment of the hospitality industry.

Tse surveyed the HFTP membership in 1989, covering three specific areas as follows:

- Demographic information such as age, gender, and educational level
- Professional activities such as position title, years in profession, and buying authority
- Information about the respondents' companies

Her survey was not limited to members associated with the lodging industry, though hotels and resorts employed over 65 percent (648) of the respondents.

Damitio and Schmidgall updated Tse's 1989 study in 1996. Three hundred members associated with the lodging industry responded.

► PROFILE OF THE LODGING FINANCIAL EXECUTIVE

The demographic information of lodging financial executives includes age, gender, education, certification, experience, and compensation.

► Age

Three of these studies report the age distribution of respondents to their studies. The De-Veaus' respondents averaged 40 years old, and the largest group of respondents (57 percent) was between 30 and 39 years of age. Tse reported that 25 percent of her respondents were 31–35 years of age and that two-thirds were in the 26–45 age groups. She did not report an average age; however, based on her reporting of salary by age, it appears that the average age was approximately 38. Damitio and Schmidgall reported an average age of 37, with 72 percent of the respondents between the ages of 30 and 46. Thus, the trend suggests a slight reduction of the average age as the HFTP membership expanded from 1988 through 1995. This trend can be expected to continue as HFTP's membership grows.

► Gender

The three studies covering age also included gender of respondents. DeVeau and DeVeau reported 20 percent of their respondents were female, while Tse reported 25.7 percent and Damitio and Schmidgall reported 28.7 percent. This trend of an increasing percentage of females is expected to continue, as a majority of students in both accounting and hospitality programs at colleges and universities across the United States are female.

► Education

All five studies surveyed lodging financial executives with respect to their levels of education, as shown in Table 8.1. The most common degree in all studies is the four-year college degree. The DeVeaus reported 68 percent of their respondents have a bachelor's degree, while Tse reported a low of 55 percent. The DeVeau study was limited to CHAEs, while the Tse study covered members of HFTP from all hospitality segments. The DeVeaus reported only 8 percent had earned master's degrees, while later studies reveal master's recipients in double digits and increasing to 14 percent in the most recent study by Damitio and Schmidgall. Increases in graduate degrees can be expected to continue in the twenty-first century.

Three studies included the major of the college graduates. The Geller et al. studies report that 55 percent and 56 percent, respectively, have degrees in accounting, while the DeVeaus report only 37 percent. Another interesting statistic is the increasing percentage of financial executives with degrees in hospitality education. Geller and his coresearchers, in their 1990 study, suggest the dramatic

Table 8.1 Level of Education

Level of Education	High School	Major of College Grads					
		Associate's	Bachelor's	Master's	Other	Accounting	Hospitality
Geller and Schmidgall	10%	11%	61%	11%	2%	56%	8%
DeVeau and DeVeau	12%[1]	11%	68%	8%	1%	37%	7%
Tse	22%[2]	9%	55%	13%	1%	—	—
Geller et al.	7%	15%	58%	13%	6%[3]	55%	17%
Damitio and Schmidgall	15%[4]	11%	58%	14%	2%	—	—

[1]The DeVeaus reported 12 percent as "none" but did not include high school as a level. Presumably these CHAEs have at least a high school diploma.

[2]Tse reported 18 percent as having some college but less than an associate's degree. This 18 percent is combined with the 4 percent with high school diploma to equal the 22 percent reported above.

[3]Geller et al. states that in most cases "other" represents multiple degrees, such as two master's degrees.

[4]Damitio and Schmidgall combined 3 percent with high school diplomas with 12 percent of those with some college.

increase to 17 percent from only 8 percent in 1984 may be because students graduating from hospitality programs are choosing to work in accounting or because lodging companies are beginning to recognize the value of hospitality education for accounting positions.

▶ Certification

The DeVeau and DeVeau study focused on HFTP members holding the CHAE. In addition, they reported the highest percentage of certified public accountants (CPAs). The other studies suggest an increasing percentage of lodging financial executives earning the CHAE from 8 percent in the Geller and Schmidgall study in 1984 to 20 percent in the Damitio and Schmidgall study, conducted in 1996. In addition, the total certifications increased from 21 percent in 1984 to 52 percent in 1996, as shown in Table 8.2. By any measure, this is a dramatic increase. This increase clearly supports Schmidgall and Kasavana's conclusion regarding certifications:

> "... initials after one's name suggest excellence, failure to have earned the initials may well lead one's peers and supervisors to question not only one's knowledge but also abilities." (Schmidgall and Kasavana, 2000)

Most likely, lodging financial executives will continue to earn various certifications in the future as proofs of their excellence.

▶ Experience

Several studies provide limited insight into the professional work of the lodging financial executive. The DeVeaus reported that 53 percent of the CHAEs have between 10 and 15 years of work experience and that the average is 16 years.

Tse reported that a plurality (24 percent) of lodging controllers had 11 to 15 years of work experience. Geller et al. reported a median average of 10–12 years of hospitality accounting experience, while the median from the Damitio and Schmidgall study was 11–15 years. Across these four studies, the average years of experience (generally hospitality-related) is 10–15. The average years added to an expected age of 21 or so at graduation with a bachelor's degree suggests that most lodging financial executives have spent most of their professional years working in the hospitality industry, as their average age in the most recent study was 37.

▶ Compensation

A major element of each study is the compensation of hospitality financial executives. Of course, over time the average pay is expected to increase. Table 8.3 addresses increasing compensation. The Geller and Schmidgall

Table 8-2 Certifications of Lodging Financial Executives

	CHAE	CPA	Other	Total
Geller and Schmidgall	8%	13%	—	21%
DeVeau and DeVeau	100%	22%	18%	140%
Tse	14%	15%	12%	41%
Geller et al.	17%	14%	12%	43%
Damitio and Schmidgall	20%	12%	20%	52%

Table 8-3   Compensation

	Median Salary	**Bonus**
Geller and Schmidgall	$30,000–$34,999	9%–12% (median)
DeVeau and DeVeau	$49,900 (mean)	44% received benefit packages including a bonus
Tse	$30,000–$40,000	$2,000–$5,000 (median)
Geller et al.	$40,000–$49,999	11%–20% (median)
Damitio and Schmidgall	$45,001–$50,000	$6,100 (mean)

study conducted in 1984 revealed a median salary of $30,000–$34,999 and a median bonus of 9–12 percent of the controller's salary. Based on this information, the average annual bonus approximated $3,400. The 1996 study by Damitio and Schmidgall reported a median salary between $45,001 and $50,000 and an average bonus of $6,100. At the beginning of the twenty-first century, it appears lodging financial executives' median salaries are most likely to be greater than $50,000, as the last study was conducted five years previously.

► Skills and Knowledge

What skills and knowledge should the lodging financial executive have, and how have these changed over time? Geller and Schmidgall studied the technical skills and knowledge of lodging financial executives in 1984, and Geller et al. repeated the study in 1990. Table 8.4 reflects the results of these studies. The 1990 study included more skills, and the report provided results by type of controller. As expected, the percentage of respondents with technology knowledge (computers) increased, and most likely a study conducted today would result in a 100 percent response.

Other areas that more than 90 percent of respondents indicated were required skills and knowledge included cash management and internal controls.

A study by Cichy and Schmidgall in 1996 focused on leadership of lodging financial executives. Financial executives not only must know the numbers but must also lead, as they supervise several employees. The 1996 Damitio and Schmidgall study revealed that the number of employees supervised by these financial executives varied from one to more than 30. Just over one-third (34 percent) manage two to five employees, while nearly another third (31 percent) manage six to ten people. Another one out of five (22 percent) manage 11 to 30 people, and 6 percent manage over 30 individuals. They found that lodging financial executives are expected to have skills and knowledge beyond the technical skills covered in the two Geller studies. The study of lodging financial executives covered seven keys to leadership (see Table 8.5) and 17 secrets of leadership (see Table 8.6).

Lodging financial executives strongly agreed that four of the seven listed keys to leadership were important to their own leadership style. The most important key was "trust your subordinates," followed by "de-

Table 8.4 Technical Skills and Knowledge

Skills, Knowledge	Corporate	Division or Area	Hotel	Other	Total	1984 Study
Taxes	89%	77%	74%	69%	75%	60%
Computers	92	96	99	95	97	70
Personnel	81	82	84	77	82	78
Cash management	100	89	94	81	91	89
Capital budgeting	87	89	87	77	85	80
Statistics	68	81	85	71	88	82
Auditing	87	96	87	72	84	†
Internal controls	92	100	100	94	97	†
FASB* rulings	28	23	14	18	18	n/a
Risk management	55	35	36	26	36	n/a

*Financial Accounting Standards Board
†In 1984, "auditing" and "internal control" were presented as a single item. Ninety-five percent of the respondents in 1984 indicated they possessed skills in those areas.

velop a vision." Consistent with all other surveys of U.S. chief executive officers and presidents in lodging and foodservice, "be an expert" was dead last. Leaders from all segments clearly realize that being an expert is not the most essential aspect of leadership. Nevertheless, "be an expert" received a score of 4.0, indicating that respondents believe that having relevant expertise is not unimportant either. Rather, the survey results indicate that these leaders believe it is more important to surround themselves with the necessary expertise than to have the expertise themselves.

Of the 17 secrets of leadership, respondents strongly agreed or agreed that leaders in their organizations must have 14 of them. At the top of the list were dependability, credibility, responsibility, and accountability. At the bottom of the list was physical stamina, with a score of 4.4. (A score above 4.0 indicates inherent importance; in this case, the low score for physical stamina is merely an indication of its relative unimportance when compared to the other secrets of leadership presented to the survey participants.)

Table 8.5 Keys to Leadership

	Mean Level of Importance*
Trust your subordinates	5.4
Develop a vision	5.3
Simplify	5.2
Keep your cool	5.1
Encourage risk	4.8
Invite dissent	4.5
Be an expert	4.0

*The scale is from 1, "very unimportant," to 6, "very important."

Table 8.6 Secrets of Leadership

	Mean Level of Agreement*
In our organization/company, leaders must possess . . .	
Dependability	5.6
Credibility	5.5
Responsibility	5.5
Accountability	5.5
Self-confidence	5.3
Decisiveness	5.3
Emotional stamina	5.2
Loyalty	5.2
Desire	5.2
Stewardship	5.1
Courage	5.1
Empathy	5.1
Tenacity	5.0
Anticipation	5.0
Timing	4.9
Competitiveness	4.8
Physical stamina	4.4

*The scale is from 1, "strongly disagree," to 6, "strongly agree."

▶ Responsibility and Authority

Four of five of the studies focused on authority. Table 8.7 reveals the results of the two studies (1984 and 1990) conducted by Geller and others. The 1990 study divides the responses by type of controller. The vast majority (over 75 percent) of lodging financial executives have authority to sign checks, approve purchases, and extend credit. Tse found that only 56 percent of hospitality financial executives have authority to approve purchase decisions. Damitio and Schmidgall re-

ported 56 percent were authorized to make purchasing decisions without the approval of others. They indicated controllers were most involved with technology purchases (90 percent) and, to lesser degrees, guest supplies (29 percent), furnishings and equipment (44 percent), security/maintenance systems (43 percent), and fire/safety/energy conservation systems (30 percent).

The expansion of authority based on the two Geller studies is the greatest for investing funds (from 2 percent to 46 percent) and to set or change prices (from 21 percent to 41 percent).

Both the Tse and the Damitio and Schmidgall studies covered hiring and firing authority. Tse found that more than 80 percent of the respondents have the authority to hire and fire either in their own department or in their company. The percentage increased to 90 percent when only accounting personnel were involved. The 1996 study by Damitio and Schmidgall revealed 76 percent have authority to hire and fire within their own department, while 7 percent have no authority to hire or fire.

Only the two Geller studies (1984 and 1990) covered responsibility, and the comparative results are shown in Table 8.8. Again, the 1990 study provided detail by type of controller and included areas not covered by the 1984 study.

More than 90 percent of the respondents indicated they have responsibility for such standard accounting functions as general accounting, receivables, and payables. Other major areas of responsibility shared by most controllers (75 percent or more) include payroll, night and income audits, computers in accounting, and cash management.

There are indications that controllers are becoming increasingly involved with the op-

Table 8.7 Extent of Authority over Specific Functions

| Functions | Type of Controller | | | | | |
	Division or Corporate	Area	Hotel	Other	Total	1983 Study
Invest funds	70%	46%	48%	30%	46%	2%
Sign checks	79	85	88	59	79	87
Extend credit	66	85	92	63	80	85
Set or change prices	26	62	48	28	41	21
Borrow funds	36	27	20	10	20	19
Approve purchases	83	89	94	69	86	82

Table 8.8 Controllers' Responsibilities

| Responsibilities | Type of Controller | | | | | |
	Division or Corporate	Area	Hotel	Other	Total	1984 Study
Hotel security	15%	27%	25%	18%	22%	9%
Receivables	89	89	100	73	91	95
Payables	89	92	99	77	92	93
General accounting	89	92	98	80	92	91
Payroll	85	89	95	68	87	89
Night auditors	60	85	94	60	80	83
Income auditors	57	81	89	60	77	79
Cashiers	43	65	77	47	64	63
Food controls	47	77	78	44	65	53
Computers: Accounting	83	89	95	73	88	*
Computers: Front office and reservations	49	77	65	44	58	*
Purchasing	32	62	77	40	60	50
Receiving	28	54	66	36	52	50
Storage (inventory)	23	58	66	39	52	34
Tax returns	70	58	61	54	61	n/a
Risk management	51	39	37	24	36	n/a
Cash management	85	81	86	51	77	n/a
Beverage controls	49	77	81	42	67	n/a
Investments	75	39	40	27	42	n/a
Internal auditors	47	62	46	31	44	n/a

* In 1984, a single question asked controllers about their computer-system (EDP) responsibilities. Fifty-two percent of the respondents in 1984 had some responsibility for EDP.

erational aspects of their hotels. More than 50 percent of the respondents indicated that their responsibilities included purchasing, receiving, food and beverage controls, and storage (inventory). The number of respondents responsible for the storage function increased 18 percentage points from 1984 to 1990, from 34 percent to more than 52 percent, and a purchasing function was claimed by 60 percent of the respondents in 1990, which is 10 points greater than in 1984. Responsibility for hotel security, the least commonly shared function among the controllers, more than doubled in the last six years, growing from 9 percent in 1984 to almost 22 percent in the 1990 study.

The controllers' role in electronic data processing (EDP) and computer system management grew by leaps and bounds during the 1980s. In 1990, 88 percent of the respondents indicated responsibility for the computer systems used for accounting functions.

Additionally, 58 percent indicated responsibility for front office and reservations system computers—systems clearly not under the umbrella of traditional accounting functions. In the 1984 study, respondents were asked just one question about responsibility for EDP, and 52 percent of the controllers indicated that they had some responsibility for EDP. It's clear that, over the years, computer-oriented responsibilities have escalated

sharply. This trend can be expected to continue into the twenty-first century.

▶ Committee Involvement

Just how involved have lodging financial executives been on committees of their lodging businesses? Both of the studies conducted by Geller and others reported over 80 percent of the respondents were members of the executive committee, although the Tse study showed only 71 percent (see Table 8.9). The difference may be that the Tse study covered all hospitality segments employing HFTP members, while the Geller studies were restricted to the lodging industry. In addition, the involvement of financial executives from 1984 to 1990 increased significantly on both the compensation and strategic planning committees. The 1990 study by Geller and others also included involvement in training and risk management committees, and a majority (66 percent and 72 percent, respectively) of lodging financial executives revealed involvement.

A 1998 study by Woods and others surveyed general managers of large hotels (500 rooms or more). Eighty-one percent of the respondents in this study reported that either the vice president of finance or the controller of their hotel was a member of the executive committee.

Table 8-9 Committee Involvement

	Executive	Compensation	Strategic Planning
Geller and Schmidgall (1984)	82%	23%	41%
Tse (1988)	71	—	—
Geller et al. (1990)	86	75	94

► SUMMARY

Considerable research has been conducted over the past 20 years on lodging financial executives. These studies indicate that the most common title is controller and the average age is the late thirties. Males are still dominant, though females are increasingly assuming the top financial position with lodging operations. The majority of these leaders have bachelor's degrees and majored in accounting. An increasing number of lodging financial executives are certified and have 10–15 years of hospitality accounting experience.

The skill set of financial executives includes both technical and leadership skills. The technical skill set includes technology, cash management, internal controls, and statistics. The most important leadership skills are trusting subordinates, developing a vision, dependability, credibility, responsibility, and accountability.

Financial executives commonly have authority to sign checks, extend credit, and approve purchases. To a lesser extent, they invest funds, may set or change prices, and borrow funds.

Their responsibilities range from managing receivables, payables, payroll, general accounting, night and income auditors, cash, and computers in accounting to hotel security, risk management, investments, and internal auditors.

Finally, financial executives commonly serve on the executive, compensation, and strategic planning, training, and risk management committees of their hotels.

8.3 BUDGETING AND FORECASTING: CURRENT PRACTICE IN THE LODGING INDUSTRY

Raymond S. Schmidgall and Agnes L. DeFranco

Financial forecasts and budgets can strengthen management's control of hotel operating expenses and help determine the profitability of the property (Chamberlain, 1991, 89–90; DeMyer and Wang-Kline, 1990, 64; and Karch, 1992, 21–22). Specifically, forecasts give owners a projected level of sales, while budgets alert owners and operators alike to significant expenditures that are on the horizon or predictable shortfalls in revenues. Used together, forecasts and budgets can provide a benchmark for sales-incentive programs, executive-compensation bonuses, incentive-based management fees, and capital expenditures (Temling and Quek, 1993).

A major difference between forecasting and budgeting is that budgeting is normally viewed as a process that covers a longer period of time than forecasting. Budgeting often results in a formal, long-range plan, normally expressed in terms of dollars over time—for example, the predicted revenues and expenses of a hotel for 24 months (Schmidgall, 1997, 369–372, 411–413). On the other hand, forecasts are generally prepared by hoteliers to establish staffing levels and may cover a period of just seven to ten days (Schmidgall, 1989, 101–2, 104–5). Long-range budgeting, therefore, is a form of strategic planning. It may entail several years' financial projections, a coordinated management policy, and a control-and-correction mechanism that allows actual results to be compared to estimates and followed by corrective steps, if necessary (Coltman, 1994).

▶ THE CURRENT STUDY

Our study serves the following purposes:

- to determine the purposes, methods, and procedures in performing an operations budget,
- to determine how an operations budget is used in budgetary control, and
- to determine the techniques used in forecasting revenues in the various operating departments in lodging properties.

Limitation. Our study used a random-sampling technique to select 600 samples that yielded 171 responses (almost 30 percent of the sample). As a result, there may be respondents who belong to the same national chain and thus represent the same set of corporate operating procedures. In addition, with the full-service and luxury segments of the hotel industry constituting more than 90 percent of our responses, the results are likely more applicable to those two groups than to limited-service hotels. Thus, although more than one-quarter of the hotel executives solicited by this study responded, it may not be useful to generalize the study's results (particularly beyond full-service hotels).

The instrument. We designed a four-part questionnaire with the assistance of a number of lodging controllers and by modifying a survey previously used in 1995 (Borchgrevink and Schmidgall, 1995). We also employed a pilot study in which other lodging controllers offered comments and allowed us to fine-tune the final survey. Part I of the questionnaire included six questions that collected demographic data about the respondents and their lodging operations. Parts II and III consisted of 14 questions regarding the procedures and methods used to develop an operations budget, and about how the budget is used for financial control. Finally, the last part of the questionnaire asked respondents to provide information regarding their various operating departments' forecasting techniques.

Sampling. As mentioned, a simple random-sampling technique was used to select our study's population. Six hundred financial executives who are associated with lodging operations were chosen from the 1997 membership list of the association of Hospitality Financial and Technology Professionals (formerly the International Association of Hospitality Accountants).

Data collection and analysis. We first sent the survey in October 1997 to each of the 600 executives, requesting them to participate in our study. To ensure a good response rate, we sent a second copy of the survey to everyone in January 1998, as a reminder. Data received were analyzed using the software package SPSS for Windows.

▶ RESULTS AND DISCUSSION

Of the 600 executives who received our survey, 171 responded, yielding a 28.5-percent response rate. The majority of the respondents held the title of hotel controller (147, or 86 percent), while the others reported such titles as assistant controller, regional controller, corporate controller, VP-controller, executive VP-CFO, and director of accounting. Respondents were mainly associated with full-service hotels (72 percent). Together with those from the luxury segment (21 percent), those executives constitute well over 90 percent of the responses. As for affiliation, the majorities (62 percent) were part of a national chain, and 29 percent reported working for independent lodging properties. International chains accounted for another 7 percent, while 2 percent of the responses came from franchisees. Most of the properties reported having more than 250 rooms (71 percent) and enjoyed 1996 annual gross revenues of at least $10 million (also 71 percent). Figures 8.1 and 8.2 show the details of the lodging-property size.

Preparing the budget. The operations budget is an integral part of the financial operation of a lodging property, and virtually all

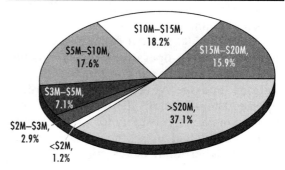

Figures in U.S. dollars (millions). Profile of properties represented in this study.

of the respondents reported that they prepared an operations budget for the year—only three reported not preparing a budget. Moreover, almost 60 percent indicated that they set a tentative financial goal prior to developing the operations budget. The majority of those (64 percent) related that tentative financial goals were based on either sales (33 percent) or net-income (31 percent) levels. (In this case, sales equals revenues, while net income refers to the financial statement's bottom line.) Other financial executives' financial goals were based on gross operating profit, net operating profit, EBITDA, debt-service coverage, occupancy percentage, RevPAR, or some combinations of those.

We presented five possible reasons why an operations budget might be prepared, and we also offered the fill-in-the-blank answer "other." When asked to give one major reason why a budget was prepared, 45 percent selected the option that stated "It is used as a standard by which the lodging operation is

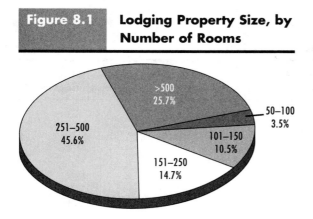

Profile of properties represented in this study.

managed." Another 28 percent chose the answer "It is a planning tool." About 15 percent of the respondents gave more than one reason, and their responses almost always noted a budget's value as a standard of comparison or as a planning tool.

More than 90 percent of the respondents reported that a co-operative effort among hotel departments was used to prepare the operations budget. Nevertheless, 73 percent reported that the controller was the one who held the main responsibility for preparing the operations budget using the input provided by other department heads and the general manager.

Only five respondents indicated that the controller prepares the budget with little input from others. Thus, in more than three-quarters of the hotels surveyed, the controller was primarily in charge of budget preparation. In another 5 percent, the lodging units' controllers and general managers jointly prepared it, and in 12 percent of the hotels, the general manager coordinated the budget-preparation process with the various department heads. Other responses indicated that budget-preparation responsibility fell to an executive committee, department heads, the general manager (with input from the owner), or a budget team (for example, a team might comprise the general manager, owner, and controller).

While all but three of our 171 respondents confirmed that they prepared an operations budget for the year, less than half prepared a long-range budget (i.e., for more than a year at a time). Of those who prepared long-range budgets, more than three-quarters used a five-year time span for future planning.

Making adjustments. Only one in four of the respondents revised their budget at any point during the operating year, with the most common frequency of change being monthly (40 percent). Other responses to this question included "as needed" (21 percent), "quarterly" (16 percent), "semiannually" (12 percent), "bimonthly" (3 percent), and some combination of the above (4 percent).

► BUDGETARY CONTROL

The majority of the respondents who used budgets declared that the operations budget

Table 8.10 Cost Tolerances Between Budget and Actual Costs

	Food cost	Beverage cost	Labor cost	"Other" operating costs
Less than 1%	11.5	14.3	8.2	8.2
1%to 1.9%	33.8	33.3	26.5	16.3
2% to 2.9%	29.0	23.1	25.9	21.1
3% to 3.9%	10.1	13.6	16.3	14.3
4% to 4.9%	6.1	4.1	12.2	17.0
5% to 5.9%	6.8	8.2	6.8	17.0
More than 5.9%	2.7	3.4	4.1	6.1
Median	2.2%	2.1%	2.6%	3.3%
*Median, 7996 Study**	*1.9%*	*1.9%*	*2.8%*	*3.7%*

*R. S. Schmidgall and C. P. Borchgrevink, 1996.

was used for budgetary control, with 90 percent reporting that budgets were prepared for all of the hotel's operations, versus just for selected departments. Next, we asked what level of variance between the budget (original or revised) and actual performance is permitted before corrective action is taken. The results for this question are summarized in Table 8.10. About a third of the respondents try to hold food, beverage, and labor costs within the range of 1 to 2 percent of the budgeted amounts. One-fifth of the respondents hold "other" budget items within a range of 2 to 3 percent. (The median of the responses for food and beverage costs was about 2 percent, with the medians for labor and "other" costs at about 3 percent.) Compared to responses to a similar question in a 1996 study, it appears that hotels today are slightly more tolerant in food and beverage cost variances and slightly less tolerant in allowing labor and other operating costs to deviate from the budget (Schmidgall, Borchgrevink, and Zahl-Begnum, 1996).

► FORECASTING TECHNIQUES

The last part of our questionnaire outlined in a grid presentation seven forecasting techniques, ranging from simple to complex (i.e., smoothing-constant method), and five principal hotel revenue-generating departments. We also allowed space so that respondents could write in other techniques. Respondents were then asked to reveal the methods they used for forecasting department revenues (see Table 8.11).

From this exercise, we find that some hoteliers used more than one technique for each department and that the methods used varied among departments. More than 40 percent of the restaurant and beverage departments, for example, appear to favor the use of "number of guests by expected spending per guest." While the chief technique applied to the rooms department was "expected units to be sold multiplied by the expected average

Table 8.11 Various Departments' Forecasting Techniques

Techniques	Rooms	Room Service	Restaurant	Banquet	Beverage
Prior year's budgeted dollar amounts multiplied by $1 + X\%$	10%	8%	9%	10%	10%
Number of guests by expected spending per guest	7%	28%	46%	25%	41%
Expected units sold by expected average price per unit	73%	27%	27%	26%	21%
Change in advance bookings from prior year	27%	6%	4%	22%	5%
Last year's actual revenues	16%	18%	16%	19%	16%
Last year's actual revenues adjusted subjectively	20%	24%	25%	33%	29%
Average of several past years' revenues multiplied by $1 + X\%$	5%	6%	5%	6%	6%

Source: R. S. Schmidgall and C. P. Borchgrevink, 1996.

LITERATURE REVIEW

*A*ccurate budgets are considered essential to profitable hotel operation. Yet obtaining reliable data is a problem. Smith and Lesure state that perhaps the greatest problem with forecasting and budgeting is the number of widely varying forecasts that are regularly published side by side, without question or support, and in some cases making all predictions vague.[1] Moreover, business prejections and financial trends are often published without any explanation of the underlying assumptions. Smith and Lesure contend that perhaps the way to construct reliable forecasts and budgets is to build a statistically reliable industrywide database that can be regularly updated with and compared to new economic and financial information. Those numbers can then be used to develop a short-term outlook for the industry as a whole or various geographic and market segments.

Hoteliers' desire and need for accurate budgeting and reliable data are not new. In 1989, hoteliers reported being generally satisfied with their forecasting accuracy, and yet they desired improvement.[2] Just one year earlier, Lasky noted that budgeting was one of the factors hoteliers ignored when opening a hotel. Thus, he wrote, he was personally involved in rescuing 130 hotels and motels from bankruptcy due to this oversight.[3]

Besides the budget's role as the business plan for owners and operators, Temling and Quek discuss the importance of hotels' budgets to lenders.[4] The budget is important to this group, as it can indicate a lodging company's potential for success. It also lets the officers of financial institutions know about the financial health of the business.

As the lodging industry's competitiveness increases, so does the interest in budgeting practices, as indicated by studies that appear biennially, on average. In 1995, 122 U.S. lodging properties were asked about their budgeting practices.[5] The areas of investigation included: budget development processes, budget reforecasting procedures, and budgetary control methods.

To further investigate the budgeting process, 140 U.S. lodging controllers were asked in 1997 about their use of forecasting and budgeting at the department level.[6]

That study reported that controllers rated "proper staffing" as the main benefit of preparing forecasts and "strategic planning" as the main benefit of budgeting. That study's results also showed that a hotel's size (as measured by the number of rooms) did not significantly influence the perception of the usefulness or the practices of forecasting and budgeting.

Some years earlier, Records and Glennie provided insights to the Boca Raton Resort and Club's budgeting and business forecasting processes.[7] Forecasting business volume and scheduling the required labor to serve its customer are crucial steps in maintaining an operation's quality. Thus, using a relatively simple computer network and basic software, the Boca Raton Resort and Club ensured it could control budgets, forecasts, and labor schedules.

[1] R. A. Smith and J. D. Lesure, "Don't Shoot the Messenger—Forecasting Lodging Performance," *Cornell Hotel and Restaurant Administration Quarterly,* Vol. 37, No. 1 (February 1996), pp. 80–88.

[2] R. S. Schmidgall and J. D. Ninemeier, "Budgeting Practices in Lodging and Food Service Chains: An Analysis and Comparison," *International Journal of Hospitality Management,* Vol. 8, No. 1 (1989), pp. 35–41.

[3] M. Lasky, "An Rx for Hotel Health," *Lodging Hospitality,* Vol. 44, No. 6 (May 1988), pp. 75–77.

[4] W. P. Temling and P. Quek, "Budget Time," *Lodging Magazine,* Vol. 19, No. 3 (November 1993), pp. 21–22.

[5] C. P. Borchgrevink and R. S. Schmidgall, "Budgeting Practices of U.S. Lodging Firms," *Bottomline,* Vol. 10, No. 5 (August–September 1995), pp. 13–17.

[6] A. L. DeFranco, "The Importance and Use of Financial Forecasting and Budgeting at the Departmental Level in the Hotel Industry as Perceived by Hotel Controllers," *Hospitality Research Journal,* Vol. 20, No. 3 (February 1997), pp. 99–110.

[7] H. A. Records and M. F. Glennie, "Service Management and Quality Assurance: A Systems Approach," *Cornell Hotel and Restaurant Administration Quarterly,* Vol. 32, No. 1 (May 1991), pp. 26–35.

price per unit" (reported by 73 percent of respondents), the banquet department was the high user of "last year's actual revenues adjusted subjectively" (33 percent).

► THE EFFECTS OF AFFILIATION, SALES, AND PROFITABILITY

To see whether a property's (1) affiliation, (2) size in terms of sales, and (3) profitability have any effect on its budgeting practices, we used the chi-square statistic. The properties' budgeting practices were reflected in the answers to eight questions that asked about the procedures and methods used to develop operations budgets and how those operations budgets were used in budgetary control.

We first classified the responses according to the properties' affiliation. A chi-square was then calculated by cross-tabulating the affilia-

tion on one hand and the eight questions on the other. Next, the same procedure was used to classify the responses according to sales level, and then by profitability. If an effect has a probability value (p-value) or a significance level of less than 0.05, it is significant. That means, in general, the effect happens due to chance less than 5 percent of the time. As seen in Table 8.12, two of the practices were affected by property affiliation, one was affected by sales, and one was affected by profitability (see those data marked with an asterisk).

When the chi-square test was performed based on annual sales, a significant difference ($p < 0.05$) was found in the preparation of long-range operating budgets (Table 8.13). That is, the higher the sales level a property enjoyed, the greater the likelihood that the property prepared a long-range operations budget.

Our second set of cross-tabulations determined whether differences occur between

Table 8.12 Property Characteristics Correlated with Budgetary Practices

	Selected Property Characteristics		
Budgetary Practices	**Chain Versus Independent Operation**	**Size (sales)**	**Profitability**
Major reason for having an operations budget	0.009*	0.015*	0.017*
Tentative financial goal set in advance	0.018*	0.562	0.156
Base for the tentative financial goal	0.116	0.292	0.202
Long-range operating budgets prepared	0.062	0.008*	0.067
Revision of operating budget	0.252	0.914	0.675
Monitoring food costs	0.440	0.516	0.398
Monitoring beverage costs	0.535	0.342	0.447
Monitoring labor costs	0.447	0.299	0.416

*Significance level is less than 0.05.

Table 8.13 The Effect of Annual Sales on Long-Range Planning

Annual sales	Percentage of respondents who prepared long-range operatons budgets
Less than $5 M	28%
$5 M to $10 M	28%
$10 M to $15 M	37%
$15 M to $20 M	48%
Over $20 M	74%

Figures in US dollars (millions).

branded lodging operations and independent properties (Table 8.12). We noted two statistical differences, namely (1) the major reason for having an operations budget and (2) whether a tentative financial goal was set in advance.

First, it appears that national-chain hotels cited different reasons for having an operations budget than did the independent properties, as shown in Table 8.14.

Hoteliers affiliated with national chains tend to have more than a single reason for creating an operations budget. In addition, it appears that national chains prepare the budget to be used for comparison purposes more often than do the independents, and that the independents prefer to use the operating budget as a planning tool (compared to the national chains).

Second, 65 percent of the chain properties responding to our questionnaire established tentative financial goals prior to developing their operations budgets compared to only 45 percent of the independent properties. This difference is most likely due to pressure from chains' corporate offices on individual properties to deliver the required "profit" to meet the chains' overall financial objective.

The last step of our research was to test for differences according to profitability. The profitability of each respondent was determined by dividing the net income reported by each hotel by its total sales. Respondents were then divided into four categories according to their profitability: less than 11 percent, 11 to 20 percent, 21 to 30 percent, and over 30 percent (Table 8.15). The greater the respondent's profit margin, the more likely that a single reason was cited for having an operations budget.

Table 8.14 The Effect of Affiliation on Budget Usefulness

Affiliation	Major reason for having an operations budget		
	Planning tool	Use as a standard	More than one reason
Chain property	26%	53%	22%
Independent property	48%	48%	5%

Note: Totals may not add to 100 due to rounding.

Table 8.15   The Effect of Profit Margin on Budget Usefulness

	Major reason for having an operations budget		
Affiliation	**Planning tool**	**Use as a standard**	**More than one reason**
< 11%	45%	52%	4%
11% to 20%	46%	46%	9%
21% to 30%	36%	44%	20%
> 30%	10%	60%	30%

Note: Totals may not add to 100 due to rounding.

► SUMMARY AND FUTURE RESEARCH

Operations budgeting is an important part of U.S. hotels' financial planning. The majority of hoteliers set tentative financial goals prior to preparing their operations budgets. The goal for the majority of hoteliers is based on either sales or net income. Most hoteliers indicated that the major reason they used budgets at all was as a standard for comparison to actual performance figures. The second most common use was as a planning tool. At the majority of hotels, a cooperative effort among departments was used to produce the budget. In a clear majority of those hotels, the financial executives coordinated this process. Less than half of all respondents prepared long-term operations budgets, and less than a quarter of all respondents indicated that their budgets were revised during the year.

All but two of the 171 respondents indicated that their operations budgets were used for control purposes. For all departments, the mean of the allowable deviation between the budget and actual performance ranged near 2 to 3 percent. That range is slightly tighter and smaller than the range measured in a similar study in 1996 (Schmidgall, Borchgrevink, and Zahl-Begnum).

Respondents' revenue-forecasting techniques varied by department within individual hotels. A number of respondents reported they used multiple techniques for a single department. The most commonly used technique was "expected units sold by expected average price per unit." Other techniques that were used by more than 20 percent of the respondents included "number of guests by expected spending per guest" and "last year's actual revenues adjusted subjectively."

Our research uncovered several points that deserve attention. First, virtually all hotels use an operations budget and yet less than half of the hotels budget beyond one year at a time. Future researchers might explore the reasons why more hoteliers don't prepare long-range operations budgets. Second, few hoteliers revise their budget during the year (only about one in four). Budgeting is not an exact science, so regular adjustments should be expected and planned. Third, for most hotels, the largest single cost is labor. Yet our research shows that hotels' food and beverage costs appear to be more closely controlled than are labor costs.

Future research could also focus on specific control techniques to monitor hotels' costs and to determine whether more-profitable hotels use different techniques than less-profitable hotels. Finally, further study could examine closely the forecasting techniques actually used by the operating departments. For example, in our study, the technique "last year's actual revenues adjusted subjectively" was rated high, and future research could explore exactly what "subjective" adjustments are being used.

8.4 AS I SEE IT: THE HOTEL CONTROLLER

Mike Draeger

The controller is the manager with overall responsibility of the accounting department. This executive is credited with having his or her hand on the purse strings, eye on the bottom line, and ear of the general manager, all while counting the beans and balancing the books. In fulfilling this role, the controller must know the hotel operations and be familiar with what goes on in each department. As is the same with all other managerial roles, the controller must have many skills that are used daily.

Obviously, the controller is an administrator. He or she supervises the accounting functions, including payroll, payables, receivables, purchasing, and auditing. The controller wants to know that procedures are being followed and deadlines are being met. He or she questions what is happening in each hotel department. Is all the money getting to the bank, and is there enough to pay all the vendors and staff? That large group function in the ballroom is being extended 30-day credit; have their references been checked? Are purchase orders on file in the receiving department?

Do the actual payroll tax deposits equal what is reported on the IRS form? Accounting affects almost every aspect of the hotel operation, and the controller is the one looked to when it comes to the proper functioning and conduct of this department.

The controller is an advisor, meaning he or she provides information and recommendations to every department in the hotel. Regarding giving information, accounting generates more reports than any other department. Daily reports to management showing sales, labor, and purchases are a must in any business, with comparisons to budget and/or last year. The financial statements, including the balance sheet and income statement, are periodically produced in accounting. The controller is expected to be prepared to discuss these types of reports with managers and owners, and to make sense of all the numbers and percentages. A hotel holds any number of meetings where the controller discusses the financial or operational results. At these meetings, the controller is a part of the process of generating recommendations and suggestions to improve operations in areas the reports might point out. Often, a morning operations meeting finds the controller addressing labor costs that are creeping higher than appropriate given current levels of business, or the monthly manager's meeting starts with the controller giving an overview of last month's financial results and the hotel's year-to-date standing. When the owners visit the hotel, they usually attend a meeting to discuss financial results and what is being done to ensure profitability expectations are being met. The controller might even be asked to sit in on a specific department's staff meeting as its members brainstorm ways to reduce departmental costs. As others digest the information accounting provides, the controller offers advice and counsel on its significance.

The controller is also a technician. He or she must have a foundation in the debits and credits of accounting. Regardless of whether the accounting department is staffed with one person or two dozen, the controller is prepared to jump in and do the work. A tight labor market and staff turnover sometimes necessitate that the controller assist in every function. There are always balance sheet accounts to reconcile, budget variances to explain, and journal entries to post. It takes a lot to keep an accounting department functioning.

Very early in my accounting career, I began working in a small accounting department of a regional restaurant chain. Due to state laws, the restaurants could buy alcoholic beverages with cash or check only, and never on credit. To facilitate purchasing, the restaurant general manager was provided an imprest checking account for purchasing alcohol. (An imprest account is one that has a specific amount of money in it, and money replaced with precise amounts checks are written for.) This account had $1,000 in it, and each week

the manager called the home office and have deposited into the account the amount equal to the checks written in the previous week. Then the invoices for what had been purchased were forwarded to the home office, which supported the amount of the transfer. In theory, the account balance never exceeded $1,000. The bank statements were sent to the general manager of the restaurant to balance and send completed to the home office.

Because I was the new guy, I was given the task of balancing the checking account of one restaurant, which had not been balanced in over two years. It was well known that this restaurant's manager, an exceptional people person, wasn't good with numbers and never found time to balance that puny checking account. So I went to work ticking off the checks and deposits and trying to make the account balance to the $1,000 imprest amount. There were several irregularities, and, of course, many documents (cashed checks) were missing. I worked with the bank to recreate copies and research the irregularities, of which there were many. When all was finished, I had discovered the manager had embezzled over $18,000! This manager had actually been a very astute numbers person and had found ways to divert extra funds into the account and then wrote checks to himself and others for personal use.

It was a technician who caught him. But had a technician balanced that checkbook monthly and always verified the purchases through the invoices, it never would have happened in the first place. Procedures were wrong and not enforced, and the climate was ripe for trouble. A good bookkeeper or accountant is primarily a good technician in accounting aspects, and a good controller does not lose sight of this ability as his or her career develops.

Most successful businesses create a financial plan or budget to operate by. The more honest and detailed this plan is, the better one can gauge actual performance. Most budgets are prepared annually, with monthly detail breakdowns. The controller is a planner and is usually the one who prepares the budget—or, better yet, coordinates the hotel's efforts in preparing departmental budgets to consolidate into one master document. I worked for a company that provided major cash incentives for meeting and exceeding the annual budgeted bottom-line numbers. Budgeting was taken very seriously, and each member of management had a vested interest in all departments' performance. Budgeting is not hard to do, but it can be time-consuming.

Over the years, I became a detail-oriented and effective budgeter, although my first budget review taught me the most. My hotel and I had spent weeks and months preparing the next year's budget. All the numbers had been gone over, comparisons completed, and volumes of expense and revenue backup catalogued and bound in three-ring binders. The general manager and I flew 3,000 miles, with our binders, to present the budget to our area and regional vice presidents and receive the company's stamp of approval. We were scheduled for a five-hour review session, if that much time was needed. As the GM and I came into the review room, the vice presidents were already seated and waiting. They stated that this could be a short and productive meeting. If we would only commit to increasing our bottom line by $200,000, we could all be out of there in five minutes. No way! The GM and I had solid defendable numbers, and we weren't going to let months of everyone's hard honest work get blown away. Needless to say, the review lasted the entire five hours, our budget was ripped to

shreds, and the GM and I were verbally bloodied, bruised, and beaten at the end of it all. Oh yes, our bottom line increased $350,000, and we did not make budget or our bonuses that year. A good manager should always know what the people above him are looking for and then strive or rather plan to produce it, and this includes budgeting.

Additionally, the controller is an educator. All managers have a responsibility to instruct and train others, and the controller is no exception. Obviously, the accounting staff must be proficient in their duties to perform their jobs, and the controller must ensure this is happening. However, to the majority of the hotel, what accounting does and how they do it can be quite a mystery. Controllers should demystify the role of accounting. Managers with an understanding of accounting find they have more tools to work with in the operation of their departments after they have been involved in just one year's budget process. The controller can be building public relations for accounting by using opportunities to develop others' financial awareness and expertise.

Finally, controllers should be mentors. They should be involved in the development of people. The accounting staff should experience new challenges to keep them interested. Cross-training in other accounting or hotel positions can give staff perspective on areas not previously understood. This aids staff in developing their careers and additionally helps within the department when staff is short.

There was a time when this backfired on me, though. My accounting department had a staff of 14, and each was cross-trained to perform at least part of a job besides their own. My general cashier was responsible for counting the previous day's receipts and preparing the bank deposit. Additionally, she replenished the cash banks used in the restaurants and stores and at the front desk. She was responsible for maintaining a safe in her office that contained close to $400,000. Sadly, her father passed away and she needed to leave town for a week or so. No problem! We had someone in accounts receivable that had cross-trained in the cashiering position and was able to step in immediately. The cashiering temp completed her first week without a hitch. We left work for the weekend feeling all was well. On Monday, my cashiering temp didn't show up for work. She also didn't call. In fact, I have never seen her since. Over the weekend, she had taken advantage of procedural flaws and helped herself to $30,000 of the hotel's money and fled.

When I was able to step back and take a broad look at what had happened, I realized the problem. The accounting procedures were such that one person could steal from the safe and not be questioned. Not only was this an opportunity for a dishonest employee, but it placed an honest employee in danger! One employee had both the combination and the key to the safe tumbler. One employee could go into the accounting offices alone on a day when the entire hotel knew the accounting department was closed. One employee could go into the cashier's office alone with a backpack and exit the office, department, and the building without anyone asking to see inside the backpack. A single employee could be in physical danger if others knew all of this and were hard up for cash. Needless to say, procedures were changed immediately and policy manuals were rewritten with haste.

The controller should be on the lookout for promising managers who show potential. Managers enjoy taking a few minutes over coffee or lunch or even just sitting in the office to talk about their objectives and goals.

Often the controller can facilitate a manager's accomplishments by being a friend and being aware of the manager's professional developmental needs.

Mentoring and educating can benefit the controller in many ways—maybe, most interestingly, his or her personal advancement and compensation. Several hotel companies evaluate and offer incentives to the back-of-the-house departments for criteria previously reserved for more service-oriented or revenue-producing departments. As a controller of an accounting department, I am measured by the service my department provides to the hotel operation—our internal customers. Accounting becomes a support department and the rest of the operation its customers. In this way, accounting offers products and services, and it works to satisfy customers. The manager and even staff can establish quantifiable objectives focused on the department's product. These become the criteria for performance evaluations, bonuses, and other incentives and rewards.

Current objectives in accounting might now include:

- Working professionally with all other departments.

- Meeting deadlines and issuing timely reports.

- Achieving superior results on internal and external audits.

- Training operational managers in the financial aspects of their departments.

- Stocking storerooms at appropriate par levels.

- Keeping the accounting offices neat, orderly, and presentable.

- Being willing to answer questions and assist with problems.

With this type of product and service attitude, there is no limit to what a department might do for its customers.

It is not easy to describe the controller's job as a daily routine. However, the position does call for skills and traits that are continually in use. Just as with all other aspects of the hotel, the scenery is always changing, guests are constantly arriving and departing, restaurants open and close, telephones ring 24 hours a day. Each day brings new challenges and opportunities, and the controller, as part of this, must embrace the many facets of the hospitality industry.

8.5 THE HOTEL PURCHASING FUNCTION

C. Lee Evans

The hotel purchasing function did not change very much from 1970 to 1990. Until the late 1980s, various tax advantages and benefits were the primary reason for the construction of U.S. hotels. Providing a substantial return on investment was not expected or required.

In our current economy, expectations of hotel profitability have changed. Profitability is now required, along with maintaining the established level of quality. This has brought about a new level of interest in the purchasing function and greater importance placed on cost savings.

The financial aspects of the hotel business changed in the 1990s. Hotels enjoyed the longest boom in revenues and profitability over the previous 40 years.

Today, however, in the slump following the terrorist attacks of 2001, hotel managers realize that true cost savings generated in the purchasing department are dollars that drop directly to the bottom line without associated incremental cost. It is not difficult to generate arbitrary savings; the true challenge is to create cost efficiency utilizing a standard specification.

Purchasing for the hotel requires much more than obtaining three bids and circling the lowest price. The true definition of *purchasing* should be "purchasing the right product, at the right price, at the right time."

The statement sounds extremely simple, but when it is applied to the thousands of items a hotel purchases, it presents a great challenge for the purchasing manager. The hotel purchasing function supports virtually every department within the property, whether purchasing chemicals for housekeeping or stewarding, office supplies for marketing, computer supplies for accounting, or food and beverage products for the restaurant outlets.

The purchasing manager usually reports to the hotel controller or the hotel's financial control division, but I am convinced this will change. There is a need for a more operational approach to managing the purchasing function. We need to build a team that is committed to the common goal of servicing our customers and maintaining established quality standards. The reporting structure will begin to shift to operations, with the purchasing manager directly reporting to the general manager or, in larger properties, to the executive assistant/operations manager. This will help promote the philosophy of team building and support and service customers directly. As matters stand now, purchasing is viewed as a support department.

With the increasing importance of the purchasing function, the mission of the purchasing manager is to procure products and services cost-effectively that will meet or exceed the customer's expectation. The purchasing manager must continually evaluate product specifications to incorporate new products and technology. Reviewing the specific need based on the expectation of the customer helps product evaluation.

The purchasing function is changing for several reasons. In the past five to seven years, the hotel industry has undergone tremendous consolidation. With this consolidation have come economies of scale for support areas, which include marketing, accounting, purchasing, and reservation systems. Many of today's hotel companies have centralized the purchasing function to some extent. They negotiate purchasing agreements with producers and processors and distribute products and supplies through predetermined distribution channels.

| Figure 8.3 | **Partial Hotel Organization Chart** |

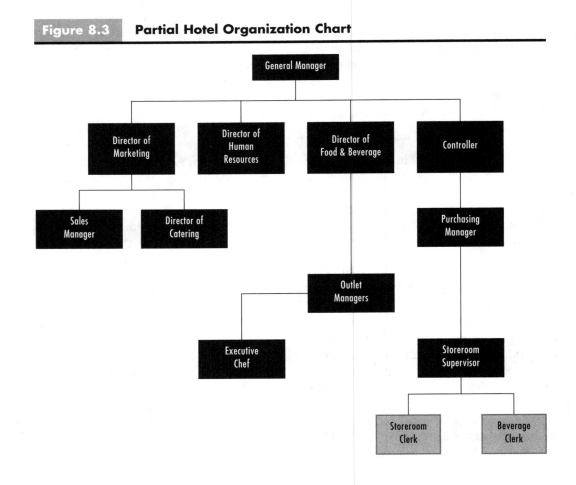

▶ PURCHASING ORGANIZATION

The purchasing department can be organized into three basic areas:

- **Administrative:** This area consists of pricing, vendor selection, and the purchase of nonstocked items. Nonstocked items are products purchased for immediate use or held in storage in other departments throughout the hotel.
- **Receiving:** There are two categories of receiving: (1) hotel goods that are placed in storage in the purchasing area or are immediately issued to the requesting department or guest/group; and (2) items that have been shipped to a registered guest or expected guest/group.
- **Issuing:** Product issuing falls into two categories: (1) consumable food and beverage supplies consisting of all food items and liquor, beer, wine, and mixes to be held in the purchasing department storerooms; and (2) office supplies, printed forms, and linen. This is just a small listing of items, depending on the physical layout of the hotel.

The staffing and segregation of duties varies from hotel to hotel depending on the property size and physical layout of the back-of-the-house areas. A partial organization chart is shown in Figure 8.3. See sidebar, "Sample Job Descriptions."

▶ INTERDEPARTMENTAL RELATIONSHIPS

It is essential that the purchasing manager develop close working relationships with key managers within the hotel. These relationships should build and demonstrate trust, confidence in judgment, and integrity. Key managers include the following:

- Corporate purchasing manager
- Hotel general manager
- Executive assistant/operations manager
- Director of food and beverage
- Executive chef
- Director of housekeeping

Interaction between the purchasing manager and all other departments occurs regularly. Spoken interaction, either by telephone or in person, is the most frequent. With the technological implementation of the Internet and email, the communication process has become more efficient. Communication can be accomplished quickly with large numbers of people.

Most day-to-day interactions of the purchasing manager involve the following key managers and issues, among others:

- **General manager/executive assistant manager:** Issues relating to quality changes and all discussions regarding capital expenditures (defined as equipment or renovation purchases exceeding $2,000).
- **Director of food and beverage:** Unresolved food purchasing issues and information related to wine, liquor, and beer purchases.
- **Executive chef:** Issues relating to food purchases. This area requires close communication with respect to vendor performance, food markets, quality, and availability information.
- **Director of housekeeping:** Coordination and purchase of linens, paper goods

SAMPLE JOB DESCRIPTIONS

Purchasing Manager

POSITION TITLE: Purchasing manager

DIVISION/DEPARTMENT: Administrative and general

REPORTS TO (TITLE): Controller

DIRECTLY SUPERVISES: Storeroom supervisor, beverage clerk, storeroom clerk

NO. OF EMPLOYEES SUPERVISED: 3

BASIC FUNCTION OF POSITION: To support the hotel department with dependable sources of materials and services; to buy competitively; to control inventories; to develop and train personnel; to implement planning to avoid emergencies; and to implement and supervise all procedures and staff in the purchasing department.

EDUCATION AND EXPERIENCE OR SKILLS NORMALLY NEEDED: College helpful but not required. Previous buying experience a must. Food and beverage buying necessary. Accounting background needed. Extraordinary organizational skills required. Must display excellent management skills and a great deal of diplomacy.

TYPE OF GUIDANCE REQUIRED TO DIRECT THE ACTIVITIES OF THE POSITION AND MAGNITUDE OF INDEPENDENT DECISION-MAKING RESPONSIBILITY: Must have the ability to function independently within the parameters established by the controller and other upper management in the hotel. Has the authority to hire and terminate.

FUNCTIONS:

20%: Develop and monitor policies, procedures, and performance objectives for the purchasing team.

30%: Solicit competitive price quotation.

40%: Supervision of purchasing staff.

10%: Miscellaneous duties (O-G = ongoing):

O-G: Review par stock levels.

O-G: Schedule storeroom hours.

O-G: Develop employees for supervision position.

O-G: Maintain high levels of employee motivation.

O-G: Insure proper handling of receiving, storing, and issuing.

O-G: Assure accurate and timely preparation of daily records for purchases and issues for food and beverage forms.

O-G: Visit surveyors and stay abreast of market trends.

Storeroom Supervisor

POSITION TITLE: Storeroom supervisor

DIVISION/DEPARTMENT: Purchasing

REPORTS TO (TITLE): Purchasing manager

DIRECTLY SUPERVISES: Beverage clerk, storeroom clerk

NO. OF EMPLOYEES SUPERVISED: 2

BASIC FUNCTION OF POSITION: To supervise the storeroom staff and resolve day-to-day problems in food and beverage storerooms. To assist in the procurement of all consumable food and beverage items assuring that they are of the right quality and right quantity. To maintain minimum investment and reduce unnecessary expenditures to maintain high sanitation standards and enforce all hotel policies relating to the food and beverage storerooms.

EDUCATION AND EXPERIENCE OR SKILLS NORMALLY NEEDED: College degree helpful but not required. One to two years' prior food and beverage background required. Must be able to read, write, and speak English fluently. Must have good organizational skills.

TYPE OF GUIDANCE REQUIRED TO DIRECT THE ACTIVITIES OF THE POSITION AND MAGNITUDE OF INDEPENDENT DECISION-MAKING RESPONSIBILITY: Must have the ability to act as administrator of the purchasing department in the absence of the purchasing manager. Must have the ability to function independently within the parameters established by the purchasing manager. Has the authority to hire and terminate.

FUNCTIONS:

50%: Supervise food and beverage clerks and provide assistance when necessary.

5%: Prepare daily food order.

5%: Prepare semiweekly food order.

5%: Maintain perpetual inventory (liquor, beer, wine).

2%: Assist purchasing manager in placing orders.

5%: Prepare weekly food bid sheet.

5%: Prepare monthly food bid sheet.

2%: Maintain accurate food and beverage vendor files.

2%: Assist in monthly inventory.

2%: Prepare monthly Food Dead Stock list (raw materials for which there is no finished product) for chef.

2%: Prepare monthly Beverage Dead Stock list for director of food and beverage.

10%: Assign miscellaneous duties (O-G = ongoing):

    O-G: Product quality inspection.

    O-G: Communication with the chef.

    O-G: Keep abreast of industry trends and information.

    O-G: Maintain accurate and organized filing system.

Storeroom Clerk/Beverage Clerk

POSITION TITLE: Storeroom clerk/beverage clerk

DIVISION/DEPARTMENT: Purchasing

REPORTS TO (TITLE): Storeroom supervisor

DIRECTLY SUPERVISES: None

NO. OF EMPLOYEES SUPERVISED: None

(continues)

SAMPLE JOB DESCRIPTIONS (continued)

BASIC FUNCTION OF POSITION: To receive, store, issue, rotate, and secure merchandise as outlined in the storeroom procedures. To accurately record transactions and to follow written policies and procedures relating to purchasing and the food and beverage storerooms.

EDUCATION AND EXPERIENCE OR SKILLS NORMALLY NEEDED: Prior experience in food and beverage consumable receiving. Prior storeroom experience in issuing stock, and inventory control. Must have math aptitude and be detail oriented.

TYPE OF GUIDANCE REQUIRED TO DIRECT THE ACTIVITIES OF THE POSITION AND MAGNITUDE OF INDEPENDENT DECISION-MAKING RESPONSIBILITY: Must have the ability to function independently within the parameters established by the purchasing manager and storeroom supervisor.

FUNCTIONS:

25%: Responsible for the second thorough inspection of the product as it is being stored and rotated; assure proper stock storage location on shelving units.

10%: Maintain high standards of sanitation and inventory organization.

10%: Participate in monthly inventory.

40%: Insure completion of paperwork in a timely manner:

A Form (daily record of purchases and issues of food).

B Form (daily record of purchase and issues of beverage).

Issue recap food.

Issue recap beverage.

Perpetual inventory, beverage.

Perpetual inventory, paper.

Food stock levels.

Beverage stock levels

15%: Miscellaneous:

To complete projects in a timely manner.

(toilet paper, facial tissue, paper towels), uniforms, and laundry and cleaning chemicals.

A good purchasing manager bases purchasing decisions on the same criteria as all business decisions: data. One cannot be an expert on every product available. This is where purchase specifications come into play. Written specifications must be developed for all key products. These products should be tested periodically to verify that they meet or exceed specifications. Examples of testing: a monthly butcher yield test on specific meat cuts; a yearly test of terry linen by an independent laboratory.

▶ PURCHASING SOURCES

There are many sources of information about producers, processors, and manufacturers. Technical data are also available. Suppliers are the best source of information. The listings in the sidebar "Purchasing Sources" are a small sample of material available to the purchasing manager. The latest and greatest means of identifying product sources has to be the Internet.

▶ THE PURCHASING MANAGER'S DAY

7:00 A.M. Inspect the quality of food and beverage consumables as they are delivered to the hotel. This includes rejecting incorrect or inferior products and then contacting the appropriate vendor(s) to rectify issues or determine another source, if necessary. The average daily purchase cost could vary from $3,000 to $50,000, depending on the size of the property and level of business.

9:00–11:00 A.M. Attend daily meeting with catering department, chef, stewarding, and banquet departments to review upcoming banquet business. Review the room setup for each scheduled function, menus, and, most important, the guaranteed attendance numbers.

12:00 noon. All food and beverage purchases have been received and issued. Inventory is now taken on all items in storage to determine the next day's needs. After reviewing the current levels and calculating banquet business requirements, select the vendors and place orders with suppliers, which may range in number from 1 to 25.

Spend the rest of the afternoon on purchasing nonconsumable food and beverage items, obtaining bids, and following up on outstanding purchase orders overdue for delivery.

The average workweek for the purchasing manager is 50 to 60 hours and may include weekends. For the most part, normal business hours are 7:00 A.M. to 6:00 P.M., Monday through Friday, and 7:00 A.M. to noon on Saturday.

▶ CORPORATE DIRECTION AND INTERACTION

Corporate direction and control varies with each hotel company. As a general rule, though, hotel companies that manage rather than franchise their properties are more involved in setting policies and procedures. The minimum standards of the purchasing manager vary by hotel company as well.

The corporate purchasing function is still viewed with skepticism, although not as much as in the past. Today, purchasing is nonprofit and established to benefit managed properties. The idea of doing more with less applies at the corporate level as well as to the individual properties. The most efficient method of purchasing systemwide is targeting where dollars are spent and creating the most cost-efficient way to purchase high-volume expense items. Corporate hotel purchasing offices are currently working to accomplish this goal. Examples of items that could be considered for systemwide agreements between corporate and property purchasing offices are uniforms, flatware, paper goods, laundry supplies, and food products; these, too, vary by company.

PURCHASING SOURCES

The Meat Buyers Guide (1988)
by National Association of Meat Purveyors
8365-B Greensboro Drive
McLean, VA 22102
(703) 827-5754

Fresh Produce Manual (1989)
by the Produce Marketing Association
P.O. Box 6036
Newark, DE 19714-6036

The Food Professional's Guide
by Irena Chalmers
American Showcase, Inc., New York

Quantity Food Purchasing (2d ed.)
Lendal H. Kotschevar
John Wiley and Sons, Inc., New York

The Encyclopedia of Fish Cookery
by A. J. McClane
Holt, Rinehart, and Winston, New York

The Advanced Seafood Handbook
Seafood Business Magazine
P.O. Box 908
Rockland, Maine 04841

The Packer 1990
Produce Availability & Merchandising Guide
Vance Publishing
7950 College Blvd.
Overland Park, Kansas 66210

▶ CASE IN POINT

The company I worked for out of college and until 1995 had its own in-house profit-driven purchasing company. This approach was not unique to this company; many of the large hotel companies had their own profit-driven purchasing arm, subsidiaries that, from a hotel owner's standpoint, could be considered double dipping, as the owner was already paying the hotel management company a management fee. In the late 1980s and early 1990s, many hotel owners were looking for a greater return from their management company. I had the privilege and opportunities to be involved in the overthrow of the company's internal purchasing subsidiary. At that time we had been sold to foreign investors, and they were looking at every function and subsidiary

in the company. With some prodding directly at the hotel company's new owner by one of the senior management, we were able to demonstrate that the days of double dipping had to go and that the individual properties would recognize and support a corporate-level purchasing function whose only mission was to generate benefit for the properties. My boss and I succeeded in accomplishing what was once thought could never be done due to politics.

▶ CONCLUSION

Hotel purchasing must focus on and utilize resources in the most efficient manner today. In the past, a heavy-handed approach was used to resolve issues with suppliers. As we move toward building partnerships with key vendors today, a teamwork approach provides an environment to build on the strengths of both the hotel and the vendor. This is now called *supply-chain management*.

Another key component in business today is communication, both internal and external. One of our national suppliers has the capability to link their customer service for placing orders with our domestic properties through a mainframe computer network linked to each property by PCs. Our hotels can place orders directly with the supplier through the network system and receive immediate confirmation from the supplier. This nationwide system allows both our properties and the corporate office to access pricing, availability, and consumption.

To succeed, we must resist the confines of our traditional paradigms. We must continually examine the ways we conduct business and strive for new and innovative approaches.

8.6 DATA MINING FOR HOTEL FIRMS: USE AND LIMITATIONS

Vincent P. Magnini, Earl D. Honeycutt Jr., and Sharon K. Hodge

In the hotel industry, knowing your guests—where they are from, how much they spend, and when and on what they spend it—can help you formulate marketing strategies and maximize profits. Fueled by the proliferation of centralized reservation and property-management systems, hotel corporations accumulate large amounts of consumer data. This information can be organized and integrated in databases that can then be tapped to guide marketing decisions. However, identifying important variables and relationships located in these consumer-information systems can be a daunting task. The relatively new process known as data mining can be instrumental in overcoming such obstacles. [For a discussion of the use of compiled data, see Robert K. Griffin, "Data Warehousing: The Latest Strategic Weapon for the Lodging Industry?" *Cornell Hotel and Restaurant Administration Quarterly* 39, no. 4 (August 1998), pp. 28–35. For a discussion of the use of guest-history data, see Paula A. Francese and Leo M. Renaghan, "Database Marketing: Building Customer Profiles." *Cornell Hotel and Restaurant Administration Quarterly* 31, no. 1 (May 1990), pp. 60–63.] From stores of information, data mining technology extracts meaningful patterns and builds predictive customer-behavior models that aid in decision making (Kamrani, Rong, and Gonzalez, 2001, 361–377).

Data mining is a largely automated process that uses statistical analyses to sift through massive data sets to detect useful, non-obvious, and previously unknown patterns or data trends (Frawley, Piatetsky-Shapiro, and Matheus, 1992, 213–228). The emphasis is on the computer-based exploration of previously uncharted relationships (i.e., using "machine learning" methods that typically require only limited human involvement) (Peacock, 1998a). Without data mining, valuable marketing insights about customers' characteristics and purchase patterns may remain largely untapped (Shaw, Subramaniam, Tan, and Welge, 2001, 127–137). By uncovering such previously unknown relationships, managers have the potential to develop a winning marketing strategy that increases their hotel's bottom line.

Hotel managers understand the importance of adapting to the changing business environment not only to remain competitive, but merely to survive. As a result, technology has become a large and growing expense for many hotel corporations. Under such a technology framework, data mining is a valuable competitive tool being adopted by hotel corporations in an effort to create customer value. However, given the importance and complexity of data mining, senior hotel managers report a low level of understanding about data mining's capabilities, how it works, and what value this technology contributes (Dev and Olsen, 2000, 41–47). The purpose of this paper is to educate hotel managers about the benefits and application of data mining on the properties they oversee.

▶ DATA MINING VERSUS STATISTICAL MODELING

Data mining differs from traditional statistical modeling in a variety of ways. Data mining focuses on machine-driven model building, while statistical modeling stresses theory-driven hypothesis testing. Data mining techniques build models, whereas classical statistical tools are supervised by a trained researcher who possesses a preconceived notion of what to examine. With statistical *a priori* analysis, relevant associations may be overlooked. By building dependency hypotheses instead of merely verifying them, though, data mining techniques reveal important links. For example, Marriott Vacation Club International reduced the volume of direct mail it needed to reach target sales levels by correlating response rates to specific vacation offerings and specific customer characteristics (Peacock, 1998a).

Data mining also offers enormous gains in terms of performance, speed of use, and user friendliness (Le Bret, 1997). While data miners must understand statistical principles, highly specialized statistical knowledge is not necessary to study, understand, and improve decision-making processes. Data mining helps managers to spot trends more quickly.

Because researchers may ignore the assumptions and limitations of a theoretical model, traditional statistical analyses in customer-satisfaction research are often biased. Satisfaction research includes measures of the importance that customers place on product and services attributes. Typically, these measures are highly correlated, which can dramatically bias the statistical values that determine attributes' importance rankings. Also, statistical analyses usually assume that relationships between independent and dependent variables are linear—which is often not the case. Therefore, violation of these assumptions can result in biased and misleading statistical outcomes. Data mining techniques (e.g., neural networks) overcome these limitations and outperform traditional statistical analyses in cases where such assumptions do not apply (Le Bret, 1997).

Another considerable advantage over traditional statistical models is data mining's ability to easily handle large and complex datasets (Peacock, 1998a). Data mining techniques are not hampered by large numbers of predictive variables, and that feature makes data mining

A DATA MINING TOOLKIT

- *Association rules:* Information from customer-purchase histories is used to formulate probabilistic rules for subsequent purchases.

- *Case-based reasoning:* Sets of attributes from new problems are compared with attribute sets from previously encountered problems (called cases) to find one or more boilerplate examples that provided good outcomes or solutions.

- *Decision trees:* Automatically constructed from data, these yield a sequence of step-wise rules; good for identifying important predictor variables, non-linear relationships, and interactions among variables.

- *Descriptive statistics:* Averages, variation, counts, percentages, cross-tabs, simple correlation; used at the beginning of the data mining process to depict structure and identify potential problems in data.

- *Genetic algorithms:* Use procedures modeled on evolutionary biology (e.g., selection, mutation, survival of the fittest) to solve prediction and classification problems or develop sets of decision rules.

- *Neural networks:* Applications that mimic the processes of the human brain; capable of learning from examples (large training sets of data) to discover patterns in data; can combine information from many predictors and work well even with correlated variables, non-linear relationships, and missing data.

- *Query tools:* Provide summary measures such as counts, totals, and averages.

- *Regression-type models:* Ordinary least-squares regression, logistic regression, discriminant analysis; used mostly for confirmation of models built by "machine-learning" techniques.

- *Visualization tools:* Histograms, box plots, scatter diagrams; useful for condensing large amounts of data into a concise, comprehensible picture.—V.P.M., E.D.H., and S.K.H.

useful for selecting variables, that is, identifying those within a set that are most relevant. The ability to handle large numbers of variables also makes data mining more realistic than statistical models in representing the complexity of a typical business environment.

While many analytical techniques can be classified as data mining tools, opinion has not coalesced regarding exactly which techniques should be considered part of the data mining toolkit. The tools listed in the sidebar "A Data Mining Toolkit" almost certainly belong, however.

Looking at that toolkit, decision trees, association rules, case-based learning tools, neural networks, and genetic algorithms are categorized as machine-learning methods, while the others can be thought of as machine-assisted aids to support human learning (Peacock, 1998a).

EXAMPLES OF THE USES OF DATA MINING INFORMATION IN HOTEL MARKETING

- Create direct-mail campaigns.
- Plan seasonal promotions.
- Plan the timing and placement of ad campaigns.
- Create personalized advertisements.

- Define which market segments are growing most rapidly.
- Determine the number of rooms to reserve for wholesale customers and business travelers.

With data mining techniques, levels of *a priori* specification can vary. In some cases, certain independent variables and dependent variables may be specified for examination, while predictor variables in other cases may be uncovered only by the data mining tool. The point remains, though, that in comparison with traditional statistical methods, data mining techniques invariably are more data driven than they are user driven.

We have observed that some hotel corporations are attempting to harness the power of information by investing in data mining technology that exploits consumer information. Hilton Corporation uses E.piphany E.4 software at its Beverly Hills headquarters, for instance (Stevens, 2001a, 35–38), and Starwood Corporation recently invested in Unica Corp's Affinium software (Tischelle and Maselli, 2001, 31–32). Such data mining technology allows hotel corporations to predict consumer-behavior trends, which are potentially useful for marketing applications. For example, Starwood's marketing staff can run reports and analysis on customer and occupancy data stored in a data warehouse that combines customer and transaction information from all company properties. Such infor-

mation indicates where customers who visit a specific hotel live. If the data reveal that the Sheraton Fisherman's Wharf in San Francisco experiences a surge in visitors from Fort Lauderdale in April, for instance, hotel marketers can increase promotional efforts in Fort Lauderdale during the late winter months (Tischelle and Maselli, 2001, 31–32). The sidebar "Examples of the Uses of Data Mining Information in Hotel Marketing" lists examples of how information gleaned from data mining can be used in a hotel corporation's marketing activities.

▶ HARRAH'S DATA MINING SUCCESS STORY

In 1997 Harrah's hotels and casinos introduced a trademarked loyalty-card program, "Total Rewards," which tracks customers' purchasing activities and provides rewards that encourage spending at Harrah's properties. Rather than build glitzy properties with eye-popping attractions, Harrah's pursued a customer-service-oriented strategy centered around data mining techniques. Harrah's used an information system called WINet to link all its properties, allowing the firm to collect and share customer information company wide. The process effectively changed the corporate culture from an every-property-for-itself mentality to a collaborative, customer-focused enterprise (Levinson, 2001).

The WINet system connects and consolidates customer information from all of the company's transaction, slot-machine, hotel-management, and reservation systems. Key pieces of information—gender, age, place of residence, and types of casino games played—help predict which customers are most likely to become frequent users. Based on this information, Harrah's designs marketing strategies to retain those customers. Customers' purchasing and gaming patterns are tracked, too, so that the company can target its customers with the most appropriate incentives. For example, customers who reside outside the local area receive complimentary hotel rooms or transportation, while drive-in customers receive food, entertainment, or cash incentives (Nickell, 2002).

Data mining techniques help to reveal data patterns and relationships that can be used to develop strong models for predicting the potential value of each customer. Given that retaining a customer is less costly than attracting a new one, building strong relationships with valued existing customers can boost profits. Having information regarding such things as the customer's birthday, anniversary, and favorite foods and drinks allows a hotel to provide excellent, tailored customer service that cements brand loyalty. Harrah's discovered that the 30 percent of its customers who spent between $100 and $500 per visit accounted for 80 percent of company revenues and generated nearly 100 percent of profits. In the first two years of its rewards program, Harrah's saw a $100-million increase in revenue from customers who visited more than one property (Nickell, 2002). Currently, Harrah's ranks first in the industry in profit growth (Levinson, 2001).

Because the WINet system can consistently identify which customers will be most valuable over the long term, data mining is also useful for determining when to avoid offering incentives to customers who are not lucrative. Harrah's estimates that it has saved some $20 million by withdrawing incentives from customers who are not likely to return (Levinson, 2001).

Despite Harrah's success, some remain skeptical of data mining's customer benefits and long-term financial payoffs. As an example, Susan Dobscha, co-author of "Preventing the Premature Death of Relationship Marketing," advises hotels that giant central databases "are not where customers want a relationship forged. A customer would probably prefer a lower price over, say, having their beverage choice anticipated" (Mining Hotel Data, 1998).

Another important caveat regarding data mining is that any relationship discovered must be valid to benefit a company's performance. When British Columbia Telecom tried to reward 100 of its best customers by inviting them to a Vancouver Grizzlies basketball game, for instance, it selected customers from the database comprising frequent 900-number users. After sending invitations to the printer, the marketing staff realized that those 900-number users included a large number of sex-line enthusiasts. The company avoided a serious gaffe by refining the criteria to create a list of truly loyal guests (Press, 1998, 58–61).

▶ DATA MINING APPLICATIONS FOR THE HOTEL INDUSTRY

The tasks performed by data mining can be grouped into the following five categories.

1. Classification arranges customers into pre-defined segments that allow the size and structure of market groups to be monitored. Also, predictive models can be built to classify activities. An illustration of such a model is one that predicts which segment's usage rate will experience the largest decrease when a particular promotion expires. Classification uses the information contained in sets of predictor variables, such as demographic and lifestyle data, to assign customers to segments.

2. Clustering groups customers based on domain knowledge and the database, but does not rely on predetermined group definitions. This function is beneficial because it aids hoteliers in understanding who are their customers. For example, clustering may reveal a subgroup within a predetermined segment with homogenous purchasing behavior (e.g., a subgroup of holiday shoppers within the transient segment) that can be targeted effectively through a specific ad campaign. (The idea is that the members of the subgroup will increase their number of stays or become more loyal.) On the other hand, clustering may indicate that previously determined segments are not parsimonious and should be consolidated to increase advertising efficiency. Information such as demographic characteristics, lifestyle descriptors, and actual product purchases are typically used in clustering.

3. Deviation detection uncovers data anomalies, such as a sudden increase in purchases by a customer. Information of this type can prove useful if a hotel corporation wants to thank a guest for her or his recent increase in spending or offer a promotion in appreciation. Marketing managers may also attempt to draw correlations between surges in deviations with uncontrollable business-environment factors that are not represented in the database (e.g., a sharp increase in gasoline prices).

4. Association entails the detection of connections between records, driven by association and sequence discovery. For example, a possible detected association may be that a particular segment's average length of stay increases after a specific advertising campaign. Another association task could be employed in an effort to determine why a specific promotion was successful in one market, but ineffective elsewhere. Specific information regarding customer-purchase histories is necessary to formulate probabilistic rules pertaining to subsequent purchases.

5. Forecasting predicts the future value of continuous variables based on patterns and trends within the data. For instance, the forecasting function can be used to predict the future size of market segments. With forecasting one can also use data trends to project which hotel amenities are of growing importance to consumers and will be key drivers of the consumer's future perception of value.

In the hotel industry, the most common sources of data are CRSs and PMSs. Some hotel corporations also use information that resides in guest-loyalty-program databases. Hilton, for instance, analyzes data contained within its trademarked Hilton Honors database (Stevens, 2001b, 29–30). Another potentially important source of data is the information provided by guest-satisfaction surveys.

► GUIDELINES FOR EFFECTIVE DATA MINING

When properly employed, data mining is a powerful and valuable marketing tool. However, simply investing in data mining technology may not guarantee success. As presented below, seven guidelines influence the effective management of data mining technology.

Guideline #1: *Match your IT priorities with an appropriate provider.* There is high demand for and low supply of data mining expertise as more companies realize the potential value of the information residing within their databases. To capitalize on this demand, a number of second-tier research firms now provide data mining services (Brandel, 2001, 67–70). However, providers offer a wide range of skill levels. The most-skilled providers can turn data into useful information. Companies that initially set clear priorities have a greater chance of reaping maximum benefits from data mining projects than do firms that are unsure of their goals (Stevens, 2001). Clear priorities include goals about what the firm would like to achieve through data mining and when it will be achieved. Without goals and objectives the hotel corporation is uncertain about what it is shopping for when seeking a data miner. It is also important to communicate these goals to prospective providers. When selecting a provider, ask the following six questions:

- *Does the provider have experience setting up predictive models with marketing applications?* Data mining has applications other than marketing. Data mining's ability to detect patterns in data is used extensively in criminal justice and anti-terrorism efforts to anticipate illegal activity, for instance. Wall Street also employs data mining to predict moves in the financial markets. Large global corporations use data mining to gain efficiencies in purchasing and production throughout their networks. Therefore, it is not enough to have a data mining consultant, but one must find a provider that has experience in marketing. Building models to predict consumer behavior is a form of data mining that requires specific expertise. For example, a data miner with marketing-applications experience would know to replace a zip code with resident characteristics, such as median income (Brandel, 2001).

- *Does the provider have experience in creating models within the hospitality industry?* Marketing applications of data mining are employed across diverse industries. Building predictive models for a grocery store, a furniture chain, an airline, or a hotel is different in each case. It is beneficial to find a provider that has experience in setting up models in the hotel industry. Such a provider would more clearly understand hotel-guest-segmentation processes, for example.

- *Is the provider reputable?* Because many second-tier companies provide mining services, it is important to check the credentials and reputation of the vendor.

- *Does the provider offer the latest technology that is appropriate?* Because of the wide range of products available, it pays to do your homework. It is crucial to invest in the latest appropriate technology because it is extremely expensive and time consuming to switch products after one is installed—in no small part because switching products requires retraining the IT and marketing staff.

- *Does the provider offer a product that has visual-exploration capabilities?* Cutting-edge data mining software has visual-exploration capabilities, which means that data patterns can be viewed as three-dimensional objects that can be rotated or zoomed for detailed analysis. In addition, pixel-oriented technology assigns colors to data values so that patterns and trends can be examined. Visual exploration is an immense aid to managers and marketers because it often serves as a preliminary tool in selecting the appropriate variables for data mining tasks (Shaw *et al.*, 2001).

- *Is the provider willing to provide a custom contract?* Contract negotiations are a critical step in initiating a successful data mining program. The contract should be as precise as possible and should abstain from nebulous clauses discussing partnership (Lacity and Hirschheim, 1995). Moreover, the vendor's standard contract should not be used, because the standard contract does not customarily include specific performance standards or penalty clauses if the vendor falls short of requirements. Worse, payment schedules in standard contracts may favor the vendor (Lacity and Hirschheim, 1995). A custom contract should be written to include service-level measures and a termination clause. The buyer should be particularly suspicious of so-called change-of-character clauses, which state that the buyer may

have to pay for any changes in "functionality" throughout the life of the contract. Change-of-character clauses have caused many disputes because of the ambiguous nature of the term "functionality" (Lacity and Hirschheim, 1995).

Guideline #2: *Build segmentation and predictive models.* Building appropriate segmentation and predictive models necessitates an extensive knowledge of the hotel business. The sidebar "Examples of Hotel-Guest Segments" provides examples of some of the many ways that hotel guests can be segmented (Kotler, Bowen, and Makens, 1999). Transient hotels, convention hotels, extended-stay hotels, and resort properties all segment guests differently. Furthermore, guest segmentation is distinctive for most hotel properties. Hilton's and Marriott's property-management systems segment and code markets at the property level, for instance, since each location has its own particular segments. A given property may serve a set of corporate clients, a group of government clients, and social clients (e.g., weddings and reunions). The segment categories contained in the sidebar can be strung into a large set of combinations. Furthermore, a guest could potentially fit into several categories, which poses a challenge for current data mining techniques (Shaw *et al.*, 2001). As a consequence, finding a provider that has experience creating models in the hotel industry is a major benefit. Additionally, even if the provider has hotel experience, it is critical that IT and marketing managers work closely with the provider to segment the market and build predictive data mining models.

Once a data mining model is built, confirmatory testing must be conducted to assess its predictive accuracy. For instance, a model designed to predict who will respond to a pro-

EXAMPLES OF HOTEL-GUEST SEGMENTS

Geographic

Nations
States
Counties
Cities

Demographic

Age or life-cycle stage
Gender
Income

Psychographic

Social class
Life-style

Personality
Behavior
Occasion of purchase decision
Occasion of use
Benefits sought
User status (e.g., potential, former, first time)
Usage rate
Loyalty status
Buyer-readiness stage

Source: P. Kotler, J. Bowen, and J. Makens, *Marketing for Hospitality and Tourism,* 2nd ed. (Upper Saddle River, NJ: Prentice-Hall, 1999).

motion should be based on a prior offering in which it is known who did or did not respond. After the model is constructed, a "holdout" group from a previous promotion can be analyzed to verify reliability. If the holdout predictions do not replicate the results of the past promotion, then the model may not be significantly predictive. To further enhance accuracy, a score can be assigned to the model based on the level of agreement between the holdout group and the entire group. Subsequent refined models can then be tested and scored. Another standard approach to model validation involves drawing two random samples from the data. The first sample is used as a calibration sample to build the model, while the second is used as a holdout sample to evaluate the model built from the calibration sample (Peacock, 1998b, 15–25). The validation process requires a knowledgeable IT professional, because when data subtleties

that arise only in the sample are used to build the model, the model may be highly predictive of the sample but biased with regard to the population (Shaw *et al.,* 2001). This is called overfitting the data. To avoid creating a biased model, the IT professional must be knowledgeable of the analytical procedure and possess a basic understanding of the hotel segment and promotional scenario from which the sample was extracted.

Guideline #3: *Collect data to support the models.* Accurate data collection is critical for successful data mining. The major obstacle to effective data mining, however, is inadequate data gathering and input (Smith, 2001, 36–37). Data problems lead to a decrease in the value of any data warehouse, in addition to diminishing the value of proposed models (Shaw *et al.,* 2001). Problems with data are related to one or more of at least three different shortcomings.

The first possible difficulty involves missing or inaccurate data. For example, when occupation information is available for only 15 percent of a data set, it is difficult to create a profile of customer occupations. Then again, it's a problem if the data file contains occupation information for 90 percent of the population, but the accuracy of the information is poor. Hotel corporations can reduce inaccuracy of this kind by asking guests for their current occupation.

A second obstacle is poorly coded data. Databases must have standards regarding data formats, text case, and redundant codes (Stevens, 2001b). Although some software automatically formats the data properly, most do not. Problems then occur when data-input sources are added over an extended time and no one has ensured that the data entering the warehouse is properly formatted. This would occur, for instance, if, when original data mining technology was installed, predictions were made based on the reservations system and the property-management system, but then a subsequent decision was made to input data from guest-satisfaction surveys. Problems would transpire when additional data inputs are not standard or are coded improperly. For example, some models require continuous and ordinal data, while others demand categorical data fields or binary constructs (Siragusa, 2001).

A third potential problem involves using homonyms (that is, putting the same label on two or more different data elements) and synonyms (that is, using two different labels for the same data element) (Chopoorian *et al.,* 2001, 45–51). While it may seem tautological to advise precluding this occurrence, the most common culprit is a new user on the system. It is common for hotel and IT professionals to change companies from time to time.

Turnover causes coding problems when new employees bring their old labels and fail to use their new employer's framework.

Guideline #4: *Select the appropriate tools for analysis and prediction.* Numerous analytical tools can be employed to transform data into useful information. Some of the less-common analytical tools used by data mining software include regression models, factor analysis, cluster analysis, structural equation modeling, and self-organizing maps. On the other hand, the most common statistical methods used in data mining applications are decision trees, neural networks, and genetic algorithms. As previously mentioned, a decision tree is a rule-based model constructed of nodes (decision points) and branches (connections between nodes) that reach numerous outcomes based on traveling through two or more nodes. A neural network is a nonlinear predictive model that resembles a biological neural system and has the ability to learn through training. Last, a genetic algorithm is a learning-based model founded on the concept of evolution. That is, partial solutions to a scenario compete with each other, and then the best solutions are used for further problem solving (Hair *et al.,* 1998).

Most of the statistical methods employ techniques that achieve a desired outcome. Likewise, each methodology has strengths and weaknesses, and each is appropriate for a specific scenario. Therefore, the most effective results emanate from data miners who have the expertise to select the most appropriate statistical method for a given scenario and the hotel's intended goals (Siragusa, 2001). For instance, a positive attribute of genetic algorithms is that they converge on an optimal solution, but the method is most applicable to large databases since arriving at a valid outcome may require many generations of competing solutions. Likewise, there are also pros and cons associated with neural networks. They are beneficial in analyzing complex data because of their ability to discover unusual trends, but monitoring accuracy is difficult because many intricate relationships are handled invisibly by the methodology (Hair *et al.,* 1998).

Guideline #5: *Demand timely output.* Timeliness is critical in making marketing decisions. The length of time required to produce output varies widely among data mining packages. Before Hilton Corporation upgraded its data mining technology, for instance, the reports that managers requested from IT would take three to six weeks to arrive. "By the time they'd get the report, it was often too late to act on it," said Joanne Flinn, vice president of leisure marketing. With the new technology, managers receive reports in 30 minutes or less (Stevens, 2001b).

Guideline #6: *Refine the process.* By its nature, data mining involves knowledge that evolves over time. Never complete, data mining involves a continuous cycle of inputs and outputs based on models that must be modified and refined as conditions change in the competitive environment. Flexibility is needed to adapt the established models and processes to changes that occur (Cline, 2000). Refinement consists of three actions:

1. Chart progress toward initial goals. Use the forecasting function of data mining to regularly set new goals.

2. Compare and contrast the characteristics of the clustering output with the attributes of the classification output. When necessary, modify predictive models based on changes in the size or structure of customers' market segments. For instance, notable variances in purchase patterns in one segment and similarities in purchase patterns among other segments may lead to refinement of the segment, usually by adding a new criterion or dimension. This action can result in the discovery of previously undetected segments with homogenous characteristics.

3. In addition to clustering and classification features of data mining, also use the associations and deviation-detection functions to assess the effects of promotions. Maintain a promotional history table in the database to use as a learning tool for future campaigns and models (Siragusa, 2001).

Guideline #7: *Hire a well-trained staff and a knowledgeable IT manager.* Information technology was initially viewed by the hotel industry as a back-office function that supports the finance and accounting areas (Cline, 2000). The industry has advanced far beyond this view during the past decade. In two sessions sponsored by the International Hotel and Restaurant Association (IH&RA), one in Singapore in 1997 and the second in Nice, France, in 1998, hotel-industry leaders pondered the role of technology. Among the conclusions reached were: "Going forward, technology will be the most competitive weapon for any hospitality company. If hospitality organizations want to compete successfully, they must do so by using technology to drive value to both the customer and to the firm" (Olsen and Connolly, 1999, 29). However, implementing such recommendations at the property level can be a difficult task.

Training is a key to effective implementation of data mining systems. Productive data mining requires two-fold proficiency among both IT managers and those who interpret the outputs.

The hotel's IT managers must also be proficient with the data mining system because the system requires continuous refinement. Just as market segments, sources of data, and property goals change, so must predictive models and analyses be modified and refined. It is an unsound policy for the IT staff to be totally dependent on the provider's recommendations for refinement and alterations. Instead, the IT staff and data mining provider should work together, with their common goal being to maximize the technology's effectiveness. The most effective data mining projects occur when IT managers and providers collaborate and share project information.

Second, adequate training must be provided to all potential users of data mining outputs. At the corporate level this includes the marketing staff, operations managers, and those developing new properties. Users at the property level include general managers, directors of sales and marketing, and the sales staff. Users must be instructed about the available reports and how to properly interpret the information. Since the information is used for decision making, it is important for users to understand the boundaries and limitations of the information.

▶ BOUNDARIES AND LIMITATIONS

Technology must serve managers' purposes, rather than dictate processes (Chudnow, 2001, 28–29). Along that line, data mining cannot capture all the information relating to what drives consumer behavior. Data mining is simply one of a number of research methods that help predict travelers' demand trends. Therefore, data mining technology should be used in conjunction with other forecasting and research techniques. With this in mind,

managers should be aware of the following four limitations of data mining technology.

Limitation #1: *Data mining analyzes only data collected from existing customers.* Data mining software generates information by analyzing data patterns derived from the company's reservation, property-management, and guest-loyalty-program systems. Patterns thus detected can help predict the actions of current guests in the system and of those with similar needs and wants. Data mining technology does not, however, provide information about market segments not found in the company's databases. Moreover, a market segment that is currently small but is on the verge of experiencing substantial growth may not be detected by data mining.

Another blind spot is the data in competitors' reservation systems. A key question in planning a marketing strategy in the hotel industry is: Who are my competitors' guests and where are they coming from? Data mining technology is unable to answer those questions.

Limitation #2: *Databases used in the mining process are often hotel-brand specific.* Just as data mining cannot analyze competitors' markets, it also creates prediction models that are brand specific. Thus, corporations that operate multiple brands often must create a data warehouse and conduct data mining for each brand. This is also true for the franchisees that may have a portfolio comprising, say, six Holiday Inns and four Marriotts.

Brand-specific marketing information is useful for the brand's corporate office to plan marketing programs, which is largely what franchisees purchase. Conversely, brand-specific marketing information may not be helpful if the hotel corporation that franchises numerous brands wants to predict customer demand based on a multiple-brand portfolio.

PSYCHOLOGICAL DETERMINANTS OF DEMAND

Education
Escape
Family bonding
Prestige
Relaxation
Self-discovery

Sexual opportunity
Social interaction

Source: P. Kotler, J. Bowen, and J. Makens, *Marketing for Hospitality and Tourism,* 2nd ed. (Upper Saddle River, NJ: Prentice-Hall, 1999).

Limitation #3: *Data mining may not segment travelers by psychographic traits.* Segmenting consumers based on psychographic traits, such as personality and lifestyle, can be useful in the hotel industry. This is because psychology and emotion play significant roles in the hotel guest's decision process. That is, as seen in the sidebar "Psychological Determinants of Demand," a traveler may select a destination for a variety of psychological reasons (Kotler *et al.,* 1999). One limitation of data mining is that common system inputs do not account for psychological factors that influence a traveler's purchase decision.

A time-tested tool used in understanding hospitality demand trends is Stanley Plog's psychographic scale (Plog, 2001, 13–24). Many key drivers of demand identified by Plog, such as personality distribution among travelers (e.g., dependables, venturers, and centrics), are not common inputs into data mining systems. Hotels can acquire this information from customer surveys.

Limitation #4: *Data mining does not provide information about consumers' thought processes.* It is important to engage consumers in research to better understand their thinking. Information generated by data mining does not account for the fact that approximately 80 percent of human communication is nonverbal (Zaltman, 1997, 424–437). Interviews and focus groups are both useful methods for gathering information about the needs and wants of hotel guests. The insight gained from those techniques is difficult to capture in the statistical data mining outputs. That is why it is important to step back and ask what the hotel guest's inherent needs are and what the product is really about. This involves conducting in-depth conversations with guests. At times, improved insight and perspective are gained from talking with three customers for two hours rather than by surveying a thousand customers (Ohmae, 1999).

► CONCLUSION AND MANAGERIAL IMPLICATIONS

Data mining technology can be a useful tool for hotel corporations that want to understand and predict guest behavior. Based on information derived from data mining, hotels can make well-informed marketing decisions—including who should be contacted, to whom to offer incentives (or not), and what type of relationship to establish.

Data mining is currently used by a number of industries, including hotels, restaurants, auto manufacturers, movie-rental chains, and coffee purveyors. Firms adopt data mining to understand the data captured by scanner terminals, customer-survey responses, reservation records, and property-management transactions. This information can be melded into a single data set that is mined for nuggets of information by data mining experts who are familiar with the hotel industry.

However, data mining is no guarantee of marketing success. Hotels must first ensure that existing data are managed—and that requires investments in hardware and software systems, data mining programs, communications equipment, and skilled personnel. Affiliated properties must also understand that data mining can increase business and profits for the entire company and should not be viewed as a threat to one location. As seen in the Harrah's example, implementing a data mining system is a complex and time-consuming process.

We advise hospitality managers to adopt a data mining system and strategy if they have not done so. Guidelines presented in this paper—including how to select and manage the data mining provider—offer guidance for implementing a viable data mining strategy. Since data mining is in its initial stages in the hotel industry, early adopters may be able to secure a faster return on investment than will property managers who lag in their decisions. Hotel corporations must also share data among properties and divisions to gain a richer and broader knowledge of the current customer base. Management must ensure that hotel employees use the data-management system to interact with customers even though it is more time consuming than a transactional approach.

REFERENCES

Borchgrevink, C. P., and R.S. Schmidgall. 1995. "Budgeting Practices of U.S. Lodging Firms." *Bottomline* 10(5):13–17.

Brandel, M. 2001. "Spinning Data into Gold." *Computerworld* (May) 26:67–70.

Chamberlain, D. 1991. "A Written Budget Is a Valuable Tool for Tracking Your Meeting Dollars." *Successful Meetings* 40(6):89–90.

Chopoorian, J., R. Witherell, O. Khalil, and M. Ahmed. 2001. "Mind Your Business by Mining Your Data." *S.A.M. Advanced Management Journal* 66(2):45–51.

Chudnow, C. 2001. "Knowledge Management Tools." *Computer Technology Review* 21(11): 28–29.

Cichy, Ronald F., and Raymond S. Schmidgall. 1996. "Leadership Qualities of Financial Executives." *Cornell Hotel and Restaurant Administration Quarterly* 37(2):56–62.

Cline, Roger. 2000. "Hospitality 2000: The Capital." *Lodging Hospitality* 56(7):20–23.

Coltman, M.M. 1994. *Hospitality Management Accounting,* 5th ed. New York: Van Nostrand Reinhold.

Damitio, James W., and Raymond S. Schmidgall. 1996. "A Profile of the Lodging Financial Executive." *Bottom Line* (September): 9–11.

DeMyer, J.P., and D. Wang-Kline. 1990. "What's On the Books? A Practical Guide to Forecasting and Budgeting." *Hotel and Resort Industry* 13(1):64.

Dev, C.S., and M.D. Olsen. 2000. "Marketing Challenges for the Next Decade." *Cornell Hotel and Restaurant Administration Quarterly* 41(1):41–47.

DeVeau, Patricia M., and Linsley T. DeVeau. 1988. "A Profile of the CHAE: Gaining Strength in

Numbers." *Bottomline* (October/November): 18–19.

Frawley, W., C. Piatetsky-Shapiro, and C. Matheus. 1992. "Knowledge Discovery in Databases: An Overview." *AI Magazine* (Fall):213–228.

Geller, A. Neal, and Raymond S. Schmidgall. 1984. "The Hotel Controller: More Than a Bookkeeper." *Cornell Hotel and Restaurant Administration Quarterly* 25(2):16–22.

Geller, A. Neal, Charles L. Ilvento, and Raymond S. Schmidgall. 1990. "The Hotel Controller Revisited." *Cornell Hotel and Restaurant Administration Quarterly* 31(3):91–97.

Griffin, Robert K. 1998. "Data Warehousing." *Cornell Hotel and Restaurant Administration Quarterly* 39(4):28–35.

Hair, J., R. Anderson, R. Tatham, and W. Black. 1998. *Multivariate Data Analysis*, 5th ed. Upper Saddle River, NJ: Prentice-Hall.

Kamrani, A., W. Rong, and R. Gonzalez. 2001. "A Genetic Algorithm Methodology for Data Mining and Intelligent Knowledge Acquisition." *Computers and Industrial Engineering* 40(4):361–377.

Karch, R. 1992. "Streamlining Your Hotel Cost." *Hotel and Resort Industry* 15(11):88–90.

Kotler, P., J. Bowen, and J. Makens. 1999. *Marketing for Hospitality and Tourism,* 2nd ed. Upper Saddle River, NJ: Prentice-Hall.

Lacity, P., and R. Hirschheim. 1995. *Beyond the Information Outsourcing Bandwagon.* New York: John Wiley and Sons.

Le Bret, C. 1997. "Have You Heard About Data Mining?" *Science Tribune* (October).

Levinson, M. 2001. "Harrah's Knows What You Did Last Night." *Darwin* (May).

"Mining Hotel Data." 1998. *Data Warehouse Report,* October 20.

Nickell, J.A. 2002. "Welcome to Harrah's." *Business 2.0* (April).

Ohmae, K. 1999. *The Borderless World.* New York: McKinsey and Company.

Olsen, M., and D. Connolly. 1999. "Antecedents of Technological Change in the Hospitality Industry." *Tourism Analysis* 4:29.

Peacock, P.R. 1998a. "Data Mining in Marketing: Part 1." *Marketing Management* (Winter): 9–18.

———. 1998b. "Data Mining in Marketing: Part 2." *Marketing Management* (Spring):15–25.

Plog, S. 2001. "Why Destination Areas Rise and Fall in Popularity." *Cornell Hotel and Restaurant Administration Quarterly* 42(3):13–24.

Press, S. 1998. "Fool's Gold?" *Sales and Marketing Management* (June):58–61.

Schmidgall, R.S. 1989. "While Forecasts Hit Targets, GMs Still Seek Better Guns." *Lodging* 15(3):101–102, 104–105.

Schmidgall, R.S., C.P. Borchgrevink, and O.H. Zahl-Begnum. 1996. "Operations Budgeting Practices of Lodging Firms in the U.S. and Scandinavia." *International Journal of Hospitality Management* 15(2):189–203.

Schmidgall, R.S. 1997. *Hospitality Industry Managerial Accounting,* 4th ed. East Lansing, MI: Educational Institute of the American Hotel and Motel Association.

Schmidgall, Raymond S., and Michael Kasavana. 2000. "Certifications by HFTP." *Bottomline* (April/May):20–22.

Shaw, M., C. Subramaniam, G. Tan, and M. Welge. 2001. "Knowledge Management and Data Mining for Marketing." *Decision Support Systems* (May):127–137.

Siragusa, Thomas J. 2001. "Implementing Data Mining for Better CRM." *Customer Inter@ction Solutions* 19(11):38–41.

Smith, M. 2001. "Refining Raw Data." *Printing Impressions* 43(9):36–37.

Stevens, L. 2001a. "CRM Analytics—CRM by the Slice—Running Analytics Is Expensive, So Companies Are Focusing on Areas with Customers." *Internetweek,* April 9, pp. 35–38.

———. 2001b. "IT Sharpens Data Mining Focus—Instead of Building Data Mining Applications with No Clear Goal, Companies Are Setting Priorities Up Front to Maximize ROI." *Internetweek,* August 6, pp. 29–30.

Temling, W.P., and P. Quek. 1993. "Budget Time." *Lodging* 19(3):21–22.

Tischelle, G., and J. Maselli. 2001. "Hotels Turn to

IT to Stem Losses." *Informationweek,* December 17, pp. 31–32.

Tse, Eliza C., 1989. "A Profile of the IAHA Member." *Bottomline* (October/November):12–18.

Woods, Robert H., Denney G. Rutherford, Raymond S. Schmidgall, and Michael Sciarini.

1998. "Hotel General Managers." *Cornell Hotel and Restaurant Administration Quarterly* 39(6):38–44.

Zaltman, G. 1997. "Rethinking Market Research: Putting People Back In." *Journal of Marketing Research* 34(4):424–437.

SUGGESTED READINGS

Books

Jagels, Martin G., and Michael M. Coltman. 2003. *Hospitality Management Accounting,* 8th ed. New York: John Wiley and Sons.

Schmidgall, R.S. 1997. *Hospitality Industry Managerial Accounting,* 4th ed. East Lansing, MI: Educational Institute of the American Hotel and Motel Association.

Articles

Borchgrevink, C.P., and R.S. Schmidgall. 1995. "Budgeting Practices of U.S. Lodging Firms." *Bottomline* 10(5):13–17.

Cichy, Ronald F., and Raymond S. Schmidgall. 1996. "Leadership Qualities of Financial Executives." *Cornell Hotel and Restaurant Administration Quarterly* 37(2):56–62.

Damitio, James W., and Raymond S. Schmidgall. 1990. "Internal Auditing Practices of Major Lodging Chains." *Hospitality Research Journal* 14(2):255–268.

Dubé, Laurette, Cathy A. Enz, Leo M. Renaghan, and Judy Siguaw. 1999. "Best Practices in the U.S. Lodging Industry—Overview, Methods, and Champions." *Cornell Hotel and Restaurant Administration Quarterly* 40(4):14–27.

Schmidgall, R. S., C. P. Borchgrevink, and O.H. Zahl-Begnum. 1996. "Operations Budgeting Practices of Lodging Firms in the U.S. and Scandinavia." *International Journal of Hospitality Management* 15(2):189–203.

SOURCE NOTES

Chapter 8.2, "The Lodging Chief Financial Executive," by Raymond S. Schmidgall.

Chapter 8.3, "Budgeting and Forecasting: Current Practice in the Lodging Industry," by Raymond S. Schmidgall and Agnes L. DeFranco, is reprinted from the December 1998 issue of *Cornell Hotel and Restaurant Administration Quarterly.* © Cornell University. Used by permission. All rights reserved.

Chapter 8.4, "As I See It: The Hotel Controller," by Mike Draeger.

Chapter 8.5, "The Hotel Purchasing Function," by C. Lee Evans.

Chapter 8.6, "Data Mining for Hotel Firms: Use and Limitations," by Vincent P. Magnini, Earl D. Honeycutt, Jr., and Sharon K. Hodge, is reprinted from the April 2003 issue of *Cornell Hotel and Restaurant Administration Quarterly.* © Cornell University. Used by permission. All rights reserved.

chapter nine

HUMAN RESOURCES POLICY MANAGEMENT

9.1 INTRODUCTION

In the third edition, this section on human resources (HR) became a different creature than it had been in previous editions. It used to be called "The Management and Processes of Human Resources" and included several how-to articles. I now believe the reader will be better served by contemplating broad strategic policy considerations.

Part of this shift in focus grew out of recent research that strongly suggests the future health of any organization will be based on human resources—that is, of course, if HR is called upon by top management for advice on legally and functionally delivering hotel services. A well-managed hotel HR department will be a competitive advantage.

Among observers and participants on the hotel management scene are those who compare human resources, formerly personnel management, to the weather: Everyone talks about it, but no one does anything about it. This is a problem faced by a good many managers. If an HR department is to be effective in dealing with the people they recruit, hire, and train, they need a strategic view of the future and strategies to achieve that view.

It has been said we should be very interested in the future, for that is where we are going to spend the rest of our lives. It has also been said, "Predicting is difficult, especially about the future" (Berra, quoted in Woods, 1999). That was the premise of the lead article in this section of the third edition, by Bob Woods. Now a professor in the Harrah College of Hotel Administration at the University of Nevada, Las Vegas, Woods suggested that for this edition he convene a select panel of his colleagues at UNLV and, using a variation of a predictive model, discuss the future based on what these researchers and teachers know about present and foreseeable trends. Their wide-ranging and instructive discussion of the future challenges to HR is presented in 9.2.

Perhaps the most insidious and pervasive human resource challenge the above-mentioned group addressed was turnover. For whatever reasons, lots of employees leave hotel companies, and whenever they do, it is expensive—not only to the hotel but also to the employees. That is why Riegel's presentation of a conceptual model of turnover is an important inclusion here. This material updates research he and two colleagues did among foodservice employees, but the conceptual model holds equally well for hotel employees. It is included here because in many ways the strategic concepts of legal environment, HR professionalism, and management respect are avenues to control or reduce turnover.

In a series of guest lectures in my class at Washington State University, Jim Treadway, formerly president of Westin Hotels and Resorts—North America and currently president and CEO of MTM Management L.L.C., outlined how he sees the job of hotel general manager. Among the components of his "job description" is "to keep the owners out of jail," by which he means the GM must manage the business without incurring legal trouble and must avoid all possible risk of liability. The essay by Murrmann and Becker on the legal environment discusses the realms of risk facing hotels and their human resources departments. Increasingly, hotels are finding themselves at legal risk for hiring "high-risk employees." The most professional HR departments are aware of and prepared to ad-vise their internal customers (department heads and the GM) how to employ the best people without running afoul of the ever-increasing regulatory and liability environment. See also the essay by Melissa Dallas in Section 5.

Reinforcing the importance of considering the HR function in a strategic light rather than an enabling one is the article included here by Tracey and Nathan. They argue that because human capital considerations are top-of-mind in research and trade publications, leadership still fails to consider HR when making strategic plans and that many firms are still mired in archaic policies and practices that threaten business activities in the business and regulatory environment. They argue their position cogently and with vigor; see if you agree with them.

There is no lack of research and commentary in hospitality publications, both academic and trade, that deal with human resources. Many of the articles and essays in this book could be and should be looked at with an eye toward their implications for the management of human resources in a hotel. Perhaps second only to marketing, human resources is the most written-about topic in not only the academic but also the trade press. Readers are encouraged to find publications that offer solid, practical, objective, and legally valid advice for aid in determining their individual model of how a human resources philosophy and its resultant practices should be designed. A good place to start is the list of suggested readings and references at the end of the chapter.

9.2 DRIVING HOSPITALITY INTO THE FUTURE[1]

Christian Hardigree, Ellis Norman, Gail Sammons, Vince Eade, William Werner, Robert H. Woods[2] and Cheri Young

It has been five years since the publication of "Predicting Is Difficult, Especially About the Future: The Future of Human Resources in Hospitality Management," the journal article used in the third edition of this book (Woods, 1999). As Yogi Berra would say, since then, the future has changed. Indeed, the future has changed, and it is time to attempt to forecast it once again.

Time flies. Ten years ago, decoding the human genome was a pipe dream (Mack, 2005). Five years ago, terrorism was something that people outside the United States had to worry about. As Mack noted, "Imagine if you could have understood the potential for such monumental changes before they happened" (Mack, 2005). The value of predicting the future is evidenced by the fact that major corporations spend millions of dollars annually on studying the big picture, or macroenvironmental analysis, as most strategic planners call it. Futurists, those who predict the future, often call this a *six-sector analysis,* but it's the same thing. A six-sector analysis uses trends and forecasts in technology, economics, environment, society, demography, and government to predict the future. One can easily imagine the changes that have occurred in these six sectors since 1999.

In this article, we use what might be called a seven-person analysis—that is, the insight of seven experienced professors from the University of Nevada—Las Vegas to predict the future. These seven professors have experi-

ence in a wide range of areas and were asked to lend their expertise to predicting the future of HR in the hospitality industry. What follows is an edited transcript of a lengthy discussion among these seven professors on this subject. We start with a discussion of the impact of unions in the hospitality HR future and range widely from there.

Note: This chapter has seven authors. Each is identified by name, and quotes are associated with each throughout. For instance, the first quote is from William (Bill) Werner, the second from Cheri Young, and so on. Topics are presented in random order.

Werner: One of the big issues human resources managers will have to think about in the future is whether health care is or is not a natural right of every employee. Recently there was a merger between the hotel employees union and the restaurant employees union. The resulting merger is a union of about 500,000 members. One of the big discussions between these unions has been about even trying to merge with more unions and to follow the current corporate pattern of merger and acquisition. Employers are going to have to find a way to find a middle ground with the union stance that employees pay nothing for health care benefits, no matter what other bargaining positions the unions might assume. Eventually, this is something with which every employer is going to have to come to terms. Health care among union workers has become an expected normal benefit of employment, but the cost is rising so fast, basically out of control, and employers are going to have to come to terms with this.

Young: Only 8.2 percent of the private sector employees are unionized in the United States. Union membership has steadily declined from its peak decades ago and is at an all-time low. One question to ask of the future is whether this trend will continue. Mergers among unions may be able to counter that decline, or the decline in union membership may continue.

Werner: The political power of unions is the one thing that they still have to hang on to, and their political strength in Washington particularly really is the one thing that unions are still able to claim, despite their declining membership. Even if unions do not increase membership, they are likely to be able to hold on to what they have through amalgamation and mergers. The question is, will unions be able to turn declining membership into increasing membership? The only way to do this is through union organizing efforts. Therefore, we are likely to see more of such efforts in the future. Unions are not likely to continue to decline without a fight, and that fight comes through organizing efforts. This means human resources departments and managers are more likely to need to address union issues in the future than they have in many years. Because unions have steadily declined, many human resources managers may not ever have had to address this issue in the past. Since hospitality organizations (and hospitality human resources professionals) today have little experience with unions because they have not played a major role in recent years, they are likely to have to devote time and money to learning how to address such needs in the future.

Eade: In the 1940s, unions represented about 30 percent of the workers in the United States. According to the Bureau of Labor Statistics, today unions represent about 12–14 percent of workers in all industries.

Norman: According to statistics recently released, unions now represent only about 12.9 percent of the workers in the United States.

Eade: While unions have been declining, cooperation between unions and hospitality organizations may not be headed in the same direction. There might be more cooperation in the future. There is significant evidence of this here in Las Vegas, where one can find several models of training and development cooperation between organizations and unions. Such mutually beneficial developments might hinder the growth of union membership in the future, or it might result in more growth. At any rate, such cooperation might mean there are fewer, not more, union organizing efforts in the future.

Werner: These cooperative efforts are interesting. The largest hotel and restaurant workers' unions have recently noted that they actually have a dual agenda—that is, working cooperatively with organizations that are good to their employees and fighting like dogs with those which are not. In 2004, for instance, we saw the demise of the Golden Horseshoe hotel and casino in Las Vegas. This demise began with a culinary union strike 11 years ago over health benefits. The union kept up their efforts for 11 years! When unions are pushed to the wall, they will fight.

The interesting part about the mergers we are seeing, however, is that unions with different special skills are merging. In hospitality, we have seen the merger of a union with special skills in organizing with one that has special skills in striking employers.

To me, this means that unions are likely to start going after companies which have been traditionally non-union in the past.

Young: It is my understanding that at one time unions fought against open immigration laws because they believed that immigrants would take jobs from union workers. However, in recent years some unions have adopted a policy of welcoming immigrants. For instance, UNITE here in Las Vegas is largely made up of recently immigrated Latinos and Asians. The rapid population growth of these two ethnic groups would seem to indicate that some unions are likely to be able to exert more pressure on hospitality organizations in the future.

Woods: Much of the future on this topic might be attributed to the outcome of current political efforts to extend amnesty to illegal immigrants already in the United States. If this is done, are we not more likely to see an increase in hospitality industry union membership?

Werner: This does seem likely, doesn't it?

Eade: Many recent immigrants working in the hospitality industry have jobs in departments such as housekeeping in hotels. Because of this, some form of amnesty for illegal aliens certainly seems like it might affect how hospitality human resources managers work with employees in such departments.

It seems to me that one of the big issues in the future for hospitality unions will be outsourcing of jobs.

Young: Yes, I read recently where some California hotels were sending their laundry to Mexico, having it washed and shipped back, thus outsourcing jobs. When we think of outsourcing we typically think of this happening in manufacturing sector jobs, but this example indicates how it might happen in service industries as well.

Norman: There are already hotels that outsource all of their food and beverage operations, not to foreign countries but outside the organization nevertheless. This is a different type of outsourcing, but an important one to unions, as non-union companies are providing the food and beverage operations. This means a net loss in jobs for unions.

Eade: The point is that in the future these will be life-and-death issues for unions. We tend to look at issues such as this from the organizational viewpoint. From that perspective, such developments might be relatively small issues. However, for unions they are life-or-death issues.

Werner: The bottom line is that unions in the hospitality industry will be forced to attempt to increase membership. Some hospitality unions today have almost as many retirees as members as they have currently employed workers. Some unions seem to have taken the position today that they can get more new members by attempting to decrease the workload of employees. For example, would union efforts to reduce the workload of housekeepers from an average of 16 rooms cleaned daily to an average of 12 rooms lead to increased membership, or would attempting to maintain health care benefits for members be better for increasing membership? The unions deal with strategic issues such as this all of the time; they are always trying to predict what will be important in the future for their members. It may be that more immediately tangible efforts such as reducing workloads would lead to more new members than benefit extensions.

Sammons: An issue that concerns unions in the casino industry is the rapid and continuing development of casinos on Native American land. My understanding is that National

Labor Relations Laws do not apply to such locations because they are on Native American land. Interestingly, unions fought against Native American casinos because they believed that such organizations would take away union jobs. Now that this fight is lost and these casinos are growing rapidly, unions would like to be able to organize their workers. Politics breeds strange bedfellows, doesn't it?

Hardigree: Actually, some of the casinos that are being built on Native American land may have to adhere to NLRB (National Labor Relations Board) requirements. For instance, they do not if they are wholly owned tribal entities, but they do if they are a partnership with a gaming organization such as Harrah's or MGM.

Actually, I want to make sure that there's a difference between what laws apply to a wholly owned tribal entity versus a partnership with a Caesar's or a Harrah's or something like that. Because if there is that partnership, they do have a requirement to adhere to the NLRB. This also applies if the manager is employed by a non–Native American organization.

This is significant to unions because 5 of the 25 top-grossing casinos in the United States are tribal facilities, but some of them are partnerships with nontribal companies.

Young: This brings up a related issue because the human resources skills needed to manage in Native American casinos may be somewhat different than the HR skills needed in other sectors of the industry. Human resources professionals would have to understand the importance of tribal cultural and work ethic issues, for instance. These casinos are providing jobs to some Native Americans who have not worked in years, for instance. The HR challenges that might be

faced in such an environment are new for most managers.

Hardigree: Such issues are not limited to Native American casinos. For instance, I did some work on employee training in St. Croix, U.S. Virgin Islands. In the island culture, as many people know, time is not as important as it is here on the mainland. One of the training issues that I faced was training employees that they had to show up for work at a specific time. In some cases I found properties that were not opening on time simply because their workforce had not showed up yet. People unfamiliar with human resources in the islands will have to learn how to address such issues in the future.

Woods: The responsibility of human resources departments and managers to address the culture of their workforce seems to be a pervasive issue. This is as true in the United States today as it is in foreign countries. There are many hospitality properties in which the employees are predominantly from another culture and even speak another language. I remember a few years ago talking to a general manager from a hotel in Toronto who said that there were 60 different languages spoken by employees in his hotel. This is certainly a problem that hospitality companies did not have to address 20 years ago.

Norman: I agree, we sometimes forget to think about the impact of subcultures here in the United States. Some employees from other cultures do things a certain way before they eat and before they work and they don't show up when you want them to for various reasons. A question for human resources in the future is whether or not the organization can prescribe strict rules and absolutes as they have in the past. First you have to understand the way things work within the subculture, then you can attempt to effect policies that apply. This means that human resources will become more complicated in the future. This becomes an issue of addressing the diversity of all employees, not simply those who are obviously from another country. In the past employers have been able to say simply, "This is the rule for everyone." In the future this may not be so easy to do, as it has become incumbent on organizations to think about the individual diversity of its employees, too.

Hardigree: This is the issue in many "English-only" cases. English-only refers to organizations that prohibit employees from speaking their native language while at work. To managers this might seem logical—that is, employees speaking a different language might be threatening simply because you don't know what they are talking about. Whether or not the same rules will be applied for everyone in such cases might lead to significant HR issues in the future as well.

Woods: I recently read an article from a futurist who believes that the clash of cultures in organizations—that is, the clash between the cultures of so-called native (or American) employees and managers and foreign cultures—could easily destabilize organizations in the future.

Young: It seems obvious that, in the future, hospitality managers will certainly need to be more culturally sensitive and flexible than they have in the past. Hospitality organizations will be challenged to get the most out of their human capital but within the parameters of the cultural values of their employees. This brings up some interesting challenges. For instance, our notions about motivation are based on our model, the American model of motivation. Some might call this the white Anglo-Saxon motivation model because this is who it has applied to in the past. Much has been written about motivation with this set of employees. However, in the future managers will also need to know how to motivate employees from culturally diverse backgrounds as well. This means that managers and HR professionals will need expertise in areas that they are not today prepared to deliver. This, of course, will mean training in these (and perhaps other) areas will become more important in the future. Whether this means hospitality organizations will have to spend more time and money on training in the future is not clear, but it certainly seems that is the case.

Werner: When I was in grade school, we used to hear a lot about America as the melting pot of the world. The American ideal then seemed to be that anyone could come to this country and start over. However, the significant thing about that phrase is that it meant that those people would be gradually melted into the mix and everyone would come out the same. We thought then about a "typical American." There is much more appreciation today for diversity, and that has been a significant change in American society during my lifetime. Today there is more emphasis on diversity and less on assimilation through melting peoples together.

Corporate cultures appear to have emphasized the melting pot approach for many years. Everyone wanted to create a corporate culture and assimilate everyone into that one culture. Now we see the reverse of that at work. In the future we may see people believing that the best approach is to forget corporate culture. Instead we may see people thinking of corporations simply as legal entities without personality. If so, the emphasis then will be on employee personalities, not corporate personalities.

Young: I disagree on that because I think organizations do have a personality. We call it corporate culture and it ends up being a social organization. There's a whole social system in there and how people relate and get their needs met and power and politics and you name it. Looking at culture as something you created as a corporate control mechanism might have been prevalent at one time but not today or in the future. I believe that we have finally acknowledged this as a myth, that we have finally come to realize that we actually do have all these subcultures in organizations. Today we should think not of a melting pot but of a soup or stew. Now we see all these identifiable pieces floating around in the stew. Now and in the future HR people will have to peer into that soup and figure out how to make things work for all the ingredients.

Norman: For instance, in Native American and Latino cultures, family is more important than it is in what has been known as the mainstream culture in the past. Family is the number-one priority in these and other cultures. Family is more important than work. The impact of this on work-based motivation practices in the future will be interesting to see. In the traditional theory of motivation we have understood that certain practices by employers will lead to improved work performance by employees. This is not necessarily true for all cultures.

Young: The same thing could be said about Generation X. Much has been written about the failure of Generation X to put work first in their lives. Quality of life appears to be more important to this group than to past generations. Quality of life is a priority over work in some cases. This group wants to believe that quality of life is more important than some work-related issues.

Woods: This all seems to tie together for HR in the future, doesn't it? Whether or not employees will be unionized might depend on

organizational approaches to diversity and cultural awareness, or even on how employees are motivated to work. It is a big challenge for HR.

Norman: What is interesting to me is that in some organizations training seems to focus on do's and don'ts pretty exclusively. Attempts to match the employee with the organizational culture are not as prevalent as trying to make employees behave in organizationally specific ways. For instance, I recently worked with an organization on casino card-dealer training. In this instance, the organization was spending quite a lot of time training dealers in technical skills that they will seldom use. For example, dealers are taught how to perform card tricks like fancy shuffling and things like that. They will never use these skills in most cases, but this is the emphasis in training. In comparison, orientation for these groups consists primarily of a discussion of what actions will get you fired. In effect, there is no effort to attempt to identify the person with the property and its values.

In the casino industry, most managers came up the old way, the "hard way," as they describe it. This means that they started as an employee, worked their way up to supervisor and then to manager. These people have good technical skills; that is likely why they were promoted. However, they may never have had any experience or training in interpersonal skills—that is, managing people. Yet, how the human capital of the organization will be managed and motivated will likely determine the company's future success. The HR department of the future will likely have to address more managerial training than it has in the past.

Woods: For several years we have been seeing and reading about the lack of employee and managerial loyalty in organizations. Most predictions are that people will bounce from company to company in the future. In the past, of course, managers and employees worked for one organization most of their lives. Predictions are that people will probably follow a pattern of working for one organization for five or six years, then moving on to another. In some cases these people will move from one industry to another, taking time off between the two to retrain. Since most current employees and managers produce at higher levels than new employees and managers, this becomes an issue of how to make work interesting enough for people to stay. Getting people not to quit then will become a focus of HR in the future.

I'm glad you brought up managers, Ellis. I think the human resources department of the future will spend more time on managerial human resource issues that aren't employee human resource issues because of the changing nature of the managerial workforce. All the predictions are, and we see this already, that people will not stay in the same job their entire career. They will probably follow a pattern of working five or six years in one organization, then may take a sabbatical for six months and retrain for another career or retrain for another year. So, I think what we'll see is more people moving from career to career—maybe not in the same industry—and that poses interesting problems for the human resources department.

Hardigree: And this might mean that HR personnel will be training older and older workers and managers in the future. It might become more common for HR people to have to know how to recruit, hire, and train employees and managers who are older in the future as a result. As these people bounce from career to career, they will need additional training at ages we are just not used to training.

Woods: When you combine this movement between jobs with retirement issues for baby boomers, the problem becomes exacerbated. The baby boom population is starting to retire now and will retire in greater numbers in the future. HR people will need to decide how to address that issue in the future as well. This means not only how to address retirement issues for managers and employees but also how to address replacing that worker. Will it lead to downsized organizations, which cannot find enough employees in the future, or will the employees simply change dramatically as we have discussed earlier—that is, will workers from other cultures predominate? It seems that organizations will have to make a decision about which direction to go and, either way, more training will be required. It could also lead to increased job design changes, too. Will we change how work is done to accomplish it with fewer people, or will we simply employ a different type of worker?

Young: I know of one 82-year-old cocktail server at a hotel. Think of the problems associated with working with this type of workforce when you are accustomed to working with a young workforce.

Norman: In the past, we read predictions about how baby boomers were going to have such a huge impact on leisure and hospitality industries, and we have certainly seen this. More and more people are taking advantage of leisure activities today than in the past, and this has certainly helped to increase revenues for hospitality companies. However, there are also indications that baby boomers will not necessarily opt to retire for many reasons, from personal to economic. One characteristic of the baby boomer population is the active lifestyle of its members. Some people are working out more, exercising more, and working later into life. The rapid changes in medical care and life expectancy are affecting this too, of course. Some people simply work longer because they live longer.

Woods: This might certainly mean that eldercare issues will become more prevalent for HR, too. We think of eldercare today as how to address the issues of older citizens, but these people may also be employees. HR will have to deal not only with how to address the challenges employees face from taking care of both elderly parents and children, but also the issue of how to make work accessible and meaningful for a more elderly population.

Hardigree: HR already has to address the issue of younger workers who believe they are ready for management, or managers who want to move up but can't because the baby boom population is blocking their path. Baby boomers are not leaving these positions as quickly as predicted, and as the next generation is coming of age they feel they are entitled to move up—but those positions are not opening up. I think this also contributes to people moving back and going into different careers and reeducating themselves as they move. This also leads to disgruntled managers and employees, some of whom have come to think of older employees as roadblocks to their own careers.

Young: The impact of baby boomers on retirement issues is still four or five years away, but not long. What will happen when this population attains retirement age will certainly impact hospitality.

Werner: This issue of moving from job to job and career to career will depend on the rate of unemployment prevalent at the time. People who once enjoyed the opportunities associated with jumping from job to job and telling their employers to take this job and shove it will be greatly influenced by the impact of unemployment issues. That approach is okay with low unemployment, but what happens with high unemployment? You can't jump from job to job as easily when unemployment is 10 to 12 percent.

In the future, HR people may need to adapt to their organization rather than vice versa. I think of this like coaching basketball. There are coaches who are very well known for their strategy, and they create a program and then they find people to put in it. Then there are other coaches that take whatever talent they have and make the most of it. I think that continues to be just different managerial skills and techniques. It will be interesting to see which type of manager, or coach, prevails in the future. One would think that those who can adapt will succeed more.

Norman: I recently read a book about going from good to best. According to this, the enemy of best is good. It reminded me of Steve Wynn, the casino icon in Las Vegas. You ask Steve Wynn if he's got a mission statement; he doesn't have one. What he does do is get the right people on the bus to begin with. His approach is to find the best possible people and go with that instead of attempting to force everyone into one mold.

Young: Some people see human capital as an asset worth investing in because they believe that the employee is capable of generating revenues in the future. One thing that organizations must surely do in the future is develop ways of accounting for the value or worth of employees on the balance sheet. Because people in organizations make indirect contributions, most companies do not do this today. The HR people have stomped their feet up and down and said nobody thinks that we're important, nobody thinks we're important. The problem is that HR has not been able to equate human capital to dollars, so the people making decisions today in organizations cannot relate. HR people are finally figuring out that if they compute human capital in financial terms, they will get more. One mission of HR in the future is to learn how to do this better.

Eade: Work performance will be a more important term in the future. The human performance of people can make a difference in organizations, and HR is finally figuring that out. Organizations need a department of human performance that spends all of its time assessing performance and figuring out how to do things better. This is not just performance for the bottom line but performance for and by people.

Some organizations are doing this through training programs such as how to manage your household, or parenting skills, or how to plan retirement. It comes down to organizations showing that they care about employees. They have to show that they are attempting to improve performance in all areas, not just in the bottom line. These are likely the organizations that will attract and keep the best people in the future.

Young: Organizations need to assess and define the benefits of such programs. They need to answer the question of why they should train people in parenting skills, for instance. The answer is in empowerment. As people learn how to better manage their lives, they gain a sense of control over their environment, and that helps them to perform better. Hopefully these same employees will make the connection between what the organization is doing for them and commitment or loyalty to the organization.

Eade: It's either this or move to inde-

pendent contractor status with employees, and that seems worse. We seem to be moving toward the independent contractor type of relationship between organizations and employees.

Woods: I read recently that the half-life of an engineer's knowledge is now six months. This means that college freshmen will have to renew their knowledge base five or six times during their college careers. Just think how this might affect the workplace. I wonder how true this is for hospitality management education?

Young: Another issue for hospitality is how women are treated. Housekeeping is a female ghetto in many organizations. Let's get a woman to be the director of rooms or the CEO or the VP of finance.

Norman: In the 1980s, the executive housekeeper reported not to the GM or the executive committee but to a person three or four rungs below. We have made progress, but it's slow.

Hardigree: We still use lots of sexist terms in hospitality. We also have jobs reserved for one gender or another. For instance, we still use cocktail waitresses in most properties, and too often they are still hired on the basis of height and weight. Not everyone is five foot nine and 125 pounds, and hospitality needs to address that in the future. Many customers today want to see a diversity of employees in places they frequent, partially because they, too, are diverse. Customers like to see employees who look and act like they do.

Christian: From an Asian standpoint, am I discriminating against Asians because I require all my dancers to be five foot nine or taller?

Young: Now are there lawsuits coming up about this?

Christian: I've seen a few claims. I don't know if they've resulted in full-blown litigation. Cosmetic practices, such as use of terms like *cocktail models* to avoid the gender-specific term *waitress,* just do not do the trick.

Werner: The average hospitality discrimination case results in a judgment of only about $7,500. As a result, many companies are not too concerned about this issue. Most customers believe that the awards are much higher. This is an example of a fundamental philosophy that needs to change in hospitality.

Eade: This issue of segmenting women for certain types of jobs, even specific shifts, needs to change to satisfy the customer base. For years companies got away with saying that women could be security guards, but not at night . . . and things like that. In fact, one case that did go to court resulted in a win by the company, which said they were only thinking about the safety of the female guard in question. Today we have female soldiers dying in war, and this has forced some companies to rethink their position on such issues.

Hardigree: In some cases, changes in this type of issue must wait for the courts to catch up. For instance, in one case a man with disabilities wanted to do a job that the company thought was too dangerous for him. He sued, and the company won. The court believed the company was only trying to protect the employee from himself.

I strongly believe that one of the changes we will see in the future is more acceptability of sexual orientation issues. Today, there are only about 12 states that protect employees based on sexual orientation. Some of these may actually repeal their laws on this issue, sensing that the public mood has changed. The public mood may or may not have changed, but what companies need to be afraid of is using gender discrimination to bootstrap a sexual orientation claim.

Young: The whole issue of whether or not to extend benefits to gay partners really raises the larger issue of who should receive benefits. What do you do about two heterosexuals who have lived together for 15 years? Many people today are living together and having children outside marriage. They are going to start screaming for benefits as well, and this may be a significant issue in hospitality.

Woods: We may find that the more we disenfranchise people, the more viable they become as a political entity. I expect this to happen within hospitality due to the large number of gays and lesbians employed there.

Sammons: One of the cultural issues we are likely to deal with in the future is the growth of spirituality in the workplace. I don't mean just religious spirituality, but all kinds. As more and more people serve in overseas positions, they are likely to bring back new and different kinds of spirituality to their workplace.

Woods: I read the same thing in a futurist publication recently. Many futurists believe that organizations will be forced to address the spirituality of their employees soon.

Sammons: One issue I see being more important in the future is that of training. I mean who and what we train. Some companies are outsourcing training; others are keeping it inside their companies. Organizations will decide which approach they want to pursue. The objective for most companies will be how to acquire needed training at the lowest cost. Sometimes this can be done through third parties.

Woods: An issue for hospitality will be what happens to the HR department if you outsource some aspects. Does the department become more or less fundamental to the company, and, if it becomes less fundamental, who in the corporation will look after the rights and issues of employees that we have been talking about?

Would companies hire human capital agents, or would they simply ignore employees more than they do today?

Sammons: In some organizations, HR has been included on the executive committee and is respected as an important strategic partner in the company. Others see HR as functional only and not part of strategic development. Which method a company employs will likely have a major impact on how their employees view the relationship. Hence, it may drastically affect the performance of employees and companies.

Hardigree: I wonder what impact outsourced training may have in the future. Few employees view training programs as something that they want to do today; perhaps that is because of how the training is approached. What happens in the future when you have an outsider come in and attempt to conduct training sessions? My guess is that some employees will resent this and others simply won't care.

Sammons: Some outsourced training may be acceptable and other types may not be. For instance, we have outsourced food processing in hospitality for years. At one time, of course, most food processing occurred on site. Today we commonly see packaged products. Training in how to handle this type of product might be acceptable to employees because the processing is done outside, while training on other issues may not be acceptable. Sometimes the cutting edge of technology is outside the corporation, of course, and organizations need to take advantage of that. This occurred back in the 1980s when point-of-sale technology arrived in hospitality. Or-

ganizations learned that the training from outsiders didn't really stick with employees until they, themselves, understood the processes.

Young: What if we think about the outsourcing of the entire HR program? I don't think that's a fantasy; it could be a reality. It kind of follows along the lines that we don't see HR as strategically critical to the organization because HR hasn't been at the executive committee table for that long. What if hospitality companies outsource the entire HR department? I see that as being a bad thing because we know that human capital or human performance and the ability to get the most out of your employees is one of the only sustainable competitive advantages out there. If it's true that HR has a sustainable competitive advantage, then typically you're going to want to do it in-house because you do not want it replicated. Unfortunately, I don't believe many hospitality executives agree with us on this issue. While we see it as bad in the long term, they see it as good in the short run. They also can always bring HR back in-house. We can probably expect those companies on the top, the really great companies in our industry, to never outsource HR because they believe it is too important. Others will outsource.

Sammons: Outsourced HR has grown from a $2.5 billion industry in 2002 to what is expected to be over $15 billion in 2005. However, I agree that what we are likely to see are outsourcing of some processes, not whole HR departments.

Young: Some processes do not have strategic advantage. For instance, everyone does fire safety training, and it is pretty much the same in most companies. This type of HR training does not increase strategic advantage and could, and perhaps should, be outsourced in the future so that HR departments can concentrate on more important issues.

Sammons: The issue is money. Outsourcing saves money. If it didn't, third-party companies would not exist.

Werner: I think the future of outsourcing can be anticipated. Ten years ago we didn't have this word in our vocabulary. Today we all use it.

Eade: However, we have always outsourced jobs. We called it *subcontracting* for many years, now *outsourcing*. It is the same thing. In the 1970s, many hospitality companies subcontracted many parts of their HR departments. Then they mostly brought the processes back in-house, so it's back to the future for hospitality.

Young: Hospitality owners today are expecting more. They expect every department to make money. Food and beverage was, at one time, viewed as a service, an amenity for guests. This is no longer true. Today every department has to make money or it will be outsourced or closed. Hotels learned a long time ago how to turn a food and beverage operation space into retail shops because they make more money. Mean, lean, and flexible, that's what owners expect today.

Sammons: How people are trained has an impact on outsourcing. In 2001, for example, using a lead instructor in a classroom-like environment completed 77 percent of training. Two years later this had dropped to 69 percent of training. We are replacing people-led training with Internet and computer training because it is more cost-effective. We may never see the day in hospitality where less than 50 percent of training is done through some means other than instructor-led, but it is likely to be close that percentage. It may well depend on the age of the employees and managers being trained. Some age groups are more amenable to computerized and Internet training than others.

Another issue of interest to HR in the future might be how part-time workers are used. We now have on-call boards in most hospitality organizations for most revenue-producing positions. We are likely to see that expand to security issues because of the increased criminal and terrorist threat.

Eade: How to address the needs of part-timers and on-call personnel will be a big issue in the future, and we have not even talked about it. What do you do about those on-call steady extras working for you, building loyalty? The question for organizations will be how to keep them on board. This is only one of the many issues that may be important in the future.

► CONCLUSION

Some people say the best way to predict the future is to look at the past. Others believe that paying attention to the past simply restricts one's thinking about the future. No one really knows.

"The future" does not spring on us all of a sudden. Instead, it takes its time and eases over us. Today's trends predict tomorrow's events. The problem is knowing which trends are important and will affect the future and which are not. One cannot track all trends, and even if you could, this would not necessarily help predict the future. Some trends become future events and some do not. Sometimes the trends are obvious and sometimes they are not. Thus, predicting is difficult, especially about the future. The past is easier to predict.

What we have done in this chapter is attempt to analyze the current trends and events we see in hospitality human resources and use them to predict the future. We hope you enjoyed reading our thoughts on this subject. Remember, the past is history; the future is a mystery; today is a gift. That is why we call today the "present."

CHAPTER 9 ■ ENDNOTES

1. The title is based on a quote from Marshall McLuhan, "We drive into the future using only our rearview mirror."

2. Corresponding author, Harrah College of Hotel Administration, UNLV.

9.3 THE CAUSES AND CONSEQUENCES OF TURNOVER IN THE HOSPITALITY INDUSTRY

Carl D. Riegel

Turnover is and has been a pervasive problem for the hospitality industry. Substantial anecdotal evidence suggests that turnover rates can reach as high as 200 or 300 percent in rank-and-file positions, and management turnover, at least at the operations level, can approach 100 percent in some organizations. While the importance of turnover as a problem for our industry was somewhat obscured by the recession of the early and mid-1990s, it has moved to the forefront with the advent of unprecedented full employment.

A low unemployment rate presents a three-pronged challenge for the industry. First, the number of workers in traditional target markets for hospitality is decreasing. This is likely to remain this way for some years to come. Second, unless the industry can present opportunities for meaningful advancement in pay and responsibility, it will continue to attract, in large measure, a transient workforce—that is, employees will view working in the industry as something to do while they prepare to do something else or while they wait for "something better" to come along. Unfortunately, at the time of this writing, "something better" can easily be found by talented people who are not happy working in the industry. Finally, despite unprecedented efforts to change its image, the industry is frequently perceived as the employer of last resort rather than the much-touted employer of choice. Although this perception is probably not deserved, it acts to make the current labor shortage much worse for the hospitality industry than for many other fields of employment.

For service industries like hospitality, turnover is a serious problem. It makes an existing workforce shortage worse, and in some cases it can be argued that turnover is a symptom of an insidious organizational disease. More important, however, is that recent research has established a strong link between employee satisfaction and overall profitability. In this article we examine the concept of turnover in detail—what it is and why we should care. Next, we examine what many believe to be the causes of turnover, and we then turn our attention to emerging areas of concern about the real costs of employee turnover. Finally, we examine what some researchers believe will help stem excessive turnover.

► WHAT IS TURNOVER, AND WHY SHOULD WE BE CONCERNED?

In general, *turnover* refers to either voluntary or involuntary separation from organizations (Bluedorn, 1982). Involuntary separations (firings) can be a problem if they occur frequently, but the focus of this article is primarily on voluntary separation from organizations—that is, the process by which people quit their jobs.

Historically, hospitality organizations have perceived turnover in two ways. First, many companies are concerned that turnover costs the organization money and, because of that, unacceptable levels should be avoided. Turnover costs money for a variety of reasons, including:

1. The actual costs related to separation
2. The cost of replacing employees, such as advertising, interviewing, and moving expenses
3. Learning curve inefficiencies by new employees

4. Costs associated with the temporary disruption of the work force
5. Nonquantifiable costs due to diminished image, customer loyalties to previous employees, and so forth

Some hospitality firms take the view that turnover is not necessarily undesirable because performance and longevity have an inverse U-shaped relationship. As Figure 9.1 suggests, performance increases over the short to the intermediate term but decreases or stagnates over the long term—that is, the longer employees stay, the less likely they are to demonstrate increases in performance. More importantly, the longer they stay, the more they cost in raises and increased benefits. Firms adopting this tenure/performance position are concerned primarily with the distribution of tenure throughout the organization and more likely to concentrate on *appropriate* rates of turnover rather than *reduced* rates of turnover. For many firms holding this philosophy, turnover control strategies may be viewed as not worth the effort when pay raises are combined with antic-

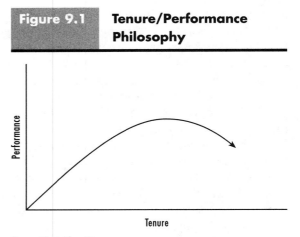

Figure 9.1   **Tenure/Performance Philosophy**

Source: Adapted from Staw.

ipated future performance. The problem with both of these philosophies, as we show later in this article, is that they are limited. They view turnover as an event or phenomenon rather than a process. Thus, it is the event that managers must control rather than the process. A more expansive and probably a more effective approach does not focus on the turnover event per se; rather, it comes from a process perspective that views turnover as but one outcome of a sequential chain of events. Before we discuss this notion of phenomenon versus process, let us turn our attention to the causes of turnover.

► THE CAUSES OF TURNOVER

Many researchers (March and Simon, 1958; Porter and Steers, 1973; Price, 1977; McFillin, Riegel, and Enz, 1986) believe that turnover occurs as a result of a complex series of

---

Figure 9.2 **Model of Turnover**

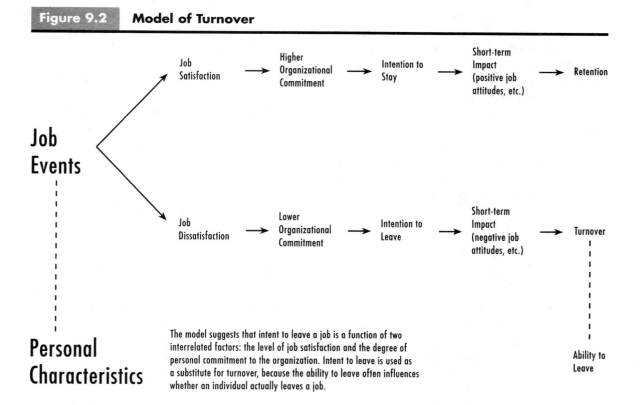

The model suggests that intent to leave a job is a function of two interrelated factors: the level of job satisfaction and the degree of personal commitment to the organization. Intent to leave is used as a substitute for turnover, because the ability to leave often influences whether an individual actually leaves a job.

Source: Adapted from McFillin, Riegel, and Enz, 1986.

factors that influence employee attitudes and eventually affect employee behavior. Models sometimes oversimplify the processes they represent; however, a model is useful to provide a reasonable approximation of reality and is, therefore, useful in assisting our understanding and predicting outcomes.

The model shown in Figure 9.2 uses "intent to leave" as a measure for actual departure. Intent to leave is a surrogate or stand-in measure; however, it has been well substantiated in previous research as a proxy for actual departure. As the model suggests, intent to remain in or leave an organization is a function of two related factors: the level of job satisfaction and the degree of an employee's commitment to the organization. Job satisfaction is also influenced by individual personality traits and specific job events. If the level of job satisfaction is high, then the employee's commitment to the organization tends to be strong and he or she will hold positive job attitudes and can be expected to stay on the job. On the other hand, if the level of job satisfaction is low, commitment decreases, job attitudes decline, and the employee, if given the opportunity, leaves the organization. This gives rise to new areas of concern.

► NEW AREAS OF CONCERN

We previously explored two of the traditional philosophies that describe how hospitality organizations view turnover. While these philosophies point out reasons for organizations to control or reduce turnover, they offer a limited perspective of the potential damage excessive turnover can have. As we discussed earlier, a more comprehensive model views turnover not as an isolated event but as a process. This process views turnover as a series of related events, and each of these events can have negative consequences for employees as well as for organizations. A closer look at Figure 9.2 demonstrates this. According to the diagram, turnover results from negative attitudes toward the organization and occurs only if an employee has the ability to leave. This means that he or she must have other job options, not need to work, or not care to work. If employees have limited or unacceptable options and do not have the ability to leave the organization, they may adopt other withdrawal behaviors such as complaining, absenteeism, poor performance, or unacceptable customer service behavior. This implies that turnover is only one choice of a variety of withdrawal behaviors available to disaffected employees, and disaffected employees can act out these behaviors either as isolated occurrences or as a set of behaviors. Furthermore, the individual choice of withdrawal behavior depends on a variety of other factors such as degree of unhappiness, perception of self-worth, and, most importantly, the ability to find acceptable alternative employment.

Given this view of turnover, companies with high rates of turnover are likely to experience a variety of negative outcomes. One way to categorize these outcomes is to look at how they affect individual employees as well as how they affect the organization in both the short and the long term. Figure 9.3 indicates that both organizations and individual employees suffer from the effects of high rates of turnover including attendance problems, decreased cooperation, decreased work performance, and even sabotage. In the longer term, however, the effects are more systemic and potentially more devastating.

For example, high rates of turnover can worsen existing turnover rates, contribute to system problems such as poor customer relations, and even eventually limit a firm's ability to develop and implement strategy. The potential dollar cost of this is incalculable but potentially enormous. A question of major importance for firms with high turnover rates is not only who leaves but also who stays. In some cases, it may be that employees who stay with an organization are not necessarily the ones the organization wants to keep and those who do leave are not necessarily the ones the organization wants to see go. In

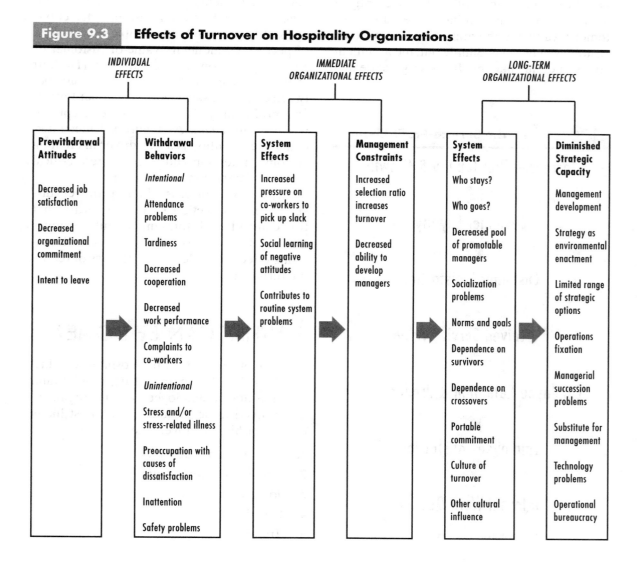

Figure 9.3   Effects of Turnover on Hospitality Organizations

some cases, outstanding employees find the organizational environment so dissatisfying they opt to separate from the company, and those who remain are those who can adapt to a dysfunctional environment or those who have no choice but to stay.

In addition, there is evidence that excessive turnover rates can have a substantial and negative impact on profitability. Recently, a great deal of discussion has centered on customer loyalty and the importance of avoiding customer defections. Simply put, the argument goes something like this. It costs a great deal to create new customers. The costs associated with advertising, promotion, and other marketing efforts are staggering. Thus it is wiser to try to retain existing guests than to create new ones. Furthermore, the longer customers stay with a company, the more they are worth. Generally, they buy more, buy more frequently, and are less price-sensitive. In fact, one management writer (Reichheld, 1996) suggested that decreasing customer defections by as little as 5 points can double profits. With respect to the monetary value of customer or guest loyalty, several researchers (Heskett et al., 1984) suggested a strong relationship between employee satisfaction, customer loyalty, and profitability. They call this concept the *service-profit chain*. As Figure 9.4 illustrates, employee retention is a key driver in creating customer retention and is therefore a critical factor in determining profitability.

The new concerns about turnover discussed in this section strongly indicate that the conventional thinking about turnover may capture just a small portion of its devastating effects. Now let's look at ways of reducing turnover.

Figure 9.4   The Service-Profit Chain

Increased Profitability & Growth

Customer Loyalty

Customer Satisfaction

Perceived Service Value

Employee Retention & Productivity

Employee Satisfaction

Internal Work Quality

Source: Adapted from Heskett et al., 1994.

▶ WHAT CAN BE DONE?

A study of turnover in the hospitality industry (McFillen, Riegel, and Enz, 1986) found that hospitality employees in one organization ranked these reasons as the most likely causes for high turnover rates:

1. Treatment by superiors
2. Amount of work hours
3. Job pressure
4. Scheduling
5. Training

6. Fringe benefit packages
7. Better opportunities elsewhere
8. Physical demands of the job

A short-term strategy would be for managers to focus on these reasons—in other words, working on fair treatment of employees, creating fair and reasonable schedules, and so forth. However, these strategies do not necessarily address the causes of excessive turnover and are likely to have limited effectiveness and to be short-lived. A longer-term solution would take into account the causes of worker dissatisfaction and attempt to deal with these in a comprehensive and continuous manner.

Frederick Herzberg (1976) suggests that dissatisfaction occurs as a result of a lack of what he calls "hygiene factors" and that satisfaction occurs as a result of what he calls "motivators." While there is not necessarily any linkage in the organizational behavior literature between job satisfaction and job performance, a substantial body of theory does suggest that satisfied employees adopt pro-social and, therefore, committed behaviors toward the organization. Herzberg says hygiene factors that can cause dissatisfaction among employees include salary, working conditions, fringe benefits, and job security. While paying a fair salary or providing job security decreases dissatisfaction, it does not necessarily create satisfaction in employees. Motivators or satisfiers recognized by Herzberg include achievement, recognition, challenging work, responsibility, and advancement. These factors, if provided for by the organization, create satisfaction and therefore commitment. Thus, hospitality managers who are concerned about turnover as an insidious disease process should not only take care of the extrinsic job factors, such as job security and salary, they also must pay a great deal of attention to providing opportunities for advancement, challenging work, and so forth.

In addition to attending to environmental factors in the organization, paying attention to the selection of employees in the first place goes a long way toward quelling dissatisfaction and, therefore, diminishing turnover. An axiom in the human resource field is that the goal of selection is not to hire the best-qualified employee but rather to hire the best employee for the particular job, the point being that it is important to match prospective employees to the organization and the position. Similarly, efforts to select employees who will be successful in a particular job as well as successful in the organizational culture enhance the likelihood of their retention. Selection is an important human resource function that is worthy of substantial effort and care.

► SUMMARY

Turnover is a problem of longstanding significance for the hospitality industry. The effects of high turnover rates on hospitality businesses are substantially greater than many existing philosophies suggest, and dealing with turnover as an isolated event fails to acknowledge its causes and, therefore, is likely to have limited impact as a turnover control strategy. Comprehensive approaches that attempt, on the one hand, to eliminate sources of dissatisfaction and, on the other hand, to promote employee satisfaction and retention have greater potential to strengthen commitment and, therefore, encourage a wide variety of pro-social behaviors that will strengthen organizational effectiveness, eliminate withdrawal behaviors (of which turnover is one), and, ultimately, contribute to guest loyalty and profitability.

9.4 CURRENT ISSUES IN HOSPITALITY EMPLOYMENT LAW

Suzanne K. Murrmann and Cherylynn Becker

Fairness in the workplace is a significant issue affecting the productivity, loyalty, and commitment employees have to their organizations. The treatment an employee receives from his or her supervisor affects the worker's motivation to provide excellent service to customers, ultimately affecting the bottom-line profits of the organization. Many factors influence workplace justice. These include the voluntary human resource management policies that organizations put into place to provide fair and equal employee treatment. In addition, a significant number of federal and state laws and regulations protect employees from various forms of discrimination, provide employees with certain rights, and specify actions employers must take when hiring and managing their workforce. Such laws may vary in their wording and coverage from state to state. However, they generally mirror law at the federal level. These laws, which significantly affect the human resource function in hospitality organizations, fall under four general categories:

- Those governing equal employment and opportunity and nondiscrimination
- Those governing compensation and working hours
- Those governing the health and safety of workers
- Those governing labor relations and collective bargaining (Jackson and Schuler, 2000)

The judicial process is a dynamic one.

Continual changes occur in laws and regulations due to amendments to existing laws, enactment of new laws, and interpretations made by courts and regulatory agencies. It is mandatory for managers to keep up to date with the status of laws that affect their HR activities. Even with appropriate legal counsel, day-to-day activities of supervisors and managers are often where organizations run into legal problems. Therefore, it is necessary that managers be aware of their legal obligations.

Because space does not permit a full discussion of all relevant employment laws, the following text concentrates on federal laws that have seen significant changes in the last decade as well as those that are forecasted to change significantly in the next several years (Flynn, 2000; Goldberg, 1998). They include sexual harassment and employer liability under Title VII of the Civil Rights Act, the Americans with Disabilities Act, the Family and Medical Leave Act, and the Immigration Reform and Control Act. A discussion of these laws and implications for hospitality managers follows.

▶ SEXUAL HARASSMENT

In general, *sexual harassment* is defined as unwelcome sexual conduct in the workplace that is a term or condition of employment. Complaints of sexual harassment fall under two categories: quid pro quo and hostile work environment. Quid pro quo harassment is said to occur when submission to or rejection of unwelcome sexual conduct by an individual is used as a basis for employment decisions affecting an employee. In other words, when a supervisor demands sexual favors from his or her subordinate and either promises an employment benefit, such as a raise or promotion, or threatens the employee with loss of such benefits, quid pro quo harassment exists. Such activities may be subtle or overt, and the employee must show that he or she belongs to a protected group, was subject to unwelcome harassment that was based on his or her gender, and that acceptance or refusal resulted or could result in tangible changes to the working conditions.

While quid pro quo harassment implies an exchange of sexual favors for work benefits, *hostile work environment harassment* refers to the overall working environment in which employees function. Hostile work environment harassment is conduct that unreasonably interferes with the ability of an employee to perform his or her job properly or creates an intimidating, hostile, or offensive working environment. This may be so even if it does not lead to tangible or economic job consequences. As in quid pro quo harassment, the activities or conduct in question are unwelcome by the employee and are based on gender. The employee must also show that they are sufficiently pervasive and severe as to have caused an abusive working environment and that the employer is liable for these activities. Typical examples of this type of harassment include unwelcome physical touching; whistling, leering, improper gestures, or offensive remarks; unwelcome comments about appearance; sexual jokes; and the use of sexually explicit derogatory or otherwise offensive language.

Sexual harassment in the workplace continues to be an important discrimination issue, particularly with recent Supreme Court rulings (Goldberg, 1998). Two of particular note, *Burlington Industries v. Ellerth* and *Faragher v. Boca Raton,*[1] have significantly shaped the obligations of hospitality managers. In them, the Court clearly articulated the liability of employers for the actions of their harassing supervisors. First, in cases in which an employee has suffered tangible, detrimental employment actions, such as demotion, termination, or loss of benefits, the employer is strictly liable regardless of fault. Strict liability is premised on the fact that the supervisors are acting for the employer (company), and regardless of whether or not the employer can show it has an antidiscrimination policy, final responsibility rests with the company. In cases, however, where the employee has suffered no loss of tangible job benefits, the employer can avoid liability by showing that reasonable care was taken to prevent and promptly correct any sexually harassing behavior. Documentation that the harassed employee subsequently failed to take advantage of any preventive or corrective opportunities provided by the employer further minimizes the likelihood of employer liability for harassment charges.

For hospitality managers to protect themselves against charges of sexual harassment, they need to focus on three major areas: (1) implementation and dissemination of antiharassment and complaint policies, (2) training of personnel, and (3) complaint investigation.

Though the Court has not specifically ruled that companies must have policies specifically targeted to sexual harassment, many human resource management professionals feel employers can more easily demonstrate their "reasonable duty of care" by developing separate antiharassment policies. Such policies should explicitly define sexual harassment, both in terms of quid pro quo and hostile environment harassment, and give specific examples of inappropriate conduct. Though this point seems obvious, the policy should also unambiguously prohibit such conduct. It should also indicate protection for employees from retaliation for reporting harassment. Numerous studies have shown that employees are often afraid to report inappropriate activities because of fear of retaliation by their supervisors. Managers should develop and include in their policy multiple avenues for filing harassment complaints. One such avenue would be to start with the employee's immediate supervisor; however, an additional route would be to bypass the supervisor and complain to an individual outside of the supervisor's direct chain of command. Assurance of prompt and thorough investigations and privacy are equally important components of an antiharassment policy.

As necessary as a well-developed and well-written policy is, it is also important that the policy be disseminated in such a way that all personnel in the hospitality organization are aware of it. Merely including it in an employee handbook may not be sufficient. Antiharassment policies should be posted in locations regularly visited by employees as well as discussed with new employees. This is especially important in an industry where a significant part of the labor pool is composed of employees who do not read and speak English as their primary language. The company should also attempt to keep written acknowledgment that each employee understands the policy.

Periodic training in what constitutes sexual harassment is essential for the prevention of misconduct in the workplace and the de-fense of the employer against liability in court. The purpose of such training is to make supervisors and employees aware of conduct that constitutes harassment and provide them with mechanisms for effectively dealing with it. Training must be tailored to the individual workplace and take into account the diversity of the workforce; however, a number of key components should be common to training in this area. Though all employees should attend training, separate sessions should be held for supervisors and managers to instruct them in their obligations to subordinates and their responsibilities for investigating harassment complaints. The language and the customs of employees should always be taken into account when developing training materials, particularly when such activities as role-playing are used. Training in the hospitality industry should take into account the interaction of employees with third parties such as customers and outside vendors. Managers must be aware that the employer has an additional duty of care in the area of customer harassment of employees, and they should be trained to delicately but effectively deal with such situations. Finally, care must be taken to select an appropriate resource for carrying out training. This may be an in-house trainer or an outside individual or firm. In any case, the individual selected should have recognized expertise in the area of sexual harassment.

The final area of concern for managers is prompt investigation of harassment complaints. The employer who fails to document fair investigation of employee complaints will more than likely be found liable for harassment. All complaints should be investigated as swiftly as possible by an unbiased investigator who is sensitive to the privacy concerns of the complainant. If, during the course of the investigation, there is sufficient reason to believe the complainant and the accused should be separated, the complainant should not be assigned to a lesser job. Such action could be seen as retaliation for filing a complaint. Relevant material and information should be obtained, in private, from the accused and additional witnesses. Based on this, immediate and appropriate corrective action should be taken by doing whatever is necessary to end the harassment, to make the employee whole by restoring lost employment benefits or opportunities, and to prevent the misconduct from recurring. If appropriate, disciplinary action should be taken against the offending supervisor or employee, ranging from reprimand to discharge. Generally, the corrective action should reflect the severity of the conduct. Document the findings and subsequent steps taken, if any, and place this documentation in a confidential investigation file. The Equal Employment Opportunity Commission policy guidance on sexual harassment suggests that follow-up inquiries be made to ensure that harassment is not resumed and that the employee does not suffer retaliation. Finally, use what was learned from these investigations to streamline or customize future training and policy restatements in this area to more closely align with specific company needs.

► AMERICANS WITH DISABILITIES ACT

The Americans with Disabilities Act of 1990 (ADA) prohibits an employer from discriminating against a qualified individual with a disability with respect to job application procedures, hiring, advancement, discharge, compensation, training, and other "terms, conditions, and privileges of employment." The Act has undergone almost a decade of interpretation by the courts, which continue to refine and define its coverage and the responsibilities of hospitality managers. As noted by many professionals in human resource management, these rulings at times leave as many unresolved questions as they answer concerning employer responsibilities.

Under the ADA, a qualified individual is defined as "an individual with a disability who, with or without reasonable accommodation, can perform the essential function of the employment position that such individual holds or desires."[2] There are two questions the manager must ask when determining whether an individual is qualified. First, does the individual satisfy the prerequisites for the position, such as the appropriate educational background, employment experience, skills, or licenses? Second, can he or she perform the "essential functions" of the position with or without reasonable accommodation? The former is answered by comparing the qualifications of the individual to job-related requirements and production standards traditional to the industry—for example, number of rooms cleaned per day. When identifying requirements, employers should use those used for other employees in the position and not those selected to intentionally exclude the disabled person. The latter question may be answered by defining the fundamental job duties of a position in a well-constructed written job description. Factors suggested for identifying essential functions include the amount of time spent performing the function, the number of employees available to perform the task, the work experience of past incumbents and present employees in the position, and the consequence of not performing the function. For instance, several courts have found attendance to be an essential function of the job because the inability to maintain regular attendance creates an undue hardship upon an employer.[3]

A disability is defined under the Act as (1) "a physical or mental impairment that substantially limits one or more of the major life activities of such individual," (2) "a record of such an impairment," or (3) "being regarded as having such an impairment."[4] Impairments may include physiological disorders or conditions, cosmetic disfigurements, and anatomical loss affecting one or more major body systems. Before 1998, it was generally accepted that for an impairment to be covered under the definition of a disability, it needed to be a permanent condition that, if uncorrected, substantially limited a major life activity such as walking, seeing, hearing, or speaking. Several Supreme Court rulings have limited this definition, stating that "an individual's corrections, medications, and even subconscious mechanisms for coping with an impairment are to be considered when assessing whether that individual is disabled" and covered under the ADA (Sherwyn, Eigen, and Klausner, 2000). These rulings, though limiting the definition of a disability in one respect, in no way clarify the issue of what is considered a disability, nor may they actually limit the number of individuals claiming discrimination if managers continue to perceive individuals impaired even with corrective devices.

Traditional human resource functions and employment decisions can be considered discriminatory under the ADA. These include such activities as recruiting, advertising, and the processing of applications for employment, hiring, updating, promotion, termination, compensation, job assignment, and the like. In other words, the ADA mirrors, to a great extent, the rights of protected groups under Title VII of the Civil Rights Act. Hospitality managers should be aware of a number of issues unique to disability law. An employer risks violating the ADA by asking about medical conditions and disabilities in a preemployment situation. Questions at this point should be job-related, with inquiry limited to the applicant's ability to perform the essential functions of the job as described in the written job description. Preemployment medical examinations and tests, with the exception of testing for illegal drug use, are also seen as discriminatory in the hospitality industry. The ADA also prohibits disparate treatment discrimination—that is, limiting and segregating employees in a way that affects their opportunities because of a disability. A hospitality employer that demonstrated a pattern of hiring disabled job applicants for back-of-the-house, non-customer contact positions, though such applicants were able to perform effectively in customer contact positions, would be demonstrating potentially discriminatory behavior. The use of employment tests or other selection criteria that are not job-related to screen out disabled applicants is prohibited under the ADA. For example, if an employer requires an interview that is job-related and consistent with business necessity as part of the application process, it would not be legal to reject a hearing-impaired applicant solely because he or she could not be interviewed.[5] Finally, failure to reasonably accommodate disabilities of either job applicants or employees constitutes discrimination under the ADA.

Accommodation for individuals with disabilities is at the core of the ADA. By law, *reasonable accommodation* mandates employers to accommodate qualified individuals who can perform the essential functions of a job, unless this causes significant difficulty or expense—that is, undue hardship.[6] Accommodations can be modifications or adjustments (1) in the job application or testing process that allow a qualified applicant with a disability to be considered for a position equally with other applicants; (2) in the workplace or in the manner or method in which the job is performed that allow the employee to perform the job; or (3) that enable the disabled employee to enjoy the benefits and privileges of the job equally to those without disabilities. Types of accommodations may include but are not necessarily limited to the following:

1. Modifications of existing facilities (ramps and entrances, bathroom facilities, workstations, etc.)
2. Job restructuring
3. Modified work schedules
4. Reassignment to vacant positions
5. Acquisition and modification of equipment or devices
6. Adjustment or modification of examinations or training materials
7. Provision of qualified readers and interpreters (for preemployment activities, etc.)

The EEOC has issued guidelines for employers to follow for compliance. Hospitality managers should follow these procedures. Using the interactive process outlined in the following guidelines should increase the likelihood of employees viewing a manager as reasonable and concerned about their needs.

1. Notify employees and job applicants of the employer's obligation under the Act to make reasonable accommodations.
2. Wait for a request for a reasonable accommodation by a qualified individual with a disability.
3. Analyze the particular job to determine its purpose and essential functions. Communicate to the employee your understanding of the essential functions of the job and the abilities needed to perform them.
4. Consult with the disabled individual to ascertain the precise job-related limitations imposed by the disability and how those limitations can be overcome.
5. With the disabled individual's assistance, identify potential accommodations and assess the effectiveness of each in enabling the individual to perform the essential functions of the job.
6. Consider the disabled individual's accommodation preferences and select and implement the accommodation most appropriate for both the employee and employer. This is a final decision that should be made by the manager.

Given the relative youth of the ADA, it is anticipated that interpretation of even the most basic areas of the law—for example, the definition of a disability—will continue to evolve. There are, however, certain steps that many feel to be appropriate for managers (Sovereign, 1999). Facilities should be made as accessible as possible. This is particularly true of the hospitality industry, given its public accommodation requirement. Because the concept of reasonable accommodation is based on a clear understanding of the essential functions of the job, well-written job descriptions are extremely important in managing liability associated with the ADA. With the exception of drug testing, all preemployment medical inquiries and examinations should be eliminated. Always attempt to accommodate a qualified disabled individual. A case of undue hardship can be made after accommodation is researched. Finally, in organizations that are large enough to support service staff, an individual should be designated as the ADA resource for other managers and used when accommodations are requested.

► FAMILY AND MEDICAL LEAVE ACT OF 1993

All hospitality employers with 50 or more employees are covered by the Family and Medical Leave Act of 1993 (FMLA). The FMLA was passed in an attempt to balance the demands of the workplace with the family and medical needs of employees. Employers both in and outside of the hospitality industry expressed grave concerns over the impact of the law on workplace productivity and employer compliance. Many of these fears proved unfounded; many, however, were not. Compliance with the law has proved cumbersome, given its technical recordkeeping nature. Since the enactment of this act, the Department of Labor (DOL), which oversees the FMLA, has seen thousands of complaints filed and has changed the guidelines and directives to comply with dozens of court rulings.

The FMLA allows employees up to 12 weeks of unpaid leave during any 12-month period to deal with family and medical issues. Companies that employ 50 or more people (within a 75-mile radius), including part-time and temporary workers, during each of 20 or more calendar workweeks in a year are covered. In order for an employee to be eligible

for leave, he or she must have worked at least 1,250 hours for the employer. An eligible employee may take unpaid leave for the following reasons;

- The birth of a child
- The placement of a child with the employee for adoption or foster care
- A serious health condition of a spouse, child, or parent
- The employee's own serious health condition

The DOL regulations define *serious health condition* as any illness, injury, impairment, or physical or mental condition that involves:

- Any period of incapacity or treatment involving inpatient care in a hospital, hospice, or residential mental care facility
- Any period of incapacity requiring absences from work, school, or other regular daily activities of more than three calendar days that also involves continuing treatment by a health care provider. (*Continuing treatment* means either treatment two or more times by a health care provider or one treatment that results in a regimen of continuing treatment. A *regimen of continuing treatment* includes only those treatments that cannot be initiated without a visit to a health care provider, such as taking prescription drugs. It does not include taking over-the-counter medication, nor does it include therapy such as bed rest, drinking fluids, and exercise.)
- Continuing treatment by a health care provider for any period of incapacity due to pregnancy or for prenatal care, or for a chronic or long-term health condition that is incurable or so serious that, if not

treated, would likely result in a period of incapacity of more than three calendar days

As a general rule, ailments such as the common cold, the flu, earaches, upset stomach, minor ulcers, headaches other than migraine, routine dental or orthodontia problems, and periodontal diseases are not serious health conditions unless complications arise.

Employers covered by the FMLA must post notice of the Act and their obligations as well as provide additional information to employees concerning their entitlements and obligations through standard mechanisms such as employee handbooks and manuals. An employee requesting leave is required to give 30 days notice to his or her employer, if possible. If such notice is not possible, the employee must provide "such notice as is practical" so that the employer has an opportunity to plan for the employee's absence. As little as one to two days' notice (or less) may be sufficient in emergency situations. Employers may require a medical certification, such as a doctor's statement, from a health care provider to support leave requests. Additional opinions concerning the employee's condition and periodic reports from the employee on leave regarding his or her status and intent to return may also be required. During the time of the leave, the employer must continue existing health care benefits.

Leave can be taken intermittently or on a schedule that reduces the typical number of hours per workday or workweek when medically necessary. Incremental leave may be taken in increments as short as one hour.

Under the FMLA, the employer is obligated to place the employee, once returned from leave, in the same position he or she left. If this is not possible, the employee must be placed in a position equivalent in pay, benefits, and other terms and conditions of employment. Based on rulings to date, "equivalent" appears to be construed as "identical" by the DOL.

A number of significant compliance issues cause difficulty for human resource professionals and employment law attorneys. Due to their technical nature, they are not discussed here. However, several issues are worthy of note because they affect hospitality managers and supervisors in general.

While attendance has been successfully defended by several employers under the ADA as an essential function of a job, FMLA leave absences cannot be used in discipline and termination decisions. Therefore, it is particularly important in intermittent leave situations to record the reasons for absences. Supervisors should be encouraged to document "verbatim reasons" for absences. This information allows a manager to conduct an "FMLA audit" of employees who may be undergoing disciplinary action for excessive absenteeism.

Though the FMLA does allow for managers to require medical certification from employers for leave purposes, as well as second opinions, overuse of such information could open up liability under the ADA (Shea, 2000). Managers must be wary of asking for more medical information than is necessary for the purposes of granting FMLA leave. Medical certification is a useful tool to employ if there is doubt about the existence or extent of an employee's health condition. However, it is not necessary as long as the absence has been noted as FMLA leave.

A "serious" health condition under the Act may include many "minor" illnesses and conditions of short duration. Absences of less than three days may also be considered legitimate reasons for leave. This is due to the interpretation of the FMLA-specific wording. Indeed, many experts in the area agree that regulations have gone beyond the intent of the legislation in terms of interpreting what a serious illness should be. Managers should be aware that, at this point, a liberal interpretation must be placed on this definition.

▶ IMMIGRATION REFORM AND CONTROL ACT OF 1986

In 1986, Congress enacted the Immigration Reform and Control Act (IRCA) in response to significant increases in undocumented immigration and vocal concerns from unhappy voters. This law was an attempt to control undocumented immigration in a number of ways, including the imposition of sanctions on employers for knowingly hiring undocumented workers. In addition, the law provided for amnesty for undocumented immigrants who could demonstrate a record of continuous residence in the United States for a designated period. These regulations, along with increased support for border patrol activities, were thought to significantly diminish the attractiveness of U.S. jobs for undocumented workers, thereby protecting jobs and wages for legal workers in the United States.

Critics of the IRCA argued that it would encourage employers to engage in greater discrimination against U.S. citizens and legal aliens based on their appearance and cultural background, and safeguards against such discrimination were included in its content. However, several studies to date have shown that even with these safeguards in place, a pattern of discriminating against individuals based on physical appearance or accent exists (Phillips and Massey, 1999). Such discrimination includes the denial of jobs as well as paying lower wages to undocumented workers. This decrease in pay, below legal minimum, is thought to take place to compensate for the risk involved in being sanctioned under the Act.

The IRCA requires employers to verify the employment eligibility of all employees hired by and working for the organization and to complete and maintain eligibility paperwork. This paperwork, commonly referred to as *I-9 forms,* must be maintained on all employees, U.S. citizens as well as aliens authorized to work in the country. The Immigration and Naturalization Service (INS) is charged with enforcing the IRCA. However, any number of other federal agencies, including the EEOC, the Justice Department, and the Department of Labor, may request a review of the eligibility documentation records of a company. Employers must verify an employee's or applicant's identity and eligibility to work by requesting proof of both within three days of hire. Documents that can be used to verify identity include a state driver's license, state or school I.D. card, and a voter's registration card. Eligibility to work may be established using a number of documents including a Social Security card, birth certificate issued by a U.S. state, county, or municipal authority, or an unexpired INS employment authorization. Some documents, such as a U.S. passport, establish both identity and work eligibility. A complete list of all appropriate documents is provided on the back page of the I-9 form.

As mentioned earlier, the Act contains antidiscrimination provisions that are in addition to and do not change discrimination under Title VII of the Civil Rights Act. The

IRCA bans discrimination against legal aliens or people intending to become U.S. citizens. An alien has employment rights equal to a U.S. citizen, unless citizenship is a bona fide occupational qualification. If an alien is authorized to work in the United States, an employer cannot give preference to a U.S. citizen who is less qualified.

Employers have several responsibilities under the law:

1. Employers cannot request more or different documents than are required under the provisions of the law. Though it is often easier for managers to require specific, approved documentation such as a driver's license or Social Security card, they must accept any qualified document from the I-9 list if it appears to be valid.

2. Employers cannot knowingly use, attempt to use, possess, obtain, accept, or receive any forged, counterfeit, altered, or falsely made documents. It is often extremely difficult to identify counterfeit documents. However, managers should closely scrutinize the documentation of all applicants for obvious falsification—for example, multiple individuals with the same or similar Social Security numbers.

3. Employers cannot backdate or otherwise falsely make I-9 forms appear as if they are or have been in compliance with the IRCA. Individuals responsible for hiring on an ongoing basis should perform eligibility verification. Paperwork should be kept up to date.

4. Employers must have new employees complete Section 1 of the employment verification I-9 at the time of the hire by filling in the correct information, signing, and dating the form.

5. Employers are responsible for reviewing and ensuring that the employees fully and properly complete Section 1 of the employment verification I-9. Applicants who do not fully complete this section should not be hired.

6. Employers must examine the original documents(s) (the only exception is a certified copy of a birth certificate) presented by the employee and then fully complete Section 2 of the employment verification I-9.

7. Employers must keep the employment verification I-9 for three years after the date employment begins or one year after the person's employment is terminated, whichever is later.

In order to avoid penalties under the IRCA, hospitality managers should use the following checklist:

- Verify employment status of every person hired.

- Employ only U.S. citizens and aliens authorized to work in the United States.

- Verify employees' status within three days of their being hired to work.

- Inform each new job applicant, either orally or in writing, that you hire only U.S. citizens and aliens lawfully authorized to work in the United States and that you require all new employees to complete the designated verification for I-9.

- Examine documentation presented by new employees, record the information on the I-9, and sign. Retain these documents for three years.

- Do not ask for proof of citizenship or authorization to work before deciding to hire the applicant.

- Do not refuse to offer employment to anyone on the basis of foreign accent or appearance.
- Do not discharge present employees based on foreign appearance or language.

The above discussion of these key issues only scratches the surface of the legal challenges facing hotel HR managers. When you consider that the 535 members of Congress and the members of 50 state legislatures are constantly proposing laws that result in regulation, it is easy to see why HR managers can face daunting tasks in assisting the organization and its managers in staying out of legal trouble.

CHAPTER 9 ■ ENDNOTES

1. *Burlington Industries v. Ellerth:* 524 U.S. 742; 118 S. Crt. 2257 (1998); *Faragher v. Boca Raton:* 524 U.S. 775, 118 S. Crt. 2275 (1998).
2. 42 U.S.C. §1211(8).
3. *Tyndall v. National Education Centers:* 31 F. 3rd 209 (4th Cir. 1994); *Earl v. Mervyns Inc.:* No. 99-4264 (11th Cir. 2000).
4. 42 U.S.C. §12102(2).
5. 29 CFR Part 1630, Appendix § 1630.15(a).
6. Undue hardship is assessed by reviewing the nature and cost of the accommodations needed; the financial resources of the employer; the size of the company and the number of its facilities; the financial resources of the facility itself; and the effect of the accommodation on the expenses or operations of the facility, on other employees' ability to do their jobs, and on the facility's ability to conduct business (ADA Sec. 101[10], 42 U.S.C. 12111[10]; EEOC Sec. 1630.2[p]).

9.5 THE STRATEGIC AND OPERATIONAL ROLES OF HUMAN RESOURCES — AN EMERGING MODEL

J. Bruce Tracey and Arthur E. Nathan

Effective human-resources management is one of the most important considerations in creating and maintaining a competitive advantage for a hotel (or, for that matter, any hospitality organization). Indeed, human-capital considerations top the list of current managerial concerns in the hospitality industry (Enz, 2001, 38–45). Despite the industry's concern with human resources, however, the HR function is oddly disconnected from the line function. That disconnect is evident on two primary levels. First, we argue that many business leaders fail to fully consider HR influences when making long-term plans. While most executives acknowledge the importance of HR for implementing strategic plans—

"making it happen"—we have seen few who formally incorporate HR concerns when developing a strategic direction. While the predominant framework requires consideration of HR strengths and weaknesses during the strategy-formulation process, HR is primarily viewed as an "enabling" function, responsible for implementing "the plan," and thus largely ignored during the initial planning stages.

Second, we argue that many HR departments fail to execute even the most basic functions effectively. Many firms' policies and practices are archaic, inflexible, and do not directly benefit those who are most keenly affected by HR actions. Based on those concerns, we advocate the need for a new model of HR—one that should be used as a guide for developing vision, values, and goals, and one that creates a more effective and efficient function for attracting, developing, and retaining quality employees.

To explain our model, we will first discuss the manner in which HR can contribute to the strategic-planning process. We then present data that demonstrate the link between HR practices and systems on important business objectives. Finally, we offer some ideas that may change the prevailing paradigm and the operational role of HR in hospitality organizations.

▶ HR AND STRATEGIC PLANNING

Our observations are that HR suffers from a negative image in many hospitality organizations and that, sadly, it has earned that negative image. The following views of HR may be familiar: HR is basically an employee-advocate function and represents the "soft"

side of the business; HR is a cost center since it does not generate revenue; HR serves as an administrative-support office and organizes the company picnic; and HR is responsible for implementing strategy, not developing strategy. We could go on, but the point is made: human resources gets much lip service but no respect.

One of the reasons for this negative image may be the narrow application of the strategic-planning process taken by many business leaders. Too often, the human-resources function is left out of key planning steps. The following comment illustrates our point. A successful hospitality executive and colleague of ours maintains that his primary function is to determine the vision and direction of the firm, and then it's up to HR and other departments to "make it happen." This statement summarizes his views:

HR as a function does not *per se* have a dedicated role in the strategic-planning process. Corporate strategic planning begins with an external assessment of opportunities and threats and an internal assessment of firm strengths and weaknesses. This process is not driven by a function or discipline formula, but rather by an evaluation designed to determine the relative importance and veracity of assumptions management has made about the industry and the firm. Management combines its fact-based knowledge with its assumptions and beliefs about the business it is evaluating. Strategic planning, at its core, is the process by which the veracity of these assumptions and the relative importance each has to the overall outcome are revealed. Functional executives confound and corrupt the initial stages of the planning process by becoming caught up in interdisciplinary issues that should be subservient to the strategy process they aspire to influence. As such, the

CEO is forced to pull the process of formulating strategy away from these executives and rely more heavily on his or her own judgment or a formal strategy group of executives without discipline responsibilities.[1]

In this leader's view, HR plays a subservient and reactionary role in the business-planning process. While this is only one individual's perspective, we've encountered many who share similar views. We contend that HR considerations must be taken into account not only during strategy implementation, but also during the process of developing that strategy. Indeed, the prevailing models of business planning support this contention.

Several approaches can be used to predict a firm's competitive position and develop strategic plans. The traditional SWOT model (i.e., strength, weakness, opportunity, and threat) is based on a matching process such that a firm's strategic direction is based on the fit between external conditions (i.e., opportunities and threats) and internal capabilities (i.e., strengths and weaknesses). Based on this assessment of fit, leaders can then take actions intended to achieve a sustained level of competitiveness—for instance, by using internal strengths to exploit external opportunities and taking advantage of opportunities to motivate change and fix internal weaknesses. Another popular framework, VRIO analysis, extends the SWOT model and maintains that competitive advantage is gained by identifying and exploiting the rare, distinctive competencies of the firm (Barney, 1997). The VRIO explanation considers a firm's resources—understood in terms of value, rarity, imitability, and organization—as keys to long-term effectiveness. In simplified terms, value is characterized by the firm's internal resources that can be used to respond to external threats;

rarity is associated with the scarcity of such resources in the external environment; imitability is based on the ability of competitors to acquire, duplicate, or substitute valued resources; and organization is associated with the firm's structure and systems that are used to extract the greatest degree of value from a given resource.

These and other models (e.g., portfolio assessments, competitor ranking) that can be used to analyze strategic positions and develop plans have at least one thing in common: the human element is central to an analysis of internal strengths, resources, and capabilities. Technology, in contrast, is quite imitable and thus should not be considered as a source of competitive advantage. Human capabilities, and the social context in which such capabilities are applied, are difficult and perhaps impossible to copy or transfer to settings outside the focal context. While access to capital, relative market share, brand image, and service quality are all essential to a hospitality business, such concerns would be largely irrelevant if the appropriate human resources were unavailable. Therefore, while HR may not be the most important consideration during the strategic-planning process, this factor cannot be ignored when developing long-range plans.

► EVIDENCE FOR THE STRATEGIC IMPORTANCE OF HR

Despite HR's apparent image problem, it remains an essential function. Much has been written about the critical role of HR for achieving business goals and objectives, and there is a growing literature that shows HR policies, practices, and systems are related to a variety of financial and operational success indicators.[2] Indeed, there is some rather compelling evidence that the proper alignment between HR systems and business strategy will enhance a firm's performance.[3] We will complement this literature by presenting two hospitality-specific examples that support the strategic importance of HR for not only implementing long-range plans, but also developing such plans.

Example 1: Compensation and turnover. The 2000 Lodging Compensation and Benefits Survey, conducted by Realtime Hotel Reports (now part of Smith Travel Research) and sponsored by the American Hotel Foundation, provides direct evidence for the need to consider HR factors throughout the strategic-planning process. In addition to compensation levels and benefits offered by over 2000 hotels, the survey also gathered information about employee turnover. Turnover is a key concern to many hospitality employers. It can be quite costly (Hinkin and Tracey, 2000, 14–21) and has been shown to be related to many important outcomes, including profitability (Simons and Hinkin, 2001, 65–69). As such, understanding HR policies and practices that can contribute to turnover can lead to more insightful strategic and operational decision-making.

An analysis of the relationship between compensation level and total annual employee turnover (Table 9.1) yielded statistically significant results for the following positions.[4]

While the magnitude of the correlations demonstrates that a great deal of variance in the compensation-turnover relationship remains unexplained, the data suggest that compensation does have an effect on intentions to stay or leave—a finding supported by related research (Simons and Enz, 1995, 20–27).

Table 9.1 Analysis of the Relationship Between Compensation Level and Total Annual Employee Turnover

Position	N	X
General manager	363	−0.24
Director of sales and marketing	172	−0.20
Sales manager	145	−0.19
Reservations manager	94	−0.19
Controller	125	−0.19
Front-office manager	220	−0.17
Restaurant manager	109	−0.17
Chief engineer	252	−0.11
Executive housekeeper	311	−0.10

Example 2: Training, turnover, and sales. The second example is based on an analysis of training, employee turnover, and sales data gathered from a privately held restaurant company that currently owns and operates approximately 115 restaurants and franchises an additional 70 throughout the United States. Complete data for 96 corporate-owned stores were gathered over a 12-month period beginning in January 2001. The primary proposition was that investments in training and employee turnover would be significant predictors of net sales. The training variable was expressed as the number of hours per month dedicated to skill-based programs (e.g., new employee training) and development-based programs (e.g., interpersonal customer service) for line staff. Employee turnover was also measured on a monthly basis (i.e., number of new hires divided by the total number of employees at the end of the month), as was net sales.

After accounting for store-specific effects (e.g., location, size) and time effects, the results from regression analyses of the panel data showed that both training and turnover accounted for significant variance in store sales.[5] These results suggest that if sales are influenced by training and employee turnover, then long-range plans for growth must consider the consequences of HR decisions regarding employee development and retention.

These two examples demonstrate the effects that HR can have on strategic and operational goals. Although researchers and practitioners have yet to fully understand the process by which the various HR policies, practices, and systems might influence long-range effectiveness, the data presented here reinforce the need to consider HR throughout the planning process. However, it's not enough simply to incorporate HR influences more broadly—the HR function must also be reconsidered. We contend that a holistic and collaborative approach to HR is required, one in which the HR function is closely integrated within the strategic and operational elements of the firm. Thus, HR plays a critical role in designing structures, facilitating change, and evaluating progress. This objective requires that firms embrace a new model of HR to achieve and sustain a competitive advantage.

▶ A NEW MODEL FOR HUMAN RESOURCES

The traditional role of HR is more appropriately termed "personnel." In this role, personnel professionals were responsible for recruiting and hiring, compensation- and benefit-program design, negotiating and administering collective-bargaining agreements, policy development, personnel recordkeeping, and serving as a conduit for employee

views and concerns. Over the years, personnel was renamed human resources, and its role in the organization (in addition to its existing functions) became one of integrating people, policies, and cultures. To meet the needs of this role, HR practitioners' responsibilities were expanded to include communications, training, safety, employee relations, and recognition and reward programs. Along with those additional responsibilities the HR department became responsible for the organization's legal compliance in the ever-expanding area of employment law.

The expansion of the HR function resulted from changes in the way businesses were managed. One such change was the explosion of mergers and acquisitions in the hotel and restaurant industry. In the past 20 years mergers and acquisitions have tested HR practitioners' ability to be flexible, detail oriented, and expeditious in both their support of other business functions and in the decisions they make related to HR issues. These increases in responsibility, occurring alongside changes in the business, transformed HR professionals from generalists to specialists. This metamorphosis also fostered the perception—often promoted by HR—that only "specialists" could handle such complicated issues. The HR model that emerged was one based on the centralization of knowledge, responsibility, authority, accountability, and control within the HR department.

Even as all this was taking place, however, business practices were changing. As a colleague of ours succinctly put it:

As organizations began to realize that different businesses needed and could afford different types of HR programs and benefits, even within the same corporation, HR began to decentralize, replicating the centralized HR structure at division and even business-unit levels. This had the advantage of supporting differentiated HR for each business, but its redundancies cost a lot of money and the specialist jobs got smaller (i.e., they supported smaller groups of employees) and thus attracted less capable or experienced people.[6]

Added to the complexity of this decentralized approach is the fact that business leaders are under extreme pressure to reduce expenses, increase productivity and revenues, and realign their organizations to become focused on core issues. In the last five years, these changes have led to enormous pressures being placed on businesses to reevaluate the HR function, its role and responsibilities, and how these integrate with the rest of the organization. High-performing organizations today are looking for ways to transfer authority, responsibility, and accountability for HR-related transactions and decisions to line managers and, in some instances, employees. The ramifications of this are enormous. Ironically, we see the most resistance to this change often coming from HR itself.

► A DECENTRALIZED FOUNDATION

The underlying premise of our model is that all decision-making authority, responsibility, and accountability should be vested in the person who supervises the employee. Thus, decisions related to hiring, promotion or demotion, training, work actions,[7] pay, and scheduling can and should be made by the immediate supervisor of the affected employee. In many cases actions of this kind do require additional approvals from the company's upper echelons. However, the farther away from

the source that these decisions are actually made, the less likely it is that real-time and relevant information about the decision and its outcome will be available for the decision maker. It is also important to note that the time it takes to complete the decision-making process is extended in direct proportion to the distance it has to travel through an organization's bureaucracy.

One key construct in our proposed HR model is that HR practitioners will no longer make operational decisions, but rather act as consultants to other business functions by designing, developing, and delivering programs that give line managers the tools and training they need to effectively perform their responsibilities. The following scenarios represent common decisions made by HR practitioners.

Scenario 1: An employee resigns and the manager needs to fill the vacancy. The process will probably include deciding whether the open position can and should be filled, locating and interviewing applicants, determining whom to hire and how much to pay that person, assigning a start date, conducting training, and determining whether to retain the new employee. In the real world the immediate supervisor will know the most about everything relating to those issues and be in the best position to make the most appropriate and timely decisions. The need for direct HR intervention should be minimal.

Scenario 2: A service employee is not performing up to expectations in spite of being trained and supervised. The organization has documented policies and practices relating to progressive discipline and the issuance of notification to the employee. The supervisor should have full authority to determine the need, timing, wording, and level of notice to be given. While it's practical to assume that this type of decision might require some additional approvals, the managers directly related to the employee's performance are best suited to understanding the issues and nuances involved.

In these situations, usually there are policies and processes that require the involvement of the HR department. Yet in most organizations these decisions are best made in a timely manner by the individuals who know the most about the issues. HR specialists should be involved in this decision-making process, but final decisions would ultimately be made by individuals outside of the HR function.

Our model has drawbacks, perhaps, but some of that relates to the fact that HR information is not always shared with line managers. One drawback is line managers' potential ignorance of the fine points of HR practice and law. The centralization of the HR function occurred in part because there was a belief that the legal and organizational issues involved in making HR decisions were so complicated that it would not be prudent to trust non-HR supervisors to make them.

Moreover, the decentralized model's redundancies could be costly. Under the new HR model the power to make decisions is entrusted to line managers. In this model it is the role of the HR practitioners to assist companies in training managers how to make and implement business decisions and then entrust them with the authority to do so. If such decision-making power is not distributed to line managers, they will not gain the necessary skills to be able to effectively perform their duties. In contrast, if line managers are supported in the HR function, the necessary information will be spread throughout the organization.

The examples in Table 9.2 illustrate how HR practitioners can use the constructs of this new model.

The responsibilities identified in Table 9.2 follow the functions that are traditionally found in HR departments. Organizations with centralized HR functions adopt these "traditional practices" on the theory that they are specialized and should only be conducted by those who are trained and skilled. That approach presupposes that being in HR is the only way to gain that expertise, and further, that this expertise is more important than understanding the operational nuances that exist at the line level. We suggest that HR expertise can be gained by those at the line level more easily than can the nuances of departmental activity be understood by those in HR. The key to transferring these responsibilities to the line level is training the supervisors in how best to perform these duties, providing them with the tools and technology to effectively and efficiently carry out these responsibilities, supporting them with advice, and monitoring their performance. This means that the role of HR changes from gatekeeper and decision maker to trainer and supporter.

Additionally, management should put in place strategies that reinforce the performance of managers who adopt and successfully handle these duties. Indeed, that should be tied to their reviews and total compensation. This is consistent with the goals of (a) the organization to have better-trained and -performing managers, and (b) most HR professionals to be more of an internal consultant and strategic partner than mere arbiters of proper practice. This new construct allows the line managers to achieve new competencies and control, while giving HR professionals the chance to become more of what they want to be—and should be. The organization benefits from using this new model, because decisions are made more quickly and appropriately, allowing the business to be

Table 9.2 Examples of the New HR Model in Operation

Traditional Practice	Suggested Practice Under the New Model
Recruitment HR departments have become gatekeepers for whom and how many to hire.	As part of the strategic planning and budgeting process, departments should be responsible for determining and justifying staffing levels. Once identified, decisions on whether to fill positions, and with whom, should be left to the department. The role of HR should be to establish suggested sources for obtaining applicants (both internal and external), designing methods for communicating with applicants using those sources, and developing an applicant tracking system. HR should also assist line managers in developing appropriate interviewing methods and materials, train the managers to use them, and monitor the process for legal and policy compliance. Information technology now exists to provide managers with self-service capabilities to find and track applicants. At Bellagio, for example, HR designed a self-service system for applicants, which eliminated the need for data input by HR staff and allowed applicants (both internal and external) to update and monitor their application information and status. These systems are always available and can help reduce the workload of the HR staff.
Compensation HR departments control both the design and administration of the compensation program.	Salary administration can be managed by line departments through technology, such as the web-based models developed by Melon's HR Solutions group, that provides managers with the data and analytical tools that they need. This gives the responsibility and accountability for these decisions to the departments; HR's role is to provide advice and establish proper control mechanisms to prevent the inexpert (non-specialist) manager from making inappropriate decisions. In this role, HR facilitates the gathering of competitive data and then provides it directly to line managers so they can do their own payroll modeling.
Job Training New hires attend an orientation conducted by HR, and then they are given some form of on-the-job training.	All new employees attend a general company orientation that is designed by HR and presented by fellow employees. This will give the new hires a peer perspective and help them to develop relationships with other employees. Department and job training should be conducted by a trained trainer from the new employee's department or job. This trainer should have the added responsibility of evaluating the new employee's performance and conducting any retraining that may be required. HR's role should be helping to create the training materials, training the trainers, and implementing a tracking system to allow managers to monitor course attendance and related performance. Park Place Entertainment, for instance, has developed this type of employee development system. The HR department has developed scripts and protocols that serve as templates for all training and development efforts. Line managers are primarily responsible for content, giving them more control over the job- and department-specific training needs. An example of this decentralized approach to development is PricewaterhouseCoopers, which has developed online knowledge management systems that give consultants access to problem solutions that have been identified from prior projects and that may have relevance for current client needs. This type of real-time learning enhances the quality and efficiency of project work.

Table 9.2 (Continued)

Traditional Practice	Suggested Practice Under the New Model
Record Maintenance Managers fill out work-action documents (e.g., wage and job changes, disciplinary notices, and performance reviews) and submit them to HR. These are then checked for accuracy and keyed into a database, and the originals are placed in file folders. Employees also submit information that initiates actions such as vacation requests, address changes, and other general requests. These are routed through MR in a similar manner as the management documents.	Using self-service technology, managers and employees fill out and submit transaction data directly to HR or the database, where they are ultimately stored and used. Starwood's online "executive dashboard," for example, provides the corporate office with continuous information about a wide range of property-level data that are directly related to strategic goals—from employee and guest satisfaction data to occupancy and rate information. In addition, operations managers have direct access to the data, thus freeing HR from the responsibility of facilitating access requests and generating reports. HR should learn about technology and actively participate in the development of these self-service tools, and then train managers how to use them. Many organizations today are outsourcing HR, payroll, and benefits administration, and are using Internet connectivity to facilitate transactions and maintain access to their data. Many are also adopting shared-service approaches that are designed to bring more functionality and service capabilities to line managers and employees.
Management Policies Most companies have handbooks and policy manuals that strictly define legal concerns and consistent policies and processes. These materials are often printed and distributed in hopes that employees will keep them in an accessible place and read them when needed. They seek to cover every conceivable circumstance with carefully written rules, policies, and practices.	Replace companywide rules with concepts that are consistent with local and departmental concerns. Involve line managers in the process of determining these concepts to ensure that they are applicable to the department's needs and concerns. Base the concepts on values and principles rather than rules. Policies and practices should focus on being fair rather than merely consistent. Workers in the 21st century expect to be treated as individuals, and when presented properly these practices have greater acceptance than those that treat everyone identically in every circumstance. Practices of this kind will be easiest for managers to understand, use, defend, and enforce. For example, Le Parker Meridien in New York City has a long history of focusing on values—from "frank and fearless feedback" to "happy but never satisfied"—which are the primary drivers for individual behavior and set standards for accountability and performance. HR should also monitor competitive practices and provide this information to managers. In some cases, this benchmarking information is also available online.
Organizational Structure Most companies have a hierarchical design in which decisions are made at the top and then implemented at the bottom of the supervisory structure. While empowerment as a practice has been widely debated, most organizations still maintain practices where authority is vested at the highest levels of this hierarchy.	Companies such as Winegardner & Hammons are flattening their organizational structures and giving line managers the flexibility and authority to make decisions. In other organizations, such as The Boulders in Carefree, Arizona, self-managed work teams are obviating the need for supervisory interventions and allowing trained employees to set the tone and monitor the behavior of their teams. Within both structures, decisions are made in context, with a focus on what is most relevant and important to those involved.

more focused on its core responsibilities of production and service.

► ENABLING TECHNOLOGY

Public and private companies alike are driven to make effective decisions and to improve performance through expense control and revenue improvement. Over the past 20 years, tools have been developed to help organizations achieve these goals. This trend began when financial departments discovered online analytical processing (OLAP) tools that allowed them to collate and query information from all of the disparate files in their databases and develop queries therefrom. This ad hoc interactive querying capability allowed them to conduct complex multidimensional analyses and more rapidly discern issues that needed to be addressed. This practice provided a means for organizations to control expenses more effectively and thus improve their bottom lines.

The next challenge involved improving revenues beyond the normal realm of sales and marketing. Those same OLAP tools, when applied to complex and disparate customer databases, allowed companies to target their efforts and dollars in ways that maximized revenue opportunities. Today, customer-relationship-management (CRM) systems are helping these companies to better use their resources to satisfy their customers and increase revenues. Much has been written about these practices. For example:

> The new cross-departmental imperative for companies in virtually all industries is to empower decision makers to obtain quick answers to their business questions by immediately acquiring the information they need. The effective sharing, distillation, and analysis of information among such an array of departments—customer relationship, sales, product planning, marketing, and finance, for example—coalesces into an enterprise-wide intelligence that is greater than the sum of its informational parts (Liautaud and Hammond, 2001, 5).

As these practices become perfected, organizations will look for additional ways to improve performance, and we suggest that HR is the next area to which these might be applied. Adding employee-activity data to the practice of interactive and multidimensional analyses will help organizations to truly get the most out of their human resources. To gain this capability, human-resources departments in highly successful organizations "will understand how to use systems and software to solve business problems and will exploit technologies to achieve their business goals" (Boyett, Boyett, Henson, and Spirgi-Hebert, 2001, 28). The decision makers in this instance are the line managers, and the decisions are related to the management of their employees; giving line managers the use of a system like this will increase their access to data and give them the ability to make better decisions. This technology will assist them in converting those data into intelligence. It is expensive to store and maintain all of these data, and "until it is put in the hands of business users and brings real value to these business users, the value obtained from that information does not compensate for the cost of maintaining that data" (Liautaud and Hammond, 2001, 38). While the initial capital investments required to develop and implement decision-support technology may be high, the operational savings[8] and improved decision quality more than justify the investment.

The appropriate use of technology is critical to the successful transfer of responsibility from HR to the line managers and departments. The use of business-intelligence technology and tools will enhance line managers' skills and decision-making capabilities by giving them the same view that was once reserved for HR staff. Again, the key to this will be the training and support provided by the HR staff.

► SOME ADDITIONAL THOUGHTS

We would be remiss if we didn't offer some thoughts related to the tragic events of September 11, 2001, which occurred during the conceptualization and writing of early drafts of this manuscript. The pressure on management to react to the terrorist acts and their effect on the hospitality industry has been intense. The range of responses to the plunge in business levels was varied and is not germane to our discussion. What is important to note is that swift, intelligent, and decisive actions were required in the wake of the attack. That supports the need to adopt new roles for HR and line managers.

A company's ability to adapt to changing conditions depends not only on its policies, but also on the tools that it provides to those responsible for deciding and implementing its strategies. HR departments worked with their management teams to define the strategies to address issues relevant to the attacks and then helped to implement them. Line managers needed accurate information about business and staffing levels, staff skills and abilities, and financial-modeling capabilities. Having HR and line managers in possession of and

trained to use the most effective tools available will ensure the organization's capacity to meet its needs. This enlightened division of responsibilities will result in the most orderly and informed execution of each group's tasks, and promote teamwork.

It seems to us that the best part of a line manager's job is having the ability to make decisions that are most critical for a department's success. Conversely, the things that managers dislike have to do with the HR department's always telling them what to do. In truth, there are probably times when it would be convenient to pass certain responsibilities to HR, so that line managers don't have to make those decisions or would at least have someone to point to as the culprits. In the end, however, the role of a manager is about responsibility and accountability, and the adage that "the buck stops here" seems to have been written with that in mind. The following requirements will help line managers feel most comfortable in this role:

a. They have some say in the development of a company's policies and practices;

b. The company provides them with the tools and training to perform at this level;

c. There is a clear definition of HR's and line managers' responsibilities;

d. They are recognized and rewarded for good performance relative to these issues; and

e. There are programs in place to help when mistakes are made.

If it is true that our future success both at the business level and as HR practitioners lies in the adoption of new ideas and technologies, and that leaner, more focused organizations are the ones that succeed, it is imperative that this transition to a new HR model occur. To assure that the transition is smooth, we will need to learn from others' errors as well as our own mistakes, and we will need the steadfast support of the organization in maintaining this new set of roles and responsibilities.

CHAPTER 9 ■ ENDNOTES

1. Statement made by the CEO and chairman of a medium-size management company of mid-price hotels.
2. For example, Paauwe and Richardson reviewed nine studies that yielded 22 significant empirical relationships between various HR policies, practices, and procedures, and several measures of firm performance. See: J. Paauwe and R. Richardson, "Strategic Human Resource Management and Performance," *International Journal of Human Resource Management,* Introduction to the Special Issue, Vol. 8, No. 3, pp. 257–262.
3. Youndt, Snell, Dean, and Lepak, for instance, found that different types of organizational strategy moderated the relationship between two types of HR systems and firm performance. Specifically, Youndt et al. found that a "human capital enhancing" HR system (e.g., selectivity in hiring) was most effective in organizations that incorporated a quality-based strategy (versus other strategies). They also found that an "administrative" HR system (e.g., policies and procedures training) was most effective in organizations that employed a cost-based strategy. Thus, this study provided convincing evidence that organizational effectiveness is contingent on the proper alignment

of HR systems and overall business strategy. See: M.A. Youndt, S.A. Snell, J.W. Dean, and D.P. Lepak, "Human-Resources Management, Manufacturing Strategy, and Firm Performance," *Academy of Management Journal,* Vol. 39, No. 4, pp. 836–866.
4. All significant at p < .05.
5. Overall F = 44.32, df1 = 123, df2 = 1085; R2 = 0.82, p < .01; standardized beta weights for training and turnover were 0.031 and 0.032, respectively, p < .01. These and related results were presented by J. Bruce Tracey and Michael J. Tews at the 2002 Meeting of the Society for Industrial and Organizational Psychology, Toronto, Canada.
6. As related by Andrew Geller, principal, organizational development, Unifi Network, a former subsidiary of PricewaterhouseCoopers LLP, Teaneck, New Jersey, April 26, 2001.
7. These are defined as disciplinary actions, commendations, granting of leaves, and the completion of related paperwork.
8. Alanna Klaussen, senior analyst with Radiant Systems, Inc., has demonstrated that a 2-percent to 10-percent savings in payroll expenses can be realized by adopting decision-support technology.

REFERENCES

Barney, J.B. 1997. *Gaining and Sustaining Competitive Advantage.* Reading, MA: Addison-Wesley.

Bluedorn, Allen C. 1982. "Theories of Turnover: Causes, Effects and Meaning." In *Research in Sociology of Organizations,* S.E. Bacharach and E.J. Lawler (eds.). Greenwich, CT: JAI Press, pp. 75–128.

Boyett, Joseph H., Jimmie T. Boyett, Row Henson, and Heidi Spirgi-Hebert. 2001. *HR in the New Economy: Trends and Leading Practices in Human Resources Management.* Pleasanton, CA: PeopleSoft, p. 28.

Enz, Cathy A. 2001. "What Keeps You Up at Night? Key Issues of Concern for Lodging Managers." *Cornell Hotel and Restaurant Administration Quarterly* 42(2):38–45.

Flynn, G. 2000. "Predictions About the Future of Employment Law." *Workforce* 79(1):78–80.

Goldberg, A.C. 1998. "Top Employment Law Issues for 1999." *HR Focus* 75(12):1–3.

Herzberg, Frederick. 1976. *The Managerial Choice: To Be Efficient and To Be Human.* Homewood, IL: Dow Jones–Irwin.

Heskett, J.L., T.O. Jones, G.W. Loveman, W.E. Sasser, and L.A. Schlessinger. 1984. "Putting the Service-Profit Chain to Work." *Harvard Business Review* (March–April).

Hinkin, T.R., and J.B. Tracey. 2000. "The Cost of Turnover: Putting a Price on the Learning Curve." *Cornell Hotel and Restaurant Administration Quarterly* 41(3):14–21.

Jackson, S.E., and R.S. Schuler. 2000. *Managing Human Resources: A Partnership Perspective.* Cincinnati, OH: South-Western College Publishing.

Liautaud, B., with M. Hammond. 2001. *e-Business Intelligence: Turning Information into Knowledge into Profit.* New York: McGraw-Hill, p. 5.

Mack, T. 2005. "Forecasts for the Next 25 Years." *World Future Society Special Report* (Winter):2.

March, J.G., and H. Simon. 1958. *Organizations.* New York: John Wiley.

McFillen, James M., Carl D. Riegel, and Cathy A. Enz. 1986. "Why Restaurant Managers Quit (and How to Keep Them)." *Cornell Hotel and Restaurant Administration Quarterly* 27(3): 36–43.

Phillips, J.A., and D.S. Massey. 1999. "The New Labor Market: Immigrants and Wages after IRCA." *Demography* 36(2):233–246.

Porter, L.W., and R.W. Steers. 1973. "Organizational Work and Personal Factors in Employee Turnover and Absenteeism." *Psychological Bulletin* 80:151–176.

Price, J.L. 1977. *The Study of Turnover.* Ames: University of Iowa Press.

Reichheld, Frederick F. 1996. "Learning from Customer Defections." *Harvard Business Review* 74(2):56–67.

Shea, R.E. 2000. "The Dirty Dozen." *HR Magazine* 45(1):52–56.

Sherwyn, D., Z.J. Eigen, and A.A. Klausner. 2000. "Interpreting the ADA and Civil Rights Law." *Cornell Hotel and Restaurant Administration Quarterly* 41(1):85–93.

Simons, T., and C.A. Enz. 1995. "Motivating Hotel Employees: Beyond the Carrot and the Stick." *Cornell Hotel and Restaurant Administration Quarterly* 36(1):20–27.

Simons, T., and T.R. Hinkin. 2001. "The Effects of Employee Turnover on Hotel Profits." *Cornell Hotel and Restaurant Administration Quarterly* 42(4):65–69.

Sovereign, K.L. 1999. *Personnel Law,* 4th ed. Upper Saddle River, NJ: Prentice-Hall.

Woods, Robert H. 1999. "Predicting Is Difficult, Especially About the Future: Human Resources in the New Millennium." *International Journal of Hospitality Management* 18(4): 443–456.

SUGGESTED READINGS

Books

Jerris, L.A. 1999. *Human Resource Management for Hospitality.* Upper Saddle River, NJ: Prentice-Hall.

Sovereign, K.L. 1999. *Personnel Law,* 4th ed. Upper Saddle River, NJ: Prentice-Hall.

Tanke, Mary L. 2000. *Resources Management for the Hospitality Industry,* 2nd ed. Albany, NY: Delmar.

Ulrich, D., M.R. Losey, and G. Lake (eds). 1997. *Tomorrow's HR Management.* New York: John Wiley and Sons.

Woods, Robert H. 1992. *Managing Hospitality Human Resources.* East Lansing, MI: Educational Institute of American Hotel and Motel Association.

Articles

Knicely, H.V. 1997. "The Future of Human Resources: Superhuman Resource Leadership in the Twenty-first Century." In *Tomorrow's HR Management,* D. Ulrich, M.R. Losey, and G. Lake (eds.). New York: John Wiley and Sons, pp. 111–118.

Sherwyn, D., Z.J. Eigen, and A.A. Klausner. 2000. "Interpreting the ADA and Civil Rights Law." *Cornell Hotel and Restaurant Administration Quarterly* 41(1):85–93.

Woods, R.H. 2000. "Predicting Is Difficult, Especially About the Future: The Future of Human Resources in Hospitality Management." In *Hotel Management and Operations,* Denney G. Rutherford (ed.). New York: John Wiley and Sons, pp 459–469.

SOURCE NOTES

Chapter 9.2, "Driving Hospitality Into the Future," by Christian Hardigree, Ellis Norman, Gail Sammons, Vince Eade, William Werner, Robert H. Woods, and Cheri Young.

Chapter 9.3, "The Causes and Consequences of Turnover in the Hospitality Industry," by Carl D. Riegel.

Chapter 9.4, "Current Issues in Hospitality Employment Law," by Suzanne K. Murrmann and Cherylynn Becker.

Chapter 9.5, "The Strategic and Operational Roles of Human Resources—An Emerging Model," by J. Bruce Tracey and Arthur E. Nathan, is reprinted from the August 2002 issue of *Cornell Hotel and Restaurant Administration Quarterly.* © Cornell University. Used by permission. All rights reserved.

INDEX